how to ORGANIZE
and OPERATE
a SMALL
BUSINESS

PEARCE C. KELLEY, *Ph.D.*

PROFESSOR OF MARKETING, UNIVERSITY OF OKLAHOMA
SMALL BUSINESS AND RETAIL CONSULTANT

KENNETH LAWYER, *Ph.D.*

PROFESSOR OF MARKETING AND MERCHANDISING, HEAD OF
DEPARTMENT, WESTERN RESERVE UNIVERSITY

how to ORGANIZE *and* OPERATE *a* SMALL BUSINESS

3rd Edition

PRENTICE—HALL, INC.

Englewood Cliffs, N. J.

Dedicated to

FREE ENTERPRISE

• Preface

For many years the opportunity to become an independent business or professional man has been excellent for the well-prepared individual but hazardous for one having only the bare desire and no other qualifications. Whether or not the person is a college graduate, this is true. This book aspires to show a person how he can succeed as an independent enterpriser, as well as to help him decide whether he would be happier as an employee or in self-employment. Financial success, though important, is not the only factor in a full and useful life.

Selection of the appropriate field of endeavor, or kind of activity to enter, is as important in small business ownership as it is in big business employment. Many factors that need to be considered in making this decision receive attention in the text and accompanying case problems. The degree of financial success achieved, as well as one's health and happiness, may depend as much on choosing the right career as on mastering business techniques.

Present and prospective employees in big business usually realize that most of their customers or suppliers are small businessmen. The more the former know about the characteristics and problems of small enterprisers, the more effectively they can deal with them. Economists, bankers, career counselors, and those charged with the determination of public policy are also interested in small as well as large businesses. Independent enterprise occupies an important place in our economy; this book seeks to describe and to place it in its proper perspective.

Good judgment, analytical ability, creative imagination, enterprise, and a well-balanced foundation are important to every individual. Decision-making, which recognizes these relevant factors, is one of the major goals of the book. Modern business requires more than unguided employment experiences, no matter how extensive. The ability to make intelligent decisions in our complex economy is influenced both by a broad background and practice in decision-making. Liberal arts graduates who succeed in business may illustrate the former; science or engineering graduates, the latter. To integrate the benefits of both types of background, and to furnish the factual basis needed for important business ownership decisions, are goals of this volume.

This book is intended to be of continuing value to all persons interested in the field of small business. It may be used for independent reading or as a basis for college or adult courses for students who later plan to go into business for themselves, as well as for owner-managers who desire to increase their knowledge of modern small business operation. Salesmen and purchasing agents who deal largely with small independent businessmen should find the book helpful in understanding the independent's viewpoint and problems. The earlier editions were widely used for each of these purposes as well as in orientation, or Introduction to Business, courses. It is hoped that this new edition will be even more useful because of the additional material.

In the process of compiling material for training and counseling present and prospective small businessmen, several extensive surveys were conducted. Follow-up surveys and new research also have been undertaken. The authors have had the advantage of access to the excellent material on small business released by the United States Department of Commerce and the Small Business Administration, by trade journals, and by the publishers of many books and pamphlets on different aspects of the subject. The authors wish to acknowledge indebtedness to each of these sources of information and ideas. In all cases where material or assistance was requested, the co-operation received was most generous. Throughout, many references are cited, and the selected bibliography at the end suggests excellent collateral readings.

The book follows a sequence recommended by the authors for persons interested in small business. The importance of small business, its status, problems, and requirements for success, are discussed. Then topics are considered in the order they would ordinarily occur to the reader. First is to decide between entrepreneurship or employment and the occupation in either case. Next is to examine the preparation needed, the choice of how and when to become an independent, and the methods of launching an enterprise on a sound basis and keeping it operating profitably. Separate chapters are then devoted to each important management function involved in operating the enterprise. In all cases attention is given to the relatively greater importance of personal factors in small, as compared to big, business. Chapter 25 considers independent practice in the major professional fields and also discusses certain interrelationships, as well as signficant contrasts, between professional and business practice. Concluding chapters deal with self-employment for older folks and with the future of the small independent enterprise, both on a national and international scale. A comprehensive checklist for organizing and operating a business is presented in Appendix B.

In scope, the text recognizes three main fields of small business: merchandizing, including retailing and wholesaling; manufacturing; and service businesses. In most chapters, following a general treatment of the topic, special applications to each of the three main fields are considered in turn. This organization helps to stress the fundamentals basic to all three fields while recognizing variations in application suited to particular needs. At the end of each chapter questions, projects, and problems are suggested for review and discussion as well as to guide individual research and application. Case problems are also included for practice in decision-making.

Excellent co-operation and much valuable information have been received from editors of trade journals, trade association officials, Department of Commerce, Small Business Administration and other Government representatives, Directors of Industrial Development Agencies, officials of the member schools of the American Association of Collegiate Schools of Business, former students who are now independent businessmen, many owners and managers of small businesses, and other authorities on small business. Officials of Dun & Bradstreet, Inc., the National Retail Credit Association, and National Cash Register Company have contributed generously of their time and material.

The authors gratefully acknowledge the assistance that was given them by their respective institutions, and by students and colleagues, in the preparation of the manuscript.

PEARCE C. KELLEY
KENNETH LAWYER

• *Table of Contents*

18 · Sales Promotion   382

19 · Advertising for Profit   400

20 · Pricing for Turnover and Profit   423

21 · Expense Control   442

how to ORGANIZE
and OPERATE
a SMALL
BUSINESS

1 • Small Business: Free Enterprise

ORIGINS, MOTIVES, AND HAZARDS

Interest in small business has grown and expanded enormously during the last few decades, and the number of articles and books on the subject has increased greatly. But interests are varied, and the expression "small business" means different things to different groups. Opinions and attitudes also vary widely because of the diversity of concepts embraced by the term.

Let us attempt an orientation in the great world of business. The economy of the United States, and of the world, is made up largely of small businesses. In fact, there are really very few large businesses if we consider the total number of stores, plants, offices, farms, and other enterprises. The great majority of these achieve much less that $100,000 in sales each year and employ fewer than ten people. Only two per cent of all businesses employ more than 50 people and reach $1 million or more in annual sales. While the large business attracts more attention, it is the exception rather than the rule.

The desire to start a small business is a human and natural one, for the entrepreneur seeks to secure his material needs through self-expression and with independence. In this way, the purely economic needs of the individual are supplied in a manner emotionally pleasing to him. These motivations make up the backbone of business. To be an independent business operator is the inherent ambition of millions of men and women in every land, of all ages, and of varying backgrounds, intentions, and qualifications. This fact is economically fortunate for all of us.

Some businesses, by their very nature, can never become large—the many small repair shops, for example. Others start small in order to introduce a new idea or a new product or service. They may grow as the idea, product, or service grows, or they may fail. Many, however, are small-scale operations in industries where the size range, as well as the efficiency of operation, varies greatly. This latter group exerts a major influence on the statistics of small business, and when the relative efficiency of small business is discussed, these are the firms being considered.

1

Every year thousands of men and women, most of them already employed by existing concerns, venture forth with their accumulated job know-how, capital, and judgment in search of the income and independence they believe to be associated with going into business for one's self.* [1] And the number of enterprises thus begun increases annually. However, statistics show that a large number of these fledgling small businesses are relatively short-lived. The question is, why? The authors assert that it is their weaknesses as businesses, rather than their small size or lack of maturity, that cause these undertakings to fail. In the highly competitive arena in which all businesses contend, poor judgment, careless handling of detail, or other incompetencies in management bring fast reaction. The trouble usually lies in the new owner-managers' limited preparation, lack of administrative experience, and failure to apply the easily understandable principles and methods of business operation which have always characterized the successful firm.

The fact that many of these business casualties were founded by persons possessing unusual mechanical aptitudes, manual skills, and artistic or other talents is significant. The cost of failure is increased by their loss of capital, investment, and of hard-won status in their previous occupations, as well as attendant injuries to their personal pride. The problem is this: they had never encountered, as employees, workers, or colleagues, the difficulties they encountered as owner-managers of their own businesses. The point here is that business *management* calls for a wide variety of talents far beyond those of the person performing—or in charge of—any single business function. Many persons who know their jobs do not know the businesses of which those jobs are a part.

CONTRIBUTIONS OF SMALLER FIRMS

The development of an idea into a business, the exploitation of a patent into an industry—these successes typify many successful products familiar to all of us. Significant innovations almost invariably have been pioneered and often invented by small-scale enterprisers. As each industry has grown to maturity accompanied by continuous scientific and technological progress— and usually a long series of interrelated patents—it is natural that further innovations, whether patented or not, that merely represent improvements on existing products and processes would come largely from within the industry. But radically new innovations continue to appear from outside the organized research programs and laboratories of giant corporations.

Every major invention of the past—the steam engine, automobile, flying

* Footnotes include readings on the topic as well as credits. The bibliography at the end of this book consists of general references and a few important ones on certain topics. It is not a compilation of footnotes.

[1] See: *The Persistence of Small Business* (Kalamazoo, Michigan: W. E. Upjohn Institute for Community Research, March 1958).

machine, telephone, electric light, and so on—was at first considered worthless. It was not until their economic value was proved by their pioneers that they became "worth" anything. The same is true for many innovations in marketing —the chain store, department store, automatic merchandising, and other ideas of widespread acceptance today. The authors see considerable merit in encouraging the type of free enterprise represented by such innovations. But this is not a blanket endorsement of all small businesses merely because those mentioned in the foregoing two groups were once small. In these categories the enterprises sometimes tend to be small because large, well-established corporations have not as yet chosen to launch big concerns in these fields. Enterprisers who do undertake such pioneering usually are less wealthy but ambitious beginners. The very nature of many projects indicates small-scale beginnings until the idea proves successful.

The small businesses serving as sources of supplemental income or means of livelihood for older people, widows, and many "unemployables," need comment only because many people carelessly judge these entrepreneurs by the standards of economic efficiency used in big business. Although this group is not our primary concern in this text, the social and economic contributions made possible by such activity are briefly discussed elsewhere.

ASSUMPTIONS OF THIS BOOK

In summarizing these introductory comments, let us say that almost every business was once a small business and that the forests of industrial strength have grown from such a seed bed. The desires to be creative, independent, and wealthy are very human ones, and without them the economy would not exist as it does. Yet these desires, or even the possession of outstanding personal productive ideas, talents, or skills, are not in themselves sufficient in the cold and cruel world of business as it exists today. The dynamics of creativity must be tempered by the statics of economic reality—the never-changing and increasingly important rules of the business "game." And a game it is, in many respects—a game requiring intelligence and ingenuity. But it is not a pastime.

These sobering restrictions need not be feared, but they must be observed. They are intelligible to those who seek to understand them. Although it is growing increasingly important, formal education has never been a prime requisite of the successful entrepreneur. Yet recognition of the many facets of business—of the importance of each as a functional part of business operation —and a willingness to respect each enough to master it, either personally or with the help of associates, has ever been a requisite. This book is written with emphasis on that respect, with an assumption that the reader is willing to learn, and with a deep conviction that, under normal circumstances, basic principles combined with modern methods, serving as rules, can aid in assuring success.

DEFINITIONS AND CONCEPTS

"Small business," "independent enterpriser," and "self-employed" are terms which will be used interchangeably throughout this book. Each expression implies some aspect of the institution with which we are concerned. In this chapter, the usually popular concept of small business will serve our needs: the independently owned and managed retail stores, service establishments, wholesale houses; small factories, plants, or shops with fewer than 100 employees; locally owned motels and various drive-in businesses; equipment rental; independent real estate and insurance agencies; local contractors; and the independent practice of accounting, law, and similar professions.

Probably the most fundamental definition ever given is the following statement by the Committee for Economic Development:

Usually a small business will show two or more of the following characteristics:

1. *Management is independent.* Usually the managers are also owners.

2. *Capital* is supplied and ownership held by an individual or small group.

3. *Area of operations* is mainly local. Workers and owners are in one home community. Markets need not be local.

4. *Size within the industry is relative;* the business is small when compared to the biggest units in its field. The size of the top bracket varies greatly, so that what might seem large in one field would definitely be smaller in another.[2]

The most widely used measures of size are number of employees and dollar sales volume. The U.S. Department of Commerce suggests: manufacturing plants with 100 employees or less; retail stores, service establishments, hotels, places of amusement, and construction companies, with annual net sales or receipts of less than $100,000; and wholesale establishments with net sales of less than $500,000. Definitions formulated by the Small Business Administration stress nondominance in the field but larger quantitative measures.

In the opinion of the authors, a qualitative definition such as that of the Committee for Economic Development is the most satisfactory. It is the four attributes therein cited—independent management, owner capital, local area of operations, and relative size within the industry—that give rise to most of the problems and special needs of the small, as compared to the large, business unit. In general, this qualitative concept will be the one used throughout the text, unless otherwise stated.

Other definitions may also be considered—especially numerical standards, some of which have been widely used for certain purposes. Assets, investment required, number of employees, and dollar volume of sales are the most important of these.

[2] The Research and Policy Committee of the Committee for Economic Development, *Meeting the Special Problems of Small Business* (policy report of the Committee for Economic Development, New York, June 1947), p. 14.

The beginning small enterprise is, therefore, of special interest to us because (1) the great majority of businesses must be classified as small, hence (2) small businesses characterize our modern economy; (3) successful enterprises that start in a small way tend to expand and grow into big businesses; and (4) the new enterprise pioneering some innovation has occupied a unique and extremely valuable place in the development of our economy.

A publication of the U.S. Chamber of Commerce recently stated:

> Except in a few industries, the concentration of business in large-scale enterprises was probably never as great as commonly assumed. Contrary to the opinions of many people, the evidence today indicates a declining concentration in American business. This means that smaller firms are increasing their share of the market at the expense of the large ones.[3]

RISE OF BIG BUSINESS

Big business in the United States is less than a century old, but small business antedates the Union itself. In 1858, R. H. Macy was still trying to start a successful retail store and to avoid "closures," and Henry Ford's struggle to build his first "gas buggy" by hand foretold little of the present-day mass production and big business that the name "Ford" now symbolizes throughout the world. As late as 1900, the steel industry consisted of numerous small firms, and only after 1900 did department stores come to be identified by their present designation. Chain stores were "syndicates" in 1911-1912 when the first study of their growth was made by the staff of *Printers' Ink*. And the newly developed monopolistic tactics of the large concerns in steel and similar industries did not receive public attention until 1914, when the Federal Trade Commission Act and the Clayton Anti-Trust Act became law.

Without exception, every one of our present-day examples of big business started in a small way. Railroads, telegraph, telephone, automobile, steel, oil, department stores, chain stores, cut-rate stores, discount and mail-order houses were all introduced by individuals with an idea and not much else. Often these businesses were begun under the shadow of considerable public opposition and ridicule. But this is not unusual. The resistance faced by the innovator of business methods by those whose domain he invades is the natural reaction to change. Each newcomer, if he succeeds and remains, appears to go through a cycle of (1) resistance and criticism, sometimes with legislative restriction brought about by his competition; (2) emulation by others, including eventually the injured and resentful competitors; (3) acceptance of the method as the way of proven efficiency, as a reputable contributor to the economy, and as the predominant type in the industry. Various writers have observed this sequence.

The 50 years preceding World War I saw the development of giant corpora-

---

[3] *Small Business, Its Role and Its Problems,* a Report of the Committee on Economic Policy, Chamber of Commerce of the United States (Washington, D.C., 1958).

tions, trusts and monopolies, and mass production, but while they are significant in percentage of total productivity, it is small business that actually constitutes the backbone of the world's economy.

STATUS OF SMALL BUSINESS

Throughout most of the world small business is representative of the economy of its nations. "Mama and papa" stores, tiny handicraft or "job" shops, laundries, bakeries, footwear, houseware, blacksmith and general repair shops are fair examples, as they have been for centuries. The family enterprise tends to be dominant in many countries. But in forward-looking areas, small business is not destined, except by the owners' choice, to remain small or to fail to make important contributions in a wide scope of fields. The fact that the little fellow has problems should not blind us to his present and future importance. All businesses have problems. However, the emphasis on the importance of small business does not imply an underestimation of the contributions of big business. Nor is it a recommendation that all interested persons should become independent enterprisers. Small and big business have their place and are interdependent. Moreover, the requirements needed for success as an independent enterpriser are rarer than some people believe.

The above comments seek not only to re-emphasize the opportunities in small business, but also to dispel any impression that the authors, as a matter of principle, are "against" larger firms. Furthermore, they assume that the student, or any other reader, is academically interested in the role of small business in the economy as well as in considering practically his personal potential as an entrepreneur. The purpose of this book may as well be to warn away the unqualified as to encourage those who should become owner-managers of small concerns. In fact, both authors, as instructors and consultants, take some pride in having influenced individuals in both directions. Both aspects of the problem will be elaborated upon later but deserve mention here to lessen possible misunderstanding.

Rise of Dependent Employment

A century ago, 80 per cent of our productive workers were self-employed. As late as 1880, almost 75 per cent were self-employed—about 62 per cent in farming and 38 per cent in merchandising and neighborhood industries. By 1960, however, only about 20 per cent were self-employed, while 80 per cent were in dependent employment. This shift has magnified the personal hazards of business cycles, has increased the burden of public support for social security and anti-depression measures, and has distorted our perspective from "working to live" to efforts to maintain employment at all costs. It has also led to the erroneous belief that the small or independent enterpriser has left the public scene. Nothing could be further from the truth. The independent enterpriser is more important today than he has ever been at any time in our history.

It seems paradoxical to claim that in America and elsewhere small business occupies a more favorable position today than it did 50 to 100 years ago, knowing that self-employment has declined from about 80 to 20 per cent of the total, and that very large corporations—though relatively few in number—account for a large portion of manufacturing output and of total paid employment. Yet it is easy to establish the numerical importance of the independent enterpriser and his ability to maintain this status, because the number of business units has increased more rapidly in proportion to the growth of total population. Over 85 per cent of these business units are proprietorships and partnerships—often with three or more part-owners per establishment—indicating that self-employment has increased even more rapidly. In 1960 there were estimated to be over 26 firms per 1,000 population compared to 22 in 1900.[4]

A major factor that accounts for the reverse in the ratio of those in self- and in dependent employment has been the relative drop in the percentage of our population who are self-employed in small-scale farming. Another factor is the great increase in the number of workers in large-scale industry that has accompanied the rise of mass production and industrial concentration. These types of industry, less than a century old in this country, have in a sense developed markets for employment that never before existed, just as the automobile built its own market for long-distance pleasure travel—a market which did not exist during the period of railroad monopoly. For almost a century the numerical increase in large-scale industrial employment and its allied occupations has about balanced the decline in agricultural workers. From 1880 to 1956 the number of persons employed or engaged in agriculture declined from 8.6 million to 6.5 million (most abruptly since 1945—from 8.58 million) and this trend continues.[5] Applications of power machinery and modern technology to agriculture have further reduced the ratio, as well as the importance, of family labor on the farm.

Manufacturing employment increased from about 3.0 million in 1880 to 14.4 million in 1950, and to an estimated 18.0 million in 1960. Workers in wholesale and retail trade have increased from approximately 5 million in 1920 to an estimated 12 million in 1960.[6] To these figures should be added the increase of women in the labor force from less than 3 million in 1880 to almost 20 million in the non-agricultural labor force alone in 1957.[7] All occupations of significance involving paid employment of women except teaching, had their expansion after 1880.

---

[4] *Statistical Abstract of the United States* (Washington, D. C.: U. S. Department of Commerce, 1957), pp. 482-483.

[5] *Statistical Abstract of the United States* (1957), p. 199 (Table No. 242).

[6] *Statistical Abstract of the United States* (1957), p. 202 (Table No. 247).

[7] *Ibid.*

Mass Production and Modern Marketing

The phenomenal rise in our standard of living was made possible by the high productivity of power-motivated industrial mechanization. Our average annual increase in productivity per worker of over two per cent, accompanied by a decline in working hours of over 33 per cent, and an increase in leisure time of over 40 per cent[8] has furnished both purchasing power to buy the expanded output of our manufacturers and the leisure time to use it effectively. This is one of the most significant developments in the world's history—a mass market for all the former luxuries and "class" products of other generations and nations which has opened up opportunities greater than ever before for independent enterprises of all sizes and types. As least half of our gainfully employed are engaged in producing or marketing goods that were unknown 50 years ago.

In manufacturing, most of these gainfully employed are in dependent employment; but in marketing and services, the situation is reversed. All important service fields excepting the public utilities, have developed within the past 50 years. About 99 per cent of all service establishments are small businesses. Although large-scale retailing had its growth during this half century, independent merchants also increased in number and importance.

A fundamental but widely misunderstood fact is the relationship between primary production and marketing, including the marketing of services. Just as the standard of living or extent of industrialization in a country can be measured quite accurately by the smallness of its agricultural contribution—the higher the standard of living, the lower the proportion of total national products contributed by agriculture—so both the standard of living of the masses and the extent of industrialization can be measured very accurately by the relatively greater proportion of the country's gainfully employed engaged in marketing and the services, including the professional fields.

This fact has a dual significance for prospective enterprisers: (1) most small enterprises are in the marketing, service, and professional fields, and (2) the much greater productivity per worker in capitalistic production requires expanded markets that can be secured *only* by intensive efforts on the part of those engaged in marketing. Thus marketing has increased responsibilities in the new era of independent enterprise: to distribute the goods of quantity production; to market services to meet certain needs of large-scale industry, such as auxiliary services, market information, or business forecasting; and to satisfy consumer wants, such as for recreation and entertainment. And as automation expands in manufacturing, the importance of marketing is further enlarged.

[8] Pearce C. Kelley, *Consumer Economics* (Homewood, Illinois: Richard D. Irwin, Inc., 1953), pp. 73-74.

Revival of Independent Enterprising

Two other developments help to explain some of the expansion in small business: (1) the higher economic status of labor, and (2) certain features of our Federal income tax system. The former has influenced many craftsmen in the building trades and repair fields to launch their own businesses as contractors or repair and servicemen. High wages during World War II and post-war years, with intense consumer demand, encouraged many ambitious craftsmen to try self-employment. Except for numerous contractors who lacked managerial ability and ample working capital, these ventures met with apparent success.

Opportunities for legally valid income tax deductions when certain expenses were incurred in self-employment, but not allowable for the same expenses to wage earners, expanded this trend. In many communities, some of these newly rich, independent businessmen own beautiful homes in the better residential districts, have two cars or more, are good customers of the local banks and other businesses, and in similar ways are symbolic of the recent trends toward affluence and economic equality.

Education for Small Business

A very important source contributing to the recent interest in independent enterprising has been college graduates—especially those from our university schools of business. During the 1930's, many graduates became self-employed because no other employment was available. Some found such ventures to their liking and remained independents. Since then, courses in colleges and schools of business have paid increasing attention to the advantages of independent enterprising. Also business has gained a prestige hitherto accorded only to the older "learned" professions, and many college graduates have taken over family enterprises.

Courses in small business operation are now offered in some 150 American institutions of higher education. Additional evidence of the interest of colleges and universities in training and education for small business are the many conferences, institutes, and seminars they have held in recent years. Some of these, covering specific topical areas, have been attended by specific trade or industrial groups; others have been general in nature. Many have been sponsored or encouraged by the Management Research and Assistance Division of the Small Business Administration.

Surveys conducted by the U. S. Department of Commerce and other agencies continue to reveal this greatly increased attention by schools of business to preparation for entreprepeneurship and the self-improvement of existing entrepreneurs, in contrast to what has long been considered an overemphasis on training for big business employment.

Current Interest in Small Business

The interest in small business in recent years is the result of many causes, among which the following are important: increasing recognition of its economic and social importance, a growing fear of concentration of economic power, and a recognition by big business of its dependence upon many small firms. As we have already indicated, a shift in educational emphasis to give greater attention to the problems and needs of small business has accompanied this interest.

During and since World War II, successful efforts have been made by the government to assist small business in securing a fair share of defense contracts, in obtaining financial assistance in certain cases, in procuring critical materials in short supply, and, in general, seeking to protect smaller firms under conditions that are normally harder on the little fellow than on his big business brother.

We believe that this interest in the small independent businessman is likely to be permanent. Experiences during wartime have repeatedly demonstrated the value of subcontracting and of close co-operation among all firms in an industry, regardless of size. As the Committee for Economic Development states, the basic fact is the interdependence of all business.

IMPORTANCE OF SMALL BUSINESS

Let us attempt to appraise the importance of small business in our economy. Later the advantages and limitations of business ownership will be cited and discussed.

The importance of small business may be reviewed in summary fashion according to the ways in which it contributes to our economy:

1. It is necessary to maintain dynamic competition as well as our system of free enterprise.
2. All businesses and segments of our economy are interdependent.
3. Most large businesses were once small.
4. It is essential to keep free enterprise *free*.

Competition and Growth

If a truly free competitive economy is the desired goal of a nation, the continued existence of independent enterprises is imperative. Modern competition appears in many forms: in price, credit terms, service, product improvement, inter-industry struggles concerning substitution and replacement, innovations as to method, and so forth. Basically, it is rivalry for consumer patronage. The history of the railroads before the advent of motor and air transportation illustrates the economic and social hazards of monopoly that only the effective competition from newer carrier enterprises could control.

Chain stores afford another example. Before the many independent retailers learned how to compete effectively, several chains had become somewhat autocratic in their treatment of labor, suppliers, and even of customers by restricting services and assortments to the bare minimum for maximum sales and immediate profits. Effective competition, much of it independent, swung the pendulum back.

Even such a highly competitive field as automobile production furnishes examples of the regimenting effects of big business before the appearance of competition. Witness the Model T Ford "in any color as long as it was black," any model as long as it was the model T, any accessories as long as the customer added them himself. In the oil industry, despite some opinion to the contrary, the 13,000 large and small companies think and act differently. So do the thousands of large and small banks, although they are more closely regulated than most other industries. In nearly every field where large and small units compete, different policies and attitudes toward production, research, financing and expansion, pricing, service, market development, and other functions, are found. Such diversity is basic to free enterprise competition.

The foregoing are but a few of hundreds of examples that illustrate how free enterprise, competition between new or old small businesses and established big ones, as well as between the giants in the field—such as Ford and General Motors—are essential to maintain competition, to avoid the tendencies of big business or big government to carry standardization and regimentation to excess, and to help maintain diversity and a wide range of consumer choice. Others include: telegraph vs. telephone vs. radio; stage plays vs. movies; high-fidelity phonograph vs. radio vs. television; pre-1950 American automobiles vs. foreign models vs. post-1950 American sports models; larger cars of the early 1950's vs. 1960 compact cars. A steady influx of new independent enterprises is so important to insure all-around competition that Professor Sumner H. Slichter of Harvard University has suggested that more big-business executives be encouraged to launch enterprises of their own to keep our economy competitive.[9] This thought has since been echoed by other authorities, and evidences that the idea is taking root appear to be plentiful as certain "adoptive" mergers have taken place. We suggest here that the challenge of making a company in difficulties succeed may be fully offset by the tax advantages accruing.

Competitive capitalism insures freedom of enterprise and provides an outlet for individual creative impulses and abilities, as well as a livelihood for a large segment of the total population. It is the safest insurance that our economy will remain dynamic and provide a continuous stream of innovations, new ideas, experimenting, and pioneering.

[9] "Why is United States Industry so Productive?", *Management Review* (December 1951), pp. 731-732. From an address by Sumner H. Slichter before the School of Banking, University of Wisconsin.

Major Sources of New Business Ideas

Individuals and small business provide the major fund of new ideas and inventions. Records of the U. S. Patent Office show that from 1921 to 1938, 43 per cent of the patents were issued to individuals, and 34.5 per cent to 17,500 small- and medium-sized business establishments.[10] This trend has continued. Many patents, whether issued to giant corporations, to the government, or to individuals, may never be put to effective use. This is indicated by recent efforts of the U. S. Department of Commerce to encourage prospective enterprisers to exploit several thousand different patents on a free or royalty basis. Thus, in fact, any economic scarcity is due to a lack of business enterprisers rather than of inventors.[11] Moreover, as we shall discuss later, competent authorities have conceded that our current patent system is in need of revision, for some inventors prefer the short route to immediate gain by assigning their patents to large corporations. The *fact* remains, however, that the majority of fundamental innovations of modern times originated with individuals.

Many innovations originated because (1) alert and sympathetic individuals realized a need for them when unusual conditions were encountered, and (2) parents and others sought relief from some problem formerly accepted as inescapable. A few illustrations of each type will prove interesting as well as suggestive of other possibilities. Later, additional examples originating from business motives will be presented.

In 1851, Gail Borden on a transatlantic trip observed that the milk supply was not refrigerated and that many babies aboard ship died. This led him to develop canned condensed milk which did not require low temperatures for preservation. A mild winter in 1890 reduced the supply of natural winter-cut ice upon which families and industries dealing in perishable products, such as meats, had formerly depended. This launched efforts to manufacture ice by mechanical means that before long eliminated our dependence upon nature. The Hygeia nursing bottle was invented by a physician in general practice to help curb infant cholera that often resulted from the use of unsterilized containers for babies' milk. Quick freezing of perishable foods was developed by Clarence Birdseye in the early 1920's to preserve the natural flavor of fresh foods that were out of season or were shipped great distances from their points of origin.

In the border area between our two groups of illustrations is that great dish for all—ice cream. Prior to the mid-nineteenth century, ice cream was an ultra luxury served only at the most elaborate functions of royalty and other

[10] Emerson P. Schmidt, "Small Business, Its Place and Problems," *Post-War Readjustments*, Bulletin No. 7 (Washington, D. C.: Chamber of Commerce of the United States, December 1943).

[11] Pearce C. Kelley, "Producer Aids to Consumer," *Consumer Economics* (Homewood, Illinois: Richard D. Irwin, Inc., 1953), pp. 309-311.

potentates. In 1846 Nancy Johnson, a housewife, contrived a simple hand-cranked freezer which she considered to be too obvious to patent. In 1851 a Baltimore milkman started quantity production and marketing of ice cream at popular prices. By 1890 the "industry" was established and selling a million gallons a year, all hand-cranked. By 1900, with the aid of electric power machinery, 25 million gallons of ice cream were sold annually. In recent decades progress has been rapid and expansion virtually continuous. The development of "frozen custard" and similarly competitive frozen concoctions has expanded the industry to the far corners of the world. Ice cream is now a staple food and total American production of frozen dairy products now approaches 750 million gallons annually.[12]

Our second group illustrates how many innovations originate in efforts to solve personal problems and later become the basis for business enterprises. For centuries, mothers had been laboriously squeezing and straining foods—especially vegetables and fruits—and extracting juices from meats to feed their infants before the young hopefuls had teeth. The medical profession had more or less accepted these few years as ones of anemia until the child could masticate the natural sources of blood-building foods such as liver, beef, and certain other foods rich in minerals and vitamins. In one of the typical family scenes about a generation ago, Dan Gerber was prodding his wife to hurry or they would be late for an engagement. In desperation she said, "Here, smarty, *you* strain the baby's peas!" Dan's first attempt did not set any speed record, but it did lead to the first factory production of prepared baby foods in his cannery in Fremont, Michigan. Thus our current multimillion-dollar baby food industry was launched less than a generation ago.

In the 1930's, Mrs. Margaret Rudkin started another outstanding example of the development of a traditionally "home-cooked" product into a national brand. Her Pepperidge Farm, Inc., established in Fairfield, Connecticut, baked and sold a whole-wheat bread. Mrs. Rudkin originally prepared this bread to alleviate her son's asthma, and it was produced according to an old family recipe. The business, with annual sales amounting to 40 million dollars, is now nationwide and markets 57 different bakery products which are made in six plants employing a total of 1,500 people.

Mrs. Rudkin's success is attributed in part to her departure from accepted rules of business conduct, and in part to her strict adherence to them. Departures included the establishment of a price originally far above that of competitive products and depending largely, at first, on word-of-mouth advertising. Adherence included strict quality control, direct contact with distributors, and careful cultivation of physicians, food authorities, and others whose recommendations of her product were vital.[13]

Other parent innovations of current importance include: the Cradle Gym, developed by Vernon Eisel, a government worker, from scrap in his basement

[12] Based on figures from *Statistical Abstract of the United States, op. cit.*, p. 685.
[13] See *Time* (March 21, 1960), p. 90, for details.

in order to get his four-month-old daughter to take the exercise she needed to become healthy and normal; the Jonny-Jump-Up toy exerciser to pacify crying children; the Folda-Rola baby carriage and general utility carriers; the Kiddy-Koop, Dryer Panty, and so on. Within a few years over four million Cradle Gyms had been sold, and other parent inventions have had similar business success.

Small business often serves as the proving ground for such new ideas and products, patented or unpatented. Many of these may never achieve public acceptance, but they must be given a trial before it is possible to know their future. Big business tends toward conservatism in this respect, and some of our cherished products of today would still be in the "science fiction" stage but for the daring pioneer efforts of small businessmen with confidence in a new idea. Small enterprise is the backbone of America, and it exerts a stabilizing influence on our social order.

Even in well-developed fields the most creative thinking is likely to come from freelance innovators. Mr. F. B. Jewett, former president of the Bell Laboratories, Inc., stated: "Fundamental patents which mark big changes in the arts are more likely to come from the outside than from the inside. I think in the majority of cases, the chances are ten to one that the fundamental idea will come from outside the big laboratories." [14] Even in chemistry and physics the most valuable processes have started with small laboratory experiments.

Initiative, Self-Expression, Independence

The desire to experiment, to test one's strength, to prove one's ability to master a situation and thus to gain all the emotional and material benefits to be derived therefrom, is inherent in most of us. The entrepreneur, by nature, is most willing to take a risk if he can see such opportunities for gain. The existence of these opportunities is a characteristic of democracy, a free society, and the free world. One speaker has expressed it as follows:

> . . . Freedom of enterprise is more than the freedom to succeed. At the core, it is the freedom to fail. This country owes its greatness to men who are free to take chances and who dare. We can stick our chins out, we can take risks . . . and we get the reward for doing it if we are right. Our cold war opponents have no such latitude. . . .[15]

As yet no substitute has been found for the incentives provided by free enterprise. Dean Donald Kirk David of the Harvard Graduate School of Business aptly calls free enterprise the "nuclei of initiative." The history of the typewriter illustrates the power of free enterprise. During the 154 years prior to 1868, seven men in foreign countries had invented "writing machines,"

---

[14] *Small Business, Its Role and Its Problems* (Washington, D. C.: Chamber of Commerce of the United States, 1953), p. 16.

[15] Ray R. Eppert, President, Burroughs Corporation, in an address before the Boston Conference on Distribution (October 20, 1959).

but not one was marketed. Christopher Sholes, an American, perfected a typewriter in 1868 and produced and marketed his product so successfully that before long it was in use throughout much of the civilized world.[16]

For the development of self-reliance, for making men as well as money, small business excels. It suits the personality and independent attitude of many. Thousands of individuals who would chafe under the restrictions of employment find business ownership to their liking. It is the channel through which thousands of individuals rise to fame and fortune. Small business offers the opportunity for self-employment to hundreds of thousands—some with technical and professional training, others with business experience, and large numbers who are outside the employable standards set by many concerns, especially big business. Men past middle age, those with physical handicaps, and others who for various reasons are not attractive as employees, find self-employment their principal method of living a productive life. Widows lacking previous business training or experience, housewives desiring to supplement the wage earner's income, and young married couples before family responsibilities keep the wife busy at home often find small business ventures attractive and profitable.

Several other groups have found small businesses a welcome source of supplemental income. These include retired people, most of whom also desire to continue working—but at a more leisurely pace; school teachers, college professors, and some political office holders often have a small venture of their own which they operate three or four months each year in some resort area. Recent professional school graduates who enter practice have found that a side-line business undertaking can furnish satisfactory income for the family living expenses during the three to five years before their professional practice is self-supporting. Cases known to the authors include attorneys, dentists, accountants, and psychologists; and others have been disclosed in alumni surveys. Not infrequently undergraduate business students operate their own enterprises in lieu of taking part-time jobs to earn their expenses.

If the intense competition for jobs appears during the 1960's, as some unhappily predict, we may again witness, as we did in the 1930's, numerous graduates immediately becoming self-employed. Those who start planning early for this contingency should have the best opportunities for success.

Interdependence in Our Economy

Small business performs at least three basic functions for big business: (1) facilitation of concentration in the most effective areas, (2) propagation and rearing of future business adults, and (3) compensation for the limitations characteristic of bigness.

Big business is most effective for natural monopolies and in well-established industries where large markets for low-unit-cost products exist; where con-

[16] Burlington Mills' advertisement, "Who Deserves the Credit for the 'Writing Machine'?" *Time* (June 14, 1948), p. 7.

siderable experience has developed technology and mechanization to a high degree of efficiency, but huge capital investments are required; where standardization and simplification (limitation of variety) are desirable and acceptable policies; and where concentration on one function—production, marketing, or finance— is preferable. In all of these cases, except the first, with qualifications to be discussed later, numerous small enterprises are essential to enable a few large ones to concentrate on those activities where their efforts are most effective.

These small satellite concerns function in four main areas: (1) as suppliers of materials and parts—often as subcontractors in defense work; (2) as service agencies to the large firm and its employees; (3) as dealers or distributors; and (4) as customers who use, rather than distribute, products of the large corporation. No comprehensive data are available on the number of satellites attached to each big corporation, but exploratory analysis indicates that the numbers are large, probably averaging at least 500 suppliers and several thousand distributors for each large producer. Advertisements in general magazines during the 1950's claimed that General Electric had 33,000 suppliers and subcontractors, of whom 82 to 92 per cent were small (500 employees or less). Of these suppliers and subcontractors, 12,500 were for normal work and over 19,000 for defense work. Jet engine production for planes by Lockheed required over 4,000 independent suppliers, including 2,835 small firms. R.C.A. uses over 5,000 suppliers for defense and consumer goods, of which 70 per cent are small and 50 per cent have fewer than 100 employees. Ford spends $700 million a year for the products of 7,200 independent firms. Another automobile company has 21,074 suppliers distributed throughout 48 states.

Some observers comment that our large mass production industries are essentially assemblers of the products of thousands of small specialized manufacturers. Mass-produced goods such as motor vehicles, planes, refrigerators, radios and so on, have from a few hundred to several thousand parts, indicating that, on the average, each large concern buys materials and parts from small firms in several hundred different fields. One big producer may use from one to over ten different suppliers for each part purchased. Census data for manufacturers supports this reasoning, since less than 2,000 firms employ over 1,000 workers each, and probably not over 500 of these are in mass-production industries. Over 236,000 firms have less than 500 employees, so a crude ratio would be 472 small manufacturers to one in mass production.

A somewhat similar analysis for retail dealers is as follows: 85 per cent or over 2,380,000 of our retail establishments are small-scale independents. Each store handles from a few thousand to well over 20,000 different items (over 600,000 in very large department stores), or a crude approximation of about 5,000 items made by almost 1,000 different producers. Using aggregate census figures, over 2,380,000 small independent retailers distribute the products of 4,664 large manufacturers (500 employees or more), a ratio of 509 stores per manufacturer, which obviously grossly underestimates the number of retail dealers for the average large producer. Thus, until a comprehensive study becomes available, our conclusion that, on the average, at least 500 different suppliers and several thousand retail dealers serve each large manufacturer is probably very conservative. In addition, most consumer goods go through wholesale establishments, the majority of which are small businesses, and each large producer buys services from numerous small and mostly local establishments.

Since industrial decentralization has gained impetus, another aspect of small business assistance to large organizations has gained greater attention. It is the ability of a new community to provide adequate auxiliary services to the big industry, and also attractive merchandising, personal, and amusement services for the employees of the large concern. The large firm moving to a smaller town, or opening a branch there, needs both types of assistance that small independent enterprisers are better able to render. Alert communities today recognize this fact. If local people are unable to establish and operate modern service establishments, retails stores, and places of amusement, there always seem to be plenty of "camp followers" anxious to do so—a fact that slower moving local businessmen often learn to their loss.

Small Origins of All Business

Almost all our giant corporations of today had small-scale origins. This is true of the mass production industries such as automobile, aircraft, and radio; of heavy industries such as steel, aluminum, and chemicals; of communications industries such as the telephone and broadcasting; as well as of retailing and other fields.

The small independent enterpriser will always be important in pioneering some innovation and proving its worth on a small scale until the growth stage, if there is to be one, is reached. At this point the small enterprise changes to large-scale techniques if the necessary capital can be secured, or sells out to a larger firm more able to finance such a shift. The latter has occurred so frequently recently that it has often been misinterpreted as an attempt by big business to absorb all small competitors. The basic reasons are, in the opinions of most authorities, our tax system, that virtually prevents the small enterprise from accumulating funds for major expansion, and the greatly increased investment required. It is hoped that some legislation may somehow ease this discouraging situation in both respects.

There are many who believe that only the younger small businessman, with greater inquisitiveness and flexibility and less inhibition, offers industry much of its modern initiative. Old as well as large bodies (both human and corporate) move slowly; and great numbers of personnel tend to effect a slowing down in both imagination and decision making. It may be said that we need more of an "accent on youth" in both business and its management. Several developments have resulted in the accent-on-youth movement as symbolized by the "Young Presidents Club," which features the extraordinary youth of certain college and company presidents and other achievements formerly considered to be in the province of maturity that usually comes with age. An interesting offshoot of the Young Presidents group is the "Pioneers of New Industries," an organization, with headquarters in New York City, encouraging the promotion and development of new business concepts. This agency currently seeks to identify characteristics common to successful small firms, in order that this knowledge may be disseminated among those who contemplate establishing such small businesses.

Evidence of this emphasis-on-youth movement presents itself in at least three ways, all of which are gaining in acceptance: early start, side-line ventures, and retirement entrepreneurship. The first is for those who "have what it takes" to become independent enterprisers as quickly as possible. Thus, economic security for life, rather than just for a short period of paid employment, is insured—as nearly as security can be assured. A health factor may exist. Very likely these "natural entrepreneurs," were they to enter dependent rather than self-employment, would augment the already large number of emotional and mental cases and premature deaths of many big-business executives.

While this statement cannot be proved with data available, it is based on a few apparently well-established facts. In self-employment a man can set his own pace and is not under constant pressure from superiors to achieve certain goals. On the other hand, he may be able to move ahead more rapidly. Some men are happier, worry less, and achieve more with less emotional and mental strain in self- than in dependent employment. As his own boss, a man can exercise *all* his faculties and abilities, thus avoiding the irritating and repressive effects of enforced conformity in becoming an "organization man." The point here is that pressure from within, in its psychological effects on the individual, differs from pressure from without. Also, most men want to continue in useful productive employment long past the usual compulsory retirement age, and they can do so more easily if they are self-employed. Thus small business provides many valuable opportunities for self-employment after retirement.

The Part-Time Small Business

While it is a basic conviction of the authors that ownership of a firm obligates most operators to devote their full attention to it—at least until it is well established—there may be circumstances under which a business can be begun as a side line. Sometimes an employee of a large company buys or launches a small enterprise that he can supervise or operate without encroaching upon his employment duties. Likewise, members of professions such as accounting and teaching, as well as employees of large city hotels and merchandising concerns, often establish side-line enterprises. These may add as much net income as the primary "bread-and-butter" job, furnish legitimate income tax advantages under current legislation and regulations, provide a hedge in case of unsatisfactory developments with the enterpriser's employer, and lead to a post-employment occupation of well-established and proven value.

Upon retirement, many people prefer to remain in their home towns; others find it necessary to do so because of family or similar obligations. When the town is fairly small or nonindustrialized, opportunities to secure well-paying jobs or to expand an independent enterprise may be limited. The flexibility of free enterprise has solved this dilemma for many small-town and home-town people by allowing multiple enterprises. Thus, a physician owns and operates a service station, drugstore, and grocery store in one small southern town, and a practicing attorney in the Southwest is the owner-operator of a self-service automatic laundry and a maintenance and repair service (he also sells reconditioned automatic washers and plans to expand into the automobile service station, grocery, and enough other fields to give him control over ten separate small enterprises—all within his home town of about 30,000 population).

Women with managerial or merchandising ability often operate small establishments of their own and make more money than they could as employees under our double-wage standard. In addition, they have greater flexibility and more control over their own time and responsibilities than they would have as employees. Conceivably this development may help to reduce or even eliminate the double-wage standard—at least for the better qualified women.

CONCLUSIONS

Free entry into small business is an essential feature of the American way of life. Opportunities for reward in proportion to effort and contributions have always made independent business ownership or professional practice attractive to energetic individuals. In recent years, additional aspects of independent enterprising have appeared that are, in part, responsible for renewed interest in the subject. Among these are knowledge of the need for both small and large businesses, recognition of unique contributions that can be made by enterprises in each group, and a realization of their interdependence.

During the present century, giant corporations have developed in the mass production and heavy industries, in public utilities, and in mass retailing. In less than one century our gainfully employed population has risen from 20 to 80 percent in dependent employment. These events have misled many people to conclude that small business has greatly declined in importance; this fallacy has been explained at length in this chapter. The large proportionate increase of those in dependent employment has resulted mainly from new markets for employees created by our giant manufacturing industries and public utilities, accompanied by a pronounced decline in the need for workers in agriculture.

Small independent enterprises are more important today, both in number and in the essential contributions they make to our way of life, than at any time in our history.

Many college students and others have available to them only those textbooks that take the viewpoint and discuss the problems and methods of large corporations. To them this chapter may appear to be unduly laudatory of small business—especially independent enterprising. One stated objective of the authors is to compensate for some of the neglect of the place and contributions of small business in many college courses and texts—at least up to very recent years. Since this is a book concerning small business, we have naturally directed attention to the advantages and contributions of small enterprisers. All other texts do the same in their respective subjects. We consistently recognize that small and big business are interdependent; each has its appropriate place, and each has made its unique contributions to our economic world supremacy.

Within the area of small business we have differentiated among several groups and commented upon the strong and weak points of each. We have thus discussed the types of small business and the need for their development from economic, social, and psychological viewpoints. We have also discussed the small origins of big business, the interdependence of all business, and the kinds of people who enter into and are successful in small-business operation. That big business has made enormous contributions to our high standard of living is too obvious to warrant mention, but that small business is equally essential, we have endeavored to make similarly obvious.

There is considerable evidence that new businesses established in recent years are sturdier than were some of their predecessors. In the first quarter of 1960 it was noted that three per cent fewer businesses were being forced to discontinue than in the same period of 1959. And in 1959, business mortalities were 11 per cent lower than in 1958. These figures are interesting and significant, although the periods noted were of short duration.[17]

We can safely estimate, guided by the following statistics, that there will be 5 million businesses in the United States by 1965. There has been an increase of roughly 100,000 per year: 4,232,300 in 1955,[18] 4,301,000 in 1956, 4,375,-000 in 1957, 4,450,000 in 1958, 4,600,000 in 1959, and an estimated 4,700,000 in early 1960.[19] Any serious recessive activity or other untoward economic upheaval would, of course, alter these predictions.

The problems of small business are those of all business. This summary, as published in a popular booklet on small business, may serve to review certain items in this opening chapter and to point the way to further discussions in the text.

---

[17] From an article by J. A. Livingston, Financial Editor, *Philadelphia Bulletin* (published in the *Cleveland Plain Dealer*, April 3, 1960), p. 17B.

[18] *Statistical Abstract of the United States, op. cit.*, p. 482.

[19] J. A. Livingston, *loc. cit.*

SUMMARY

1. The American economy is composed primarily of small business firms. There is no valid basis for belief that large business threatens the survival of small business.

2. The small business has a definite place and function in our economy. It is largely complementary to so-called large business, and for the most part operates hand in hand with it as an essential part of our economic system.

3. The primary problems facing small business are the lack of adequate management and the high levels of taxation which hinder the accumulation of capital. In many respects these are problems of all business.

4. While the problem of obtaining financing is a problem of small business, it is not a problem that is peculiar to small business. Sources of credit, although inadequate in some cases, are probably more numerous and liberal today than at any previous time.

5. Although raising capital is a problem that confronts all business, a small growing business may have its growth seriously impaired by the reduced opportunity to plough back earnings.

6. High progressive taxation retards capital accumulation and growth of small business, syphoning off earnings as well as reducing the sources from which equity financing is available.

7. Further revision of tax laws to facilitate continued and controlled ownership in a successful business would help bring about a more liberal supply of capital and credit available to small business.

8. Since one of the primary problems of small business is inadequate management skill, methods for improving managerial know-how are fundamental in any constructive effort to aid small business.

9. Increased management counseling by business associations, lending institutions and other qualified organizations, and better management training by schools and universities will help materially in solving the problems of small business.

10. Better understanding of the functions and problems of all business—large and small—will contribute to the development of sound policies that are essential to the welfare and continued progress of the American economy.[20]

QUESTIONS AND PROBLEMS

1. Why is the beginning small enterprise likely to be of greater interest to us than the typically established small business?

2. In the past nearly all businesses in all fields had small-scale origins. Is there reason to believe that in the future a greater proportion of new firms will be launched as very large corporations? Discuss.

3. Evaluate the discussion in this chapter that big business in America created its own market for employees.

4. Justify the claim made in this chapter that small independent enterprises are more important now than at any time in our history.

5. Explain the relationships that exist between the standard of living in a country and the proportion of its agricultural to total production.

---

[20] *Small Business, Its Role and Its Problems, op. cit.,* p. 36.

6. Why is the percentage of the total gainfully employed who are engaged in marketing and the services an excellent index to the standard of living in a country?

7. Summarize the reasons given in the chapter for the revived interest in small business, then suggest and justify additional reasons.

8. In your opinion, are there valid reasons for the government to assist small business and attempt to regulate and control certain activities of big business? Explain.

9. Since competition among big businesses in America is so keen, how can you justify the need for small enterprises to maintain our type of dynamic free enterprise?

10. How do you account for the general tendency for innovations to be met by opposition or ridicule, even by otherwise well-informed people? Has this tendency virtually disappeared in recent years?

11. Distinguish carefully between innovations likely to come from large laboratories and those from individuals or small enterprisers at the present time.

12. Should many college women who plan on successful marriages prepare for small business owner-management?

13. How has small business made it possible for big business to achieve such a high degree of efficiency?

14. What industries composed of small units today are most likely to be big business within the next few decades? Why do you think so?

15. How does small business compensate for inherent limitations of big business?

16. Select some product turned out by one of our mass production industries, and determine the parts that are or could be made by independent firms for several different mass production companies.

2 • Characteristics and Problems of Small Business

Small business is ubiquitous—even in fields dominated by a few giant corporations—and you will find it in highly industrialized countries as well as in those that are less developed. The field is enormous. Just as the application of basic principles to, and the needs and problems of, small business differ from those of big business, so variations exist within the different segments of small enterprise, and between new and well-established firms in the same field. Some additional variations are found for self-employed professional practitioners.

TYPES OF SMALL BUSINESS

Small independent enterprises may be divided into seven major classes, on the basis of *reasons* for their small size, as follows:

1. Newly organized business to be expanded
   (a) in an established field
   (b) pioneering a new product or service.
2. Newly acquired business to be expanded
   (a) nonfamily
   (b) family enterprise.
3. Professional practice
   (a) beginning
   (b) well established but limited in size by standards in the profession.
4. Limited market.
5. Size relative to giants in the industry—chiefly important for political consideration, defense contracts, fair competition, etc.
6. Size limited by
   (a) needs and resources, technical or managerial ability, available

capital of owner-operators—retired persons, widows, "papa, and mama," personal satisfaction or "own boss" types

(b) choice or preference.

7. Side-line ventures with various goals and objectives.

CHARACTERISTICS OF SMALL ENTERPRISE

The characteristics discussed here are merely a few that appear to be distinctive of all small undertakings.

1. *Independence.* By accepted definitions, independence, or no outside control, is a feature of all small business. It leads to many problems when carried to excess, but it is also a highly valued, desirable attribute. It needs qualification in some cases because many small ventures are not entirely independent of some control by supporting family members or close associates, and at times by outside creditors.

2. *Enterprise.* Every type of self-employment demonstrates some degree of enterprise, risk-taking, adventuring, or pioneering, even though it may be forced in some cases because of the absence of acceptable alternatives. For example, during hard times a large company might cut salaries drastically. Two employees in such a situation may react entirely differently. One lacks enterprise and accepts the salary reduction meekly; the other resigns and launches out on his own even though he would have preferred to remain employed, and may later return to dependent employment when salaries return to near their former level. Our primary concern is with small business where enterprise appears in a more positive or voluntary form, such as a desire to put one's own ideas and abilities to effective use.

3. *Personal factors.* In many small concerns personal factors, usually non-financial, dominate the impersonal profit-seeking motives. Home-town or family ties may often be the primary consideration in deciding among alternatives; in other cases the owner-manager's age, health or desire to be free of additional responsibilities so he can enjoy his family, hobbies or more recreation, may outweigh prospects for greater profits. In still other situations an intense urge to prove that a new product or idea has great future possibilities may overshadow all thought of immediate gain. Some important consumer goods of today owe their existence to this early zeal of their originators. Even for the less idealistic cases, the importance of the personal factors should not be depreciated.

PLACE OF SMALL BUSINESS

In general, the small enterprise has inherent advantages, or is otherwise the more appropriate, under such conditions as the following:

1. For new ventures, because: (a) the soundness of the idea and the ability

of the management require proof before much capital is invested; (b) efficient machinery and a body of technology must be developed before great volume of operations is feasible; and (c) probably 99 per cent of all new enterprises would never be launched if more than the limited resources available to almost all new entrepreneurs were required.

2. Where a high degree of flexibility is required because of: (a) frequent demand changes; (b) demand for small quantities in a wide variety of styles; and (c) rapidly developing techniques of production.

3. Where manual labor and personal attention to details by the owner-manager are of dominant importance. This criterion embraces the professional fields and most semi- and nonprofessional services, such as interior decorating, durable goods repairing, and all personal services such as beauty and barber shops.

4. Where demand is definitely local because of the nature of the product, such as residential real estate, or because of high transportation charges, such as for concrete blocks.

5. Where both raw materials and finished products are perishable, such as cut flowers and most dairy products.

6. Where the market is very limited, as for neighborhood grocery stores, drugstores, and extremely specialized services, such as custom tailoring.

7. In many cases where personal, in contrast to financial, considerations are of dominant importance. This category includes a broad area—"dyed-in-the-wool" hometowners, older people who desire a comfortable income for their remaining years and nothing else, young college graduates who prefer to be their own boss at all costs, and numerous others. It is the most confusing segment of small business for the average business-school student to comprehend and appreciate. The best explanation in this case is that man does not live by bread alone.

For measuring the extent of economic concentration and trends toward or away from monopoly, numerical criteria of relative size are essential. They should not, however, be used alone. Fairly representative of American industrial history is the obscure pioneer (Hall, in aluminum, for example) who "discovers" something almost universally available to all other less enterprising people. The discovery results in a new "industry" that at first may have a monopoly in its field. Decades later others enter the field and the concentration ratio begins to decline. Eventually monopolistic competition, or rivalry among several large corporations, is representative of the field. Most of our new industries—aluminum, electric light and power, automobiles, radio, and others have demonstrated this pattern.

Our concern is primarily with small or independent enterprises that have good profit potentials, rather than with those with limited prospects or the so-called "thousand businesses that can be started with less than a thousand dollars."

PROBLEMS OF SMALL BUSINESS

Small business has its problems, just as does big business, but small business is no more a "bundle of problems" exclusively than is any other type of human activity. Our interest in the problem approach is mainly threefold: (1) to caution prospective entrants into the fields; (2) to seek a classification of these problems that will be of practical use to prospective small businessmen; and (3) to suggest certain areas where remedies in the form of public action may be needed.

No doubt some of the problems of small business are purely relative. This makes it difficult to generalize, especially since our definitions are rather arbitrary and loose. For this reason it will be necessary to visualize a typical small business—one representative of its class. It seems desirable to attempt a classification of the problems if our threefold purpose is to be effected. The following two-way division appears to meet this need: (1) problems characteristic of most small businesses because of the type of individuals who frequently enter these fields; (2) problems resulting from conditions at any period of time, such as laws unfavorable to the little fellow, discriminatory financial policies, and unfair competition that could be remedied to lessen the burden on small business.

Problems Due to Smallness and Limited Resources

In small business the man *is* the business. The typical small businessman lacks the broad, well-rounded experience desirable in modern business. In most cases the business is started by a man experienced in one function, usually either production or selling, and he is likely to slight the other function, as well as accounting, personnel, policy formation, and similar activities. As long as nearly all of these functions are activities in already highly developed fields of individual concentration and specialization, it is obviously impossible for one or two men to be experts in all of them. Nor can they afford to hire a specialist for each function.

Retailers in small towns often fail to appreciate the need to keep up to date, and many are less well informed about new merchandise and materials than are their customers. The radio and national magazines keep customers alert to new developments and create new wants which, if not satisfied by their home-town merchants, are taken care of by mail order or out-of-town shopping trips.

In many cases it takes competition from outside to jar the local merchants out of their lethargy. Retail history is replete with examples of how innovators forced this change. Less familiar are examples such as the following, encountered by the authors early in 1954. An independent merchant in the Southwest opened a branch store, 30 miles from where he lived, in a town of 3,000 population. Although opened in an old building, the new store had a modern all-glass front, color, air conditioning, and other similar features of modern stores. Within six months five other stores modernized and seven installed air conditioning—the first changes made in the business district by local merchants since before Wold War I. All merchants who modernized are well pleased with the results, and two who failed to do so went out of business within less than a year after the new pacesetter opened for business.

Selection of the best location, determination of initial capital requirements, and even the wise choice of an appropriate kind of business to enter are difficult for persons lacking adequate training and balanced experience. Personal preferences, likes and dislikes, influences of family members or close friends, and limited perspective often lead to unwise business ventures. If outside capital is required even for a sound undertaking, it is difficult for such enterprisers to present a convincing case to possible lenders. If the basis of their project is something new, no matter how sound it may be, the idea is hard to sell for one lacking training and experience in marketing. Former salesmen may encounter unexpected difficulties in production and other functions. And in all cases where an employee shifts to self-employment without a balanced background, the big surprise is likely to come in achieving self-discipline, time management, and similar directions formerly provided by his employer.

Before an enterprise is launched with reasonable prospects for success, a genuine business opportunity must be discovered and its possibilities appraised. This is not easy for a person lacking imagination and training. Most people think of opportunities only as other concerns similar to ones already in operation, and would have difficulty even in determining whether another similar unit could be justified. Two true stories will illustrate these points. A man wanted to enter business in a town of 30,000 population, to have his firm making a moderate profit quickly, and to keep his investment modest. A small furniture and home furnishings store was for sale at an attractive price, but the town had more than its normal quota of such stores as well as two other more expensive establishments. Personal investigation showed, however, that all stores that would be his likely competitors were following traditional practices and policies. He purchased the store and opened with two ideas different from those of his competitors—quick turnover at reasonably low prices, and treating every person who entered the store as a most welcome guest. Neither idea was new, but so far the store has been successful in achieving all of its new owner's objectives.

About the same time our furniture store owner started, the president of a bank in the same town, in talking with one of the authors, expressed a desire to help finance justifiable small enterprises but asked, "What opening is there for another business in town? Every field is well taken care of." There was no doubt about his sincerity; he is reliably reported to have helped finance many small ventures from his own funds for a total of close to a quarter-million dollars. The next day the same question was put to students in the author's small business class. Within 15 minutes we had seven concrete suggestions for new businesses, only one of which was currently operating in that town although several had proved successful elsewhere. The one mentioned had been launched a few months earlier by a member of the class and was currently operating successfully and expanding rapidly. Our furniture store owner is a college graduate who belongs to the new school of creative imagination in business. The bank president is not a graduate, although he is a successful member of the old school of business enterprise.

Capital, even when accompanied by a desire to be one's own boss or to help prospective enterprisers, is not enough today. Imagination plus managerial ability in all its aspects is far more important, as illustrated by the two case histories just described. Much broader experience proves this point. The American Research and Development Company, an organization formed to render financial and managerial aid to *new* ventures, reports no case of lack of venture capital, but great difficulty in locating justifiable ideas and competent operating management for ventures it would like to finance.[1] A more controversial example of problems encountered by small businessmen of the old school is the plight of most retail stores, many hotels, and other formerly prosperous businesses in the small towns of the country. There is no doubt that lack of progressiveness and good management on the part of most small town merchants provided the opportunity for the mail-order houses and many chain stores to get their start. Decades later when good roads, automobiles and busses made it easy for small-town residents and farmers to shop in the larger towns and cities, most small-town merchants were unable to stop this trend. In a few cases where new and well-trained managers took over the old stores and modernized them in all respects they *have* been quite successful. Usually such cases have occurred where other conditions have also been favorable, which reflects the good judgment of the new management in selecting these locations. On the one hand the continuous decline in economic importance of rural areas and movement to the cities has lessened the importance of small towns; on the other hand the trek to the suburbs and industrial decentralization have increased the importance of small towns.

It has often been said that the chief problem of the independent businessman is his independence. Small business ownership does attract an independent, self-reliant type of person—one less likely to seek advice and assistance from those of greater experience and know-how. Often the biggest problem is to get the independent to appreciate his need for outside assistance, and then to be willing and able to take the time to profit by it. The Honorable William C. Foster, who was Undersecretary of Commerce at the time, stressed this point in suggesting ways colleges of business could assist the small business population.[2] Years of experience with the Distributive Education Program by

---

[1] George Howard Allen, ed., *Individual Initiative in Business,* "How to Initiate a New Business" (Cambridge, Mass.: Harvard University Press, 1950), pp. 155-180.

[2] William C. Foster, "What Government and Colleges Can Do for Small Business," an

the authors lend further support to this problem. It is always the small distributors, who need the free training, that are the hardest to reach.

Fear of losing control over their enterprises causes many small businessmen to resort to short-term borrowing when their real need is for permanent capital. This is because they fail to realize that majority stock ownership of a corporation, or contractual arrangements with a silent partner, leaves the owner in control just as effectively as if he provided all the capital from his own resources. Actually risk of losing control may be greater when reliance is placed on short-term borrowing.

Prosperous times, such as those following the recent World Wars, attract many entrants into the fields of small business who misinterpret the easy going as a sign of success. Many do not know the price trends and are unable to make accurate forecasts. When the inevitable readjustment comes, the casualties are heavy. Even their few years of experience are of little help because they do not equip them for operations when the going gets tough. Further aggravating the problem is the fact that many have paid inflated prices for goodwill, leaseholds, fixtures, and merchandise.

Emotional decisions to become one's own boss also occur more frequently during prosperous times. An employee with some savings becomes angry at his boss and decides to become independent. The first vacant building looks like his opportunity, and he learns only too late that it is easy to enter small business but difficult to get out without a loss of some sort.

A condition existing in many large cities, often referred to as the "business opportunities racket," helps to increase the number of small business disasters. This "racket" is mainly the practice of selling unprofitable businesses to unwary, new enterprisers instead of permitting such firms to go out of existence. Especially in the retail field, a single business unit often wrecks a dozen or more owners through successive sale and resale to a steady stream of newcomers, each confident that he can succeed where others have failed. Naturally, the brokers who promote these sales make more commissions the more frequently the business unit changes hands. Sometimes they are not too careful to disclose all the facts or to inform each new gullible loser as to how many of his predecessors have failed. While there are several reliable business brokers in the country, we have as yet no system for securing unbiased ratings, and the prospective entrepreneur needs plenty of training and ability to keep out of the group of "suckers" immortalized by the late P. T. Barnum.

Two major reasons have prompted many unqualified persons to undertake business ownership overhastily: a sudden desire for independence, and the appearance of an unexpected business opportunity that must be taken advantage of at once or lost. The usual result in either case is for the would-be businessman to realize too late the amount of managerial ability required for success.

Often problems related to incompetence can be traced to the fact that small

address delivered at the 29th annual meeting of the American Association of Collegiate Schools of Business, St. Louis, May 16, 1947. Reproduced as a mimeographed News Release.

business ownership for many is an unplanned occurrence. In other words, these individuals are in business as a result of inheriting a going concern, because of some event that left them with a business to salvage, or owing to the necessity of making a living to support the family when an attractive job was not to be had.

The inheritance of a business does not necessarily mean poor management, as illustrated in the following example. A survey of small business owners conducted by the authors disclosed the fact that four had taken over a family enterprise. In each case the individual had grown up with the business. One had worked in the family enterprise for several years before recognizing his need for college training. All four planned their college courses to be of greatest benefit to them later as managers of their particular businesses. In one additional case a former student married into a business partnership, and he reports his college training as invaluable. Several cases not included in the survey, known personally to one of the authors, include: (1) former students who majored in marketing so as to be better prepared to take over a family business, which they have since been operating successfully for from five to ten years; and (2) a few recent cases where students purchased a business with parental assistance while still in college and then planned the balance of their courses with this owner-manager objective as a goal. (The incentive of ownership has resulted in a noticeable increase in students' interest in courses relating directly to their future business.)

The smaller the business, the greater the tendency to rely upon the owner's knowledge, experience, and limited resources. With increased size comes a recognition of the value of seeking advice and co-operative assistance from others.

Small business is likely to be the victim of schemes or hoaxes more frequently than is big business. Many rackets seem to thrive on the inexperience and gullibility of small businessmen, especially newcomers in the field. Veterans intent on owning their own business were victimized so frequently that the Better Business Bureau published booklets warning them of the more common schemes and rackets.[3]

To compensate for the natural tendency toward overemphasis on self-reliance by the small businessman, the following suggestions deserve consideration.

1. No one can be expected to know all things about buying a business. Therefore it is well to hire a competent lawyer, or to discuss your problem with the local bank or other "knowing" individuals or concerns to help determine the true value of the property you are about to purchase.

2. If you know that some day you will inherit a going business, begin now to learn the business by actual work in the establishment and by supplementary training related to that business.

3. Make a *habit* of seeking advice and discussing your ideas with others.

[3] *Facts You Should Know About Schemes,* a booklet (Boston: Educational Division, The Better Business Bureau, 1939, rev. 1946).

4. Practice organizing your work (job, studies, and so forth) so as to have "free" time for self-improvement activities and participation in community projects.

5. Talk with successful alumni enterprisers and seek their advice, or study results of alumni surveys reported by the authors and others.

6. Emphasize such courses as accounting, taxation, business law, English, business communication, typing, salesmanship, basic marketing, retailing, consumer problems, and—if available—courses in small business or the independent enterpriser.[4]

7. Enroll in courses where practical case problems on the local-independent-enterpriser level are discussed. Participate actively in the discussion. Earnestly seek to learn the techniques of problem solving, of exercising your imagination, of *profiting from the experience and ideas of others,* and learn all you can about the important sources of information and the kind of data each provides, for later use when and as you need it. The appendices included in this text contain a wealth of such material and should be used as a continuous source of reference for many years.

Since the war, considerable attention has been given to the need for management aids and practical current information for the small enterpriser *who will take advantage of such assistance.* Those of major value will be discussed in later chapters.

Problems Due to Existing Conditions

Changing conditions are accompanied by legislation, variations in taxation, unusual economic conditions, and many other developments that often impinge more heavily on small business. It is primarily those amenable to change that we are interested in here.

Concentration of economic power has many facets. As noted earlier, it has been declining for several decades in some long-established industries such as steel, primary aluminum, and the manufacture of electric light bulbs and similar products. In newer industries, pioneered by small enterprisers, concentration naturally increases as the more successful competitors expand, technology develops rapidly, capital investment increases, and the less-successful and less-progressive competitors fall by the wayside. This happened during the early days of automobile production and somewhat later in radio and other industries—fields generally conceded to have been highly competitive. Several dynamic decades usually result in these "new" industries moving into the area characterized as big business. A few very large firms account for the major proportion of total output, but each big company has hundreds of small suppliers and thousands of small distributors. At some stage near the transi-

[4] Courses listed in 6 and the suggestions offered in 7 are mainly those recommended by alumni enterprisers for *emphasis* in preparation for entrepreneurship. It is understood that cultural courses should not be slighted. Nonbusiness students would naturally take most of their work outside the business school, and students in accredited business schools are required to take 40 per cent of their hours in nonbusiness subjects.

tion from small to large size no doubt some firms have "squeezed" smaller or weaker competitors, as our history of antitrust and unfair competition cases indicates. Also, as discussed later, some large corporations have at times abused their powerful positions, resulting in certain legislation such as the Holding Company Act, Securities and Exchange Act, and Robinson-Patman Act. That such practices have been increasingly widespread during recent decades as a planned effort of big business to eliminate small competition cannot be supported by the facts. The opposite has been more nearly true, largely because of the vigilance of the Federal Trade Commission and organizations of smaller businessmen. That concentration of economic power has been significant and of general public concern is well known and was mentioned earlier as one reason for the recent expansion of interest in small business. There have been mergers, absorptions, abuses of patent rights, and expansion of large companies through branches entering into direct competition with small business. In general, however, small and very large business are not in many fields in direct competition. There are five important exceptions reflecting existing conditions: (1) banking, (2) patents, (3) employees, (4) vendor relationships, and (5) controlled shopping centers.

Banking. Probably the most significant and dramatic recent example of concentration of economic power eliminating small competitors has been in banking. This is especially serious because (1) banking holds a strategic position in our economy; (2) it has been a government sponsored program; (3) if continued, it will shift one more traditionally small-business field into the camp of exclusively big business—more amenable to government control; and (4) it is likely to lessen the ease with which numerous small enterprises have, in the past at least, been able to get a start. The core of this trend has been a decrease of 25 per cent in the number of unit banks during the 25 years up to 1953, when in nearly all other fields the number of establishments increased; and the dominant reason seems to have been the preference of state banking authorities for granting charters to large city banks to establish branches in preference to authorizing independent banks.[5] In many cases the smallest independent bank in a town has been "absorbed" by a larger local bank or become a branch of a big city bank.

Whether this trend is the result of permanent factors that make banking more desirable socially and economically when concentrated in a few large firms (as in automobile production), or the result of conditions during recent decades when government has distrusted private enterprise and sought increasing domination of it, could conceivably be debated.

Patent abuses. Small business problems related to patents also may reflect more basic factors in our highly technological economy, or conditions during a period when long-overdue revision and simplification of our patent system and procedures gain recognition. The interests of free enterprise, especially the

[5] *Bank Supervision,* Proceedings, Federal Reserve Relations Committee, Third Federal Reserve District, Philadelphia (April 25, 1952), p. 53.

creative small-business segment that has contributed so much to humanity, would be enhanced immeasurably if the patent system were simplified and modernized. In our highly complex, technological, free-enterprise economy, it is understandable that radically new inventions might be more difficult now than prior to our Industrial Revolution. Scientific and technical developments, however, might just as easily make even more unique ones possible. When an early patent, granted before later discoveries were made, covers a broad enough area to hamper some new ideas, or when patents on minor changes in the original basic patent idea are granted almost continuously, the situation approaches hopelessness for the young, imaginative, prospective enterpriser. Until some relief is obtained in this area both the public and many creative prospective enterprisers will continue to be deprived of favorable opportunity to progress. Our present patent system is one of the serious and, we hope, temporary problems of prospective beginning small businessmen.

At least three alternative solutions are available in many cases. One is to employ a patent attorney (possibly one recommended by the inventor's local attorney or some fellow inventor), secure the patent if possible, and go ahead with production and marketing hoping for the best. If capital and experience are limited, the inventor might do better to team up with an experienced and better-financed individual or group. The added protection might be worth the sacrifice of sharing future profits, at least for the first invention. A third alternative is to take up the proposition with some reliable organization such as the American Research and Development Company, or possibly the Gadget of the Month group, or some large corporation likely to be interested. The last proposal would be more logical if the invention consists of a product superior to one already produced by a large company, but serving the same purpose. Either this company or a likely but equally strong competitor could be consulted. If the invention represents a major improvement on an already patented article, but the existing patent prevents production of the new one without serious danger of infringement, there is no apparent alternative for the little fellow other than to sell out to the present patent holder—if he can. When an invention is discussed with other companies before a patent has been secured, or if patented, before production begins, the inventor's attorney should be able to advise on reasonable safeguards to be taken.

According to the late Professor Floyd L. Vaughan, well-known authority on patent history, an increasing number of patents have been assigned to big business by outsiders and employees in recent decades. The little man lacks the funds needed to carry his patent through to successful production and marketing. It is so much easier for him to sell to the big company for a few thousand dollars cash and a royalty on production. Employees often have no choice but to assign their patents since this has become part of many employment contracts.

Employee problems. During a tight labor market normal competition between big and little business for competent employees is intensified. This is especially true for college graduates and certain types of skilled workers. During World War II many small concerns were unable to obtain *any* employees. Their owners had to choose between closing up or operating on a restricted basis doing all of the work themselves. In postwar years a situation apparently new in our economy developed as a result of a combination of factors not likely to reappear very often. The strain on big business executives during the depression and war years was terrific, resulting in abnormal casualties of all types. Military demands during the early 1940's made it exceptionally difficult to groom younger men for executive replacements, and, apparently, many large companies had not planned far enough into the future to be ready, personnel-wise, for the postwar expansion. Another factor that further aggravated these conditions was the aging of the founder or initial management group in many medium-sized corporations. Organizations that were started during the beginning years of the century often found in postwar years that their top management was composed of men in their seventies or even older, with no qualified replacements having been trained. The Korean War made the situation even worse. One final development has been more important than is generally recognized—the increased number of college graduates who are determined to become independent enterprisers.

A major result of these combined shortages of qualified executive personnel, coming at a time of peak peacetime business activity, has been the greatest competition between big and little business for future executive material the country has so far experienced.[6] College recruiting has been stepped up, executive training programs streamlined, almost fabulous beginning salaries plus numerous fringe benefits offered, new inducements devised such as postgraduate training at company expense, and extensive advertising used in leading magazines and college papers. The competition seemingly has been too great for the small employer to meet, although most have never been sufficiently aggressive in their recruiting activities. It has, however, had little effect upon the determination of many graduates to become self-employed, other than causing some to defer launching their own enterprise for a few years. This interval is expected to furnish an opportunity to obtain experience and some additional capital, but in particular to result in launching their own venture at a time when qualified employees should be more abundant on reasonably competitive terms.

Established small businessmen during postwar years have frequently mentioned the near impossibility of securing satisfactory employees as one of their major problems, often equal in importance to heavy taxation and government regulation. With business conditions unusually favorable for the little concern, the employee problem goes deeper than an alleged inability to pay the high wages of big employers. Certainly the relative wage-paying ability did not decline for the small independent as compared to prewar years. Three condi-

---

[6] "The Great Man Hunt—Industry Needs More Good Executives," *Time* (October 12, 1953), p. 98.

tions appear to have been primarily responsible: (1) the general decline by most employees in a willingness to do a fair day's work when jobs are plentiful; (2) big business attracting the more energetic and ambitious employees; and (3) others willing and able to work hard choosing self-employment. Solutions for this problem of the independent enterpriser will be considered later, especially in Chapters 9-11 and 16.

No doubt the most serious problems of a small enterprise, which most businessmen hope are due to temporary conditions, are those of greatly increased government regulation and taxation.

Certainly small retailers, caught in the maze of complex, confusing, often contradictory and unintelligible regulations during price control and rationing, were the innocent victims of such conditions.

Many other types of government regulations are intended to be permanent, although they had their origin during the 20 years following 1933 when the general attitude of government seems to have been anti-business and pro-labor, pro-farmer, and pro-other specially privileged groups. Both direct government regulations imposed on business and the indirect results of special concessions to labor and similarly privileged groups have added to the already ample problems of operating a small enterprise successfully. Some of these are wage and hour laws that blanket supervisory and technical personnel; numerous records and reports required solely to serve as possible proof of violation of some probably obscure legal provision; social security records, reports, tax deductions, and payments to the government; sales tax collection, recording, reporting, and payment; abiding by agreements made by labor unions with big business on an industry-wide basis; incurring potential liability for some wage-hour law infraction incurred years before a small firm had been purchased, and so on.

Vendor Relationships. During the 1950's, considerable attention was directed to "the right to buy." [7] This is a modern version of the original monopoly of supply—with some differences. Earlier supply monopolists emphasized high prices and buyer discrimination or even favoritism. The recent problem has focused on refusal by primary producers to sell to certain potential buyers, especially fabricators and independent contractors. It is often associated with vertical integration where the primary producer owns or controls fabricating plants or particular distribution channels or outlets. Thus it is within the law that recognizes a vendor's right to select his vendees, and avoids prohibitions of the Robinson-Patman Act against price discrimination among buyers. However, even when the product is one enjoying patent monopoly privileges, there are valid questions regarding the desirability of excluding able and willing buyers from participation in efforts to bring the benefits to consumers. When an integrated producer sells to independents as long as they do not compete

---

[7] *The Right to Buy — and Its Denial to Small Business,* Document No. 32 by the Select Committee on Small Business, United States Senate, 85th Congress, 1st Session (Washington, G.P.O., 1957).

with his own outlets but cuts off their supply when they do, or during periods of supply shortage, the practice is open to serious question and public concern.

Another aspect of this problem is that of producers imposing undue burdens on their dealer outlets—often shifting the results of erroneous producer forecasts to the shoulders of dealers. This problem became so acute among automobile dealers during the late 1950's that they were able to secure some relief through Federal action.

Controlled Shopping Centers. Controlled shopping centers are a recent development. One organization owns and controls the center with its parking facilities and other services and screens tenants to be admitted or granted leases. Controlled centers are of the community or regional type, in contrast to both downtown and neighborhood retail districts. They are larger than earlier shopping centers or retail districts where land ownership tended to be multiple, with each landowner selecting his own tenants. Thus controlled centers require a large capital investment of the type desired by the big insurance companies. Aside from stringent government regulation, insurance companies usually seek long-time investments in enterprises of *proved* financial stability. Other agencies responsible for the prudent use of public funds, such as the Small Business Administration, also do so.

A serious problem for the local independent—principally the retailer—arises from these conditions. For example, the fourth annual survey by the *American Druggist* shows that the majority of shopping center drugstores are located in the community type of center having less than 15 stores.[8] Logically, financial backers have valid reasons for insisting upon "big name" tenants, strongly intrenched financially, before they will finance these new controlled shopping centers. Just as logically, the Federal government could earlier award its production contracts solely to a few giant corporations. Subcontracting helped in this case, as did the commendable programs of the Small Business Administration in reserving certain contracts for small businesses and in devising ways for small enterprises to pool their facilities. Now ways should be found to meet the valid needs of controlled shopping center promoters and financiers that also permit qualified independents to participate in this recent development.

Taxation

Many small employers have complained that high postwar taxes prevented their paying adequate salaries and wages. Since the 1930's, taxes, especially *the Federal income tax, have kept small business small.* Excessive taxation and government regulation of the type developed from 1933 to 1953 are considered a threat to all free enterprise and impose unreasonable burdens on the new small concerns. High personal income taxes during periods of inflation and business uncertainty made it doubly hard for prospective and incumbent small businessmen to acquire initial capital and funds for expansion once an

[8] "Shopping Center Druggists Now Total 3,270 . . . Up 37%," *American Druggist* (August 24, 1959), pp. 5-7.

enterprise was in operation. On the average, the initial capital required to start a small concern doubled from prewar to early postwar years. The cost of living also nearly doubled. Although wages and salaries increased slightly more, personal income taxes rose very much more. The results were that employees found it unreasonably difficult to save their initial equity capital in the traditional American manner; potential private investors were unwilling to furnish funds on an "all risk and no gain" basis—taking all the usual risks of financing a new enterprise but paying practically all of any possible gains to the government in taxes. For example, a 10 per cent return on $25,000 invested by a single person would leave after taxes only 2.5 per cent for the individual with a $50,000 income, or only 3.5 per cent with an income of $25,000.[9] All losses had to be absorbed by the investor; so many played safe by putting their funds into tax-exempt government securities. Rigid government regulation of banks has removed this traditional source of funds from practical consideration.

Since the vast majority, probably well over 98 per cent, of all new enterprises are not incorporated at first, their owner-managers suffer the handicaps just mentioned for individuals attempting to build up capital for expansion. Even those started as small corporations have had heavy tax burdens and such uneconomic legislation as the excess profits tax to contend with. Even after paying high Federal income taxes, the corporation risked a tax penalty of 27.5 to 38.5 per cent if it failed to pay out as dividends a large portion of its profit after taxes. What the government agents consider a reasonable amount to retain in the business without penalty is usually thought by the management to be inadequate. Certainly management, not the government, should be the one to decide on this amount. An "accumulated earnings credit" or amount retained for reasonable needs of the business may be excluded from the taxable base for that year. In 1958 this amount was raised from $60,000 to $100,000.

Dividends are again subject to the individual income tax or the double taxation so often criticized. Fortunately the government attitude begun in 1953 is more favorable toward business, and many of the tax handicaps mentioned have already been removed or lessened.

Problems Due to Size of Small Business

In this section two factors influence much of our discussion. First, "small" is a relative concept. Second, many of the problems exist because the size of firm under consideration is small relative to something of significance to it, such as competition, and so on. Reference to our seven types of small enterprises discussed earlier in the chapter should make these points clear.

A major problem characteristic of small business is the importance of *time* to the owner-manager. With so many essential duties to perform, or to supervise, and only the same amount of time available as is used by each of a

[9] *Small Business, Its Role and Its Problems* (Washington, D. C.: Chamber of Commerce of the United States, 1953), p. 26. Reprinted from the Patman Hearings.

number of persons in big business, the number of hours in a day is usually the most serious problem of the typical small businessman.

The great demands made on the owner-manager lead to the problem of lack of free time, once the business is in operation, in which to study and improve his business methods through self-development. If he does take the time after attending to all essential business duties, he is likely to be so tired and worried as to experience difficulty in learning effectively. The solution, at least for the prospective small businessman, is adequate preparation in advance.

Closely related are the limited opportunities to specialize management, to subdivide work for specialization of labor, and to make effective use of efficient machinery and modern technology. A shortage of capable management personnel permeates most small enterprises. Although good management is not a defect inherent in the small enterprise, it is difficult to achieve. In the beginning of a very small concern one man is likely to bear all managerial responsibility without an understudy or assistant manager. With increased size, some opportunity appears to share responsibility and to specialize the management functions, provided a willingness to do so exists, and the company is able to attract qualified personnel. Modern methods for achieving these objectives are explained in detail later. Managerial ability is a rare quality commanding a high price that in turn requires a large income-earning base or unusually good prospects for advancement.

Unless modern methods are used it is difficult for the small enterprise to solve these problems. First, the entrepreneur must recognize the need to delegate authority and share responsibility. Then, advantage should be taken of all timesavers: policies, organization, supervision, standard procedures, simple methods of reporting only essentials and consulting top management only on unusual points—in general, application of the *exception principle of management*. Advance planning and preparation, with adequate reminders and follow-up, are modern methods that can be applied simply even in the one-man business.

Opportunities for the most efficient use of labor subdivision and machinery tend to vary directly with the size of the establishment. Modern methods of management in the small firm have been developed, however, that overcome many disadvantages. The major problem lies with management that is unable or unwilling to learn and apply new techniques. Methods analysis, work organization and scheduling so as to take maximum advantage of the basic principles of specialization can be applied to the smallest enterprise. But planning and system are required. Small jobs can often be accumulated and done in larger batches. Even the railroads use this system when they delay l.c.l. shipments until a carload is accumulated. Automobile manufacturers run all of one variety through before shifting to another. Department stores do not send their trucks out to deliver each sale as it is made but carefully route and schedule deliveries. In the small concern with ten employees and 40 tasks it is often possible to have each employee specialize on four duties and shift time and operations to secure a major portion of the advantages of labor subdivision. In the use of machinery the small firm is less able to use highly efficient single-purpose machines, which may be as much of an advantage as a disadvantage under capable management. Greater flexibility and more efficient use of capital investment are advantages, provided the machines are carefully selected and used most effectively.

Technology, know-how, or science applied to industry and business may be more highly or more rapidly developed in big organizations, but the little fellow can profit by any progress. Only certain very restricted phases of technology are appropriate exclusively to the giant enterprise. The first atomic drugstore, described in Chapter 1 of the second edition is a fine example of technology being pioneered by small independent enterprisers. In most cases the basic problem is, again, the attitude and training of the small business owner-manager. College of business students contemplating self-employment are exposed to the same technical training received by future executives of big business. Those who have imagination and initiative and an opportunity to take small business or independent enterpriser courses have no reason to be at a disadvantage when they become entrepreneurs. It is the man rather than the size of the establishment that makes technology a problem in some cases but not in others.

Lack of research facilities and access to sources of information on new products, materials, and methods is associated with the independent nature and unorganized status of most fields of small business. To inventory research and facilities available to small business and to inform small businessmen of these aids was the purpose of the White House Conference held in September 1958, and discussed in Chapter 10.

Market analysts and industrial engineers are too expensive for the very small operators. One proposal to aid small establishments of this type is to subsidize technical specialist services through public funds, which is now being done through the SBA field offices.

Postwar developments indicate that private enterprise may be able to meet the research needs of small business, with government functioning only to provide basic factual information such as census data. In the early 1950's, Sinclair, and probably other large corporations, were advertising the availability of their extensive research facilities for the individual or small enterpriser with an idea to be developed. American Research and Development Corporation and other private organizations have assisted many innovators in developing their "brain children" to commercial status. In Chapter 10 the outside staff services available to the small enterpriser are explained. Many of these include aid in research.

In many fields big business concentrates on products with a steady or predictable demand, leaving to the small operator the slower sellers and more risky items. This makes effective use of advertising harder for the little fellow, but appropriate methods for meeting this problem are covered in later chapters. For many small concerns it also raises the problem of obtaining adequate volume to justify the business. The question of inadequate sales ranks high as a cause of discontinuance among many small firms, but this is likely to be misleading. The beginning enterprise pioneering a new idea naturally does not have a product or service of proven demand; neither would big business if other small firms had not done the pioneering. Building adequate sales for something new is so universally underestimated, in terms of the time and expense required, that frequently several pioneers go bankrupt in the process before one finally succeeds. Thus this problem distills to lack of knowledge by the beginner and its companion, inadequate finances. Big business, though possessing both of these features, conservatively holds back until small independent enterprise has developed a proven market for the innovation.

At the other extreme is the marginal small firm, or "papa and mama" retail store. Inadequate sales to support a typical family may mean a decent living to many self-respecting people who would otherwise be forced on relief because of lack of employment opportunities.

The most serious matter of inadequate sales results from poor management, as do practically all the fundamental problems of small business. This is not a problem inherent in the small enterprise but in the enterpriser. Ample facilities are available today for any prospective small businessman to develop managerial ability, but none in this group takes advantage of them. As in most other fields, the greatest task is to get those most in need of help to accept it when offered.

One final problem in this area is the strong probability, almost a certainty, that the beginning independent will make one serious error in judgment during his first year, which usually leads to sales inadequate to meet expenses. A friend of one of the authors, after 25 years of successful experience as buyer and merchandise manager of several department stores in three states, decided to have a business of his own. He took two years to make the best market analysis and prospectus for his enterprise that has come to our attention. His family living expenses would not need to draw upon his business capital for the three years estimated to have his enterprise self-supporting. He waited nearly two years for the right location. He built up proper bank "connections." He erred in only one respect: he concentrated on the "in-between" markets of big business. However, a bad combination of unseasonable weather and advance buying would have put him into bankruptcy in nine months if his bank connections had been "typical." His most recent employer weathered the freak weather easily because of diversified markets and ample finances, but failure to recognize that *most beginners make one serious error during their first year* almost resulted in disaster.

Small business is weak in coping with vested interests or monopolistic practices, even though some of the latter may be illegal. Also, it is harder for the little fellow to deal satisfactorily with representatives of organized labor or even with his own local government. It is more difficult for the small businessman to secure the best brands and exclusive agencies. Selective selling policies of vendors plus the fact that established dealers often have already secured the favored lines make this a serious problem in starting a new retail store. A small firm may encounter greater problems than its big brother if it becomes involved in some controversy over its product. Also the little fellow often has trouble presenting a convincing case when seeking assistance from state agricultural and industrial commissions accustomed to dealing mainly with large industries.

Problems related to monopolistic practices have been the main reason for our early antitrust laws, and protection of the little fellow is still a major concern of government for maintaining fair competition. Better Business Bureaus will usually assist any firm in coping with unfair practices that may not be actually illegal. Probably in most cases the small independent having problems of this sort should discuss them first with his local Better Business Bureau. The latter will know what action to take.

Small business is more sensitive to economic fluctuations than big business. The primary reason is lack of liquid reserves. Often a firm is forced to cease operations just before changed conditions would have made the business profitable. However, firms launched shortly before the upturn of the business cycle may be the most favorably situated. Not only do they start at bargain prices for buildings, equipment, fixtures, materials, and supplies, but, with the right timing, a short period of loss will be quickly compensated for by one of increasing profits.

Small business is at a disadvantage in securing high quality employees. A well-managed small firm can often cope with this situation and even take advantage of it. This may be accomplished by "selling" desirable prospects on the advantages of employment experience in the small concern as preparation for entrepreneurship or for preferred executive employment in big business. In postwar years several large corporations in various fields both at home and abroad have established small subsidiaries for the primary purpose of testing and training future executives for the parent company.[10] Experience has taught them all too often that promising executive material becomes submerged in the complex specialized duties of the large concern. In the past big business has often employed men trained in small firms, and still does so. The well-managed independent affords an ideal opportunity for the ambitious man man or woman to learn all the functions of management and to develop managerial ability more rapidly than could be done in a large organization.

The beginning small enterprise is at a disadvantage in paying the high wages characteristic of most big business, and rarely can it guarantee employment like a few big corporations do. This problem has been met successfully by many small enterprisers through profit sharing, closer employee relations, and even partnership plans. While these techniques have little appeal to the

[10] Bill Davidson, "Are You The *New* Executive Type?", *Collier's* (February 5, 1954), pp. 58-61.

employee interested mainly in the highest possible immediate and certain wages, they do attract the more desirable men who want their incomes to be in proportion to their contributions and ability, and those anxious to become business owners. In other cases the small independent has obtained good employees by selecting the physically handicapped and older workers.[11] Both groups are not generally wanted by large firms, although recent experience indicates that in many ways they are superior to the typical employee of big business. For years the small-scale employer has been unable to compete with big business on many employee services and fringe benefits. In postwar years several agencies have developed plans suited to the needs of the small enterprise, such as group insurance, retirement benefits, hospital and medical care, recreational facilities, and others. Progress is being made.

Financing

For at least three decades adequate financing of small business has been losing ground as compared to big business. In at least three respects small business has a serious financial problem: (1) in securing long-term equity capital, in contrast to short-term working capital loans; (2) in obtaining greater protection from the calling of loans or stoppage of credit during trying times when outside financial aid is most direly needed; and (3) in securing funds in small amounts at lower rates.

It costs just about as much for a banker or other lender to investigate and evaluate a loan application for $1,000 as one for $1,000,000. The former may cost more because the applicant for the large loan is often more helpful in providing significant information. So long as the failure rate is higher for small than for big business, the risk of financing and the resulting costs will be higher, unless subsidized in some way or at least aided by some development not yet proved. One recent approach was authorized in the Small Business Investment Act of 1958 discussed in Chapter 11. Others involve proposals to change the Federal income tax regulations to encourage more equity financing.

A lender or investor insists on a much greater degree of control of the enterprise when financing a small business. This often hampers the management of the small firm and keeps many independents who are unwilling to share control from obtaining the finances they need. When accompanied by high taxes and the antibusiness philosophy so general up to 1953, it becomes a serious question for the little fellow.

Whether or not adequate facilities have been available for financing small business in recent decades is one of the most controversial topics. Numerous investigations seeking the facts have been conducted by government committees, the Federal Reserve Banks, and the Chamber of Commerce of the United States. Their results are not conclusive. In general, studies by bankers reach the conclusion that ample financing is available for all "creditworthy"

---

[11] William A. Ulman, "They May be Disabled—But Man! Can They Work!" *Saturday Evening Post* (October 20, 1951), pp. 20 ff.

enterprises. The creditworthiness is, of course, decided by the bankers, so this conclusion is understandable.

Bankers also call attention to relatively new devices, such as floor plan financing and installment loans to small concerns, as further evidence that the financial needs of small business are better provided for now than in former years. They claim that providing equity capital has never been a function of commercial banks, although in practice many banks in small communities did so until the practice was stopped by government regulation.

Several banks have been expanding their services to small business in recent years, however, indicating the existence of an unsatisfied want. The Commercial National Bank of Peoria, Illinois, has pioneered some of this work, and the Chase Manhattan of New York launched a nationwide program in co-operation with its correspondent banks to help finance small business ventures that individual local banks were unwilling or unable to handle alone. The Metropolitan Life Insurance Company has indicated a desire to enter the field of financing small enterprises but so far has had difficulty in securing the necessary amendments to the New York code regulating insurance company operations. After reviewing developments such as those just briefly mentioned, the Chamber of Commerce of the United States concluded that a gap does exist between the needs and facilities for financing small business.

Certain principles of insurance and basic concepts of free enterprise suggest that the solution to the problem should be found in private enterprise rather than in more government in business. Pooling and diversification of risks, taking advantage of the law of large numbers, and applications of principles from other fields indicate that small business could be financed on a national or regional basis with an actuarial precision approaching or equal to that of casualty, hospital and medical care, and similar forms of insurance. Despite considerable misleading publicity, the failure rate of American business concerns has been phenomenally low for well over 50 years—much lower in fact than that of almost any other type of human endeavor. Criteria for appraising the probable success of a new business are at least as reliable as those available for marriage, driving, employment, and similar ventures having a much higher mortality rate. Preparation for self-employment is also usually better than that for these other fields, and incentives to succeed are very strong. There seems to be no basic reason why standards of eligibility could not be established and procedures simplified so that the financing of small enterprises could be handled economically and efficiently. Financing the consumer-buyer on such a plan is already in operation in many cities and is expanding steadily, as explained in Chapter 23.

SANE VIEW OF SMALL BUSINESS HAZARDS

The anti-independent enterprise critics have been so vociferous for so long that a few cold, hard, factual comparisons are necessary at this point to orient students in the facts of life that will so vitally affect their entire future. Emphasis should now be placed upon each student: (1) comparing for himself the advantages and disadvantages of self-employment, (2) determining whether he is better suited to independent or dependent employment, (3) selecting the appropriate field in either case, (4) ascertaining the risks, problems and requirements for success in his chosen occupation, and (5) preparing adequately for success and happiness in a planned future career.

Various Human Failures

Success, failure, or merely average achievement in small business depends more upon the individual than upon anything else. Business failures are human failures, as are those in most other lines of activity.

Although divorce rates do not measure all failures in marriage any more than technically defined commercial failures measure lack of success in business, they furnish one objective criterion. Official data show that the divorce rate per 10,000 married males increased from 40 in 1900 to 104 in 1950 and averaged 96 for the 50 year period. Business failures declined during the same interval and averaged only 76. The postwar high failure rate in 1958 was only 56. Yet who would be foolish enough to advise young men against marriage because of the "high mortality" involved?

The failure to complete correspondence courses is notoriously high. Even resident college students fail to achieve many goals. When these data are computed on the same basis as the business failure rate of 76, we have the following:

> Failure to graduate from college—6,666
> Failure to complete courses started—714
> Failure to pass courses completed—650
> Failure in business—76.

Yet who would be so foolish to warn young people against enrolling in college because the "mortality is so high"?

The failure rate for small business is not higher but is actually lower than that for any comparable field of human endeavor—76 per 10,000 on the average for half a century and under 35 in most post-World War II years.

Dun & Bradstreet Reference Book

Business enterprises listed in the *Dun & Bradstreet Reference Book* include manufacturers, wholesalers, retailers, building contractors, and certain types of commercial service establishments including public utilities, water carriers, motor carriers, and airlines. This count by no means covers all the business enterprises of the country. Specific types of business not listed are financial enterprises including banks; mortgage, loan and investment companies; insurance and real estate companies; railroads; terminals; amusements; and many small one-man services. Neither the professions nor farmers are included.

New enterprises. A concern is listed in the *Reference Book* as a new enterprise when the first credit report on it is written. While a majority of the names thus added will be new concerns, it is possible for a period of time to elapse between the establishment of a business and the first request for a credit report.

A mere change in name with no accompanying change in internal organization is not included, nor is a move from one location to another within the same community. A removal to a new community causes a new listing, but such cases are relatively few.

Successions. A change in ownership or legal form of organization constitutes a "succession," that is, a business unit which continues its existence, although for credit purposes it is the discontinuance of an old concern and the establishment of a new one, since financial responsibility has changed and new credit relations have to be established.

Business failures. Business failures are concerns involved in court proceedings or voluntary actions which are likely to end in loss to creditors. These include discontinuances following assignment; voluntary or involuntary petition in bankruptcy, attachment, execution, foreclosure; voluntary withdrawals from business with known loss to creditors; firms involved in court action; and, since June 1934, reorganization or arrangement which may or may not lead to discontinuance, as well as businesses making voluntary compromises with creditors out of court.

Discontinued enterprises. Names removed from the *Reference Book* include most of the failures, all voluntary liquidations in which there is no indication of loss to creditors, and all changes in ownership and legal form of organization, plus moves to another community. Mere changes in name or trade style, or changes in location within the same community, are not included.

A change in ownership or legal form of organization is listed both as a discontinuance and new enterprise.

BUSINESS FAILURES

Table A-1 (appendix) shows the failure rates from 1900 to 1959, many of which have been used in earlier discussion in the chapter.

Table A-2 shows the high mortality of concerns during their early years. The vast majority of those that failed, as well as those that did not, were small concerns. As shown in this table, among concerns that failed during 1958, 57.2 per cent had been in business five years or less. Failures were highest for two- and three-year old concerns which together accounted for 33.6 per cent of the total. Only three per cent failed within one year.

Reasons for Failure

Two groups of reasons for failure always appear—the owner's explanation and that of outside agencies.

Table A-3 classifies the reasons for failure by underlying and apparent causes in great detail. *Changing Times* summarizes the cause of failures under the following seven headings: (1) They don't sell enough; (2) they lack experience; (3) they are incompetent; (4) they start with too little capital; (5) they choose poor locations; (6) they give credit too loosely; and (7) they neglect the business.[12]

Obviously failure means a situation where available capital is insufficient to pay all the obligations of a business. No matter how large or how small initial capital may have been, incompetent management has not only exhausted it but incurred debts beyond ability to pay. To the failing entrepreneur the most obvious reason is lack of capital, regardless of how inefficiently he has managed his former capital.

Failure statistics reported by Dun & Bradstreet include data on the liabilities of failing concerns. No corresponding data are available on losses incurred by the owners of concerns that failed or merely discontinued because of unsatisfactory returns. In a letter to the authors, Dun & Bradstreet explained how difficult it would be to obtain such information, partly because the owner at the time of ceasing operations does not know how much he may secure from certain assets, such as fixtures, machinery or remaining inventory, nor how much he may eventually be able to collect on his receivables. It may be several years before this information is available to him. Since these are mainly personal losses to the entrepreneur, there is no compulsion to make them public, and as yet no significant research on the subject has been undertaken. This is a topic of considerable interest to prospective enterprisers and others concerned with small business, and it would be a valuable contribution if such research were undertaken and the results published.

CONCLUSION

The small enterprise has certain characteristics that are very different from those of big business in spite of the mutual interdependence of large and small concerns. Personal, largely nonfinancial, features are far more important in small business. For many people independent enterprise is as much a way of life as it is a means of livelihood. To others it is the main opportunity to achieve important goals both financial and personal, such as promoting an important innovation.

As do all fields of human activity, small business has its problems, but no more so than any other field. As developed in this chapter, the major problems amenable to solution are those characteristic of the enterpriser himself, al-

[12] "Why Businesses Fail," *Changing Times* (March 1960), pp. 14, 15.

though some are imposed by government. All can be solved by intelligent action. In other cases there is no justification for making a fetish of "small business" and attempting to preserve this institution if it becomes no longer desirable. Our economy is dynamic, and as part of the economy, small business must adjust to changing conditions for survival.

Although many small businesses do not succeed and are discontinued or transferred, the actual failure rate is *much* smaller than many alarmists have indicated.

QUESTIONS AND PROBLEMS

1. What are the seven classes of small business based on the reasons for size? What others can you suggest?

2. What benefits would result from a classification of small businesses according to the suitability of the enterpriser to entrepreneurship?

3. State the conditions where an enterprise remains small due to the owner's preference. Criticize any of these you do not approve of and explain your reasoning.

4. Name the three distinctive characteristics of all small enterprises and illustrate each. Suggest, if you can, any other universal characteristics and illustrate each.

5. Discuss the statement in the chapter that "small business is no more 'a bundle of problems' than other fields."

6. Which of the three classes of problems warrants most attention? Explain.

7. What major conclusions for the prospective enterpriser do you draw from the discussion of small business problems?

8. How would you define "a genuine business opportunity"?

9. Which is basically more important for success in small business, capital or managerial ability? Explain.

10. What likely developments do you predict for business in the small towns of the country? Discuss.

11. In recent years several business brokers, operating on a regional and national basis, have appeared. Is the wider scale of operations likely to influence the quality of the brokers' services? Discuss.

12. What limitations are there to the prospective entrepreneur learning from the experience of others?

13. Trace the usual progression from a small enterprise pioneering some innovation to the transition into big business.

14. Present both sides of the controversy that concentration of banking may help or hinder small business in the future.

15. Are opportunities for inventing potentially useful products in the future as promising as they have been in the past 50 years? Discuss.

16. What are the major problems relating to patents faced by the individual inventor? Suggest solutions for each.

17. What are the advantages and disadvantages to society in the trend toward increasing numbers of individuals assigning patents to large corporations?

18. Suggest solutions for the employee problem of small business.

19. In what practical ways could small business problems connected with government regulations and taxes be reduced? Discuss.

20. How can problems relating to the limited time available to the small business-man be solved?

21. Discuss the statement in the chapter that most beginning enterprisers make one serious mistake during their first year of operations.

22. Suggest solutions for problems resulting from potential lenders insisting on control of small businesses they help finance.

23. Find out all you can about the Small Business Administration and its approach to solving problems such as those discussed in the chapter. Consult well-informed businessmen and reliable publications, then summarize and report your conclusions.

24. Talk with several small businessmen regarding their "problems" and report your findings. How would you classify these problems according to the three groups given in the chapter?

25. Fred bought a small but successful store near his college, hoping to earn expenses for his three remaining years in school. The business is profitable when-ever Fred devotes full time to it, but Fred has been unable to secure competent employees to do any of the work although he pays more than the going wages. Is Fred's venture sound? What should he do to complete his college education?

3 • Factors in Business Success

To be successful today an independent enterpriser must have an understanding of fields the previous generation never even heard of. In addition, he must be proficient in traditional business and management practices. New products and processes, keener competition, and new managerial techniques are all involved.[1]

TRENDS IN BUSINESS MANAGEMENT

Tremendous strides have been made in business management during recent years. The more important trends bearing on small business are summarized first. Naturally every trend is not of equal significance in all fields. These major trends are:

1. Increasing size accompanied by greater attention to employee and public relations.
2. Decentralization—management from a distance.
3. Greater interdependence of all business.
4. Closer control and co-ordination.
5. Increased accuracy of the measurement of operations.
6. "Professionalizing" of management.
7. Expanding use of machinery and technology.
8. Greater reliance on research.
9. Greater use of mathematics and findings of the behavioral sciences.
10. Automation.

For over half a century business units in many fields increased in size, with a corresponding increase in the use of management methods suited to operating these larger units. Later, in manufacturing and some fields of merchandis-

[1] *So You're Going Into Business* (Washington, D. C.: Domestic Distribution Department, U. S. Chamber of Commerce, 1956), lists various factors to consider and sources for further information.

ing, the establishment of branches began. This in turn required special techniques for so-called "management from a distance," or centralized administration with decentralized (branch) management. This latter trend has special significance for the independent small business operator because it shows how the best management principles and methods developed by large concerns can be used in the small unit.

Although the areas of emphasis and methods of application have varied to some extent from field to field, the general trend has been to seek closer coordination through better direction, supervision, and control over the activities of the business. Improved direction has stressed careful planning and policy formation. Better supervision has resulted from emphasizing the positive approach and developing impersonal supervising aids. Closer control has been developed over an increasing range of functions.

Trends in Manufacturing

Prior to 1900 America had no organized training for business, and most business methods were based on rules of thumb or the limited experience of the manager. But pioneering efforts were under way in several fields. In industry, notably in the steel industry, a small group of experimenters led by Frederick W. Taylor was seeking the "one best way" to do each job. This movement was later called "scientific management." However, it was not until 1912 that public, and even international, attention was directed to the progress of these early pioneers by the railroad rate hearings of 1911-1912. Cost accounting as an integral tool of managerial control made its debut at this time. Time and motion studies (now called methods studies), planned layout, routing, scheduling, production control, stores control, standardization, and the basic pattern of all modern managerial devices were also introduced as part of this development.

This movement toward greater accuracy of measurement of industrial operations and closer control over an increasing range of activities has been an important trend in management. It spread from the steel industry to other lines of production and later to merchandising and the service fields. Something comparable to a profession of management has developed, as represented by the Society for the Advancement of Management, emphasizing the formulation of management principles, and the American Management Association, concerned more with the application of these principles. A tremendous body of publications dealing with almost every aspect of management, except its applications to the small business, has been developed. During recent years a beginning, at least, has been made in seeking adaptations of this knowledge to the small enterprise. This, and professionalizing management in the new small enterprise, are major objectives of the Society for the Advancement of Independent Enterprisers (Iota Epsilon), organized in 1953 at the University of Oklahoma.

The increasing use of machinery in industry has been accompanied by further specialization and subdivision of labor. Standardization has been applied wherever possible. In certain fields mass production methods have been highly developed—notably in the automobile and other durable goods industries, and in meat packing. Continuous straight line production has been the goal in these industries. A logical result of such developments has been a tremendous increase in productivity per worker. Output per industrial worker increased steadily until 1939, when a reversal of this trend took place. From 1939 to 1947 output per worker declined while hourly wages increased. Naturally labor costs increased. To counteract this unfavorable trend, management has endeavored to "sell" itself more aggressively than in the past. Therefore, during this same period industrial management gave increasing attention to relations with both labor and the public, and this is a trend that may be expected to continue. Industry, as well as other areas of business, can well afford to do an improved job of selling itself to employees, the public, and government agencies.

Another trend in management has been the increasing use of research—both technological and market. During World War II a great many new industrial plants were built under conditions where construction costs were of little concern, but maximum volume of production with a scarce labor supply was of paramount importance. Ideas that might not have been introduced into factory management for decades of peacetime production were launched within a few years. Although they do not as yet constitute definite management trends, some of these new ideas are certain to start new trends in industrial management.

Mathematical models have been used increasingly in operations research, computer programming, and game theory applied to management decision-making. Although they are still largely in the ken of big business, some uses of these newer techniques are often found in progressive independent enterprises.

Recent emphasis on interdisciplinary training of business executives has also been adopted for entrepreneurs. Both the Ford Foundation and Carnegie studies have pointed to the need for greater understanding of human relations and all the social sciences. Small businessmen of the future must meet this challenge.

Automation, or machines that direct and control other machines, may not find direct applications in small business for some time, but its indirect effects are being felt in distribution, servicing, and repair fields. Electronic data processing has already found a place among groups of small-scale independents for inventory control and some paper work.

Increasingly, both automation and electronics will find applications in the smaller enterprise and owner-managers will need to understand these developments.

Trends in Merchandising

In distribution, the rise of large-scale retailing, paralleled by the decline in relative importance of wholesaling and the extensive use of national advertising, was the outstanding development affecting management during the period up to World War I. More recently these have been recognized as the logical developments of mass marketing to accompany the rise of mass production, although at the time they were merely the results of profit-seeking businessmen aggressively searching for and promoting new ideas and methods to increase their competitive position and resulting profits. However, in each field —national advertising or retailing organized along chain store, department store, or mail-order lines—specialization naturally resulted in the development to a high degree of perfection of certain techniques, methods, and policies of special importance to a given field. Later, from 1920 on, these results of progress were shared by businessmen in other fields.

In wholesaling the powerful position once occupied by a few large firms has been lessened in relative importance owing principally to: (1) the rise of large-scale integrated retailers like chain stores, department stores, and mail-order houses; (2) the increased number of small wholesalers located closer to their retail customers; and (3) the increasing importance of fashion or rapid change in many lines of merchandise. For the large wholesalers, and many medium-sized firms, this has resulted in management emphasis on closer working relationships with retailers—such as the organization of voluntary chains, or efforts to reduce operating costs to meet the lower price standards set by integrated retailers.

This brief discussion of management trends in wholesaling is not meant to imply a decline in the total importance of wholesaling. In high fashion lines the wholesaler has lost ground. In most other lines he has merely adjusted organization and management methods in order to meet changed conditions.

Trends in Service Fields

Although both manufacturing and distribution have developed a body of management principles in their respective fields, this cannot yet be said for the service industries. This may be explained in part by the great diversity of activities included among the "services," but especially because no comprehensive study of the field as a whole has yet been made and the results published. At first glance it may appear that professional services like accounting, law, medicine, or cosmetology have little in common with insurance, commercial amusements, appliance repairing, laundries, drive-it-yourself auto agencies, or rentals, plumbing, and construction. However, research by the authors suggests that much the same over-all pattern may develop here as appeared in both manufacturing and in merchandising. Within each of the well-established service fields, such as laundries, beauty parlors, insurance or accounting services, tourist facilities, and repair services, well-accepted principles and standards have been developed. It seems likely that these basic principles, standards, and policies may be generalized, at least for each of a few broad divisions of the service fields. In each major field the trade or professional association has developed management principles, methods, and operating standards on a par with progress in manufacturing or merchandising. Since no large units operate in the service fields, this is a logical development.

BIG BUSINESS MAY BE MORE EFFICIENT

Business is not necessarily more efficient because it is big. Often the over-all or net efficiency is less than that of small units in the same field. However, analysis shows that many large concerns have developed a high degree of effectiveness in certain fundamentals such as the seven M's of management: men, money, machines, materials, methods, markets, and minutes.

Efficiency in Manufacturing

In manufacturing efficient use of labor results from the large firm's ability to subdivide the work for greater specialization, and provide machinery developed especially to increase the productivity of each type of labor. This is true for office work as well as for the common and factory labor, but it is in actual production that the tremendous increase in worker productivity resulting from machine methods has taken place. The trend in many businesses has been toward single purpose machines in spite of the heavy initial cost. In other industries where models are changed and new designs are introduced frequently, the preference is for general purpose machines although they are not so efficient.

Capital may be used more efficiently by the large firms as a result of their ability: (1) to employ specialists like economic advisors and investment counselors; (2) to establish better systems of forecasting and budgetary control; and (3) to keep all funds working constantly because of the many opportunities for use, such as in product development, market research, and so on.

The large concern's huge purchasing power makes it easier to buy and use materials more efficiently, usually through purchase according to specification and often on an extended contract basis. Such materials may be carefully engineered to the machine processes to be performed and to requirements of the finished product, which constitutes another advantage. More efficient methods are not an inherent advantage of the largest concerns, but are likely to be sought more aggressively in the medium-sized and very large organizations.

In market research and in market promotion, companies beyond a certain size can be more comprehensive in their surveys. Especially are they in a favorable position to use product differentiation and large-scale promotion through national brand advertising.

The time factor is often utilized to greater advantage by big business. Work is planned and scheduled more carefully; through methods studies and time studies less idle time is permitted; and great effort is made to keep employees working.

Notwithstanding all these advantages of large over small business, the former is not necessarily more efficient; it has not been possible to prove it scientifically, but there is reason to believe that small business, well managed, can compete successfully with big business in all fields except those where expensive machinery dominates the productive process.

Efficiency in Merchandising

Efficiency in merchandising is difficult to measure, partly because of the number of rapidly changing variables involved, partly owing to the more intangible nature of marketing activities, and also owing to the important part played by human beings rather than machines. Most marketing functions are still performed "by hand." However, a relatively free competitive economic system has provided us with some guides.

Contrary to popular belief, *all* types of present-day large-scale retailing started as very small businesses that later expanded. Chain stores were the first to start but about the last to receive public attention. The history of most present-day chain store organizations is well known. Each was started as a single small store; success there led to the opening of a second, third, and many more stores. Buying power developed much later. But efficient management and reinvestment of profits started with the first store.

Efficiency of chain store operation in many respects resembles that of mass production. Both make effective use of standardization. Chains concentrate on fast-selling, standard merchandise; they apply standardization to their store fronts, equipment, and layout; even their personnel are somewhat standardized. Large savings are made through standardization.

Field supervisors are on the alert to discover improvements, which are sent to headquarters and then relayed to all stores. Whereas new ideas may die in unorganized independent stores, this loss is not permitted in chains. The following example comes from the experience of one of the authors. In the process of organizing material for the teaching of a course in chain store management it was discovered that one of the most widely used books in the central libraries of many chains was Clyde Bedell's *Seven Keys to Retail Profits,* a book written to teach independent merchants how to compete more successfully with the chain stores!

The ability and willingness to use thoroughly trained, well-qualified specialists wherever their services are needed, and employees of less experience and minimum ability elsewhere, is another important source of chain store efficiency. Large numbers of men and women need work who are not well qualified by training, experience, or native ability, or who lack interest to develop themselves. The wisdom, and often the justification, of using low-paid help may be questioned. However, recommended modern personnel practice tends toward job analysis, classification of jobs according to the skill and ability required, evaluation of each such category according to its relative importance to the firm, and selection of employees who qualify and who are paid accordingly—to do otherwise is economic waste. To overpay an employee gives him a false sense of his importance and lessens his incentive to improve. Under keen price competition it means job instability and possible unemployment.

Chains often secure lower prices for their merchandise because of one or more of the following reasons: expert buyers, larger volume of purchases of the same merchandise, and integration—or performing for themselves most of the functions performed for the independent retailer by the wholesaler. At least since the passage of the Robinson-Patman Act, uneconomic price concessions resulting from bargaining power and high-volume purchasing have been greatly lessened, if not eliminated. Briefly, this law provides that the difference in prices between large and small orders of similar goods must not exceed the difference in costs of producing, selling, and handling orders of each size.

Dealer co-operatives, voluntary chains, and corporate chain store agency and franchise systems owe their efficiency to the same factors just discussed for chain stores, plus the added incentives that may result from individual ownership of each store, or to the motives prompting the sponsor. In the case of voluntary chains the sponsoring wholesaler has a direct incentive to improve the management of his co-operating retail stores for his own survival. Corporate chains that sponsor agency or franchise stores probably have a combination of the following three major types of incentives for insuring the success of independently owned co-operating merchants: (1) desire for greater market coverage, such as having representation in towns too small for company-owned stores; (2) desire to secure greater volume, which is especially important when the chain manufactures a substantial portion of its merchandise, as does Walgreen's; and (3) desire to hedge against anti-chain store measures and criticism, such as discriminatory taxes or charges of monopoly.

The efficiency of department stores results from their ability to distribute overhead expenses over a large number of departments, to use advertising and other sales promotion effectively, to capitalize on their reputation and their location in the central shopping area or through branches in suburban shopping centers to be readily accessible to all their customers. Relative to the small independent, they can employ more and better trained specialists, can seek out merchandise resources more thoroughly, and can organize plans and policies on a more long-time basis. Like the chains, the larger department stores are integrated and can secure lower prices for their merchandise chiefly through performing some of the wholesale functions and by the use of better buyers. Their "buying power" is often less than that of much smaller specialty stores since it is distributed over such a wide range of producers.

The mail-order house is in a unique position in the field of retail distribution.

It can utilize many of the methods that make large-scale American industry so efficient—methods studies, straight line layout of the warehouse, standardization of procedures, forms, and routines, mechanical handling, and production control—because it operates as a "factory" that fills orders rather than as a customer reception area, like the over-the-counter retail store. Also, the large mail-order house uses the most efficient form of mass selling—advertising.

That mail-order marketing is not ordinarily a cheap method, and that some strictly mail-order houses have found it desirable to open chains of retail stores may be explained as follows. Costs of impersonal selling through catalogues or direct mail tend to be high, and transportation costs on small shipments are usually very high. The time factor of waiting for the arrival of goods ordered by mail is risky in that it discourages a great many consumers. Also, the relative inflexibility of pricing, policies, and merchandise selection is greater for strictly mail-order concerns.

Supermarkets, the latest type of mass retailing to prove its place, originated during the depression of the 1930's as "cheapies," or stores selling staple foods at low prices on a cash-and-carry basis with no services. They combined chain store limited services and low prices with department store one-stop shopping, and expanded with increased use of the family car for shopping trips. Supermarkets have made effective use of all major promotional devices. By concentrating mainly on foods bought and sold in large volume in one location they have made use of most of the recent progress in mass retailing on a very narrow margin. Chain stores, independents in the food field, and even department stores, are tending increasingly to adopt and adapt supermarket methods.

American consumers usually compare the quality of a product with the high standards established by large manufacturers, and approve or condemn it accordingly. Chain stores, department stores, and mail-order houses have led to an upgrading throughout all retailing.

Big business in both manufacturing and in distribution has contributed immeasurably to our present high standard of living. A small business must justify its existence in terms of needs and wants, as well as in terms of its ability to furnish these on an equal competitive basis with other concerns, whether large or small.

Efficiency in the Service Fields

Although the contrasts between large and small units in the service fields are less pronounced than in manufacturing and retailing, there are some contrasts worthy of comment. Large auto laundries and one-day auto paint shops operated in some of the large cities are examples. When the volume of business is large and regular enough for automobile cleaning and repainting, as it is in several of the large cities, work can be subdivided, straight line process layout adopted, and many specialized tools and equipment employed. The relative efficiency of these large units as compared to the small concerns manifests itself in the form of somewhat lower prices, quicker service, and quality of the work performed that is equal to, or sometimes better than, that obtainable in small shops. However, the work is so organized that it is impractical to give special attention to certain jobs where individual care may be needed for satisfactory service.

In one other area of the service fields the large units may be more efficient than the small. Where the task of diagnosing the trouble involves the use of expensive, highly technical equipment, this condition is likely to exist. The most obvious example is the large medical clinic, although similar examples exist among service establishments specializing in the repair of complicated electrical devices such as radio and television sets. Although the latest scientific equipment may be needed to diagnose the trouble in complicated cases, the well-trained practitioner equipped with the normal tools of his occupation can successfully handle the vast majority of service needs in any of these fields.

INTERDEPENDENCE OF ALL BUSINESS

The basic reality of modern economic life is the interdependence of all business.[2] All use the same basic elements: money, men, material, space, time; all require management and markets; and all must work together within the law and according to established trade customs and business ethics. Money is a highly flexible and mobile instrument. It functions equally well in small or big business, in financing a drugstore or an automobile factory. The same is true of men, materials, space, and time, although to a lesser degree. No modern business is an entity in itself. It must buy from other firms and sell either to different businessmen or to consumers in competition with a great many other businesses.

SUCCESS VERSUS FAILURE

Make or Break Factors in Business—Early Axioms

The principles of business have been developed from the beginning in terms of plain common sense and therefore are not difficult to understand. Their practice, however, is another matter. Knowing what to do is very different from knowing how to do it. Still harder is to do it the best way. The farmer who wrote to the Department of Agriculture, "Please quit sending me any more bulletins, I'm not farming half as well as I know how now," is a case in point.

1. Business opportunity. Too often an idea plus ambition are mistaken for a business opportunity, or maybe a vacant store is so interpreted. A genuine

[2] The Research and Policy Committee of the Committee for Economic Development, *Meeting the Special Problems of Small Business,* policy report of the Committee for Economic Development (New York, June 1947), p. 9.

business opportunity means a need for the proposed good or service in sufficient volume and at a high enough price to operate at a profit. Of course, the demand will not always be ready and anxiously waiting for the newcomer. Often it will have to be stimulated or developed. Especially will this be true when the embryo businessman has something new to offer.

An indefinite but very large number of businesses fail because they never should have been started. There is no justification for their existence. Notice how thoroughly big business goes about launching a new product. Laboratory experiments, product analysis, market surveys, and pilot operations are often conducted for several years before the newcomer is announced to the public. Although big business could afford to make a few mistakes, it seldom does; but small business, where a single major error is fatal, makes many.

2. Trade experience. Obviously if it were contended that personal experience in the actual trade is indispensable, then no novel or unique businesses would ever be created. Many businesses have been successfully started and successfully operated by novices, with little capital and without apparent proof of business acumen. But these are indeed exceptions, for the paths of commerce are strewn with the bones of businesses that started out thus ill-equipped.

Since perhaps no one knows what a beginner's problems will be, he cannot be expected to know them. His ability to anticipate them, to surmount them, to make the best decisions, to "do the right thing at the right time" will depend on his general business experience and how closely this is related to the new business.

In beginning a business in a well-known field, one in which many others are already engaged, the need for experience in the trade is apparent. In retailing, for example, the grocery business has certain well-established practices that make for efficiency in handling goods, reducing expenses, and building goodwill. In the service occupations there have been developed—for example in the gasoline business the laundry or dry cleaning trades, and repair shops of most kinds—certain ways of "cutting corners," improving service, and protecting materials and equipment. These would be unknown to the beginner. In small manufacturing establishments certain organizational routines, order-of-work patterns of production flow, and methods of buying and of caring for materials are essential to success and profit.

The extent to which trade experience must be acquired by the slow laborious process of firsthand personal experience depends on the individual. The modern trend, for college graduates at least, is to shorten the time spent acquiring personal experience and devote much more attention to learning from the experience of others. A properly trained analyst can learn much more from the experience of numerous other successful operators in one month than he could in two years or more of normal personal experience. In 1942 the most successful operator of the largest supermarket in one city opened his own grocery store without any personal experience in the field. He has pioneered more new methods and launched more innovations in his store than have the other five supermarkets in town combined, and one of these is owned by the second largest chain in the country. Before every new move this man has spent from two to six weeks making an intensive study of the latest and best methods in various parts of the country. What he could not have learned from years of personal experience he has mastered in a few short weeks devoted to absorbing the years of experience of others.

3. Enough money to carry through. The beginner will require adequate capital for equipment, fixtures, materials, or merchandise, plus rent and overhead, salaries, and incidentals until he can make a profit. He must make provision for his own and his family's human needs. This topic is covered in greater detail in Chapter 11.

4. Managerial ability—a "must" item. Every individual is more or less business-minded, but most of us are less so. In everyday living as consumers, only a few seem naturally to take a businesslike approach to matters of shopping, banking, property management and the buying of services.

Bankers are of necessity good judges of business aptitude. When reviewing the possibilities of extending a loan to an operating or prospective business-man, the banker will frequently inquire as to his client's personal business habits. He will find significant, perhaps, the fact that overdrafts are frequent in the applicant's checking account record.

A sure way to ruin the business is for the short-funded owner to draw from the business more than it is earning; that is, to draw from operating capital rather than from income.

The man or woman who has no standards of dollar-for-dollar values in goods, services, or manpower will also be a hazardous business operator. The person who is continually being sold "gold bricks" in the form of unneeded frills and useless gadgets cannot be expected to exercise sound judgment in the markets of his trade.

The little business may some day be a big business. Until it is larger, it had best copy its progressive elders as to behavior. Its elders are successful, or else they would not be in existence. They have followed successful ways of operation and have proven them to be successful. The fledgling should carefully study these proved successful methods. In the retail field, according to Department of Commerce figures, almost 60 per cent of the nation's business is done by less than 20 per cent of the stores; similar figures prevail in manufacturing. The moral is evident.

THE WAY IT IS DONE

Granted that the small business operator has experience, capital, and judgment, he should be able to organize and establish his business with some degree of success. Keeping it going will depend on how well he conducts it, once it is well launched. General conclusions may be reached as to how he may conduct it to the best possible advantage—to derive the maximum return from his investment and his effort. The following are drawn in terms of successful principles and practices as applied to large and small businesses alike, but as developed largely by the bigger operators and through which they have generally made their progress:

1. Careful study of markets.
2. Wise planning of activities.
3. Vigilant control of investment, merchandise, personnel, equipment, and buildings to insure maximum use for production.
4. Adequate expense records.
5. Thoughtful selection of goods.
6. Strategic location with particular reference to the market, but also bearing in mind resources and transportation of goods.
7. Sound policies, unalterable in general objective, but flexible and adjustable to meet obvious business expediencies.
8. Strong working relationships with resources as well as with customers on a co-operative as well as a competitive basis.
9. Judiciously controlled credit.
10. Customer selection and market concentration.
11. Skillfully selected personnel.
12. A well-planned sales promotion program.

Modern Methods in Retailing

Perhaps the small retailer, more than any other businessman, can profitably bring his methods up to date and get in step with modern business.[3] Manufacturing generally has made greater progress than distribution in streamlining operations and thus reducing costs. Although this movement has been led by the large manufacturers, their competitive price challenges have entered the markets of all productive enterprises, no matter how small. In contrast, many small stores have never felt genuine competition, owing to their locations in spots lacking attractiveness to chains and other large operators. Yet efficient methods would have prevented many of their failures, would have insured greater profits for small store owners, and would bolster them against the day when stiff competition becomes a reality.

A typical example was the neighborhood grocer after an arterial highway was rerouted past his door. Business boomed, but from a new class of cash-and-carry trade that interfered with service to his old customers. Soon a modern supermarket opened up across the street and most of his newly acquired customers shifted their patronage. Old customers used his charge and delivery service during bad weather but took their profitable business to the modern "super." An effort to offset lost sales by remaining open nights

---

[3] See: *Essential Personal Qualities for Small Store Managers,* Small Marketers Aids No. 46 (Washington, D. C.: Small Business Administration, July 1959).

after competition had closed helped somewhat, but involved excessively long hours.

When the situation looked hopeless a wholesaler's representative suggested a plan of modernization and concentration of purchases with his house under agreements typical of the voluntary chain plan. Shortly after putting the new cash-and-carry, semi-self-service plan into operation in the enlarged, modernized building the grocer was back in the profit-making class again. His intimate knowledge of customers' needs and preferences was put to good use. Close co-operation with the wholesaler in buying and merchandising proved advantageous to both.

This case is only one of many examples of how the present-day merchant or shop owner must adjust himself to the times. Although new ideas are not always successful, the world thrives on change. It may be sound judgment to play safe and go slowly, but when the public clearly indicates its wants, it is the alert merchant's duty to provide services or goods as wanted. Otherwise he cannot long exist.

Modern Methods in the Service Business

The same principle, of using the proved methods of successful operation as demonstrated over the years by the big operators, applies in any branch of business. The difficulty is that so few small operators will admit their weaknesses and seek the needed information until it is too late. A laundry owner in a small mid-western community was an exception.

The owner had inherited a successful laundry business from his father, who had built it up over a period of 30 years in a town of 6,000. When the young man took over, the business was paying no great profit, supposedly owing to the general depression. As business conditions improved the laundry did not. After he had studied the situation carefully it dawned upon the owner that perhaps he was doing things too carefully and too much as his father had done.

He joined the laundrymen's trade association, from which he gained figures on operating expense that differed so greatly from his own that he was alarmed. He visited a fellow member who was known as a successful operator. After seeing his neighbor's business and restudying his own situation he started making changes.

Within three months he had reduced his operating cost 22 per cent, while his production potentials were increased 18 per cent. He found that he had had poor management controls in different operations; no standards of performance; no idea of relative costs; that accounting for bundles was outmoded; equipment was behind the time; and his handling of customer accounts was inefficient and costly. The business is now thriving. Its adjustment to the times did not come from the integrity established by the owner's father, or from industry alone, but he combined them with open-mindedness and willingness to adjust to change.

Modern Methods in the Small Factory

A small machine tool factory just outside an eastern metropolitan city had been established during the war, and while on subcontracted war orders it had been able to maintain a payroll of 36 men and produce an adequate product at a profit. When the war ended, efforts to find peacetime uses for the company's facilities were unsuccessful because prices quoted were too high. Lacking management aid from the prime contractor that had been utilized repeatedly during the period of war production, the owners now secured assistance from a management consultant. Modern methods of inventory and storage control, tool checking, purchasing, and personnel management soon put the company in a favorable competitive position and enabled the management to engage successfully in peacetime production.

The results were only those to be expected from reorganizing in terms of proven methods. Acknowledged improvements included the reduction of operating costs by 17 per cent and the increase of production potentials by 26 per cent, in addition to the improvement in personnel relations and the fact that the plant continued to exist at all. There were principles and methods available that would make this plant a success—the success of others proved their existence, and it was only necessary to seek them out and apply them. Small business generally can profit by such examples.

Our discussion so far should serve to emphasize three outstanding conclusions: (1) competition and changing conditions set standards that the small businessman must and can meet; (2) larger businesses usually have developed methods that can be successfully adopted and adapted by the small operator; and (3) basically, requirements for business success are the same in all fields regardless of the position held or the size of the firm in that field.

LESSONS FROM FAILURES

One reason why personal experience is valued so highly is that it "drives home" mistakes in the application of sound principles, or cases of poor judgment, usually before the learner has assumed full responsibility for the outcome of his acts. Another reason is that many people learn better, or at least remember longer, by doing than by reading or hearing about how something should be done. Thus, prior to the present century nearly every occupation was entered by the apprenticeship method, serving years of long hours at tedious routine "to learn the arts and mysteries of commerce" so common in training for retail and wholesale careers in the "old country." Even in America this method was common prior to the advent of scientific management and collegiate training for business. It is still used by many chains to train their future managers. So long as no body of analyzed and recorded knowledge was available, the long hard road of apprenticeship by each generation was almost a necessity. Today such conditions no longer exist, except possibly in such radically new fields as to be beyond the scope of this book.

Both the underlying and apparent causes of failures in business as discussed in Chapter 3 and presented in detail in Table A-3 deserve consideration. The distinction resembles that between the cause of an ailment and its symptoms. Particular attention should be given to the four major underlying causes that account for 89 per cent of all failures and are evidenced in such conditions as inadequate sales, heavy operating expenses and the like. Most of the remaining chapters of our text will be devoted to a discussion of how these common causes of failure can be avoided by developing proficiency in all the factors required for success. These are fundamentals applicable to any kind and size of enterprise.

CONCLUSIONS

American business is highly dynamic, competitive, and interdependent. Free enterprise encourages innovation and pioneering, as well as adopting, adapting and improving developments made by others. We have few, if any, of the old-time trade secrets. Several results significant to small business follow from these conditions.

In all major fields of enterprise great progress has been made in recent decades. The general pattern has been for small independents to pioneer innovations in all fields—production, merchandising, and service—and for big business to develop the successful ones that have potential mass markets to a high degree of efficiency. Since the 1920's widespread interest in the functioning of our economy resulted in greater publicity of business trends, publication of census of business and other business research reports, efforts by many individuals and agencies to aid segments of business in need of such help, a rapid expansion in collegiate training for business, and revival of interest in the independent enterpriser segment of our economy.

QUESTIONS AND PROBLEMS

1. Which of the trends in business management mentioned in the chapter have had the greatest effects on raising the requirements for success? Explain.

2. Do you think there is a valid place for the Society for the Advancement of Independent Enterprisers, or Iota Epsilon, mentioned in the text? Is there a chapter at your school?

3. What significant trends in management in any of the main fields should be added to the brief discussion of this topic in the chapter? Explain why you consider those you mention as significant for small business.

4. If big business is not always more efficient than small business in the same field, how do you account for the presence of large units in these fields?

5. What, if any, similarities account for the relatively greater efficiency of large concerns than of small businesses in some lines of manufacturing and distribution?

6. What conclusions important to the small merchant do you draw from the brief account of the rise of mass retailing?

7. How is a "genuine business opportunity" defined in the chapter?

8. Explain the statement "A number of businesses fail because they never should have been started."

9. Is it necessary to acquire trade experience through actual employment or work in the trade? Explain.

10. Is there any connection between the way a person handles his own or family finances and his likelihood of success in a business of his own? Discuss.

11. Name the first four of the 12 steps given for launching a business successfully. Are these four of greater importance than the others? Discuss.

12. Is personal experience in business *more* or *less* important today for success as an owner-manager than it was a generation ago? Explain.

13. Is a man better off if he learns through personal experience and goes through one failure in the process, or if he avoids failure by learning from the experience of others who have failed? Are you sure? Discuss.

14. Explain the distinction between underlying and apparent causes of failure in business.

15. How should each group of causes of failure be used by the prospective and beginning enterpriser?

16. Talk with a few progressive bankers regarding the factors they would consider before making loans to prospective or fairly new enterprisers, and report the results.

17. A 40-year old former Seabee and construction supervisor wants to buy a small, but successful, hardware store near where he is graduating from college. A banker and another hardware store owner advise him to get at least two years experience working in a store before becoming an owner-manager. Evaluate this advice and advise what he should do.

4 • *Self-Employment or Dependent Employment?*

Whether to be self-employed or a dependent employee is a major decision for many individuals. It warrants careful consideration.

As part of the process of planning your future, you should compare the advantages and disadvantages of both employment and business ownership with your individual personal traits in mind. If you decide you are the type to operate your own business, then survey the opportunities, risks, and requirements. Next, begin your planning and preparation as considered in Chapter 5. Finally, before launching out on your own, study the principles and modern practices discussed in the balance of the text. Your full understanding of all aspects of the subject will be more complete if you will follow the sequence suggested.

Although conditions at certain times may alter the situation temporarily, in general a person must earn what he receives whether as an employee or an independent enterpriser. But the effort and other requirements differ, as does the nature of returns. Our objective in this chapter is to analyze these differences so as to enable each individual to make an intelligent decision.

EMPLOYMENT CONSIDERATIONS

Many individuals would rather be employees, especially wtih large, well-established concerns. Some of the alleged advantages are security, the prestige that goes with working for a "name" business, the receipt of unemployment insurance and other benefits, greater regularity of income, a more limited area in which knowledge and ability are expected, less annoyance from shifting frequently from one type of work to another, and less worry outside of business hours.

Other advantages of employment are the absence of risk of capital or personal savings, or of personal reputation or the success of the business; shorter hours, regular vacations, and pay for overtime; larger initial income; more limited responsibility; less planning of tomorrow's work; and in general a more regular routine.

DISADVANTAGES OF DEPENDENT EMPLOYMENT

That salaries and wages paid by big business are good, and that even be, ginning salaries for college graduates in recent years have risen very highly, are well known. In terms of purchasing power, however, big business executives lost ground from 1939 to the early 1950's relative to wage earners and independent enterprisers. Because of high income tax rates and inflation, executive purchasing power declined 59 per cent from 1939 to 1950, whereas that of the other two groups increased.[1] Independent enterprisers with incomes in the same brackets as higher paid executives have been able to take business deductions not allowable for employees, and to reinvest a reasonable proportion of their earnings for expansion. Big business has devised many ways of rewarding their better paid men so that such a large proportion of their income is not currently drained off by excessive personal income taxation. In general, these plans involve some deferment of raises or bonuses until after retirement or at such time when conditions taxwise may be more favorable.[2]

Employment opportunities and inducements offered by large companies fluctuate according to economic conditions fully as much as the prospects for success in independent enterprising. In recent years offers have been excellent. The mild recession of 1958, however, caused pronounced slackening of college recruiting. Many firms even cancelled interview dates made earlier. However, during the three worst years of the depression of the 1930's, when the aggregate of corporate income showed a loss of several billion dollars, business made strenuous efforts to retain as many employees as possible. During 1955 organized labor campaigned for a guaranteed annual wage, and this emphasis on security for dependent employees is likely to continue. How such activities will affect the incomes and tenure of employees is problematical, but it is difficult to visualize how all employees could be assured of steady jobs unless salaries and wages fluctuate even more drastically than economic conditions in general. The "accent on youth" movement discussed in Chapter 1 may have significant bearing on those already employed at a time when business activity declines.

In recent years many big businesses have changed their top management rather frequently. Such changes may ignite a chain reaction involving the security of positions of numerous executives on down the line. In other cases certain positions seem to be highly volatile, such as department store buyers, sales managers and general managers of large corporations. Mergers also tend to disturb the security of many executives.

[1] "Executive Pay, The Great Game of Gimmicks," *Time* (August 24, 1953), p. 74.
[2] Prentice-Hall Loose-Leaf Services, *How Top Executives Increase Their Personal Incomes* (Englewood Cliffs, N. J.: Prentice-Hall, Inc., 1953).

"Most big corporations have long believed that the best way to get executives is to take the most promising men from the work bench or college, and set up a systematic program to turn the brightest of them into bosses. . . .

"Many of the systems put a premium on conformity, and the best executives are frequently non-conformists." [3]

Many employers want "organization men" who can fit nicely into any niche and be content not to overstep its predetermined boundaries. Such positions received considerable attention in management literature but no satisfactory solution has appeared. In fact it is difficult to conceive of a topflight specialist in some limited functional area of big business having an opportunity to exercise all of the faculties of a well-trained graduate from a school of business. If and when such an individual becomes president and general manager, or a member of the board of directors, his comprehensive training and all of his abilities will be needed but, of course, not all business executives reach these positions.

Criticism of the usual policy of big business to claim prior rights on all innovations made by employees has been growing. The subject is highly controversial. To the person with a creative mind a condition of employment that forces him to relinquish his constitutional right to seek and exploit a patent on his own ideas must be quite distasteful. No doubt some employees have taken unfair advantage of their position which gave them access to information belonging to their employers, and others may have failed to reveal discoveries made on the job for which they were being paid to seek. But the exact origin of ideas that lead to inventions and other innovations is often obscure, and employment contracts that give the employer prior claim to these may at times be unfair. It is significant that by 1952 engineers employed in industry were organizing for the purpose of securing better patent protection for themselves.[4]

Executives in big business necessarily have heavy responsibilities. Many drive themselves even harder than do the self-employed. For others the constant pressure from top management is a terrific strain. "In General Motors alone, 189 of its top management group died in five war years. . . . And the American Fidelity & Casualty Co. had found that the average businessman dies six years before his time, thus losing for the company a sizeable investment." [5] In periods of economic stress, such as the depression of the 1930's, the suicide rate of business executives rises alarmingly. Early enforced retirement seems merely to hasten mortality, as those retired do not live out their remaining life expectancy nearly as often as other people. No wonder big business is having increasing difficulty recruiting qualified executive material as facts such as the foregoing are discovered and publicized.

[3] "The Great Man Hunt—Industry Needs More Good Executives," *Time* (October 12, 1953), p. 98.

[4] "Why Engineers in Industry Are Organizing," *Management Review* (December 1952), p. 788.

[5] "Management, The Pace That Kills," *Time* (March 30, 1953), p. 78.

Another factor has an important bearing on the decision between self- and dependent employment. The alleged advantage of employment resulting in less worry than being one's own boss is not always true. It depends primarily on the individual. Three university school of business alumni surveys made by the authors disclosed several cases of graduates who worried less as their own bosses than as employees. In our Oklahoma University survey, 21 reported they worried less as their own boss, 47 worried more, and the experience of 10 was the same in either case. Successful small businessmen who have been speakers in the authors' classes have stated that they worried less.

The essence of the matter seems to be that a competent and conscientious graduate who finds himself working under a careless, incompetent, or inefficient boss, tends to fret and worry because of the neglected opportunities he sees but feels unable to correct as an employee. This is not a new situation in business history. It was the report of similar conditions found by co-operative trainees in the Antioch College program that led the staff of that institution to investigate and publish their findings over 20 years ago.[6] It was similar conditions found in some of our most "progressive" industries that motivated Frederick W. Taylor's pioneer efforts in the steel industry during the 1880's, Harington Emerson's "efficiency" campaign in the railroad industry after 1910, and Frank Bunker Gilbreth's work in the building trades at about the same time. From what we know about worry this condition is not surprising. Some individuals suffer when they encounter inefficiency and become worried when they are unable to change conditions. In self-employment, conditions are almost completely under their own control; therefore, the major cause of frustration that led them to worry is removed. The fact that they may not achieve a high degree of efficiency on their own is not in question in this case. The important point is that they can exert all their efforts to do so. For the majority of people, however, especially for those best suited to dependent employment, this condition is not too important. Most people worry more when their own capital is at stake than they do when only that of their employer is involved.

ADVANTAGES OF BUSINESS OWNERSHIP

Once established, small business ownership offers security comparable to employment, and for a much longer period of time. There is also the satisfaction of being known in the community as an independent businessman and not as merely an employee who takes his orders from others, as does even the manager of a branch house or chain store. The college alumni survey by *Time* found that 83 per cent of the top positions held by alumni in each community were in business ownership and independent professional practice. Incomes of

[6] Stanley B. Mathewson, *Restriction of Output by Unorganized Workers* (New York: Viking Press, 1931).

these groups were double the national average.[7] Median net worth is also highest among the self-employed, $15,000 in 1953 compared to $4,100 for all spending units included in the Federal Reserve Board survey.[8] Noncorporate business and professional practice and other forms of self-employment as sources of income are greatest in the highest income bracket.[9] Self-employed businessmen with incomes of $10,000 and over for 1956, 1957, and 1958 comprised respectively 33, 27, and 24 per cent of the total. In 1958 only two groups had larger percentages in the $10,000 and over bracket: managerial with 26, and professional and semiprofessional with 27 per cent.[10]

The small business owner and independent professional man are not subject to the same time limitations on their earning power as are employees who must accept retirement at a certain age because of company policy. Some prefer to get the entire profit from their own efforts, ideas, judgment, and skill, saving or investing as they choose and retiring when they please.

If a person owns his own business, he cannot be fired, except by customers—his real bosses. He need have little fear of petty jealousies, factions, internal politics, or favoritism; instead, he has the forces of competition to be met successfully. This may not always be easy, but at least it is usually above-board, ethical, and available to all competitors equally or according to their ability.

If an individual has ideas and wants to try them out, he can do so as his own boss to a far greater extent than as an employee. If he likes to pioneer, small business is a natural for him; if he likes to carry a job once started through to successful completion even if it means working overtime, he should enter business for himself. If he enjoys a line of useful work, is good at it, and is not afraid of hard work, he will probably make much more in this type of business for himself and will be happier than he would be working for the other fellow. If he wants to secure all the profits from his efforts and will take the risk of loss, if he wants to do something differently from the way it is being done, or if he is unhappy working for others and feels restrained from the opportunity for self-expression, he should make sure first and then start on his own business. If an individual really wants to go into business for himself but is afraid to start because of the many risks involved, he should plan definitely to do so anyway, waiting only until he has an even chance for success. The large number of today's businesses that passed through several stages of failure during their beginning years include those of F. W. Woolworth and R. H. Macy.

---

[7] "A Letter from the Publisher," *Time* (March 24, 1952), p. 17.

[8] *1953 Survey of Consumer Finances,* reprinted from the *Federal Reserve Bulletin* (September 1953), p. 3.

[9] *1956 Survey of Consumer Finances,* reprinted from the *Federal Reserve Bulletin* (June 1956), p. 563.

[10] *Federal Reserve Bulletin* (September 1958), p. 1052, and *1959 Survey of Consumer Finances,* from the *Federal Reserve Bulletin* (July 1959), p. 713.

An excellent commentary on the satisfaction resulting from business owner-ship appeared in a 1949 survey covering 64 college graduates who had entered business for themselves over a period of 23 years. Only two of this group stated that they would take a job instead of again becoming business owners immediately if they were entirely free and had no financial ties in any business. Even these two stated they would become entrepreneurs again as soon as they had acquired certain desired experience as employees.

Our University of Oklahoma alumni survey, conducted late in 1953, showed similar results in that 80 of the 93 entrepreneurs would not remain employees compared to three who would. Nine would do nothing differently. Fifty-one would not wait so long before becoming independent; nine would wait longer. Twelve would be better prepared by planning and experience, and seven would be better financed.

As his own boss, the individual has fewer restraints on his actions, is able to express himself more fully, and can develop any creative idea he has to the limit of his ability and resources, no matter how "harebrained" it may seem to others. He is not restrained by precedent, regulations, and limitations of the past, or the conservatism characteristic of big business employment. Among the bases of modern successful enterprises that were once considered hare-brained ideas, we find the railroad, photography, the automobile, telegraph, phonograph, dictaphone, typewriter, calculating machines, electric light and power, metal boats and steamships, radar, and atomic energy. Modern prac-tices such as a one-price store policy, the returned-goods privilege, women in business and professions, the manufacture of standard interchangeable parts, honesty as a policy in business, the generation of cold heat, and others too numerous to list were once-upon-a-time strange ideas.

An employee who suggests something new that is not given a trial may be disturbed by the thought that it might have worked if tried. When later the same idea is announced with credit given to his "boss," it is quite disappoint-ing. The authors have seen numerous examples of this situation.

It is well known that college graduates in particular frequently have too many ideas for a big company. The presence of a research division tends to aggravate rather than alleviate this situation because it seems to obstruct the constructive urges of employees outside its department.

Business ownership gives a person a chance to exercise all of his abilities, skill, knowledge, energy, and desire for pioneering and adventure. This fact is not only especially important for the college graduate in capitalizing fully on his investment in a broad education, but also emotionally in providing expression for the entire personality. Chances for recognition are better so-cially, politically, and economically. Opportunities for social contribution are much greater because of the scarcity of entrepreneurial ability relative to those suited to employment. There is no need to share profits, if any, with anyone except the federal, state, and local governments. Of course, a businessman will be expected to make greater contributions to charity and various community activities, and to belong to more associations and possibly more civic clubs. His returns will be more nearly equal to his efforts than if he were dependently employed.

Freedom of action is greater. If an owner wants to slow down a bit or take a vacation, that is his business. Recently one of the authors had some pictures of his daughter taken at a studio noted for high-quality work. After several weeks he received notice that the pictures were ready, only to be greeted the next day by a sign on the door "Gone Fishing. Open in Two Weeks." As Professor Converse said about the relief from pressure:

> A successful chain store executive lost his health largely because of such pressure, and later started a manufacturing business of his own. This business grew into one of considerable size. He regained his health in spite of the fact that he worked more hours each day than he did as an employee.[11]

The proprietors of many small businesses admit that they could make more money if they would work harder, but they do not want to. From one point of view this is a weakness of small business, since many proprietors, in the absence of any prodding from higher-ups, show a tendency to loaf. From another standpoint, however, this is really a good thing, for life certainly should have a meaning other than continual hard work under pressure.

Since it is the most obvious as well as the most common reason for entering business for oneself, the opportunity for greater profit is discussed last. This aspect includes the negative factors of not working to help pay the salary of high-priced top executives, not sharing profits resulting from one's efforts with absentee stockholders, and the positive fact that a man is worth more as his own boss. Since World War II the Federal income tax provisions have made it highly advantageous financially for men of ability to operate their own enterprises rather than to remain in dependent employment. The authors' surveys of the reasons why school of business graduates entered business for themselves disclosed that desire for greater profit was the dominant motive. Professor Converse considered it to be the foremost reason for starting a business,[12] and other authorities usually accord it first place in order of importance. As far as small manufacturers are concerned, a recent survey made for the Committee for Economic Development shows this reason to be unimportant because it influenced only one out of ten. The main reason given was to be able to create, to develop, to invent; and fourth on the list was a desire to be their own boss.[13] As with most human conduct, the "reason" for going into business rather than employment probably consists of many components,

[11] P. D. Converse, "Should I Start My Own Business?" University of Illinois Special Bulletin, No. 5 (April 10, 1945), p. 8.

[12] *Ibid.,* p. 6.

[13] Doland R. G. Cowan, *The Small Manufacturer and His Specialized Staff,* Small Business Management Series No. 13 (Washington, D. C.: Small Business Administration, February 1954), pp. 10-11.

opportunity for greater profits being merely one of the more obvious and less controversial.

Although statistical data dealing with the reasons for business ownership are limited, the results of two recent surveys furnish information on this topic, at least for the group included. Replies were obtained from 250 commerce majors of the University of Mississippi who had been graduated from 1923 through 1948. Approximately one-third were business owners. This group stated the following reasons for entering business for themselves:

Reason	No. stating each reason	
Desire for independence; to be own boss	20	
To go in business with father	11	
Inherited family enterprise	3	
To expand business started by brother	1	
To locate at or near home	3	
Total personal and family reasons		38
More rapid advancement as own boss	8	
Make more money	7	
Capitalize own experience	4	
Take advantage of a good opening	4	
Steadier and more secure	3	
Unable to find position at satisfactory salary	2	
Total economic reasons		28
Grand total		66

Although this list emphasizes the importance of personal reasons as factors leading to entrepreneurship, greater profit certainly is apparent as a major motive.

Of this same group of commerce graduates, nine-tenths of those who were employed stated that they wanted their own business some day. These employed persons gave the following reasons why they had not as yet undertaken business ownership:

Reason	Number of Employees	Percentage of Total
Need more capital	68	27.6
Need more experience	56	22.8
Waiting for right opportunity	52	21.2
Not suitable for my type of work	12	4.9
Risk too great	12	4.9
Prefer employment	12	4.9
Worry less as employee	10	4.0
Miscellaneous	24	9.7
Total	246	100.0

A survey of College of Business alumni of the University of Oklahoma conducted in 1953 showed that 93 self-employed had 145 reasons for becoming independent enterprisers, as follows:

Reasons (not separately ranked)	*No.*	
More income, profit, opportunity, receiving all gains, reward proportionate to effort, ambition, accumulating and investing savings	49	
Dissatisfied with employment and lack of progress	10	
Greater security	6	
Total primarily financial reasons		65
Desire for own business, independence, freedom, initiative, challenge, prestige, applying ideas and being own boss	44	
Personal satisfaction, contentment, leisure, health, being with family ...	8	
To settle down in one place	4	
To practice profession	2	
Hobby interest	1	
To provide jobs for others (depression years)	1	
Total largely personal preferences		60
To enter Dad's or family business	14	
Depression, no jobs, fired	6	
Total due to circumstances		20
Grand total		145

As shown in the foregoing table, 65 of the reasons, or 44.0 per cent, were concerned primarily with the financial advantages of being independent. Considerable data from other sources indicate that the advantages are based on facts. Independent businessmen do have higher money incomes and especially larger disposable incomes (after taxes) than dependent employees. *Fortune* reports that more than 50 per cent of the 70,000 individuals with incomes in excess of $50,000 per year in 1952 were independent enterprisers.[14] Professional men in self-employment had average incomes of $7,395 compared to $5,078 for those in dependent employment.[15] Financially at least, all reliable evidence points to the superior advantages of independent business or professional practice. When the entire period of gainful employment is considered, there is no iota of doubt—independent enterprising is vastly superior on a purely financial basis.

The University of Oklahoma survey[16] showed 93 self-employed and 89 in dependent civilian employment. Forty, or 45 per cent, of the latter had definite plans for becoming independents. Eighteen of the remaining 49 gave the following reasons for not planning on self-employment:

[14] "The Private Enterprise Revived," *Fortune* (June 1953), pp. 115, 234.
[15] Sylvia F. Porter, "How Does Your Income Rate?" *Look* (October 20, 1953), pp 85-90. From 1952 Bureau of Census.
[16] See page 70.

Reasons	*No.*
Satisfied with their jobs and feelings of security	5
Security of employment	2
Would lose retirement benefits (Civil Service and education)	2
Risks too large, lack capital, job O.K.	2
Scared	1
Restrictions on small business too great	1
Total risks and security	13
Too late, 15 to 20 years in dependent employment	3
Lack of opportunity so far	2
Total lack of opportunity	5

DISADVANTAGES OF BUSINESS OWNERSHIP

Attractive as your own business may seem, the attractiveness is not without its limitations. Risk is probably the greatest of these—risk of financial loss, of the loss of your business reputation, and of personal prestige. Actually, loss of business reputation is not great, as most small businesses that do not succeed fold up quietly with plausible excuses given to the public. Usually no serious financial loss results, especially to creditors. Only the supersensitive individual unsuited to business ownership is likely to suffer development of a serious inferiority complex. In a surprisingly large number of cases one or two failures are followed by success that eventually leads to an outstanding business. Again Woolworth and Macy may be cited as examples, although the number is legion.

Most of the alleged disadvantages of business ownership are traceable to: (1) lack of personal aptitude; (2) lack of proper qualifications; (3) inadequate planning and preparation; and (4) poor judgment, incorrect timing, or choice of the wrong kind of business. A careful study of the field of small business, such as that aspired to in this book, will enable a larger number of individuals to make the right choice for their future and to succeed in direct relation to the accuracy of their decision.

The following are usually given as the disadvantages of small business ownership:

1. Greater risks, financial and personal; some may be covered by insurance *if* the owner has a policy, but many he must bear himself. Among the latter group are: errors in forecasting, demand and price changes, obsolescence, changes in government policy, changes in taxation or in the international situation, inventions, ideas launched by competitors, changes in traffic routing or rates.

2. Longer hours and, sometimes, more worry.

3. Entire responsibility for all decisions, and for meeting payroll and other expenses.

4. Irregular income since all business is subject to continuous ups and downs.

5. Responsibilities to self, family, employees, and creditors.

6. Bosses are not one but several: the public, customers, creditors, the government, and other social groups.

7. Income is usually small, especially at the beginning.

8. Many agencies, in addition to those already mentioned, will regulate activities and reduce independence. Some are the requirements by insurance companies of minimum standards, the local fire or police departments, health authorities, labor unions, and quite possibly others—depending on the type of business.

Until the hoped for relief is obtained, the following are additional disadvantages of business ownership: (1) the burden of numerous government reports and investigations that make heavy demands on the owner's time and resources, and (2) taxation that bears especially heavily on the beginning small enterprise. It seems that government investigators have refused to deal with anyone but the owner in the small firm, thus diverting the owner-manager's already limited time and energy to what in many cases are simple routine inspections for safety provisions, and adequate records for required reports.

As we review and compare the foregoing arguments, our individual reactions will differ. Family matters and financial conditions will influence some decisions. Differing personal characteristics in terms of courage (or foolhardiness) versus timidity (or conservativeness) will evoke various responses. The thrill of going into business and banking one's capital and reputation against the ability to produce independently may be the determining factor for some. Others, on recognizing the hazards, will conservatively withdraw. All of which prompts the question, "What kind of person does it take to be a good operator in the field of small business?" Certain authorities believe that only one out of twelve or fifteen individuals has what it takes to be in business for himself. In 1954, we had nearly 4.3 million business establishments and a total of about 60 million gainfully employed. Thus, the ratios mentioned agree closely with existing conditions.

WHAT IT TAKES

The successful independent in business or professional practice exhibits many desirable traits in addition to those generally conceded to be important for success as an employee. Important among these are (1) enterprise—a self-reliant attitude supported by confidence in one's ability to take risks, make decisions, assume responsibility, and pioneer; (2) determination—a driving urge for success as an independent and persistence and stamina enough to carry through in spite of obstacles; (3) balance and control in self- and time management; (4) ingenuity or creative imagination—constantly seeking new and better ways to do things, to outdo competition, to determine and control one's own progress; and (5) honest self-evaluation and constant efforts to improve. Notice that these are all stimuli provided for employees in varying degrees by the employer, if and when they are wanted, which must originate with the individual himself when on his own. They do not exhaust the list, but they are of outstanding importance.

A decision so important and so complicated as whether or not you should enter business for yourself deserves a multiple approach. In general, the procedure is to study what different authorities consider to be prerequisites for successful business ownership, and then to compare or evaluate yourself in terms of these requirements. In this section several groups of requirements are given. Although they overlap to some extent, the duplication is not serious. All should be used before reaching your final decision.

The person who fails to grasp opportunity fails in business; and the person who characteristically permits others to overrule, override, and overrun him will just as characteristically be ridden, ruled, and run out of the business world. Business is not unethical, but some businessmen are. The fact of the existence of such business hazards, plus the fact that business is, above all, sometimes cruelly practical, will soon be evident to the naïve beginner.

What are typical reasons for personal success in small business? Among the most common attributes we may include:

> Ability to handle money wisely.
> Ability to inspire and instruct others.
> Ability to make sound decisions.
> Knowledge of modern business methods.
> Knowledge of merchandise and materials.
> Knowledge of laws and restrictions.
> Willingness to accept responsibility.
> Willingness to work hard and long.
> Willingness to wait for results.

Note that these are all abilities (skills), knowledge, and willingness (attitudes). As previously stated, certain *skills, knowledges,* and *attitudes* are essential to success in any occupation. The above are representative of those required in small business.

The following advice published by the U. S. Department of Commerce under the caption "Are You the Type?" may also aid you in deciding whether you should be your own boss.

Your entire mental make-up has a direct and important bearing on whether or not you should go into business for yourself. A practical way to judge this matter of traits is to compare yours with those of the typical independent businessman who succeeds.

First and foremost, he is the leader type and gets a big kick out of being independent. He has ambition and initiative, energy and good health. He isn't afraid of hard work.

He likes people and he knows how to get along with all kinds and all ages. He is a firm boss but a fair one.

He thrives on responsibility. He takes the bad breaks and the good breaks in his stride. He has the knack of sizing up a situation accurately and making quick decisions. If his judgment is wrong he isn't sunk. Rather he swallows his medicine and determines not to make the same mistake again.

He is honest and pays his bills promptly. His word is as good as his bond. He is businesslike—a good manager. He watches details and knows at all times the state of his business and where it is headed.

He knows when to borrow money in order to take advantage of cash discounts or quantity buys. He also knows when to expand, when to draw in, when to risk and when not to risk.

He gives his customers their money's worth in goods and services. He studies their likes and dislikes; strives to satisfy them without giving away his profits.

In other words, he keeps his eyes wide open, is smart enough to seize a good bargain and honest enough not to take an unfair advantage of anyone.

Lastly, the successful independent businessman feels a definite sense of responsibility to his community. He has a civic pride, takes an active part in co-operative efforts to make his town a better place in which to live and work.[17]

It's a big order. Can you fill it? To those who answer "Yes" the following suggestions are offered:

Sit down with yourself for an honest analysis of your own history, your likes and dislikes. What did you do as a boy—deliver groceries after school for regular pay, or run your own lemonade stand, your own paper route, or similar business venture? How did you react? Did you envy other boys who chose the opposite approach to yours? Carry this analysis right down to the time when you began to consider starting your own business. What gave you the idea in the first place? Was it some friend's unexpected success as his own boss? Was it a reaction to taking orders with no chance to talk back, such as many veterans experienced during and after both World Wars? If so, maybe another employer could be found who would be easier to get along with. In some cases at least, an individual's family situation may have a bearing on the right decision. We are not thinking now of family financial status—just of personalities.

Rating scales are used by employers in evaluating prospective new employees. Consider that you are employing yourself to manage your own capital, reputation, and future when you use such a scale. Be honest with yourself. It is your own future you have at stake.

[17] *Establishing and Operating Your Own Business,* Industrial (Small Business) Series No. 19 (Washington, D. C.: U. S. Department of Commerce, U. S. Government Printing Office, 1945), pp. 3-4. See also rev. ed., 1950, and Wendell O. Metcalf, *Starting and Managing a Small Business of Your Own* (Washington, D. C., Small Business Administration, 1958), pp. 1-8.

Later consideration will be given to selecting a kind of business, evaluation of specific requirements for success that may be acquired, and points to evaluate relating to finances, location, and similar factors. It may be helpful to draw up a blank, listing the qualities that are considered important for success in business. You should rate yourself on each trait, comparing yourself with someone who has that trait in a highly developed form. In addition to rating yourself, you might ask some of your friends to rate you. If they know you intimately and are willing to judge you frankly, this may be very helpful. It should be remembered that many men succeed because they have some traits in a high degree; very few possess a full measure of all these character traits.

Such an analysis will possibly show that you are weak in some of the important character traits. Once you are aware of your weaknesses you can set to work to eliminate them.

Too many prospective enterprisers fail to realize the range of abilities and skills required for success. In response to an inquiry about a course in small business given by the Armed Services at the close of World War II, the following interesting answer was received:

> At Shrivenham we gave the students some factual information about opportunities and possibilities. Most of the boys knew pretty well what businesses they were interested in, however. Then came the disillusioning part—we went over, one by one, all the functions of business. About half of the students finally decided not to start a small business; they had not realized it was necessary to know so much about so many subjects! For those who were serious, we had frequent personal conferences to try to help them with their individual problems. I believe the courses were successful, but the man who did most of the work in that field over there was Professor D'Alton B. Myers, Washington, D. C. His connections with the Department of Commerce Committee on Small Business gave him a wealth of material and experience.[18]

FIELDS OF SMALL BUSINESS

As already noted, in each field or kind of business it is possible to have a unit that is small relative to others in the field, and yet very large when judged by the usual standards set up for small business. An outstanding example today would be automobile manufacture by minor companies. Of greater practical value in keeping with the purpose of this text is size relative to the average, individual prospective businessman, especially the college student and recent graduate.

Small business, like any heterogeneous group, may be divided into various categories—dependent upon such factors as size, location, volume of business, nature of activities engaged in, goods or services offered. Some classification of these enterprises is desirable. For our purposes, it may be well to consider

[18] Excerpt from letter of June 17, 1946, from Professor Wayne L. McNaughton, University of California, Los Angeles, California.

them from the viewpoint of activities engaged in or functions performed. Merchandising, service, and manufacturing are the three major fields.

In the late 1930's retailers accounted for about 58 per cent of all firms.

If only the four main fields of small business are considered, in 1959 retailers comprised 57.3 per cent and service establishments 24.1 per cent of the total. Much more important than relative numbers, however, are the unique contributions of the small enterpriser in manufacturing—pioneering new products and innovations, and rendering specialized production services for large industrial corporations.

Small and independent enterprises predominate numerically in (1) merchandising, both retail and wholesale; (2) certain fields occupied by functional middlemen, such as agents and brokers; (3) services, both professional and nonprofessional; and (4) manufacturing. Independent professional practice is unique enough to warrant a separate chapter later in our text and will be referred to only incidentally in the other chapters. The service fields in general have received far less attention in most college books and courses than the others listed.

The merchandising businesses have as their objective the selling of goods at a profit. They buy finished products from wholesalers or manufacturers and retail (or wholesale) them to others for consumption (or resale). They are all merchants, whether retailers or wholesalers. Most retail stores are small businesses.

Functional middlemen perform one or a limited number of marketing functions for goods they do not own. Many small independents operate in (1) selling—brokers, manufacturers' agents, advertising agents, local window display companies and sales consultants; (2) buying—resident buyers for both retailers and consumers, and merchandise brokers; (3) transportation —local cartage, short-haul truckers for hire, taxicabs and limited service buses and airplanes for hire. Many individuals operate on a full- or part-time basis in these fields in the broad zone that overlaps professional and nonprofessional services, such as accountants, and market researchers.

For our purposes any business may be considered as manufacturing that is engaged primarily in receiving materials in one form and, after working on them, distributing them in an altered form. This would include processors of farm products, local craftsmen or artisans, bottling plants, and similar enterprises regardless of size. It would exclude the accepted "service" industries, such as laundries, cleaning establishments, and repair shops, where work is performed on goods owned by the customers; and beauty parlors, dentists, and the like, where work is performed on the person of the client.

The service businesses offer trade-specialist services to consumers, merchants, or even to manufacturers. They are staffed by technicians with skills for hire.

As a class the service industries have risen to a position of national importance only since 1920. They were not included in the census until 1933, although many larger units now listed in this category—such as large power laundries, for example—were included previously in the census of manufacturers.

Most of the common types of service establishments perform work on goods owned by the customer or upon the person of the client. Many others perform services of a different kind, such as rendering special advice, but for these their patrons are also willing to pay a fee.

For our purpose a more precise definition of service is important because the very nature of services has an important bearing on factors like policies, location, financing, market promotion, and other management factors. We are also seeking a better understanding of the status and opportunities of small business in this second largest field. A "service" may be defined as an intangible economic good, nonreversible or nonreturnable, whose value does not depend primarily upon some material article that may, or may not accompany the rendering of the service. It is an economic good because: it requires productive effort of a type that must be paid for directly or indirectly; it has utility or want-satisfying power which users are willing to pay for if necessary; and is available free, if at all, in such limited amounts or inferior quality as to command a price from users. This limits our definition to the commercial of business service fields.[19] The qualifications are necessary because: (1) many services are offered free of charge in connection with the sale of tangible commodities, such as the retailer's free credit and delivery; and (2) certain other service fields have self-appointed experts. This is where the quality aspect comes in. On the one hand it constitutes the major problem of service institutions in these fields, whereas on the other hand it is serious enough to require legal protection for the public in fields like the practice of medicine or public accountancy. As to the "advice experts," giving advice, regardless of the advisor's qualifications, seems to give some people so much pleasure or satisfaction that, unless restrained by law or other devices, they often force their unwanted and incompetent advice on their victims; moreover, they expect no direct payment from the public.

The second characteristic of a service, namely, that it is nonreturnable or nonreversible, is of great importance to the businessmen in the service fields. Some services once rendered may be destroyed and their value consequently eliminated, but they cannot be returned. An example would be a fancy "hairdo" exposed immediately after completion to a deluge or hurricane.

Illustrative of the nonreturnable characteristic would be a train passenger who, after arrival at the station of departure, changes her mind and decides she does not want to take the trip. Of course the property right evidenced by the ticket, merely a claim good for the transportation service not yet rendered or received, may usually be returned for a refund. Some other passenger may later utilize the opportunity to receive the forfeited transportation service.

---

[19] The definition would also include professional services, such as law and medicine, but these are beyond the scope of this section.

The professional advice of the railroad agent in this case may have been destroyed, but returning the unused ticket does not return the service the agent rendered. This is one reason why most service fields operate on a pay-in-advance basis. In recent years two modifications have been made in this policy. One is the promotion of greater use of certain services like tourist travel through the arrangement of pay-later credit plans. The other is a policy of "money back if not satisfied," occasionally used in a few entertainment or advisory service fields. Both examples have their counterparts in the sale of tangible goods. Credit extension is an accepted fact in retailing, as is the returned goods privilege.

Although the value of a true service does not depend primarily upon a tangible article that may in some cases accompany the rendering of the service, it is important to understand the relationships between the service proper, the material object, and the reasons for use of the latter. On the one hand some record or evidence of the transaction may be necessary, or convenient, for the service-rendering agency, while on the other hand such a material object often enhances the value of the service to the client or patron. Professional men often accompany oral advice with either a prescription written in Latin, or a "brief" that elaborates on certain unique features of the case before stating the suggested remedy.

The convenience or economy aspects are illustrated by the use of tickets entitling the purchaser to a seat on a train, in a theater, or other service. Such a procedure may be necessary to prevent promises to render the service later in excess of the capacity of the train, theater, and so forth. It may be a device to sell particular positions, such as reserved seats, or it may be merely a convenience. It is often desirable to separate the cashier who sells the ticket and receives the money from the ticket collector. It may also be an advantage to the customer who prefers to purchase and pay well in advance for the right to receive the service. Certain repair shops use this device, with something else added, by selling coupon books calling for particular repair services later as needed, or even a "packaged" job. The last named may cover inspections, tune-ups, and all repairs needed to maintain the article in good working order for a specified period of time.

The various service fields, some as diverse as medical care, transportation, and maintenance of the family radio, have found the same management devices useful. These are often devices previously developed in different fields like commodity marketing and manufacturing. This further illustrates the importance of understanding our thesis of the basic fundamentals regardless of their main association with a particular business field.

In general, it is not our intention to study functional middlemen or professional and semiprofessional service fields, especially not those that require highly specialized training and have few of the problems and functions, such as financing, selection of location, layout, vendor relations, and the like, typical of other small businesses. In Chapter 25, however, independent practice in the professional and semiprofessional fields of interest to business school graduates is discussed. Certain topics discussed throughout our book will have a bearing, and may be usefully applied.

The importance of the fields of independent enterprise may be suggested in two ways: by a study of the fields entered by college of business students after graduation, and by an analysis of census data. Data on the former are limited to the results of four surveys of state institutions of medium size. The percentage of small business alumni for each school by main fields was as follows:

| School | Per Cent | | | |
	A	B	C	D
In retailing	26	45	40	29
In wholesaling	7	16	4	3
In manufacturing	7	13	10	7
In real estate and insurance	29	13	16	18
Practicing law and accounting	7	3	7	12
In other service fields	19	10	16	22
In farming and ranching	5	..	7	9
Total	100	100	100	100

Because the samples used in each survey were small, these distributions should not be considered as representative, but merely as the only data available on this topic. The Harvard Graduate School of Business in 1953 was in the process of developing records of alumni that could be used to identify entrepreneurs from employees, and found that among 16,000 graduates 3.3 per cent were in one-alumnus enterprises covering a wide diversity of occupations.[20] Stanford University Graduate School of Business, in a survey of 2,000 alumni found 34 per cent of the 1927-1941 graduates to be entrepreneurs and 18 per cent of the total of 1927-1952 to be self-employed, but did not publish the occupational distribution of the entrepreneurs.[21]

CONCLUSIONS

One of the major decisions many people must make is whether to choose dependent or self-employment. For those who are well suited to being their own boss, financial and other advantages are *much* greater than in dependent employment. But evidence indicates that only seven to eight per cent of our gainfully employed are suited to independent enterprising, and probably from 17 to 55 per cent of business school graduates would be happier and would achieve greater financial success and other recognition as independent enterprisers. On purely financial grounds the advantages of self-employment for

[20] James W. Fitch, "A Study of Employer Companies," *Harvard Business School Bulletin* (Winter 1953), pp. 216-218.

[21] Carlton A. Pederson, "Twenty-five Years of Business School Graduates," Stanford Business School *Alumni Bulletin* (July 1953), pp. 3-10.

college graduates, at least in recent decades, have been clearly established.

Neither independent nor dependent employment is any guarantee of security or happiness for the misfit or the indolent. Both have their price. The intelligent approach includes an appraisal of all advantages and disadvantages of each method of earning a living, a study of the requirements for success in each, a self-analysis by the individual as to which group he belongs, followed by adequate planning and preparation based on the results of these steps.

QUESTIONS AND PROBLEMS

1. What sequence of steps is recommended in the chapter in preparation for your future career?

2. State and evaluate the advantages claimed for big business employment.

3. How do inducements for employment offered to college graduates by big business fluctuate as compared to opportunities for self-employment? Discuss.

4. Is a typical executive in a large corporation likely to be affected by frequent changes in top management? Explain.

5. What feature or attitude has been stressed in recent years by college recruiting scouts for big business? Is this good or bad for the college senior? Discuss.

6. Suggest how large corporations should deal with inventions and other innovations made by their employees.

7. How do you account for the abnormally high death rate, mental and emotional incidence, and shorter life span of big business executives compared to entrepreneurs and the entire population?

8. Is a conscientious and ambitious business school graduate likely to worry more as an employee or in self-employment? Explain.

9. Compare the financial security of big business employment with that of self-employment for the college graduate.

10. Evaluate the nonfinancial advantages of dependent and self-employment.

11. On a purely financial basis, is it true that big business executives are better off than independent enterprisers?

12. Summarize the major advantages of entrepreneurship for the typical business school graduate.

13. Why do the majority of college graduates *not* become self-employed since the advantages appear to be so great?

14. State and briefly describe the five major characteristics of the successful independent enterpriser.

15. How can you determine whether or not you are the "own business type"?

16. How do you account for the decline from the late 1930's to the early 1950's in the percentage of total business concerns engaged in retailing?

17. In relative order of prominence, what major fields account for the largest percentages of small concerns?

18. Describe a "service" as explained in this chapter. What are the essential features of the service fields compared to merchandising and manufacturing?

19. From limited data presented in this chapter, and from census of business data, how are self-employed school of business alumni distributed by main occupational fields as compared to total population?

20. What significance do you attach to the fact that the two leading graduate schools of business have begun to survey the occupational distribution of their alumni?

21. Secure three to five copies of an appraisal scale such as the one discussed in the chapter; ask close friends and acquaintances in business and finance to rate you and to get their ratings to you without identifying themselves. If you consider yourself to be the own business type, but others rate you low in this respect, try to develop the qualities that caused your unfavorable appraisal.

22. Two years after his promotion from a junior to senior executive position in a big company Joe develops insomnia, loses weight, and becomes irritable. His salary is good, and prospects for further promotion are excellent, but he is unhappy and worried. A month's vacation ordered by his physician affords no relief. His wife advises him to resign and enter business for himself although, even if success-ful, this would reduce their income by over half for several years at least. What should Joe do, and why?

5 • Pre-Ownership Planning and Preparation

The greatest assurance of success in entrepreneurship is adequate planning and preparation. This should include experience and knowledge and their applications. One of the more pathetic situations has been the polished college graduate forced on family or government dependency because of failure to plan and prepare for a probable need. This applies especially to women.

BASIC DECISIONS

Two decisions are basic, careerwise, to future success and happiness:

1. First is a careful analysis of all factors that determine whether an individual is better suited to self- or dependent employment. This is the time when preconceived notions or snap judgments should be avoided by an honest evaluation. At one extreme is the man who decides he wants to be his own boss before considering what it takes and whether he is willing to make the necessary sacrifice. Many failures can be traced to a hasty decision, as illustrated by the high percentage of failures due to personal causes. The other extreme appears most frequently among young women who "just know" they could not operate their own business successfully. Almost invariably they have no basis for their "knowledge" on this point. Many obtain jobs and use only part of their potential ability and superior education to make money for their employers, while others may be obliged later to enter self-employment because of circumstances beyond their control. How much better it would have been in either case if adequate planning and preparation had been made.

In the past, vocational guidance or career conferences have given inadequate consideration to independent enterprising. Fortunately, this situation is changing. Business orientation courses in progressive schools are devoting increasing attention to the opportunities in, and advantages of, self-employment in both business and professional fields for those capable of becoming independents. It is no more difficult to measure and predict capacity for success in owner-management than in executive employment. Probably it is easier. Some of the modern small business courses devote considerable attention to this point. The approach is sound because extensive experience indicates that despite many similarities the same individual may be very successful and happy as an independent operator but a near failure in dependent employment, and vice versa. The college student who has an opportunity should enroll in at least one of the small business or independent enterpriser courses even though at first he may not be seriously considering self-employment. This should enable him to make a more thorough appraisal of the two careers, dependent and independent employment. In dependent employment many of his business contacts will be with smaller concerns, distributors, suppliers, and service establishments; so the better he understands their characteristics and problems the easier it will be to deal with them effectively.

2. The second basic decision is the choice of an appropriate field of activity, or career, whether for self- or dependent employment.[1] In this respect consideration should be given to the major fields of retailing, wholesaling, manufacturing, and servicing; to choice of function, such as accounting, advertising, personnel, purchasing, and the like; as well as to the commodity or service to be handled, such as groceries or wearing apparel, personal or maintenance service. Not only are many individuals likely to be better suited by temperament and other personal traits to one of these alternatives than to the others, but there are often significant differences in techniques involved. In student counseling the authors have encountered many such problems. One graduating senior, an accounting major, who had taken none of the merchandising courses offered had two attractive job opportunities. One was with a large industry in which her accounting training could be used to maximum advantage, though working in the office of a large manufacturing concern did not appeal to her. The other opening was in the controller's division of a leading department store where, of course, the Retail Method[2] was used. This position appealed to her but she knew virtually nothing about the Retail Method and felt uncertain about starting in this field. Fortunately, the girl had ambition and ability and by intensive study of material recommended by the author and sympathetic encouragement by the controller she was able to make good in the position to her liking. But six months of uncertainty and intensive extra effort could have been avoided if adequate attention had been given earlier to the probability of such a development.

In several cases known to the authors, girls have stopped their formal education by dropping out of college as soon as they became engaged or married.

---

[1] See: Ed and Reed L. Cunningham, *Your Career; How to Choose a Profession and How to Prepare for It* (New York: Simon & Schuster, Inc., 1949) ; *Career for the College Man: The Annual Guide to Business Opportunities* (New York: Career Publications, Inc.) ; Dun & Bradstreet, Inc., *Getting Ahead in Small Business* (New York, 1954) ; *Retailing Has a Career for You* (New York: National Retail Merchants Association, 1954).

[2] See Chapter 24 for discussion of the Retail Method of accounting control.

The fallacy involved in such cases is the assumption that marriage, even a potentially successful one, guarantees financial security for the wife, and she need not prepare for the possibility that some day she may have to become an income earner for the family. Sometimes this need is temporary, to supplement the family income during periods of relatively heavy expenditures or when the husband is temporarily disabled. In other cases the difficulty of maintaining a desirable standard of living under current conditions with only the man working causes many wives to remain employed almost continuously. Since the war, two-income families have become common among wage earners and college faculties. During the early 1950's, married women in the labor force outnumbered single women about two to one. Although fewer in number than families with two wage earners, there are many notable examples of side-line family enterprises bringing in as much or more income than that of the chief wage earner. Local political office holders and teachers are prominent in this group.

Two contingencies that no beginning family can forecast accurately deserve consideration. One is permanent disability of the husband; the other is divorce. Especially for the mother with younger children an opportunity to support the family by operating a small business often has many advantages over employment. Her hours can be more flexible; the children may at times accompany her to the shop; or the enterprise may even be operated from the home. Your authors know of several cases of this sort, and a few less fortunate. In one city a neighbor purchased a beautiful home and maintained her family, including two school age children, on a very satisfactory standard of living, all from income earned in her own small business. In the same city at the same time another woman in essentially similar circumstances, except that her business venture was having trouble, finally sought professional counsel. Investigation disclosed that several unwise decisions, all traceable directly to lack of business training, had resulted in exhaustion of her original capital, and a shift from a moderately profitable beginning enterprise to one in hopeless difficulties. Although a college graduate, this woman had taken no business courses and had to learn the hard way, and too late, that operating a small business successfully requires more than a college degree and initial capital. A moderate amount of preparation while still in college, or seeking professional counsel before committing her enterprise to a hopeless position, would have meant so much to this family. But it was the old story—no need to prepare for income earning if marriage is in the picture.

One final contingency is at least more pleasant to contemplate than those just discussed. It is the probability that the mother may want to demonstrate her ability to contribute to the family income when the children are old enough not to need her at home continuously, or to "fill the void" when the children are married and set up their own families. Small business is a natural recourse in such cases, especially for the college woman who is adequately prepared. Similar in many respects is the operation of a small independent enterprise during retirement years, for which adequate planning and preparation should begin early.

PLANNING AND PREPARATION

Before proper steps can be taken to become adequately prepared for the future, the college student must accept the probability that he or she may someday be obliged to enter self-employment. For those who contemplate becoming independents soon, some rational choices must be made and specific preparation undertaken.

Probability of self-employment. It is shortsighted for any college student, regardless of major or any other factors, to neglect at least a minimum of preparation for self-employment. Our society has become highly complex, interdependent in all spheres, and definitely a pecuniary market-economy. We buy our living in the market place. While in college the engineer, education major, home economist, physical education major, journalist, fine arts student, and all others, should enroll in several business courses including one or more dealing specifically with the independent enterpriser.

The future is uncertain at best. Extensive experience shows that many college graduates do not remain with their majoring subject for their careers. Individuals and economic conditions change; some occupations decline in importance and new ones appear. Unpredictable events may indicate the desirability of changing occupations or of shifting from employment to self-employment, or vice versa. One way of being better prepared for such developments is for the nonbusiness major to include a few business courses in his curriculum, and for all students to enroll in a small business or independent enterpriser course. The last suggestion may furnish information that need never be put to actual use in later life, but how can the student know this? Also, the broader outlook obtained should make for a more intelligent choice between dependent employment or independent enterprise, as well as furnish a basis for a better appreciation of our complex economic system.

Minimum of experience. In addition to taking business courses every student should endeavor to obtain some employment experience in the field selected for a career or one closely related to it. It is difficult, if not impossible, to provide conditions on the college campus that are truly representative of full-time postgraduate employment. Learning what an employer expects in return for his investment in wages, and how to get along with co-workers and customers are objectives difficult to achieve in the classroom. Vacation work and part-time employment, especially that in connection with a co-operative or in-service training program sponsored by the school, may serve two of the purposes desired: (1) actual work for pay in the environment representative of a chosen career; and (2) learning to work with and for others on an income-earning basis. The first of these objectives may result in disillusionment or deglamourization of a previously selected career, because many vocational choices are made on scanty knowledge of the field. But how much better it is to discover this while still in college, with an opportunity to change goals and prepare for another occupation, than in the traditional manner—several years after graduation. Since a man's future happiness depends primarily on his occupational fitness, this objective warrants emphasis.[3] College men are often unduly influenced in their career choice by current salaries being paid or a misconception of what an occupation involves. Many college women select their majors largely because the field is currently glamourized. The fashion fields, advertising, and personnel are modern examples. These are all desirable lines of activity, but each has its special requirements for success, which include certain abilities and, usually, hard work—features that should be understood and appreciated rather than submerged in a sea of glamour. Just as the ambition of the vast majority of men is to own their own enterprise (and many change their goals when they understand the abilities and effort required for success) so it is with the glamour careers. We can't all be small businessmen or there would be no big business; we can't all be leaders or there would be no followers.

PRE-OWNERSHIP EXPERIENCE

Students often ask about the amount and type of experience that will best prepare them for operating their own enterprises. Some believe it is better to learn the best methods developed by big business; others feel they can learn all the functions of management and get broader experience by employment in a small concern. The beliefs are more widespread than well founded that experience needs to be obtained in a firm similar to the one a person plans to operate, and that it must be firsthand experience. Our use of the term "experience" in this section includes actual paid employment, as well as work analysis of the type described later.

Balanced experience. Top-ranking experience should be balanced and include managerial responsibilities. Balance refers principally to including all of the major functions, such as selling, buying, production, personnel, finance, accounting, and communications. Balance is also involved in some cases where concerns of appreciably different size operate in the same field. The man with several years' vacation and part-time experience in all divisions of a small store should consider seeking his additional experience in one or two functions that the large companies are known to have developed efficiently, such as merchandising and accounting in chain stores. Conversely, the former chain or department store employee should obtain experience in a smaller independent concern to get the over-all viewpoint of managerial duties and to learn what the owner-manager has to do for himself that is normally done by headquarters for the manager of a chain store or for a buyer in a department store.

[3] "A Man's Happiness Depends First on Career," *People Today* (November 18, 1953), pp. 24-25.

It is sometimes difficult to obtain exactly the type of experience desired, but planning and control are as important in this as in other activities. Certainly it is well to know the type of experience needed, to realize when you have learned as much as possible in one job, and when to move on to another. If at this time your employer is unable to transfer you he may make it possible for you to learn something about the other function in various ways. A former student of one of the authors did just this, with permission, by working on his own time at night with the manager of another department. Before long he was offered a position as assistant to this manager. Sometimes you may need to change jobs to round out your experience. Our survey of Oklahoma University alumni enterprisers already mentioned showed that the representative alumnus worked for one or two employers before becoming his own boss. Some of our alumni surveys, however, have disclosed very little connection between the type of jobs held and kind of business ownership later undertaken. In such cases the beginning years as an independent have been much rougher than for those with well planned pre-ownership experience.

If an in-service training course is offered by your school there is an excellent opportunity to obtain desirable experience and to multiply its benefits. In such a program the trainee is recognized by his employer as such, rather than as just another college student working part time. Job experience is usually rotated or diversified and the trainee has access to management for questions and consulation. Often in larger concerns he is invited to sit in on junior executive meetings. The fact that the student's grade depends upon his work analysis report, ratings by his supervisor, and participation in seminar discussions, add greatly to the benefits obtained. Many students who have worked part time for several years in the same firm learn much more about the business during their one semester as a trainee. With 20 students all in different training stations meeting to exchange experiences and discuss problems during their seminars, each one has his own perspective vastly enlarged. Questions raised during a seminar stimulate each trainee to seek an answer from his employer.

Managerial experience. Actual managerial experience is not so easy to secure within the few years which ambitious prospective enterprisers allow for pre-ownership employment. However, a student working part time may sometimes act as relief manager during the vacation period, if he is capable and willing. If the average of five years of full-time employment after graduation is allowed some managerial experience may be obtained. Over 50 per cent of alumni enterprisers started on their own within five years after leaving college. The next most common interval is one year or less, representative of somewhat older graduates with considerable pregraduation work experience and above average capital and credit status. These averages emerged from surveys by the authors of the case histories of alumni of two state universities, covering their graduates in business from the early 1920's to the early 1950's.[4]

---

[4] University of Oklahoma, 1953 and University of Mississippi, 1949. Supply of survey reports exhausted.

The fact that two independent surveys yielded similar results on this point suggests that on the average five years is the maximum time needed by most graduates to acquire pre-ownership experience and to secure the minimum capital and credit reputation needed. None of the alumni had had the advantage of enrollment in an in-service training program or in any of the modern independent enterpriser courses, both of which could have reduced the postgraduation time devoted to acquiring experience.

Managerial job analysis. When actual managerial experience is not obtainable on the job, there are several devices that have proved their usefulness. They fall into two classes—work analysis and similar experience. Analysis involves critical observation of the management, determination of just what management activities are performed and why, the reasons they are done in a certain way, appraisal of their effectiveness and possible improvements, checking on the soundness of ideas for improvement and urging the learner to visualize how he would carry out each managerial responsibility. These steps call for keen observation, creative imagination, discreet questions, and discussing ideas or suggestions with the manager and co-workers. If handled tactfully with a proper display of interest, and well timed, an inquiring mind is certain to be approved by progressive management. In fact it is one of the key criteria in the newer methods of selecting future big business executives. Even though it often happens that an employee's ideas for improvement may be impractical because they neglect something he does not know about, making suggestions may be the best way to learn of factors not readily apparent, and imagination is still considered by management as indicative of promising executive ability.

Testing managerial ability. The value of similar experience rests on the fact that management functions and principles are universal. What is managed may call for some modifications in application or emphasis and magnitude of responsibility, but that is all. This fact helps to explain the success of Junior Achievement Clubs and the general transferability of managerial skill from field to field. It is also an important factor in the recent establishment of small-scale plants for executive training by huge corporations. The seven M's of management were discussed in detail in Chapter 3, but those of greatest significance for our present purpose are: minutes (time), money, materials, markets, and men.

Every prospective enterpriser has ample opportunity to test his managerial ability and to develop proficiency in management, even while in college.

Time (or minutes) management stands out like the proverbial sore thumb at the dinner table in differentiating competent, self-reliant students from their weaker sisters. This is also the top ranking managerial prerequisite for successful independent enterprising. Time is the most fixed or absolute of the elements that enter into a task. The whole field of scientific management originated with Frederick W. Taylor's efforts to ascertain the time required to accomplish different tasks. Taylor in turn got the idea from his mathematics teacher in school who always seemed able to assign problems that required exactly the same amount of time to solve regardless of whether two or 29 were assigned. With a little analysis, any student should be able to determine the time he needs to complete assignments in each course and then budget his time accordingly. The same idea applies to getting to classes on time and to all other activities. Yet in any group there are always those who are chronically late for class, finishing assignments, keeping appointments, and everything else. Others under similar circumstances are always on time and still have more free time than the chronically late ones.

Money management for the individual's personal affairs should be easier than for the family or business enterprise. Income tends to be more certain than in the small business. Expenditures are more nearly under the control of the individual than in the family or business. But enough of the elements of uncertainty, choice and need for control are present in all three situations to permit developing and testing managerial ability. Yet students have been known to pay fines for not paying school fees on time, and student clubs always have some members who fail to pay their dues on time.

Materials, merchandise, or raw materials in business, and personal effects for the individual or family, are capable of equally effective management in the two areas of activity. Decisions must be made regarding wearing apparel, food, shelter, recreation, and so, in terms of needs, alternatives, values, results desired—all factors similar to those in business. This is one reason an increasing number of men are enrolling in consumer economics or consumer-buyer courses. Spending the individual's or family's income for best returns, and making most effective use of goods purchased both on a short-time and long-time basis is fundamentally a function of money and materials management.

For the management of markets and men our analogy is not quite as close as for the first three factors. Many students, however, work part-time. Some wait until the last minute and grab the first job available. Others make a market study, plan well in advance, select a job to their liking with above average pay and with opportunities to learn while earning, "sell" themselves to the employer and do a superior job of market management. A student of one of the authors, after analyzing the public transportation facilities near the campus, convinced the transportation company officials that they needed a new service that he had devised, and sold himself as the part-time manager while in college at double the going rate of student wages. He made good and was offered a full-time job with the company at graduation time.

Man, or personnel management, is discussed later, especially in Chapters 9 and 16. In essence, it consists of getting others to want to do what you want them to do, and to do it efficiently. Unless a student operates his own business on the side, or has a part-time job involving the management of others, most of his efforts in this area will be for nonfinancial goals. Roommates and other fellow students may at times be influenced to assist, or at least not obstruct, one's work. Club affiliations and other extracurricular activities afford opportunities to develop and test leadership ability. Even classroom activities, oral reports, class discussion, committee or panel memberships, and the like afford similar opportunities. Many students are very proficient in managing their instructors—learning the latters' pet ideas, idiosyncrasies and motivation—and using this knowledge effectively. The average student who attempts this form of "man management" is just "politicing" and is soon known among his professors as another "operator" or "big blow." He is lucky if his pseudo-management does not actually harm him. So it goes in business. The manager who considers his employees as easy prey, or dumb, proves his lack of leadership or managerial ability.

An almost infinite number of capsule or pilot plant projects are available to any student who cares to make an honest test of his managerial ability. He can play his hobby for a potential profit, become a freelance agent for some large concern, or act as a resident buyer for out-of-town, usually rural or small-town consumers. The idea is to set up an actual business venture—accurate in every detail except size, like the scale models of navy ships and airplanes—then manage the venture profitably. Dollar profits may be small but they must be earned profits.

Three points of major importance warrant emphasis here: (1) good management is basically the same in a drugstore, automobile factory, or the family enterprise; (2) one *can* learn from the experience of others; and (3) it is humanly impossible for one person to acquire all the knowledge and skill needed for entrepreneurship from personal experience alone.

Special applications. Management involves four basic functions: direction, supervision, control, and co-ordination. Practice can be used to develop skill and ability in any one of these. In large organizations managerial responsibilities are commonly specialized so that different individuals or groups are responsible for only one of the basic functions. A prospective manager can test his ability and develop proficiency by taking one function at a time and practice performing that function as applied to almost any type of activity. It need not be in the field of business, as our earlier discussion of student activities illustrates.

Direction may be used as one example. Direction involves planning, forecasting, deciding what is to be done and how it is to be done—in terms of guides or standards rather than details. Policies and executive decisions are elements of direction used in business. A policy is a guide to action based on anticipated future conditions and the predetermined reputation desired. An error in forecasting the conditions upon which a policy is formulated is almost certain to result in failure unless the policy is changed in time. Skill in forecasting can be improved through practice. In training assistant buyers for retail stores, one technique is to have them practice estimating the cost of merchandise, then analyze why their estimates are too high or too low. So with forecasting. Predict the outcome of any activity, then analyze the bases for your prediction and why the outcome is different from what you expected. What factors did you fail to take into account? Could these have been anticipated had you understood their importance? Try this for new products, new store locations, some policy change announced by business, a new service being offered, a new course announced by your college, or new models of different products. Select things for which you will be able to determine the reliability of your forecasts within a reasonable time, then conduct your post-mortem seriously and profit by your experience in later forecasts.

A similar project is part of the content of one of the authors' classes. In a town of 30,000 a new residential area of above average homes was developing two miles from the central retail district. There were no retail stores nearer than downtown. The residential area was bounded on one side by Main Street, and on another at right angles to it by a street that led traffic from the new district, as well as from several older residential districts, to Main Street en route to the central retail district as well as to a new superhighway to a large city 20 miles away. A centrally located grocer decided to build a medium-size supermarket on part of this vacant space.

Our project was to predict the outcome of these developments. Most of the students considered the supermarket project a good move and predicted it would be successful. A few, however, thought it should be much larger and provide greater parking facilities. They suggested a location one block away which was not yet built up. Within a few months the second largest supermarket in town announced that it would construct a new, much larger, and more modern building, with very generous parking facilities, just one block from the new store but on an intersection currently occupied by older houses. The students had not given adequate weight to the tendency of retail districts to move toward the better residential districts and had not foreseen the trouble and expense that progressive merchants will incur to obtain the best possible location and customer facilities. Students who participated in the project have learned by "experience" with no personal loss of funds or time. The project is being continued, and we are building our new forecasts on lessons learned from previous experience.

Control is another function that can be practiced in a wide range of activities. It involves a predetermined but possible achievement, current information or checking to see that progress is satisfactory, and prompt corrective action if it is needed. Try it in some course—any course—just for practice. Pick your final grade in the course, then exercise control. How? How does modern business control expenses, sales, or desired profit? Not by waiting until the week before the end of the accounting period to determine its progress and to take whatever action may be needed. Not by trying to talk the accountant into showing a profit because the business needs it to float a securities issue. Instead, control starts even before the beginning of the accounting period and is continuous throughout, sometimes on a daily basis. The final goal, say a net profit of five per cent of sales, is broken down into its major components, gross margin of 30 per cent, total expenses of 25 per cent. Gross margin and expenses are further subdivided and scheduled on a time basis.

Some of these are more amenable to control by management than others and consequently are watched more closely. The result is that management knows in advance what must be accomplished each day, week or month, if the final objective is to be achieved. It also knows the factors that can most readily be manipulated to achieve its objective. By continuous comparison of actual with standard, significant deviations are caught in their incipient stage and corrected.

Conceding that the student does not have the authority possessed by management to require frequent and detailed reports does not lessen the usefulness of our example, unless he picks an unusual course where no measures or clues to progress are indicated, and only the final course grades are announced. In a representative case he will have several guides to his progess, including one or more tests before the final; class discussion with questions and answers; announced policies regarding factors included in grading, such as attendance; possibly some written or oral reports; and, finally, the "grapevine" reputation of the instructor as to his method of grading. All of these are likely to be fully as reliable as the guides used in business management. The public is notoriously fickle in its demand and preferences, and employees in recent years seem to be trying to outdo the public. College students change and even professors do sometimes, but more slowly and less drastically than the consuming public and business employees.

Co-ordination in modern functionalized management is our current version of the entrepreneur's traditional goal of obtaining the optimum combination of resources. Co-ordination may also be likened to driving a three-horse team, or keeping a limited budget properly divided as to essentials, luxuries, and savings. The *auria mediocritas* (golden mean), wisdom, judgment, temperance, and similar guides to balance preached throughout the ages, show that even the individual in his personal affairs must co-ordinate many diverse forces that often tend to pull in conflicting directions. Thus, co-ordination, though specialized as a function of higher management in modern big business, is basic to success in every type of human activity no matter how small or how personal.

As the top management function, co-ordination usually involves appropriate use of direction, supervision, and control. In securing pre-business ownership experience, or in testing and practicing co-ordination, almost any project may be used. One encountered recently by the authors should illustrate this point. The authors know a young family who, to acquire certain durable goods they wanted, stretched their resources to the limit expecting to receive $400 extra income in one payment that failed to materialize. The man's regular income could make up this deficit in six months, or in four months with extra care. The family decided on four months but did not want to sacrifice on the more important elements of their standard of living. A bank loan was arranged to carry them for the four months needed. Regular expenses were reviewed for opportunities to economize during the period. Spending and living habits were likewise examined and a four-months' plan developed that would meet their needs if operated as planned. Thus the usual steps involved in direction were taken. A simple recording procedure was set up to keep them informed twice a month as to goals that should be met as against actual accomplishments. Since several habits would have to be changed during the interval, each parent agreed upon certain ones to supervise. During the first month unexpected emergency expenses for their child made it clear that larger economies for the remaining three months would be required. Reconsideration of expenses showed that a shift to certain less expensive but equally nutritious foods and a similar change in entertainment would provide the extra savings needed. These were agreed upon and their schedule revised accordingly. Each remaining reporting period showed progress being made as planned, so control indicated no need to change their plans. The bank loan was repaid when due and all other obligations were met on time. Had difficulty been encountered in changing certain habits, supervision would have detected it in time for any necessary adjustments. Thus, co-ordination was obtained through effective use of direction, supervision, and control, making adjustments needed in time to achieve their final goal in spite of the unexpected extra expense. Incidentally, the family learned the importance of a contingent reserve to meet unexpected expenses.

AVENUES TO INDEPENDENT ENTERPRISE

Many prospective enterprisers may choose between starting a new concern, buying, or buying into an established one, and a few may have a fourth alternative of entering or taking over a going family business. Chapter 6 deals with buying a going concern, especially from strangers. Chapter 7 considers starting an entirely new enterprise. Our interest now is with the remaining alternatives, where preownership experience is more directly involved.

Much may be said for, and a little against, buying a controlling interest from one's employer. By working in the business you plan later to own, the major dangers of buying a going concern from strangers are avoided. You have an opportunity to study strong and weak points of the firm that could easily be missed by an outsider. You can learn all the details of operation, study methods or policies that you might be able to improve under your own management, and get much better acquainted with the personnel, customers, and suppliers than would be possible otherwise. You may be able to take over managerial responsibilities gradually, profit by the experience and knowledge of the retiring management, and transfer to yourself most of the goodwill associated with the personality of the former owners.

It is probably this last advantage that makes this method preferred by those planning to enter professional practice for themselves. A recent graduate in medicine, dentistry, law, or accounting usually finds that the endorsement of the well-established, reputable practitioner with whom he becomes associated is accepted by the clientele, and he has an opportunity to prove his own ability much sooner than if he were to attempt to practice alone. Even in nonprofessional fields the method has similar advantages though to a lesser degree. A unique feature about many small businesses is that their goodwill is directly related to the personality of the owner, rather than to the brands or company reputations of large corporations.

In taking over the owner-management of a family enterprise much of our previous discussion applies, except that emphasis shifts from verifying the honesty of the retiring management to proving the managerial ability of the new owner-manager. In some cases there may be a valid need to appraise the soundness of the enterprise and to decide whether it would be worth taking over in preference to other alternatives; but such cases differ little, if at all, from the continuous need for management to appraise its position and future prospects. More important is proving the managerial ability of the heir. So many case histories are known in which a founder built a successful enterprise whose profitable operations were enjoyed without effort by his son, only to have the grandson ruin the business by his incompetence, that the expression "three generations from shirt sleeves to shirt sleeves" has gained widespread acceptance. Employees, and sometimes other family members, tend to resent and suspect the boss's son who steps into a top management position right out of school. Thus we have both a potential lack of managerial competence and a need to prove one's ability to others where a family enterprise is acquired.

To avoid the dangers just mentioned, several methods have proved their effectiveness. Most common is for the boy to work in the firm during vacations and part time during the school year. If his work is co-ordinated with business courses it can be extremely valuable experience. Principles and methods discussed in class can be considered closely as to their application to the company. One difficulty in the case of many college courses taught in terms of big business is to appreciate applications to the small independent concern. The very effort of seeking to find ways to utilize those that are appropriate can greatly enhance the value of the course work and indicate possible ways the family concern might be improved. This is not to say that the company's methods and policies should be changed as each new topic is developed in class. Rather it is an exploratory exercise to determine what would be necessary to make any indicated changes and the probable effects such moves would have. The process resembles class discussion of a case problem.

A second method is for the son to learn the business through part-time work while still in college if possible, but as soon as feasible on a full-time basis as an understudy to the management. He is upgraded in stages as he develops proficiency. This plan may be successful even when the son does not start to work in the company until after graduation, but is usually better if pregraduation experience in the firm is obtained. While he is still the boss's son, and considered by other employees to be a favored person, he does have an opportunity to make friends and demonstrate his ability. It is far better than coming in as a total stranger to the organization and starting in a top management position.

A third and final method is for the son to prove his ability in an outside organization before becoming associated with the family enterprise. Although more time-consuming than the other plans, it does reduce the danger of an incompetent person becoming the owner-manager purely by inheritance, and tends to reduce employee feeling of favoritism. It also has an equally important advantage, that of bringing in an outside viewpoint. The dangers inherent in inbreeding are reduced. Just as many large companies often employ executives from other concerns to keep a flow of new blood and outside ideas coming in, so it is with this method. Probably the more serious limitations upon a college graduate going directly into the family enterprise center around this danger of inbreeding. It is also the major disadvantage of buying the business from an employer in a nonfamily enterprise.

In the final analysis a decision should be based on circumstances in the particular case. No two family enterprises will be identical in all factors, such as attitudes of other family members, possible rivalry for control of the business, ambitions and attitudes of employees, qualifications of the prospective owner-manager at the time of graduation, or needs of the business. The basic guide in all cases is adequate planning and preparation far enough in advance to make it really effective.

CONCLUSIONS

The strong probability that even college women may someday need or want to operate a small business venture was discussed at greater length than it has been in the past because our knowledge in this area has expanded greatly in recent years. No college student can safely assume that he or she may not someday find independent enterprise to be the only satisfactory alternative to support by the government, or by relatives, or to a life devoid of purposeful activity—one of the greatest tragedies that can happen to a healthy intelligent person today.

From the time of graduation, about 50 per cent of the college men who become entrepreneurs have in the past taken up to five years to do so. Survey results indicate that often these years have not been used effectively either to secure related preownership experience or to acquire adequate initial capital. Only very recently has the value of planned preownership experience received the attention it deserves. With logical planning it may well begin while a student is still in college, and need not involve spending much, if any, time in actual paid part-time employment.

With the premium placed on time by modern society, and especially by the small enterpriser, planning and preparation that may easily result in over 50 per cent more effective utilization of a prospective enterpriser's time is of major importance.

No reference was made directly in this chapter to accumulating adequate initial capital. This topic has been so grossly overemphasized relative to managerial competence that it is handled later in Chapter 11. Also, acquiring capital is an integral part of planning and preparation.

QUESTIONS AND PROBLEMS

1. What two career decisions are basic to adequate planning and preparations? Why is each so important?

2. Discuss the recommendations in this chapter for college women who plan on marriage as a career.

3. Compare our ability to predict the probable success of college students in dependent employment with those in self-employment.

4. If a college student has definite plans for employment in a large corporation, what, if any, benefits could be gained by taking a "small business" or "independent enterpriser" course? Discuss.

5. Why is it advisable to consider the field of business as well as commodity or service and type of employment (dependent or self-employment) when deciding on an occupational career? Illustrate.

6. Discuss the place of side-line or part-time independent enterprising in career planning for both men and women.

7. For a mother with young children to support compare the advantages of and limitations on dependent with self-employment.

8. What likely developments might result if many women college graduates who usually take jobs were to become independent enterprisers?

9. Compare the logic of present college curricula that require all business majors to take several liberal arts courses with the absence of any business courses required of most nonbusiness majors. Discuss.

10. Specifically, what does a college graduate need to learn from employment experience that could not be obtained from college courses? Are you sure? Discuss.

11. Do you agree with the survey conclusion cited in the chapter that a man's future happiness depends primarily on his occupational fitness? Does this also apply to women? Discuss.

12. Discuss the ways many college students select their careers. How could this situation be improved?

13. Discuss the desirability of big or little business employment for preownership experience. Which do you prefer for yourself?

14. Why do all business schools not offer in-service training courses? Should they do so? Explain.

15. Explain how analysis can be used as a substitute for, or supplement to, actual managerial experience in preparation for business ownership.

16. Discuss the nature of, and limitations on, similar experience in lieu of actual managerial experience in business.

17. Which is more important in preparation for business ownership, proficiency in time or money management? Prove your answer.

18. What, if any, elements are common to both good consumer economics and able entrepreneurship?

19. How is man, or personnel management, defined in the chapter? Comment on this definition.

20. Briefly summarize the discussion in the chapter of preownership managerial experience.

21. Name and briefly describe the four basic functions of all management.

22. Describe how practice can be secured in the exercise of supervision while still in college.

23. Compare buying a concern from strangers with buying into the concern you are working for.

24. Discuss the problems and other relevant considerations in taking over a family enterprise upon graduation.

25. What basic principle represents the thesis of this chapter?

26. Outline a practical one-semester side-line project for yourself to achieve the best possible test of your managerial ability. Would you be afraid to try it? Explain.

27. Two Korean War veterans in their early twenties called at the home of a business consultant in 1955 seeking financial aid to start their own radio and television repair shop. In lieu of dollars they were offered free consulting service, which they promptly declined in a highly resentful attitude. Evaluate the attitude of both parties. Why would the consultant offer advice valued on a time-only basis at over twenty times the "contribution" requested?

6 • *Appraising a Going Concern*

To enter business for yourself you may buy a going concern or begin a new one. Even if you plan to start an entirely new business it will be worth your time to study methods used in appraising a going concern for possible purchase. In starting a new business you may not be able to secure contracts restricting competition, such as exclusive agency rights, as you can in buying a going concern, but you may investigate the likelihood of such developments for the future.

The Need for Evaluation

Frequently the beginner prefers to buy a business already in operation. In most instances the business will have been offered for sale, but in some cases the prospective purchaser, on seeing a given establishment operating in a certain location, makes an offer. In either case the value of the business must be determined by buyer and seller alike before an agreement can be reached. Both parties are anxious to secure full value in the exchange.

Points to Consider in Appraisal

A going business can be appraised with reasonable accuracy. The problem is, first, to have a check list of considerations and, second, to be able to recognize good points and bad, or advantages and disadvantages as they appear. The great deficiency in amateur business buyers, as with amateurs in any market, is that they usually fail to recognize certain vital factors when they are present. Successful analysis of the value of any business requires the following qualifications on the part of the analyst:

1. Enough experience in the trade to recognize obvious points against, and points in favor of, the business as it stands.
2. Knowledge based on well-kept personal records or other sources of

101

information as to past performance and probable future developments and trends.

Any list of considerations for appraising the average business would include the following questions:

1. Has it been consistently profitable?
2. Is business volume increasing or decreasing? Why?
3. Are overhead expenses in line with the volume of business?
4. If the profit ratio is not satisfactory, could it be improved?
5. Is the inventory well balanced? Is it new and timely?
6. Is the equipment modern, and in good condition?
7. Is the lease satisfactory? When does it expire? Can it be renewed?
8. Is the competitive situation healthy? Is any new competition developing?
9. Are relationships with wholesalers satisfactory? Are there any franchises expiring?
10. What is the buying public's attitude toward the business?
11. What is the business community's attitude toward it?
12. Are there any new or proposed community developments that will affect the business?
13. Is the personnel situation satisfactory? Are key people efficient and willing to remain?
14. Are there any personal, religious, or political reasons why a successor would be unable to carry on this business successfully?
15. Why does the present owner desire to sell?
16. What occupation will the present owner follow when the business is sold?
17. How does this business, in its present condition, compare with one you could start and develop yourself within a reasonable time?

There probably are more such questions that could be asked by the prospective purchaser. Buying a business is a serious matter, involving substantial financial investment as well as having certain other implications in terms of personal satisfaction and occupational enjoyment. A business bought at the wrong price, which despite much work never becomes successful, costs the purchaser and his family far more than the dollars invested and lost.

The more important factors to consider in appraising a business may be grouped under four main headings according to objectives and process of evaluation. These are: (1) profits, (2) tangible assets, (3) intangibles, and (4) estimates. Several aspects of each deserve consideration. With sufficient care, both the profit aspects and the tangible assets can be appraised objectively and quite accurately. Intangibles include attitudes of the public and the trade as well as goodwill. They may be more difficult to appraise accurately, yet they are real and often are of great importance in determining the true value of a going business. Estimates deal either with probable future developments or with comparisons of alternatives: whether to buy or to build "from scratch."

In buying a business, as in buying a house in which to live, the question alway arises, "Is it better to buy or to build?" In this connection, a ledger-like pattern for comparing pros and cons might be followed to determine on which side the balance may be:

Arguments for buying an established business	*Arguments for starting an entirely new business*
Proved location	Can select own lines
Resources known	Can plan own layout
Equipment available	Can hire own employees
Stock already selected	Can select own clientele
Established clientele	No precedents to follow

PROFITS

Profitability

A study of the authentic records of the business will quickly reveal whether or not it has consistently paid its owner a reward for his efforts. The prospective purchaser must weigh the question of whether or not this income would be satisfactory to him and his family, and if not, whether it could be increased. He will want, therefore, to study the records of operating expenses, comparing their percentages with those of efficiently run enterprises, in order to detect opportunities for reduction or extension. Among bankers, suppliers, and lawyers, most of whom deal frequently with problems of business failure, there is a common acceptance of the principle that most failing businesses do so for lack of intelligent management. Those who are accustomed to studying the records of bankruptcies and other discontinuances can as quickly spot the discrepancies causing the failures as a physician diagnoses the common human ailments that cause most illnesses and deaths.

Profit Trend of the Business

A study of the records of any business will indicate whether or not volume is on the upgrade or downgrade. If it is going up, it is worth while to know which departments or items are bringing the volume, and whether or not there is profitable volume. If it is going down, a similar determination of areas of lost volume should be made. Many businesses have failed after selling great quantities of goods at such low margins as to make net profits impossible. Some of these have allowed their competitive lines to crowd out their profit lines.

If the volume is decreasing, the question may arise as to whether it is due to failure to keep up with competition, inability to adjust to changing times, or simply lack of energetic sales promotion. A familiarity with the trade plus a few pertinent questions put to bankers, suppliers, and others will usually bring out the facts.

The Expense Ratios

For every size and type of business there are generally recognized ratios of expenses to sales that are accepted as proper throughout the trade. Some of these are collected and consolidated by trade organizations, such as the National Retail Hardware Association or the National Association of Retail Grocers. Others are developed by interested manufacturers, as Eli Lilly and Company has done for the druggists, and Butler Brothers for independent variety stores. Figures for manufacturing concerns have been collected by Dun & Bradstreet, Robert Morris and Associates, and others. Operating figures for some businesses have been determined by Westinghouse (radio repairs and appliances), the American Foundry Institute, and the National Association of Dyers and Cleaners. Dun & Bradstreet operating ratios for retail concerns are the standard for this field. Useful figures are also available in books on the subject and government bulletins that may be secured in most public and school libraries.

A study of the figures of any concern offered for sale, compared with standard ratios for the trade, will quickly bring out any discrepancies. In the course of explanation of these by the seller, the intelligent buyer will quickly become aware of operating problems that may be important factors in helping him make up his mind to buy, or how much to pay for, the business. Some conditions are due simply to poor management. An excessive operating cost may be caused by carelessness, and a less than normal expenditure may indicate laxity in attention to a particularly vital activity that would bring results if properly financed. Frequently if the same amount of money is intelligently spent on one activity, instead of being misspent on another, desirable results in volume and profit promptly appear. The following is a simple illustration of how operating ratios are used in appraising a business.

A grocery store offered for sale has had average annual net sales of $70,000 for the past three years with no appreciable increase or decrease. Analysis of the company's records discloses the following operating ratios expressed as a percentage of net sales, for the preceding three years.

	19—	19—	19—
Total expenses	15.8	16.2	16.5
Wages other than owner's	4.0	4.5	4.9
Rent	3.5	3.5	3.5
Advertising	0.5	0.3	0.1

Dun & Bradstreet standard operating ratios for this kind and size of store for the years covered were as follows:

Total expenses 15.9

Wages other than owner's 4.1

Rent 2.6

Advertising 0.6

Certain comparisons significant to the prospective purchaser may be noted from these ratios. Obviously the rent is too high. Possibly a talk with the landlord would result in a new lease that would bring this expense into line. The payroll has increased steadily. Why? Investigation would probably disclose a situation that could be corrected by the new owner, such as carelessness in employing more help than needed, or laxness on the part of certain employees. Further analysis shows that both total expenses and payroll were close to the standard ratios the first year; total expenses increased each year by approximately the same amount as payroll. If the new owner could bring payroll into line, total expenses would be satisfactory. However, if conditions are such that dollar payroll could not be reduced enough to adjust the ratio, there is still another possibility. Notice that total sales remained constant over the three-year period while advertising expense declined from 0.5 per cent to 0.1 per cent. By increasing this item it is quite likely that total sales could be increased enough to bring both payroll and total expense ratios into line.

Even the casual reader will notice the frequency with which "if" was used in the preceding illustration. Operating ratios are standards or guides. Their effective use depends upon the ability of the new owner to change conditions that have caused any ratios to be appreciably different from the standard.

TANGIBLE ASSETS

The Inventory

A wise buyer's stock of goods is made up of timely, fresh, well-balanced selections of materials or merchandise, which in the well-managed store will consist of those items the public wants—in the proper sizes and designs and colors, priced to fit the local buying power and purchasing habits. In a well-run factory there will be a representative collection of raw materials and supplies that will surely be used up within a reasonable period of production. Seldom will quantities of metals, lumber, oils, compounds, or other ingredients be found on hand that are no longer used or for which there is no reasonable expectation of future use. "Close buying" is as essential to profit in one line as in another.

In the mercantile line there is an old saying that "goods well bought are half sold." Goods well bought are those for which there is a proved demand, or which the seller wisely buys to meet the requests of customers whom he knows well enough to anticipate their needs.

Every bankruptcy sale brings bad buying to light—one crossroads store in a recently electrified community was found to have six gross of chimneys for kerosene lamps. Another had four dozen pairs of specially constructed, expensive miner's gloves to meet the needs of six local men who were infrequently employed in a mine 12 miles away. Another store had drawer after drawer full of yellowing stiff collars, and numerous boxes of one-piece men's underwear long after their popularity had waned. Not only had they been poorly bought but they had not been "cleared" in time to prevent a substantial loss.

A small factory had forty cases of wooden toy wheels when metal toys had displaced the demand for which they had been bought six years before.

One of the classics among thousands of such examples is a grocer who, after an ocean voyage, developed a taste for exotic sea foods that caused him to pile his shelves high with cans, jars, and bottles of marine novelties, of which his agricultural customers would have none.

The purchaser of a going business is not particularly concerned with the errors of his predecessor, except as an object lesson. His concern is that he does not become the loser on an aggregation of "dead" stock that the seller has listed as worth its original value—the loss is rightly the original buyer's, and the new buyer must beware that the loss is not passed on to him. "Age" an inventory before appraising it.

The Equipment and Fixtures

Because of the rapid mercantile and industrial progress in recent years, it is important that the modern business be equipped with machines and fixtures that are efficient. A row of punch presses that made a substantial profit twenty years ago may not now compete with those that produce several times as many units in the same time, nor can those old machines even be made to produce at the greater speed. Office equipment must be investigated very closely, since obsolete calculating, addressing, or duplicating devices are almost worthless; to use them is generally inefficient, and parts and supplies may be unobtainable. This is particularly true of little-known makes.

Fixtures that dignified the store and pleased the customers a few years ago are now as out of date and uneconomical as carbide lamps for automobiles. A cash register for the bookkeeping requirements of 15 years ago will usually not give the information now required for computing figures for taxation. This entire picture of obsolescence is one that is all too characteristic of the business about to be sold, for in many cases the usefulness of these items, representing a substantial capital investment, has been outlived long ago, and their cost has long since been written off. The owner has delayed so long in replacing them that they have no trade-in value, with the result that now, in considering their replacement, he finds the prices of new equipment to be exorbitant. Hence he decides to sell the business—any financial realization he makes on the fixtures and equipment is now clear profit, an extra bonus on his period of operation.

Other Assets

Certain assets in addition to the more obvious physical goods and equipment have a real value to the purchaser. Among these are the following:

Lists. Mailing lists, general lists of customers, lists of customers interested in certain products and other lists have very definite value. Selective lists may often be sold or rented. A veterinarian's list of wealthy dog owners, for example, could bring a good rental fee from a store introducing a new line of accessories; a custom tailor's list of customers would be worth money to a seller of made-to-order shirts.

Credit Records. These, if carefully kept, are of high value to the buyer of a business; without them he may lose heavily in granting credit or be forced to pay for credit reference information.

Sales Records. Carefully kept records that show normal seasonal demands are a valuable insurance against under- or overstocking.

Franchises. These have a sale value even if they were granted without cost. Even informal franchises have value if the supplier will continue delivering to the new owner.

Contracts. Favorable leases and other advantageous contracts are worth real money. In the winding up of many profitable businesses, the sale of leases has produced unexpected profits for the owner.

Incidentally, purchasers of businesses should have their attorneys make sure the foregoing assets are included in the sale. There is at least one instance in which the sales agreement did not include the list of customers; the seller came around the next day and got his own price for the list from the helplessly stymied buyer.[1]

INTANGIBLES

The Public's Attitude

All of us know of business concerns that have existed for years without ever establishing sufficient goodwill to be regarded favorably by the average customer. These stores and shops and manufacturing plants do business, to be sure, but it is done *in spite of* their policies, their goods, their service, their handling of customers. Strong competition would have driven them out of business long ago. Their position in the public mind, from a preference standpoint, is at the bottom of the scale.

[1] "Business Assets in Addition to Stock and Good Will," *Small Business Aids*, No. 2 (Washington, D. C.: U. S. Department of Commerce). Extracted from "Many Assets in Addition to Stock and Good Will Can Be Built, Increasing Dollar-and-Cents Values of Business Enterprises," by Elmer Roessner, *Small Business Today* (August 3, 1946), McClure Newspaper Syndicate, New York.

This public attitude cannot be changed quickly. Most observers will agree that it takes far less time to ruin a good name than it does to make a bad one good.

A successful business has goodwill as an asset. The point of discussion here is that ill will is a liability. Taking over a popular business may bring with it public acceptance that has been built up over a period of many years, and which is therefore valuable. Taking over another that is unpopular may mean that it will take years of promotional effort to remove the taint of unsatisfactory customer relationships, accumulated over as many years, before valuable goodwill can be acquired.

Because many sellers of businesses seek to place a premium on goodwill that really is ill will, care should be taken to determine whether or not the business in question is selling an asset or a liability. This may be done by questioning unbiased persons, including customers, bankers, and others who will have bases for an opinion. Statements obtained from such individuals may then be compared with the ledger entries to support conclusions regarding the status of the business in the public mind.

This Thing Called "Goodwill"

According to Webster's Dictionary, goodwill is "the favor or advantage in the way of custom which a business has acquired beyond the mere value of what it sells." Most books on the subject describe it as a value placed upon certain business benefits and advantages, such as public recognition and patronage, that a given business has acquired through the years and which, therefore, must be regarded as an appraisable asset when the business is sold. Methods of evaluating goodwill will vary, whether the business wishes only to show it as an asset on the records, or whether it becomes a factor in the sale of the firm.

The buyer of the business must be very realistic in determining what he can afford to pay for goodwill. It will reflect itself in the excess of selling price over the objectively appraised value of goods, equipment, and supplies, after liabilities are deducted. Actually it will be the price, above cold appraisal of the balance of assets as against liabilities, paid by the new owner for his old owner's constructive efforts in developing the business to its present condition. The amount to be paid for goodwill will depend on:

1. How long it would take the new owner to set up a similar business and at what expense and risk.

2. The added amount of income possible through buying a going business as against starting an entirely new one.

3. The relative prices for goodwill asked for other businesses of similar type with similar advantages.

4. The extent to which the old owner agrees by contract to remain out of the same business within a competitive area.

What is the value of goodwill on a statement of assets and liabilities? The prospective buyer had best regard it as valueless, as such, rather considering any premium he must pay above true "book value" as (1) compensation to the owner for his losses on beginning mistakes the new buyer himself might have had to make instead, or (2) payment as an investment for the privilege of carrying on an established and profitable business.

In either case the premium paid should be small enough that it can be made up from profits within a relatively short period. Excessive amounts paid for goodwill are most common where competition for the purchase of a business exists; and frequently, for various reasons, the "other fellow" can stand the excessive beginning costs better than the enthusiastic but unanalytical novice. Goodwill, in the usual sense, can be lost overnight; an opportunity, a proved one, may be worth paying for.

The Business World's Opinions

Occasionally businesses, like people, have dual personalities—one for home use, and one for work and the public. Some enterprises, too, have more than one pattern of behavior—one for customers, and another for employees and business firms. The attitude of the average employee is important to business success; the attitudes of suppliers or contemporaries can make or break any business at critical times. A firm that has the reputation of underpaying employees, of overworking them, or of failing to promote the proper individuals is weakened in its operations. The business that has broken contracts, schemed to get advantages, or has generally established itself as a hard bargainer with no sense of co-operation or loyalty is in an unfavorable condition for sale.

Resources and Franchises

Every manufacturer and wholesaler has among his accounts many whom he considers for one reason or another to be undesirable. If there are favors to be granted, some customers receive them automatically and others on request, while a third group receives as few "breaks" as possible. This last group represents the marginal customers, or those who the supplier has decided are not worth the effort to keep. In fact, they may eventually be displaced in communities where other outlets promise more satisfactory volume. Occasionally a business owner, knowing that he is soon to lose this resource contact, desires to dispose of his business. This is most frequently true in the case of a franchise or a restricted representation for strong lines of goods that in the opinion of the suppliers has been abused. The buyer should, in any case, obtain satisfactory assurances, and new contracts if necessary, with the supplier if a franchise is involved.

Why Is the Business Being Sold?

When the owner of a business decides to dispose of it, the reasons he presents to the public may be somewhat different from those known to the business world, and both of these may be somewhat different from the actual facts. As a rule, there are numerous contributing factors in business sales as well as in business discontinuances and bankruptcies. There may be considerable difference in emphasis, however. The businessman who is about to lose his contract or franchise for a strong line of merchandise, or who knows a new law or civic development that will affect him unfavorably, will not tell his prospective purchaser all that he knows. Nor will the man whose business is threatened by intensive competition usually explain such reasons for selling. If he also "needs a rest," or if owing to his wife's illness she needs a change of climate, he may decide to emphasize these reasons to the total exclusion of the really decisive factors.

The Seller's Personal Plans

Although there is no intent here to cause the prospective purchaser of a going concern to feel that all sellers of businesses are subject to questionable ethical and moral principles, *caveat emptor* has through the years been a reliable maxim for buyers of horses, used cars, and going businesses. There is just enough ignorance on the part of the average buyer and just enough avarice on the part of the typical seller to make buying a business somewhat hazardous. True, there are laws against fraud and misrepresentation, but such cases are usually very difficult to prove in court. Also, pride and the desire to avoid publicity frequently prevent the injured purchaser from taking any legal action.

A few years ago in a small midwestern city an enterprising young man bought what had always been a prosperous men's wear store. The seller took his check and left for Florida to retire. Six months later the new owner received notice to vacate, for the building was to be torn down by order of the state. At about the same time, a new clothing store opened across the street, financed and supervised by the former owner of the old store. Strangely enough, also at the same time, another unfortunate event took place. A second new store was opened one block away by the manufacturer of the line of clothing that the purchaser had hoped to distribute at a profit. Needless to say, the new owner suffered considerable loss.

This is not a typical case, but merely an example of what may happen. Most such calamities can be avoided by careful study of leases and franchise contracts, and by writing protective clauses into contracts of sale. Any hesitancy on the part of the seller to bind himself against undesirable later behavior or consequences may be regarded as indicative of some danger from that source.

ESTIMATES

Competition

Healthy competition is most desirable where there is an ample market. In manufacturing businesses the nearby presence of a competitor improves labor resources, and the two organizations working together can obtain concessions from railroads, utilities, and others that neither could get alone. Since their markets are not entirely local, the fact that they are near together is not a handicap. In the mercantile field the effect of competition, even in areas where the market is large, will vary according to lines of merchandise carried. In staple goods, such as notions, groceries, drugs, and small hardware, close proximity of large-store competition is often undesirable, since trade will be limited to the particular area and there may not be anough to go around. In regard to shopping goods, like furniture, appliances, and apparel, the fact that two stores are side by side is in favor of both, for people will go a great distance to buy shopping items and will go more readily if there are two or more stores in which to shop.

Service industries depend entirely upon the local market and share available business with competitors in proportion to the reputation, aggressiveness, and goodwill of each establishment. Ordinarily the advantages just mentioned resulting from locations near competitors do not apply to service industries; however, the presence of progressive retail stores in the vicinity is usually desirable.

The only dangerous competition in most cases is unscrupulous competition, and that type of business is usually short-lived as compared with longer established, more ethical concerns. Occasionally, however, unethical practices can be carried on over a long enough period to make business impossible for the smaller, legitimate operator. The presence of any such competitors, or the imminence of their presence, should be carefully determined and considered if the business is in a highly competitive trade.

The Manpower Situation

Businesses generally are made up of four elements—materials, money, machines, and manpower. When a business is being purchased, manpower must be considered as of equal importance with profits and production, for it will usually be desirable to retain certain key people to keep the business on an even keel. New people who are both properly trained and steady workers can seldom be secured readily. The prospective buyer will want to know:

1. Are all duties provided for with qualified people?
2. Will any of these people depart with the old owner?
3. Are there any key individuals among the workers who will for any reason be unwilling or unable to continue working indefinitely for the organization under new ownership and supervision?

ADVICE TO THE NOVICE

Check and Double Check

It is recommended practice to make several independent appraisals and then to compare each appraisal with others arrived at through different methods. "Check and double check" is the formula to use.

Unfortunately for the prospective buyer, as was mentioned earlier, something approaching a "business opportunities racket" has developed in many cities. Brokers may advertise and sell the same business time after time to a succession of newcomers, each of whom lasts only long enough to lose his accumulated savings. Naturally this does not mean that all businesses advertised for sale are necessarily white elephants.

Nearly every city has one or more leading business brokers, and some, like Charles Ford and Associates, have several hundred branch and affiliated offices throughout the country. There are over 6,000 business brokers and many deal in other income property. A few, like Ford, reportedly inspect and appraise every business before listing and advertising it, and some also assist a buyer in financing the purchase. The National Business Brokers' Clearing House located in Wilmington, Delaware, publish the monthly *National Business Brokers Journal.* Business brokers normally receive their commission from the seller, but a well-established, reputable broker can be helpful to a prospective buyer, can assist in locating a suitable business offered for sale at a fair price, and aid in negotiating terms and similar matters.

Considering that it is not easy to find a profitable business with good future prospects on the market at a reasonable price, a good broker may be very helpful to both buyer and seller, but the basic advice contained in this chapter still should be followed—check and double check, and take nothing for granted.

An interesting postwar development is the *UI Buyers Digest,*[2] formed in Los Angeles in 1948. This is an advertising and marketing service agency to bring prospective buyers and sellers of businesses, farms, and other income property together through national advertising. Their *Digest,* published monthly, is sent free on request to prospective buyers who indicate the kind of business they are interested in purchasing, and is also used by business brokers. The *Digest* contains descriptions, frequently illustrated, of several thousand businesses and income properties for sale. Headquarters does not do the selling but through field men assists sellers to prepare good advertising copy and sends them lists of prospective buyers. Individual sellers or their brokers then deal directly with the buyers. To the authors' knowledge no claim is made regarding approval of asking prices, although such could be part of the assistance rendered by field representatives. Developments such as

[2] A Universal Interchange, Inc., publication, Interchange Building, Los Angeles 27, California. Formerly, National Business and Property Exchange, Inc.

this, of which there are a few others, should nationalize the market for transactions too often in the past excessively localized. The burden of proof and major risks, however, still rests with the buyers.

The seller's books should not be taken as proof of sales or profits stated therein. Insist upon seeing the record of bank deposits for at least five years or for the length of time the business has been operated by the present owner, whichever is shorter. If possible, obtain the deposit records of previous owners in case the present one has been in business only a short time. Ask to see the owner's copy of his income tax return, which any honest seller should be willing to show. Inspect all bills paid to suppliers and reconcile purchases with sales and markup claimed. Do the same for sales tax receipts. Be sure fixtures and equipment are fully paid for and know any debts you assume. Make certain all back taxes have been paid. It is better not to include any delinquent customer accounts in the purchase price unless they are heavily discounted.

Ask to see the owner's insurance policies. Is his coverage in line with assets claimed?

Experienced business buyers often investigate the reputation of the seller, in addition to the public's attitude toward the business. Talking with customers may furnish information of both types.

Next consider the reasons for selling the business. If poor health is mentioned, determine whose health is poor and verify the claim by consulting the physician in charge. Often the druggist can furnish clues to alleged "illness." What does the owner plan to do after the business is sold? Be sure you receive an agreement in writing that he will not enter the same kind of business as a competitor for some reasonable number of years.

Ask him about any franchises he has for preferred merchandise lines, then verify his statements by writing directly to the firms concerned. Find out if they will continue the franchise if you buy the business, and if they know of any competition about to begin in the district. Also consult the Chamber of Commerce and local bankers on the latter point. If a permit is required to start a business in the town, consult the government officials in charge for clues of new competition.

The city planners may give information about proposed changes in streets or routing of transportation lines that might have a serious effect upon the business in the near future.

An individual should make checks on customers to be sure they are not fakes and should be suspicious if customer traffic increases every time he appears at the store. He should also do some secret checking for at least one week, talking to any suspicious customers and following up on the information they give him.

There are many other schemes used to defraud innocent buyers, such as falsification of inventory figures, solvency, and sales and other records, to mention only a few. It is well to check with several of the owner's more important merchandise resources to see if all bills are being paid when due and to verify his statement of current balances due to vendors. The prospective businessman should familiarize himself with the provisions of the Bulk Sales Law if one exists in the state and take adequate steps to protect himself against future loss resulting from the protection this law gives to creditors.

We quote selected items from a published list of fact-founded admonitions by the Better Business Bureau:

1. *Advance Fee.* If your business needs financing, don't fall for an unscrupulous promoter who offers to arrange a loan if you first pay his expenses. Front money operators may offer to incorporate your business and assist in selling stock. But, when advance fees have been paid to them or their associates, service usually stops or is found to be worthless.

2. *Business Brokers.* Some business brokers, in acting as agents for sellers of businesses, are irresponsible, unfair to prospective purchasers, avoid all liabilities, and are interested only in collecting a fee. Do not be rushed into a deal. Get all verbal understandings in writing from the seller. Put the deal in escrow with a third, reputable, disinterested party. Before you sign an agreement to purchase, have all papers checked by your attorney and all books and records showing earning capacity, past profits, inventory, equipment, obligations, etc., checked by an accountant.

3. *Buy-Back Contracts.* Buy-back contracts, like money-back guarantees, are no better than the guarantors. They are frequently worthless promises made by dishonest promoters.

4. *Job Investments.* Invariably large earnings or a better than average weekly salary are offered to those who will "invest" in the business of a promoter who misrepresents.

5. *Listing Fee.* This is a variation of the Advance Fee Scheme. The fake business broker gets you to pay a fee for listing your name with him for finding the type of business you wish to engage in. Listing fees are sometimes disguised as expenses for advertising or circularizing prospects.

6. *New Promotions.* Decide whether you can afford to lose before you invest in any new enterprise. A large number of new enterprises fail.

7. *Partner Wanted.* Partner-wanted propositions are sometimes nothing but deceptive frauds to get your investment in a supposedly profitable business claiming the need of new funds. In a partnership each partner is responsible for all the debts of the firm. *Know* your partner.

8. *Patents and Inventions.* Investments in new inventions, patents, or patent litigation ventures are usually risky speculations and sometimes frauds.

9. *Territorial Rights.* Should a high-pressure promoter lure you with the right to sell his product in exclusive territory, reserve your decision until you possess the facts. Some promoters misrepresent their products to get quantity orders and often sell several people the same territorial rights.[3]

Although there are many opportunities to mislead or defraud an inexperi-

[3] *Facts Veterans Should Know Before Starting a Business,* a booklet (Boston: Educational Division, The Better Business Bureau, 1944, revised 1946), pp. 8-9. For a discussion of the Bulk Sales Law, see Chapter 12.

enced business buyer, a man who really knows the field places more weight on his ability to analyze the market, judge the competitive situation, uncover adverse future developments, and estimate the profits he could make from the business, than upon the present owner's reasons for selling. These "reasons" are too hard to verify.

CONCLUSIONS

Buying a going business is risky at best. One may not secure all the benefits anticipated, even if they are honestly presented by the seller, but a person will inherit all ill will and other handicaps the business has acquired. Do not be rushed into a decision to purchase on inadequate information, for there are so many difficulties in securing legal satisfaction in case of deception. *Once the business is purchased, it is yours for "better or worse."*

Whether or not to deal with a broker is less important than verification of all aspects of the transaction, using your own lawyer or accountant as needed. Remember that in a small business even genuine goodwill may attach to the owner-manager rather than to the business or its location. Be certain *you* can earn the goodwill and retain it if you must pay for it.

QUESTIONS AND PROBLEMS

1. List all the sources of information you could use to double check a seller's statement as to the value of machinery, or fixtures and equipment.

2. How could the amount of insurance carried by a seller be used as a guide by a prospective business buyer?

3. List the various ways a dishonest seller could create the impression of having a larger volume of business than he actually has. For each method, suggest how you could check on it.

4. Name and briefly explain each of the four groups of important factors to consider in appraising a business.

5. What precautions should be taken if the business offered for sale is a partnership?

6. Examine the provisions of the Bulk Sales Law to see how the buyer should protect himself.

7. What factors warrant special attention in appraising (a) merchandise inventory; (b) fixtures and equipment; and (c) accounts receivable? Explain.

8. Discuss the advantages of and precautions to take when dealing through a business broker.

9. Make a few tests of your ability to appraise certain going concerns. Include one or two that are offered for sale, then follow up later on what actually happened and report your findings and conclusions.

10. Make at least one test case of the comparative costs of buying a going business and starting a new, but similar, concern.

11. A business broker in Pat's city advises him to invest his $8,000 in a business for sale and to borrow the $2,000 balance from his bank. The broker says he would make the loan himself but has too many such requests. Pat figures he could launch a similar business for $11,000. What should he do, and why?

7 • Justifying the New Business

Many small businesses are successfully started "from scratch." It is our purpose in this chapter to examine the justification of starting a new business in a given location, and that the proposed business venture is sound. A genuine business opportunity may be defined as a need for the proposed good or service in sufficient volume at a high enough price and low enough cost to operate at a profit.

The entrepreneur considering a radically new product or service should make a realistic appraisal of the time, effort, and cost of gaining acceptance for his offering. He may also be faced with stubborn opposition and even ridicule that could discourage certain beginners before their proposition has a chance to prove its merits.

Justifying an idea as a genuine business opportunity furnishes the basis for the general policy, at least as far as the aim or purpose of the business is concerned.

Often a genuine business opportunity is uncovered as a result of making a location study. This close relationship will be more apparent later when we consider the new business that is justifiable because of locational shifts.

Most situations involving "justification" will require action in one of three major categories: appraising the need for another business similar to those already established, testing an idea for a new type of business, or shopping to discover a genuine business opportunity. The last represents the typical situation of a young, prospective small businessman who has decided he "has what it takes" to be on his own but has not yet decided what kind of business to start or where to begin.

ROOM FOR ANOTHER SIMILAR BUSINESS

There are two typical situations in which another business similar to those already present may be justified: (1) an expanded market; (2) the presence of inefficient management of existing firms.

Four means are used, usually together, to determine whether or not there is room for another small business in a given community as a result of an expanded market. Three are based on statistics or averages, the other on personal investigation. These data and sources of them are discussed in Chapter 13, "Selecting the Profitable Merchandising Location." It is better to use several methods when the data needed are available because it will give you a sounder judgment.

Assume that a community of 150,000 persons has 14 stores of the type a young man is interested in starting; census data show an average of one store for 9,000 population. Experts calculate that this type of business requires an average of 10,500 in the trading area. Apparently there is such a slim margin that another store would be quite a risk. This is where additional guides are needed. If an index of sales potential shows the town to be well above average, this may be sufficient justification. More important for most lines of small business is the fourth method, the personal investigation. Assume for the foregoing example that this method reveals an increase in population from 120,000 to 150,000 during the past few years; no new stores in this line have been opened, and those already in existence are rushed and apparently very properous. The conclusion is obvious. Select a location carefully and get started in your enterprise.

The second situation—poor management of similar enterprises—justifying another business requires firsthand familiarity with the local situation. Some of the usual symptoms will be evident if it exists: high prices, extensive out-of-town consumer buying, poorly kept stores, shoddy merchandise, frequent out-of-stock conditions, incompetent clerks, slow service and poor quality of workmanship in service establishments, high business turnover, lack of customer loyalty, prevalence of consumer gripes, and exaggerated advertising. Where these conditions abound, there is a "natural" for a progressive, alert newcomer. This is the situation that has given birth to our newer forms of large-scale, modern retail and service businesses.[1] No need exists to worry about stores per 10,000 population or similar averages in a situation like this—there may already be twice as many outlets as the national average, yet one good store is needed. Consumer surveys, if available, are often useful in such a situation to reassure the new enterpriser that his disapproval of the management of existing stores is shared by the local population and evidenced by its buying habits.

Consumer Surveys

Often independent surveys of consumer buying are made in the community by organizations such as schools, clubs, and chambers of commerce. The authors as well as faculty members of other schools of retailing have conducted such studies and published the results which may be available to the

[1] For recent changes that businessmen have been slow to adjust to, see: *The New Era of the Sophisticated Shopper,* New York: Doyle . Dane . Bernbach, Inc. 1960.

enterpriser by consulting publications listed in the footnotes. Usually such surveys indicate the preference for certain stores, reasons for patronage and for shifting trade from one establishment to another.

From such a consumer survey an analysis should be made of the reasons certain businesses acquire patronage. In a particular business one may plan to draw trade by making needed goods available, especially popular goods and exclusive brands. He should determine the potential demand for his product and study his competition. Perhaps he plans to offer unusual value in terms of price. Here he must consider the factors of buying at low prices and operating at low cost in order to be successful. The offer of services of repair or maintenance may be another drawing point, but he must know whether there is a need for such special services and whether he will have a sufficient volume of business to support them.

The amount of out-of-town consumer buying and the reasons people travel to shop should be studied. Capturing this out-of-town trade might be the justification of a business. Surveys conducted in Fayetteville, Arkansas,[2] Portland, Oregon,[3] and several towns in Oklahoma disclose both the extent and reasons given for this out-of-town buying. The extent of shopping away from home is a rough measure of the lack of alertness of hometown merchants to customer wants, although it is also influenced by factors such as buying incidental to trips. Customer beliefs and preferences regarding prices, merchandise assortments, and quality, services, credit terms, advertising, the newness of merchandise, and modern store facilities are usually disclosed as major reasons for out-of-town shopping. Although the tendency is for trade to gravitate toward the larger cities, this is not always true, especially among nearby towns that differ in size by not much over 100 per cent. Our Oklahoma studies disclosed a few examples of towns attracting a sizable amount of trade from others having double their population, mainly as a result of more wide-awake and aggressive management. This leads to another viewpoint that often warrants analysis.

In some small towns the level of management of local businesses may be obviously low and out-of-town shopping extensive. This does not *always* indicate a genuine business opportunity for a newcomer. Whether such an opportunity exists depends upon the need for the proposed venture to attract customers from the surrounding territory, attitudes of local businessmen, and size of town relative to accessible larger cities. If under efficient management the business contemplated could be profitable entirely from resident trade a genuine business opportunity is apparent. When customers must be attracted from out of town, whether from rural areas or nearby towns, our Oklahoma

[2] Pearce C. Kelley, "Buying Habits of Fayetteville Women," *Arkansas Business Bulletin,* The School of Business Administration, University of Arkansas (January 9, 1933), Vol. 1, Supplement, p. 4.

[3] N. H. Comish, *Small Scale Retailing* (Portland, Oregon: Binfords and Mort, 1946), p. 143.

studies[4] show that the quality of management of leading retail and service establishments is more important than what one small enterpriser can do alone. Unless the other businessmen will co-operate in a self-improvement program to make the town a more attractive shopping center, the new business is likely to be short-lived. If they will co-operate under the leadership of the newcomer an excellent opportunity may exist with the entire town supporting the enterpriser who can reverse a trend of declining business. Several small towns have been revived in this manner.

One variation of lack of awareness to needs is traffic congestion and lack of customer parking faciiities. Established firms may be reluctant to move out of the congested business districts so long as their concerns are profitable. A new firm that provides adequate customer parking and locates not too far from the central district may easily obtain a generous share of the business quickly and even start a secondary business district. Although more easily copied than solving customer parking problems, other opportunities may be found, such as being the first to provide air conditioning, self-operating doors, and other types of customer convenience and comfort or saving time and energy.

Seeking Justification for a Unique Idea

From a virtually infinite number of sources individuals secure ideas for a new business, including from deliberate search for business opportunities as discussed in our third group. However, some ideas may be practical from a technical standpoint but impractical either in terms of use value or cost-price relationships. Many ideas are based on known facts and may seem practical until put to the test of justification: Does it promise a sufficient volume of business at a high enough price and low enough cost to yield a profit?

Since a large proportion of our currently important goods and services were unknown or considered impractical a generation ago and many fortunes have been made by exercising creative imagination, this topic warrants discussion. One aspect is the origin of practical ideas for new goods, the other is how to capitalize on the new idea. Both contribute to the important but expensive function of independent enterprise pioneering new fields.

Contrary to popular belief, the practicability of an idea often depends more on its market acceptability than on technical aspects of production. The latter can almost always be solved if demand or potential customer acceptance is strong enough. Thus, ideas that meet a widespread basic need or solve some recognized consumer problem are almost certain to succeed even though some may require more technical research than could be provided by the average prospective enterpriser. Ideas for basic innovations occur most often to the alert observer with a creative mind. He need not at the time be seeking a business opportunity but is alert enough to recognize an unsatisfied basic need and some possibility for meeting it. Probably Gail Borden was not seek-

---

[4] Business Extension Service in co-operation with the Marketing Department; results not published.

ing an innovation when he observed the infant mortality aboard ship because the milk supply was not refrigerated, or young John Wanamaker when buying a birthday present for his mother and felt the need to "make shopping a pleasure," or Dan Gerber when "drafted" by his wife to strain peas for the baby. Yet the resulting innovations—canned milk, the modern customer service department store, and canned baby foods—represent new business opportunities of the type that have contributed so much to our material progress. They have been repeated in many other business case histories and will continue to be an important source of progress.

Procedures for the discovery and development of new product or service ideas are described in several excellent books on the subject referred to in the footnotes. Recommended steps are: (1) Record and file examples encountered where a widespread need is not currently provided for, or where annoying experiences or hazards are encountered; objects slip out of hands, containers topple over and spill contents, bottles drizzle or drip, people often slip and fall, objects are burned (the proverbial burned toast and cigarette-marred furniture), fires are started from smoking in bed or wearing inflammable clothing, certain foods are easily spoiled, certain household or business duties become chores, needed objects are too heavy to move or difficult to store, or mar the floor or spoil the appearance, and so on. (2) Mull over the problem at odd times and record *every* idea for a possible solution for later testing and development. (3) Keep alert to observe developments in other fields or ideas encountered anywhere that might furnish a solution and record them. When James Ritty observed the mechanism for recording the revolutions of a ship's propeller, he recognized that the idea could be adopted to recording sales transactions in a business, a problem he had long been seeking to solve, and thus laid the foundation for the modern cash register.[5] (4) Relax occasionally and let your subconscious make suggestions. Experiment with possible solutions, test their practicability, seek advice, and stay with the search until a solution is found that meets the test of a genuine business opportunity. Guides such as those listed in the bibliography should prove helpful.

In addition to the need for justification of radically new ideas as just discussed, another broad group of ideas are those representing a new combination or adaptation of businesses already in existence, a restaurant in New York that combines service in order of arrival with entertainment and advertising. As soon as a customer takes a seat a number is automatically lighted showing the order in which he is to be served, and, simultaneously, an individual, commercially sponsored moving picture starts its showing for his exclusive attention.[6]

Usually, it will be easier to justify the need for a new project based on a combination of two existing types of business or an adaptation of some kind

[5] M. Weisinger, "Romance of the Cash Register," *Coronet* (March 1954), pp. 156-61.

[6] Committee on Consumer Relations in Advertising, "Lunch Counter Patrons Watch Ads on Screen," *Consumer News Digest* (October 1947), p. 7.

now operating than for one based on a radically new idea. If average business judgment is used in selecting types of business to combine, or adaptations to be offered are decided upon only after an analysis of customer needs, the chances for success are good. Of course, as before, the test of volume, costs, and price must still be met in every case. This situation may be summarized for the prospective businessman under the following five headings:

1. He can offer a new service to the community.
2. He can offer a new line of goods to the community.
3. He can offer a new service with an established line of goods.
4. He can offer a new line of goods with established services.
5. He can offer a new line of goods and new kind of service. One approach is to test the proposed business in the light of known consumer motivation.

What the Market Wants

The study of buying motives may well be considered as vital to the establishment of a business. Certainly if the people in the community in which the concern is to be established have no particular motivation for buying certain goods, or, if those motives or their relative strengths are unknown, selling, displaying, and advertising efforts will be wasted in almost all cases.

People want many things, and nearly everyone wants the same things, although in varying degrees, to satisfy his needs of living. The presence of many individuals with similar preferences in the same community makes it a good or a poor market for specific goods and services, depending on what a firm has to offer.

Buying motives, as generally listed, include the following satisfactions that people seek, thus determining their needs, which usually can be met with business offerings of goods or services:

Comfort—the desire for physical or mental ease and well-being.

Convenience—the desire for a minimum of effort, for saving of time and energy.

Security—the desire to know that the future is predetermined with their welfare assured.

Prestige—recognition of the individual as personally outstanding or a member of a desirable group.

Health—the desire to look and feel physically fit.

Economy—the desire to secure full value for each penny spent, to save money.

There are many other reasons why people buy things, including the desire to gain and hold the affections of others, the desire to belong to the crowd, the desire for recreation and amusement, and so on. The six that have been listed, however, will serve as a guide for our discussion of buying motives as influencing the justification of a business within any community or market.

Groups and communities differ. Certainly a traditionally low-paid group would respond to any offering stressing *economy;* they might forego the *convenience* and *comfort* of certain services to achieve this *economy.* Others will buy exotic and otherwise unusual goods to secure *prestige,* which may be more important to them than *economy.* These preferences will differ among people of different incomes and ages and sexes. If the good or the service contemplated offers *health* or *security* with *economy* as well, then the prospective operator will find ample business volume in communities containing many older people living on limited incomes.

Market Analysis

Market analysis is not a practice limited to large organizations. The businessman contemplating the establishment of a small concern also has a job of market analysis to do. To him, this job of analyzing his potentials is vital, whether (1) as to what a given comunity wants so that he can offer the right thing, or (2) as to which community wants the thing or service he is capable of offering.

Such analytical procedure is customary in large businesses, where it prevents many misplaced stores, shops, and plants. The thousands of dollars spent for this purpose are considered good investments. The lack of such precautionary measures is one important reason for small business failures.

The absence in small business of adequate studies concerning consumer needs, location, sales appeals, and similar factors is doubtless due to (1) the lack of trained specialists among small operators, (2) the lack of funds and time for adequate programs of research, and (3) the small operator's impatience and stubbornness that are natural corollaries of his economic independence.

With particular reference to the third item, it is unfortunate that the beginner in business on his own is inclined frequently to choose the business *he likes,* and the goods or production methods or standards of service *he likes,* and the location *he likes* without enough objective thinking in terms of what the *customer likes and wants and is willing to buy.*

Market analysis is not necessarily complex.[7] It is essentially logical. There are many variations of a basic pattern or procedure, but in general they will follow a scientific approach involving steps such as the following:

1. State the problem or question clearly.
2. Get the facts; insist on adequate information.
3. Organize and study the facts as secured.
4. Develop possible actions; review pros and cons for each.
5. Select the best procedure, and start using it. Adjust as required.

[7] An excellent reference is: Robert G. Seymour, *How the Small Plant Can Analyze Old and New Markets,* Management Aids for Small Business No. 9 (Washington, D. C.: Small Defense Plants Administration, 1952). See also our Chapter 10, "Management Research, the Outside Staff."

6. Observe progress alertly and adjust as necessary.

7. Use results.

The problem of market analysis for the manufacturer of a set product for which he seeks a market will be different from that of the producer who seeks to find out what the public wants in design and performance and then makes his product accordingly. The procedure, however, will be similar in both cases.

Let us assume that a manufacturer has available various types of woodworking machinery with which he could, given designs and plans, make any one of many wooden items—even items with which he is not now familiar. He has previously turned out toys, but demand for them is slackening; he fears he may have to stop making them altogether. His question is one of finding employment for his machinery and manpower. He will not want to change the equipment or the people involved, but he can choose his materials and his product. The problem, thus, is to choose the product under the conditions described.

Getting the Facts

He goes about getting information with a series of questions such as:

1. Is there any product I have previously made for which there is now a demand?

2. What requests for goods that I could make have I had recently?

3. What items now made of other materials might be made either better or cheaper of wood?

4. What items are my competitors making and selling?

5. For what items that I can make are stores and wholesalers being asked?

6. Is there any other material that can be handled like wood, which I might use to make new items?

7. What are the actual facts as to why my old product is not selling as it did?

To get the facts he want with which to answer these questions, he consults: (1) his own records, (2) retail buyers, (3) wholesale buyers, (4) trade journals, (5) trade associations, and (6) users of various products.

Organizing the Facts for Study

After the various facts are organized, and irrelevant and uninteresting findings have been eliminated, he notes the following results from his study:

1. He has had requests for:
    a. Other kinds of toys.
    b. Improvements in toys he has made.
    c. Toys of other materials.
    d. Miscellaneous kitchen items.

2. The toys he has been making are too bulky and heavy.

3. The sides of many of the toys he has made have split.

4. A new kind of wallboard is replacing wood in kitchen equipment.

5. One manufacturer is making toys of a kind of cardboard that is lighter than wood, but is not sturdy enough.

6. Retail and wholesale buyers could sell his wooden toys if they were lighter and sturdier.

7. He has many friends and a good reputation in the toy field.

8. His status-of-sale and discount arrangements are not so good as those of his competitors.

Reviewing the Possibilities

After studying the findings of his records, interviews, questionnaires, and correspondence, he finds that the following possibilities present themselves:

1. He can start making kitchenware instead of toys.

2. He can make kitchenware to supplement his toy business.

3. He can make a new kind of toy, of wallboard.

4. He can make the same toys, with material currently popular or recently developed.

5. He can sell his goods on terms to meet competition.

Reviewing each possibility he builds his business plans accordingly. He feels that since he knows the toy business, has an established reputation in it, and knows the people to whom he sells, he had better not try the kitchenware. He adjusts his terms to meet competition and starts out on his new program. Now, as always, his trouble is that toys are seasonal. Soon, however, he finds that he can make and sell a beach toy of wallboard and tin that will give him a summer business. He also discovers an export possibility through the U. S. Department of Commerce.

Trying Out the Plans

After six months he has settled down to routine business, with a year-round program that keeps his plant busy. One final adjustment is to contract for two years' full production of his major item, the entire output to be sold to a large mail-order chain. This transaction will give him broad distribution, does not cost him much to sell, and assures steady production and income for a long period. Contact with the buyer for this mail-order chain came about in the course of his inquiries about his product and prospects.

SURVEYING BUSINESS OPPORTUNITIES

This is one of the most intriguing of our three situations, especially for the younger prospective businessman. Even though he has made a tentative selection of a kind of business to enter, the survey approach may prove valuable either as a test of his present idea or in suggesting more promising alternatives

Various motives in addition to those mentioned prompt different individuals to survey the opportunities available for launching a new enterprise. Most of these will fall in one or more of the following categories:

1. Seeking a large and continuous profit—King Gillette's safety razor needing frequently replaced blades.

2. Making profitable use of an inheritance—Eugene Shireman's problem of putting "gold" into goldfish.[8]

3. Capitalizing on trends to "get in early" such as the do-it-yourself and self-service shops.

4. Putting a hobby to productive use—some handicraft, flower or Chinchilla raising.

5. "Cashing in" on special abilities or training—store buyer launches own resident buying office.

6. Seeking to solve widespread consumer problems as already discussed.

7. Wanting to help minority groups—Goodwill Industries and concerns to employ the handicapped.

8. Putting new discoveries into use—the "atomic drugstore" already discussed.

9. Meeting wants resulting from population shifts, changing age composition of the population, and changes in economic conditions.

10. Seeking to put new materials or waste products to profitable use.

11. Meeting wants neglected by monopolies or big business—usually for minority groups or those desiring individualized attention, an example of dovetailing by small enterprisers.

12. Seeking to be of public service—providing employment during hard times or promoting ideas for greater safety, sanitation, and self-development.

A prolific source of ideas and products available to a prospective enterpriser is the U. S. Department of Commerce promotion of patents available for free use, license, or other applications. Several thousand are available and a real need exists for competent business enterprise to make these inventions available to consumers. Both profit to the entrepreneur and benefits to society should result from effective use of this mine of new business opportunities.

To discover an opportunity for starting a new business, seven methods of approach are suggested. You may think of others, but these will serve to illustrate the process.

1. Start with what you are prepared or equipped to offer. What can you do with your preparation and equipment? Who wants the products or services you could offer? In what form? Where? When? How? At what price and volume?

2. Analyze expansion trends of a community, suburb, and industry. Find

[8] Robert D. Wilcox, "Goldfish Made Him a Millionaire," *Saturday Evening Post* (May 5, 1951), p. 17.

new uses for zippers, staples, and other common products. Study communities in different stages of development, such as larger cities and smaller towns. What businesses exist in the cities that the town will soon need? Compare classified sections of the telephone directories or business directories. Make personal observations. The same approach can be made by comparing communities in different sections of the country.

A study of the community might reveal particular enterprises that are needed. Perhaps there is no sporting goods store in the town and the population is sufficient to support one. Or a particular service may be needed. Find out why people go out of the community to have certain services performed. Perhaps what is needed is improvement of existing business establishments. Furthermore, a study of existing businesses in the community might suggest a new business that would dovetail with them—perhaps a small manufacturing industry making products local businesses have to import.

One of the most significant trends affecting modern business is that of population moving to the suburbs. The result is that new and active shopping centers have been growing up on the outskirts of the big towns. Even smaller cities are finding it desirable to plan for a more decentralized growth, with new neighborhoods being developed as "semi-self-contained" entities each served to a considerable degree by its own community shopping and service center. It may be important for a prospective businessman to watch developments of large-scale housing projects. These will create new business opportunities, but will also cancel some of the present ones. Another trend to watch is the changing age composition of our population—some 16 million senior citizens with money to spend, and the increasing market domination of teenagers.

A further study of industries in the community may lead to other ideas for a small business. The use of waste products or by-products of other industries offers many opportunities in the manufacturing field. Examples of products using waste materials are Celotex, made from sugar cane stalks, and pressed wood, made from sawdust. In a lumbering area, opportunities may exist to use bark or other parts of trees considered waste. In a citrus fruit area, the peelings of fruit might be made into a profitable product. Certain plastics can be made from waste or by-products.

The use of local products or raw materials in industry is becoming increasingly important. In an agricultural region find out who is processing the commodities that local farmers grow. If this processing is not done locally, find out why. In a predominantly forested region there might be opportunities in the chemical treatment of wood, in charcoal and wood distillates, in pulp mills and paper mills, in toys, in handicrafts, or in Christmas greens. Plywood fabrication is another industry upon which there has been much emphasis because of prefabricated housing and new uses of such wood in product manufacturing.

In an agricultural area there may be a need for custom-built farm equipment, for a parts and service agency for farm machinery, for apiarists', dairymen's, and poultrymen's supplies, or for rental and operation of farm machinery. In an industrial region opportunities may exist in the operation of small shops for custom welding, in custom built shop equipment, in research laboratories for industrial use, in machine tool service and repair, or in materials, parts, or containers for the local industries.

New outlets for manufacturers or wholesalers may be needed in a particular area. It might be well to contact the maker of a new product, with a good future, having few outlets at the present. Wholesalers are a good source of information regarding needed outlets in their trading area.

3. Analyze each market: children, newlyweds, home seekers, businessmen, professional men, single women, home owners, bachelors, students, working women, older people. The presence of these and many similar groups in every community constitutes markets within the market. Consider how the occupation or other characteristics of the group may give rise to the need for special goods and services. A large majority of working girls might welcome a personal shopping, meal planning, housekeeping, or similar service.

Jobs related to family or personal living that are of necessity neglected perhaps will provide opportunities in the service field. Reminder services for appointments, birthdays, anniversaries, and similar occasions; or labor-saving services, such as paying the family's monthly bills and yard or house maintenance, would be examples. Services to professional men might include co-operative buying of supplies; office layout counsel; specialized employment service; secretarial or accounting, tax, and social security service; or servicing, renting, and repairing recreational equipment. Supervision of recreation, speech correction (by experts), care of children with transportation provided, and bicycle and scooter rental services, are but a few services that can be made attractive to mothers of small children.

The small businessman might get in touch with retailers, wholesalers, manufacturers, and institutions to see what products they have to import. He could find out why these products are not manufactured locally. After a definite need in the community for your type of business has been established, the population trend and major type of industry in the community should be considered. Preference should be given to a growing town that has stable industries.

4. Find out the dislikes, complaints, problems, jobs that are avoided, and so forth, for each class of businessmen and for other groups (such as housewives and professional women), with reference to goods and services available to them in the community. If consumer buying habit surveys are available, these may suggest consumer complaints to be investigated further. Another fruitful source of ideas may be found in publications that often list ideas for new or improved products.

5. Study the existing products, merchandise assortments, stores, service establishments, and other business offerings for possible improvements or com-

binations that would make for greater convenience, comfort, utility, or other desirable factors. Opportunities may exist even though people are not complaining and may not even have thought of some improvement.

6. Observe people's habits of living: leisure time activities, hobbies, amusements, recreation, modes of transportation, methods for care of the home and business premises, group meetings, and the like, with an eye to possible business opportunities. Is a catering service, or box lunch or packaged picnic outfit supply needed? Naturally these are only illustrative suggestions.

Why not put idle equipment into use? Occasionally owners of partially used, high-cost equipment will help set up an individual in a separate business. Or leased departments or concessions may be obtained in retail stores or markets.

Hobbies have often led to ideas for a small business. A photography shop might be needed in a community, or a small machine shop specializing in custom made tools or miniature locomotives might be profitable. In a tourist region opportunities may exist to retail local handicrafts, or to provide especially good cabin developments and eating places. Appeals to special tastes may lead to ideas for small business.

Otto F. Reiss offers a number of methods of developing new ideas. He says, "Why not ask yourself why a thing is the way it is today—why not change it by making it larger or smaller or by changing its shape?" [9] He suggests taking a cue from the past and adding a new twist to a product or service. Or the combination of two things might lead to a profitable idea. Study emotions and habits of people. Many want to own useful things, and a study of public facilities like those at municipal parks that could be furnished to people as their own might lead to a good opportunity. Private swimming pools are a good example. The discovery of unuttered desires and the satisfaction of them has proven itself to be a profitable idea.

7. Capitalize on some trend by getting in on the ground floor. Demand is dynamic, always changing. Certain periods of our economic history have seen the rise of entirely new industries—several of major importance, such as the automobile, radio, and aviation. Many more have been of lesser importance, sometimes fairly short-lived, but have provided opportunities for small business to expand while enjoying the higher profits of the early years. For some years following World War II many such new industries developed.

To carry out some of the foregoing suggestions may necessitate keeping an

---

[9] Otto F. Reiss, *How to Develop Profitable Ideas* (Englewood Cliffs, N.J.: Prentice-Hall, Inc., 1945). See also: George Howard Allen, ed., "How to Initiate a New Business," in *Individual Initiative in Business* (Cambridge, Mass.: Harvard University Press, 1950), pp. 155-180; Prentice-Hall Editorial Staff, *Business Ideas Handbook* (Englewood Cliffs, N.J.: Prentice-Hall, Inc., 1949); "The Creative Urge," from the Royal Bank of Canada Monthly Letter, in *The Stove Builder* (June 1953), pp. 49-69; Cyril C. Herrmann and John F. Magee, " 'Operations Research' for Management," *Harvard Business Review,* Vol. 31, No. 4 (July-August 1953), pp. 100-112; Alex F. Osborn, *Applied Imagination, Principles and Procedures of Creative Thinking* (New York: Charles Scribner's Sons, 1953); James Webb Young, *A Technique for Producing Ideas* (Chicago: Advertising Publications, Inc., 1951).

idea file, considerable clipping of news items on new developments, visiting and talking with people, doing a little "snooping" and note taking, or other procedures such as these. It may take time and lead to several false starts before the big idea is discovered. But it should be fun and good training and will provide a waiting period while you accumulate adequate finances and make connections of future value. Remember, test each idea by the standards of justification—volume, costs, and profits—as well as by those of Chapter 11, "Financing and Organizing the Business," before making your final decision.

CONCLUSIONS

The objective of all business is to give the public what it wants, at a profit. Everyone generally wants the same things. Buying motives thus are well established. Different people like different things to different degrees, however, and in many cases competition already has taken care of certain needs.

The newcomer's concern is with the unfulfilled needs as related to what he wants to offer and is able to offer at a profit. His procedure in testing an idea for a business must equal, in the detail of analysis, that of his big business rivals and contemporaries. The approach consists merely of getting the facts, studying them, making a decision, alertly following it up and changing it as required.

This procedure is the salvation of the beginner, for the lack of it represents the greatest weakness of all small business; with it, the other advantages claimed by the large-scale operators are easily offset by the human elements of personality and personal service so characteristic of the little fellow. Whenever possible, check results arrived at by one method against those derived from a different and independent procedure.

Suggestions and advice given in this chapter for the development of radically new enterprises should appeal to those gifted with imagination or a love for pioneering. This is the area where the greatest opportunities exist for making a fortune while performing a valuable service to society, but it requires entrepreneurial ability of a high order, not just daydreaming.

QUESTIONS AND PROBLEMS

1. Distinguish carefully between justifying and appraising a business. Show any interrelationships.

2. How does the text define a genuine business opportunity? Comment on this definition.

3. What special considerations are important in starting a radically new kind of business? Discuss.

4. How is justifying the opening of a business related to location, and to policies?

5. How would you expect justifying a business to be related to financing, and organizing a business?

6. State and briefly explain the three major categories embracing most cases of justifying a new business.

7. Analyze the test of justification given in this chapter and show certain ways in which it is unsatisfactory. Then suggest a better test.

8. How could you determine whether another similar business would be justified in a given situation? Sate your assumed conditions.

9. Discuss inefficient management of established concerns in a community as a basis for justifying a new enterprise.

10. How can a small businessman with limited capital make a consumer survey? What use should he make of the results?

11. Cite examples from business history where the founder would have had difficulty in justifying the new business at the time. Discuss.

12. How is marketing likely to be the factor determining the practicability of a radically new idea? Discuss.

13. What steps are involved in the discovery and development of ideas for new products or services?

14. Name a few of the 12 motives listed as prompting an individual to survey the opportunities for a business, and illustrate each.

15. If you know that a town of interest to you has a very large amount of out-of-town shopping, how would you use this information to locate a genuine business opportunity?

16. Show how some of the guides and methods useful in appraising a business for possible purchase would be useful in justifying a proposed new business.

17. Give several examples of how the inherent characteristics of *small* business would preclude the justification of certain types of business ideas. Discuss.

18. Study the seven ways used to survey opportunities for a new business and see if you can suggest additional different, yet practical, methods.

19. Suggest some idea for an entirely new business and apply the pertinent sections of this chapter to justify it or to reject the idea.

20. Locate, in the library or elsewhere, case histories of some products launched during the present century; study the problems encountered, and the time and capital required to put these products on the market in profitable volume. Report your findings and conclusions.

21. If there is a suburban shopping center in your home town, find what types of stores and shops are included in this center. Is there a demand for another type of store or shop? Talk to the owners of the various businesses on their opinions as to whether another kind of store or shop is needed. Discuss your findings and draw your own conclusions.

22. Locate published suggestions for several new or improved products or services and select a few promising ideas for a new business. Explain how you would justify each.

23. Bill had just completed experiments on an electric bed cover that could be plugged into regular house outlets and could furnish air conditioned sleeping comfort to its users. Initial prices to consumers would be double that for heating blankets but probably could be reduced later. All bankers and other commercial lenders flatly refused any financial aid. Bill's college professors advised him to forget such an impractical idea. His wife's parents offered to supply the 30 per cent of initial capital needed to supplement his own savings, but this would exhaust their resources and provisions for retirement. What should Bill do, and why?

8 • Establishing Business Policies

Modern business operates in a complex and continuously changing environment. Change is the only constant factor. Daily the businessman is faced with new conditions and questions requiring decision and action. Some stabilizing force must be present to guide all the activities of the business in one direction or it will flutter around aimlessly like a leaf in an autumn breeze. This stabilizing force is policy, without which a business is like a mariner without a compass or an automobile tourist without a road map.

Modern business success depends upon the firm's reputation. This may be for any one of a variety of desirable features: low prices, exclusive merchandise, customer service, rapid delivery, reliable quality, freshness of stock, always having something different, and numerous others. Whether it plans one or not, every business acquires a certain reputation. Policy enables it to build the particular reputation desired. All other activities of the business are related to its policies and dependent upon them. The very idea that later results in the establishment of a new business is the kernel from which develop major and minor (that is, departmental) policies, an integrated set of guides expressing the purpose, objectives, and principles of the concern. The owner and all his employees use these policies to guide their actions.

Webster Robinson defines policy as "an accurately determined directive control which is based on definite and adequate knowledge and which designates the aims of the business and the approximate methods to be used in their accomplishment." [1] A policy directs the business and controls its activities to keep them in line with objectives set. To be worthy of the name it should be based on definite and adequate information. Policies should be definite and stable, yet flexible enough to be adjusted to meet fundamental changes.

Policies enable the small businessman to conserve his energies and resources by directing them consistently toward an established goal. This concentration

[1] Webster Robinson, *Fundamentals of Business Organization* (New York: McGraw-Hill Book Company, Inc., 1925), pp. 1-2.

in itself increases his effectiveness and chances for success by lessening dissipation or dilution of effort. Experience can be utilized to the greatest extent, because policies show what not to do as well as what should be done to accomplish a particular purpose.

The elimination of inconsistencies by a well-regulated set of policies results in less lost effort and less working at cross-purposes. Each policy should be selected in relation to the general policy and to all other policies. For example, the temptation to invest in a very efficient machine that would treble a firm's output immediately would require careful consideration if production policy stressed volume, whereas financial and expansion policies stressed growth from profits only.

Policies should capitalize all advantages a business may have, including special skills and knowledge the owner or firm members possess. Limiting factors may at times require the rejection of an otherwise attractive-appearing policy. Financial resources are usually a major limitation for small businesses. Also, character and abilities of personnel available and various forms of social control must be considered.

Written policies are more definite and can be followed more easily, but unwritten policies in the small business may be equally effective. The most important requirement is that the policies be understood and followed by all members of the firm. Customers, competitors, and other groups that look to a firm's policies to know what they can expect from it should be informed of all policies that affect their dealings with the company.

Policies are of three types—general, major, and minor. General policies relate to the business as a whole and include the over-all purpose and aims of the business. They define what the business is to accomplish and what success is desired for it. These policies must be the result of much forethought and planning, and they may still have to be changed somewhat with time.

Illustrations of general policy that show changes in even the basic idea behind the birth of new small businesses that have subsequently become leaders in their fields are the following familiar examples: Henry Ford's original "economical transportation," and Frank W. Woolworth's "all merchandise that could be sold profitably for ten cents."

Major policies include the formulation of guiding principles for each important long-range activity, including department co-ordination. Examples of such activities are finance, expansion, personnel, and public relations. Major policies also cover such things as: what type of merchandise is to be sold; what customer services are to be rendered; what customer relationships will be; what the relationship between management and employees will be; and how the firm should participate in community activities. Minor, or departmental, policies are those affecting the actions of various departments directly. They include decisions regarding the use of newspaper, radio, or enclosure advertising, if not all three; the extension of open-account credit, installment credit, or perhaps both; and similar procedures. All three kinds of policies are vital to a business and must be formulated carefully according to its needs.

In the launching of an entirely new business, there is always an experimental or pioneering period during which initial policies will be on trial. Two dangers are to be guarded against. First, after every reasonable effort has been made to justify the need for the new business as recommended in Chapter 7, and after the real opportunity has been defined, great care should be taken to formulate policies most likely to enable the business to satisfy this need at a profit. All too often a small business is started not only with little serious attempt to justify its need, but also with only vague ideas as to how the assumed need can best be satisfied. It is better to formulate the policies one considers desirable, even though later experience proves the advisability of changing them, than to have no policies at all. Thus, one will at least profit by directed experience. Changes can be made as required and the firm will be basing on proved experience a co-ordinated set of policies that will continue to develop as the business progresses.

Second, well-conceived policies should not be abandoned before they have had a fair chance to prove their worth. A beginner often fails to realize how long it may take people to become familiar with something new and to approve of it. As the sponsor of the idea, the proprietor is understandably enthusiastic about it. When potential customers fail to show their interest and appreciation, it is natural for him to become discouraged. Again, unduly slow progress may make the enterprise seem hardly worth the effort. At this stage it is easy to be tempted by some other, more attractive venture. A change in general policy, the basic idea upon which the new business was founded, will probably cause it to lose whatever progress it has made, and the new line may very likely be even harder to pioneer than the first.

It is admittedly difficult to tell at just what point a general policy proves unsound and should be abandoned. However, the danger of early discouragement is so great that every reasonable effort should be made to give a carefully selected policy sufficient time to prove itself. About the only guides that can be offered as to when policy abandonment is desirable are: (1) if experience shows actual errors of fact or judgment in formulating the original policy; (2) if unforeseen changes destroy the soundness of the policy; and (3) if the time required to establish the business on a paying basis is greater than the owner is able to stand financially.

This discussion relates primarily to the general policy of a new business. During the experimental period it is to be expected that some major and departmental policy changes will be made as the business finds its place and tests the desirability of minor variations in policy. For example, although a policy of accepting no special orders may have been decided upon at the start, an adjustment would be called for if it developed that only a few requests for special orders were received, that these came from some of the most profitable customers, and that the trouble and expense of handling special orders was less than had been expected.

As we have said, most successful businessmen have the faculty of making prompt decisions. Since well-formulated policies guide these decisions, in one sense the decisions were all made well in advance, at the time of policy formation. In most cases the businessman tests each problem as it arises in the light of his policies and decides accordingly. This is one of the big advantages of having a good set of policies.

Occasionally the proprietor is required to make a hasty decision of far-reaching importance without having time to investigate all the ramifications of the question or to deliberate upon the possible effects of his decision. In such cases his established policies are the safest. No matter how attractive a proposition that violates his policies may seem, he should reject it without hesitation if he does not have time for an investigation at least as thorough as that involved in establishing the policies.

POLICIES APPLICABLE TO ALL FIELDS

In addition to a general policy, certain major policies deal with such fundamental matters that they are likely to be very similar, at least in basic content, for all lines of business. These major policies involve basic business principles and experience which cannot safely be slighted by the small businessman regardless of his choice of field. Deviations must be justified by unique circumstances and should be recognized as exceptions. They should be labeled "handle at your own risk." Differences in policies necessary to individualize each business undertaking and to suit each different set of circumstances can usually be made in the departmental policies.

The following major policies are basic to every business: product, finance and expansion, and personnel or organization.

Product Policy

Decisions governing products to be made, merchandise to be handled, or services to be offered should be guided by what is variously referred to as the product, merchandise, or merchandising policy. Merchandising in a policy sense deals with designing, adapting, or selecting the goods or services to be offered by the business. Naturally the producer designs or adapts the goods; whereas the merchant selects goods to suit customer demands. Although closely related to general policy, which defines the field in which the business will engage, product policy goes beyond this by designating a particular area of operation as well as the methods to be followed. For example, a small factory that plans to make furniture must ask itself: What kind? For what customers? What principles will be followed as guides in designing and restyling? Will it cater to custom designs or work toward standard articles? Will it attempt to introduce or pioneer new concepts of style, such as improvements in functional design? When will designs formerly made be abandoned? What standards will be used in making these and other decisions affecting the goods to be offered?

Similar questions must be decided in the merchandising and service fields. In retailing and wholesaling, merchandise selection rather than product design is involved, although this difference is less significant than is commonly assumed. Actually some retailers have secured manufacturers who would make products according to specifications or designs dictated by their customers' needs. Also, some small "manufacturers" merely submit their product designs to private label firms or subcontractors for actual production.

In the service fields competition, new developments, and market strategy are continually raising questions of adapting present services to customer needs, of adding new services, and of dropping old ones.

Two other policy guides may be suggested. Especially in the initial selection of products to make, merchandise to carry, or particular services to offer, a decision must be made as to whether to enter an already established though possibly crowded field, offering goods or services the same as those of competitors, or to differentiate the new firm's offerings in some way. The latter policy is usually better, if practical, as it gives the company a new market within the already established field, a strong claim for patronage, and a good talking point for its advertising. Too many beginners merely copy the policies of firms already established, often without investigating how successful these have been.

There is one situation in which adopting policies similar to those of established firms may be justified. If careful investigation shows these policies to be the best for the conditions and if the newcomer has a good chance of competing successfully, these would be the logical policies to adopt. When existing firms are lax or careless in following stated policies or have other obvious weaknesses, the new entrant would have a good chance for success. Policies are often publicized in general terms with principles phrased for public approval rather than as guides that the business sincerely intends to follow. Many real business opportunities are found through investigations that readily disclose this to be the situation.

Finance and Expansion Policies

Policies regarding finance and expansion are so closely related for the small business that they may well be considered together. Two diverse viewpoints of considerable merit appear: namely, the conservative and the adventurous. In most other fields of policy it is possible to state well-established principles that have very few exceptions. Maybe underneath the surface even these apparently different expansion policies will display common principles.

The adventurous or heavy-risk-taking attitude is based on premises like the following: any business ownership is a risk; if the risk is worth taking at all, it should be exploited to the limit. That some limit exists is implied, but it is accepted only when necessary. Waiting for a conservative opportunity or condition is likely to defeat the very purpose of independent business ownership. By the time a person has accumulated adequate capital and experience and a good business opportunity occurs, he is too old and too much saddled with family responsibilities to take advantage of it. A small business waiting to expand conservatively may sit by and see competitors become entrenched before conditions arise to permit its expansion by conservative standards.

Since numerous examples can be cited of success on a shoestring, of fortunes made from expansion against conservative advice, and of hundreds of thousands of individuals who waited too long to satisfy their business ownership ambitions, as well as of conservative small businesses that are still small, this adventurous policy must be recognized as having merit. However, it is to some extent a matter of individual attitude and ability, and it varies so greatly with circumstances that probably the best approach is to use the more conservative principles as a starting point. After that, each individual may proceed at his own risk.

The financial policy should state the amount of the concern's total capital the small businessman plans to own or what his equity will be at all times. Advice varies from half to over three-fourths as the minimum safe owner equity. Of course, in a corporation, 51 per cent of the voting stock will give the holder control of the business, but a powerful minority can be annoying. From what sources and under what terms will the businessman secure funds needed for initial capital, fluctuating amounts of working capital, and future expansion? Initial capital secured from the outside should be on terms that allow more than ample time for repayment out of reasonable expected earnings from the business. A serious danger to most small businesses is the need to finance fixed capital from short-term loans. Even if renewal is promised orally, it may not come as expected when needed. One form of fixed capital is that invested in fixtures and equipment. Since both of these may usually be purchased on installment, the temptation to overspend is great. A better policy might well be to follow recommendations of authorities in the field as to the approximate amount of capital to invest in fixtures and equipment. Adequate depreciation should be taken each year in order that a reserve for replacement when each item wears out may be accumulated. The policy should provide for comparing vendors' installment prices with their cash prices and the terms upon which a bank loan could be used to buy for cash.

Working capital is usually the easiest to secure for a sound, going business. The principal problem for small business seems to be securing favorable terms or a low interest charge when funds are borrowed from lending institutions. When a business is once established, vendor credit is an important source of working capital. Comparison should again be made of prices quoted on credit and cash prices with payments made from funds borrowed from your local bank. Often the latter policy will save money.

Although the soundest policy is to expand from earnings only, this is not always the most profitable. It "takes money to make money," but carefully borrowed money works just as well as owned capital. There is always the possibility that many excellent opportunities will be lost if expansion is based solely on accumulated surplus. Expansion from borrowed capital, however, should be as much guided by adequate information and good judgment as initial entry into business. Two policies especially important during the early years of a business career are paying off all indebtedness in the shortest possible time and leaving as much of the total profit in the business as possible. This means that the owner's drawing account, or "salary," should be as small as possible. It should definitely be much less than what he could earn working for someone else.

The monetary factor is the common denominator or thread connecting various activities of the business through the same measurable unit. Sales volume is related to production or merchandise needs by furnishing the dollar revenue with which to pay all expenses and costs of materials or merchandise sold. The financial budget is the device used by business to bring all its activities into close co-ordination over a period of time. Policies should be formulated covering the scope of budgetary control, major steps in developing and administrating the budget, and the extent to which a long range budget, a five- or ten-year plan, will serve as a guide for future expansion.

One final point to be covered in the financial policy will be the reputation desired regarding payment of bills and the taking of discounts. At one extreme is a policy of paying cash for every purchase and seeking the largest allowable discounts. The average small business will usually take advantage of regular credit terms, however, because this is an important source of working capital. Too many are careless about taking advantage of cash discounts, and some tend to be slow in making payment even when bills are due at the net amount. A reputation for paying all bills promptly is a valuable business asset. Always taking advantage of cash discounts gives the business an even better reputation. In addition, cash discounts alone amount to important savings in most fields. The typical terms "2 per cent, 10 days, net 30" are equivalent to an annual interest rate of 36 per cent when cash discounts are taken. For example, an invoice dated January 1, amounting to $100 with terms of 2 per cent, 10 days, net 30, would carry a 2 per cent discount of $2.00 if paid on the 10th. If it were paid twenty days later, on the 30th, the gross amount, $100, would be due. Assume it is necessary to borrow from the bank at 6 per cent to discount the bill. Interest on $100 (actually only $98 would be needed) at 6 per cent would be due for only $\frac{20}{365}$, or approximately one-eighteenth, of a year to secure $2.00 or 2 per cent of the principal. The annual rate would be 18 times 2 per cent or 36 per cent. Thus by borowing at 6 per cent to discount the invoice the businessman actually makes 30 per cent interest. A bill with terms of 5 per cent, 10 days, net 30 would net him an 84 per cent return on a bank loan at 6 per cent; one with terms of 6 per cent, 10 days, net 40 would give him a gain of approximately 72 per cent on a 6 per cent loan.[2]

The policy should be emphatic about paying all bills promptly when due.

[2] The examples assume continuous discounting of invoices throughout the year. Other similar qualifications have been omitted to keep the illustrations simple.

If cash discounts are used by vendors, the policy should provide for taking full advantage of every cash discount. In both cases standards or procedures to follow in case funds on hand are inadequate to discount bills should be formulated. These may include short-term bank loans, special sales, use of a revolving reserve fund set up by the business for such emergencies, special efforts to collect accounts due to the business, and sometimes others.

Personnel or Organization Policy

Personnel and organization policies in the small business could hardly be considered separately, except possibly for the one-man business in which there is no personnel and organization is confined to a systematic distribution of the owner's time. An organization policy should cover the way in which responsibility and authority are distributed to different members of the firm. Decision must be made as to the extent to which authority of various sorts is to be delegated to others by the proprietor and as to the particular types of authority that he will retain for himself.

An axiom of good organization is that responsibility and authority must always be equal. No person should ever be held responsible for a job unless he has the authority to do it, nor should an individual, even a relative, be given authority in a business unless he is held fully responsible for the results. Unless a policy is absolutely clear and definite in this point, it will lead to confusion and low morale.

A common weakness in many small businesses is failure to delegate sufficient responsibility and authority to leave the owner free to devote his time to the more important management functions. It is this same condition that discourages good men from staying with a small business. A correct balance between delegating enough authority of the right type to relieve the owner and furnish incentives to employees, on the one hand, and actually losing control over the business by unwise delegation, on the other hand, is the ideal of good organization in the small business. In most cases the owner will want to reserve final authority over all major expenditures, the employment of persons for important positions, and final settlement of especially difficult customer or vendor complaints. Naturally, at least final approval of all policies above the minor or departmental level will be the prerogative of the owner. The burden of final decision in all important matters relating to labor and public relations will also be the proprietor's.

Because the human element is a factor common to all businesses regardless of type, basic principles of human relations are equally good in any business or other organization. Two standards of paramount importance in any personnel policy are: fair treatment and the recognition of each employee as an individual human being, not as a mere cog in the machine. Fair treatment is not easy to define, but its absence is quickly detected by employees. Giving promotions and pay raises to a few favorites when they are denied to others equally deserving is one of the rankest forms of unfair treatment, disliked alike by both groups. Some employees tend to "politic the boss" instead of devoting their efforts to worth-while production. Policies that permit discriminations among employees for reasons other than merit tempered with a moderate amount of seniority soon become known and increase the difficulty of securing and retaining valuable employees.

Personnel policies can at least assist executives and top management in meeting the second standard. By encouraging bosses to discuss workers' problems with them, by basing advancement in part on ratings of each individual, by provisions for giving each worker individual personal credit or acknowledgment for contributions, and by many similar devices that can be stated in the personnel policies as the desired company attitude, executives may be continuously reminded of their responsibility to recognize and treat each employee as a self-respecting human being.

A policy regarding promotions and standards to be followed in making promotions should be a part of every firm's personnel policies. Practices usually accepted as desirable are: to promote from within the organization whenever possible; to base promotions on certain factors of which employees have been informed and which are in general accepted as fair; and to promote a good man out of the organization or department when he has reached the limit of the company's ability to give him further promotions within the organization. Certain small companies have acquired an enviable reputation in this last respect. Once a man has developed to a point where he is capable of handling greater responsibilities than the firm can provide, a position is virtually secured for him in some larger concern. This policy attracts a constant stream of high-class personnel to the small company and accumulates a larger and larger number of their "alumni" in big competitors. Reciprocity in many respects is the natural result.

Another aspect of the personnel policy deals with the type of person to employ, as defined by such factors as age, sex, schooling, previous experience, appearance, health, handicaps, marital status, financial status (sometimes), and others considered important in certain cases. Until recent years surprisingly few companies had formulated any clear-cut policies in this respect, especially for executives, although each department head had his own unwritten guides, usually prejudices, that he observed.[3] Observation will show that all the salesgirls in one store are, say, redheaded, whereas a competitor will employ only dark-eyed brunettes. Why? The answer is personal liking or preference of the employer. Likewise we often find only very young employees in one firm and only older workers in another concern that operates under similar conditions.

The modern approach to this problem is one of job analysis and description. What type of employee is best suited to each job? What nonbasic factors, if any, like color of hair, political belief, or possibly looks, are important in

[3] For further study see: Pearce C. Kelley, "Selecting Executives," *Personnel* (August 1933), pp. 8-26.

terms of their effect on other members of the organization? A somewhat neglected field for the small business is to employ persons who do not meet certain arbitrary standards of most large companies, such as men over forty, those lacking formal schooling, or those physically handicapped in certain respects that would not interfere with the work or be a hazard to themselves or others. Experience shows that often such individuals are more reliable and steadier because they are not constantly seeking better jobs elsewhere and are so appreciative of an opportunity to earn a self-respecting living that they are actually more efficient in their jobs than their more physically perfect and well-equipped fellows.

In one other respect the small business has an advantage in securing high-class employees: namely, by being able to select those with potential ability who lack actual experience. Often the small firm is attractive to these people, or could be made so with the right publicity, because it offers a wider range of opportunities to develop well-rounded abilities. A policy seeking to attract persons of this caliber should be accompanied by a policy of promoting out of the organization after the employee has developed beyond the capacity of the small firm to utilize his abilities fully.

Although the close contact between employer and employee in small firms should be an advantage in training, actually the training done in small companies is often weak because of two prevalent conditions: (1) lack of time by the owner to do the training, and (2) lack of knowledge and of ability to train. To meet this need the federal vocational laws have been passed. Starting with the Smith-Hughes Act of 1917 and the George-Deen Act of 1936, Federal aid has been provided in the training of both small business managers and their employees. Certainly a small firm should utilize this aid and provide for it in its personnel policies.

There are many other respects in which the small business should formulate its personnel policies to capitalize on its size, as well as to compensate for both the few inherent advantages of employment by big business and the over-publicized advantages claimed for such employment.

Personnel may be as important as finance for expansion. As explained in Chapter 16, a small firm should plan the development of personnel, as well as source of funds, for future expansion. Policy statements covering executive development and expansion serve to attract and hold good employees and to stimulate expansion.

Since the middle 1930's many personnel policies have come increasingly under government regulation. State and Federal minimum wage and maximum hour regulations, management's recognition of unions and collective bargaining, safety provisions, and such socio-economic provisions as minimum employable age, required schooling, and unemployment and old age insurance have become law and must be observed by personnel policies. These vary from time to time, but absolutely must be considered in the formulation of the major personnel policy.

Although personnel policies have been considered as sufficiently basic to the three major business fields for general consideration, important aspects of the human element in each of these fields will be touched upon further as we now examine policies which are of particular importance in each of these fields.

POLICIES IN RETAILING

Successful retailers do not leave the treatment customers receive to the whims of employees. Rather, they are careful to establish and enforce a policy specifying the attitude the store desires to maintain toward its customers. Usually this covers the type of greeting customers are to receive as to friendliness, intimacy, or formality; limitations to be placed upon the alleged "policy" that "the customer is always right"; procedures for handling troublesome customers and embarrassing or ticklish situations; employee conduct while in the presence of customers; meeting unusual customer requests; and type of selling to be used and not to be used, sometimes including particular expressions considered objectionable by the management. Among the last might be certain references to competitors.

An important policy for any store is that dealing with the class of trade desired. It is usually difficult for a store to cater successfully to more than one major income group—high, middle, or low. Sometimes catering to particular age or occupational groups is desirable. This policy should be consistent with the store's location, the class of merchandise carried, and related policies such as sales promotion and customer services.

In general, three types of stores are recognized on the basis of the aggressiveness of their sales promotion: promotional, semi-promotional, and non-promotional. Promotional stores rely heavily on advertising and special sales; semipromotional are represented by the average store; and nonpromotional stores rely upon their regular customers, using a limited amount of more dignified advertising and very few, if any, special sales.

Successful stores usually cultivate some outstanding point of superiority over competitors as a result of consistently following a policy emphasizing this particular point. It may be complete assortments, new things first, fashion leadership, fashionable merchandise at popular prices, always lower-than-average prices, more helpful personnel, certain guarantees, or unusual customer services. There is almost no limit to the range of such points from which an imaginative retailer can select his particular one. Of course it should have customer appeal and be practical in application.

In selecting policies regarding customer service, at least the following should be provided for: credit, delivery, guarantees, returns, adjustments, allowances, telephone and mail orders, clerk or self-service, C.O.D. sales, layaways, cashing customers' checks, discounts, special orders, alterations when required by the kind of merchandise, and possibly others. This does not mean that all the services mentioned should be granted, but rather that a definite policy about each should be stated and adhered to in practice. If there are to be exceptions, such as monthly open-account credit to fellow businessmen or free deliveries on all orders over ten dollars, these should also be stated and observed—with no exceptions. If the policy is too strict, change it, but *never* make an exception so long as the policy is in force.

Certain factors will influence the selection of the best customer service policies in each case. One group relates to what services will be demanded or expected of the retailer. Factors like customs, customers' shopping habits, occupation, competition, location, nature of the merchandise (necessitating delivery of furniture and heavy appliances, for instance), and similar ones operate on the demand side. Offsetting these are what the retailer is willing and able to furnish. Credit may be customary in the area and expected by customers, but the merchant's financial resources might prevent him from offering this service.

Many beginning retailers make the error of merely copying the services of their competitors. A certain service is not necessary just because it is customary and expected. In some cases it may even be undesirable. A former student of one of the authors recently purchased a general store in a town of 2,000 where liberal credit had been the custom for the past thirty years. Most of the trade, which is rural, expected the kind of credit his only direct competitor and all other stores in the town continued to grant. The new owner started immediately with a strictly cash policy and no exceptions, expecting to lose about one-third of the customers and one-fourth of the sales volume of his predecessor. Results during the first year were interesting: for the first month about half of the customers objected to the new policy, but less than 5 per cent (almost all of it low-income trade) shifted to the competitor's store. Instead of declining 25 per cent as expected, business increased slightly. A later remodeling job increased total (cash) sales an additional 10 per cent. The competitor acknowledged receiving the new credit customers—with regrets. Of course, one case does not prove a principle, but it does show that long-established customer service policies *can* be changed. The question of the need for credit extension, as well as certain advantages and disadvantages of granting credit, are discussed in Chapter 23.

Another policy of special importance to the retailer is his price policy. Two price policies often confused are the one-price and the single-price. The latter, which is of limited application, relates to stores that handle merchandise at only one retail price, such as $5.00 shoes or $6.00 hats. The one-price policy means that goods are plainly marked and are sold only at the one price marked, regardless of who the customer is. It implies no bargaining over the price, but does not preclude policies giving special discounts to institutions or other large buyers. A one-price policy is representative of most retail stores in this country. However, a small retailer selling higher-priced merchandise having a short selling season, like fashion goods, is often tempted to deviate from this policy. Since markdowns must be taken on some of his merchandise, price shading can be easily rationalized as reducing necessary markdowns. Such a procedure will soon be discovered and the retailer will then find it difficult to follow the one-price policy at all. The better practice is to refuse all attempts to get the price cut. A policy is not like a rule to which exceptions can be made. Under no circumstances should even a single exception be made to a policy.

Other aspects of the price policy relate to the markup taken, the number of different prices for each line of goods, and the general level of prices or price zone. Low markup and large volume or rapid turnover at low prices go together. Nature of merchandise and clientele desired are the principal factors governing the markup policy to follow. Averaging markups within a department instead of trying to set a fixed markup on all items is usually necessary. For "shopping goods" and some other lines in which numerous grades exist, price lining (that is, maintaining only a few best-selling prices in each line) is usually desirable. A policy of concentration on about three prices within a zone or range of prices suited to the store's class of trade is recommended. Selection of the zone is determined by the income of the class of trade desired. Obviously men's shoes at prices of from four to ten dollars would not appeal to the top income group in most cities.

An important decision for many retailers is whether to affiliate with some buying and merchandising group like the voluntary chain or to buy independently. The advantages and limitations of each plan are discussed in greater detail in Chapter 17. If a retailer decides to affiliate with one of these groups, his policies should be formulated to capitalize on all the advantages it offers. Concentration of buying and full co-operation with the group is usually desirable, if the affiliation is one worth forming.

If buying is to be done independently, policies should be formulated to cultivate vendor goodwill. Fair play, prompt payment of bills, and courteous treatment of salesmen are important. The buying policy should also cover extent of quantity buying, attitude toward "free deals," selection of resources, brands to be carried, and similar important factors. Whether to use a resident buying office may be a consideration for medium-sized department stores. Most small stores need some guides to make their buying more efficient. If possible these should be covered in this policy. Buying guides are of two general types—those relating to quantity, such as the merchandise budget, and those relating to quality, or what to buy. Policy provisions covering the latter might consider the relative weight to be given advice from vendors, advice from a resident buying office, and suggestions found in the trade press or from local surveys; and when, if at all, to use professional forecasting agencies like Amos Parish's.

POLICIES FOR THE SMALL FACTORY

A manufacturer's production policy should define the extent to which he will make or purchase various parts and fabricated materials. At one extreme is the use of private label firms to do all the actual manufacturing. This policy has many advantages for the beginner with limited resources, even though he may plan at some future date to do the manufacturing himself. Private label firms have machinery and "know how" not available to the beginner. They can furnish advice on design and production methods that would be almost impossible for the small manufacturer to obtain independently. The real disadvantage in using these firms is that the beginner is not gaining experience as a manufacturer, but is merely a sales and distributing organization posing as a factory.

Sources from which raw materials and parts will be secured, and under what conditions, must be covered in the purchasing policy. The basic principle of concentration should be considered here, even to the extent of buying all parts at first and concentrating on their assembly into the company's finished product.

For the beginner especially, the type of production to use is often a matter of policy. Once a firm is well established, production methods are likely to be determined by considerations of relative costs. How rapidly should processes be standardized and machines substituted for hand labor? What quality of labor should be used? This will depend to some extent upon the degree of standardization, upon volume of production, and especially upon the nature of the product, whether highly standardized or custom-built. The previously determined expansion policy will probably have a bearing on such questions. Usually a business planned for rapid expansion will lean toward standardization of processes and introduction of machine methods as quickly as feasible.

Two cases of small manufacturers following widely diverse policies of production standardization may be used to illustrate the factors involved in this policy decision. They have in common the facts that they produce novelty or fashion goods, tried the wrong pricing policy during the 1930's and have profited by this experience, and are single-owner concerns. In other respects they differ widely.

The Lee Skirt Company of New York City, with an eighth-floor loft "factory," manufactures women's and misses' all-wool and rayon skirts to retail at $1.99 and $2.95. The firm has experienced a phenomenal demand for its low-priced quality products. In 1939 the concern had difficulty in selling higher-priced goods and turned to low-priced products. A flood of orders started the owner on his present policy of low-cost "fashion" merchandise. The policy is to dodge most of the costly style changes by concentrating on "what most women want most of the time." Inflationary conditions have forced the company to adopt policies of production simplification and standardization. Increased volume has made possible, and necessary, the adoption of policies for quantity buying and advance ordering.[4]

In contrast to this example of simplifying and standardizing production

---

[4] "What Most Women Want," *Time* (August 16, 1948), p. 86. Copyright by Time, Inc., 1948.

methods is the case of a small artificial flower shop. This business, located in the Southwest, produces an artistic product unique in its field. During the 1930's a policy of selling at low prices was unsuccessful. Department store buyers "snooted" the product. During 1948, with a product of slightly better quality, still using raw materials purchased during the 1930's but with new policies, the company was far behind on production. Orders have come in without the use of paid advertising. The new policy is to price the product at about ten times its 1930-1940 price, stress individual artistic production, and sell direct to users or individual gift-givers. Proposals to standardize the product and use mass production and mass marketing have been rejected.

These examples of small manufacturers' sales, price, production, and related policies demonstrate the necessity of integration. No one factor, such as luxury nature of the product, economic conditions, or location of the plant, should dominate policy decisions. The examples are concrete cases that could be duplicated many times over. The important point is to study each individual situation from every possible angle before adopting what seem to be the best policies to follow. Spurious reasoning in the matter of policy formation is a serious error for the small manufacturer.

Production standards regarding quality of materials, workmanship, inspection, and packaging or packing will be related to the policies governing the class of customers desired and level or zone of the company's products. Policies must be consistent, and the basic one here is the class of trade desired. Production and management standards will be set to serve this market.

Distribution, selling, and advertising policies must be consistent in turn. Present and future costs of marketing the company's product, as well as market strategy, will be influential in this regard. Unless production is under contract for one or a few large distributors, marketing will probably be local at first, expanding gradually as the firm increases in size. Soon the question of what channels of distribution to use must be decided. It is better to study such problems before they arise and formulate tentative policies to be followed rather than to develop them haphazardly even during the beginning years.

Product identification should be considered early in the life history of the business. At first the company name may suffice, but a suitable brand name should be sought and adopted early enough to be exploited in the firm's advertising, packaging, and other sales promotion. Hints for the brand name and themes for advertising may be secured from the particular selling points of the product, the way customers identify it.

Manufacturers of consumers' goods sold through retail stores find that all practical steps taken to help the dealer resell the product are well worth the effort. At first the small producer will be limited in what he can do. Attractive packaging and appearance of the product, even though it adds nothing to its utility, will be the first step. Later, advertising and dealer aids like signs and display racks may be used. The main point is to keep the dealer's problem of reselling the product in mind at all times. Provision should be made in the policies to see that this is done. Detailed methods to use from time to time and special activities and objectives not herein discussed are also problems for management.

POLICIES IN THE SERVICE BUSINESS

Policies in this field should stress the basic nature of the business—service —and emphasize those particular aspects of the service that (1) are most desired by customers, and (2) the company is best equipped to furnish. The common human resistance to paying for such intangibles as service should be overcome by giving something extra or unexpected, if possible.

Since customers are less qualified to judge most services than they are to evaluate physical goods, the policies of the service business should stress reputation. To achieve this reputation, product and inspection standards to maintain the desired level of quality should be provided for in the policies and rigidly adhered to in practice; in addition, the quality of the service should be publicized continuously. Accordingly, this need should be mentioned in the publicity policy. Trade journals in each service field are a mine of ideas or themes to use as a basis for developing a desirable reputation. However, the quality of the basic service must be right, even if some unusual theme is selected for publicity purposes.

In some service fields a quality symbol is used and extensively advertised, such as *Sanitone* in the dry cleaning industry. Such a possibility should be investigated and evaluated.

When the nature and variety of services to be offered are clearly stated in the service operator's policy, the shop is enabled to plan all activities in such a way as to accomplish the stated purpose. For instance, a beauty parlor can offer general service or some type of specialized service for which it would seek a reputation of leadership. General service includes all branches of the beauty business, such as hair work, scalp and facial treatments, massaging, and manicuring. Any one of these services can, of course, become a specialized one, constituting in itself a main source of income. Whichever service policy is adopted, the shop facilities and personnel must be planned accordingly.

A somewhat different policy is that of giving each patron complete individual service. When the business is large enough, one person can act as receptionist and beauty consultant. This person's duty is to receive the patron, examine her hair, scalp, and skin, find out her needs, and advise her with reference to the appropriate beauty service. Then skilled operators who are trained for specialty work give her, in the shortest possible time, the treatment indicated. Not only are the patrons willing to pay a higher fee for this type of service, but they are delighted to find a shop where they can obtain particular and specialized attention.

Before the product or service policy is adopted, at least three groups of factors should be investigated—the market or potential demand for the type of service contemplated, the availability of adequately trained personnel competent to render this kind of service, and the owner's financial resources. Naturally the nature of existing competition would always be studied. In a community where all shops offer general services it might be better to concentrate on hair and scalp treatments or on skin care and make-up, including the sale of proper cosmetics for individual needs.[5]

Repair shops also differ in range of services offered and reputation desired for specialization. Automobile repair shops are classified by types of service. A general shop, for example, does all kinds of repair and maintenance work. Other shops specialize in one or two forms of such repair as brake work, wheel aligning, body repairs and fender straightening, and radiator repair. In addition, there is the superservice station, which most authorities define as a well-managed shop offering complete maintenance and repair service, and equipped also as a drive-in type of filling station.[6]

In many types of service business, policies to guide the relative emphasis on the sale of service as compared to the sale of related merchandise are desirable, at least until the shop is well established. At first there is the danger that a division of resources and effort between these two activities may result in doing a poor job of both. Also, it is much easier for the small operator to gain a reputation for one specialty than as being outstanding in all lines. For example, a skilled watch repairman who started in business during the war when this type of service was in great demand quickly established a reputation for quality of workmanship throughout the community of about 15,000. To handle his growing business he moved the shop from the basement of his house to a secondary retail location in town. Starting first with the sale of "reconditioned" watches, he was soon handling a general line of related jewelry items in competition with several other jewelry stores. Thus he has "just another jewelry store" with no distinctive reputation either as a merchant or as a repair shop.

CONCLUSIONS

Policies are basic to every business, whether put in writing or formulated only in the mind of the owner. The general policy and usually certain provisions of the major policies should be formulated before a new business is actually started, although many modifications may be required later to keep the policies flexible enough to meet changing conditions. Policies constitute one management control that should be followed without any exception. Change the policy, if necessary, but never make an exception or the policy is

[5] For further study see: "Types of Service," Industrial (Small Business) Series No. 25, Bureau of Foreign and Domestic Commerce, *Establishing and Operating a Beauty Shop* (Washington, D. C.: U. S. Department of Commerce, 1946), pp. 54-57.

[6] "Nature of the Automobile Repair Business," Industrial (Small Business) Series No. 24, Bureau of Foreign and Domestic Commerce, *Establishing and Operating an Automobile Repair Shop* (Washington, D. C.: U. S. Department of Commerce 1946), p. 2.

automatically destroyed. *All basic, long-run phases of the business's activity should be guided and controlled by policies.*

Through appropriate policies a business develops the reputation desired, capitalizes on its own strengths and avoids the errors of others. A progressive small firm can attract and hold qualified people by developing them for co-ownership, by both financial and nonfinancial incentives, by learning why better employees prefer the small concern and meeting these preferences.

QUESTIONS AND PROBLEMS

1. Why are policies important even in the small firm?

2. Make a list of the basic concepts underlying all policies. Discuss.

3. List the important factors limiting or governing policy formation. Explain each.

4. Why is a corporation an unlikely form of organization for a beginning small business? Explain and qualify.

5. Why must both major and minor policies in a business be formulated? How do minor policies differ for each of the three main fields of small business? Discuss.

6. Why must policies be based on factual information? In what sense is this information "factual"?

7. When should policies be changed? Differentiate between the policies of a new and of a well-established business.

8. Explain and illustrate applications of the product policy to each main field of small business.

9. Discuss the two types of finance and expansion policies—conservative and adventurous. Which do you prefer? Why?

10. What are the major weaknesses of the personnel and organization policy of many small concerns? Suggest practical ways to correct each weakness.

11. Compare and contrast the basic policy aims of small retailers, manufacturers, and service establishment operators.

12. If you owned a shoe store in a small town of 12,000, selling men's, women's, and children's shoes, what service policies would you establish? Explain.

13. Why is quality of performance so important to a service business?

14. Compare and contrast buying policies for a retail, a service, and a manufacturing business.

15. Select some kind of business, assuming a particular location, and formulate an appropriate general policy and the basic major policies you would recommend.

16. Interview several small businessmen in the same kind of business to learn all you can about the policies of each. Analyze and report your findings and conclusions.

17. Late in 1954 two partners disagreed on a policy of continuous expansion for their chain of three variety stores all in nearby towns. A policy of training assistants to manage new stories, as well as favorable conditions, explain their success so far. Finances are as good as most fairly new small enterprises. Should they continue to expand by opening new stores when a manager is ready and a suitable location available? Discuss.

9 • *Management and Leadership*

IMPORTANCE AND SCOPE OF MANAGEMENT

It would be hard to name a human activity in which the quality of management is not a primary factor in determining the degree of success. Both the need for and principles of management are universal. But the application of principles and scope of activities managed differ considerably by size of the enterprise, field, and other factors.

Leadership increases in importance with the number of people involved. Our concern in this chapter is with the internal management aspects of leadership for the other members of an organization. Leadership is currently a highly prized quality in the successful management of men.

Management in the new small business differs from that in a large established one in length of experience and in specialization. Experience naturally increases with time, and, partly, the repetition of given activities. The larger firm having the same operations performed frequently—such as erecting displays in a chain store system, the same mechanical or assembly operations in mass production—has a broad basis for analyzing each one and developing it to a high degree of perfection. Management specialization is the application of labor subdivision to the management functions. Because of the longer period of training required for specialists in management functions such as in accounting, advertising, methods analysis, market research, and personnel work, a still greater degree of efficiency may be achieved.

The small businessman has had less specialized experience than his big business brother, and must rely more heavily on his own limited experience in all the management functions. This is a major weakness of the small enterprise, but it can be corrected by special training of its owner-management.

Since most business courses devote major attention to the needs of the established larger company and disregard those of the small-scale beginner, in this chapter we will consider some of these neglected topics. Sources of information and assistance available outside the small enterprise are considered in Chapter 10.

It is top management's duty to see that a satisfactory return is obtained on the investment, that the business has an opportunity to continue as long as desired by its owners, that goodwill is maintained with employees and with the public. These are easier to list than to achieve.

A small enterprise pioneering some innovation, even when operated by a hired manager, may well be concerned more with gaining customer acceptance and proving the future prospects for the innovation than with immediate profits or a continuity of the enterprise under its current ownership. Other small businesses are organized to secure only a modest immediate financial return, but many future nonfinancial benefits. These are unique features of some small concerns that require no further elaboration at this point.

Management consists of a series of decisions dealing with planning and operation of the entire enterprise and each of its components. Thus management begins before the enterprise is launched, and includes such pre-operating decisions as selection of the kind of business, suitable location, provision of personnel and facilities, formulation of policies and initial organization. It includes operation of functional divisions or departments, such as buying, producing, advertising, accounting, expense and inventory control, as well as protection and provisions for the future. Many of these applications of management to special activities are fully discussed in Chapters 11 through 27. Our scope in the present chapter is limited to (1) some guides especially appropriate to the beginning enterpriser; (2) top management considerations; and (3) the basic management functions of direction, supervision, control, and co-ordination.

MANAGEMENT GUIDES

Time management is always important, but especially so to the small-scale beginning enterpriser. It has two major elements, (1) ranking the importance of duties, and (2) making effective use of timesavers. With all of its advantages, even being one's own boss has a maximum price in terms of time that can be devoted to it, and still permit the enterpriser to live. A major goal of time management is to keep this price for success reasonable. It may be less than 40 hours per week in some cases and well over 70 in others, but it has a definite limit in all cases.

A major weakness of the ambitious beginner is to glorify his unusually long hours devoted to achieving success—a modern version of the martyr complex. Good *time* management in most such cases could reduce these long hours from 25 to 35 per cent and produce better results.

Time is limited, fixed within absolute and reasonable limits. Managerial and other duties are virtually unlimited for the small-scale beginner. Choice is essential, and ranking is the only intelligent approach. "First things first" should be the guide, but like other maxims it is often difficult to accomplish mainly because of lack of planning. Which should come first, serving a customer when all other employees are busy and you, the manager are doing essential paper work that must be completed before tomorrow? The customer situation could not have been predicted a few minutes earlier, but your essential paper work was known in advance for days or even months. You be the judge—it's your enterprise.

The first steps in time management are: (1) to rank the various jobs in order of importance; (2) to divide them into at least two classes based on the manager's ability to control the time when they will be performed; (3) to decide which ones can best be delegated to other members of the organization; (4) to determine those where time can be saved in the long-run by adopting suitable procedures; and (5) to select or formulate all suitable aids to time economy. Each of these needs some explanation.

Ranking involves valuation. First are those mandatory duties required by law: keeping adequate records for income tax, sales tax, social security, excise and other tax reports; filing all tax reports and making payments according to times specified for each; and maintaining any other legally mandatory records, reports, permits, and payments. Next are provisions necessary for protection: appropriate insurance with its necessary records and payments on time; adequate safety provisions for the premises and property against accidents, theft, and so on; meeting contractual obligations for the payment of interest and principal on loans, rent and other current operating expenses, and for merchandise and other purchases.

The foregoing are nearly all dated obligations, most of which can be taken care of at any convenient time up to the dead line. To avoid a last minute rush and possible penalty for tardiness they should be cared for as time permits, well in advance of the dead line. This method also permits planning in advance so as to be adequately prepared, doing much of the work during slack periods, interrupting such work temporarily to take care of an emergency or immediate need—such as service to a customer when all other employees are busy—and doing a more thorough job on each activity by allowing ample time for it. A simple device to use is a tickler or reminder file or desk calendar. For every duty at least two dates are recorded, the dead line and beginning or warning date if ample time is to be allowed. Most businessmen take these steps, but do so mentally instead of recording the dates on a calendar or setting up a card file. The result is that frequently important duties are overlooked in the rush of day-to-day tasks. Even the tickler file will be of little value unless it is used constantly, consulted each day or often enough to insure its effective use.

A second group of managerial duties consists of all acts necessary to maintain continuous day-to-day operations. Most of these are routine, recurring regularly: opening and closing the shop; maintenance of the premises, mer-chandise or machinery, and adequate personnel; operating the enterprise by serving customers or maintaining production; and conducting such activities as advertising and communications. They should be performed in a systematic and businesslike manner, but need not require the personal attention of the owner-manager except in the one-man enterprise. Most can and should be delegated to other members of the firm so as to economize the time and effort of top management. Adequate guides can be formulated, such as policies and regulations, and limits to authority clearly defined, so that only unusual or exceptional cases need be taken up personally with the manager. This is the very important *exception principle of management.* Failure to apply this principle is a major weakness of the management in many small concerns, and the chief reason the manager is so busy with day-to-day tasks that he lacks time for planning, deliberation, and attention to important duties that he alone can perform satisfactorily. The difficulty usually results from one or both of two causes, an unwillingness to delegate authority and uncertainty as to how it should be done.

In the one-man enterprise it is, of course, not possible to delegate duties, just as in the two- or three-person firm the owner-manager is likely to bear some responsibility for routine tasks. Time management is important, however, even for the lone operator. Routine duties are not all of equal importance, nor do they all have the same degree of urgency from a time standpoint. In a customer service type of enterprise the shop must be open for business at regular or announced times even though some maintenance may have to be deferred. Also in other respects serving the customer properly takes precedence over all other duties except extreme emergencies such as fire or serious misfortunes. But serving customers on the premises is usually irregular and difficult to predict. All time not required for customer service should be used most effectively for other duties in the order of their importance. These other duties include the dated ones discussed earlier, as well as daily tasks. A useful device is a daily memorandum, or "order of work," that lists the important jobs to be done, if possible, during each business day. This list is prepared in advance, away from the pressure and interruptions of business hours, and is partial protection against two dangers—failure to complete essential work on time, and dissipation of available customer-free time on odd jobs that appear continuously but are less important than those on the "do today" list.

In deciding what duties should be delegated factors such as the following require consideration: size of the enterprise, legal form of organization, abilities of available personnel including top management, legal responsibilities and possible penalties involved, purpose or justification for the enterprise, current conditions, and possibly others in certain cases. Most of these are self-explanatory and those that warrant elaboration will be discussed later.

Long range timesavers especially are a form of intangible capital. Although Americans tend to worship capitalistic machine production, many small businessmen are woefully weak in their appreciation of the value of intangible capital. Witness the widespread lack of system and adequate records in most small enterprises. This condition results from the general human tendency to undervalue intangibles, from lack of adequate business education, and from the normal urge of aggressive individuals to get going as quickly as possible.

Whenever data from records must later be compiled for reports, such as income taxes and financial statements, setting up the record keeping system so as to facilitate these uses, not only saves considerable time later but gives more accurate results. A printed form lessens the danger of omitting essential information. Merely checking appropriate blanks replaces repetitive writing.

In connection with sales checks in retail stores several timesavers are being developed. Cash register receipts are suitable for cash-take transactions where it is not necessary to identify by name each of several items purchased, and where trade-ins or other allowances are not involved. Modern registers are available that give the store a record of identification of each transaction by salesperson, department, and classification number. Additional data may be recorded manually on tally cards for a limited number of topics, specific items, price lines and the like, or duplicate unit control labels may be accumulated where several variations (size, color, style) are involved for each item sold. These are all devices to save time and reduce errors likely to be made when writing out information at the time of each sale. They do not eliminate the need for some writing for send or charge transactions. In communities where the bank credit plan described in Chapter 10 is in operation, where a name and address charge authorization plate is employed, the plate may serve as a stencil to print this information and thus save time-consuming writing.

In service enterprises the trade association in the field, and sometimes the vendors, have developed procedures and forms that may be utilized to great advantage by the beginner. In other fields of small business the outside staff discussed in Chapter 10 provides similar aids. In such cases time, effort, and expense may be reduced by taking advantage of these aids, even if slight modifications are needed.

Filing. In two other respects considerable time may be saved by a little initial planning, with regard to storage and routines. The guide is "a place for everything, and everything in its place"—if you must keep it. Studies by the National Records Management Council show that for the records of an average business: less than 10 per cent must be kept permanently, 20 per cent retained currently, 30 per cent should be transferred to inactive status, and 35 per cent should be destroyed.[1] Alphabetical, subject, and chronological bases for filing will serve most purposes at first until more specialized needs become apparent. Certain financial records used in reporting taxes must be retained as specified

[1] *A Basic Plan For Record Retention and Destruction* (New York: Remington Rand, Management Controls Division, n.d.), p. 2.

See also: Edward H. Hempel, ed. *Small Plant Management,* American Society of Mechanical Engineers (New York: McGraw-Hill Book Company, Inc., 1950); Robert S. Holtzman and A. Kip Livingston, eds., *Big Business Methods, For the Small Business* (New York: Harper & Brothers, 1952); J. K. Lasser, *How to Run a Small Business* (New York: McGraw-Hill Book Company, Inc., 1955).

by law at the time. Purchase and sales records tend to go through three stages: active, reference, and dead. If the use to which they are put during each stage is considered in planning the filing system time and space will be economized, particularly in the reference and dead stages.

Once invoices have been paid they may be useful for a few months to a year in analyzing past purchases by kinds of goods, vendors, price and terms, delivery dates and services, and any significant differences between goods purchased from different suppliers. After they have served such purposes there should be some important reason why these records are retained, and dead storage means disposing of them permanently. In most cases sales records should also be retained long enough for careful analysis to aid in future buying, sales promotion, and customer control as described in later chapters. After this period of reference use they should be disposed of. Records of physical inventories should receive similar treatment. After their active period of verifying the book inventory and preparation of financial statements, they should be analyzed for management action to put the stock in order and to guide future buying, then held in safe dead storage just long enough for emergency use in case of fire or other insured loss. The two extremes that cause most beginners trouble are: the discarding of records before analyzing them adequately during the reference stage, and the storing of all records indefinitely without making effective use of them once they become inactive.

Storage. Storage of goods is somewhat different for each of three broad classes: (1) merchandise or materials currently used in the business, (2) equipment of various sorts temporarily not in productive use, and (3) miscellaneous used containers and odds and ends. Inventory or stores control is the subject of Chapter 22. Equipment not currently being used is either of a reserve stock type or just being held on the assumption that it may some time be useful. Fixtures in reserve should be easily accessible with a minimum of time and effort when needed, without occupying valuable space. Fixtures, often damaged or obsolete, often become a problem in some types of production. They are kept for spare parts, but it is often more economical in the long run to avoid such storage entirely. Miscellaneous used cartons, bits of paper, wood, and so on, are kept in case they may be useful in the near future; systematic storage of these may be made provided that they are put in a safe place as they constitute a great fire and accident hazard.

Aids to time economy include those applicable to the firm's planning, policies, organization, routines or procedures; good layout, fixtures and equipment; and certain aspects of self-management. Those not discussed in this chapter receive adequate consideration elsewhere in our text.

Planning. Planning is basic to all good management. Even the elaborate division into eight functions for factory management devised by Frederick W. Taylor put four of these in the planning group. "Use your head and save your feet," epitomizes one value of planning, and equally important ones are available for time saving and other benefits. Make each trip serve several purposes, and reduce empty return trips. Do all similar jobs at one time instead of skipping about aimlessly.

Lack of long-range planning accounts for the untimely death of many businesses which made spectacular starts. Failure to insure a reliable source of raw materials or parts, an adequate volume of repeat sales to justify high initial promotional costs, or loss of customers (say in a retail store) when changes in traffic or competition take place that could have been predicted with logical planning, are typical examples that occur frequently. A simplified application of Benjamin Franklin's ledger, in which was recorded all factors to consider before making an important decision is helpful. The essence of this procedure is to list *every possible factor* that may have a bearing on the enterprise or project, study and evaluate each, then base decisions or plans on the results—the broadest possible base of available information.

As applied to the beginning small enterpriser this procedure calls for a planning pause before launching, and periodic deliberations during operations concerning events two or more years in the future that might influence his success. He should also seek for information and ideas from his friends, other businessmen, his barber, local political office holders and employees, and every other possible source. One of the most fundamental principles of this procedure is to secure the widest possible diversity of viewpoints, interests, backgrounds, beliefs, and knowledge. Druggists may contribute valuable ideas for a proposed or operating ceramic plant, professors of philosophy may provide significant pointers on running a beauty parlor, or mathematicians may solve a costly operation in some handicraft enterprise. There are no known limits to the peculiar combinations and apparent lack of direct connections between occupation or specialty of the person consulted and the value of his ideas. The two important points are to secure as many ideas as possible, and from the greatest possible diversity of contributors. Then *use* your compilation of opinions and suggestions.

Short-run planning includes control through budgets and schedules as well as through less formal procedures. The former will be considered later as applied to important operations. The latter or informal planning is usually slighted in college courses and texts, but is important for our use at this point. For both types it is important to see the complete picture, to visualize all relevant factors, the effects of possible changes, and in general to make effective use of your imagination. The basic guides are that *nothing in business is static, and everything can be improved.*

For current operations, likely places where improvements may be made include: all frequently repeated activities, all traditional methods and procedures, all areas where no deliberate effort has been made to eliminate nonessentials, and all distributions of responsibilities and duties that have not been planned and delegated. In addition, any of the foregoing that represent large proportions of total expense, or that have a significant bearing on profits, should receive major consideration. Suggestions such as these embody the typical approach of the management consultant, who in addition has the advantage of an objective or outside viewpoint.

A practical procedure when several people are involved is to study the jobs each one performs in relation to the others. If properly handled, regrouping of assignments will often result in greater productivity, a better balance of work assigned to each person, and reduced payroll. It is wise to group jobs requiring (1) the same mental and physical ability, (2) the same safeguards and safety protection, (3) the same tools or equipment, and (4) the same type of operations. If the redistribution results in freeing part or all of the time of certain workers, other necessary duties should be assigned to them if possible. After jobs have been regrouped conditions should be reviewed periodically to see that the plan is working successfully, and to make changes as needed. It is much better to maintain a fair day's work continuously for each employee than to impose sporadic reforms only when the level of productivity falls too low.[2]

Probably every business has continuous problems or areas where existing conditions never seem to be entirely satisfactory. A few of these are: building goodwill, making most effective use of personnel, location, physical facilities and finances, and achieving the best rate of expansion.

Whatever the more important continuous problems may be, it is advisable to devote some time for deliberation and planning under conditions that are free of the pressures and interruptions characteristic of a normal business day. As the results of time economy procedures become effective, much of the planning can be provided for during business hours by proper organization. These planning periods should be respected by other employees as essential managerial activity.

Both time management and self-discipline are important. We refer to personal habits of the owner-manager. We all sometimes dissipate time on such things as idle conversation, newspaper reading, or just daydreaming. A businessman must keep up with important news events that might affect his business or family life, but many spend more time than necessary in the process. Conversation also is needed to spark fresh ideas, to make new friends and to build goodwill, but a lot of time is often wasted on unimportant exchange of comments regarding the weather, storytelling and the like. Of course, time consuming habits such as these are often relaxing and enjoyable. The main point is that unless controlled they frequently use up the only time the enterpriser could use more effectively in deliberation and planning. Experience shows that from one to two hours per day can often be obtained from these sources alone.

Protection. Consultation with a reliable insurance agent and other members of the outside staff will disclose the types of insurance coverage needed. A major goal is protection against serious losses. A minimum of insurance should usually include fire, public liability, key-men, and burglary insurance. Further-

2 "Job Grouping Key to More Productive Manhours," *Management Review* (February 1954), p. 108, from W. S. Lienhardt, *Supervision* (October 1953), p. 4:2.

more, whether or not they are covered by insurance, certain situations also warrant special attention; they are accidents, theft, and—in retailing—shoplifting.

Most accidents are avoidable through training and constant vigilance. Serious accidents, whether to employees or outsiders, happen quickly. Conditions conducive to accidents should be remedied immediately.

Theft of cash or merchandise often involves trusted employees—even relatives. Spot checks of the cash register, or inventories at irregular times, may disclose "overages." Errors, especially in the records, is one cause. Another is an attempt by a dishonest employee to build up enough surplus to warrant a theft—even amounts of money such as $10 or $20 bills, or a car or truck load of merchandise.

Shoplifting can easily wipe out any potential profit—particularly in retail stores using open displays. Shoplifters come from every economic and social class. In addition to the small number of kleptomaniacs—or those constitutionally unable to resist stealing—shoplifters are either professionals or amateurs.

Professionals often work in pairs. One creates a commotion to distract employees while the other takes the merchandise and leaves. At least one employee in every selling area should remain on duty to supervise customers regardless of any disturbance and to take appropriate action if shoplifting is detected.

Amateurs usually work alone. They tend to lack finesse and may display signs of nervousness visible to experienced supervisors. Children comprise a large segment of amateur shoplifters.

Formerly a shoplifter could not be accosted while still on the store premises. Since 1950, several states have passed laws that permit retail personnel to detain a suspect until a law officer can be obtained. These laws also lessen the danger of the retailer being sued in case of error. Regardless of these laws, however, the merchant should exert great care in handling suspected shoplifting.

TOP MANAGEMENT CONSIDERATIONS

Even the smallest business needs good organization. Basically, organization involves two steps: a division, by analysis, of the particular business into the functions or activities that must be performed, and assignment of each to certain individuals. It is one of the most powerful tools of management. Organizing ability is universally accepted as a characteristic of the successful manager.

A simple approach to organization is to write down what the business must accomplish to be successful, and from this to subdivide or list *all* the activities that *must* be performed. These should then be grouped in *related* activities commonly called "functions," such as selling, producing, and recording. For a new business, effort should be made to secure individuals well qualified to perform each of these functions. For an established business, the job is to assign functions and subfunctions to members of the firm according to their respective abilities, capacities, and interests, being careful not to overload the better-qualified individuals.

In assigning duties to individuals, there are certain principles that extensive experience has proved to be of vital importance. Authority and responsibility should always be assigned equally. If you make an individual responsible for a certain job, give him the authority necessary to do it. Also, as was stated elsewhere, do not permit any individual to exercise authority—that is, to give orders or make commitments *for the business*—unless that person is held accountable for results. One's own relatives should never be excepted from this rule.

Division of authority and responsibility in the small business is especially important in the case of a partnership, since the acts of either partner with respect to outsiders are usually legally binding. Also, employees recognize each partner as an owner and will take orders from him. If no agreement has been reached between the partners as to their division of authority, conflicting orders often result.

However, a principle useful in securing employee loyalty and cooperation is to give each member of the firm *some* authority and responsibility. This helps to build men as well as business. In the small business the tendency is for the owner to retain all authority, thus truly making it the so widely criticized one-man enterprise. The successful manager constantly considers his responsibilities (1) in terms of those which he can delegate whenever possible, and (2) with respect to the effect of his actions on his own work, on his assistants, and on the rest of the organization.

In practice, organization must be the answer to a particular problem. This means that the conditions existing in the business are more important determinants of the setup than arrangements illustrated by generalized organization charts. Even big business has started placing less emphasis on formal organization as depicted in charts and is paying greater attention to informal organization that always seems to develop, largely as a result of employees selecting their own authority and responsibility according to preferences and abilities. Very often it is the informal organization that actually functions most fruitfully.

One of the author's former students and his brother bought a small town general store. Three main classes of goods were handled: foods, hardware, and apparel—the third consisting mostly of men's and women's work clothes—but divisions or departments were not clearly recognized. One brother was experienced in food merchandising but had not had business training or executive experience; the other had college training in marketing and accounting. Neither of the men had had experience merchandising hardware or wearing apparel. The two were able to employ a lady familiar with the women's wear lines, who was put in charge of that merchandise division. The college-trained brother had done enough rough carpentry work to be fairly well acquainted with the general line of hardware items and work clothes carried, so he took over the merchandising of these lines. Naturally his brother took charge of the groceries and meats. A "typical" organization would have consisted of three (or four) merchandise departments—foods, hardware, and apparel—whereas the practical solution in this case is more truly typical of most small businesses in that the organization is built around the abilities of the individuals.

As co-owners with different training and experience, the two men divided the other management functions accordingly. Both determined store policies after consulting their banker and their major suppliers and after discussing each question with the manager of the women's department.

The college-trained brother is an extrovert, aggressive, and very likable. Within a year after taking over the business he organized a local chamber of commerce. He was elected its first president. Within six months after its formation the chamber of commerce succeeded in attracting new industries to the town, and promoted other civic developments.

Since the net profits and other achievements of this partnership have been well above the usually optimistic estimates of beginners, its organization and the policies followed have been discussed at some length.

Special Problems

The founders of the partnership just discussed were more fortunate in one respect than many small businessmen who may be under pressure to employ in-laws, or a particular type of worker who has become traditional for certain jobs in the community.

Sometimes the small business manager feels the burden of contributing to community activities to be relatively heavy. As a businessman he wants to participate in civic development and belong to local service clubs. Often these activities consume a large amount of his time. Also, because he is known personally in the town, he may be called upon quite frequently for donations toward community development. Whereas the larger organization with sales of $200,000 might contribute $20 to some "cause" and feel virtuous about it, the little fellow with $40,000 sales would probably feel ashamed to contribute only $4.

Although there is no single solution for such problems, there is a plan that, if followed tactfully, will solve most such difficulties. First, the manager, in conference with specifically qualified individuals, should formulate policies covering each of these situations. Then (to cite one case in point) the owner may truthfully say to a job-seeking relative that on the advice of his suppliers and banker he has adopted a policy of not employing relatives. Similarly, to the friend soliciting contributions he may reply that on the advice of the chamber of commerce (or some other group) his firm has adopted a policy of making contributions in the same relative proportion to those of large concerns in the same field on a corresponding ratio of sales volume. It is much easier to handle these situations in this way than to give direct, impulsive personal decisions. Many small businessmen have found this plan to be very satisfactory.

BASIC MANAGEMENT FUNCTIONS

Four functions basic to all management are direction, supervision, control, and co-ordination.

Direction is concerned with setting the objectives and guides to be followed. Policies, executive decisions, instructions, and "orders" given by management are examples. (Modern management recommends *suggestions rather than orders*.) A case in point is a retail store which stated that its policy was to serve young people with "fashion right" merchandise. The manager declined an invitation to stage a private fashion show for a matron's club because this would have been inconsistent with the company's policy. To accept would have meant special purchases of merchandise appropriate for matrons, thus diverting the business from its predetermined goal.

Supervision has at least three aspects that are important even in the small business. First, to supervise implies observation, to see that duties are being performed or that work is being done correctly. This means that jobs or responsibilities have been assigned to individuals and that the supervisor knows the correct way of doing the work. For example, the manager observes a salesgirl demonstrating an article to the customer. Was the demonstration correct? To answer intelligently he must know the most effective or approved ways of demonstrating this particular article. This example suggests the other aspects of supervision; assume that the girl used a method of demonstration totally new to the manager. If so, it was either good or bad. If bad, the manager would take the first opportunity to discuss it with the girl and show her the correct or more effective ways to demonstrate this merchandise. This is the second aspect of supervision, the training or remedial phase. In the absence of supervision, the girl's sales record would eventually show that something was wrong (see "Control"), but it would not disclose the reason for lost sales.

If the new demonstration had been especially effective, the manager would have complimented the girl and adopted her method for future use, also telling all the other salespersons about it. This illustrates the third aspect of good supervision—"upgrading" of work by making all improvements general practice.

In all but the one-man enterprise some responsibility for supervision should be delegated. The modern trend is to use more supervisors and to treat them as members of management, encourage them to operate their divisions with initiative and ingenuity, and to experiment with promising new methods. Top management should go to the supervisor and discuss operating problems with him in his familiar environment instead of calling him to the manager's office.

The supervisor's authority and prestige among his men should always be respected. It should provide him with incentives and recognition for good work. Our immediate concern is with know-how supervision.

Supervisors deal chiefly with men, materials, methods, and machinery or equipment used by the men whom they supervise. Men are most complicated, unpredictable, difficult to handle. Personalities, emotions, and conditions outside the business affect most workers and cause many intangible elements to become important in achieving effective supervision. Family problems loom large with many workers. So do details of their jobs. A good supervisor understands the place of these personal factors in his workers' lives and is alert to detect symptoms of what may cause trouble later unless corrected. He strives for the confidence and co-operation of his people and succeeds as a supervisor in almost direct ratio to earning this confidence and co-operation.

The basic characteristics of a good supervisor are presented in most management texts. A supervisor must first instruct, explain, train, and sometimes demonstrate what his workers are to do. In some cases an explanation of the reasons is needed, especially for anything quite new. Close observation and follow-up are needed as soon as the worker is on his own. This is the crucial stage—the experienced supervisor knows it but the beginner does not unless adequately warned. Communicating instructions and ideas correctly takes time and skill. Five fundamentals are important: (1) emphasize the use and job applications of information given; (2) stir the learner to activity, get him to take part; (3) give the employee time to digest what he learns; (4) help him to see what is especially important; (5) help him to understand the meaning of what he is learning.[3] When the worker has demonstrated his ability and willingness to do the job as requested, the supervisor need only make periodic checks to see that no deviations are beginning.

When several workers are involved, some will work better together than others. The alert supervisor pairs off or groups his men on this basis. Individual abilities, attitudes, and ambitions also differ, and the good supervisor makes the most effective use of these differences both in assigning work and in spotting men for promotion or other recognition. All people like praise, recognition, and treatment as individuals. Praise and encouragement stimulate and inspire workers and constitute a part of the modern positive type of leadership. When criticism or correction must be given, real tact is needed, but it is better to "help the worker to help himself" in such cases early than to delay remedial action too long. This is, at times, one of the unpleasant but essential duties of a good supervisor.

Achieving worker participation and distributing some responsibility among as many as possible usually enlist support and co-operation and lead to other objectives—to make workers conscious of the importance of costs, quality,

---

[3] *Getting Work Done with Fewer People; Suggestions to Supervisors,* Training Manual No. 8 (Washington, D. C.: U. S. Department of Health, Education. and Welfare, Division of Personnel Management, 1954), pp. 12-14.

safety, and preventive maintenance. Sometimes these goals may be achieved by a challenge to the workers, such as contests or awards which are significant as recognition symbols but need have no monetary value. An important order dependent on meeting quality and cost standards as well as a specific delivery date is a good example, if the workers are consulted first. At times fabulous achievements result from this technique, and the workers seem to enjoy the importance of their part in the project. Some small companies keep all workers informed on the competitive position of the firm, enlisting worker co-operation in meeting stiff competition, or in checking any possible decline in the concern's competitive position.

The "suggestion system," in the small firm may serve many objectives under a supervisor who has know-how. Worker conferences in the big organization to stimulate two-way communication serve this purpose. The more personal nature of the small outfit can be used to advantage in getting employees to express themselves, to offer suggestions, and call attention to opportunities for improvement. Recognition is still important even though ideas are communicated informally and often conversationally. Also, the supervisor must be particularly careful to give the worker full credit when reporting to top management. He must be certain that nothing he does can be interpreted by his men as an attempt to steal their ideas or any rewards rightfully due to the contributors.

Control requires three steps: setting standards or objectives for accomplishment, maintaining current operating records for comparison with standards set, and acting promptly when operations deviate too much from the goals established. Control systems deal with the measurable quantities like money, units of production, or sales. Managerial control requires an appraisal of the *reasons* for operating results being different from those planned, and intelligent decisions as to what action is needed. Example: Production control in a small factory plans a daily output of thirty units, based on anticipated sales department needs. Daily reports show actual production to be averaging only twenty-five units. Investigation discloses recurring delays because of repeated breakdowns of one machine. Review of sales estimates verifies the need for thirty units daily. Immediate action by management will prevent an increasing amount of back orders, broken promises, and lost sales. If possible, the defective machine should be repaired or replaced at once. Otherwise it would be better to slow down on sales immediately so as to meet current ability to produce than to have disappointed customers and the other likely results of failure to co-ordinate sales and production.

Co-ordination is both a basic function of good management and an *ideal* seldom, if ever, achieved. Management is always striving, however, through direction, supervision, and control, to secure the maximum possible co-ordination of all the activities of the business. Each important decision must be made in the light of its effects on all divisions of the business. Policies are important co-ordinating devices because they set common goals or objectives toward which various departments work. Budgets, schedules, and other types of control assist in securing co-ordination because they help management to plan and secure a balanced relationship between the operation of different divisions of the business. Co-ordination represents the culmination of effective management—nearly perfect balance between the elements of sales and production, of expansion and resources available, and of revenue and expenses plus profits.

LEADERSHIP

Modern management stresses leadership and the human element. Recognition of good work by the manager usually does more to encourage employees than incentives that are less personal. Criticisms, when necessary, should be made privately, sympathetically, and constructively for each employee. Great care is taken by the real leader to treat all employees fairly and understandingly, as individual human beings. Employee suggestions are welcome; they are actively sought by alert managers. In the more progressive organizations employees are consulted on management problems, and they are furnished with management information formerly of a confidential nature. This employee-management co-operation is one way for the small business to attract and hold personnel of excellent quality.

Sometimes owner-operators of small businesses have the capacity for leadership, but do not exert it. Usually the reason for this is that they are too concerned with minor details, are unable to see their opportunities, or lack the energy that forthright leadership demands. To expand, or even protect, their businesses under such conditions becomes almost impossible.

The Leader's Guide to Human Relations

Mr. B. W. Elsom, Personnel Superintendent, the Boston Store, Milwaukee, Wisconsin, offers the following excellent advice:

1. The most dangerous policy in handling subordinates is to ignore them.

2. The "mental wage" is low if the employee is not interested in his job.

3. There is more "mental wage" in a request than in an order.

4. The "mental wage" is low when the worker's suggestions are ignored.

5. Prompt decisions by supervisors add to the "mental wage."

6. "Mental wage" goes up as working conditions are improved.

7. Workers are hungry for commendation; a "pat on the back" stimulates effort.

8. An indirect method of praise is to ask the worker for his opinion as to the methods or progress of a job.

9. One of the most potent forms of "mental wage" for employees is the certainty that they can have a sympathetic ear for their grievances.

10. People resist change. Tell workers of [impending] changes which will affect them. Surprises upset people.

11. Intelligent employees have the right to know the reasons that lie behind rules and company policies and organizational set-ups.

12. Tell employees as much as possible about department plans and results. This adds interest and stimulates a sense of responsibility.

13. Give each worker an answer to his ever-present question, "How am I doing?"

14. It is better not to have a rule than to permit frequent violations of one.

15. Every employee is entitled to thorough instructions in the duties he is to perform; best methods to use; standards his work will be judged by.

16. Corrections should be made with fairness and consideration.

17. Criticism in the presence of fellow workers is unnecessarily embarrassing.

18. Ambitious employees are eager to broaden their knowledge . . . storewide.

19. Belief that the boss shows favoritism is highly destructive of morale.

20. Wholehearted employee co-operation is never built on a foundation of fear.

21. We all want "a place in the sun." Every employee should have a feeling of pride in the worthwhileness of his contribution to the business.

22. No promise that the boss makes is unimportant.

23. Discipline should be consistent.

24. "Mental wages" pick up when the worker is given more responsibility and a chance to show initiative.

25. The worker's sense of security, his knowledge of reasonable regularity and continuance of employment, is essential to personal efficiency.[4]

CONCLUSIONS

Good management is the key to success in business. In the small business, management—the owners—formulates the policies, arranges the initial financing, selects the location, building, and fixtures, and determines layout, besides operating the business. Throughout the book more than twelve special aspects of management, such as those just mentioned, have been recognized as important enough to warrant discussion in a separate chapter. Yet they are all special phases of management.

When the wide range of duties required of the manager of a small business is considered, the need for some outside aid is apparent. He must balance every division and activity of the business; plan for the future while busy with pressing matters of the present; provide the right insurance; select, train,

[4] B. W. Elsom, "25 Ways to Build Sales Morale," an address delivered before the National Marketing Conference, U. S. Department of Commerce, Washington, D. C. Reproduced as an article with the same title in *Home Furnishings Merchandising* (April 1947), p. 94.

and supervise employees; conduct or direct research; and *manage* all activities of the business. Surely our two basic statements regarding small business may well be used here to emphasize the need for careful attention, namely: (1) good management is the one essential for success, and (2) time is the number one problem of the small business.

The opinion is widespread that success in small business requires long hours of hard work, and most enterprisers do put in long hours. Others equally successful, however, through adroit time management accomplish just as much and achieve the same results in more nearly normal working hours. In some cases, learning more rapid ways to perform essential tasks may be indicated. In other cases the time needed may involve sacrificing some social amenities, aimless scanning of the daily paper, or similar uneconomic, though pleasurable, activity. An employee has his time managed for him by company regulations, but the entrepreneur must do his own time management for success at a reasonable price.

Management has been developed to a fine art, and organization to a near science. Each has a body of well-established principles, practicing specialists, professional organizations, and literature comparable to that of the other recognized professions.

Management deals with the *direction, supervision, control,* and *co-ordination* of all activities of the business. Organization deals with the *structural arrangement* or *interrelationships* between different parts of the business. Since a business organization is operated by individuals, most of the important principles of organization are expressed in terms of the human element. We think of managing a group of people, rather than of running a machine. The group of people may be well organized, the machine well built.

Since management is a highly skilled art involving a range of knowledge and abilities infrequently found in the average small businessman, many proposals have been made, and some steps taken, to assist the little fellow to improve in this respect. The "outside staff" discussed in this chapter is a step in the right direction. The subject is more fully dealt with in Chapter 10, which follows.

QUESTIONS AND PROBLEMS

1. How could you prove that management is the most important factor governing the success of an enterprise?

2. Explain and illustrate how management specialization may result in greater relative efficiency than specialization of labor.

3. How do you account for the tendency of the small enterpriser to rely more heavily on his own limited experience than do executives in big business?

4. Is efficient management of the small firm always concerned primarily with maximum profits and expansion? Discuss.

5. How is the term "management" used in this chapter?

6. Why is a discussion of time management more appropriate in a small business text than in one for future big business executives?

7. Briefly describe each of the five steps in time management.

8. Since recordkeeping is time-consuming, how can you justify the emphasis placed on adequate records as timesavers?

9. Suggest ways the owner-manager can "do first things first."

10. Explain how neglect of the exception principle of management results in many small enterprisers being too busy to do adequate planning and reviewing.

11. Describe several forms of intangible capital discussed in the chapter and explain why they are examples of capital.

12. Describe several ways the small business can save time safely by reducing or eliminating frequent writing.

13. Describe appropriate applications in the small enterprise of the guide, "a place for everything and everything in its place."

14. Explain efficient records management for (a) sales records, (b) purchase records, and (c) inventory records.

15. What are the two major weaknesses concerning records of many small businessmen?

16. How is planning related to good management? Illustrate.

17. Explain the objectives and techniques of Operations Research and its applications to the independent enterprise.

18. Which of the following could make useful Operations Research contributions: (a) A plumber for a publishing project? (b) An author for a watch repair shop? (c) A public school teacher for a proposed garage? (d) A local politician for a firm of consulting engineers? (e) A baker for a hardware store?

19. As the new owner-manager of a ten-year-old retail store and repair service enterprise employing 40 people, where would you look for the best opportunities for improvement? Explain.

20. Explain "job grouping" and what guides to use.

21. Illustrate how time management often requires self-discipline for a beginning enterpriser.

22. Explain the major guides to effective internal organization and illustrate each.

23. Distinguish the formal from the informal organization within a business.

24. Why is organization an aid to management?

25. Illustrate how "organization is an answer to a particular problem."

26. Name the four basic management functions and briefly describe and illustrate each.

27. Describe supervision, the right and the wrong way.

28. Explain know-how supervision.

29. Why do some owner-managers who have leadership ability fail to exercise it?

30. Analyze the "leaders' guide to human relations" presented in this chapter for the few basic concepts or principles involved. State and briefly explain each.

31. How can a business organization be "audited" to find its weak points? Discuss.

32. How, specifically, is the present chapter related to the topic of personnel? Explain.

33. Select two independent enterprises where you will have an opportunity to

observe the managers for a reasonable period of time, choosing one that appears to be very well managed and the other poorly managed. Record, analyze, and report on your observations.

CASE PROBLEM

STONE ENGINEERING COMPANY: MANAGEMENT PLANNING

The Stone Engineering Company, started in the Midwest in 1941, is a small concern in its field. The company operations are diverse. The shop is not departmentalized, but is flexible enough to adapt itself so it can do any of the following:

1. Design and produce dies for manufacturers and fabricators.
2. Produce parts or subassemblies for manufacturers.
3. Manufacture and assemble finished products for established concerns.
4. Manufacture and assemble patented products for inventors, under contract. Before accepting a contract, product analysis and market analysis are conducted to determine acceptability.
5. Manufacture its own patented products, such as metal baskets, sporting goods items, etc., for distribution through jobbers.

Operations 1, 2, 3, and 4 are carried on whenever orders for the type of work involved are accepted. Operation 5 is continuous, although the production of individual items will vary from time to time.

For operations 1 and 2, no market studies are made, since Stone Engineering Company does not work on the final product. For operation 3, no market studies are made, since it assumes that the contracting concern knows the marketability of the product. The procedure followed in determining market possibilities in operations 4 and 5 will vary with the product to be manufactured, depending on the type of customer, the usual channels of distribution, et cetera. The technique followed with its most recent product, a plastic item of marine equipment, is illustrative of the detail into which Mr. Stone goes.

Product Analysis. The company secured sales literature, prices, and delivery schedules from all competitive manufacturers. These were studied, with particular attention to prices and potential markets. It analyzed the competitive products, itemizing their advantages and disadvantages. It then listed in parallel columns the advantages and disadvantages of its own product and proceeded to weigh the selling points thus revealed.

A survey was also made of all state laws to learn the permitted uses and types, and the standards of safety and construction that must be met. To permit complete market coverage, specifications must meet the most rigid standards.

Market Analysis. Next, it proceeded to make an estimate of the size of the total market. Lists of dealers were obtained from trade publications and directories. Personal contacts at trade conventions with dealers, representatives of other manufacturers, and sportsmen provided additional names.

Ten per cent of the better class dealers were selected for purposes of a canvass of market possibilities. They were chosen because of their known success and because they were progressive, had high credit ratings, advertised extensively, and sold only nationally advertised competitive products. The outlets approached included mail-order houses, jobbers, sporting goods stores, and similar firms. Mr. Stone believed that these dealers would know the market and trade possibilities. He also felt that information obtained from these sources would be more valuable than available statistics of sales, because it was up to the minute and included the best judgment of the trade.

By mail, telephone, and personal interview, the distributors were asked what their total sales of this class of marine equipment were likely to be in the following year; their opinion of products already on the market; the advantages and disadvantages of these competitive items; their reaction to price level, and what the difference in sales might be at various prices.

The replies provided information on the demand for the marine items in those outlets. Allowance was made for dealers not contacted by estimating the share of the market they represented and then discounting that portion to avoid inflating the calculation. A total annual market of 200,000 units was thus estimated.

Mr. Stone further concluded from the response that he could capture one-twentieth of the total, or 10,000 units, if his product proved to possess the major advantages of the competitive items, with none of the disadvantages, while still selling for a comparable or reduced price. This decision was not influenced to any great degree by an offer from one optimistic dealer to purchase the first 12,000 units produced. Nor was the order accepted, because Mr. Stone preferred to sell through a number of dealers, thereby giving wider distribution.

Testing the Market. Forty models were made, and careful cost records maintained. Some of the models were displayed at the New York Sportsmen's Show, and in other similar shows across the country. The salesmen took orders, and noted the type of comment passed by observers. They were also expected to observe and to report the interest shown toward competitive products. Other models were made available to a number of large dealers who agreed to display them for the purpose of taking advance orders and testing customer reaction.

From these orders and the observed market interest, the development budget and production schedule were set up.

The cost of introducing this product was substantial. For smaller and less expensive products, the cost would be much less and might represent a small proportion of estimated sales. Mr. Stone feels, nevertheless, that if a product is worth introducing at all, it is advisable to plan carefully, and to ascertain as fully as possible what the reception will be.[5]

Assignments

1. Discuss the strong and weak points in the organization and management of this company.

2. Explain and justify the different attitudes toward operations 1, 2, and 3, compared with 4, and 5.

3. Analyze and evaluate the procedure followed in launching their plastic item of marine equipment.

[5] Adapted from "Measuring Potentials Before Introducing a New Product" (Case Study), Small Business Aids, No. 273 (Washington, D. C.: U. S. Department of Commerce, U. S. Government Printing Office, May, 1947).

10 • Management Research: Outside Staff

The President's Conference on Technical and Distribution Research for the Benefit of Small Business was held in Washington, D. C. during September 1957. The Conference disclosed the great range and variety of outside staff services available to small businessmen.[1] This conference of leaders was followed on the local level in many states where small businessmen comprised the audience and chief beneficiaries.

Big business has subdivided and specialized management as well as other functions but still employs outside staff assistance. Why should the small independent be deprived of these benefits? In recent years outside aids have been made available to him, but here the major requirements are (1) a recognition of need, (2) knowledge of the availability of outside staff aids, and most important, (3) willingness to use them.

Importance of Outside Aids

Lack of managerial ability and lack of sufficient time to perform all of the activities of management have been proven beyond any reasonable doubt to be the outstanding weaknesses in almost all small business failures. Adequate planning and preparation greatly lessens these weaknesses but cannot for long remove them entirely as long as the enterprise remains small. Although the well-prepared manager has a big initial advantage over the typical beginner, conditions change so rapidly that unless he keeps abreast of developments even a good start is soon lost. Until a business becomes large enough to employ its own management specialists and staff experts it must make use of outside staff or eventually lose out in the competitive struggle.

Clarification of Terms and Concepts

Many specialists in big business have line rather than staff authority, but specialists in the same line functions who are not members of the firm may be

[1] *Proceedings of the President's Conference on Technical and Distribution Research for the Benefit of Small Business* (Washington, D. C.: U. S. Department of Commerce, 1957).

utilized as outside staff. The sales manager of a large corporation is a *line executive,* a specialist in his function, but when sales consultants are employed they normally serve in a staff or advisory capacity. A small firm may have a man responsible for sales and still make effective use of many outside agencies to further the success of this function. The latter are specialists in a line function but serve in a staff or professional advisory capacity. Only in some dire emergency would the typical independent grant full, or line authority, to an outsider, as to a creditors' committee to ward off bankruptcy. Our interest in this chapter is in assistance from outside a firm's own organization where final decision to use or reject such aid rests with the management of the firm.

Scope of the Outside Staff

Outside staff assistance can be obtained by the average independent in every area or function where similar assistance is furnished to executives of our largest corporations. Some types of assistance are more appropriate than others for the small enterprise, such as a simple but sound procedure for selecting employees intsead of an extensive battery of scientific personnel tests that must be administered and interpreted by experts. Some are too expensive in one form but available in other suitable but less expensive forms, such as a large firm of management consultants instead of a part-time small business consultant. Some render individualized services for a substantial fee whereas others furnish basic data of a general nature with special applications to be made by the management of each firm, a detailed market analysis of a particular company's product and its competitive position compared to basic statistics and trends affecting that class of products.

There are several bases that could be used to classify outside staff services:

1. *Price*—fee per assignment, retainer, subscription, nonprofit cost only, gratis.

2. *Type of agency*—governmental, suppliers, equipment manufacturers, lending agencies, trade and professional associations, trade press; professional practitioners, lawyers, accountants, management consultants, insurance counsellors; credit and collection agencies; protection services, property, employee honesty, private policing and watchman services; parcel delivery companies; window display, store cleaning and maintenance services; advertising and sales promotional agencies; university research bureaus; university short courses, home study courses, business clinics, and faculty consultations; vocational schools, state and local departments of vocational education; fashion forecasting agencies; consumer panels; and so on almost indefinitely.

3. *Management function*—production, marketing, finance, research, accounting, personnel, buying, pricing, policy supervision, public relations, maintenance of plant and equipment, government contacts, reports and regulations.

4. *Purpose or objective*—aid to all businesses, aid to small independents in

particular, aid to self-improvement of owner-managers, protection needed more by small independents than by large integrated concerns; goodwill and sale of related products or services; consumer movement goals, as more reliable buying information and better customer services.

Extensive as they may appear to the neophyte, the foregoing do not exhaust the bases upon which outside staff aids may be classified. They should, however, suggest how really comprehensive these services are, and the need to limit our discussion to those of greatest practical significance to the representative beginning young entrepreneur. Our plan is to give separate primary consideration to (1) private company services where the service is "free" but tied-in with obligations to favor the purchase of certain products, and (2) governmental services at all important levels. Cross references and similar techniques will be adequate to provide for cases that may appear to be slighted by this pragmatic approach.

PRIVATE COMPANY SERVICES

Several of the agencies discussed here provide many outside staff services with some overlapping, but usually one type of agency will have advantages in a particular case.

Trade Associations

Every field of business interest has some trade or professional associations. In contrast to chambers of commerce and other civic groups that cut across occupational boundaries, trade associations function in one field, such as hardware retailing, dry goods wholesaling, bolt and nut manufacturing; or in one function, such as direct mail advertising. The U. S. Department of Commerce has published directories of trade and other business associations, the most recent of which may be purchased directly from Washington, D. C., upon request. In general terms the following list refers to many, but not all, of the activities of interest to small enterprises. Several call for additional discussion. Here are some of the things trade association executives consider most important:[2]

1. Promoting better accounting and record keeping methods.
2. Sponsoring industry-wide meetings and developing leadership within the industry.
3. Operating a liaison service between Federal agencies, the Congress, the industry, and its individual members. Some trade associations also provide liaison service for their members with state and local governments.

[2] Reuel T. Elton, *How Trade Associations Help Small Manufacturers,* 2nd ed., Management Aids for Small Business No. 32 (Washington, D. C.: Small Business Administration, July 1953), p. 204. Also: Walter Mitchell, Jr., *How to Use Your Trade Association* (Englewood Cliffs, N. J.: Prentice-Hall, Inc., 1951).

4. Providing publicity and public relations programs for the industry.

5. Fostering industry-wide technical research.

6. Maintaining a labor relations service within the industry designed to prevent work stoppages and promote industrial harmony.

7. Issuing special information bulletins to their members. These bulletins report on current affairs affecting the industry, on government orders and legislation, and other, similar matters.

8. Gathering statistics for the industry.

9. Publishing specialized data concerning their industries. Many of these relate to such activities as promoting sales, educating the public to possible uses of the industry's products, or attracting qualified individuals into employment within the industry.

10. Offering training courses to employees of member companies.

11. Supplying other services to the industry such as credit reporting services, savings on the purchase of insurance, and varied economic studies.

12. Furnishing the industry with specialized technical advice that few small members, individually, would be able to afford.

Trade associations[3] are typically membership organizations financed by dues that average a small fraction of one per cent of members' sales volume. Most associations limit their services to members, except for co-operation with educational institutions and government agencies, and in certain cases advice or assistance requested by persons considering starting a business in their field. When the association has open membership, a request from a nonmember is usually answered accompanied by an application for membership blank and descriptive material regarding the advantages of belonging to the association. In a few cases one requirement for membership is being in business in the field for one or two years, as the National Food Brokers' Association (one year), the National Wholesale Furniture Association, and the American Warehousemen's Association, Merchandise Division (two years). Some of these restricted membership organizations lend whatever aid they can to beginners, and a few, such as the American Warehousemen's Association, have prepared kits to help newcomers get off to the right start. Frequent inquiries are received from beginning and prospective nonmembers by most associations and these are answered as completely as possible, except for material and services restricted to members. Nearly all associations accept subscriptions to their official periodical and sell their publications to libraries and nonmembers with a price differential in favor of members.

Because trade associations are concerned with the needs and problems of firms operating in their field, their services are naturally designed more for the established than for the beginning or prospective enterprise. The latter groups, however, can often make very effective use of the wealth of information and

[3] Most of the material in this section is based on direct correspondence by the authors in late 1953 with headquarters executives of 24 national associations representing all four major fields.

analyzed experience available from these agencies. A dramatic illustration tells how a veteran purchased some trucks hoping to enter the trucking business only to learn later that a certificate of necessity or similar license is required, which may not be obtainable at the time. A simple letter of inquiry to the American Trucking Association, Inc., or one of its affiliates, would have resulted in warning him of this situation.

National associations in most fields have developed uniform accounting systems, standard record forms, and standard expense classifications. These range from the long established plans of the National Retail Merchants Association to a costing system launched in 1953 by the National Potato Chip Institute. One group at least, the National Shoe Retailers' Association, encountered so much difficulty in getting small merchants to understand and use their uniform record keeping systems and forms that they now advise members to consult with the local manager of the National Cash Register Company.[4] This exception to the general trend may be the result of special conditions in shoe retailing, but it also emphasizes a point basic to our book, that often the small independent needs help in applying the best practices to his own concern.

Compiling statistical data and other information for use by members is a valuable service of at least one national association in each major field. Uniform expense classification and accounting is essential to render such data useful for developing standard operating ratios, and for individual members effectively to compare their operations with others in the field. Annual cost of doing business and similar surveys are conducted by the national association in the hardware, dry goods, men's clothing and furnishings, laundering, and other fields. Progressive small independents make effective use of their associations' cost and expense surveys to check on their own operations, to locate danger spots, to take appropriate management action promptly that might otherwise have been slighted until conditions became really serious. Thus an important advantage heretofore held by integrated and affiliated retailers is now available to independents through their trade associations. Data on operating results of the industry are also valuable when managerial decisions involving a new enterprise, department, or other activity is concerned.

In many fields of small business, cost studies and operating ratios are assembled by other agencies often with trade association co-operation, as producers, university research bureaus, accounting firms, Dun & Bradstreet, and the U. S. Department of Commerce. The trade association interprets such data, reports to members pertinent conclusions and often the entire survey report. This type of activity—keeping in touch with all studies and developments of concern to members, and analyzing and reporting on them in terms understandable and applicable to members—is one of the major managerial aids to small independents. It is mainly when certain topics are limited in

[4] From correspondence with L. E. Langston, Executive Vice President, National Shoe Retailers' Association (November 4, 1953).

their applications to one field that the association is likely to conduct its own special or continuing research. Example: the Circles of Information, a panel of 80 experts, serve the special needs of members of the Direct Mail Advertising Association.

Education and training of members, their employees, and sometimes outsiders, is another group of important association services. Training is presented through conventions, field contacts, booklets and periodicals, visual aids, correspondence and short courses often in co-operation with some university. Increasingly, national associations have been publishing *Management Handbooks,* or *Manuals,* often with distribution limited to members.

The National Retail Furniture Association and others assist members through store visitations, and all associations welcome member visits at headquarters to discuss their individual problems. Executives will assist and advise on proposed layouts, and some will even originate layouts from information furnished by members. Aid in modernization of building, fixtures and methods is provided by leading associations, sometimes through their own staffs or from specialists approved by headquarters. The major method for receiving individual assistance is naturally by correspondence. Large, well-established associations can answer many inquiries by sending some of their published material, but all endeavor to make the service as individualized as may be needed.

On the local level, agencies in the larger cities have quite an array of services to members, such as about thirty furnished by the Cleveland Retail Grocers' Association. Many locals are affiliated with the national trade association in the field, and some of the services already discussed for the nationals are carried out through the local association. This seems to be a recent trend for state and local managerial training conferences. Conditions often differ in various cities and among the states, so trade association services adapt to local needs as well as participate in assistance on a national basis.

Interindustry competition has increased so much that is is often more important than competition among concerns in the same field. Nearly every industry serving consumer wants with goods and services competes with all the other industries for its share of the consumer dollar—movies with television, food with drugs and hardware, clothing with automobiles and jewelry, and so on. Members of each industry can compete for their share better through trade association participation than as individuals. If an industry retains or increases its share of consumer spending each firm comprising the industry will be better off than it would be by losing out to other industries because of concentration on competition among concerns in its own field. Both types of competition work together and complement each other, since healthy competition within an industry improves its competitive position relative to other industries, but overemphasis on rivalry among firms in the same field is dangerous today. This means that so-called competitors must subordinate their individual rivalries and pool their efforts at times to retain their combined position in total consumer spending.

Many trade association services to members require pooling information, statistics, ideas and improvements, for the good of the entire industry. To obtain maximum benefits from his association a member must give as well as take. The decay of industries in many foreign countries that had carefully guarded secrets is mute testimony to the obsolescence of this attitude. In America the opposite results may be seen in patent pooling by our automobile manufacturers, acceptance of the idea of standard interchangeable parts, simplification projects, and our open membership trade association activities.

In addition to sharing information and furnishing statistical data requested by one's association, it is advisable for more small businessmen to attend their trade association conventions and participate actively in discussions. A familiar vocational conference technique should emphasize this point. An independent owner-manager who takes a week away from his business to attend his trade association convention may share in and profit by the experience of 50 others having an average of ten years experience or a total of 500 years of diversified experience in his line of business. In addition, he meets men who are superior in certain activities and can learn much from them by personal conversation. When meetings are not in session, stores or other types of business of interest in the convention city may be visited to advantage, sometimes including his own resources. Conventions are planned and conducted by experts to emphasize topics of current importance. Trade association officials understand the needs and problems of their members and are glad to talk about them. Many associations maintain model stores, complete libraries and other facilities well worth study by visiting members. Time away from one's own business premises often leads to a "new look" approximating that of the outside viewpoint upon return from a trip.

Trade Publications

For the independent enterpriser starting on a small scale, active participation or membership in his trade association may be difficult at first. Familiarity with the trade publications in his field, both before launching his enterprise and continuously thereafter, is of the utmost importance. Even college graduates need advice on this point. Trade publications in college libraries are nearly always neglected by most students due to course emphasis on mastery of the books and lectures, and the pressure of social activities. Yet both books and lectures are prepared largely from material presented in the trade press, but from one month to several years earlier.

Trade publications constitute one of the most economical sources for the small independent to use in keeping abreast of developments in his field. This category includes the official publications of trade and professional associations that are usually available to nonmembers by subscription. Both association publications and commercial trade and business periodicals are available in many libraries and these sources may be useful at all times. As a minimum, however, every small businessman should subscribe to at least one good trade journal in his field and to one good general news periodical, newspaper or the like that carries significant reports on business developments and topics affecting the class of trade or industry with which he is concerned. Retailers should also subscribe to the leading magazines consistently read by their customers and use them. Failure to do so results in the situation already mentioned where customers are often better informed about new styles, merchandise or materials than are many small merchants. In the fashion fields a few periodicals have retailers' editions that contain advance notices to the merchant of what his customers will soon be demanding.

Management Consultants

Only recently have increasing numbers of small businessmen come to realize the assistance they can obtain from management consultants or "business doctors," as more and more consultants are tailoring their services to the needs of small firms. This trend is likely to continue because it is the result of fundamental conditions. Management is becoming increasingly complex, specialized, scientific, professionalized, and distinct from the unique idea or motivation characteristic of a particular business. Operating management of the firm is intensely concerned with promoting its basic reason for existence or unique idea that justifies continuing the enterprise. Whereas the concern's own management is thoroughly familiar with this aspect of the business, much more so than an outsider could be, it often lacks the expert skills and experience needed successfully to manage *any* business including its own today. It is this latter need that management consultants are equipped to meet. Many small businessmen fail to appreciate the place and value of outside consultants, but those who utilize management counsel give five general points in its favor:

1. It provides an outside point of view.
2. It is based on wide experience.
3. It applies specialized knowledge to the problem at hand.
4. It emphasizes the scientific approach to problems.
5. It saves time.[5]

In individual cases there may, of course, be other more specific reasons in addition to these five for calling in consultants.

In many small concerns problems requiring the special abilities of a consultant are intermittent and of short duration. It would not pay such firms to have management specialists continuously on their payroll any more than it would pay an individual to employ a physician full-time when his services are needed only occasionally to help prevent or remedy an illness. A large corpo-

[5] Robert E. Williams, Executive Secretary, Association of Consulting Management Engineers, *How Management Consultants Help Small Manufacturers,* Management Aids for Small Business, No. 26 (Washington, D. C.: Small Business Administration, April 1953). See also: Donald R. G. Cowan, *The Small Manufacturer and His Specialized Staff,* Small Business Management Series No. 13 (Washington, D. C.: Small Business Administration, February 1954).

ration might be able to afford both kinds of "doctors" as a permanent part of their organization because of continuing needs in different departments and because of their numerous employees.

What most small firms need are (1) specialized assistance when some serious difficulty is encountered, and (2) periodic check-ups to detect hidden dangers that may be avoided if corrected in time.

There are over 15,000 management consultants operating as firms and individuals in both general and specialized areas. Although some limit their services to a special phase of management, plant layout, location, or communications, most of them are able to service the needs of the average business, and specialize mainly in the sense of acquiring greater experience with firms of a certain type and size. Part of this results from the way consultants are often selected, by personal recommendations of satisfied clients. The Association of Management Consulting Engineers, Inc., maintains a file of information about firms that furnish the necessary data, but reports that only a small fraction of the total number of consulting firms do so.[6]

Choosing the right consultant for the small enterprise should receive careful attention. In sizing up a particular consultant it is worthwhile to get answers to these ten questions:

1. How long has the consulting firm been in business?
2. What is the background of the principals (partners)?
3. What is the firm's financial status?
4. What companies has it served?
5. What do its clients say about the technical quality of its work?
6. How much of its business is "repeat" business?
7. How well does the firm get along with people—its own employees as well as outsiders?
8. How much time do principals spend on the job?
9. Has the firm had experience applicable to your problem?
10. Has the firm a recognized expert on your kind of problem?

You can get help in answering some of these questions, but others you will have to decide on the basis of your own judgment. There are a few rule of thumb measures that can be applied. They are not infallible; they are only indicators. But, as a rule, you should be suspicious of a consultant who deviates from the normally accepted pattern.

Be wary of the fellow who employs high-pressure salesmen and high-pressure advertising. Broadly speaking what is meant by "high pressure" is this: the fellow who *promises* benefits from his counsel, who urges you to sign up *now*, who hints at dire consequences if you fail to follow his advice, or who advertises a special *limited time* offer.

---

[6] Letter to the authors, dated October 28, 1953, from R. E. Williams, Executive Secretary.

Stay away also from the man who offers cut-rate services or promises results before he has had a chance to make a thorough study of your business.

Avoid the fellow who offers to make a study and a report on your business for a fixed fee, usually a couple of hundred dollars. He cannot possibly know how much work would be involved before he even starts on the job.

Don't expect much from the person who offers consulting services contingent upon the purchase of certain machines or merchandise.

Be cautious of the man who asks for payment in advance.

Look out for the tricky financial arrangement. Insist that the consultant tell you in writing precisely what he proposes to do, about how long it will take, and about how much it will cost, as well as what he thinks he will accomplish by doing it.[7]

Once a consultant is employed it is of the utmost importance to co-operate with him in every possible manner, both during and after his employment. His work consists of two major parts: diagnosis of the trouble or weakness, and recommendations for improvement. His recommendations are of no value unless followed. In some cases it may be necessary to have the consultant carry through with his recommendations, install more efficient methods, better quality control, or a new layout. This need occurs when a recommendation calls for some technical job beyond the ability of the concern's own management.

Management consultants are relatively expensive but may represent an excellent investment. A small firm or individual may charge $100 per day or more but may be needed for only a short time to remedy some trouble that would otherwise result in loss of profits far in excess of the consultant's fee.

A limited service type of management consultant is the small business consultant. He is often currently employed by an educational institution or large corporation and does consulting work on the side. Progressive colleges and universities encourage their faculty to engage in a reasonable amount of such private practice in their professional specialty. Many of these men have had exceptionally fine training and considerable practical experience in their fields. The nature of their regular position requires them to keep abreast of the latest developments, and exposes them to continuous requests for information and advice. They are obliged to observe high standards of honesty, integrity, and professional ethics.

In many cases the typical independent enterpriser will find a small business consultant better suited to his needs, and probably less expensive, than a full-time management consultant, but he should not expect cut-rate or bargain services, and certainly not the free advice that the specialists so often are asked to give. Small business consultants are more numerous in the fields populated by the largest numbers of small businessmen, retailing and service, as well as in functional areas such as market research, insurance, and public relations.

[7] Robert E. Williams, *op. cit.*

Miscellaneous Fee for Service Outside Staff

As already mentioned every activity of the management in a small enterprise may receive assistance from an outside staff. This outside assistance will be invaluable. Market research is available from firms specializing in this function, from Dun & Bradstreet, Inc., from A. C. Nielson and Company especially for advertisers, from advertising agencies, from freelance researchers, and in particular fields from many firms who confine their activities to their own field, consumer surveys and the like. Some firms specialize in making location studies, others in analyzing traffic problems, materials handling, personnel problems, filing systems, and almost every phase of management. Market information is available usually by subscription to services that specialize in reporting fashion trends and developments, shelf prices in chain food stores and supermarkets, and in other areas where sufficient demand for a service exists.

Many recurring tasks in the small concern may be "farmed out" to companies or individuals—window cleaning, setting up displays, copywriting, correspondence, employee training; maintenance of machinery, equipment, cars and trucks; parcel delivery, sign writing, or silk screen work; comparative and service shopping for retailers, checking or auditing any phase of the firm's activities. Certain tasks involving calculations, as pricing merchandise, may be simplified by obtaining slide rules, made for such calculations, from suppliers or purchasing them. Prepared tables or charts are often available from your suppliers, larger competitors, or your office supply dealer. The latter often knows where a particular type of aid may be purchased and will place an order for you if necessary.

A recent development is renting the use of electronic computers and programmers from banks or others who have such facilities. This may be to solve a complicated but infrequently occurring problem such as selection of suppliers or a location study, or for a continuous function such as inventory control. Early in 1960, "Datacenters" were being opened by International Business Machines and Remington Rand in various cities. In addition to hourly rental of machines Datacenter customers can make full use of IBM's educational facilities, experience, and library of programming aids.[8]

Staff Services of Producers and Resources

Producers of business machines, cash registers, computing and recording machines, weighing and measuring scales, often render many services gratis in an effort to build goodwill and eventually to increase sales of their products. Merchants Service of the National Cash Register Company is a good example, as the following list of subjects on which they have answered inquiries indicates:

[8] Advertisement in the *New York Times* (February 14, 1960), p. F11.

Advantages or disadvantages of partnership

Advertising: mediums, what to spend, how to handle, etc.

Bookkeeping problems

Breaking down a business by departments

Capital needed for new venture

Cash vs. credit

Collection problems

Control of inventory

Converting to self-service: groceries, drug stores, hardware, variety stores, service stations, department stores, specialty stores, etc.

Credit problems

Current business conditions

Dishonesty by employees

Diversification of lines or merchandise

Dressing windows

Getting more business

Guidance in opening new store (specific line given)

Handling of customers

Improving salesmanship

Incentive plans for salespeople

Interior display

Mailing lists

Market possibilities

Meeting cut-price and other competition

Modernizing

Operating costs for various lines

Pilferage by customers

Pricing properly

Promoting sales

Reducing expenses

Selling new products

Show card and sign writing

Sources for buying

Stock shortages

Store arrangement

Taxes and regulations

To incorporate or not to incorporate

Trade areas

Traffic problems

Training salespeople

Writing sales letters[9]

Over the years the company has gathered much data and information. Files in the Bureau are extensive, and the library in the department is well selected, including various services subscribed to and contacts with material and services from government and other agencies. A large factory library embracing over 10,000 volumes also provides a valuable source. However, considerable research and outside contact involving much correspondence are needed for a sizable number of requests.

Services are adapted to the needs of retailing in general and by lines. For example, one of the tangents that has developed into a separate service in itself is the store layout service where, through the medium of miniature grocery fixtures and photographic reproductions, they are able to offer visual layout information and suggestions. They have made suggested self-service arrangements for over 15,000 stores through this phase of Merchants Service. Companies producing floor coverings, display materials and equipment, and modern store fronts have made layout and modernization studies for different kinds of small businesses and will usually assist an independent on problems of layout and modernization. Many local public utilities have specialists available for consultation on lighting and color conditioning. Public utilities also make surveys and advise on power installations and other fuel-using appliances. Building materials dealers can often give advice on sound and color conditioning. Naturally manufacturers of machinery, materials handling equipment, and industrial installations have experts available to analyze customers' needs and recommend the proper installations.

[9] From R. H. Koch, Merchants Service, National Cash Register Company, Dayton, Ohio (May 11, 1951).

The customer's banker and the manager of his nearest branch office of Dun & Bradstreet, Inc. can render valuable assistance especially with reference to counsel on financial and credit matters. Dun's Failure Index is published monthly; their survey of the number and reasons for failures, quarterly, in *Dun's Review and Modern Industry.* It is available in many libraries or by subscription. These reports may indicate adjustments needed in management efforts and policies. Other indexes published in governmental and private periodicals include the wholesale price index, unemployment statistics, consumer disposable incomes, business inventories, bad debt losses, and many others of interest to different kinds of businesses. In particular, each entrepreneur should determine certain indexes or trends most significant for his enterprise and follow these closely.

Another valuable, but sometimes overlooked source of information for the small businessman, is any innovation by the larger concerns, especially the leaders in his field. This does not mean that the small enterpriser should mimic every move made by large companies or spend undue time watching their activities. In some cases, however, what the leaders in a field do today may be almost universal practice tomorrow. Needless delay in making adjustments can be serious. Independent retailers in the hardware and drug fields waited so long to adopt open displays and self-service that they may never recover business lost to customers who prefer these methods. In other cases some changes by large-scale competitors may open up new opportunities to small-scale independents through dovetailing operations. Many additional ways the independent can utilize observable activities of leaders in the field are explained in later chapters dealing with special phases of management. An excellent and concise discussion of some of these, and sources of information available are contained in the footnote reference.[10]

GOVERNMENT SERVICES AVAILABLE TO INDEPENDENTS

The federal and many state governments have for over 50 years been concerned with maintaining economic conditions favorable to free enterprise and competition, restricting monopolistic and unfair practices largely in the interests of small businessmen. A small independent who feels he is the victim of any such practices or conditions should consult his local Better Business Bureau or his state's Attorney General's Office for advice and assistance. In more personal or serious cases one's own attorney should be consulted, especially before any legal action is considered. These are largely negative aspects of government's relations to business, whereas our primary concern in this chapter is with positive aids or outside staff services.

Three areas of government services are of major interest to the progressive

[10] David L. Fox, *Appraise Your Competitive Position to Improve Company Planning,* Management Aids for Small Business, No. 43 (Washington, D. C.: Small Business Administration, February 1954).

enterpriser: (1) providing basic economic and statistical data and trend analyses for long-range planning and policy decisions, (2) information on current conditions and developments, and (3) assistance relative to specific individual problems or needs. The second category includes various surveys and studies that may produce results that are valuable for from one to ten years unless underlying conditions change or subsequent more refined studies are made. Sometimes the disclosure of defects existing at the time a survey is made stimulates sufficient corrective measures to render findings obsolete in a short time, as excessive numbers of brands carried by small grocers, or excessive bad debt losses due to failure to utilize the local credit bureau facilities. Such disclosures offer real advantages to the small independent who can profit by these mistakes of others. Both conditions were reported in the early U. S. Department of Commerce grocery and drugstore surveys made in Louisville and St. Louis.[11] Also in our second group are management booklets and technical aids describing the best practices up to the time of publication.

Since World War II, it has become of the utmost importance for prospective and incumbent small businessmen to be well informed on an ever increasing array of developments. These include opportunities for starting new enterprises, for diversifying operations, for shifting emphasis among various products, markets, or types of customers; knowing when to expand or contract; timing certain activities in relation to tax provisions, government purchasing plans and regulations; meeting government requirements for reports, permits, licenses and regulations; and taking advantage of improved technology and managerial developments. Firms with the best informed management are the most alert to seize opportunities as well as most likely to be prepared for adjustments that must be made to meet changing conditions. The increased rate of physical change in recent years, discoveries in science, and other innovations have intensified the need for reliable and up-to-date economic data, and for greater market information. Marketing policies and methods that were very satisfactory a few years ago may be obsolete today. Personal experience alone will not inform management of various developments in time to adjust to them. Outside information must be utilized.

More than two dozen agencies of the Federal government furnish information and data useful to the small businessman at little or no direct cost. Some also provide services that may be very helpful when they are known and used by the independent operator—assistance in recruiting employees and other personnel aids by the U. S. Employment Service field offices; parcel post, C.O.D., and many other services of the Post Office Department. Information and advice on foreign and domestic commerce is available from the Economic Co-operation Administration and especially from the Bureau of Foreign and Domestic Commerce. The Federal Reserve Board disseminates information not

---

[11] See any bibliography of U. S. Department of Commerce publications for these and subsequent survey reports for earlier years. Many are out of print, but may be obtained from libraries.

only with reference to banking and finance but also in related areas. Their annual surveys of consumer finances and buying plans are used to measure consumer economic status, distribution of income, savings, liquid assets, and intentions to purchase certain classes of durable goods. Leading Federal Reserve banks publish reports on conditions in their districts including continuing series such as sales and inventory indexes and stock-sales ratios. These reports are available in banks, many libraries, and by direct request from the Board of Governors in Washington or the Reserve Bank in the district.

The Federal Trade Commission has been assigned the task of conducting many studies concerned with concentration of economic power, monopolistic practices, unfair competition, effects on competition of various laws and possible needs for new legislation. Publications of the Food and Drug Administration catalogue actions against numerous firms for alleged violation of the Federal Food, Drug and Cosmetic Act with brief digests of each charge and actions taken. Like the regulatory functions of the Federal Trade Commission dealing with advertising, actions taken by the Federal Food and Drug Administration are of interest to small businessmen largely in suggesting what not to do. Publications of research projects by both agencies, however, as well as their annual reports often contain information and ideas of great value to the independent.

The U. S. Department of Agriculture has a large number of periodic series and many special research publications dealing directly, more or less, with agricultural products, both raw materials and foods ready for consumption, the status of farm families, agricultural co-operatives, consumer preferences and buying habits for foods and textiles, home economics topics, and fairly recently, certain phases of retail food marketing.

For special studies and statistical series relating to labor, status of wage earner families, employment and similar data, the U. S. Department of Labor and its Bureau of Labor Statistics publish material that is often helpful in appraising economic conditions and keeping abreast of developments in fields affecting labor. The *Monthly Labor Review* is available in many libraries or by direct subscription.

The ambitious enterpriser should purchase from the Superintendent of Documents, or study in his library, the latest edition of the *United States Government Organization Manual,* published by the General Services Administration, for a fairly complete listing and description of the activities of every Federal agency. Only in some such manner is he likely to become familiar with certain agencies that may be of real usefulness to him.

U. S. Department of Commerce

Prior to 1953 when the Small Business Administration (SBA) was established, the U. S. Department of Commerce was the most active government agency in conducting projects of interest to independent enterprisers. It is still the businessman's department of the Federal government. From time to time bibliographies or compilations of the publications of the U.S.D.C. are released which may be consulted in many libraries.[12] An individual may keep abreast of current publications in certain areas by asking that his name be put on the desired mailing list or by subscribing to periodic notices such as the weekly *Business Service Checklist*. The biweekly *Selected United States Government Publications* issued by the Superintendent of Documents, Washington, D. C., also lists many U.S.D.C. recent publications. The bibliography at the end of this text contains a representative selection of the major publications of the U.S.D.C. of likely interest to small independents.

During the 1920's and thereafter the U.S.D.C. conducted hundreds of studies of various management and operating functions of concerns in the major fields of small business, publishing the results as special reports or in the current periodical of the Department, the *Survey of Current Business*. Many of these studies are discussed at appropriate places throughout our text. The monthly *Survey of Current Business* is the standard reference source for data on production and distribution activities of the major industries and basic commodities. It also contains data on the business population and its changes, income and distribution, and about 2,500 statistical series covering nearly every measurable factor of significance to the national economy. Statistical Supplements and Annual Review numbers help to round out the picture.

The Bureau of the Census in the U.S.D.C. compiles data for publication in three major areas of interest—population, manufacturers, and business:

1. *The Census of Population,* taken every ten years, covers many characteristics of families and individuals in addition to age, sex, color, occupation, residence and nationality, to give a complete picture of families and households, and the official data are supplemented between census years by survey estimates. Along with the censuses of agriculture, education, and housing, nearly any data needed about the population and its trends are available. Of special significance are trends in the distribution of various age groups, peak years of births and trends in the older segments of our population. Business and professional men interested in certain age groups, occupations, changes in marital status or parenthood, and housing needs find additional uses for census data relating to their markets. Changing wants may be anticipated and opportunities for new enterprises, products, and services disclosed by careful analysis of census data.

2. *Census of Manufacturers*[13] data include shipments in terms of physical units and dollar value, cost of materials, payrolls, number of plants grouped according to number of employees, and the like. While this information covers a large variety of industries and products, its usefulness is limited by the num-

---

[12] See: *United States Department of Commerce Publications, A Catalogue and Index, 1951-1952 Supplement* (Washington, D. C.: Superintendent of Documents, 1954, and later issues).

[13] David L. Fox, *Appraise Your Competitive Position to Improve Company Planning,* Management Aids for Small Business, No. 43 (Washington, D. C.: Small Business Administration, February 1954).

ber of years which elapse between census surveys. *Facts for Industry* reports fill the gap between census years with summarized data for many of the more important census classifications. For example, manufacturers' shipments, by industry, are usually given on a monthly or quarterly basis.

3. *Census of Business*. The first census was taken for the year 1929, and others were taken for 1933, 1935, 1939, 1948, 1955 and 1958. Census of business data provide facts for all important aspects of retail and wholesale institutions, service establishments, hotels, places of amusement, construction firms, and other areas of business in contrast to manufacturing and agriculture. The latter two industries, incidentally, could not continue to exist without the services provided by business. Numerous fallacies have been exploded by the facts disclosed in census of business reports, and no really intelligent decisions by manufacturers or producers in agriculture and the extractive industries, or by government with reference to our economy, are possible without reliable data of the type furnished only by a census of business. The average small independent may underestimate his interest in this activity because he does not read census of business reports. But his trade association editors and all larger agencies with whom he has contacts study them and base their decisions and advise upon them. So, indirectly, the small businessman has a vital interest in a continuation or even an increase in the frequency and coverage of census of business data.

Probably of most direct use to many prospective enterprisers are a series of small business publications by the U.S.D.C., along with services available in their field offices. Two sets of small business publications are important, the "Establishing and Operating" series and the "Small Business Aids." The former consists of 43 paper-bound books, each dealing with some type of independent enterprise. This activity continued the wartime work of the Armed Services Institute familiar to most veterans, and was based on the experience and assistance of successful men and organizations in each field. Publications were released in early postwar years dealing with *How to Establish and Operate a Grocery* (hardware, apparel store, or other kind of business), ranging from about 20 to 100 pages and priced from 15¢ to $1.00. During the late 1940's these were the most valuable aids to the prospective small businessman; some are still useful for ideas, and all for principles and basic concepts. For future entrepreneurs it would be desirable if these books were revised, and the SBA as well as the U. S. Department of Commerce hope that they will be. Recently numerous U. S. Department of Commerce publications dealing with business opportunities in non-Communist foreign countries have been released.

The second group of publications consists of over 500 Small Business Aids, each covering in from two to eight pages some activity important in operating a small business successfully. Almost every aspect of operation—advertising, credit, personnel, production control, insurance, and so on—is discussed in one or more Aids.

Publication of this series has been discontinued by the U. S. Department of

Commerce, but another similar series is being published by the Small Business Administration and will be discussed later. However, the Department of Commerce series is available in many libraries and some may still be obtained gratis from the Department or its field or co-operating offices. A few of the Aids were revised and republished by the Small Defense Plants Administration, and others have been reprinted by trade associations for distribution to their members.

Up to 1953 the U. S. Department of Commerce maintained field offices in most cities throughout the country. As an economy measure field offices in smaller cities were replaced by co-operative offices, usually the local chamber of commerce or similar organization. Early in 1954 there were 33 field offices and over 900 co-operative offices.

The Department[14] maintains field offices for the purpose of providing ready access to the reports, publications, and services of the Business and Defense Services Administration, Office of Business Economics, Bureau of Foreign Commerce, and the Bureau of the Census. Information on certain activities of the National Bureau of Standards and the Patent Office is also available.

Experienced personnel will assist in the solution of specific problems, explain the scope and meaning of regulations administered by the Department, and provide practical assistance in the broad field of domestic and foreign commerce. Field offices act as official sales agents of the Superintendent of Documents and stock a wide range of official government publications relating to business. Each office maintains an extensive business reference library containing periodicals, directories, publications and reports from official as well as private sources.

Among the services which many businessmen have found of value are:

Wide range of census data:

Current data on employment and unemployment;
Detailed agricultural data on county basis;
Estimates on population movements;
Housing statistics;
Manufacturing output by industries;
Population count and characteristics;
Retail, wholesale and service business.

Basic records of nation's income and product:

Balance of payments and foreign aid;

Biennial volume on business statistics;
Current releases and business indicators;
National income statistics;
Regional trends in United States economy.

Marketing and distribution:

Development and maintenance of markets;
Distribution channels, facilities and services;
Facts on distribution costs;
Research sources on market potentials.

Government owned inventions available for license.

Since the SBA has been taking over much of the work of interest to the small businessman it is advisable to seek help through correspondence or a personal visit to your nearest SBA office.

[14] The description in the balance of this section is adapted from material published by the U. S. Department of Commerce.

Small Business Administration (Washington, D. C.)

The Small Business Administration, established in July, 1953, is the first permanent peacetime agency of the federal government created solely to advise, assist, and protect *all* small business enterprises. Previous agencies set up to render financial and procurement assistance to small firms were limited to helping manufacturers engaged in defense or essential civilian production. Since the SBA took over its predecessor, the Small Defense Plants Administration, it was initially more familiar with rendering financial aid to manufacturers than to distributors or service establishments, although both of the latter fields are included in its scope of operations. The SBA has 15 regional offices and about 40 branch offices. These are located in the larger cities in all 50 states and our possessions.

Our brief discussion of SBA is due to space limitations, the fact that complete and current information on any of its activities may be obtained from the field offices or from Washington, and that as a new agency in a dynamic and enormous field, its policies and services are likely to be fluid for many years. In the authors' opinion SBA has great prospects and should be familiar to all independent enterprisers, but should not be considered as just another government "handout" agency. Actually its funds are extremely limited in relation to its assigned duties, and no direct loans should be contemplated by most small enterprisers. Valuable assistance with their financial problems may be secured, however, and already SBA has aided thousands of financially harassed firms to find relief through regular channels of financing.

Three major areas of assistance provided by SBA are (1) financial, (2) procurement or markets, and (3) managerial and technical aids.

Since SBA is noncompetitive with private business, it makes no loans that can be secured under reasonable terms from regular lending agencies. It is also limited by law so that few loans unacceptable to private lenders would be made by SBA. Thus, as far as direct loans are concerned, SBA is of no interest to the vast majority of small businessmen. SBA may, however, authorize two other types of loans, deferred participation, and immediate participation, in co-operation with a local lending agency and for a maximum participation of 90 per cent and maximum loan to one firm of $150,000. Much more valuable are the advice and assistance SBA officials can render in aiding the average independent to secure loans from private agencies, what he should do anyway, if he knew how. This experience of SBA again supports the thesis of our text, that financial problems of most small businessmen are symptoms of more fundamental ailments—lack of managerial ability, or lack of information and know-how.

More important than direct financial aid is a second primary purpose of SBA, helping small firms to secure markets for their products, as government procurement orders, subcontracts, and nonmilitary orders of appropriate types. Several ingenious devices have been developed for these objectives, such as the *joint determination program,* whereby certain orders may be earmarked for competitive bidding exclusively by small firms. Another aid is the *production pool,* whereby several small firms may merge their facilities to bid on orders too large or too complicated for any of the separate firms to handle.

The third major area of SBA operations deals with providing managerial and technical assistance to small business. Staff specialists in the Small Business Administration's field offices assist with many types of management problems. Their services are available to established businessmen who have a specific problem or who want authoritative information on various aspects of management, and to persons who are considering starting their own businesses. One feature of this counseling service is a system of business reference libraries which the SBA has established in its Washington office and each of its regional offices. These libraries contain textbooks, Government and private publications dealing with business management, business papers and other helpful publications, and are available for reference use by businessmen.[15]

The Small Business Administration and leading educational institutions throughout the nation are cooperating in a program to help owners and managers of small business concerns broaden and strengthen their management abilities. The SBA and cooperating institutions sponsor courses in administrative management—planning, organizing, staffing, directing, and controlling, as distinguished from day-to-day operational subjects—open to officials of small firms. These courses, generally taught by experienced educators and successful businessmen, are usually held in the evening and run from 6 to 8 weeks.

The Small Business Administration publishes several series of management and technical publications of value to established or prospective operators of small business concerns. These are:

1. Management Aids for Small Manufacturers.
2. Small Marketers Aids.
3. Technical Aids for Small Manufacturers.
4. Aids Annuals.
5. Small Business Management Series.
6. Starting and Managing Series.
7. Small Business Bulletins.[16]

Management Research Program

There is great need—among small business owners and managers and those who serve small business—for additional knowledge concerning the successful operation of small businesses. The Small Business Administration helps here by financing small business research studies. As part of this program, the Agency arranges with colleges, universities, and state agencies for research and

[15] *Small Business Administration, What It Is, What It Does,* (Washington 25, D. C., 1959), p. 23.
[16] *Ibid.,* pp. 23-25.

studies concerning the financing and operation of small business enterprises. By law, the Agency may finance such projects up to a maximum of $40,000 per year in each of the States.[17]

State and Local Agencies

The Department of Commerce of New York State is a good example of an agency that undertakes extensive outside staff services for small businessmen other than state educational institutions. Most state officials will direct inquiries concerning their resources, license, and tax requirements, and similar matters to the appropriate department for reply, but few have gone beyond this simple step. In their efforts to attract industries, several states are expanding services designed to facilitate this objective. These are discussed later in connection with financing and industrial location.

On the local or municipal level governmental outside staff services have been limited to those connected with seeking new industries, answering inquiries regarding licenses and permits, zoning, and local traffic projects. Semipublic agencies, community development organizations, and industrial boards, however, may be found in a few cities, and the possibility of their existence in any situation should always be considered. It is consistent with the initial plans and policies of the Small Business Administration that more local governmental and semipublic organizations may soon be providing outside staff services designed to meet special local needs.

CONCLUSIONS

No matter how extensive the manager's personal experience may be, it is no longer possible to operate a progressive small business successfully if it is isolated from the information and assistance furnished by the outside staff. Conditions have become too complex and change too rapidly. As competition continues to increase both within each industry and on an interindustry basis, staff contacts outside each firm will become even more essential.

Services of a high quality on every function of management and phase of operations for the small enterprise are available from the outside staff. Many of these were discussed in the chapter in three groups: (1) commercial for a fee, (2) commercial for goodwill, and (3) governmental. In particular, strong endorsement was suggested for trade association and trade press services, and for those of the U. S. Department of Commerce and the Small Business Administration. Management and small business consultants, or "business doctors" may save a business life just as a physician or surgeon may save a human life. In both examples fees on a time basis are high but may be the best possible investment.

Aids and services furnished gratis by companies with something else to sell, may in many individual situations be of great value. Their brief treatment in

[17] *Ibid.*, p. 25.

this chapter is due to the wide diversity of such outside staff services and rigid demands for brevity in a book such as this.

QUESTIONS AND PROBLEMS

1. What are the major requirements for a small businessman to make effective use of the outside staff? Discuss.

2. Explain and illustrate how outside staff services may save time for the small operator.

3. Name, if you can, any important areas where outside aids are not available to the small independent.

4. In your own words describe the nature and purpose of a representative trade association.

5. What characteristics are noticeable in most of the services and activities of trade associations mentioned in the chapter?

6. Compare and contrast trade association benefits to the prospective and to the established independent businessman.

7. What trade association activities of great concern to the small businessman have been expanded considerably in recent years? Discuss.

8. In your opinion are standard accounting systems and forms practical for small businessmen in the same field? Discuss.

9. Explain how interindustry competition affects an independent in any field, and what he can do about it.

10. How can an owner-manager with so many demands on his time justify attending his trade association convention?

11. How should an independent use his trade publications?

12. Describe the proper use by the small businessman of management consultants and small business consultants.

13. Name the types of news reporting services mentioned in the chapter, then expand the list by naming those you know to be available and others that are needed.

14. How do you account for the numerous and valuable free staff services provided by Merchants Service of the National Cash Register Company?

15. Where would you look for advice on (a) sound, (b) light, and (c) color conditioning? Discuss.

16. What staff services are available to the prospective and new enterpriser from Dun & Bradstreet, Inc.?

17. Cite examples of how a small businessman should use basic economic and statistical data published by government agencies in policy formation and long-range planning.

18. Briefly explain the services a small independent may obtain from each of the following agencies of the Federal government: Federal Trade Commission, Federal Reserve Board, U. S. Department of Agriculture, U. S. Department of Labor.

19. What are the major small business services available from the U. S. Department of Commerce? Briefly describe each.

20. Explain the nature, purpose, and activities of the Small Business Administration.

21. Visit your nearest field office or co-operating office of the U. S. Department of Commerce and find out what assistance is being offered to prospective and incumbent small businessmen. Report your findings.

22. If an office of the Small Business Administration is accessible to you, repeat the preceding assignment for it.

23. Two veterans, seniors in business, considered buying a "Country Club" five miles from the campus but outside the city limits, to be operated as a dinner club. A nearby office of SBA could give them no useful help because the proposal was an entertainment enterprise. Where should they seek primarily nonfinancial assistance?

11 • *Financing and Organizing the Business*

The amount of capital needed should be determined as accurately as possible and the form of organization—individual proprietorship, partnership, or corporation—decided upon before any business is actually started. Financial needs of the beginning owner-manager and the form of organization selected are intimately related subjects. Whether either should be considered this early in the over-all treatment of the small business or deferred until the end after all other aspects have been considered, may be debatable. Certainly the beginner should have generally studied such things as where he wishes to locate, his prospective layout, his policies on credit, projected sales, his personnel budget, and so forth before he can arrive at any meaningful proposal for financing. Certain sources, such as banks, might even require a fairly detailed business proposal before advancing funds, and certainly the small businessman should postpone final decision regarding both financing and organizing until he is thoroughly familiar with all.

That old, inspirational institution the "challenge of success" seldom is encountered more immediately than when prospective small independents and young, college-trained enterprisers must come to grips with financial problems both before starting in business and once they are embarked on entrepreneurship. Money, either in hand or in the form of credit, is the key to profitable enterprise, but it is extremely mercurial and will not tolerate careless manipulation nor imprudence in handling. This was as true in grandfather's time as it is today. There are other conditions that affect small business: the winds and tides of inflation and recession, rising material costs, and shrinking or diffident markets. Even the tax factor has not been greatly altered, except in degree. Then there is competition, which is always with us. Hence, the method by which the beginner managers his investment capital and credit is a vital consideration for success. It is in this area that the college-trained person can show his knowledge of accounting, banking, budgetary control, business organization, forecasting, inventory control, law, personnel, sales management,

192

and other subjects by the way he handles the financing of his enterprise. It is well established that in small business financial and managerial problems are inseparably connected.

Capital and Profits

Capital, as we are using the term, means command over purchasing power—the total of owned and borrowed funds plus credit accepted. Thus, for a business that requires beginning capital of $15,000, the owner may have $8,000, secure a bank loan of $4,000, and obtain goods worth $3,000 on credit from suppliers, equipment dealers, and others. Often it is not necessary to borrow the full amount at once, but a line of credit equal to the maximum amount required should be established to be used. Bankers, prospective creditors, and other sources of further financial assistance usually agree that the owner's equity should be about two-thirds of the total capital required, but this is an arbitrary and somewhat conservative rule.

Capital must be regarded as a business tool requiring skill in its use. Pressure on the beginner's usually limited funds is so great that he is likely not to reserve enough working capital, and he seldom makes adequate provision for the one serious mistake most new businessmen are likely to make during their first year of operations. By "one serious mistake," we refer to no *particular* error, but to the fact that one is usually made, and of a costly nature, and should be anticipated. No such mistake may occur, but as it is expressed in the insurance field, "It is better to have it and not need it, than to need it and not have it." The contingency may be provided for by a previous agreement with some understanding lender or by keeping suitable assets unencumbered for possible use as collateral if and when needed. Whatever method is used, it it important to stay with the original purpose and keep the source of extra capital available strictly for emergency use for at least one year. Distinct from this one serious mistake, but resembling it, is the common experience that some beginners lack cash reserves to meet unexpected expenses during the first year. Others do not plan all their expenses carefully and find their capital gone before they have adequately set up their business. Still others go out of business partly because they are unable to take advantage of cash, quantity, and other discounts.

All money invested in a business, whether in fixtures, equipment, stock, or expenses, is expected to result in a profit. Careful management by the owner-operator should make this capital in the small business yield a higher rate of return than could be obtained from investment in government or corporate securities having a guaranteed rate of interest.

Capital and Its Uses

Capital is usually classified as fixed capital, working capital, and intermediate capital. The first two are the most widely used.

Fixed capital is money invested in the following:

1. Land and buildings
2. Machinery and equipment
3. Fixtures.

Working capital is invested in items of this type:

1. Stocked fuel, supplies
2. Materials or merchandise
3. Wages
4. Rent
5. Advertising and sales promotion
6. Living expenses (for the beginner).

Intermediate capital refers to money invested in goods in process.

The relative requirements of fixed and working capital will vary. The retail store's ratio of working capital to total assets will differ from that of the service business, and that of a factory will be still different.

In determining capital needs the small businessman must allow for a reasonable period, usually from three to six months, before income from the business will cover regular monthly expenses, and he must include in his estimated needs a minimum salary or drawing account sufficient to provide for his living expenses. A budget should be prepared even before the final decision to start the business is made. Great care should be exercised to include all expenses and needs for capital, including taxes and other less obvious requirements. The beginner's training and specific business experience, his market contacts, the community's needs, and the amount of pioneering necessary will all affect financial requirements.

Financial management. Extensive experience shows that difficulties in financing often arise from a few common causes, such as lack of knowledge of available sources of funds, inability to present a convincing case to possible investors, and failure to plan and prepare in advance for likely needs. Long before his programmed date for hanging up an "Open For Business" sign, the prospective enterpriser should get acquainted with a banker or two and with other influential people in his community who are potential sources of funds and sound advice. Many young men do not find it necessary to establish a credit rating in retail or other lines during their college years. But before starting a career as a business operator, such persons will find it wise, or even essential, to create records of their financial responsibility as a part of their business history. This may be done in several ways. One is by maintaining a solvent checking account, talking things over with an understanding banker occasionally, and negotiating a few small loans when larger-than-casual expenditures are being considered. Even the record of a small but systematic savings account may help when the need for financing arises. Today's bankers are usually congenial and reasonable people who will readily listen to a worthy person who has a worthwhile idea and project.

Another common experience of established small concerns is to find out too late that the source of funds they are seeking outside the firm is available within their own enterprise if proper precautions are taken in financial arrangement. Beginners can profit by this experience and avoid the dilemma by adroit management of assets and careful financial planning.

One source gives the following basic principles of financial management:

1. Avoid an excessive investment in fixed assets.
2. Maintain net working capital in proper proportion to sales.
3. Avoid excessive inventories.[1]

Others that might be added are efforts to expand more rapidly than the enterpriser's resources justify, imbalance in the capital structure resulting from disregarding recommended distribution of assets and financial and operating ratios, carelessness in formulating guides, and enforcing control over matters such as credit and collections, payroll, advertising, utilities, cost and quality control, excessive scrap and similar activities. The significant point here is that what appears to be a shortage of funds is often the result of unwise use of those available.

The tendency in recent years toward debt (rather than equity) financing is also the result of the changed tax structure. To the small businessman who can obtain capital on reasonable terms within approved ratios to his own equity, this situation may have advantages. He can deducts interest paid as a valid business expense, enlarge the funds under his control, retain control over his enterprise, and take advantage of conditions causing more people to be willing to lend rather than to invest their savings.

WORKING WITH THE MERCANTILE CREDIT AGENCY

Students and young businessmen often ask how they can obtain a favorable credit rating with an agency whose business it is to provide such ratings as a service to business clients. In answer to this inquiry addressed to Dun & Bradstreet, the following excellent comments were received:

> This is a little difficult to answer because a favorable rating implies that there must be an unfavorable rating. We do not have "unfavorable" ratings. There is no symbol in the *Reference Book* that indicates that an account should not be sold or that credit should not be granted. The story of the business is in the report, and if the situation is such that it is difficult to describe the case through the use of a rating, the *Reference Book* says, . . . 'Better read the report on this.' . . . This may seem technical, but it is fairly basic in understanding what the small businessman will expect when he comes in to obtain a "favorable" rating.
>
> It has been our experience that, so far as our own company is concerned, the best way to get off to a favorable start is to come voluntarily into the

[1] Ralph B. Tower, *A Handbook of Small Business Finance,* Small Business Management Series 15 (Washington, D. C.: Small Business Administration, 1957).

nearest Dun & Bradstreet office (of which there are 150) and explain the story of the new business before the enterprise is launched. It is easy at that time to work out all the details of the report.

The Dun & Bradstreet reporter will be glad to show the new business-man the report on his business so that the merchant will be fully aware of what is in our files and what will be used to answer inquiries from sub-scribers. The only things that we do *not* show him are any opinions or trade experiences that we have received from others in confidence, for to do so would be violating the confidence of those who have given us infor-mation.

Now after talking things out, it is possible that there may be certain weaknesses in the new setup. The weaknesses may consist of inexperience, lack of capital, or perhaps a location that is not too good. But through frank and open discussion, we are also able to show what are the *strengths*. In the end, therefore, we are able to present a fair and impartial report which shows both sides of the story. This information is then re-flected in the symbol, which is the rating.

So I would put it this way. When a man is going into business, he might just as well put his best foot forward. If he will provide figures showing his financial information, describe his plans, and generally discuss his affairs with us in the same way that he would talk over these things with a principal supplier, we feel that we can, in turn, give him the most favor-able send-off.

I think it might be of value to the readers of your book to know that we will provide operating statistics, if such are available, to the new man who intends to enter business. These figures will give an idea of what sales, expenses, and profits may be expected, based on the experience of others in business. We are glad to give whatever information we have gathered so that the new businessman can get off to a successful start. This is gen-erally free of charge.

How Dun & Bradstreet Operates—Margin of Error

A typical situation in reporting of a new business is this. Our reporter first makes a direct call on the businessman and asks questions regarding the amount of experience, the source and amount of capital, the legal ownership, and what the new businessman plans to do. Then the reporter will ask for financial statements, particularly a balance sheet and operating figures. If the business has not opened, the reporter will ask what sales volume is anticipated, and will try to talk out with the man how much of his capital will be going into fixtures, and how much merchandise he needs to buy.

Confirmation

After making the interview directly on the businessman the reporter then supplements his call with an investigation in outside sources. It is quite likely, for example, that he will call on the bank to ask questions regarding the name in which the account has been opened. And if loans are granted by the bank, he will inquire into the circumstances. He will also gather experiences from suppliers as to the previous payment record of the owner, and may check public records to see if any items such as chattel mortgages have been recorded.

Forming Judgments

Now with this information the reporter writes a report. He weighs the varying factors and comes up with a judgment—which is a rating. He considers the experience and background of the owners, the financial condition and payment record. In all, there are about eight major factors which go into making a composite appraisal.

The Factor of Error

All through this process the reporter is able to reduce error by recognizing inconsistencies in the information which he is receiving. Examples: A fine looking balance sheet does not tie in with slow payments to suppliers. A young man who says he is starting in with $25,000 from savings *may* have this capital, but it is unusual that a young man will have accumulated this much money. The chances are that there is a gift involved or an advance of capital from perhaps a friend or from relatives.

The second kind of checking comes from the opinion of outside authorities, that is people who have known the businessman. All these checks and balances coupled with the fact that nearly all businessmen are honest, and the reporter ends up with a reasonably small margin of error. There may be error in an individual case, but across the board, taking 10,000 ratings, the degree of accuracy is quite high in the opinion of many people. I think this will be confirmed by the experience of credit men who use the Reference Books regularly. Financing agencies, and insurance companies whose loss ratios depend in many instances upon the use of our ratings will, I think, also indicate that in the mass, the error is small.[2]

The above comments from this famous agency might be supplemented by the following admonition: Unless a business, small or large, enjoys a charmed life it will sooner or later suffer occasional reverses. There will be times when the enterpriser must walk a financial tightrope. In such instances the first persons to hear about the emergency should be the enterpriser's creditors and he should be the one to tell them. The business woods are full of "rumor birds" capable of irreparable damage to the business. The only way to silence them is by dispassionately telling the unvarnished story in the proper places. This would seem to be elementary wisdom, yet humans are stubbornly reluctant to admit they have erred in judgment or have been nipped in a vise not of their own contriving. Too many enterprisers wait until the roof is sagging before they make an effort to shore up the structure. It is then often too late.

In summary, here are the factors that are used in arriving at the Dun & Bradstreet credit appraisal:

1. Proper organization according to law, and clear identification of ownership.
2. Length of time in business.
3. History of management—successful or unsuccessful.
4. Balance of management experience.

[2] Letter to the authors dated May 3, 1955, from Mr. W. H. Kuehn, Director of Training, General Reporting Dept., Dun & Bradstreet, Inc.

5. Financial condition.
6. Trend—going ahead or going back.
7. Manner of payments. .

Thus, when all of the factors mentioned previously are strong, the rating is "High." When a little less strong but still quite satisfactory, the rating is "Good." Where there may be a deficiency, the rating is "Fair." When deficiencies have persisted, the Composite Credit Appraisal is "Limited." It is extremely important to remember that the *"Composite Appraisal"* rating is not based alone on how bills are paid.[3]

CAPITAL REQUIREMENTS FOR THE SMALL MERCHANDISING BUSINESS

In the following discussion of capital needs it will be assumed that the land and building are rented rather than purchased and constructed. Not only is this true for most beginning small businesses, but it is recommended practice in the vast majority of cases. "The smaller the capital, the greater the risk" might well be the axiom of small business. Certainly it applies to retailing or wholesaling on a small scale. The man who begins on a small personal investment with limited backing is working against many obstacles, including these:

1. Because he will be unable to afford many employees, he must run the store alone. His duties will include all store work, everything from sweeping out to keeping the store's records. This means long hours, little opportunity to leave the store, and calamity if he becomes ill.

2. Because he will be operating against stiff competition, customer credit may be a problem that requires careful handling. The added capital required for a credit business may deprive him of funds needed to pay for new goods or for goods already bought on credit.

3. The small store cannot afford to invest much in fixtures, for this money is taken out of essential working capital. Five hundred dollars spent for an unnecessary showcase represents money that could otherwise be invested and reinvested in goods, time after time, for profit.

4. The rental agreement should include provision for the landlord to do remodeling when needed, because the small operator's need for capital is so great that none of it can be spared for misuse as fixed capital in improvements if the landlord can be made to provide them. It is better to pay a small amount more per month for rent.

5. The average beginner will be so short of capital during the first few months or even for the first year or more that he will need very lenient terms from his creditors, especially suppliers. These represent a part of his provisions for working capital, because for all practical purposes he is borrowing this money from them.

[3] September 1956 issue of *Service*

The Store's Financing

Three approaches to determining capital requirements will be discussed here: income desired, rental rate, and cash available. The first is in terms of the amount of capital required to produce a given amount of personal income.

Assume that the entrepreneur has some personal funds, some good experience working for someone else, and the desire to avoid much experimental and ground-breaking work before his business can become established and profitable. In the case of a store, he might go about setting up his financial needs in this way:

Questions:	*Answers:*
1. How much income does he wish to be making when the business is established?	1. Assume .... $ 6,000
2. At the percentage rate of net profit common in this business, what volume must he "do"?	2. @ 8 per cent 75,000
3. At the common rate of turnover in this business, what stock must he carry?	3. @ 4 times 18,750
4. At the common rate of margin, what will this opening stock of merchandise cost him?	4. @ 30 per cent 13,125
5. How much will he require as a maximum in store fixtures and equipment?	5. (Estimate) 7,500
6. How much should he set aside for pre-opening expenses such as advertising and miscellaneous essential but unanticipated expenses?	6. (Estimate) 2,000
7. For what contingencies should he set aside added funds? How much?	7. Peak merchandise needs ...... 1,500 Cash funds, reserve for personal and business emergencies 2,000
8. Allowances for expenses for one turnover period	8. 2,310
	$128,185

The last item listed above refers to rent, wages, and other current expenses for at least one turnover period—in this case, three months. Enough cash should be on hand or readily available to pay these unavoidable operating expenses, leaving a maximum of working capital for stock adjustment and replacement. In this case these items might call for the following amounts over a three-month period:

Rent	$750
Wages	960
Advertising	300
Miscellaneous expenses	300
	$2,310

Thus a total of roughly $130,000 would be required.

This example assumes that a particular kind of store is under consideration. The standard operating ratios used are those typical of the field of variety goods, hardware, and drugs.

Another approach to determining capital needs proceeds on the assumption that only a limited number of appropriate sites will be available to the beginner who would like to open a particular kind of store. Each site may be had at a fixed annual rental. Since this is the only known fact, the first step is to calculate the necessary annual sales, using the standard operating rent ratio for the line of business selected. If further investigation shows this volume to be a reasonable possibility and to offer a satisfactory prospective income, the determination of capital needs is carried out in a manner similar to that described in the previous example.

An illustration should help to give this method the emphasis it deserves. Assume a women's ready-to-wear shop in a town of 50,000 population in the Southwest is under consideration. The only suitable location may be had for $300 a month for two years with a renewal option. Occupancy ratios for this kind of business in the 1950's were close to six per cent or about five per cent for rent alone. Capitalizing $300 at five per cent gives $6,000—the monthly sales needed to justify this rent—or annual sales of $72,000. Average operating expenses would be 29 per cent, or $1,740 per month for our proposed business, average inventory $12,240, and stock turnover four times per year as above. From these data, initial capital may be calculated as in our other illustrations, considering relevent factors such as opportunities to lease rather than buy fixtures and equipment, policies advisable regarding credit, seasonal aspects of sales at the time of opening, and so on.

This method enables a person to determine the required sales to justify a given dollar rental and, from the sales figure and standard operating and merchandising ratios, to calculate initial capital or any particular expense. When the initial capital required has been determined, it should be checked against other ratios, such as capital turnover, ratio of sales to investment or dollar sales per dollar invested, ratio of sales to inventory, sales to working capital, and similar ratios, many of which may be abtained from Dun & Bradstreet and the U. S. Department of Commerce.

A retail store's greatest investment is usually in its merchandise. The stock of a retail store or wholesale house will frequently represent a considerably greater investment than its fixtures and sometimes more than its building space. Complete lines of many kinds of goods call for a substantial investment. However, daily cash receipts from customers permit circulating capital to flow back into the business constantly with no long delays. Granting credit delays this flow to the extent of the credit terms, requiring further funds for investment in goods sold but not paid for. In a retail store, wages and other overhead items do not represent as large an investment as that in most manufacturing trades.

Capital requirements vary widely according to the kind of merchandise handled, price zone or income group of customers, managerial ability and trade connections of the merchant, location of the store, economic conditions and the general price level, time required to establish the business on a self-supporting basis, attitude of the enterpriser toward risk-taking, and many other factors in particular cases. Within one line of merchandise the initial capital required for the elaborate fixtures, expensive location, liberal customer services, and other requirements needed to attract the fastidious upper class trade may easily result in initial capital requirements far in excess of those considered satisfactory for less exacting lower income customers. Economic conditions and price levels existing at different times within the past few decades have caused initial retail capital under otherwise similar conditions to vary by over 200 per cent from the lowest to the highest.

In view of conditions such as these, it is obviously impossible to present an example of initial capital requirement in dollars that would be accurate as a standard for any individual situation. However, the procedure for determining capital needs, operating expense and merchandise ratios used in the computations, acceptable distribution of initial investment, and similar factors remain fairly constant for each line of business regardless of variations in conditions such as those just mentioned. It would be difficult to overemphasize the point that *it is the approach, method and ratios used, not the dollar results* given in the examples that are the *only* important considerations.

Another approach to understanding the relationships between income needs and capital requirements is to start with an amount of capital assumed to be available; the objective is to determine probable income resulting from its efficient use in terms of standard operating ratios and practices.

In the following example the most reliable guides available and the advice of competent authorities in the field have been utilized. The results have been carefully checked with the latest reliable survey reports. A conservative attitude toward distribution of initial equity capital has been taken; this results in slightly larger inventory investment (current assets) than surveys show to be representative of recently established stores in this line. Also, somewhat larger reserves are suggested than might be necessary in individual cases. A general merchandise store operating under approximately average conditions has been selected because of the widespread interest in this kind of store and the availablity of recent data and authoritative opinions regarding this line of business.

This example will reflect only modest financial circumstances on the part of the entrepreneur. Assume that, possessing experience and trade connections he has approximately $10,000 to invest in his business, and that a suitable location and store building are available at an annual rental of $1,200 with a satisfactory lease and renewal option. After consulting his prospective wholesaler, equipment manufacturers, local banker, and business friends, as well as published data in the field, his resulting esimates might be:

The bulk of the entrepreneur's investment would go into inventory. His major wholesaler suggests a balanced beginning inventory that could be purchased for $6,000 leaving $800 reserve or open to buy for reorders and to adjust stocks to current demand once the store is in operation. At a merchandise turnover of three times a year, average inventory would be $10,000 at retail or approximately $6,800 at cost, assuming a gross margin ratio of 32 per cent. Of potential sales during beginning years, $30,000 annually or $2,500 monthly, rent is consistent with the four per cent ratio in the field. Merchandise could be reordered and received on an average of twice a month and regular 30-day credit terms would be available. Thus the desired average inventory once purchased could be maintained from current sales and trade credit. It would also be consistent with an acceptable standard of approximately 65 per cent of total investment in inventory.

Fixtures and equipment may be purchased for $2,500, payable one-fourth down and the balance in 18 equal monthly installments, carrying charges included in the initial price. This amount is likewise consistent with recommended practice of spending from 20 to 30 per cent of initial investment on fixed assets. Total operating expenses at the standard ratio of 25 per cent would be $625 a month. Thus the gross margin of $800 would cover monthly expenses of $625, installments on equipment of $105, and a balance of $70 over and above the proprietor's drawing account of $200. Deducting $20 reserve for taxes would leave $50 surplus for reinvestment in the business during the first 18 months and $165 per month after that.

Distribution of initial investment under this projected program may be summarized as follows:

Beginning inventory at cost (open to buy: $800)		$6,000
Down payment on fixtures and equipment		625
License, insurance, and opening expenses (estimate)		625
Operating expenses, one month		625
Reserves:		
Merchandise reorders	$800	
Expenses, two months	1250	
Cash	400	2,450
Total initial investment		$10,000

Thus we have approached the financing of a small retail store from three points of view: (1) the desire for a given income, (2) the need to support a given rental, and (3) the availability of a given amount of capital. The third example is, of course, the smaller operation.

Use of Operating Ratios

"Ratios are devices for measuring financial conditions or financial changes. A ratio shows the relationship between two items, usually between a whole and one or more of its parts, or between two or more of the parts themselves." [4]

Although operating ratios have been developed for most established fields of business, they are probably used most extensively in retailing. These are averages or standards calculated from the experience of thousands of businessmen in the same field. They are useful to the beginner in determining his capital requirements for different items of expense, in estimating sales necessary to justify some fixed expense like rent, and as guides in operating the business once it is established. The beginning businessman should familiarize himself with the standard operating ratios in his particular field.[5] There are 137 sources of such ratios for retail and wholesale trades listed in *Guides for Business Analysis and Profit Evaluations,* published in 1959 by the U. S. Department of Commerce.

CAPITAL REQUIREMENTS FOR THE SMALL FACTORY

The approach to financing a small factory, which differs somewhat from the approach to financing a store, must be based on potential earning power, for unlike the retail store it seldom has reclaimable assets in the form of merchandise. For this reason the enterpriser's funds and those he may borrow are subject to a greater hazard. Money paid out for labor, overhead, and partly processed materials cannot be recovered readily in case of default or other difficulty. In this connection three things are generally true of a manufacturing business:

1. Real worth—that is, market value or desirability from an investment viewpoint—will depend almost entirely on its earnings, actual or potential. Obviously it cannot depend on its assets as collateral, for used machines, expended labor, and half-processed materials have little market value. Many raw materials have little value because of transportation costs and limited markets.

2. First capital, therefore, will necessarily come from those who have created the business and who may expect to participate in its earnings. The general public is hesitant about investing in an unknown quantity. Only after the project has proved successful will they seek to "get in on a good thing."

3. The length of time required for processing will be a large factor in determining working capital requirements. This fact is of greatest importance when the business is first started, growing less vital as sales become frequent and cash income becomes regular and dependable.

---

[4] *A Handbook of Small Business Finance* (Washington, D. C.: Small Business Administration, 1957), p. 23.

[5] Also see: "Operating Ratios for Forty-one lines of Retail Trade" (New York: Dun & Bradstreet Inc., 1958), "14 Important Ratios in 72 lines of Business" (New York: Dun & Bradstreet, Inc.) and *A Handbook of Small Business Finance* (Washington: Small Business Administration, 1957), *Operating Costs and Ratios—Wholesale* and *Operating Costs and Ratios—Retail* (Washington: Small Business Administration, June 1959).

The Factory's Financing

The man who would set up a manufacturing establishment might use the following "income desired" procedure in determining his financial needs:

1. How much income must he have to make this venture worth while?

1. Assume $4,000

2. At the percentage rate of net profit possible in this business, what volume must he "do"?

2. @ 8 per cent, $50,000

3. How many pieces or units must he produce to net $4,000?

3. If the piece sells @ 25¢, @ 2¢ (8 per cent) net profit per piece, 200,000 units.

4. How many machines will it take to produce 200,000 units in the course of a year?

4. 4 machines @ $1,500—$6,000
   2   "   @   750— 1,500
   4   "   @   500— 2,000
   2   "   @   250—   500

5. How much of a supply of materials will be required, assuming turnover of four?

5. Enough for 50,000 units—with supplies 2,000

6. How much will wages be for one complete turn of 50,000 units?

6. Three months for eight men ... 4,500

7. How much rental for three months?

7. (Estimated) 200

8. How much for sales expenses?

8. (Estimated) 1,000

9. How much for office expense?

9. (Estimated) 300

10. How much should be set aside for unexpected incidentals?

10.   1,000

11. How much for personal expenses?

11.   1,000
                                  _____
                                  $20,000

For simplicity's sake, we have used a small income figure above. The difference, it will be observed, between the expenditures for this manufacturing business and those of the variety store previously described is that the major item of the former is equipment which is subject to depreciation over ten years, whereas the store's major investment is in goods to be sold within three months. Obviously the financial requirements of the two are similar; yet to the potential creditor there might be a great difference in preference, depending on the nature of the goods compared with the machines or with the proposed product. Such considerations are typical of those that interest creditors. Raw materials are frequently a minor investment item for a factory, there being a fast and constant turnover. But as the length of time required for processing increases, the need for funds for working capital is expanded. It is necessary to know how long operations will take to begin to show a profit and how much capital should be allowed to meet wages, depreciation, inventory, the owner's salary, and the like up to that time.

To repeat again a general suggestion, provisions should be made to have the necessary working capital to carry operations along in many cases for at least six to twelve months to cover all contingencies until the business is established.

The advantages and disadvantages of buying instead of renting the plant or equipment should be considered.

In establishing a small manufacturing business one can either pay cash for the initial stock of materials, parts, and supplies or seek to establish credit immediately. Credit obtained for these items will greatly reduce the initial working capital needed. A small manufacturer should consider whether it would be cheaper to manufacture his own components, considering cost of equipment, space, capital tied up, and so forth, or to buy all parts and merely assemble them. Purchase of components may reduce fixed and working capital requirements. A well-established plant may be able to sell him parts for assembly at a lower cost than he can produce them.

In recent years, also, the tax structure has influenced business financing in many ways. Thus it is often better to lease than to own land, buildings, fixtures, equipment, or other assets because rentals are valid deductions as business expense. However, the Internal Revenue Service has made several moves recently designed to ease the burden of taxation through loosening of depreciation rules:

(a) It is now more a policy of the Department to take the word of the businessman as to the useful economic life of his asset.

(b) An additional 20 per cent depreciation can often be taken in the first year provided the asset has a useful life in six or more years.

(c) A new method is allowed in taking depreciation called the "double declining balance," increasing depreciation taken in the early years.

However, leasing still has certain non-tax advantages such as keeping larger amounts of funds available for working capital, permitting the small enterpriser to concentrate on his own business rather than on services offered by specialized renting companies:

The possibilities of leasing, as opposed to outright buying, must not be overlooked. Its use by businessmen has so increased in recent years that it is now estimated that half of all plants, stores, and offices in the United States lease some of the equipment used in their operation. In addition to the freeing of capital and the effectiveness of maintenance service facilities as mentioned, new models of equipment are usually more readily available to the user, and under short-term contracts the leased item is removed and no longer an expense when its use is no longer required.[6]

CAPITAL REQUIREMENTS FOR THE SERVICE ESTABLISHMENT

The problems of financing the service business will depend on which characteristics predominate—those of the merchandising or those of the manufacturing business. To the extent that it carries goods for resale it will call for

[6] An interesting article on this topic written by Frank Cameron appeared in *American Business* for December 1959, p. 21. See also: "Four Ways to Get It," *Steel* (April 4, 1960), pp. 101-104; this article discusses the advantages and disadvantages of four alternative methods—of obtaining equipment, leasing, rebuilding, buying used equipment, and contracting out—when capital is limited.

funds with which to buy them; to the extent that it sells labor or machine work it will require capital for equipment and wages in much the same manner as a factory.

These considerations may be observed: (1) The fact that most service businesses are operated on a cash basis reduces their capital requirements. (2) Because the average service business renders its service in a comparatively short period of time, no great amount of capital may be required for investment in labor and overhead between the time the job is brought in and the time it is called for. (3) A service business, because it may depend on machine operation, may justify larger expenditures in equipment to save expensive manpower. A machine that will save one man's work may cost considerably less than what that man's wages would be over a relatively short period of time.

The usual type of service business shares features of both store and factory.

SOURCES OF FUNDS

There has long been great concern in the U. S. Congress as to whether the small businessman is handicapped in obtaining capital and what can be done about it. Said Senator Sparkman in 1957 (at the time chairman of the Senate Small Business Committee):

> The future for small-business men in America should not and need not "look unpromising." We must not let the American Dream turn into a nightmare. There are economic frontiers yet to be conquered. Opportunity still beckons. Many areas of our industrial and commercial life can attract the bold, the resourceful, and those soundly schooled in the skills of business management.[7]

However, that the small businessman need not be discouraged is indicated by this statement.

> "Analysis of existing data lends little support to several widespread notions about the unavailability of capital for small business. One measure of the adequacy of financing is the health and ability to grow of small business. By this test, financing appears to have been adequate for the sector as a whole in the postwar period. Incomes of the self-employed rose at least as rapidly as did those of earnings on net worth . . . Formation of new businesses continued at an active pace; business failures were below rates in prosperous pre-war years; volume of equity investment in new and established small firms was of considerable magnitude . . . and the volume of credit made available to small firms increased very substantially."[8]

The small businessman has, therefore, a number of sources he can turn to after determining the amount of capital necessary. Before discussing the

---

[7] Senator John Sparkman, "Why a Senate Small Business Committee?" *Advanced Management*, Vol. 22 (June 1957), pp. 5-10.

[8] Irving Schweiger, "Adequacy of Financing for Small Business Since World War II," *The Journal of Finance*, 13:323-47 (September 1958).

sources of funds, it is desirable to consider financial needs and certain types of financing because of the bearing each of these has upon the sources from which funds are obtained.

As to use, three types of financial needs exist—those for initial capital, for working capital once the firm is in operation, and for expansion. Initial capital includes that necessary to get the business started and enough to keep it going until returns from operations provide sufficient funds to meet normal recurring expenses. That is, initial capital includes the beginning operating or working capital. As the volume of business increases, as it ordinarily does during the early months of operation, the amount of working capital needed tends to increase until the normal level of operations is reached. Whether this additional capital is provided for initially, is obtained from profits, or is obtained from other sources depends upon the conditions in each enterprise. Fluctuating demands for working capital, such as those resulting from peak seasons of operation once the business is in successful operation, are usually met by short-term borrowing from commercial banks.

As to source, two types of capital are recognized—equity and borrowed. Equity capital is that invested in the business with no legal obligation to return the principal, or to pay interest upon it, to another party. It is ownership capital, although in the small family-sponsored enterprise the ownership aspect is often relinquished or donated by the contributor (frequently a parent or close relative of the proprietor) to the beginning entrepreneur. Borrowed capital implies the obligation to return the principal together with some interest or other compensation for the use of the funds. In the small business this distinction between equity and borrowed capital is often blurred. Investigators have found that loans made to beginning businessmen by relatives or close friends sometimes resemble investment in the enterprise. No definite time for repayment is set; interest charges are deferred until some indefinite future date when the business can afford such payments. In most cases, however, borrowed funds used to supplement initial owner-equity capital, even when obtained from relatives and friends, are secured with the intention that both principal and interest will eventually be repaid.

Closely paralleling the two types of capital just discussed are the methods of financing. Three methods may be distinguished: equity financing, long-term borrowing, and short-term borrowing. A fourth method sometimes included, trade financing, is probably better considered in connection with the sources of funds.

The sources of capital for small businesses may be divided into five groups:

1. The owner and his associates, including his family and friends, who may or may not become partners or shareholders in the venture.

2. Partners and shareholders of a corporation.

3. Representatives of banks or other established lending institutions whose business includes making loans to business organizations.

4. Members of the trade, including suppliers of materials, such as manufacturers and wholesalers; and, in some instances, customers who prepay their contracts.

5. Miscellaneous, including other businesses, local capitalists, securities markets, community pools or groups, and various governmental agencies.

It is easier to list the common sources than it is to assess the importance of each in providing funds for small business. Most of the publications dealing with the financial problems and needs of the independent enterpriser treat the subject in general terms and furnish little if any factual data.

A study based on 1,000 new retail and wholesale concerns started between 1945 and 1947 included only completely new firms; no "buy-outs" were included. Also, no one-man concerns were included in the survey. Data on sources and distribution of initial capital were analyzed and presented by Dun & Bradstreet from information obtained by the Office of Business Economics, U. S. Department of Commerce. It was found that average initial investments of $9,500 in retailing and $22,000 in wholesaling were about double the pre-war level. The smaller the enterprise, the greater was the proportion of initial capital invested in equipment and the smaller the proportion in inventories.

Only three per cent of the firms used loans guaranteed by the Veterans Administration for initial capital. Personal savings constituted the major source of funds. One-fourth secured bank loans amounting to an average of 12 per cent of initial capital, or $3,900.[9] The major findings of this study are presented in Table 1.

TABLE 1. Sources and Distribution of Initial Capital
of New Retail and Wholesale Concerns

Sources of Funds	% Retail		% Wholesale
Personal Savings	56.1		38.1
Bank Loans	14.1		9.8
Suppliers	10.1	(60 days)	18.2
Capital Stock	7.1		21.9
Mortgage Loans	2.0		0.5
Others	10.6		11.5
Distribution of Funds	*Retail*		*Wholesale*
Inventories	28.8		41.4
Equipment	27.2		12.4
Plant	22.7		14.1
Others	21.3		32.1

[9] Dun & Bradstreet, Inc., "The Financing of New Trade Enterprises," from data of the Office of Business Economics, U. S. Department of Commerce (1949). See also R. B. Tower, *A Handbook of Small Business Finance,* comments on financial statements; bank transaction involving loans, accounts receivable, and inventory; budgets; ratios; and the S.B.A. lending program. Small Business Management Series No. 15, Small Business Administration (1957) Washington, D. C., or nearest field office.

According to initial investment, Table 2 shows the sources as reported in the early 1950's.

TABLE 2. Sources of Capital for Small Business*

| | Sources of Funds | | | | |
Initial Investment	Personal Savings	Capital Stock	Supplier Credit	Bank Loans	Other
Under $10,000	70%	1%	7%	10%	12%
$10,000-$19,999	75	2	9	11	13
$20,000-$49,999	57	8	9	16	10
$50,000 and over	42	11	14	17	16
All retailers	56	7	10	14	13

* "Changing Times," *The Kiplinger Magazine,* May 1953.

Borrowing from Friends and Relatives

Traditionally, beginning businessmen have gone to relatives and friends for financial assistance. Although this approach is considered poor business practice and is often based on erroneous assumptions, it may be necessary in many cases. Yet business and family or social relationships should not be mixed if the most desirable results are to be obtained.

Securing funds from intimates builds a highly personal financial relationship that conflicts with both independence and business. The businessman whose backing requires him to weigh personal considerations constantly is in a weak position when he makes decisions for the business itself. Furthermore, these financial associates frequently feel called upon to assert their proprietary interests by offering advice or even by insisting that certain business actions be taken, and their recommendations may not be in harmony with the wishes and objectives of the proprietor.

A *business* loan should be a *business* transaction, not a favor. One's friends and relatives may be more easily convinced of the possibilities involved, but they are seldom in a position to pass sound business judgment. The evaluation given the proposed enterprise by a business organization will be based on expert knowledge and experience and will be constructive and therefore valuable to the beginner. In the lending institution's efforts to place its trust wisely the new operator will find assistance in properly planning and soundly establishing his enterprise.

Sometimes forming a partnership or even a closed corporation is one way of securing financial aid from close acquaintances. A partnership is the association of two or more individuals who pool their capital and talents for the purpose of operating a business. All partners may invest money only, but one or more usually becomes active in running the business.

The average "going" small business in need of working capital, funds for expansion, or some special purpose should analyze its own resources carefully before seeking outside financing. Inventories are a frequent source of idle funds. Usually from 20 to over 50 per cent of merchandise and materials on hand in the average small business is in excess of needs, and often some of the surplus items are currently being reordered. When surplus stocks have been identified, dispose of them as quickly and economically as possible—but make sure they are not still being reordered.

When credit is extended by a small business in need of funds, it is very likely that too much capital has been tied up in slow or doubtful accounts. A vigorous campaign to collect all past-due accounts and the adoption of careful credit control for future operations is necessary in such cases. It might be advisable to explore the possibilities of shifting to a cash basis.

A small business may have idle assets in the form of fixtures, equipment, materials, and other "odds and ends" that could be sold without affecting business operations other than favorably. Excess space may be rented or subleased, or the firm's telephone or display facilities may be leased to secure extra income, if such does not encroach on regular business activities.

Since the usual tendency for beginners is to buy many assets, such as trucks, office machines, and other equipment, extra capital may often be secured by selling such articles and shifting to a policy of renting their services. This practice is becoming increasingly common and practical. From $2,000 to over $4,000 may often be secured in this manner, with little loss to the enterpriser other than an imaginary "prestige" of uneconomic ownership. Many rental or leasing firms are available, covering widely varied items of equipment. As noted elsewhere, tax advantages might accrue since rental is considered as an expense.

On a continuing basis some of the larger sources of capital from within the average small business are likely to be available through more effective expense control. Three aspects are of special importance: (1) owner withdrawals should be consistent with the needs of the business and can often be cut drastically when capital is needed; (2) certain operations performed in traditional ways may be shifted to less expensive methods, as personal service to self-service; and especially (3) closer control over payroll, rent, publicity, and other major expenses may be possible. This does not necessarily mean reduction of the dollar expenditures but, rather, securing maximum profitable returns from every expenditure. Procedures such as those just discussed also greatly strengthen the firm's position if outside financing may also be needed.

Financing Through Lending Institutions

Commercial banks represent a main type of lending agency used by small businessmen for borrowed capital. Some banks have consumer loan departments and many more make small loans to consumers in a manner similar to business loans. Actually, a great many small loans made to individuals as personal loans are used for small-business financing. Other banks have established small business loan departments and still others delegate the financing of small enterprises to particular officers.

An undetermined, but probably substantial, amount of semi-term loans are made by banks on a 60- to 90-day basis subject to virtually continuous renewal under favorable circumstances. As a business proves to be successful both the amount of such loans and their maturity tend to increase, and a generous line of credit usually results from such small beginnings.

Commercial banks are a primary source for loan rather than equity capital. Although short-term loans for less than a year predominate, many banks make long-term loans ranging from one to ten years with an average maturity of about five years. These term loans, four-fifths of which are secured by collateral, constitute one of the best ways for the small businessman to supplement his equity capital if he is not among the fortunate few who have relatives or friends willing to contribute with "no strings attached."

Bank loans are of two major types, character (or unsecured) and collateral—that is, secured by certain assets having a value well in excess of the amount of the loan. Although character loans tend to be for shorter periods and smaller amounts than collateral loans, so much depends upon the individual borrower that exceptions to this generalization are easy to find. A person with proved managerial ability, an excellent reputation, and a good business proposition may receive a character loan for several thousand dollars on a long-term favorable interest basis in the same bank where another, less well-known individual is obliged at the same time to put up collateral worth $500 to secure a short-term loan of $200 at the bank's maximum rate of interest.

The Loan Contract

The loan contract is drawn up by the bank. It includes all provisions which the banker feels are necessary to assure payment of the installments.

The loan contract will set forth the basic conditions of the loan and may include the following:

1. Length of loan period and schedule for repaying in installments
2. Interest and other charges
3. Provision that the entire balance of the loan be made due and payable immediately if any default is made in repayment
4. Any warranties that may be necessary
5. Requirements to maintain working capital at the proper level
6. Restrictions on other borrowing during the life of the loan
7. Description of assets, if any, pledged to secure the loan, and the terms under which they are pledged
8. Restrictions on the payment of salaries and dividends or distribution of earnings during the life of the loan
9. Miscellaneous restrictions and stipulations.[10]

Banks also make special types of loans, one of which is the installment loan, ranging in amount from $100 to $3,000 or more. Most installment loans are repayable monthly, with a maturity of one year or less. Another variety is

[10] *Term Loans in Small Business Financing,* Small Marketers Aids, No. 22 (Washington, D. C., Small Business Administration, April 1957).

loans secured by accounts receivable, which may be on a notification or non-notification basis. On the former the bank notifies the borrower's accounts and undertakes to collect from them. On the latter the borrower's customers may never know their accounts were assigned unless they fail to make payment as agreed. In such a case the bank is likely to notify the delinquent debtor and to assist in making collection.

A third variety of loan is one secured by negotiable receipts for warehouse or field warehouse stocks. These are common for manufacturers and for some dealers in furniture and heavy equipment. A fourth type is the equipment loan, which may be obtained on more favorable terms from the local bank than from the equipment manufacturer or supplier. And, finally, mortgage loans are sometimes made on the basis of either chattel mortgages or personal or business property or real estate mortgages, which may in turn be real estate owned by the business unit or by the individual enterpriser apart from his business. Since the early 1950's some efforts have been made to enable commercial banks to make more term loans ranging from two to over five years maturity and for relatively larger amounts than unit banks normally prefer.

Bankers' Bases for Lending

The following standards are considered important by bankers when making loans to small businessmen:

1. The character of the applicant; he should be an excellent moral risk.
2. The managerial ability of the applicant.
3. The productive nature of the loan, as evidenced by the past record for an established business or the banker's appraisal of profit prospects for a new venture.
4. The collateral offered to insure repayment in case the expected profits do not materialize or to protect the lender whenever the borrower's reputation has not been well established.

In making decisions regarding loan applications, the banker needs reliable facts. Usually the balance sheet and profit and loss statement will be requested for a going concern or, in the case of a new venture, a prospectus stating estimated sales, expenses, and anticipated profits. The use to which funds obtained will be put is a major consideration.

Since collateral is so often required to obtain bank loans, the small businessman should understand the nature of assets considered to be good collateral. These are usually "quick assets," or property that can be converted readily into its money value. Other things that the enterpriser often pays good money for may be poor collateral for bank loans. Among these would be items such as the following:

1. Specially made machines, equipment, fixtures, or built-in construction not salable to others in the same or similar trades. Examples: canning, wrap-

ping, labeling, or processing machines; store or restaurant fixtures built to fit particular spaces; wall decorations and floor designs.

2. Stationery, signs, wrapping paper, souvenirs, or other items carrying the name of the concern for which they were purchased and therefore salable to others at only a fraction of their cost, if at all.

3. Style merchandise or other goods likely to become outmoded; supplies of materials used in a declining industry or to meet a passing need. Examples: cast-iron items that are being replaced by aluminum; kerosene lamps and equipment; makeshift or temporary substitutes.

4. Partly finished products, such as mechanical parts and materials intended for particular assemblies, and even completed assemblies for which a market has ceased to exist. Examples: metal parts made to specifications for one buyer; automobile foot accelerators after they have become standard equipment on all cars.

There are generally accepted guides in each line of business as to the proper ratio of long- and short-term loans to owner equity and other standards. The beginner may secure advice on these ratios for his business from his banker, accountant, or trade association. There appear to be no well-established guides to the proper cost of borrowed capital. Costs vary widely and may tend to be high and even excessive.

Small Business Administration—SBA

Under section 207 of the Small Business Act of 1953, as amended in 1955, SBA is empowered:

> to make loans to enable small business concerns to finance plant construction, conversion, or expansion, including the acquisition of equipment, facilities, machinery, supplies or materials: or to supply such concerns with working capital to be used in the manufacture of articles, equipment, supplies, or materials for war, defense, or essential civilian production or as may be necessary to insure a well-balanced national economy.

However, under the Act, SBA cannot consider an application for financial assistance unless there is evidence that the desired credit is not otherwise available on reasonable terms." [11]

The SBA may participate up to 90 per cent of the amount of a loan needed, with a bank or other financial institution providing the remainder. However, the amount the SBA may lend to any one borrower cannot exceed $250,000, and the maturity may not exceed ten years, except for construction loans. The SBA may also make nonparticipating loans under the same terms.

A study of the 11th and 12th semiannual reports of the Small Business Administration reveals that during the fiscal year ending June 30, 1959, 10,213

[11] Ralph B. Tower, *op. cit.*

applications for $591 million were received and 5,582 for $267 million were approved. From its beginning in 1954 through that period, 12,914 general business loans amounting to $582.4 million had been approved and made.

"G.I." loans secured by the Veterans Adminitsration must be made by an authorized private lending institution, in constrast with the former Reconstruction Finance Corporation which made direct loans to business and to the SBA.

G.I. loans may be made through approved private lending institutions, such as banks, or by an individual, but maximum amounts, interest rates, and the attitude of many leaders seem to have restricted their use. A loan to an eligible veteran may be guaranteed when it meets all requirements and regulations— whether made by an institutional lender or an individual. The insurance of a loan in lieu of a guarantee is available only to approved financial institutions. The government may also insure or guarantee loans.

The difference between a guaranteed and insured loan is that the guarantee expires with the loan guaranteed while the insurance accumulates to improve the protection to the lender on all insured loans. For example: A $4,000 nonreal-estate loan may be guaranteed up to $2,000. The Veteran's entitlement is charged with the $2,000 which exhausts his entitlement for business purposes —both real estate and nonreal estate. If the loan is paid by the veteran, the Certificate of Guaranty is canceled. Had the loan been insured, the veteran's entitlement would have been charged with 15 per cent of the amount of the loan, or $600, and an account in the name of the lender would have been credited with that amount. This would leave the veteran with unused entitlement for nonreal-estate purposes in the amount of $1,400 or $2,800 for real-estate purposes. When the loan is paid, the $600 credit to the lender's insurance account remains in that account.

The Small Business Investment Act of 1958

The establishment of privately owned small business investment companies was made possible by the Small Business Investment Act of 1958. These firms supply long-term loan and equity capital on a profit-motivated basis, as with a bank, although tax benefits and public loan provisions do provide an element of subsidization.

The bulk of funds is intended to come to these small business investment companies from private investors, but they may be assisted at their beginnings by the Small Business Administration, and on other occasions when funds are not available from private sources. The investment companies may make loans on various bases of from 5 to 20 years.

These investment companies can borrow up to 50 per cent of paid-in capital and surplus, and the other 50 per cent can be obtained from the Small Business Adminstration. There are very definite upper limits on the size of firms which the companies can use as outlets for funds. There are a number of tax advantages for these investing companies and their securities are freed from certain SEC rules. A borrower from such a firm would pay 7-8 per cent on loans received or 6-7 per cent on convertible debentures sold to them.[12]

These new lending facilities are now in process of establishment, development and adjustment to their problems in various areas of the country. At this point there is some question as to their profitability as lending agencies, and conflicts of jurisdiction exist to a degree between Federal and other agencies as to certain procedural matters. However, the concept and the program do appear to have great promise as the "shakedown" period is passed. Some authorities predict that they may not survive without some basic changes.[13]

It is likely that this act could be a boon to the small businessman. Its provisions meet bankers' recommendations, and therefore should aid in attracting the financial circles' investments:

1. The act should stimulate availability of capital funds for small business.
2. Taxpayers money should be used to the least extent possible.
3. The banking system should participate in any financing program as much as is consistent with sound banking principles.[14]

One example of these lending agencies is the Cleveland, Ohio, Small Business Investment Company, founded early in 1959. Licensed under the SBA Act it accepts convertible debentures in exchange for loans, amounting to an investment in the futures of the borrowing firms. Thus, in the spirit of the act, they seek to provide funds to types of smaller concerns that are frequently unable to secure funds through normal channels. They will work closely with banks and other existing financial agencies.

There are many additional lending agencies available to the small enterpriser, such as commercial credit companies that make loans on manufacturers' or wholesalers' accounts receivable, sales finance companies that specialize in buying dealers' installment account paper at a discount, and others for special types of loans. Factors have recently expanded beyond their original financing of textile companies and now include other manufacturers and wholesalers.

[12] A number of recent articles have discussed this law. These include "New Outlet for Smart Money," *Business Week* (October 11, 1958) ; Edward N. Gadsby, "The SEC and Small Business Investment Companies," *Commercial and Financial Chronicle* 188:2405 (December 11, 1958) ; Carl M. Flora, "The Small Business Investment Act of 1958, Its History and Provisions, *Banking* 51:38-9 (October 1958) ; Wendell B. Barnes, "How the Small Business Administration Will Administer the Small Business Investment Act," *Commercial and Financial Chronicle* 188:2528 (November 18, 1958).

[13] Two of the most comprehensive recent discussions of the problems involved here are presented in *"Equity and Loan Capital for New and Expanding Small Business,"* prepared by Harold T. Smith for the W. E. Upjohn Institute for Employment Research, Kalamazoo, Michigan (November 1959) ; "SBIC's Seek Changes to Survive," *Business Week* (April 9, 1960) ; and *Equity Capital and Small Business,* Small Business Management Series No. 24 (Washington, D. C.: Small Business Administration, April 1960).

[14] Flora, *op. cit.*

Trade Financing—the Use of Credit

Trade financing is essentially a method of buying materials, merchandise, or equipment on credit. Equipment manufacturers and dealers know that the average small businessman is not financially able to pay cash for expensive installations and may have difficulty in securing local bank loans for this purpose. All major companies have financing plans to stimulate the sale of their equipment. Usually a down payment of from 20 to 30 per cent is required, the remainder to be paid in monthly installments over a period of one to two years or more.

Credit from resources for the purchase of materials, merchandise, and supplies is the most common and most widely used type of financing in the small enterprise. It often provides a major part of the small businessman's working capital needs, especially in the retail fields. The beginner should exercise judgment in selecting his resources. The wise business operator is careful of his credit and his stocks, and the wise supplier is cautious in his selling, but many instances are on record where both are shown to have become neglectful and careless, having taken too much for granted for too long.

Miscellaneous Sources of Funds

A few firms exist primarily for the financing of new businesses. The largest of these is the Walter E. Heller and Company of Chicago. It has helped in the opening and development of more than 13,000 small and medium sized businesses—over 4 per cent, in fact, of all United States corporations. Often this firm will assume risks that banks will avoid. In addition to giving the availability of funds, this firm also provides counsel and assistance in the starting of a business organization.

The organization is primarily interested in helping businesses which can, in their opinion, show promise to get started, make progress, and prosper. Occasionally, it becomes interested in a firm which has been mismanaged and which may be as a result suffering from over-extension, excessive inventory, or bad contacts. Mr. Heller, himself, has a broad knowledge of a wide variety of businesses and is backed by 400 experts in every phase of business operation. This staff is not only utilized in the appraisal of business opportunity, but it also serves as a means of advice and counsel during the progress of the company's growth.

As a means of financing the firm to which he lends money, he frequently accepts the company's accounts receivable as collateral. Although the interest rates he charges his clients are as high as 12 per cent, the companies he has financed have seldom complained. For while the rates are higher than those of banks or other lending institutions, the services the organization furnishes the client are unusual in the extreme and very valuable. His aim apparently, is to help the firm he has assisted financially to grow and prosper to the point that they will no longer need his financial backing.[15]

It is sometimes possible for an enterpriser to find other businesses that would profit by financing his venture. This may happen when a manufacturer is seeking a dealer outlet in a certain town, or when the established industries in a community feel the need for a new enterprise, such as a specialized repair shop or other type of facilitating industry. Many small businesses have been started in one of these ways.

People with property interests may be induced to aid beginning enterprisers, and often to construct buildings for them and to help secure initial financing of equipment and fixtures. Real estate agents, especially developers, and shopping center promoters have occasionally aided in financing small businessmen who buy or lease through their agencies.[16]

Many large distributors have financed small manufacturers to produce staple articles like work clothes or other items for private-label merchandising. An interesting case known to the authors, though from the service field, shows what can be done when a city needs a certain type of enterprise. A prospective enterpriser with practically no capital, but with a strong conviction that a certain town needed a modern hotel, "sold" the idea so thoroughly to local citizens that the capital needed was eventually secured locally.

The emphasis in this chapter has been on providing edequate capital for a new small business. Specific figures mentioned have, as stated, been for purposes of illustration and might be quite different in years with a different price level or under other conditions, although percentage distribution and operating ratios will be fairly constant.

Although the analytical procedure presented is the sound approach to be recommended in a vast majority of cases, another viewpoint that deserves mention permits starting a business with less capital than the minimum usually considered necessary for success. There are always a few businessmen, including some successful ones, who believe the essentials of starting out are the idea, the desire, and the opportunity, with the fact of having less capital than the estimated minimum acting as a secondary consideration. They admit the going will be hard, but claim the experience will be worth the effort and the limited funds available will be used much more carefully than if the business were more adequately financed. They further observe that if one keeps waiting for a safe margin of finances, his opportunities may be lost or other conditions may later prevent him from starting on his own. There is much evidence in

15 For further information, see *Time* (February 15, 1960), p. 98.

16 See also: "The Need for Risk Capital: Where is the Small Investor?" *Time* (July 27, 1953), p. 80, and Progress Report—First Session, Select Committees on Small Business, House of Representatives, 83d Congress, 2d Session, "Venture Capital Companies and Regional Financial Groups," Progress Report—First Session, Select Committees on Small Business, House of Representatives, 83rd Congress, 2nd Session (Washington, D. C.: Government Printing Office, 1954), p. 39.

their favor. They cite many examples of successful businesses that were grossly undercapitalized at the start. Certainly not all successful firms have met the theoretical requirements.

The authors hold no brief for or against this viewpoint except to admit a measure of truth for each of the claims. Certainly overcapitalization is not to be recommended. Also, it is probably better in rare cases to be opportunistic and, if it is "now or never," to make the plunge. But at least one should do so with his eyes wide open and be willing to accept the greater risks and harder work required.

SELECTING THE FORM OF ORGANIZATION

In deciding what form of organization to adopt, several aspects should be considered. Since each has both advantages and limitations, a good plan is to weigh these in the light of one's needs and objectives. At least the following aspects deserve consideration: (1) A need for additional funds may sometimes be met better by forming a partnership or corporation than by borrowing or using mercantile credit. However, either of the forms of organization means sharing profits as well as risks and losses. (2) A need for certain managerial abilities or experience may be met by taking in one or more partners possessing the requisite qualities. An alternate method of securing these benefits without sharing ownership is to affiliate with a voluntary chain or similar organization in the retail and service fields. In either case the additional abilities are secured at the expense of sharing authority and placing some restrictions upon one's "independence." (3) The choice of organization form to use may be influenced by the desire to achieve such objectives as limiting liability, distributing the risks involved, and taking advantage of the tax structure in operation at the time and place where the business is to be started.[17] Federal and state income tax laws may make one form of organization superior to others for the small businessman; profits from a corporation, for example, may be taxed doubly, once as corporate profits and again as individual income, whereas the proprietorship or partnership may be exempt from this double taxation. Sometimes one form or organization is given advantages by particular laws or regulations such as those limiting the power of a corporation to engage in certain activities open to the proprietorship or partnership.

As the best form of organization to use, the final decision will probably be a compromise based upon weighing the relative importance of certain needs against the limitations of each suitable form of organization. The person in business must be familiar with these pros and cons for his own welfare and protection in order to take full advantage of his rights and at the same time

---

[17] E. L. Anthony and A. B. Comstock, *Choosing the Legal Structure for Your Firm,* Management Aids for Small Business, No. 8 (Washington, D. C.: Small Business Administration, 1957). This work studies the various types of organization structures and discusses taxes, costs, and procedures in starting and continuing the operation of a firm. Explains the risks involved, necessity of capital, administration difficulties, and effects of law.

avoid undesirable consequences due to his ignorance of his exact status. For these reasons it may be desirable to review these three types of organization.

The Single Proprietorship

The simplest way to go into business is to rent space, buy goods and equipment, and start working. Except where federal, state, or local licenses or permits are required, only that is necessary for the single proprietorship. This form of organization has numerous advantages:

1. Organization entails no formality.
2. Ownership has perfect freedom of operation. When business decisions are made or moves taken, it is not necessary to get the consent of anyone else in the organization.
3. All profits are the property of the owner and need not be shared with anyone else.
4. Earnings may be retained in the business for its improvement and expansion.
5. Business losses are deductible from personal income when federal income tax is determined.
6. As compared with the partnership:
    (a) Liability is limited to the owner's errors or obligations.
    (b) There is no danger of loss resulting from the death or withdrawal of a partner.
7. As compared with the corporation:
    (a) No double tax when profits are distributed.
    (b) No capital stock tax.
    (c) No corporate reports or inspections.
    (d) No restrictions on the nature of business.
    (e) No penalty for retaining earnings in the business.

There are, however, certain disadvantages in the one-owner type of organization:

1. The many abilities required for successful business operation (selling, bookkeeping, production methods, administration, and so forth) are seldom all possessed by one person.
2. Limited personal assets do not encourage lenders and cannot always provide the required capital to meet unusual needs.
3. In case of business failure the owner's personal assets, including home, automobile, and other properties, are subject to claim by creditors.

The Partnership

Certain conditions accrue when a partnership is formed, some favorable and some definitely undesirable. Arguments in favor of the partnership include the following:

1. "Two heads are better than one." Two viewpoints, although they clash, may result in a very desirable compromise.

2. Personal abilities are complemented. The salesman and the bookkeeper, with different personalities and abilities, may succeed together when neither could alone.

3. Added capital is made available by combining the assets of two or more partners and less borrowing is necessary.

4. Business losses are deductible from the personal income of each partner for income tax purposes.

5. As compared with the corporation:

    (a) There are no state taxes, no capital stock tax, and no double tax on dividends.

    (b) Income may be divided through "family partnership" or on bases other than investment, such as talents or time spent in this business.

    (c) Partners' "salary" is not subject to payroll taxes.

    (d) No penalty results from retaining earnings in the business.

Among the disadvantages of the partnership are:

1. Each partner is liable for all debts incurred by the business.

2. Each partner is responsible for the action of all other partners that creates an obligation for the business.

3. The partnership is automatically dissolved by the death or voluntary withdrawal of a partner, except as noted later.

4. Profits must be shared among the partners.

The Corporation

The corporation is a legal form of organization made possible by state laws that govern the provisions under which its charter, or authorization to operate as a business entity, is granted. Since the corporation is a creation of the law, it is impersonal and exists without reference to the particular individuals who may share its ownership and direct its activities.

Advantages may be summarized as follows:

1. Legal liability of owners or stockholders for suits for personal injury or other activities connected with operating the business is limited to the amount of funds invested in the business.

2. The corporation is long-lived, being able to continue in existence up to the time limit granted in its charter, whereas the proprietorship ceases with the death of the owner and a partnership with the death of any partner (except as noted later).

3. Capital may be accumulated from many sources: sale of common or preferred stock, loans made by issuing bonds, exchange of assets, and reservation of profits from the business.

4. Ownership in a corporation is easily transferred merely by sale or ex-

change of stock and entry of the new ownership on the books of the corporation. Permission of other stockholders is not required except in rare cases of separate contractual agreements.

5. Management of the business may be concentrated even though ownership is widespread.

6. A large number of owners may obtain for the corporation a considerable amount of free publicity and goodwill.

A corporation has certain disadvantages, however:

1. Its activities are limited to those specifically granted in the charter. A firm incorporated to engage in the retail dry goods business could not legally handle groceries or engage in manufacturing unless "catch all" clauses granting almost unlimited scope had been included in the charter.

2. Its geographical area of operations is limited to the state granting its charter until permission is secured from each state in which it desires to operate. This means also that additional license fees must be paid and regulations observed.

3. If active management is employed in lieu of owner-management, the personal interest and incentive associated with ownership are lessened.

4. The corporation must make numerous reports for taxation and other purposes to each state in which it does business.

5. Federal and state regulation of corporations has been increasing for some time.

6. A corporation is subject to more taxes than is the proprietorship or partnership.

7. More paper work for reports and records is necessary, and the amount increases greatly as the corporation grows in size.

8. In the small corporation the advantage of limited liability is often circumvented in the case of business debts by the custom of requiring major stockholders to guarantee or endorse notes due to banks and to major merchandise suppliers.

TAXES AND THE FORM OF ORGANIZATION

Since taxes, especially Federal income taxes, have become a major business and personal expense, the form of organization may be the deciding factor between profit or loss to an enterpriser. In addition, the tax structure has become so complicated and subject to so many changes that it is difficult to make a wise choice of form or organization. In all but very simple cases expert legal or accounting advice should be obtained. Our remaining comments are presented with the foregoing basic advice as of major importance.[18]

[18] The balance of material in this section, except as noted, is adapted from Houstin Shockey, *Tax Factors in Selecting the Form of Business Organization,* with modifications for the 1954 and 1958 revisions of the Internal Revenue Code (Englewood Cliffs, N. J.:

For income tax purposes two basic forms of organization are recognized, the corporation and the partnership, the sole proprietorship being subsumed under the latter since both are treated as income to individuals. The basic distinction is that corporations are taxed as separate entities whereas other forms of organization are not. The 1954 revision, however, gives proprietors and partners the option of being taxed as corporations, and defines a partnership as an income-reporting but not a taxpaying entity. There are advantages in some cases in permitting the income from a business to be subject to the various federal taxes imposed upon corporations, to keep it out of the owner's taxable income. In other cases the corporate form may be undesirable.

One of the most important practical features for small companies is the extent to which the owners can obtain income in the form of salary, or in some other manner which represents a deduction for corporate tax purposes. If all corporate income could be paid out to stockholder operators in this fashion, corporation taxes would not be a factor for closely held companies in which the shareholders are active. The most immediate way to narrow the effect of the artificial tax discrimination against corporations is by compensating the owners from company income. If salaries, rentals, stock options and pensions to the shareholders are validly deductible items for the corporation, the double tax resulting from dividend payments is reduced to that extent.

This is an obvious device to minimize corporation income tax and it has been abused by taxpayers through the use of inflated and fictitious claims. The taxing authorities are alert to guard against that kind of tax evasion and with the courts have worked out various standards of a general character as a guide in testing the validity of different forms of compensation. Under the general tests, deductions for officers' salaries and bonuses are allowable if the compensation is reasonable in amount, and payment was for services rendered.

The ultimate feasibility of the corporate form for small, closely owned organizations depends on the measure to which the shareholders may benefit from corporate income in ways other than through dividend payments. Aside from salaries or other compensations from current income, the chief benefits to shareholders arise from appreciation in the value of their stock, and its eventual sale either before or after their own deaths. The appreciation in value depends in practically all cases upon the growth of the company. Growth and reasonably anticipated needs are the primary reasons for justifiable retention of corporate earnings in the business, in excess of the $100,000 allowable without question under the 1958 revisions, without the penalty surtax on corporations improperly accumulating surplus.

The most undesirable feature of the corporate form is the fact that dividends are not deductible in arriving at the company's net income and the individual shareholder pays income tax on the dividends he receives in excess of $50,

---

Prentice-Hall, Inc., 1952). See also: Our Chapter 12, Regulations and Taxes; and *Steps Involved in the Incorporation of a Business*, Business Service Bulletin No. 24 (Washington, D. C.: Small Business Administration, May 1954).

plus a four per cent credit on the balance of his dividends. The effect of this disadvantage may be minimized, however, by judicious arrangement of the capital structure. If the interests of the owners are represented to as great an extent as is possible by bonds of the corporation rather than by stock, a substantial part of the corporate gross income may be paid out to the owners in the form of deductible interest. In computing credit based on invested capital, 75 per cent of borrowed capital is recognized as part of the invested capital.

Upon the organization of a corporation, there is nothing to prevent the "owners" from setting up their capital investment partly in stock and partly in bonds. There is no set rule on just how "thin" the ratio of bonds to stock may be. The tax advantages may be summarized as follows:

Loans	*Capital Contributions*
1. Corporation gets interest deduction.	1. Corporation gets no deduction for dividends.
2. You pay full tax on interest received.	2. You pay tax on dividends received in excess of $50, less the four per cent credit allowed.
3. You pay no tax when the loan is repaid.	3. Redemption of stock might be held a taxable dividend.
4. Should the corporation become insolvent, you get a full or limited deduction.	4. Insolvent corporation leaves you with only a limited loss deduction.[19]

The mechanics and the immediate tax effects of creating a partnership are more simple than in the case of a corporation. The principal problems are: the validity of the partnership form for tax purposes; the selection of the type of partnership—whether it should be general or limited; the formulation of provisions for acquisition of a decedent's interest; and the anticipation of the effect of the partnership form upon the basis of assets.

In almost all states there are statutes allowing the creation of limited partnerships, usually requiring at least one general partner who has unlimited liability. The limited partnerships may have quite a number of corporate characteristics: the limited liability of some members, transferability of interests, or survival of the partnership entity on the death of members. Under the laws of some states a partnership may continue for a period after the death of a partner if the agreement so provides.

Under the Federal tax law, the limited partnership may be treated as a partnership if it does not embody so many of the corporate characteristics that it comes within the Code definition of corporations as "associations."

To illustrate the effects of corporate and individual income taxes, Table 3 shows that the corporation may be advantageous for a large (small) business; whereas a partnership may have tax advantages for a smaller enterprise. In

19 *Eight Keys to Bigger Tax Savings for Smaller Companies and Their Owners* (Englewood Cliffs, N. J.: Prentice-Hall, Inc., 1953), p. 17.

the example the principals are unmarried, have no dependents, take a standard personal tax deduction, and receive income from no other sources.

TABLE 3. How Tax Payments May Vary For Proprietorship, Partnership, or Corporation*

	FOR A $10,000 BUSINESS			FOR A $75,000 BUSINESS		
	Prop.	*Part.*	*Corp.*	*Prop.*	*Part.*	*Corp.*
Net income before salaries ..	$10,000	$10,000	$10,000	$75,000	$75,000	$75,000
Salaries to principals	10,000	{ 5,000	8,000	75,000	{ 35,000	30,000
		{ 5,000			{ 40,000	30,000
Net income after salaries ...			2,000			15,000
Personal income taxes	2,096	{ 818			{ 15,370	12,228
		{ 818	1,540	44,874	{ 18,636	12,228
Corporation taxes			500			3,750
Total taxes	2,096	1,636	2,040	44,874	34,006	28,206
Income after taxes	7,904	8,364	7,960	30,126	40,994	46,749

* From: "Changing Times," *The Kiplinger Magazine* (June 1951), pp. 15-16. Changes made in the tax laws in 1954 and 1958 are discussed elsewhere. See also: Arthur W. Hanson and Jerome B. Cohen, *Personal Finance; Principles and Case Problems,* Ch. 16 (Homewood, Illinois: Richard D. Irwin, Inc., 1954).

CONCLUSIONS

Although there is no one best way to finance or to organize a business under all conditions, *great care should be exercised in determining capital needs, sources from which funds are to be secured, and the form of organization that best suits the particular circumstances.* Personalities and attitudes as well as character and ability play a large part in determining the success of a partnership.

For the foreseeable future, the tax situation in relation to income brackets and objectives of the owners must be considered, and may be the dominant factor in selecting the best form of organization to use at a particular time. Legal and accounting counsel is often desirable in making the right decision.

Although financing is usually associated with securing funds external to an enterpriser's own resources, discussion in this chapter is intended to demonstrate that often internal sources of capital are overlooked and how important it is that this aspect of the question receive major attention.

The form of organization is not only closely related to the problems of financing, but very often also affects the financial liability of participants and the transfer of equities. It also affects taxation, regulation, and various management practices. We must therefore conclude that the various considerations reviewed here tend to be inseparable.

QUESTIONS AND PROBLEMS

1. List the advantages and disadvantages of securing additional initial capital through: forming a partnership, making bank loans, borrowing from friends, obtaining vendor credit.

2. How do financing and organizing afford the graduate in business an excellent opportunity to apply his training?

3. Compare the merits and difficulties of securing additional capital for a new business from friends through borrowing and through the sale of stock in a corporation.

4. Why is the method of determining capital needs by starting with a fixed amount for rent more appropriate for a retail store than for a small factory or service business? Show how you could adapt this method to the determination of capital needs for a factory or service business.

5. What are the advantages and limitations of using operating ratios in analyzing capital needs?

6. What are the common financial mistakes made by many beginning enterprisers? Suggest remedies for each.

7. Explain how the average small business may secure funds from within the organization. What are the advantages of doing so as compared to outside financing?

8. How can the beginner obtain the most favorable credit rating?

9. Explain any connections between determining initial capital and budgeting in the small business.

10. List the factors that go into determining the amount of capital necessary for one to go into business.

11. For a new business in an established field, why is it desirable in calculating capital needs to use operating ratios of other concerns instead of estimates made by yourself and friends?

12. Since standard operating ratios within one line of business vary according to the profitableness of the firms, how would you decide which ratios to use? Discuss.

13. Under what circumstances could you justify a ratio for your prospective business well above the standard in the field for each of the following:

    (a) rent or occupancy expense for (1) a retail store, (2) a factory, (3) a service establishment?

    (b) total payroll, excluding withdrawals of owners?

    (c) bad debt losses for (1) a retail store, (2) a factory?

14. Discuss the thesis that it is a good idea to go into business for yourself when circumstances are right even though your finances are below those considered necessary.

15. Review the sources of funds for small business and suggest and discuss additional sources.

16. Under what conditions would the need for additional abilities be more important in determining the best type of organization than need for additional capital, assuming the latter to be present in any case? Discuss.

17. "The smaller the capital, the greater the risk." Why?

18. What is meant by "venture capital"? Do you consider it a sound basis for a loan?

19. What conclusions do you draw from survey results presented in the chapter as to the beginners' sources of initial capital?

20. How do you explain efforts to finance small businesses by:
    (a) venture capital companies?
    (b) community development or industrial funds?
    (c) insurance companies?

21. Explain how taxes affect the best form of organization to use.

22. Consider the advantages and disadvantages for the single proprietorship, the partnership, and the corporation. Explain fully which of the three forms of organization you think would be most beneficial to you.

23. Why is it desirable to put all terms of a partnership agreement in writing?

24. What provisions for possible future expansion should be made in the articles of incorporation? Should these be as broad as possible, or is it better to limit the business to certain fields of activity? Discuss.

25. Select some kind of small business and after consulting businessmen and other sources of information prepare a prospectus of capital requirements to start business.

26. If you plan to open your own business soon, assemble all pertinent information, then discuss your plans with the nearest representatives of Dun & Bradstreet and the National Cash Register Company. Analyze and report your findings.

27. Joe bought a new $3,500 car for transportation to work shortly before moving to within two blocks of his store, and has been offered $3,000 cash for the car. The store needs about $3,000 additional stock. His banker offered to lend him $3,000 repayable in 12 monthly installments of $265 each. What should he do, and why?

12 • *Regulations and Taxes*

The business community, as with any other group that must work in harmony for the common good, has need for rules and regulations concerning the conduct of its members. Two classifications of such controls exist. One type consists of those developed and adopted voluntarily by the businesspeople as codes of ethics or standards of conduct for themselves, particularly in their own interrelationships. The others are established and enforced by a legislative or other public authority and administered by properly authorized bureaus, commissions, and courts and their officers. These more generally concern business contacts with the public.

It is probably the latter that we usually think of first when speaking of laws affecting business. While codes of ethics and standards of practice as established in certain trades or industries have long been regarded as powerful forces within those groups, the increasing complexity of business operations combined with increasing tendencies toward protection of the individual citizen by governmental groups has caused the public laws to be of more interest and concern to businessmen.

Laws have various objectives as well as origins. Some are designed to prevent undesirable acts by prohibiting certain kinds of conduct. Others, such as tax laws, require particular acts and are mandatory on all concerned. A third group, permissive laws, permits individuals to enjoy certain privileges provided they meet stated requirements. Many permits to do business in particular fields or to engage in professional occupations are of this type.

The origin of laws—that is, the source of their authority—in the United States is unusually significant because of our multipower type of legal authority. Ours is essentially a constitutional type of government. The scope of the Federal and of each state government's legal authority is defined primarily in its constitution and in the amendments thereto. Thus the Federal government has been delegated in the Constitution the right to regulate commerce between the states (interstate commerce) and with foreign nations. Powers not delegated to the Federal government are reserved to the states. Each state in its constitution is delegated, or presumes the right to exercise, certain powers that are generally of state-wide interest, such as the regulation of intrastate commerce. Authority over purely local matters is usually left to the local governing agency concerned, which may be the county, township, parish (relatively unimportant today), incorporated municipality, city, or town. Other minor governing units also exist for special purposes.

Even though he may be engaged entirely in activities within the state, or even within the city limits, the small businessman is interested in certain Federal laws and taxes, as well as those of his own state and local governments because they may affect his business and personal conduct. As a broad generalization subject to certain important exceptions, it can be said that the order of precedence or authority is Federal, state, and local, although in doubtful cases it is advisable to secure competent legal counsel.

There are many other aspects of law that should be understood by the independent businessman, only a few of which can be given even brief mention here. Criminal law deals with acts (crimes) considered injurious to society for which a penalty such as imprisonment or a fine is imposed and for the enforcement of which society, through its duly authorized courts and law enforcement officers, is responsible. Civil law, in contrast, is concerned with protecting the individual, especially his rights of private property, and providing that damages for injury sustained may be secured by the person concerned through such process as bringing suit against the offender.

Almost all important modern laws are statutes—that is, acts passed by a Federal or state lawmaking body—or constitutional provisions embodied in the original Federal or state constitution and its amendments. Court decisions interpreting the various statutes and constitutional provisions provide guides to the meaning and application of every law. Trends in these interpretations tend to represent trends in public opinion with respect to the purpose or even as to the need for the law.

In recent years many important statutes have been enacted that incorporate a special board, commission, or other agency charged with the administration of the law. Examples of these administrative laws are the Clayton Act, which is administered by the Federal Trade Commission; the National Labor Relations Act, administered by the National Labor Relations Board; the Small Business Administration Act; and many state laws dealing with industrial relations, public health, and safety.

Finally, the common law, or old English guides and principles leading to justice and fair treatment, may govern in situations not covered by specific legal enactments.

As in other fields that have developed a similarly extensive body of knowledge, the independent businessman cannot hope to be an expert in law, nor can he afford to call on expert counsel for every decision. But he should endeavor to recognize those situations that call for legal counsel and be ready to secure and pay for such advice, for the investment will usually be more than repaid.

Furthermore, regulations and taxes have become so numerous and complicated that many people express the belief that they constitute the greatest hazard to the independent enterpriser. In contrast to most other areas of business, regulations and taxes are usually mandatory and carry severe penalties even for unintentional violations. Ignorance of the law is not accepted as an excuse, and even licensed attorneys are not always sure of certain provisions and their interpretations by the courts.

Certain general principles of law, important legal instruments, and particular laws that have special significance for the small businessman must be considered. An understanding of these principles, instruments, and laws should help the businessman to carry on his activities without either breaking the law or sacrificing the rights and benefits to which he is legally entitled. It should also help him to recognize when legal counsel is needed.

PRINCIPLES OF LAW

Types of Legal Transactions and Contracts

Contracts. Almost every business act is based on agreements or promises, most of which are contracts. Mutual confidence among the various parties involved in business activities is so basic to modern society that it is difficult to conceive of the continued existence of civilization in the absence of contractual relations. A contract is an agreement between two or more competent parties to do, or not to do, some lawful act for a stated consideration. Although a contract is an agreement, or meeting of minds, not all agreements are contracts. The essentials of a valid contract are:

1. agreement—an offer that must be accepted as offered;
2. true consent—not under duress;
3. competent parties;
4. some lawful objective; and
5. consideration—the value of which is immaterial.

It is important that if the person being offered the contract in any way manifests his acceptance, he may be legally required to accept the contract; it is the law that decides whether the contract exists, not the subjective intent. The offer may be made either orally or in writing. And there is of course an entire branch of law built around whether the contract is offered and accepted; the small businessman must consult his attorney in all matters dealing with contracts.

All persons are considered competent to enter into contracts except infants, married women, insane persons, drunkards, corporations, and agents, fiduciaries, and other legal representatives. The specific laws relating to incompetency to enter contracts vary among the states, and one should carefully check the local statutes applicable.

The fourth point about contracts is that they must have a valid objective. Here it is important that they not be criminal, tortious (performing some private wrong), or opposed to public policy. Examples of such laws would be usurious contracts, gambling and wagering contracts, and agreements that are injurious to the peace, health, good order and morals of the people. Later discussion will detail how legislation tending to prevent restraint of trade, price fixing, and unfair practices have made many previously valid contracts illegal.

The term *consideration,* as indicated, does not mean exchange of something having monetary value. It rather indicates the doing of something or promising to do something that one is not legally obliged to do in return for the promise of another. It is important that promises based upon a past consideration have only moral enforceability, and the promisor must be under legal contract to make his word legally binding. It can be seen that it is essential to have all important contracts in writing with definite provisions meeting the essentials of a valid contract as stated above; and according to the law in many states, certain contracts must be in writing. This is especially true of contracts not to be performed within one year and of those involving the sale of real estate. A written contract is usually desirable, even if not required by state law, whenever common sense indicates a possibility that certain provisions, or even the contract itself, may later be questioned or forgotten.

Agency. Agency implies a business relationship between two parties that involves a third party. An agent may be appointed to assume entire charge of his principal's business or to transact only certain types of business. It is best when dealing with an agent to insist upon proof of an agent's authority, or to have some evidence from the principal as to the delegated authority. The agent must "exercise good faith and the requisite degree of prudence, skill, and diligence," and is not allowed to act for a conflicting interest or for himself. Persons usually deal with the agent as though they were dealing with the company or person (principal) he represents. Since agents are usually appointed by definite agreements or contracts, the law of contracts applies to agency.

The small businessman has many dealings with agents and may have occasion to appoint his own agents or to serve as agent for some principal. The purchase of insurance, many real estate transactions (whether for lease or purchase), and the procurement of equipment, materials, or merchandise often involves dealing through agents. A small manufacturer may prefer to sell through agents rather than through his own sales force. Even small-scale retailers may secure special or exclusive agency rights for certain prestige merchandise. A very important consideration whenever agency is involved is to ascertain and clearly define the authority delegated to the agent by his principal and the agent's duties or responsibilities.

Sales. The businessman is concerned with the sale of either real property or personal property. Property in this sense is the right that a person owns in something, whether land, material, or merchandise. Ownership may be transferred by gift or inheritance as well as by purchase and sale. About two-thirds of the states have adopted a Uniform Sales Act, among the important provisions of which is the clear distinction between a sale and a contract to sell. Other points that should be clearly ascertained in any sale are: the time title passes, identification of the goods, and the right or power of the seller to transfer title. Certain sales must be evidenced by a written bill of sale. If the goods are not delivered immediately, most states require evidence of sale in writing when the amount involved is above some stated minimum, varying from $30 (Missouri) to $2,500 (Ohio). In the largest number of states $500 is the minimum.

There are so many variations of sales and payment plans that complete coverage would be impractical here. However, one question that arises frequently enough to deserve comment is the protection of the seller in case full payment is not made at or before time of delivery of the goods. For example, a retailer may buy merchandise on credit, sell the entire lot for cash to one or a few customers, and fail to pay the wholesaler or other suppliers. To protect the latter almost every state has adopted the Bulk Sales Law. This law requires advance notice (usually delivered in person or by registered mail) to each creditor before sale of an entire stock of goods; if this is not given, the creditors can bring action against the goods even though they have passed into the hands of a third party. And even if "notice has been given, the sale may nevertheless be attacked if the intent of the transfer is to hinder, delay or defraud creditors." A transfer in bulk without notice to creditors is usually declared by the statutes to be "void," "fraudulent and void," or "presumed to be fraudulent and void," but the Delaware statute makes noncompliance also a misdemeanor punishable by $1,000 fine and imprisonment for five years.[1]

A point that frequently causes confusion relates to the obligation of a business to sell goods or services to any person who may offer the full purchase price. A few broad classes of business enterprises, such as public utilities, common carriers, and hotels, are required to serve all persons alike who meet publicly announced requirements and are not obnoxious or otherwise objectionable to other patrons. The merchant is not in this class. He can refuse to sell to any person regardless of the latter's readiness to pay the full purchase price in cash. Manufacturers and other sellers not in the "public service" groups may also refuse to sell to any prospective purchaser at their discretion. The principal apparent exceptions to this rule are certain public

[1] Ronald A. Anderson and Walter A. Kumpf, *Business Law, Principles and Cases,* 2nd ed. (Cincinnati, Ohio: Southwestern Publishing Company, 1958), p. 363.

eating places where the law prohibits customer discrimination because of color or race, and situations in which the businessman carelessly makes a derogatory remark about the prospective customer in refusing to sell to him. It is the derogatory remark, however, and not the refusal to sell, that is likely to cause serious trouble.

Negotiable instruments. Business transactions have been carried on to an increasing extent by means of negotiable instruments instead of money. Both serve as media of exchange; both facilitate trade and pass freely from person to person in connection with business transactions. Money, or legal tender, is universally acceptable and is required by law to be accepted in this country as adequate settlement of financial claim. Although the same legal compulsion does not exist for negotiable instruments, custom, convenience, and confidence have all contributed to their widsepread use. The common check or bank draft is a good illustration.

Negotiable instruments may be classified into three groups: promissory notes, checks, and bills of exchange. According to the Uniform Negotiable Instruments Law, any instrument must satisfy the following requirements if it is to be negotiable:

1. It must be in writing and signed by the maker or drawer.
2. It must contain an unconditional promise or order to pay a sum certain in money.
3. It must be payable on demand or at a fixed rate or determinable future time.
4. It must be payable *to order* or *to bearer*.
5. Where the instrument is addressed to a drawee, he must be named or otherwise indicated therein with reasonable certainty.

Although the meaning of most of these requirements seems obvious enough, a few points deserve emphasis. The act does enumerate "certain exceptions to the rule that the instrument is not negotiable if it contains an order or promise to do any act in addition to the payment of money. Negotiability is not affected by the want of a date, failure to specify a consideration, failure to specify the place where it is drawn or is payable, the fact that it has a seal or the fact that it designates a particular kind of current money in which payment is to be made."

Bills of exchange consist of several forms: sight and term drafts, inland and foreign bills, and trade acceptances. The latter is important to the small businessman and is sent by a seller to a purchaser with the understanding that if the latter approves the goods purchased, he will accept the draft. An example of use of this type is in selling goods on credit. The seller draws a draft on the buyer, often a retailer, for the exact amount of the invoice. This must be accepted before the goods are delivered to the buyer. Thus a promise to pay is created. The seller or drawer of the draft can often discount this trade acceptance and so secure his own money before the due date of the invoice while at the same time granting credit to his customers. Although drafts are sometimes accepted by a bank, by arrangement and for a fee, bankers' acceptances are far less common in domestic commerce than is the trade acceptance (such as the bank arranging to pay for the purchases in the above example).

A check is a negotiable order payable on demand if it is drawn on a bank. Personal checks, bank drafts, certified checks, and traveler's checks may all be encountered by the small businessman.

Promissory notes may be: unsecured notes, collateral notes, judgment notes, mortgage notes, bonds (long-time notes), certificates of deposit issued by a bank, and conditional sale notes. The note may be payable on demand (immediately), and is, in this instance, a substitute for money. "If it is not payable until a future time, the payee in effect extends credit to the maker of the note for the period of time until payment is due." [2]

In the case of checks, a bank will ordinarily make payment unless the drawer lacks sufficient funds and has not made prior arrangements for an overdraft, unless the drawer has stopped payment on the check, or unless the bank has reason to believe the person presenting the check has no legal right to do so. (In the case of other drafts, the drawee must accept the draft drawn against him to create a liability or promise to pay.)

It is well to remember that drafts may be valuable even before they are "accepted," but acceptance creates an actual promise to pay. Time drafts, checks, and promissory notes should be presented for payment when due or as soon as possible. Even though they may be legally valid claims for a reasonable time after maturity, practical considerations of security and custom dictate such prompt presentation for payment. Special cases deserve special consideration and usually require competent legal counsel.

REGULATIONS PERTAINING TO COMPETITION, TRADE PRACTICES, AND PUBLIC WELFARE

Laws of this kind are mostly restrictive or permissive. In general the aim is to encourage competition and stimulate progress by restricting anticompetitive and antisocial acts.[3]

Competition

In most areas of business that are not natural monopolies, competition is still considered to be desirable. However, unregulated business has repeatedly shown tendencies to seek monopoly powers in varying degrees. Our antitrust laws, both Federal and state, have been enacted to protect business itself against those tendencies. The Sherman Anti-Trust Act of 1890 was passed by

---

[2] Anderson and Kumpf, *ibid.*, p. 294.

[3] For a brief digest see: Burt W. Roper, *Regulation of Trade Practices*, Business Service Bulletin No. 31 (Washington, D. C.: Small Business Administration, January 1954).

the Federal Congress after the states had tried unsuccessfully to check the growing monopolies of that time. Although not completely successful, it did make possible the dissolution of many monopolistic trusts in sugar, whisky, oil, and other industries, in addition to at least rendering more difficult certain practices commonly used to crush competition, such as combinations and conspiracies in restraint of interstate trade, tying contracts, and drastic price cutting in areas where such local price discrimination was the common method used to stifle small competitors as they were starting.

More than 45 years ago a new approach was taken with the passage of the Clayton Act and the Federal Trade Commission Act in 1914. Emphasis was now placed on preventing the growth of monopolies by "cleaning up competition," or restricting practices that would lead to monopoly. In 1938 the Wheeler–Lea Act extended the coverage of the Clayton Act, especially with reference to misrepresentations in advertising. This administrative type of law has enabled the Commission to build up a long list of unfair trade practices over the years since its inception. Among these are the following: price cutting for the purpose of eliminating competition, misbranding, secret rebates, spying on competitors, boycotts, disparagement of competitor's goods, use of misleading names, false and misleading advertising, forced-line selling, predatory practices in general, rigging production and markets, using bait advertising, bribing patronage, pirating employees, selling used items as new, cornering competitors' merchandise, merchandising by lot or chance, and offering "fake" buying advantages.

There are two FTC programs which are of particular interest to the small businessman. One is the Division of Trade Practice Conferences which reduces to writing (after due notice and public hearing) rules which interpret the laws enforced by the Commission as they apply to the individual industry. The second is the Division of Small Business, which investigates complaints of unfair practice and also will consult with small business owners regarding applicability to their own problems of laws administered by the FTC.

Although both the Sherman and the Clayton Acts were Federal laws and therefore applied only to interstate commerce, most states enacted similar legislation to regulate intrastate commerce. In addition, decisions regarding unfair methods of competition as arrived at by the Federal Trade Commission have set the pattern both for state courts and for practices approved by the various trade associations. Final authority for approving trade practices, however, rests with the Commission. Many of the prohibitions were arrived at only after extensive hearings and conferences between the Commission and trade representatives. These trade practice conferences have been developed into an important technique. Although benefits to the small businessman resulting from the work of the Federal Trade Commission would be difficult to assess directly, there is no doubt that they have been enormous.

Price Regulation

In a truly competitive market, price acts as the regulator adjusting supply to demand. Attempts to manipulate prices in various ways have existed since the beginning of our price economy. In this country, four broad areas of peacetime regulation by law have appeared: price fixing, price discrimination, price cutting, and resale price maintenance.

Under the antitrust laws prior to the 1930's, all agreements to fix or set prices were generally considered illegal. Even agreements between a manufacturer and his dealers setting the price at which the goods could be resold by the dealer were unenforceable. Then the "fair trade" acts were passed and until recently certain of these agreements (on trade-marks and brand names) were enforceable under these acts.

The FTC has issued "Guides Against Deceptive Pricing" which can be obtained by contacting the Government Printing Office. These nine guides attempt to put down the legal boundaries of pricing representations and limit price advertising claims.

Price fixing. Price fixing, under court interpretations of the antitrust laws, includes agreements among competitors engaged in interstate commerce to stabilize prices or to hold competitive prices in any fixed relationship to each other. It is not limited to the fixing of uniform prices. Also, provisions for price agreements that have been considered illegal apply to many indirect methods that, taken together, have the end result of price fixing. Thus agreements to maintain uniform discounts, markup or methods of calculating markup, delivery charges, and many similar practices among competitors may be illegal when applied to interstate transactions.

Price discrimination. In 1936 the Robinson–Patman amendment to the Clayton Act declared personal price discrimination to be illegal. Differences in price of goods of like grade and quality to different buyers in competition are declared to be illegal unless justified by differences in costs of manufacture, selling, or handling, provided such discrimination may have the effect of "substantially lessening competition, tending to create a monopoly, or injuring, destroying, or preventing competition with other persons." A seller is, however, permitted to meet lower prices of competitors in certain cases without violating the law. Burden of proof that price discriminations are economically justifiable rests with the seller, and the buyer who knowingly accepts such illegal price discrimination is made equally liable with the seller. The reason for making the buyer liable to prosecution for accepting discriminatory prices was the fact that many buyers for large chain stores or mail-order houses had formerly bargained for low prices that sometimes exceeded the economies resulting from their large orders. Methods commonly used to conceal price discriminations were also declared illegal. In particular they include the following: allowances for advertising and sales promotion that are in excess of a fair payment for services actually rendered by the buyer and that are not made on proportionately equal terms to all competing customers; brokerage fees collected from the seller when the "broker" was also acting with the buyer as principal; and services or facilities furnished by the seller to certain buyers unless made available to all purchasers on proportionately equal terms.

It should be noted that the Robinson–Patman Act did not prohibit all price discrimination but only that on similar goods to buyers who are in competition where the difference in price exceeds economies connected with the lower-priced sale. It should also be remembered that the retail or other buyer is liable for violation equally with the seller.

Price cutting. Excessive price cutting when used solely for the purpose of eliminating competition has quite generally been considered to be an unfair method of competition used especially by large concerns to drive small competitors out of business. If permitted, it is normally followed by a very high or monopoly price once effective competition is driven from the market. The temporary benefits to consumers resulting from lower prices are lost during the subsequent period of high prices.

From the 1930's on, several states have passed laws to regulate excessive price cutting. These are of two general types, unfair practice and anti-loss leader laws. The unfair practice laws prohibit below-cost selling that injures competition. Cost is defined as invoice cost plus a fair share of the expenses of doing business. Especially in merchandising, where a large variety of articles are handled, this is so indefinite and it is so impractical to determine cost when applied to individual items that these laws have been ineffective. A partial solution has been to interpret "cost of doing business" arbitrarily as some fixed markup over cost, say six per cent.

The second group of laws provides an objective and definite measure of what constitutes too low a price by setting up some nominal markup figure like six per cent above landed cost as the standard. These anti-loss leader laws are enforceable, although usually the necessary policing is done by each trade group rather than by state law enforcement officers.

Resale price maintenance. Beginning with California in 1931, 45 states enacted so-called "Fair Trade" statutes that legalized resale price maintenance contracts for trade-marked articles or merchandise identifiable as to producer. These laws permitted vertical contracts between manufacturer and wholesaler or retailer stipulating either the price at which the identifiable article was to be sold or minimum price below which it could not be sold. Contracts on the same level of distribution, between different manufacturers or different wholesalers or different retailers, to set the resale price were left unenforceable. A provision that one contract between a manufacturer or his duly authorized wholesale agent and one retailer in a state became binding on all other dealers in the state, was used up to 1951. By 1937 the majority of the states had passed resale price maintenance laws, and the Federal gov·

ernment made the practice generally legal in interstate commerce by passing the Miller–Tydings Act.

In the late 1940's, opposition began growing against fair trade regulations, a danger predicted by the authors some 15 years ago. The courts were less friendly toward such legislation, and in May, 1951, in the Schwegmann decision the United States Supreme Court decided that the nonsigner provision was not intended in the Miller–Tydings Act, thus releasing most retailers from the need to observe Fair Trade prices. Pressure was immediately put on Congress with the result that the Supreme Court decision was nullified by passage of the McGuire Act as an amendment to the Federal Trade Commission Act. The Commission was empowered and directed to enforce the Act, including the prevention of the cutting of established resale prices, an ironical situation in view of the Commission's other duties and opposition to Fair Trade laws.

Then, in state after state, courts began deciding against the upholders of Fair Trade, and when the large companies (such as General Electric and Sunbeam) which had attempted to enforce it stopped their efforts, Fair Trade was dead in 17 of the original states. The public had all along been opposed to Fair Trade and was very willing to overlook its provisions; many important retailers had refused to abide by its provisions (claiming the laws were restrictive on their freedom to operate and resulted in artificially high prices); finally the manufacturer was forced to admit defeat. Of primary importance to this development was the rise of the discount house.

Retailing history in the United States so far has demonstrated that innovations will appear and expand in "soft spots" or where existing retailing and marketing fail to meet widespread demands. Legislative efforts to block such American ingenuity have consistently failed since late in the last century; and current attempts to use Fair Trade regulation as a crutch for incompetent management appear to bear out this long time trend. Among the popular devices in recent use to bypass Fair Trade are: inflated trade-ins, $20 for an old broom, non-Fair Traded articles given free with each purchase at Fair Trade prices, sales tickets made out at Fair Trade prices accompanied by an unrecorded cash refund, and so on. No company or agency can possibly be able to detect and control all of these evasions; and even if they had virtually unlimited financial resources, the time factor alone would make enforcement impossible to achieve.

Our discussion in this section has been a deliberate attempt to warn the conscientious independent enterpriser against the long run hazards of seeking security in legal devices in lieu of competent management in the interest of his customers.

For over 3,000 years businessmen have attempted to guarantee their profits by various laws and legal props. So far such efforts have not been successful for any length of time. Especially in our dynamic, free enterprise economy efforts of this sort appear to be less desirable than rendering a genuine public service through efficient management conducted in the interest of consumers. The pros and cons of Fair Trade regulation as a device for protecting small independents from large price-cutters are given in the footnote references[4] and in various bibliographies listed elsewhere. From a practical standpoint, however, the danger is real that in the long run any legal restrictive measures that place the interests of special groups above the public interest may react unfavorably to the very groups seeking protection.

Closely resembling resale price maintenance is the revival of "guild pricing" where a state board composed of members of a trade or industry set minimum prices that may legally be charged and have the power to limit entry into the field. Usually, but not necessarily, guild pricing is used for services, such as dry cleaning, barbering and beauty parlor operation. In some cases the state supreme court has been unable to see a real relationship between the public health and welfare and minimum prices set by a self-regulating monopoly, such as for barber services. Such state boards are still in operation in many states, California having the largest number.[5]

Businessmen contemplating doing any installment selling should ascertain the laws of their own state and of any states in which they have debtors with regard to permissible interest rates. Most states have statutes providing maximum contract rate of interest (the highest annual rate that can be exacted). All states have a legal rate of interest, to be used when an agreement says there is to be payment of interest, but does not specify the rate. Penalties for charging illegal interest are very heavy, and it is important to know just what can be charged and under what sorts of agreements.[6]

Merchandise Regulation

Food, Drug, and Cosmetic Act. Laws designed to protect the health and to some extent the pocketbook of the consumer have been enacted by Federal, state, and local governments. The Federal Food, Drug, and Cosmetic Act of 1938 revised the earlier Pure Food and Drug Act of 1906 by extending the coverage to include certain curative devices and cosmetics (except soap). It also provided for testing before certain drugs that might cause sickness or death are put on the market. More complete disclosure of habit-forming

[4] See Stewart Munro Lee, "Problems of Resale Price Maintenance," *Journal of Marketing* (January 1959), pp. 274-281; also, Edward S. Herman, "Fair Trade; Origins, Purposes, and Competitive Effect," *The George Washington Law Review* (June 1959), pp. 621-652; or "Some Former Fair Traders Sound Wistful About Old Times," *Printer's Ink* (July 21, 1958), p. 10.

[5] "Regulation of Price Competition, C. Price Control," *Journal of Marketing,* October 1952, pp. 198-99; Pearce C. Kelley, *Consumer Economics* (Homewood, Ill.: Richard D. Irwin, Inc., 1953), p. 25.

[6] See also: *Retailers Manual of Taxes and Regulations,* 14th ed. (New York: Institute of Distribution, Inc., 1958); this covers up-to-date Federal and State laws concerning retailers, and includes Federal and State trade regulations and taxes on property income and profits, on state legislation on sales, chain store, and occupational and excise taxes, and on welfare fund regulations.

ingredients as well as others that might be injurious to certain types of individuals is required. Like its predecessor, the new law deals mostly with adulteration, misbranding, and information that must be given on the label. The small businessman manufacturing or handling foods, drugs, devices, or cosmetics should study and observe in detail the provisions of this law. Even if he is not engaged in interstate commerce, it will be good business to meet the requirements set forth in the Federal law. A 1953 amendment authorizes inspectors to enter any establishment where food, drugs, or cosmetic items are held and to inspect the establishment and materials and equipment therein, with proper safeguards for the owners.

A recent addition to the food and drug regulation concerns food additives. Examples of cases involving these considerations include the canned cranberry and chicken caponizing problems of late 1959. Under this legislation, manufacturers must convince the Food and Drug Administration that the additives are harmless in the intended use assuming that the product is not already in a special "exempt" or "safe" category. This is done by submitting certain required data, considerably detailed, in an application to the Department of Health, Education, and Welfare; the applicant is then advised by that body as to what he can use, in what amounts, labelling requirements, and so forth. There is also agitation for similar legislation for food coloratives and lipstick color components.

Many states and municipalities require a special permit and fee to sell cigarettes. In at least one case the courts have held that cigarettes may be classified as a drug, when the label claims they may be used for "mitigation or prevention" of various named diseases.[7] This makes them subject to provisions of the Food, Drug, and Cosmetic Act, and possibly to certain state legislation dealing with retailing of drugs.

All states and most cities have legislation and regulations dealing with the processing and handling of food for the public. Many have laws governing drugs and similar merchandise. Pharmacy is recognized in every state as a profession which should be practiced only by qualified pharmacists, but the detailed regulations are not uniform for all states. Either the manufacture or the sale of certain other products is frequently regulated by state law or local ordinances. Some of these are mattresses, bedding, eyeglasses and similar optical goods, and a long list of synthetic foods and drinks.

Wool Products Labeling Act. According to the Federal Wool Products Labeling Act, all articles made of wool, except floor coverings, must be labeled as to the percentage of virgin wool and of reprocessed and reused wool contents. If any fiber other than wool is present in excess of five per cent, its percentage must also be given on the label. It is illegal for the retailer or other businessman dealing in such products to remove or deface the label containing this information.

---

[7] "Regulation of Unfair Competition, A. Advertising," *Journal of Marketing* (October 1953), p. 198.

The Federal Fur Products Labeling Act became effective August 1951, and contains both civil and criminal penalties. The Act outlaws deceptive labeling, advertising, misbranding in invoicing of furs, assigns enforcement to the Federal Trade Commission as well as the responsibility of establishing a Fur Products Name Guide, and requires that fur products must be guaranteed to consist of the type of fur indicated on the label. A retailer may replace a label provided he complies with all labeling requirements and maintains a complete record of the substitution for at least three years.

The Federal Flammable Fabrics Act became effective June 30, 1954, and was assigned to the Federal Trade Commission for enforcement. Commercial Standard CS 191—53 developed as part of this regulation requires that five specimens of the textile concerned be tested in their original state, and in addition, in the absence of proof that a fire-retarding finish has not been added, five specimens must be tested after dry cleaning and washing. The Act affects primarily producers of apparel where any risk of injury to users from fire might cause such products to be dangerous. The flammability tests and requirements that must be met are set forth in CS 191—53.

Company and trade names. The company or firm name identifies the particular enterprise and may consist of all or part of the names of the owners or an assumed name. Sometimes a proprietor uses his first or last name only, or both, and partnerships frequently use the last names of each partner, as the Smith-Jones Company. A sole proprietor can ordinarily use his full name for his business without restrictions unless another firm in the same market and kind of business has this name well established and confusion would result if a newcomer were to use the same name. If an assumed or coined name is used, and usually when only the first or last name of a proprietor or names of partners are used, it is necessary to file with the county clerk the company name and full name of each owner. This is primarily to protect others who may deal with the concern and to have on record essential information as to who actually owns the business. For a corporation the name under which it will operate as well as the names of the incorporators are part of the application for a charter.

Trade names are used to identify a product or products sponsored, originally at least, by one firm—such as *aspirin, nylon,* and so on. For all practical purposes they may be considered as trade-mark names. A point of major importance for the small businessman is to avoid any attempt to copy or imitate a company name, trade name or mark, package design, or other device already in use that might expose him to charges of unfair competition.

Patents and trade-marks. Patents and trade-marks are regulated by federal laws administered by the Patent Office. Securing a patent is a highly complex proceeding and should be handled by an attorney trained in this specialized field. Competent attorneys should also be employed in all trade-mark matters. A patent gives an inventor the right to exclude all others from making, using, or selling his invention for the term of 17 years, and may be granted only after a determination of utility and completeness of disclosure of the invention and a search to determine its novelty. No patent is granted upon a mere suggestion or idea. The patent law affords no protection prior to the actual issue of a patent, although it is common practice to serve notice of application by stating that a patent has been applied for.

A trade-mark is a distinctive word, emblem, symbol, or device, or a combination of any of these, used in connection with goods actually sold in commerce to identify the manufacturer or seller. It must have been used in interstate commerce before an application for registration can be filed in the Patent Office. Since July, 1947, provisions of the Federal Lanham Act replace those of the Trade-Mark Act of 1905. Under the new law, registration of trade-marks on the Principal Register becomes almost essential to secure future protection. Also, a trade-mark need no longer be physically affixed to the merchandise; protection is thus given to well-advertised trade-marks for such products as brands of gasoline and to "service marks" of service establishments. In addition to federal registration, many states have passed laws concerning the protection of trade-marks used in intrastate commerce.

Advertising

Federal regulation of advertising has been administered by the Federal Trade Commission as part of its work of maintaining fair competition. In general, false and misleading advertising is condemned.[8] This includes the use of deceptive and misleading names and expressions like "Cylk" or "artificial silk." Many names formerly used to describe lower-quality furs in such a way as to suggest the genuine article have been banned. The Wheeler–Lea amendment to the Federal Trade Commission Act gives the Commission power to regulate advertising to meet the labeling requirements of the Food, Drug, and Cosmetic Act. It also gives the Commission authority for the first time to act against advertising that is injurious to the *public* even though it may not directly affect competition. Many states also have laws regulating false and misleading advertising.

Late in 1953, the Commission reversed an earlier attitude toward use of the word "free" in advertising and accepted its usage where the "conditions, obligations or other prerequisites to the receipt and retention of the 'free' articles" are clearly explained.

Labor Legislation

Federal legislation governing labor relations may be divided into three broad groups: (1) settlement of labor disputes; (2) regulations of wages,

[8] D. R. Reel, "Small Business and the Federal Trade Commission," Small Marketers Aids, No. 24 (Washington, D. C.: Small Business Administration, 1956). This booklet gives advice to management on rules and conference proceedings, prohibited practices, and services rendered by FTC to small business.

hours, and working conditions; and (3) social security, which is also an important division of business taxation.

Settlement of labor disputes. The National Labor Relations Act, or Wagner Act, of 1935 became the first important law concerned with labor disputes and is administered by the National Labor Relations Board. It provides that employees shall have "the right to self-organization, to form, join, or assist labor organizations, to bargain collectively through representatives of their own choosing, and to engage in concerned activities, for the purpose of collective bargaining or other mutual aid or protection." According to the act, certain practices on the part of an employer are considered to be unfair, including the following: (1) interfering with, restraining, or coercing of employees in the exercise of their guaranteed rights; (2) dominating or interfering with the formation or administration of any labor organization; (3) encouraging or discouraging membership in any labor organization by discrimination in regard to hire, tenure, or condition of employment; (4) discharging or otherwise discriminating against an employee for filing charges or giving testimony under the act; (5) refusing to bargain collectively with representatives of employees.

The Taft–Hartley Act of 1947 changed some provisions and interpretations of the National Labor Relations Act in an effort to correct certain undesirable conditions that had developed in labor relations. The Taft–Hartley Act represents one attempt to equalize the position of labor and management. It prohibits the closed shop, mass picketing, the used of violence in connection with a labor dispute, jurisdictional strikes, secondary boycotts, strikes against the Federal government, and any labor organization from having a standing under the Act if its officers refuse to sign statements that they are not members of the Communist Party. The Act permits a modified union shop; requires that labor be held equally responsible with management for fulfillment of the terms of a contract agreed upon; and creates a Federal Mediation and Conciliation Service outside the Department of Labor.

> The Taft–Hartley Act provides a bill of rights for the individual worker because, in addition to protection against abuses by employer bosses, it also protects him against abuses by labor bosses. . . . No longer can there be excessive initiation fees and fines.
>
>   . . . The only way a man can be thrown out of the Union today is for non-payment of dues. . . . No longer is the National Labor Relations Board investigator, prosecutor, jury and judge all rolled into one. Today it is merely a quasi-judicial board that shall pass on the evidence presented to it.[9]

[9] Honorable Fred A. Hartley, Jr., "The Truth of the Taft-Hartley Law," *Hardware World* (November 1947), pp. 74-76. See also: Claude Robinson, "Taft-Hartley Gains Ground," *Look* (February 23, 1954), p. 23; "Taft-Hartley Changes—It's a Fight Between Professionals," *Time* (February 8, 1954), p. 82; "T-H Hearings: Big Cast, No Drama," *Business Week* (January 30, 1954), p. 128.

In spite of initial opposition to the Taft–Hartley Act by union leaders, recent polls show recognition or approval of its main features by both union members and others. As might be expected, considerable opinion favors some slight modifications and these may develop as conditions indicate their need.

The most recent major piece of labor legislation is the Labor-Management Reporting and Disclosure Act of 1959 (the Kennedy–Landrum–Griffin Act) which amends the Taft–Hartley Act. The provisions of this act can be summarized under the following headings: increased union member rights, additional reports required of unions and their officers, new policing of union trusteeship over subordinate organizations, union election rule tightening and safeguards for labor organizations from certain acts of their officers. The act further prohibits extortionate picketing, prohibits agreements between labor organizations and employers which lead to secondary boycotts, prohibits picketing for recognition, restricts organizational picketing, and permits with appropriate safeguards prehire and seven-day union shop agreements in the building and construction industry. Union reaction to the law was immediate and negative. "The fact is, internal affairs of labor unions have been invaded by law to a degree never before imposed upon any other important segment of society." [10]

The act was passed in part as the result of union racketeering and mishandling of funds and of union disregard for the rights of individual employees. We may, in fact, expect from this act no interference with the basic right to organize, but rather a cleaning up of union affairs in areas which have created the unfavorable public opinion leading to the act.

Fair Employment Practice, or FEP, laws have expanded since 1945 when New York State adopted the first of the new type law. In 1958, twelve states and a number of municipalities had such laws or ordinances, and three states have expressed the desirability of ending discriminatory employment but have failed to delegate enforcement power to their state commissions. California protects the employment opportunities of minorities without an FEP statute because discrimination has been held to be contrary to public policy. The enforceable laws differ among themselves somewhat, but all of them share a basic pattern. The main characteristic is that they are not criminal but administrative laws, strengthened by court intervention as a last resort. "In a few states, a criminal penalty was imposed for the violation of an FEP law, whereas in other states, although no penal provisions were provided, a violator could be held in contempt of court or fined." [11]

Specifically, these laws provide that employers are prohibited from discriminating on the basis of race or color, religion, or national origin and ancestry, in hiring, conditions of work, upgrading, dismissal, and similar activities.

---

[10] *United Rubber Worker,* Official Organ, United Rubber, Cork, Linoleum and Plastic Workers of America, AFL-CIO, Vol. 25 (November 1959), p. 11.

[11] Irving Kovarsky, "A Review of State FEPC Laws," *Labor Law Journal* (July 1958).

Labor unions are forbidden to discriminate in their membership policies, or in their relations with employers or with non-union workers. Employment agencies are prohibited from discriminating in classifying or referring prospective employees or in obtaining information from them. All of them rely largely on education and conciliation techniques.

Small businessmen who accept government supply contracts may be governed by provisions of the Walsh–Healey Public Contracts Act, which is concerned mainly with working conditions and hours and wages of employees, and should consult sources of information such as those contained in the footnote.[12]

Regulation of wages, hours, and working conditions. Federal regulation of wages and hours is covered by the Fair Labor Standards Act of 1938, which provides for minimum wages and maximum hours. One objective of federal regulation has been to secure greater uniformity of wage and hour provisions among the various states. Groups excluded from the provisions of the act fall into three broad categories: (1) certain executive and professional employees, (2) workers engaged in occupations covered by separate laws, such as railway employees and seamen, and (3) those in distinctly local or intrastate activity, such as agricultural workers and employees in a retail or service establishment the greater part of which is devoted to intrastate business. The employment of minors under 16 years of age, with certain exceptions, is prohibited by the Act.

The various states also have laws with both fair labor standards and wage and hour provisions that apply to local problems and enterprises.

State regulation is more active in the field of working conditions, especially with reference to industrial accidents. All states but one provide by law for industrial accident compensation. Many also limit work in hazardous occupations, night work, and so-called "industrial home work." The small businessman should investigate the laws in his state governing employee relations of the type mentioned.

Social security. As amended, this law provides for three kinds of insurance: (1) Federal old-age and survivors insurance for employees, (2) the same for the self-employed, and (3) state-Federal unemployment insurance.

If you are in business and hire even one person, the first two provisions apply to you, but are handled differently. You must have a social security account number card. If you already have one secured as an employee, use it for both provisions, otherwise get one from your nearest Social Security office.

For social security purposes payroll records must show the following: The employee's name; his occupation, address, and social security number; the amount of each payment to him (including any amount withheld); the date of each payment; the period of service covered by each payment; and the

[12] Small Business Administration, *Management Aids for Small Business No. 17* (1954).

amount of social security tax deducted from the wages paid. If the employee's tax is deducted at any time other than when the wages are paid, the date of deduction must be recorded. If all or any part of the wage payment is not taxable (that above $4,800, for example), the reason must be included in your records.

From each payment of wages the employees' share is deducted up to a total of $4,800 in any one year. Four times a year these deductions are reported and payment is made for them together with the employer's matching share to the Commissioner of Internal Revenue. Each employee must be given a receipt for his payment.

Whether or not you hire anyone, and even if you are an employee yourself, if you receive less than $4,800 from wages in a covered occupation, and if you earn $400 or more in any one year from self-employment in a business or trade, excluding a few professional fields, you *must* pay a social security tax and make an annual report. Your tax rate is one-and-one-half times the rate on employees. You file and pay your self-employment tax in connection with your Federal income tax, using Schedule C in Form 1040. If you are both employee and employer, consider your wages first; if you were paid $4,800 in a covered occupation from which social security taxes were deducted, this is your maximum credit in any one year and you do not report and pay on your self-employment income. If you received $3,300 in wages and earned $800 in self-employment (net earnings from self-employment provided it is at least $400 in your taxable year), you pay tax and report on the $800 of self-employment income.

The 1956 amendments bring under the social security law many people who had not been covered before: certain self-employed persons, members of the uniformed services, and many farm people.

Tax rates are shown in the following tabulation:

	TAXES IN PER CENT		
Calendar Year	*Employer*	*Employee*	*Self-Employed*
1956	2%	2%	3%
1957-1959	2¼%	2¼%	3⅜%
1960-1964	2¾%	2¾%	4⅛%
1965-1969	3¼%	3¼%	4⅞%
1970-1974	3¾%	3¾%	5⅝%
1975 and after	4¼%	4¼%	6⅜%

The Federal Unemployment Tax applies to you only if you have as many as eight employees in covered employment on at least one day in each of 20 calendar weeks during the calendar year. Most states have laws that apply to employers with fewer than eight employees; therefore, you had better make a careful investigation of the law in the state in which you do business.

As a beginning enterpriser, you should inquire at your nearest Social Security office, Commissioner of Internal Revenue, and your State Unemployment Compensation Agency or Employment Security Agency, regarding your duties and the proper forms to use.

Restrictions and Permits

Some state laws restrict business activity (1) by permitting only licensed practitioners to engage in particular occupations, such as pharmacy, barber shop or beauty parlor operation, and public accounting, and (2) by requiring minimum equipment, facilities, or processes for sanitation and the health of employees and the public. However, in general, most regulation of this sort is local, defined by city ordinance and enforced under the police powers of the governing unit.

A license is a permit granted by the governmental power to a person or company to pursue some business subject to regulation under the police power. Licensing is used both to regulate business and as a source of revenue to the government granting the license. For example, plumbers, electricians, pawnbrokers, and auctioneers, as well as dance halls, taxi companies, hotels, amusement places, and food service and drinking places, are usually licensed and frequently inspected or supervised to see that regulations for protection of the public health, safety, and morals are observed. Other businesses, such as retail stores, may not be required to have a license but be subject to minimum regulations necessary to reduce fire hazards. On both state and local levels, license requirements and regulatory taxes have been expanding. These lines include professional services as well as all major fields of small business. Not all changes increased the hardships on independent enterprisers as some consisted of more liberal provisions.

In many cities licensing is used to enforce zoning restrictions. Licenses will be granted to operate a given type of business only in areas where zoning regulations permit this particular type. For example, a retail store will not be licensed to operate in a district zoned exclusively for residences, and a dry cleaning store may get a license to operate in a retail shopping district but the *dry cleaning plant* using certain dangerous fluids will be licensed to operate only in the industrial district.

Licensing is also used to restrict competition, as when itinerant vendors selling from temporary quarters, on the sidewalk, or from house to house are required to pay a relatively heavy license fee. Some regulation of this class of merchants is considered desirable to protect the residents or public from "gyp artists" and fly-by-night peddlers. It is often difficult to draw the line between licensing for necessary customer protection and that designed to lessen competition for the local merchants. For example, "Green River Ordinances" that prohibit all house-to-house solicitation except by personal invitation of the householder, obviously protect local merchants from competition with outside sellers, but also relieve families from many annoying interruptions, some swindling schemes and crimes. Another viewpoint, however, is the limitations placed on aggressive selling, especially the launching of new products and other innovations which can sometimes be most effectively done through such personal contact.

Many other regulations and restrictions are enforced locally, such as those pertaining to use of the business premises, alleys, adjoining sidewalks, parking spaces, store signs, wiring, plumbing, heating, delivery equipment, and similar things. In addition, the small businessman will usually find among the established businessmen certain social controls relating to store hours, acceptable types of advertising, "going" rates of pay, pricing, and expected community services. Although these lack the compulsion of actual laws, they are very powerful.

TAXES

Federal income and withholding taxes and state sales taxes are covered in Chapter 24. Social security taxes have been discussed in this chapter. Certain types of business may encounter special taxes, such as a manufacturer's excise tax, railroad siding tax, use tax, and special products taxes. A corporation will usually have taxes in addition to those of a proprietorship or partnership, such as capital stock tax and a "foreign" tax if it operates in states other than the one in which it is incorporated.

In addition to the taxes already mentioned, most businesses will be required to pay both real and personal property taxes, usually at the county or city level. These are based on property valuation rather than income or profit and have been declining in importance, especially in relation to income taxes. Various fees for inspections covering the building, exits, fire hazards, machinery, elevators, ventilation, trucks, and other sources of possible damage to employees or the public are often in effect merely additional business taxes.

There are several new laws benefiting small business:

1. One encourages investors to put money into small enterprises by allowing them ordinary loss deduction rather than restricting them to a $1000 loss.

2. A second allows small corporations (up to 10 stockholders) to report as partnerships. This allows the advantages of a corporate setup without double taxation on profits.

3. A third law allows the heirs of a small business to spread the tax over ten years.[13]

Local and state tax and license requirements, plus labor union control, are factors that sometimes upset a promising service establishment in which the operator has only a small amount of capital, perhaps only in the hundreds of

[13] *Business Week* (September 27, 1958), pp. 149-150. Also see: "Tax Guide for Small Business," GPO Annual (Washington, D. C.: Department of the Treasury, Internal Revenue Service). This booklet informs businessmen on social security, Federal income tax, and withholding tax problems involved in business, and supplies needed information concerning the starting of an enterprise, buying an operating business, and selling a firm.

dollars, and not much more to invest beyond the hours he will spend working to sign up new business, keeping a small crew working, retaining old customers, and paying current bills.

There are two examples worthy of attention in which service entrepreneurs came to grief because they lacked knowledge of requirements. One is that of a singularly gifted enterpriser who, in the Great Depression years of the mid 1930's, thought up the idea of a telephone cleaning and disinfecting service. This idea was put on a working and profitable basis and sufficient customers were signed up to make a modest profit. Telephones in offices were dusted, scrubbed and sprayed with disinfectants. This went happily until the operator of this genuinely small service business was required to get a battery of licenses from city, county, and state. Even this relatively modest bite into his net profit was discouraging. He quit. The other case is that of a prospective small businessman who may be called a pigeon eradicator. He had a tested and proved method for removing bird stains from buildings. Moreover he offered his customers the added service of keeping pigeons, starlings, and their ilk at a discreet distance from edifices. After a short while this low-capitalized venture was put out of business by license fee requirements and the building cleaners' union which required an initiation charge and dues and were prohibitive to the entire operation which had to account for wages for the operator, helpers' pay, and materials costs.

CONCLUSIONS

The regulation of business by government through laws, licenses, and taxation is probably as old as business and government. Law constitutes the organized body of rules of conduct enforceable by government agencies. We have two important levels of legal authority (federal and state) as well as many minor levels (city, county, and other political sub-divisions). Certain legal areas have developed general principles, such as the law of agency and the law of contracts. Although a great many legal documents are in use, a relatively small number are of great importance to most businessmen; among them are contracts, bills of sale, mortgages, and negotiable instruments.

With reasonable effort the small businessman can gain an understanding of the more important laws and legal documents that affect his business. He can also gain familiarity with the major forms of taxation. However, both law and taxation are complex fields requiring extensive specialized training and experience. *In all important cases it is well to see competent counsel on legal and tax matters.*

Often tax savings are possible, or penalties may be avoided, by an alertness to changes in taxes and regulations, such as longer carry-backs or carry-forwards of losses, accelerated depreciation, modifications of Section 102 on retained earnings penalties, and modifications in state and local regulations. If possible, an enterpriser should subscribe to a good tax reporting service such as that of Prentice-Hall, Inc., and have his attorney or accountant keep him posted on all significant developments.

Arbitration of business disputes should be preferred to resort to the courts. Arbitration has been well organized on a nationwide basis and should be familiar to all enterprisers.

QUESTIONS AND PROBLEMS

1. How are laws and regulations related to (1) insurance, and (2) other aspects of protection for the independent enterpriser?

2. Explain how regulations and taxes may be serious hazards to the typical small businessman.

3. What are the essential characteristics of a law?

4. What are the primary objectives or purposes of law?

5. How are laws, regulations and taxes related to accounting and to the maintenance of adequate records?

6. If business is based on mutual trust and confidence, why do we need so many laws relating to business?

7. Under what conditions would a written contract be more binding than an oral one? When is the reverse true? Explain.

8. Distinguish between an agreement and a contract.

9. What are the important provisions of the Uniform Sales Act?

10. Under what conditions is it necessary to secure a written bill of sale when the full purchase price is paid at the time of sale and delivery of the article sold? Discuss.

11. When does title pass from seller to buyer on a shipment made by common carrier on a straight bill of lading?

12. State and explain the provisions of the Bulk Sales Law.

13. How should a promissory note be worded to be certainly negotiable?

14. What is meant by endorsement? What responsibilities does it carry?

15. Discuss the meaning and purpose of discounting a note.

16. What, if any, liability does the drawee of a bill of exchange have? Discuss. Explain the same for the drawer.

17. What, if any, advantages are there to securing endorsement before accepting a negotiable instrument payable to bearer?

18. What is meant by "power of attorney"? Are the transactions carried out by the agent for the principal legally binding? Discuss.

19. What are the minimum powers of a true agent?

20. What classes of business are required to serve all persons alike? Give reasons for requirements.

21. Discuss any legal limitations on the use of company names, trade names, package designs and illustrations.

22. What non-governmental agencies are active in enforcing laws relating to business? Restrictions on unfair competition or unethical business practices? Discuss.

23. Explain and discuss "guild pricing."

24. Why is it considered more important to secure competent counsel on legal and tax matters than for other problems facing the small businessman?

25. Of what significance is the fact that many of the recently enacted laws governing business are administrative laws?

26. Explain and illustrate why every self-employed person must be familiar with social security regulations.

27. Why was arbitration mentioned even briefly in a chapter on regulations and taxes?

28. From your library or any reliable sources learn all you can about the arbitration of commercial disputes and prepare and submit a report of your findings and conclusions.

29. Select some line of business and determine the various licenses and permits required for operation.

30. After working from January through August 1955, at a salary of $400 per month, in a covered occupation, Tom Jones became a partner in a business from which his share of profits or self-employed income for the balance of the year was $2,000. What were his total Social Security taxes for the year?

13 • Selecting the Profitable Merchandising Location

In selecting the location for a small business, personal factors are of far greater importance than they are for the large concern. Pragmatically, they may limit the individual's range of choice to his immediate environment, either because of his lack of knowledge of more distant locations, or because he does not have the necessary time or funds to investigate a wider area. Of much greater importance are the highly personal factors that lead to deliberate choice. Some of these are:

1. A desire to locate among friends and acquaintances. Sometimes the opposite desire, to locate where one is unknown, prevails.

2. A personal preference for one region or part of the country for various subjective reasons.

3. A need to locate in a particular climate because of health.

4. A desire to be near family or relatives.

5. An opportunity to take advantage of established trade connections in a particular territory.

6. A personal preference for a small town or a big city, and for the latter a preference for an urban or suburban location.

7. The desirability of being able to give personal supervision to other property or interests in which one may have a present or prospective future investment. Often it is the wife's interests, preferences, or connections, like many of those just enumerated, that influence the selection of a region or a particular town in which to locate.

Although it is often considered risky to go into business in a particular town solely because one is well known there, sound business reasons often favor such a decision. Credit is easier to obtain where the entrepreneur has already established a good reputation. Friends and acquaintances will give good word-of-mouth publicity, but the beginner should not count too heavily on receiving their patronage *merely* because of friendship. The native's inti-

251

mate knowledge of the community's people, their buying habits, their likes and dislikes, and other characteristics, of trends and developments to be expected in the near future, and of other useful facts may be an asset that a total stranger would acquire with difficulty.

Towns and cities vary greatly as to desirability of locations for different kinds and sizes of businesses. Ordinarily the small businessman will be faced with either of two basic types of problems: (1) comparing the merits of a number of possible towns or cities within which to locate his particular kind of business, or (2) deciding whether or not a given town is a good place in which to enter one of a few closely related kinds of business. Usually the same selection procedures will be followed in either case.

Selecting the region and town is relatively more important in terms of economic factors for the small factory or wholesale concern than for most retail and service establishments. Conversely, choosing the district and site within a particular town is usually of major importance to the small retail store or shop.

The representative beginning wholesaler, however, envisions a modest market within his community with economical access to his customers, influenced by factors similar to those that govern the selection of a profitable retail or service location. In contrast to a factory, the other three types of enterprise are seldom sought after by communities, and have other features that warrant discussing factory location separately in the next chapter, with retail, wholesale, and service business locations chosen for our consideration in this chapter.

In most cases various towns under consideration will be evaluated in terms of economic factors, population, competition, living conditions, and any special location requirements. As an aid in rating the first four considerations a check list of important factors may be used. This rating type of check list would be especially useful in the case of retail stores and service establishments. The small businessman should be sufficiently familiar with the specific location requirements for his particular kind of business to rate each item on the list in terms of his needs. The list is merely a guide to use in choosing the one town among several that has the best over-all combination of desirable location factors and the fewest undesirable ones.

In 1946 the U. S. Department of Commerce published such a list based on locational factors of importance at that time.[1] Conditions have changed so much since then that a new approach seems desirable.

In using a check list for rating, the following comments should be helpful. The "industry" or productive resources present in each town are analyzed first in terms of three basic types—farming, manufacturing, or trading. Some cities may be predominantly political centers, and, as such, trade would be the major economic activity. Such a city probably would be subject, like a

---

[1] Helen G. Canoyer, *Selecting a Store Location*, Economic Series No. 56 (Washington, D. C.: U. S. Department of Commerce, 1946).

resort or school town, to large seasonal fluctuations. These would be rated under this characteristic of the industry.

Breakdowns used under "competition" should be rated with at least two things in mind:

1. The direct effect of competition on the particular kind of business. Many lines of business do well if located in a market or shopping center with the right type of competitors. Retail stores that handle shopping goods or general merchandise sold to customers who live in a large trading area surrounding the town are examples. Small wholesalers or manufacturers who are not dependent on the local market, such as dry goods wholesalers and furniture makers, also find that healthy competition attracts buyers from out of town as well as suppliers' representatives. In contrast to this, the small grocery wholesaler intent on serving the local market would view the presence of many alert competitors as undesirable.

2. The aspect of competition and the small businessman's own ability and ambition. Where an inexperienced and less ambitious individual might rate progressive strong competition undesirable, an experienced, well-qualified, ambitious person might welcome such a situation as assurance of a healthy condition likely to make for greater permanence and stability. He would count on being able to get his fair share of the business.

RECENT DEVELOPMENTS AND PROBLEMS

Location tends toward greater permanency than many other aspects of business. When, as usual, a lease is involved, a business must anticipate the future correctly or continuously adapt to the changing conditions affecting its site. Ownership of the site aggravates this problem. For retail, wholesale, and service establishments the following are important: (1) purchasing power of potential customers; (2) their residence, place and kind of work, mode and avenues of transportation, education, means of communication, habits affecting business, age, family status, leisure, attitudes, wants, and desires; (3) shifts in kind of business, professional and administrative locations; (4) probable technological developments; (5) transportation and communication facilities; (6) social controls, both by government and nongovernment agencies; (7) unsolved problems of various types of locations; (8) economic, social and political forces; (9) attitudes and plans of those in a position to influence the future of a given location.

Potential Customers

For several decades the real purchasing power of consumers has been rising, more widely distributed, expanding the middle (income) class, favoring wage earners and nonteaching professionals, and used more generously for current consumption than for savings. Small retail and other establishments have shared this prosperity of *their* customers with resulting increase in purchasing power.

Our long-time trend toward urban residence is continuing. The postwar move from the center of cities to the suburbs has been partially checked so far with the building of central apartment houses and urban rehabilitation. At present we have a two-way flow of travel to work—into and out from the central city. This travel is by automobile in all but the few very large cities, such as New York and Chicago.

Large postwar families with both young parents working have been typical. Millions of teenagers with their own spending money will be augmented in the youth market from 1963 on by additional millions entering the labor force for the first time. Most of our 16 million persons who are 65 years old and over have ample purchasing power derived from pensions, social security, and private investment. The grandparents among them are liberal spenders. Senior citizen or retirement colonies have been spreading in Florida and the Southwest. Close-in apartment houses for the elderly have been constructed in many cities. In December 1959, the Federal government announced programs for housing for the elderly including assistance in financing home buying, rental housing, nursing homes, and low-rent public housing.

Our steadily expanding multibillion dollar leisure market will continue to affect locations and kinds of small business opportunities. The remaining developments mentioned at the beginning of this section are best covered in our subsequent discussion of types of location and significant trends.

Basic Factors

Many postwar locational developments appear to younger people to be without precedent. Usually they are merely new forms of adjustment by business to changing conditions. If we recognize this it should be easier to understand each development as it appears and to predict probable events in the near future at least. A few of these basics will be discussed briefly before we examine the developments of locational importance. Our comments here are limited to retail, wholesale, service, and many professional locations.

1. *Business always seeks maximum accessibility to its customers in terms of place, form, and time.* Place accessibility is the usual concept of site location: neighborhood, central business district, and feeder street or highway locations. Form accessibility includes the building and its facilities and increasingly adequate nearby parking. Time accessibility is indicated by the return to night and Sunday business hours.

2. *Certain conditions attract customers whereas others repel or discourage them.* The city itself is an excellent example, where its reputation, facilities, and character have always had varying degrees of pulling power for others. Adverse conditions may cause large numbers of people to avoid certain cities or business districts whenever possible. Retail affinities and store compati-

bility, discussed later, are especially important to the small enterprise. It is well known that certain clusters of stores, especially those featuring shopping goods, attract more customers than the same stores could if they were in isolated locations. Low prices, especially for food, has strong pulling power for many consumers. So does the presence of certain services and amenities.

3. *Intersections of well-traveled routes, access points, and transfer points have always been good locations.* Cities had their origin at such points but grew mainly in proportion to the employment they provided. At first this was commercial, but in modern times it has been mainly industrial employment. Postwar highway and some shopping center locations at such points are modern versions of the corner locations in our large cities where people transferred from one public vehicle to another.

4. *Established concerns frequently seek to avoid competition and to control other conditions.* In convenience goods fields—low priced, standardized items —this is understandable, especially where the market potential is limited. What makes this general tendency of special locational importance in postwar years has been the rise of controlled shopping centers and merchant cooperation to modernize downtown.

5. *The future should not be judged by the present alone.* A business may be in one place today, another tomorrow. Prewar central business districts did move, but *very* slowly. Postwar locational shifts and relevant developments have been much more rapid.

6. *Forerunners of major future developments are often crude and unimposing.* This was true of early chain stores, mail order houses, supermarkets, and shopping centers. More recently it has appeared in highway retailing.

7. *In the last analysis, cost, profit potentials, and future prospects are the final criteria of location.* Cost refers to acquisition, maintenance, and development expense. It varies for different locations. In some, rent may dominate; in others, advertising; thus the combined rent-advertising ratio to sales is superior to either ratio alone. Other expenses also vary: taxes, cooperative maintenance and promotion, customer services and amenities. Profit potentials and future prospects are estimates but usually can be made fairly accurately for short periods of time.

Retail and service establishment locations have much in common. Even wholesale locations have been influenced by many of the same factors affecting other locations. To lessen repetition we shall first consider major developments and factors, then later consider the special needs of each of these three fields.

Types of Locations

Downtown Locations. The first division is between downtown or central business districts and others. Downtown locations may be on the main street, on side streets, and in nonretail buildings. Up to early postwar years every city had its 100 per cent block or district where the heaviest concentration of shopper traffic was present—including branches of the national variety chains. This traffic was generated by the extensive advertising and pulling power of the leading department stores. Postwar decline in the relative importance of downtown in most cities has caused many variety chains and some department stores to abandon these formerly 100 per cent districts. The department stores that remain, however, are still the chief generators of pedestrian shopper traffic.

Downtown has become increasingly important as a center for administrative, financial, and professional services, while declining in relative importance for most lines of retailing and services. It still has the major hotels and convention facilities, libraries and other cultural attractions, bus terminals, financial institutions, and office buildings. Many new office buildings and close-in apartments have been erected downtown in recent years. So long as present conditions continue in most large cities, downtown stores will cater increasingly to three major classes of customers:

1. The downtown working people, who have characteristic buying habits and practices.
2. The "cliff dwellers" (apartment house occupants), who tend toward higher style and less casual wear.
3. The regional shoppers or occasional visitors.[2]

Stores and service establishments located in the large buildings—office, medical, and apartment—are typically small-scale independents. Many that locate on the street level, either on side streets or the main street, are also small independents. The best locations tend to intercept pedestrian traffic from large buildings attracted to the department store districts. The department stores are generative of retail shoppers, the building occupants are the potential shoppers. Stated differently, the same kind and size of store located between the large building and the department stores will do much better than if located at an equal distance from the building but in a direction *away* from the department stores.

Downtown has enjoyed over a century of retail supremacy. In many cities it still has the largest assortment of offerings in merchandise, professional services, finance, and administrative and cultural establishments. Although plagued with traffic congestion, parking problems, high occupancy expense and taxation, antiquated buildings, and slum areas, it is not dead yet. It may stage a comeback, slow and expensive, but ultimate. For department stores with suburban branches, the parent store downtown is often important— although Wanamaker's in Philadelphia and other onetime leading firms have closed their downtown store. Feeble efforts in some cities to promote the breadth of downtown offerings by the slogan "Downtown has everything," prompted some wit to add ". . . all bad!"

[2] Richard L. Nelson, *The Selection of Retail Locations* (New York: F. W. Dodge Corporation, 1958), p. 326.

Strenuous efforts are belatedly being made to revive or rehabilitate downtown. Results so far indicate that a mall alone is not enough. It requires good merchandising, not complacency and living in the past. Other one-time monopolies floundered on the same rocks. In modernizing Knoxville, Tennessee, and other cities, moving sidewalks from the parking lot to store access has been tried.[3] Parking appears to be more a matter of quality than quantity. Much of it is occupied by the cars of people who work in the central business district, and by those seeking only entertainment. It is expensive for the average shopper who has free parking available in shopping centers close to home. Established stores in many cities have been reluctant to reimburse customers adequately for their parking expense. One dubious policy is to limit the maximum any store will reimburse. Thus they value a customer who spends $25 with them on one day as highly as another customer who spends $500!

Downtown in many cities is still dominated by a few big department stores and property owners. So far neither has been alert to changing conditions and willing to take corrective actions. Nor were the railroads during their similar period of change. Before a small businessman decides on a location downtown many of these intangible factors should be investigated thoroughly.

In such huge cities as New York and Chicago, access to downtown has been over 90 per cent by public transportation for many decades. In almost all other large cities, however, public transit is woefully inadequate. As a municipally franchised monopoly it is sharing the fate of all one-time monopolies—stagnation and decay. It *may* be revived through generous public subsidy, which is doubtful, or through some technological breakthrough yet to appear. Wherever public transit is important to the value of downtown, the small businessman had best wait until this new version of "splitting the atom" appears and proves itself.

Many of the factors, such as retail affinities, compatibility, and locational characterizations soon to be discussed will have applications for downtown locations. But the general admonition to seek growing rather than declining (downtown) districts for locations is still relevant.

Outlying Locations. This designation covers any location outside of the traditional downtown or central business district. If certain recent trends continue it may soon be as obsolete as the early "horseless carriage" name for the automobile. Already new highway locations in many cities have rendered the former downtown an "outlying" location, and the huge interurbias, such as the 600 mile highway development from Maine to Virginia, with its almost uninterrupted business locations, are hardly "outlying" from the downtowns of the many towns they have bypassed. But for the immediate future, and for many cases, we can still use the designation "outlying" to advantage.

Nelson[4] recognizes five types of outlying retail locations: (1) major outly-

---

[3] *Business Week* (March 19, 1960), p. 47.
[4] Nelson, *op. cit.*, p. 95.

ing shopping districts, (2) neighborhood districts, (3) large outlying shopping centers, (4) small convenience shopping centers, (5) isolated or "on-your-own" locations. This classification, however, obviously slights many aspects of location significant to the small businessman as subsequent discussion will show. In particular, shopping centers, highway, and interceptor locations call for elaboration. First, a few concepts warrant explanation.

Locations and stores may be generative or suscipient. A generative location is one to which the consumer is directly attracted from his place of residence; to shop there is the principal purpose of the consumer in leaving his residence. Such a location is selected expressly to be easily accessible to the greatest proportion of persons away from home for the primary purpose of shopping.

A suscipient location is one to which the consumer is impulsively or coincidentally attracted while away from his place of residence for any primary purpose other than shopping. It takes or receives rather than generates business.

The value of a location for retailing depends upon four factors:

1. Its accessibility to the resident population.

2. Its accessibility to people moving about or gathering together on errands other than shopping.

3. Its physical desirability from the standpoint of grade or level, appearance, size, shape, neighborhood or district environment, and other amenities.

4. Its reputation—whether the location is prominent and well-known or obscure; whether it is associated in people's minds with something pleasant or unpleasant.

In most cases some aspects of both will be present, as a drugstore close to a supermarket. The drugstore may generate some prescription business and also enjoy drug sundry and impulse buying by many customers of the supermarket.

Most small stores and service establishments have little generative power, although many independent supermarkets and discount houses do have.

Small neighborhood districts are still important, especially for convenience goods in the big cities. Here trade comes from nearby residents. Our main interest, however, is with major postwar developments—especially shopping centers and highway locations.

Shopping Centers. These may be classified by (1) character of merchandise featured, (2) degree of integration, (3) layout and facilities, (4) size, (5) extent of control, and (6) sponsorship. These are not mutually exclusive classifications. Each deals with one aspect. Thus a supermarket may open a fairly large convenience goods center with inflexible control excluding other supermarkets.

We have convenience goods, and shopping goods centers. Convenience goods tend to be standardized items of relatively low unit price. Shopping goods are less, if at all, standardized and tend toward higher unit prices.

Examples include most wearing apparel and department store types of merchandise.

Earlier shopping centers were mere clusters of stores and service establishments each independently owned and operated. These are the familiar strip centers that often lack even a name for the center. Parking, if provided at all, consisted of space in front of each store and barely out of the main flow of automobile traffic. Not all of the land was necessarily owned by one person, although sometimes it was.

By layout and facilities we also have the new strip centers that provide off-street parking. Stores and parking run parallel to the traffic artery and sometimes on both sides of it. Some are L-shaped around a corner location. In these centers the first group to appear is usually on land owned by one person or a small group. Later other developments often take place adjacent to the first center but on property owned by different people. Such centers share a common parking space, often have a name for the entire center, but do less group promoting than the controlled centers. Often tenant selection is neither planned nor controlled.

Although there are many other shapes and layout arrangements that centers have taken, the trend in larger centers is toward the mall type. The mall may be simply an area reserved for pedestrian shoppers with all stores having access and visibility along its sides; many provide amenities such as greenery, flowers, protection from the elements, and even year-around air conditioning. Parking is outside the stores that surround the mall, on two, three, or four sides. Mall centers usually have two department stores with numerous independent and chain units between them on both sides of the mall.

By size, centers are neighborhood (usually specializing in convenience goods), community, and regional. Community centers may have from about 20 to 40 stores with ample assortments of shopping and convenience goods and services to serve the entire community or the part of town in which they are located. Regional centers are the largest, with 40 to over 100 stores. They expect to draw shoppers from well beyond the city limits. Although Nelson[5] objects to the designation "regional," it is in almost universal use.

Well-planned community and regional centers separate truck or service traffic from customer automobile traffic, frequently taking all service traffic underground.

Community and regional centers are planned, usually controlled, and operated as an integrated going concern. Tenants have leases that stipulate a minimum monthly rental plus a certain percentage of sales, often also above a stated minimum. Many tenants like this arrangement. The center management strives to have minimum guarantees sufficient to cover fixed financing and, usually, maintenance expense. The center advertises and promotes as a unit even though individual stores may also do their own advertising.

It is the control aspect of many centers that is most controversial and our

[5] *Ibid.,* p. 176.

immediate concern. Control refers to tenant selection and certain provisions in the leaseholds. To appreciate certain aspects of both we should first consider the various types of center sponsors.

Most large planned centers have been sponsored by industrial real estate promoters. Many have been promoted by department stores, and a few by supermarkets, discount houses, and corporate chains.

Many controlled centers sponsored by real estate promoters and department stores excluded discount houses and sometimes supermarkets. A natural reaction was for each of these types to launch their own centers. Often such centers give the sponsor an exclusive for his type of business. Since both supermarkets and discount houses are generative of shopper traffic they tend to attract smaller stores, both independent and chain, that capitalize on the presence of these shoppers. The character of shoppers may differ, however. Those attracted by the supermarket are usually interested in convenience goods; those drawn by the discount house usually behave more like department store bargain hunters. Although there may be exceptions, centers sponsored by department stores, supermarkets, and discount houses are less likely to feel the impact of financier's demands in tenant selection than those sponsored by real estate promoters. Their established financial rating and contacts are probable explanations.

Real estate promoters who sponsor large shopping centers require generous financing available chiefly from insurance companies and similar institutional lenders. These financiers insist upon well-established, financially strong, "big name" tenants. This usually means national corporate chains and *the* dominant local department store. With the power to make or break a developing center still in the planning stage these two types of retailing are able to dictate their own terms. Apparently many have done so, in any of three ways: very low rent, exclusive representation for their type of retailing, and restrictions on the type of merchandise that other tenant stores may carry.

In one community type center opened in the Southwest in 1960, a dominant independent department store branch and a "runner up" chain are the only two department store tenants. An overgrown variety store chain that insists on exclusive representation is the sole variety store present. One nationally known and highly regarded junior department store chain was refused admission. Branches of many well-established, but local, specialty stores are tenants but with odd restrictive leases, such as a leading high-style men's clothing store that is not permitted to carry men's suits or topcoats. At least this center has admitted many tenants known only locally! Our objective in this discussion is to inform prospective small business location seekers of what they may expect in some tightly controlled shopping centers. Examples cited could be duplicated from many other centers.

Three dangers arise from controlled shopping centers: excessive competition from other centers, government intervention, and interceptor highway enterprises.

Examples of competing centers launched by supermarket and discount houses have already been mentioned. Excluded tenants of other types, with the possible exception of department stores, are less likely to launch centers of their own. But they may provide the financial and prestige backing needed by new center developers. Thus one danger of too close control is the stimulation of competing centers that may exceed the local market potential. Normal free enterprise competition could also lead to launching more shopping centers than warranted by demand. In either case, operation of competitive forces will determine the outcome, but with results weighted against the center and those tenants that sought a monopoly through their attempts to obtain exclusives. Probably more serious for most shopping centers, and of special interest to small businessmen, is the expansion of highway retailing and service establishments.

Highway Locations

As early as 1958 some observers visualized highway retailing as the next revolution, comparable to the advent of supermarkets and discount houses.[6]

The source just cited coined the term "shopulation" to dramatize the great increase in mobility of our population and the extent that shopping has become motorized.

Many workers drive 50 miles each way daily in car pools. Women are doing more taxiing of family members and more shopping by car. Earlier distinctions between urban and rural people are blurred as highway business extends beyond city limits. This "shopulation" traffic comes from all classes, ages, occupations and other groups. More night and Sunday shopping takes place, often involving the whole family.

Although independents pioneered highway retailing chains and department stores have joined the movement, "solo" locations are common, especially for department stores, furniture and floor coverings retailers, supermarkets, and discount houses. Some groupings that exist have not yet repeated the former cluster patterns or retail affinities.

Highway stores are free of architectural and merchandising restrictions, price restraints, and coercion for group efforts found in integrated shopping centers. They can often capitalize on traffic drawn by the shopping centers, either as interceptors or spill-over recipients.

More "scrabbled merchandising" is appearing in highway locations. Restaurants carry a wide range of nonfoods. Discount houses carry foods, and supermarkets carry more nonfoods than usual. Automobile supermarkets carrying numerous makes are spreading. A likely expansion is outdoor, around-the-clock, automatic merchandising of an increasingly wide range of products.

In addition to the various types of shopping centers, the expansion of

[6] Weiss, E. B., *Highway Retailing—The Next Great Retail Revolution* (New York: Doyle, Dane, Bernbach, Inc., 1958).

drive-in businesses of all kinds is noteworthy. On arterial highways and string streets mere off-street parking may be sufficient for customary retail stores and service establishments. The newer types are based squarely on drive-in service where patrons do not need to leave their cars. These include about 200,000 drive-in theaters[7] and even more dairy products stands and snack bars, auto accessory stores, banks, and various combinations of batteries of vending machines accessible from the driver's seat, to conveyor systems for dispensing foods and refreshments.[8] A "motormat" restaurant in Los Angeles is representative of the latter type. A wheel-like layout has 20 parking stalls, each served by an electrically controlled food carriage. The motorist writes his order, puts it in the carriage with sufficient money to pay the bill, presses a button, and the carriage moves off to the kitchen. There an attendant fills the order, makes change on the bill, and sends the carriage back to the car. The motormat operates 16 hours a day and can serve 960 cars in that period.

For many independents our multi-billion dollar recreation market offers numerous opportunities for highway drive-ins, motels, and many types of business located in or en route to recreational areas. Since this market has expanded greatly in recent years, and appears likely to continue expanding with favorable economic conditions, there should be relatively more consumer wants not yet adequately provided for than in traditionally "necessary" fields. But the market is tricky and great care is needed to pick the right location. For tourist regions methods of measuring market potentials have been developed, such as those tested at the University of Miami and described in the footnote.[9]

Not all small cities appear to be favorable locations for the beginning enterpriser although the major trends suggest that many should have decided advantages over metropolitan areas. At one extreme is the very small town unfavorably situated with respect to future developments, where local businessmen have long since lost any hope for the future—the modern ghost town of current business progress. More significant are towns roughly in the 5,000 to 50,000 population range that have recently been fairly prosperous due to particular types of industries, defense or textile, or agriculture. Their future may be either up or down. Some danger signals in these towns are:

1. The need for high school and college graduates to leave town to find suitable employment.
2. Inability of residents to find jobs locally.
3. Declining retail sales and industrial production.

[7] Rodney Luther, "Marketing Aspects of Drive-In Theaters," *Journal of Marketing* (July 1950), pp. 41-47.

[8] Pearce C. Kelley, *Consumer Economics* (Homewood, Ill.: Richard D. Irwin, Inc., 1953), p. 227. *Automobile Facts* (September 1949), p. 7.

[9] Reinhold P. Wolff, "Estimating the Market Potential of a Floating Population," *Journal of Marketing* (July 1954), pp. 12-17.

4. An apathetic attitude on the part of local businessmen, educational administrators, and other residents.

Favorable signs include:

1. Opening of chain or department store branches.
2. Branch plants of large companies there either taking over existing buildings or constructing new ones.
3. A progressive chamber of commerce and other civic organizations.
4. Good schools and public services.
5. Well-maintained business and residential premises.
6. Good transportation facilities to other parts of the country.
7. Construction activity accompanied by an absence of vacant buildings and unoccupied homes or houses for sale.

One approach is to determine the relationships between population and each kind of store under consideration. The number of persons required to support a representative independent store varies greatly according to how specialized or widespread is its merchandise appeal; highly specialized stores, such as toys or sporting goods, may require 100 times as large a population to draw from as those having an almost universal market, as groceries or food service.

Sample calculations using data from the 1958 Census of Business indicate that the number of persons per store increased from 1939 to 1958 for different kinds of retailing from 10 to 50 per cent, reflecting: (1) the relative stability in number of stores, (2) increased population, (3) larger disposable incomes, (4) higher operating costs and price levels, and (5) larger profit margins. Table 4 shows the population required on the average to support 13 different kinds of retailing in the early 1950's. Specific ratios for a particular kind of business and its location as of the most recent year may be calculated from U. S. Department of Commerce estimates of the number of stores and Census Bureau estimates of population. They are still averages, however, and should be treated as such.

TABLE 4. POPULATION REQUIRED FOR SELECTED KINDS OF RETAILING*

Grocery	500	Jewelry	5,000
Restaurant	800	Florist	7,000
Drugstore	1,200	Appliance store	8,000
Bakery	2,500	Sporting goods	45,000
Hardware	2,700	Photo supply store	60,000
Shoe store	3,400	Toy store	70,000
Women's clothing	4,000		

* Source: *Going Into Business For Yourself*, Kiplinger Washington Agency, Inc. (reprinted from "Changing Times," *The Kiplinger Magazine*), p.14.

Any state or city may deviate considerably from the average for the entire country; it may be difficult except for census years to secure data for a particular town; and even when data are available they indicate merely the *status quo*. Despite these limitations this approach is useful to the beginner, especially if ratios for the kind of business being considered are determined for the entire country, his state or region, and his particular town. For large cities ratios may also be estimated for the particular retail district under study. In using ratios such as these it should be remembered that different kinds of stores vary considerably in drawing power or trading area; ladies' fashion apparel may attract customers from several miles away whereas a drugstore or grocery may be limited to its immediate neighborhood. The composition of different communities may also cause deviations from the average; where most families are large and have many children, food expenditures as well as those for children's wear are likely to be well above average, just as in a district containing an unusually high proportion of sportsmen sales in this line may be substantially above average.

Methods of evaluating shopping areas include:

1. Taking license numbers from parked cars and then locating the owners' addresses from the tag registration office.

2. Checking newspaper circulation which usually covers a trading area.

3. Sending questionnaires to people to find out where they buy.

4. Interviewing local merchants.

5. Securing addresses of customers from established stores in the territory, or by interviewing customers as they leave the store.

6. Asking local bankers from what territory they draw depositors.

7. Surveys on origin and destination of traffic from city and county planning commissions or the state highway department or tourist bureau.

8. Special census surveys from the U. S. Department of Commerce or its regional offices.

9. Marking on a city map the neighborhood shopping areas. By drawing intersecting circles, the city can be divided into rough potential trading areas. Purchasing power and competition in each area then can be investigated.

The purchasing power of a trading area may be estimated by the following methods among others:

1. The volume of retail trade.

2. Number of telephones per thousand population.

3. Number and makes of cars per thousand population.

4. Data on rent paid from census reports or on the value of homes owned from real estate agents and the county assessor.

5. Number of bank depositors per thousand population.

6. Analysis of the wealth produced within the area: value added by facto-

ries and extractive industries, value of crops sold, and other sources of income.
7. School and utility figures.[10]

Certain recently published data furnish a basis for calculating income and purchasing power by towns, counties, cities and states. A study by Standard Rate and Data Service based on 1950 census of population data has: (1) adjusted the data to 1951, (2) concentrated distribution into four income groups, and (3) estimated the aggregate dollars of income in each place.[11] The annual Buying Power Issue of *Sales Management,* and other sources may at times be used.

The case study approach has also been employed to measure the trading area of a city as reported in the footnote references.[12] Five methods were used and both techniques and results reported in the two articles.

A booklet, published in 1954 to aid small businessmen and chambers of commerce in small and medium-sized communities in analyzing their trading areas, is recommended reading, especially where co-operation can be secured from the retailers in the district.[13]

THE RETAIL LOCATION

Although in retailing the major location problems of the small businessman center around the selection of the best site within a town, some consideration should be given to the choice of the town, especially with reference to its size and general character. Also, since certain types of retail districts, such as suburban shopping centers, are found only in the larger cities, an examination of the main classes of towns and what each offers in retail locations is the logical starting point.

Policies concerning the clientele desired and customer services to be offered will influence both selection of the town and the site within it. Important factors to consider include income levels, buying habits and preferences of the customers, and the character of existing stores. In general, high-priced merchandise requires a trading area of above-average income, a more refined or exclusive shopping district, and the presence of suitable environment or "atmosphere." Certain merchandising policies may dictate the need for special locations. An example is concentration on a restricted line of goods that has appeal to highly specialized groups because of taste, racial or religious beliefs, or similar factors that vary from the average town's composition.

[10] *Better Retailing* (Dayton, Ohio: National Cash Register Co., Merchants Service, 1949), pp. 2-2, 2-3.
[11] Joseph H. White, "SRDS' Estimates of Local Consumer Incomes," *Journal of Marketing* (October 1953), pp. 146-54.
[12] Edna Douglas, "Measuring the General Retail Trading Area—A Case Study: I," *Journal of Marketing* (April 1949), pp. 481-97; II, *Journal of Marketing* (July 1949), pp. 46-60.
[13] I. V. Fine, *Retail Trade Area Analysis* (Madison, Wisconsin: University of Wisconsin Bureau of Business Research and Service, 1954).

Once the policies are formulated and the region selected, the next job is to appraise the present and future prospects of each town under consideration. Wholesalers and manufacturers can often help, as can agencies of the federal, state, or local governments, chambers of commerce, local banks, building and loan associations, and real estate agencies. The activities of the larger chain stores in establishing or closing branches in the town can serve as an indirect but usually reliable indicator. A personal investigation should be made of the town to compare it with others as well as to select the area and possible sites within it. At this time the check list referred to at the beginning of the chapter should be used.

Statistics showing the breakdown of family expenditures are available for the United States as a whole and are classified by type of community, location, occupation, size of family, and size of money income. These data may be obtained from the Bureau of Labor Statistics of the U. S. Department of Labor, and the Bureau of Human Nutrition and Home Economics of the U. S. Department of Agriculture.[14]

The size of a trading area, for a community or for a store, will depend largely on competition, especially from neighboring towns or trading areas. Competition in either case will express itself in lower prices or better quality, wider assortments or greater services. In general, as towns increase in size their trading areas increase at a much greater rate than the town's population.

The kind of work pursued by the majority of the local population is an important factor in selecting a community in which to locate. A suburban area made up largely of professional leaders and business executives contrasts notably with a densely populated district located on the "wrong side of the tracks."

Both the amounts of money paid to workers in different occupations, and the regularity and frequency of payments, differ. Some communities serving farmers must expect to grant long-term credit; others do a week-to-week credit business, because their customers are paid weekly. The cash business volume of many communities fluctuates abruptly with the regular pay days of establishments in which sizable groups of citizens are employed.

Preference should be given to a growing town. A rare opportunity would be needed to compensate for a static population or one that shows a declining trend. We have reference here to fundamental, long-time trends. It is always possible that with enlightened civic leadership and favorable conditions— especially something like the rerouting of a major highway—a static or declining town may stage a rebirth.

Size of Town

For the small businessman the size of the town to be selected deserves study. The type of business may limit his choice of town size. Some kinds of

[14] See also, Kelley, *op. cit.*, Chap. 12, and other recent publications reporting family spending patterns.

stores, such as photographic supply houses, usually require a town no smaller than 50,000. Drug, stationery, and variety stores ordinarily supply customer needs for photo equipment in towns smaller than 50,000.

There are certain trades that are naturals for the small town. For each of the following more than 40 per cent of the nation's total business was done in towns under 5,000 population:

Type of Business	*Per Cent of National Sales*
General stores	92
Hay, grain, and feed stores	63
Farm implement, tractor, hardware dealers	60
Farm and garden supply stores	49
Filling stations	42
Dry goods and small merchandise stores	41
Hardware stores	41

Variety stores, lunch counters and stands, drugstores, and liquor stores appear to do equally well in both small and large communities. On the other hand, large department stores, delicatessens, optical shops, and individual stores for the sale of office and school supplies, cameras, photographic supplies, fruits and vegetables, furs, books, and cigars are likely to be missing from the small town Main Street. Most of the merchandise handled by the above businesses, however, is found in the smaller town but in different kinds of stores.[15]

Although payroll is normally the largest item of expense in all retail stores, many small-scale retailers, at least at the start, actually hire few, if any, employees. This moves rent up to first place in terms of expense items that must be paid. Data assembled by Dun & Bradstreet, by sizes of town and store sales volume groups, show that for 33 major lines of business in almost all cases occupancy expense increases as a percentage of net sales from the smaller to the larger towns. This is true for each group of stores classified according to sales volume. Also, for each trade, the rent percentage decreases with increased volume for each city size group.

When the kind of business is not an important factor influencing the size of town, there still may be other considerations. From time to time there are periods when the importance of smaller towns increases. This may occur for any of a number of reasons, such as decentralization of industry, increased public interest in small communities in general, or the prosperous conditions of a great many small towns resulting from a high level of farm incomes. As noted earlier, business expenses in most small towns are still low both on an absolute and a relative basis.

There are at least two more ways in which the size of the town should

[15] Nelson A. Miller, "Small Town a Most Important Market," *Domestic Commerce* (August 1944), p. 3.

be considered. All of the larger chain organizations have a minimum size limit such as 5,000 for towns in which they will locate. This spells two opportunities to the small businessman.

1. For the strictly independent merchant it means that he will not be forced to meet direct local chain store competition. It gives him a chance to study chain methods and other examples of modern big city retailing in larger communities and bring them to the small town, to his own, and the residents', advantage. The reason chains do not open their own stores in towns below a minimum size is based on the volume needed to support the higher total necessary expenses of a company-owned store. Thus the progressive independent is given reasonable assurance of his protected position. This does not mean that chain store competition is bad and should be avoided in all cases. It is rather a question of each type, independent or chain, capitalizing on its respective inherent advantages. Where an independent has direct chain competition, he is more likely to succeed if he fits his operations into those of the chain, rather than attempting to meet the chain on its strongest grounds. Where no chain competition is present, the field is wide open for the independent, who may later expand into his own chain store system.

2. The second opportunity arises where a small businessman would like to affiliate with a large and successful merchandising organization such as one of the chains or large manufacturers in the automobile tire and accessory fields. Several corporate chains, like Walgreen's, Gamble-Skogmo, and Schulte-United, have agency or franchise plans for independent merchants in small communities. These voluntaries have developed a system of selecting locations for affiliated stores that is comparable to corporate chain methods.

Selecting the District within a Town

In large cities there may be only one important central shopping district, but frequently there are several such districts, usually adjacent to one another, and each noted for a particular price range or kind of goods, such as the general department and specialty store district, women's department and specialty store district, women's apparel district, men's clothing district, and others. Each central area will have one or more streets parallel to the main street and several at right angles to it. The latter are the secondary retail areas. Most of the centrally located, smaller retail stores and some service establishments will be found here.

Leading out from the central district will be "string" streets connecting this district with various sources of customer traffic. Some of these streets are main traffic arteries. Specialized districts with stores and shops catering to automobile traffic grow up along these traffic lanes, frequently for many blocks outward from the central district.

In addition to the central districts, there will be outlying or suburban shopping centers that have been growing in importance for several decades. Then there are the neighborhood or convenience goods districts. A substantial portion of the total retail sales in the large city is completed outside the central shopping area, and the proportion of the number of stores in the outlying districts is even greater.

Usually the rent-paying capacity of the proposed line of business will determine whether one can afford to locate in a central retail district. Certain lines of business, such as cigar, drug, shoe, and dime stores; women's apparel and men's hat stores; auto accessories, food service, barber shops, and department stores, are able to stay in the high rent group. Furniture and furnishings, hardware, and food stores generally must stay in the low rent group. Table 5 lists important characteristics of stores suitable to each district.

TABLE 5. Factors Influencing Rent Ratios*

High Rent	*Low Rent*
1. High value of merchandise in proportion to bulk.	1. Low value of merchandise in protion to bulk.
2. Window display highly important.	2. Large amount of floor space for interior display.
3. High rate of turn-over.	3. Low rate of turn-over.
4. Low gross margin.	4. High gross margin.
5. Pick-up and convenience lines of goods sold.	5. Shopping lines sold in addition.
6. Appeal to transient trade.	6. Established clientele.
7. Little newspaper advertising.	7. Much advertising and soliciting.
8. Price and convenience stressed.	8. Uses features of various kinds to attract customers.
9. Low overhead.	9. High overhead.

* Helen G. Canoyer, *Selecting a Store Location*, Economic Series No. 56 (Washington, D. C.: U. S. Department of Commerce, 1946), p. 13.

In selecting a district within a city, factors in addition to the rent-paying capacity of the kind of business deserve attention. The more important ones are the nature of the merchandise to be carried, clientele desired, and volume size of the store to be operated. The last may manifest itself as a preference for a large volume, or a size limit imposed by financial resources.

In general, convenience goods stores locate wherever a sufficient number of potential customers have quick and easy access to the store. Usually they are large-volume units able to justify the high rents demanded for such sites. This may be on streets of heavy transient traffic, in outlying shopping centers, in well-populated neighborhoods, in industrial or other business areas, as well as in the downtown shopping center. Small food stores, notions and variety stores, small drugstores, and similar enterprises often do better outside the larger shopping centers and closer to the homes of their customers.

Shopping goods require a location in one of the shopping districts. This may be the central area or one of the suburban or outlying shopping districts or centers.

Class of trade desired. Class of trade desired influences the choice of retail district in either of two ways, with reference to income class, or according to some special occupational grouping. In most cities certain districts are more "exclusive" than others. The central shopping district formerly had three fairly well-defined sections, each patronized primarily by high-, medium-, or low-income classes respectively. Some of the more common occupational groups that often have retail subdistricts are: financial and business executives, office workers, hotel guests, and students in various types of schools.

Volume size of store. The volume size of the store to be operated has a direct bearing on selecting the retail district. Usually only large-volume stores, for each line of merchandise, can locate in the central shopping district. For the fairly small-volume stores it may be preferable to choose a central or secondary district in a smaller town rather than the relatively poor districts available in the larger cities.

Specialization by type of merchandise carried tends to be greater in the central district. The "women's" side and the "men's" side of the street are usually well defined. The individual who desires to locate in such a district must be able to justify the higher overhead characteristic of the location. He should have the advantage of merchandising experience, ample capital, and command of buying sources to a higher degree than the neighborhood storekeeper, for not only must he compete with other stores selling the same or similar goods; he also must vie for the consumer's dollar with all other kinds of stores.

Naturally the number and variety of retail districts decreases with the size of the town. In small towns there may be only one shopping district with a few grocery stores scattered around in neighborhood locations.

Selecting the Retail Site

Probably in no other field of business is the best site as important a factor in determining the success of a business as it is in retailing. Some studies have found poor location to be among the chief causes of retail failures.[16] Since the typical store depends for profit upon a sufficient number of customers coming into it or telephoning their orders for delivery within an economical radius, customer accessibility is an all-important consideration. Retail customers are creatures of shopping habits that are not easily changed.

Some merchants utilize shopping traffic where they find it; others try to attract shoppers to their stores by means of advertising. Rent and advertising expenses are often so closely related in the retail business that their relationships should be understood. We are now referring to expenses incurred for advertising in media outside of the store. This qualification is necessary here because the current tendency is to regard a store's windows as its most valuable advertising medium.

[16] Helen G. Canoyer, *op. cit.,* p. 1.

Rent is a payment for the opportunity to make a profit by selling merchandise. The highest rents are paid for locations having the greatest volume of profitable shopper traffic. Competition for these locations tends to keep the rent up to the maximum that can be paid for their most effective use by the most efficient businessmen. A profitable business may be operated in these so-called "100 per cent" locations without expenditure for external advertising. The classic example of this was the former location of chain variety stores. For years these chains have followed the location policy of selecting sites in the line of customer shopping traffic built up and maintained by the larger department stores through their established reputations and continuous advertising. The variety stores, however, do little external advertising.[17]

By contrast to variety stores, consider a specialty store, such as an apparel retailer, furniture, house furnishing, or even a hardware or complete food store located close to the large department stores or variety chains. Sufficient business can usually be obtained from the regular shopping traffic passing the store. However, these stores often find it pays to advertise: first, because they carry shopping goods that are suitable to advertising; second, because their central location makes possible effective use of the low-cost-per-reader mass media like newspapers; and third, because they can often "ride the tail" of department store advertising. Shoppers coming to the center anyway will often respond to these advertisements; they will be customers who might not make a special trip in response solely to the smaller store's advertisement.

Next consider one of these specialty stores located several blocks from the major shopping district. The lower rent paid for these locations involves higher necessary advertising expense, as well as cost of customer inducement to patronize the store. Although the returns per dollar of advertising expenditure alone may be less for these fringe stores, the combined effect of low rent and moderate advertising may be very profitable. Thus it is the rent-advertising combination that is the second largest item of expense in all retail stores.

The beginning small retailer may find the number of usable sites available to him to be very limited. This is especially true during periods of good business activity. An understanding of site selection may enable him, however, at least to choose the least undesirable location of those available. The established small retailer will usually have the advantage of the beginner in being able to wait a few years to secure a more desirable site later.

The following factors are usually of maximum importance in retail site selection: environment, accessibility, nature of the building, rent and terms of the lease, and, in older districts, history of the site. Sometimes unusual restrictive ordinances may be encountered that would make one otherwise ideal site less desirable than another, such as limitations on the hours of the day when trucks are permitted to load or unload. Zoning and similar regula-

[17] Pearce C. Kelley, "The Fundamentals of Chain Store Location" (M.A. thesis, University of California, Berkeley, 1924). Unpublished.

tions are usually of minor importance, unless an individual attempts to open a store in an area restricted against business.

Environment. A retail store, like an individual, should keep the right company. Under the broad term "environment" come the subjects of "affinities," competition, and unfavorable conditions. It is well known that certain kinds of stores do well when located close to each other. Customers who patronize stores of one type in such a group are the best prospects for others in the same "affinity" class. One study of these natural clusterings of stores of various kinds disclosed the following combinations:

> DEPARTMENT STORES—women's clothing (appear in 35.2 per cent of all blocks in which there are department stores), shoe, variety, drug, men's furnishing, and millinery stores.
>
> VARIETY STORES—women's clothing (appear in 60.7 per cent of the blocks that have variety stores), shoe, department, jewelry, men's furnishing, and millinery stores.
>
> SHOE STORES—weak affinity for women's clothing, department, variety, men's furnishing stores, and restaurants.
>
> JEWELRY STORES—no strong affinities; most frequent neighbors are restaurants, shoe stores, and men's furnishing stores.
>
> FURNITURE STORES—restaurants (found in 40 per cent of the blocks that contain furniture stores), men's furnishing, shoe, and women's clothing stores.
>
> FLORISTS—restaurants (found in 47.5 per cent of the blocks that contain florist shops), women's clothing, drug, and shoe stores.
>
> THEATERS—strong affinity for restaurants (found in 58.5 per cent of the blocks that contain theaters), jewelry, men's furnishing, and shoe stores.
>
> WOMEN'S CLOTHING—variety (found in 60.7 per cent of the blocks that contain women's clothing stores), department, and shoe stores.
>
> MILLINERY SHOPS—women's clothing, variety, shoe, and department stores.
>
> FURS—furniture stores, florists, and shoe stores.
>
> CANDY STORES—theaters, jewelry, variety stores, and florists.
>
> MEN'S FURNISHINGS—restaurants, furniture stores, theaters, and men's shoe stores.
>
> HABERDASHERY—jewelry and men's furnishing stores.
>
> TOBACCO STORES—shoe, jewelry stores, and theaters.
>
> RESTAURANTS—florists, theaters, furniture, and jewelry stores.
>
> DRUGSTORES—may appear near any stores, except furniture. (Twenty-five to 35 per cent of all central shopping district blocks contain drugstores.)
>
> CURTAIN STORES—near furniture stores.
>
> PAINT STORES—near furniture stores.
>
> SHOE REPAIR SHOPS—may appear near any stores, except department or variety.
>
> BARBER SHOPS—near florists, theaters, and jewelry stores.
>
> GROCERY STORES—seldom appear in the central shopping district.

Proximity to offices of professional men is desirable, especially in outlying shopping centers. People having appointments with doctors, dentists, lawyers, and so on, quite often will become shoppers if stores are conveniently accessible.[18]

Customers are people with habit patterns and buying needs that are often associated with other activities, as the foregoing study illustrates. The same type of analysis may disclose other natural business groupings. For example, in recent years launderettes have been established in thousands of towns. What does the woman who brings in her clothes do during the fifteen or twenty minutes while the Bendix does the work? She shops in nearby stores to fill frequently recurring needs for items such as groceries, variety goods, and possibly magazines or similar articles.

In contrast to complementary or related store groupings, certain kinds of stores do better if not located close together. For the exclusive sale of convenience goods, unless the customer traffic is unusually heavy, stores of the same kind do not locate close to competitors. An apparent exception to this generalization arises where an alert independent in the drug, variety, or similar line finds advantageous a location adjacent to a chain store in the same line. The "spillover" traffic attracted to the chain may provide sufficient business for the independent. By making his mercandise offerings fit in with those of the chain he may secure additional volume. This means that some of the chain's customers who normally buy standardized popular styles or colors will be attracted by similar goods in novel designs, unusual colors, or other variations. Good examples of this will be found in party novelties, popular-price gift items, unusual but low-price toys, and seasonal greeting cards.

The small independent's natural tendency is to want to avoid competing stores. The foregoing discussion should demonstrate that often locations close to the right kind of competitors are especially desirable.

Earlier discussion of controlled shopping centers shows that many large retailers also seek to avoid competition and the probable dangers resulting from such monopoly-seeking objectives.

In smaller cities where controlled shopping centers have not yet developed, as an aid to appraising competition a plot of the district may be made, such as that illustrated in Figure 1.

There are certain neighbors, in addition to the wrong kind of retail store, that usually are undesirable for nearly any kind of retailer. Proximity to places that are normally avoided by shoppers—funeral parlors, cemeteries, hospitals, establishments of ill repute, and industries having disagreeable noises or odors—is unfavorable. Some such environmental conditions may be temporary, such as broken sidewalks, vacant lots or stores, and construction in progress, but during the time they exist shopping traffic will shun the vicinity.

Accessibility. For the small retailer accessibility is mainly a question of the ease with which his customers can reach the store. A site with the

[18] Canoyer, *op. cit.,* p. 20.

heaviest volume of pedestrian traffic including his potential customers would be ideal except that the rent might be beyond his means. Accessibility to pedestrian traffic for other sites will be influenced by distance from the traffic generators, terrain, dangerous street crossings or other hazards, and similar factors. The nature of the entrance may be important if it is even slightly above sidewalk level, or if the store has an off-the-street location, such as an upper floor.

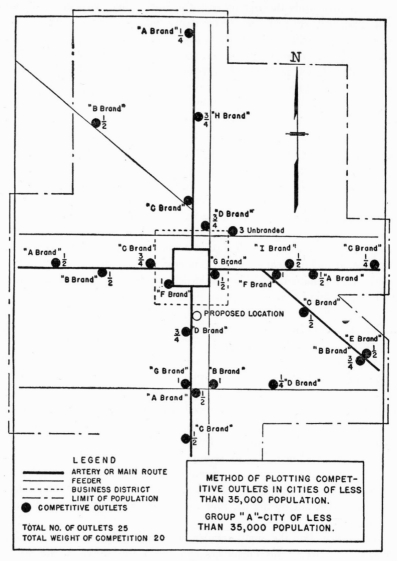

FIGURE 1. Plotting competitive outlets.
Source: Helen Canoyer, *Selecting a Store Location*, p. 28.

To an increasing extent accessibility should be considered in terms of automobile travel and parking facilities, except in the downtown districts of metropolitan centers as already discussed.

Traffic analysis. From careful analysis of experience in numerous outlets, chain stores know the approximate sales value of each pedestrian passing a given location. Pedestrian traffic can thus be used as a direct guide to the evaluation of any site. The small independent retailer can utilize chain methods in comparing and appraising various possible locations. Two factors are especially important: total pedestrian traffic during business hours, and the percentage of it that is likely to enter the store.

In making traffic counts, the checker should select a few half-hour periods, especially during the normally busy hours of the day. Only possible customers for the particular kind of business should be counted, with men and women recorded separately. Children may also be put in a separate category if they are likely customers. Even two 15-minute counts daily will enable the analyst to estimate the total eight-hour traffic fairly accurately.[19]

To estimate the probable number of pedestrians who would enter a given kind of store, sample counts may be made of the percentage of them that enters stores of the same kind in each district. The results may be checked against similar surveys made by other agencies.[20]

The mode of transportation used by customers is important. When most customers come to the store in their own cars, a site several blocks from the shopping center that has ample parking space is more accessible than a so-called "100 per cent" site. Corner locations with entrances on each street have similar advantages for pedestrian traffic.

The accessibility of a site is sometimes related to the sequence of shopping. For example, food stores located on the right-hand side of an artery leading away from a major shopping district are more accessible because grocery customers usually shop on the way home, whereas a laundry or dry cleaner located on the right-hand side going into town is more accessible because customers prefer to unload the wash or cleaning before continuing to town.

Store building. Most retailers rent rather than construct the store building. Of major importance to the small retailer is that the building be suitable to his type of business, or that it could be made so, preferably at the landlord's expense. The former will be discussed in Chapter 15; the latter is part of our next topic.

Rent and terms of the lease. Two types of lease agreements are used in retailing—the flat rate and percentage lease. Under the flat rate plan, an annual rental of a definite amount payable monthly in advance is stipulated in the lease. For each line of retailing this amount should be consistent with

[19] Pearce C. Kelley, *A Traffic Survey of Salt Lake City* (Salt Lake City: Bureau of Economic and Business Research, University of Utah, 1931).

[20] P. D. Converse, "Retail Store Location." *Opinion and Comment* (May 17, 1947), pp. 22-23.

the standard operating ratios in the field, modified according to the size of store, size of town, and the combined rent-advertising ratios discussed earlier. The percentage lease usually guarantees the landlord a minimum monthly rental, with additional payments at some percentage of sales agreed upon by both parties. For either type of lease, however, the objective is to stay in line with the standard rent ratio or to compensate for any deviation by more or less advertising, superior managerial ability, or similar considerations. Consequently, the standard ratio for the particular line of business should be known, and the rental demanded for any site under consideration should be appraised in terms of the site's potential volume of sales and the volume necessary to achieve this ratio.

Leases may be secured for from one to ten years or more. Usually it is desirable for the beginning retailer to get a one- or two-year lease with an option on renewal for five to ten years at an agreed rental. This is not always possible, but he should bargain for the best terms at the time the lease is under discussion. In newer districts where a ten year lease is involved volume estimates for rent ratios and space requirements should aim at the third year estimate.

The lease usually provides for many other important points, such as any remodeling to be done, who is to pay for it, liabilities and duties assumed by each party, permission or authority for the tenant to erect certain external signs, engage in additional lines of business, or make alterations to the premises in the future if needed. If the landlord owns adjacent property, it is sometimes possible to incorporate in the lease provisions governing the kinds of business for which these sites will be rented. A lease is an important legal document, and the small businessman should always seek competent legal counsel before entering into a formal lease agreement.[21]

Site history. At least the *recent* history of each site under consideration should be known by the prospective retailer before he makes a final selection. Although most Americans no longer believe in haunted houses, experienced merchants know that hoodoo locations do exist. These are sites that have been occupied by a succession of retail failures. Naturally there are logical reasons why the site has not been a successful one at certain times in the past, but there are also the dangers that prospective customers have formed a habit of avoiding the location, or that the next prospective renter will overestimate his ability to succeed where his predecessors have failed.

Several concrete examples of such hoodoo locations are familiar to the authors. One that was under continuous observation for over 14 years was occupied by eight different businesses in addition to one operated at a loss by the landlord, and was vacant for several years. Directly across the street was a restaurant that was in operation throughout the entire period. Within

---

[21] See also: *What Type of Lease Should You Sign?*, Small Business Aids No. 507 (Washington, D. C.: U. S. Department of Commerce, 1950); and Morton L. Leavy, *Law For the Small Businessman* (New York: Oceana Publications, 1952).

the same block with the hoodoo location were several prosperous stores. At one time, under the pressure of taking any site that would "keep the rain off the merchandise," an out-of-town merchant opened a branch store in this site. The firm remained in business for several years before finally abandoning the location but required numerous promotions and distress sales to do so.

If this guide is used carefully the chances of making a poor choice will be greatly lessened, and if a number of different sites are available, selection of the best will be assured. It is assumed that the beginner will know his business well enough to assign proper weights to each factor listed.

To illustrate recommended procedure for site selection, the following advice prepared by the trade association of independent tire dealers is presented.

> Select a site on a main thoroughfare, preferably on one of the main streets leading from the good retail shopping district to the better-class residential area of the city. Keep as close as convenient to the retail shopping district without encountering conditions of traffic congestions. Your location should be on the right-hand side of the street "going home" from work—on the near corner if there is a traffic light—on the far corner if no light. A mid-block position is not as good as a corner location except when the corner location is subject to constant traffic congestion. Be sure that the property permits easy ingress and egress and that the speed of traffic does not interfere with access to your driveways. Avoid locations where traffic speed exceeds 20 to 25 m.p.h. and give consideration to easy entrance for trucks as well as automobiles. Be sure that property will accommodate all the service facilities you propose to operate. Also be sure that the space is available to accommodate trucks. Make certain that local ordinances or zoning laws will not interfere with your projected operations.
>
> Make sure that curb passage for cars entering or leaving your establishment can be secured. It is advisable to check with the city Street Department. Do not locate too near to a firehouse where the street may frequently be blocked with fire apparatus. Guard against rear alleys which may frequently be crowded with trucks and vans from nearby warehouses. As a further consideration, keep in mind the factor of identification visibility for your establishment.
>
> Be sure that the property is large enough for your purpose and can easily be modified to meet your expanding needs in the future. Check into the building construction to make certain that it will be strong enough to stand the required load stress. Carefully investigate the condition of the heating plant, electric wiring, plumbing, roof, ceiling, basement, toilet and disposal facilities. An insurance broker should be consulted to be sure that the property is insurable.
>
> If you intend to modernize the property, permission to do so must be incorporated in your lease. The cost of such modernization should be considered as a rent expense to be amortized over the period of the lease. The rental rate should be specific and the rent you pay should range between 2 and 4 per cent of your projected sales volume—depending on the size of the market. If the landlord agrees to bear the whole or part of the modernization costs, see to it that these provisions are adequately incorporated in the lease.

Be sure that your lease does not prohibit your adding any service functions which you may want to add to your operation. Be sure that the local building and fire laws and regulations will make it possible for you to make the desired improvements or changes necessary for the operation of your business.[22]

THE SMALL WHOLESALER'S LOCATION

Small wholesalers are widely distributed over the country, many being located in very small towns in the 5,000 population class. In the long established lines—groceries, hardware, drugs, dry goods, and general merchandise —these wholesalers are relatively quite small in terms of volume of business as compared with the average in each line. In such fields, the country for some time has been pretty well provided with wholesale establishments that many years ago passed the "small" stage. These firms continue to operate in towns where they were originally established 20 to 50 years ago. Annual sales volume of many of these houses, even in towns of the 10,000 population class, runs close to the $1,000,000 mark. In some of the newer fields, such as wholesaling of electrical goods, radios, certain appliances, and various specialties, small town markets have not been so profusely supplied from local wholesale houses. In both new and old fields, however, there has been an influx of newcomers operating as small businessmen.

Selecting the Town

Usually the small wholesaler depends more on the local market; that is, retailers within his town or within a trading area radius of less than 10 miles. This means that the income in the community is of major importance in selecting a location. In this respect the small wholesaler emphasizes the same location factor as do his retailer customers, except that a wholesaler is also interested in the incomes of adjacent towns.

There are a few situations where a wholesaler's selection of the region or town is influenced by important factors other than the income of the town's immediate trading area. Four, in particular, deserve mention. If a wholesaler, even though he starts on a small scale, has definite ambitions to expand rapidly and aspires to sectional or national distribution, it would be wise for him to locate in one of the key distributing centers for his line of goods.

With the recent expansion of franchise and cooperative group plans a beginning wholesaler may wish to consider affiliation with one of them in the near future. Such an ambition may influence his choice of location.

A third example would be a small wholesaler in a specialized line where the customers are small manufacturers and manufacturing retailers located in a few well-defined market centers. At one time Southern California had

[22] *Planning Your Business* (Washington, D. C.: The National Association of Independent Tire Dealers, Inc., 1945), p. 10.

many special or custom built automobile body factories served by a few such wholesalers. Our fourth example is the middleman—a functional wholesaler, the resident buying office, or the purchasing agent. He must of necessity be located in the major markets, such as New York for women's wear or Chicago for furniture.

The small wholesaler is primarily interested in a town with stability of income, diversified industry (including agriculture) in the trading area, prosperous retail stores, and competition. The last named includes competition from other wholesalers in nearby towns. In special cases an individual may also lay some stress on availability of local financing, local taxes, and the attitudes of established businessmen.

Personal factors play a major role in the selection of the region and often the town in which many small wholesalers locate. A large majority of small wholesale houses develop in one of two ways. The first is when an established retailer experiments with quantity buying and starts selling at "wholesale" to other retailers. In the grocery field this has happened numerous times. First the retailer buys a carload of feed, flour, sugar, or other staple. Sometimes the first order is the result of pooling with one or more nearby merchants. When storage space at the retail site is exhausted, this retailer-wholesaler seeks a building for which the rent is smaller and the location is more convenient for wholesaling activities. Such cases include many other lines like hardware, electrical goods, radios and parts, automobile accessories, and seed and feed. Since the town was automatically selected by virtue of the retailer's original location, this shows the influence of the personal factor.

A second way in which many small wholesalers start occurs when a salesman for a wholesale house teams up with an experienced wholesale bookkeeper or office man, with or without additional "family" financing. The salesman spots a promising territory and may have it under observation for several years before selecting the best town in which to locate. Often the salesman has also become interested in a girl in the territory. Marriage, pooling of financial resources, and selecting the new family's home town for the wholesale location seem to go together. An example that recently came to the authors' attention was a traveling accountant who had specialized in auditing freight bills for wholesalers. After many years of this kind of experience he started his own wholesale grocery in a small town in the Southwest, where he has done remarkably well.

Well-informed persons estimate that as high as 90 per cent of all small wholesale houses are started in either of the two ways just discussed. Those resulting from a retailer's expansion into the wholesale field are said to be less likely to continue successfully than are firms started initially as wholesale houses by men experienced in wholesaling. This theory raises interesting questions concerning the selection of the town for a small wholesale business. Does it indicate that a retailer established in a town is less able to evaluate his own town as a good location for a wholesale plant than is the outsider who may visit the town from time to time as a salesman? Does it reflect the power of "first love"—retail interests, or the difficulty of successfully operating two businesses—wholesale and retail? Or does it prove that running a wholesale business is sufficiently different from retailing to require special experience? Certain established wholesalers subscribe to the last viewpoint and can cite many cases where this factor apparently was the chief reason why retailer-wholesaler businesses reverted exclusively to retailing. Probably there is also some validity to the theory that a salesman calling upon retailers in many different towns has a much better basis than any one of his customers for selecting a particular town in which to locate a small wholesale business.

Small wholesale establishments, like other small businesses, often originate as a result of family enterprise. A few of one of the authors' former students have received family backing to expand the parent's retail business into the wholesale field, the son taking over the wholesale enterprise. In one of these cases the wholesale business and the retail store were located in different towns, although in the same wholesale trading area. The location was selected only after several years of study of the economic factors involved; the main objective was to become centrally located in the trading area desired, with a good local (town) market, and without "live" competition.

Selecting the District within a Town

The average age of wholesale establishments is greater than that of other major fields of business. Most cities have wholesale districts. Usually these were in operation long before the automobile and truck appeared. Naturally they were located adjacent to water or rail transportation and frequently to both. Chicago and other cities served by both types of transportation are specific examples. In smaller inland towns the established wholesale district is adjacent to the railroad freight facilities.

In recent years there have been two significant developments leading to new wholesale locations within the town: highway transportation, and the rise of cash-and-carry wholesalers, especially in the grocery field. A third development that is having an increasing effect on intracity locations is air travel. Some cities are pushing plans to build super merchandise marts designed for use by the private planes of buyers. One authority stressed the beneficial effects of increased air travel on the location of wholesalers in smaller towns.[23] When this forecast is considered in connection with the present trend of moving wholesale plants to the edge of town, the conclusion is evident.

In many situations the small wholesaler must still decide between locating in the established wholesale district or elsewhere in the town. Usually the advantages of locating outside of the wholesale district are far more compel-

---

[23] Arthur I. Boreman, "Where Does the Wholesaler Go from Here?" An address delivered to the Wholesale Dry Goods Institute, Des Moines, Iowa (June 4-5, 1948).

ling. The principal exception occurs when the need to pick up "shorts" from other wholesalers happens frequently, as it does sometimes in the drug business.

Within the wholesale district space is limited, plants are multi-story because of high ground rents, warehousing costs—which usually constitute a major item of expense—are high, and traffic congestion is prevalent. Largely because of these conditions it is improbable that the small operator will be able to secure the street level, efficient type of plant he needs. Although rent is a relatively minor expense for service wholesalers in most fields, warehouse labor is a big item. Particularly for the small wholesaler who is not in a position to use laborsaving material-handling equipment, a wholesale district location would seem to have most of the disadvantages, and almost none of the advantages of other sites.

Selecting the Wholesale Site

Since small wholesalers serve principally the local market, their location should be selected with this fact as a primary consideration. However, there are many aspects to be considered. The rise of truck transportation and increased speed of all forms of transportation are important. For example, many small wholesale grocers located in small towns use their own trucks to deliver to customers as well as to bring in warehouse stocks. In nearly every city of 100,000 population or more there are public warehouses where commission men and brokers maintain stocks of goods. A small wholesaler located 200 miles from such a city sends his truck up to 75 or 100 miles to make customer deliveries, and the driver then continues on to the city distributing point where he picks up small lots of assorted goods from the warehouse stocks of commission men and brokers. Obviously this practice frees the small wholesaler (who could not ordinarily buy in carload lots anyway) from any dependence upon locations close to railroad facilities.

The preceding example assumed truck delivery by the wholesaler to his retail customers, location in a relatively small town, and distribution to a trading area that included out-of-town customers. There are other situations to be considered that bear heavily upon the intratown site. A primary consideration is the amount of "store" business, meaning the extent to which retail buyers visit the warehouse as compared to sale and delivery at the retailers' stores. "Store" business is of two types. The older form, still used in variety and general merchandise lines, is where the wholesaler maintains a showroom with displays from which visiting buyers make their selections. The goods may be taken by the buyer or delivered later by the wholesaler, the former practice being common with out-of-town buyers (that is, retailers located in small towns in the trading area). For this type of business a site near other wholesalers, in order to obtain the "shopping center advantages," with moderate parking facilities for customers' cars is desirable.

The second example of "store" business is the cash-and-carry type of warehouse. There are many more small wholesalers operating this type of "store" business than the other. Often one or two persons can operate a cash-and-carry plant doing several hundred thousand dollars' annual volume of business. Usually most of the patronage comes from retailers within the town. and a site of maximum convenience to these retailers that also has adequate parking and truck loading facilities is needed. This means higher rent expense. As illustrated in the following case, adapted from an earlier study by the U. S. Department of Commerce, however, the total operating expense is likely to be less. Whereas to the service wholesaler rent was 0.40 per cent of annual sales, with a total operating expense of 6.91 per cent, for the cash-and-carry plant rent was 0.57 per cent of a total of 2.90 per cent. Rent for the service wholesaler was the seventh largest item of expense, but for the cash-and-carry it was the second largest. The foregoing are figures of a small wholesaler in the grocery field relating to the main house (sales $126,000) and its cash-and-carry branch (sales $57,000) for 1939. Although they probably are not exactly accurate for current conditions, they do show the much greater importance of rent among total expenses for the cash-and-carry type.[24]

Recently small wholesalers, and a few large concerns that have built new plants, have chosen sites near the edge of town. The chief advantages are lower rent and ample space, the latter making possible the construction of the most efficient type of ground floor warehouse with transportation access on all sides. More rapid transportation and good highways, less traffic congestion, and new types of construction that provide better light and ventilation all have contributed to this trend. Probably many of these operators also have had in mind the use of some air travel to markets and air transportation to the warehouse.

Small wholesalers who make truck deliveries or whose salesmen travel, have a different problem of site selection from that of those doing "store" business. Here the relative amount of city business compared to out-of-town business is a major factor. The objective is to locate near the center of the desired trading area so as to keep the total distance traveled by salesmen and trucks at a minimum. A difference of one mile between two possible sites would be a large factor in such a case. Traffic congestion and highway facilities are important. Rent is usually a minor item of total expense, the major ones, being salesmen's expenses, warehouse expense, and delivery costs in that order. To illustrate this situation, assume there are two small wholesalers, one having 90 per cent of his business within the town, the other only 50 per cent. The former would locate in town, close to the retailers served, and at the best site available in terms of rent, traffic conditions, space, and type of building required. The other would determine toward which direction the out-of-town half of his business was concentrated, and then would logically

[24] *Effective Grocery Wholesaling,* Economic Series No. 14 (Washington, D. C.: U. S. Department of Commerce, G.P.O., 1941), p. 174.

pick a site at the appropriate edge of town or about midway between his two groups of customers.

The increase in large shopping centers affects wholesale locations in two ways. A site geographically located to serve several centers may well be in a suburban area of relatively low land value. This in turn makes possible the construction of a modern one-story economically operated warehouse with ample parking and loading facilities.

In some lines, notably drugs, retailers often want frequent emergency deliveries. One survey showed most druggists (52 per cent) gave quicker deliveries as the reason they bought from their major wholesale supplier. A limited survey conducted by the authors disclosed the same reason for patronizing a particular wholesaler, plus the following: ability to buy on a small order basis, complete stocks carried locally, preference for new one-story plants that operate on a five per cent markup (groceries). In dry goods and variety lines the retailers expressed a desire to be able to visit the warehouse showrooms conveniently. In the area where the survey was made many grocery wholesalers are operating on a six to seven per cent margin, although some of the more efficient service wholesalers have been able to reduce total expenses so as to operate on a five per cent margin.

LOCATION OF THE SERVICE BUSINESS

The general policy governing the kind of service business to be established will probably have more bearing on the requirements for a good location than in other major fields. A personal service, professional or semiprofessional, where clients call at the place of business should be as accessible as possible. This may mean an office location in the financial district or a shop location in one of the better retail districts. If the customer does not visit the business, then location as far as site within the town is concerned is relatively unimportant. An interesting characteristic of most service businesses is that a reputation for extra high quality of workmanship will attract customers in spite of a poor location to a far greater extent than is true of other kinds of business. However, since this is an exception and since it comes about only after the reputation is earned, the beginner especially should seek the best location in which to build such a reputation.

Some kinds of service businesses require a factory type of location where the actual work is performed, and a retail site for customer contact. This may be illustrated by a laundry or dry cleaning firm doing a large amount of cash-and-carry business.

Policies relating to the market or type of clientele desired will influence the choice of town and area within a town whenever: (1) a special type of customer constitutes the market, such as office workers, or automobile factories; (2) the service is one for which there is widespread demand; or (3) existing competition deviates appreciably from normal.

Both in selecting the town and the district within a large city, care should be exercised to learn the facts. Assumptions that appear to be logical are not always borne out by reality. For example, although a heavy concentration of car ownership means a good market for automobile service establishments, clean cities are better markets for dry cleaning establishments than dirty ones.

Drive-ins are important in many service fields where the customer brings the article to the shop. These include many types of repair shops, and laundry and cleaning establishments. A location close to the central business area on an automobile artery and on the side nearer the better residential districts is considered best. Delivery services are becoming increasingly costly, the present trend is toward service at the shop rather than in the home, and customers are willing to do the transporting in most cases. For these reasons service businesses not yet launched on the drive-in principle should consider this possibility whenever it is appropriate. Even some personal services like beauty parlors and barber shops are finding advantages in this type of location. As mentioned earlier in this chapter, drive-ins have expanded to nearly every field. They are best suited to services where (1) the customer prefers to remain in his own car—as drive-in theaters, restaurants and banks; and (2) where parking facilities may be dominant in determining customer patronage, as for fairly standardized services such as cleaning and self-serve laundries.

Restaurant

In selecting the actual site—the street address—for the eating place, one of the first things that must be considered is its access to transportation facilities. If customers will come by automobile, parking space will be essential. In fact, if the majority of them come by automobile, you may need your own parking area. A fire hydrant in front of the restaurant will prevent parking there, and will slow up food delivery. Lack of an alley means that trucks must take up parking space in front.

The preferred side of the street can only be decided by actual observation in the proposed location. A southern exposure gets the sun all day, it is the warmer side in cold weather, and the ice melts more quickly. On the other hand, the sun may be considered undesirable because of the effect it has in producing window glare. As a general rule, the southern exposure might be preferable in a cold climate, and the northern exposure in a warm climate.

A good location for some types of restaurants in large cities is near a streetcar or bus stop (on the stop side), not across the street beyond it. Transfer points are particularly good, as are bus and railroad depots.

In some cases, the going-home side of the street is better for dinner business, and the going-to-work side is better for breakfast business.

It is desirable also to choose the side that is easier for automobile traffic to reach, and where it is easier to obtain parking space. This is especially important for the newer highway locations where visibility from a considerable distance is also important.

More important, however, is the amount of customer traffic, especially for the "convenience" type of eating place. And for the more elaborate restaurants, the quality of the traffic is of some consequence, for one side of a street may be regarded as higher class even though the other side has a greater amount of traffic.[25]

Photographic Supply Store

The retail photographic supplier generally should locate in or near the main shopping districts. The proprietor may intend, however, to concentrate upon commercial photographic supplies and equipment, selling to photographic laboratories of manufacturing and commercial establishments. For this kind of trade the store may be more nearly of the nature of a warehouse, with most of the selling done by calling upon customers. Whatever the type of operation, it is advisable for the prospective store owner to consider location carefully as an important factor affecting the success of his business. Rentals should be closely checked against expected sales volume in each prospective location.[26]

Diaper Service

The matter of geographic location for a diaper service requires careful thought from the standpoint of potential business. The following factors are significant:

Birth rate. An average of 2,500,000 babies were born each year in the pre-war period. That number increased to 3,260,000 in 1946. Hence it would seem that the present is a good time to start a diaper service. Of course the birth rate varies in different cities, but if the rate in a particular city is climbing, that city will be a more favorable market for a diaper service than one in which the birth rate is stationary or declining.

Income level. The best prospects for diaper laundry service are in the upper-middle or middle-income groups, among native-born, white-collar families that do not have many children.

Competition. You may be faced with competition from other diaper service laundries, from large family laundries and linen supply companies that have added diaper service, and from further possible development of the disposable diaper. The number of possible customers is strictly limited by the number of infants in the community. To support a business that is exclusively a diaper laundry service, a city should have a population of at least 100,000. For two competing laundries, 150,000 population is considered necessary. Include the

[25] Mary de Garmo Bryan, Alberta M. Macfarland, and E. R. Hawkins (under the direction of Walter F. Crowder), *Establishing and Operating a Restaurant,* Industrial (Small Business) Series No. 39 (Washington, D. C.: U. S. Department of Commerce, 1946), p. 28.

[26] *Operating a Photographic Supply Store,* Small Business Aids, No. 147, p. 2. Condensed from Photographic Supply Store Operation (Albany, N. Y.: New York Department of Commerce, March 1946).

population of the metropolitan trading area (suburbs) in estimating your potential market.

Estimating sales per customer. Service for the average baby starts with 70 to 90 diapers per week, tapering off after six months to 50 or 60 per week. The price schedule will vary with the community, but assume an average price of $1.40 for 70 diapers. If you had 300 customers at $1.40 weekly, your weekly sales would be $420, your yearly sales about $22,000. An alert operator could make a satisfactory living out of a business as small as this.[27]

Radio and TV Service Business

If you do not have sufficient radio and television service work to support a small store on a side street, your logical step is to work up a clientele in the basement or in a spare room of your home before you risk too much money in the rental of a store. Many radio and television service men make a satisfactory living operating from their homes with a minimum of expense.

If you are to engage in a "wholesale" repair business, doing work exclusively for other radio dealers and service men, there would be no need for a fancy store front on or near a main street. A loft, or other cheap but commodious floor space, centrally located with respect to your dealers, would be your answer.

If you intend to service only a portion of the town or city, locate your shop near the center of this area. If you are operating in a large city and plan to confine yourself to one neighborhood, consider the location of your new shop as it relates to the district you wish to serve. Try to locate near the center of your customer area.[28]

CONCLUSIONS

To the inexperienced businessman it may seem that this chapter has been unduly long in view of the infrequency with which new locations are selected by the independent small business owner. If so, he has missed the main point. Location is so intimately, and *continuously* related to all other aspects of a small business that overemphasis would be difficult. As the reader will notice in later chapters, *nearly every phase of operating the business depends to some degree upon its location.*

QUESTIONS AND PROBLEMS

1. Why is location so important in all aspects of business? Discuss.

2. Under what circumstances should a beginner give greater weight in selecting a retail location to personal than to economic factors?

[27] *Establishing a Diaper Service,* Small Business Aids, No. 160 (Washington, D. C.: U. S. Department of Commerce, 1946), pp. 1-2.

[28] *Your Shop Location,* Small Business Aids, No. 193 (Washington, D. C.: U. S. Department of Commerce) p. 1. Condensed from Samuel C. Milbourne, "Your Shop Location," *Radio News* (January 1947).

3. What major population trends since the 1940's have influenced retail locations? Explain the effects of each.

4. List any factors not mentioned in the chapter that should be considered in selecting a location. Discuss.

5. Why is the right location so necessary to a retail store? Explain.

6. Does the rent-advertising relationship discussed in this chapter, with regard to retailing, apply to small-scale service businesses? Explain.

7. How would you expect location to be related to factors like the following for each field of small business: layout, credit and delivery policies, financing, relations with resources, customer relations and sales promotion, government regulations and taxation, and personnel? Discuss.

8. For a retail grocery store doing exclusively telephone order and delivery business (no customers admitted to the store) describe the ideal location.

9. For each of several particular kinds of small business compare the locational advantages and disadvantages of a big city with a small city or town.

10. Explain why stores specializing in merchandise like toys or photographic supplies need a much larger population than grocery or drugstores. Discuss any exceptions.

11. Analyze and explain the reasons some kinds of retailing have higher rent-paying capacity than others. Are these conditions inherent in the kinds of business in each group, high and low rent? Explain.

12. Explain the meaning of, reasons for, and uses of "retail affinities," and give several illustrations.

13. List the zoning ordinances and other legal regulations to consider for several types of businesses of possible interest to you.

14. Explain how the beginning businessman can profit by fitting his offerings into wants not already supplied by large competitors.

15. For what kind of business is the percentage lease most suitable? Why? For what kind of business is it most widely used? Why?

16. List the various conditions and circumstances under which you would prefer: (a) a percentage lease; (b) a long-term lease of ten years or more.

17. List all the kinds of businesses that could effectively use a drive-in type of location. A highway location. Explain any unusual cases.

18. What important developments regarding location do you predict for the next ten years? Discuss each.

19. Select what appears to be one of the best and also one of the poorest locations for one kind of business in your vicinity and discuss the location with each business manager.

20. For some kind of retail or service business of interest to you, ascertain, either in your proposed town or one convenient to you, all local zoning ordinances and other regulations that would influence your choice of locations. Report your findings and conclusions.

21. Mrs. Jones, a widow with two pre-school children, has a small Spud Nut shop one block from the college campus, from which she earns a modest living. A larger store downtown, one block off Main, near a conventional restaurant, is available for 50 per cent more rent. Additional equipment would be required and some modernizing needed for the vacant store. Mrs. Jones' funds are limited, but she dislikes the late night hours required at her present site. What should she do, and why?

14 • Selecting the Industrial Location

Careful examination of the map of any country and a comparison of that map with the vital statistics of the country will immediately reveal the close relationship between industry and population. Wherever there are factories, there are people—employees. To satisfy the wants of these people, there are other businesses, some of them complementary to the larger industrial concerns, some of them wholesale establishments, and many of them retail stores. To satisfy further the requirements of these industries and of these businesses, to meet the demands of these people, transportation facilities are also available. Thus, in the complex of any metropolitan area, we find the core of business to be that of production. Related with the other businesses, as well as with the people and their jobs dependent on that production, are public utilities, public education, church, and recreational arrangements. There is also the corollary matter of tax income to the community, assisted tremendously by the presence of manufacturing plants.

Probably, therefore, no type of business has been more aggressively sought after, highly praised, generously aided by various levels of government, given more credit for our high standard of living, and yet subjected to as many locational restrictions as manufacturing or nonagricultural production. Industrial growth, as observed, makes possible and necessary expansion of trade, services, research, the professions, recreation and similar activities where independent enterprise flourishes. It also provides work for the continuous surplus of farm labor, and is the catalyst necessary to lift any group above its dependence on nature. Industry, then, is the primary source of wealth above mere existence.

FUNDAMENTAL RELATIONSHIPS

With the prospective factory owner or renter, the potential manufacturer, the person who is considering a plant location, our purpose here is to review the many basic relationships which naturally exist in any business community. For example, a small business may be particularly dependent on a major industry in the community. Such an industry creates jobs, usually at higher wages than nonindustrial jobs in the community. But it can also destroy jobs by closing, reducing operations or migrating, a serious thing for those depending for their livelihood on the industry. It is immaterial that the jobs would never have existed had it not been for the factory. Once 50 or 50,000 people depend exclusively on the industry's payroll they are almost helpless without it.

Industrial plants are not always flexible as to use, therefore they are sometimes difficult to dispose of, as abandoned plants seen in various parts of the country bear silent witness.

It is usually harder when a manufacturing firm ceases operations to get another company to take over than it is to transfer ownership in the retail and service fields. A factory's plant and equipment are specialized. When conditions make it unprofitable for one company to produce in a given plant it is unlikely that new owners could make the same product profitably. Conditions making it difficult or impossible to operate a given factory profitably are likely to be beyond the individual company's control. When the market for a product evaporates, or shifts to other products, one producer is powerless unless he can shift with the market. This is a major reason for the current interest in diversification.

Locating a plant involves heavy fixed capital investment in a virtually immobile condition. The prospective manufacturer is therefore interested more in future conditions than in some immediate but temporary advantage. One city may have a below average tax cost, cheap land, and relatively low construction costs. But if its streets need repair, if the water and sewerage systems, the fire and police departments and school system are substandard, the tax advantage would certainly be temporary and may have to go well above average to bring local conditions and public services up to an acceptable level.

Furthermore, the labor supply and attitude of the community are important on a long range basis. A floating or transient population is not an attractive labor supply in most cases. Particularly in recent years prospective industrialists have been stressing the *stability* of the labor supply and a hospitable attitude by the entire community, instead of the assurances of the commonly encountered chamber of commerce secretary or industry committee chairman alone. This may be an important reason why the community-supported plans have apparently been so successful. If local property owners in town vote a bond issue to help finance the construction of a new plant it seems reasonable that *they want it*.[1]

Thus the indirect interrelationships and interdependency between all busi-

[1] An interesting article on the effect of community attitude (toward itself) is in *Dun's Review and Modern Industry* for October 1956, page 139.

nesses, large and small, in a community, as well as between certain small business and larger customer or supplier firms on whom they are directly dependent, must be carefully studied. Naturally, the small beginning manufacturer, like the larger firms we have been discussing in the long run is affected by the same conditions that promote or retard other industries. Larger, well-established manufacturers have more experienced men at their disposal and a wide range of choice in selecting their locations. Their decisions may well serve as a guide for the little man.

There are two exceptions to this general relationship between small and large industry. One is local handicraft production or making some specialized article where sentiment or folklore is associated with a certain part of the country—gold or silver trinkets in the pioneer mining regions, or Indian novelties in the plains states. The other is where an industry migrates leaving usable plant and facilities and a surplus of skilled labor. In several cases, both in New England and elsewhere, small industries have received local aid and a cordial welcome in taking over with entirely different kinds of manufacturing. Sometimes a dozen or more small producers will utilize facilities abandoned by one large firm.

Prewar Industrial Concentration

The location pattern of American industry has been changing considerably since the late 1930's. Prior to 1939, when the National Resources Committee published its findings on the structure of our economy, the vast majority of manufacturing plants, both large and small, were concentrated in the highly industrialized area of the Northeast. This concentration came about naturally as a result of the traditional combination of factors that influence plant location. Overconcentration eventually occurred in many areas, resulting in traffic congestion, high rentals, labor problems, and various other evidences of the law of diminishing returns being in operation. The serious effects of business depression on certain highly industrialized communities were evident during the depression following 1929. During prosperous times labor shortage and other difficulties lent further support to the growing realization that industrial concentration can go too far. Even before the stimulus toward decentralization given by national defense needs commenced in the late 1930's, trends away from industrial centers were in operation.

The decentralizing effects of the World War II period are too familiar to warrant further comments here. However, experience gained during this period regarding plant location, subcontracting, integration of the operations of many small plants widely separated as to location, and other developments resulting from wartime conditions, has had and will continue to have considerable bearing on small plant location.

In general, the firms located outside industrial areas are fairly large units, principally because small firms so located find it difficult to manufacture specialized or style goods, and in the production of standardized goods large units are more efficient. In other cases branch plants of large corporations could operate in many fields not suitable to the small factory.

War and Postwar Industrial Trends

From 1939 to 1959 nonfarm employment increased from less than 40 to over 60 million workers, or over 50 per cent, while total population increased only 20 per cent. The rise was caused primarily by manufacturing which accounted for about one-third of all nonagricultural employment. Although throughout the period the construction industry had the largest increases, other than government employment, most of the construction activity was for new plant facilities. The outstanding gains in manufacturing employment occurred in the West and Southwest, especially in California and Texas. All regions made some gains but the two mentioned and the Great Lakes states were above average. The latter resulted from wartime expansion that the Great Lakes states have been able to hold since then, probably in part due to the importance of abundant water.

Reports such as the foregoing, the widely publicized migration of the textile industry from New England to the South, the well-known movement of industry to the West and Southwest, and extensive decentralization could easily leave an erroneous impression. As of the early 1960's the *concentration of industrial employment* was not very different from prewar years. One-third of all *factory jobs* in the nation were still concentrated in the nine states comprising New England and the Middle Atlantic region.

The preceding discussion should emphasize several points made frequently throughout this book: manufacturing and its related industries, especially construction and transportation, provide the bulk of dependent employment. An industrial community once established tends to be self-perpetuating. New enterprises, even in manufacturing, and industries pioneering new areas tend to have small beginnings and few paid employees. Opportunities for new industries are constantly appearing in both old industrial areas (as electronics in New England, and air conditioning in New York) and in nonindustrialized areas (as petroleum products, chemicals and fertilizers in the Southwest). Industry, despite its relative immobility, follows market shifts and changes in technology and economic conditions, labor and transportation costs, access to currently used raw materials, newer chemicals and synthetics, and prospects for future growth.

In view of the foregoing account of the complexity of factors affecting industrial location, and the higher failure rate of the manufacturing compared to the retailing, wholesaling, and service trades, the still dominant preference for industry over other fields on the part of communities seeking additional businesses may seem odd, but it is a high compliment to industry's significance to a community's economy. We have endeavored here only to point out basic industrial relationship and interdependency and all that these imply in hazards as well as opportunity.

SMALL FACTORY LOCATIONS

American industrial history shows that small factories have often started in districts remote from population centers but adjacent to the type of economic activity they were to serve. Many of these have furnished the basis for major industries, remaining in their original locations long after the area's economy progressed to more advanced stages. Wisconsin is a case in point. During pioneer times zinc and lead mining attracted prospectors who needed mining tools and equipment. This period was followed by wheat farming, then lumbering, and later by dairying. During each period local factories, all started on the traditional small scale, produced tools, machines and equipment needed by the type of economic activity dominant in the area. Today, as much as a century later in some cases, Wisconsin is still an important producer of certain mining machinery and tools, saws, planers and other woodworking machinery used originally by the lumber industry, farm implements (J. I. Case Co.), and dairy machinery and containers.[2]

The logic of the origins of many industries, always on a small scale adjacent to their markets before the rise of nation-wide rapid transportation, is understandable to most students. Important opportunities still exist for modern "pioneers" to emulate such development. However, our country has developed production technology, transportation, and communication to a point where a broad long range viewpoint is desirable even in such cases today. It is advisable for the beginner to be familiar with (1) sources of assistance in selecting a location,[3] (2) the major factors to be considered, and (3) their relative importance (which may vary in individual cases) before undertaking his own analysis and decision.

Agencies Assisting in Plant Location

Nearly all states, and many cities, in both industrial and nonindustrial areas, have developed agencies to assist industries seeking new locations as well as communities seeking new industries. These may be government agencies, such as the Department of Commerce of New York State; state and local chambers of commerce or other businessmen's associations; or special agencies established for this purpose, such as the various industrial commissions and planning boards. In recent years there has been a pronounced trend for the less industrialized areas of the South and West, both states and communities, to establish agencies and seek aggressively to promote industrialization of their localities.

[2] Edward H. Hempel, ed., *Small Plant Management,* "Role of the Small Plant in the History of Communities" (New York: McGraw-Hill Book Company, Inc., 1950), pp. 36-40.

[3] *Data Sources for Plant Location Analysis,* a catalog of source materials for manufacturers for studies of prospective plant locations (Washington, D. C.: U. S. Department of Commerce, BDSA Office of Area Development, 1960).

There are three typical situations where such agencies aid industry in finding desirable locations: local concerns seeking to expand, out-of-state companies looking for sites for branch plants, and local individuals wishing to start a new factory. Types of agencies to be considered may be grouped into six classes: (1) state and city, (2) Federal government, (3) community financial organizations, (4) commercial services, (5) public utilities, (6) miscellaneous.

Most states have a Planning and Resources Board, State Planning Commission, Department of Commerce and Industry, Department of Agriculture and Industry, or similar agency. State agencies vary in the scope and nature of their activities, but in general they serve as liaison between local communities in the state and persons seeking information, whether for locational, travel, or other reasons. Usually material descriptive of the state is published and sent on request. Many maintain files of industrial prospects for use by local communities, and refer certain types of inquiries to appropriate city agencies. Although the aids rendered by state and city agencies vary widely, this source is usually a good starting point in seeking information about a particular part of the country.

Agencies of the Federal government include the Area Development Division of the U. S. Department of Commerce, discussed later, branch offices of the Department of Commerce and of the Small Business Administration. These are in addition to data published by the Census Bureau, Office of Business Economics of the Department of Commerce, Bureau of Labor Statistics, and others. In most cases a beginner should seek advice from an appropriate office of the Department of Commerce or Small Business Administration.

Community financial organizations are of three main types: (1) private venture capital companies, (2) industrial funds or foundations, and (3) credit pools. The first is concerned with new firms that show promise for the development of radically new products or processes, and would not be of locational or financial aid to other enterprisers. Community industrial foundations have engaged in the purchase, development and sale or lease of industrial sites and buildings. The foundations have also made loans to or purchased the securities of firms in the area and have when necessary offered management and technical information. Somewhat similar to the community industrial fund has been the growth of development credit corporations. During recent years they have been established in each of the six New England states and in some other areas. Frequently, after a thorough investigation by a development credit corporation, financial institutions which are not members of the organization either assume the entire loan or agree to participate. Although referred to here as financial organizations, the primary purpose of the industrial funds and credit pools is to encourage industries to locate in the state.

A recent survey of the types of public aid available to the industrialist trying to locate a plant indicated that: (1) ten states allow municipalities to issue bonds, either full faith or revenue, for erection of new or expanded plants; (2) seven states have development credit corporations employing private capital; (3) eleven states allow temporary local property tax exemptions; (4) several states have nonprofit organizations that help bring plants to the community, and (5) one state (Pennsylvania) in 1957 directly appropriated funds for second mortgages.[4]

The major commercial services to consider in selecting a plant site are real estate brokers, industrial or management consultants, and those specializing in locations, such as Fantus Factory Locating Service. Certain architectural engineering or factory construction firms could be included in this group, as many advertise both their aid in securing locations and their construction services. For most beginners a reliable broker experienced in factory locations would probably be the logical choice.

Two major public utilities have been active in assisting with factory locations: railroads, and power or fuel companies. In both groups assistance is naturally restricted to the areas served by the companies offering aid. Another source of aid that may be of worthwhile assistance in selecting locations is individuals or concerns that have a financial interest in securing new factories that will buy or use their offerings. Real estate owners and developers of industrial properties, and manufacturers of machinery and equipment needed by new factories are the major constituents of this group.

Many agencies reporting to the authors stated their desire to assist local individuals but added that few requests of this type have been received. There are at least three reasons for this: (1) individuals seeking to enter manufacturing on a small scale are not well informed about the services available through state and local industrial development agencies; (2) many such factories are started in the home community where the need for location advice is not felt; and (3) sometimes the principal need is for financial assistance.

Especially in the little-industrialized towns, there has been some tendency to use the funds of Industrial Foundations only to assist established out-of-state industries in setting up branch plants. In other situations funds are available to buy sites, construct buildings, or do other things needed by a new industry that is suited to the community, especially when it will complement already established industries, regardless of whether the organizers are local individuals or out-of-state concerns.

The prevailing attitude toward local financial assistance was aptly expressed in a letter to the authors by an official of a state chamber of commerce as follows:

In matters of financial assistance to a prospective industry we insist that all arrangements be based on sound business policy. We do not encourage any plan which involves "something for nothing." We always insist that the current interest rate be paid by the prospect for private funds invested by local citizens in constructing a plant. Local citizens are advised by us to do all

[4] "Baiting the Hook for Industry," *Business Week* (November 16, 1957), p. 86

possible to keep costs down and many services are rendered without cost during construction period by civic-minded citizens. Good co-operation and a friendly welcome is far more valuable to all concerned than free land and free rent.[5]

A liaison office, such as the agencies under discussion, needs information about communities within the state that are seeking new industries as well as data on the requirements and preferences of industries seeking sites. Information of the former type consists of complete lists of all available buildings and industrial sites, and data on basic industrial location factors. Most state and community agencies make surveys to discover available buildings and sites and relevant information about each, such as area, rental, type of building, and equipment. In recent years, according to comments made by the directors of many of these agencies, small firms seeking locations have been unduly influenced by the availability of a usable building that can be rented. This is a short-run viewpoint, and it could easily lead to uneconomic locations.

BASIC LOCATION FACTORS

The following are generally considered as basic location factors although their relative importance varies for different cases: raw materials, plant and equipment, labor, and market. These may be subdivided to indicate aspects of each to be considered, as in the following tabulation:

1. Raw materials	3. Labor
(a) Nearness	(a) Special skills
(b) Bulk transportation	(b) Female
2. Plant and equipment	(c) Male
(a) Specialized building	(d) Bulk
(b) Power	4. Market
(c) Fuels	(a) Consumer goods
(d) Processing water	(b) Specialized[6]

The most comprehensive analysis of the basic factors influencing industrial location was prepared and published in revised form by the Area Development Division, U. S. Department of Commerce, in June, 1947.[7] This is still an excellent guide for evaluating an area's resources for industrial development.

[5] Excerpt from letter of August 26, 1948, from Jefferson D. Henry, Director, Industrial Division, Alabama State Chamber of Commerce, Montgomery, Alabama.

[6] *Community Industrial Development* (Albany, New York: State of New York Department of Commerce, 1949), p. 23.

[7] *Basic Industrial Location Factors*, Industrial Series, No. 74 (Washington, D. C.: U. S. Department of Commerce, U. S. Government Printing Office, 1947). Another comprehensive list is in Oswald Stewart, "Plant Site Selection Guide," *Factory Management and Maintenance* (May 1957), pp. 180 a-f. And the Small Business Administration has issued Ronald M. Reifler, "Plant Location Factors for Small Industry," Management Aids for Small Manufacturers No. 99 (November 1958).

For 75 industry groups the report evaluates each of the 13 basic factors as "most important" or "usually important." An examination of the report supports the statements made by community agency directors that each industrial location problem is a case by itself. The following comments based on the report are generalizations. Six of the basic factors were rated "most important" for the 75 industry groups as follows: distribution facilities, 66; tax structure, 63; transportation structure, 56; labor, 39; market, 32; and location of production material, 27. This means that out of all industry groups included, 66 rated distribution facilities among the "most important" factors, and for 9 groups they were "usually important" factors, whereas location of production material was a "most important" factor for only 27 industry groups and a "usually important" factor for 48. Naturally the relative importance assigned to each of these basic factors by a particular industry will depend not only on its normal requirements (as intended in the report) but also upon the particular objective in seeking a new location at a certain time, and prevailing conditions if they are unusual.

For the purpose of encouraging local communities to conduct surveys and to do some self-appraisal, as well as to furnish information necessary to help industries make an intelligent location selection, most state agencies provide guidance to local communities. Many have issued booklets for this purpose. Others use a prepared form, as earlier noted. These forms in themselves serve as a searching checklist as to major considerations in avoiding pitfalls. One state agency official, with the results of a recent study in hand, commented on the impatience and lack of careful thinking of many would be manufacturers as follows:

> Our experience with "small business" opportunity seekers in the industrial field gives us the impression that few of them know how to gather and analyze factual data and apply their own judgment to such a problem. Far too many of them think or hope there is some shortcut, by which a central research agency such as ours can give them offhand opinions as to what field of industry or what community offers the best opportunities.

Considering the amount of investment usually involved, and the resulting risks, the importance of location cannot be overstressed. From a negative or danger-signal point of view, one author lists these pitfalls in selecting an industrial location:

1. Miscalculation of labor costs, erroneous assumptions.
2. Choice of site where the labor reservoir is inadequate.
3. Neglect to anticipate growth of the business.
4. Carelessness in checking the site.
5. Lack of distribution know-how—the marketing aspects.
6. Failure to predict the impact of the new plant on the community.
7. Neglect to check on supporting facilities (water, utilities).
8. Reliance on misinformation on utility costs and problems.

9. Underestimating the importance of taxes
10. Failure to recognize cost relationships.[8]

And many prospective small factory owners are inviting such pitfalls by neglecting these agencies as a source of assistance.

Another author lists five broad aspects of any plant location study:

1. The determination by management of the locational factors which have a bearing on the particular project and the assigning of relative degrees of importance to these factors.
2. Narrowing down the areas of choice through a careful statistical analysis of the basic economic pattern of the states, counties, and communities that lie within the region of choice.
3. Securing more detailed information from the communities and areas that have passed the tests in the preceding paragraph, analyzing and tabulating this information as nearly as possible on a comparable basis.
4. A field investigation of the communities and areas which have survived the investigations of step 3.
5. Assimilating all information gathered and evaluating it in the light of the company's criteria.

In connection with step 4, the author suggests contacting local employers, state employment offices, local assessors, city or county clerks, the local superintendent of schools, local utility and railroad officials, and someone who has inspected the site offered.[9]

With these pitfalls in mind, and considering the broader aspects as listed, the U. S. Department of Commerce has prepared a list of 150 questions, 13 of which deal with plant location:

1. Does proximity to raw materials, adequate supply of labor of required skills, or market for the product dictate your location? Generally, manufacturers seek locations that minimize the cost of raw materials carried in inventory in the plant, plus the cost of processing them, plus the cost of transporting finished products to markets. and. in addition. afford as many other advantages and as few other disadvantages as possible.

2. Do other considerations predominate? Some processes, for example, call for large amounts of cheap electric power, quantities of water, or nearness to complementary industries (e.g., tool and die shops, dye works). Some production demands a highly seasonal labor force, or prompt services of other industries that cannot be rendered from a distance.

3. What transportation, power, water supply, fuel, fire or police protection do you need, and where will you find them to be adequate? Are climatic conditions important?

[8] Leonard C. Yaseen, "The Ten Biggest Pitfalls in Plant Location." *Dun's Review and Modern Industry,* Vol. 69 (March 1957), pp. 49-50.

[9] Raeburn F. Hay, "58 Check Points for Plant Location," *Sales Management* (July 10, 1957), pp. 115-116.

4. Will your plant's processes involve unusual hazards or create nuisances in the way of smoke, noise, odor, waste?

5. Does the location have attractive places for workers and executives to live and raise families? Are housing, recreation, schools, outlets for cultural activities adequate? Will plant personnel fit into the community or may racial, religious, or social antagonisms arise?

6. Is the community—its citizens, officials, financiers—familiar with the peculiarities, if any, of your industry? Local bankers, for example, may not know how to judge the amount of credit your firm qualifies for. Does the town have a friendly attitude toward industry? Will it exploit outsiders?

7. Does location in an isolated small town, a suburb, or an established industrial center most nearly fit your needs? Land prices, taxes, and perhaps wages may be lower in small towns, but water, power, and fire protection ordinarily are limited—you may have to supplement the local resources or suffer from shutdowns or excessive insurance rates. Labor productivity varies from place to place—in many instances, high-priced labor may more than justify the cost.

8. Is the specific site appropriate to present and future needs? Will it stand the weights, vibration, etc., which it may be subjected to? Does it drain adequately? Is it filled? Will it support the landscaping and construction you desire?

9. Is it accessible to employees, suppliers, customers?

10. Does it have space for future plant expansion?

11. Is it zoned for the use to which you expect to put it?

12. Are water, sewer, electrical, and other connections already installed and, if so, are they adequate? If not, what will they cost?

13. Are local taxes in line with those of other communities? Is the site in line for special assessments due to extension of paving, gutters, sidewalks, storm or sanitary sewers, water or gas mains, street lighting or other municipal improvements? [10]

Analysis of Individual Needs

When the small manufacturer has become familiar with the basic location factors and available sources of information and assistance, his next step should be to analyze his particular business as to location requirements. His choice of region or community will be limited to those suitable to the nature of his concern. Otherwise he will weigh the relative importance of each basic factor and select the community most advantageous from the standpoint of personal preferences and future prospects. The personal aspect is the one outstanding difference between plant location for the average small factory as contrasted with the large concern. For industries in the "foot-loose" category, it may be the only consideration for the small businessman as far as region or community are concerned.

In most cases of small plant location where personal factors are not of

[10] William M. Hoad, *One Hundred and Fifty Questions for a Prospective Manufacturer,* Small Business Management Series No. 2 (Washington, D. C.: Small Defense Plants Administration, February 1953), pp. 8-10.

great importance there will be some choice as to size of the city and character of the area, such as industrial or agricultural, densely populated or average, mature or expanding regions, central city or suburban locations. Since we have eliminated personal factors, preference should be given to the newer, expanding area, and suburban rather than central locations. If other factors are the same, the small manufacturer should weigh carefully certain advantages of the agricultural region in preference to the industrial.

The small businessman is interested in two important aspects favoring rural locations. The first relates to cost. Not only is labor more loyal, dependable, and of lower unit cost (in spite of the manufacturer paying well above prevailing local wages), but other costs, with the possible exception of transportation, are also lower. Since his product is in price competition with other products, whether of the same type or not, lower total unit costs are especially important. This is particularly true during the "small" stage, when volume of output is not large and a greater margin per unit is required for satisfactory total profits.

The second aspect relates to the effects of future industrial development of the community. If the product manufactured can be sold more profitably in a local market, the more rapid expansion of demand to be expected in the agricultural community is an advantage. If the market is widely but thinly distributed over the country, however, a rapid industrial expansion of the community in which the factory is located may become an economic disadvantage by increasing total production costs per unit.

Selection of a site for the small factory within a city will be governed by the same factors that apply to larger industries: comparative cost of rent or construction, accessibility of inter- and intracity transportation, parking facilities and accessibility for workers, zoning regulations, and similar considerations. Principally to the extent that the small concern may require less land, a small work force, and other factors on a smaller scale, will the import of these be significantly different.

One other aspect of location that should be considered is visibility for mass traffic. Recent surveys by the authors have disclosed what common observation should confirm, that newly established branch plants of large corporations have been located to capitalize on this "outdoor advertising." Although the beginning small manufacturer lacks the nationwide reputation that is associated with the identification of branch plants as just mentioned, he needs this free advertising even more than the large concern does. Identifying signs, modern appearance of the building, well-kept premises, and visible evidence of a modern though small factory will all serve this end.

CONCLUSIONS

A factory location usually represents a relatively immobile heavy fixed investment. Consequently, selection of the region and community should be made with a long range viewpoint. Before making a decision even substantial immediate inducements should be appraised against the likelihood of their permanence, and the probable future developments of the prospective location and of the industry to which the new firm belongs. Locating a small plant differs from locating retail and service establishments chiefly in the much greater importance of the region and town relative to the site within a community. Personal considerations are, however, as important in factory as in other small business location decisions.

The typical prospective small manufacturer should familiarize himself with the numerous agencies available for assistance in selecting his location and for rendering additional help, should study carefully the basic location factors and how each of these may vary in importance for different cases, and should then analyze his own needs and weigh the relative importance of each before making a final decision. Material and suggestions presented in the chapter, if used, will enable any qualified beginner to make his location decision wisely.

QUESTIONS AND PROBLEMS

1. In what sense is industry the primary source of wealth above mere subsistence?

2. How and why does an industry have greater social responsibilities to its community than do retail and service establishments?

3. What factors prompt industry to migrate from one region to another?

4. How, if at all, is the quality of management more important in the success of a retail or service business than for a manufacturing establishment?

5. Why are long-range considerations more important in factory location than in other fields?

6. What two major points do industrialists nearly always look for in selecting a town in which to locate? Why is each so important?

7. What effects on geographic concentration of industrial employment have decentralization and industrial migration trends had since 1939? Explain.

8. Prior to World War II where did most small factories tend to locate, in non-industrial or in industrial areas? Explain.

9. What currently important major industries had their origins at considerable distance from centers of heavy population?

10. What current activities in remote regions might provide opportunities for new industries locating in these regions? Why are such opportunities more difficult to find today than 50 to 100 years ago?

11. Name and briefly summarize the kind of aid available from each of the five specific classes of agencies assisting in locating described in the chapter.

12. What group of agencies, in addition to the five classes mentioned, is important enough in rendering location assistance to warrant a separate class?

13. Why do industrial funds and credit pools render locational aids?

14. Should an industry long established in one town be permitted to migrate to another region mainly to secure lower labor costs? Discuss.

15. Why are large companies seeking to locate branch plants more active in securing assistance from agencies offering locational help than are most beginners?

16. Name the important industrial location factors and explain why they vary in relative importance for different cases. Illustrate.

17. Analyze the opinions presented in the chapter of state and community development agencies as to factors of greatest importance to small and medium sized firms seeking a plant location, noting points of similarity and of difference. What conclusions do you draw from your analysis?

18. What three major steps in sequence are recommended in the chapter for the beginner in selecting a plant location?

19. Why is an agricultural community likely to be more appreciative of a new industry than is a large city or industrialized community?

20. What factors influence the selection of a factory site within a city?

21. Examine several recent texts on industrial management and recent articles in trade journals for discussions of factory location. Note those that give special attention to the small, beginning manufacturer, and compare the discussion with that for the traditional giant industrial corporation. Analyze and report your findings and conclusions.

22. Select some kind of manufacturing that could be located in either a large industrial center or small town. Make a thorough investigation that would satisfy you as to which location would be preferable. Report your study and reasons for your decision.

23. Bill has perfected an economical converter for a car to permit use of 12 volt accessories on a six volt battery or generator and vice versa. He expects five years of active sales (1955-1960), during which time, he plans to develop other auto accessories. He is considering locating his plant either near his home in Oklahoma City or near Detroit. What factors should he weigh most heavily? Which location would be better, and why?

15 • Physical Plant and Layout

A good building effectively used is as valuable to an operating plant as are good home facilities for a household. As with any other tool or factory in business, such as money, personnel, equipment or materials, the building housing the operation can be poorly selected or poorly utilized. The degree to which it is properly selected or used is often a major factor in determining the amount of return on the entrepreneur's expenditure of time, effort, and money.

ADAPTING THE BUILDING

The building itself should lend itself to activities that are of greatest importance in each kind of enterprise. Three major considerations are: (1) function, (2) construction, and (3) modernization, or improvement in appearance, comfort, and effectiveness.

Function

At least seven aspects of this problem should be considered: (1) suitability, (2) cost, (3) accessibility, (4) internal transportation or traffic, (5) human aspect, (6) layout, and (7) current trends in management.

A building is good or bad in direct proportion to its suitability to the activities that must be performed. Excellent housing for one business may be next to impossible for use by some other, because of the utility factor. Simple protection from the elements and burglary may be sufficient for many lines of retailing, whereas heavy construction and solid concrete floors might be required for certain manufacturing or services industries.

The basic principle behind a good physical plant layout is to integrate men, materials, and equipment so as to move material as easily as possible over the shortest distance or to attract customers to the merchandise or service offered for sale. Either of these objectives should be accomplished by providing a natural sequence of operations, in a safe manner, and in a pleasant atmosphere.

Low cost of operation and maintenance is always desirable, provided it is not obtained at the expense of other more important considerations such as efficiency in use. Efficient maintenance and use depend upon two factors, the condition of the building and its business application. The former is obvious and does not vary according to most of the different uses to which a building may be put. The latter must be considered in relation to all the other functional aspects.

Accessibility varies by kinds of business as follows: in retailing customer accessibility is of greatest importance, but adequate facilities for receiving merchandise and making deliveries should be provided; in manufacturing easy receipt of raw materials and discharge of finished product are dominant; service industries usually require accessibility for customers or clients and often also require easy access for delivery equipment. Accessibility to a retail store building is hampered by steps, a narrow entrance, or any type of obstruction, such as a post. Steps represent an accident hazard as well as an obstacle to customer traffic. A nonskid ramp may be the best solution if no way can be found to eliminate differences in elevation.

Receipt of goods may be difficult if there is no door to an alley or if goods must be unloaded from a heavy traffic lane without an offset for trucks. Delivery through the main customer entrance is extremely undesirable. Where merchandise traffic is heavy, unloading platforms at truck level are useful; gravity chutes may be used if the receiving room is below ground level. Recently portable roller chutes that save human energy and time have come into use.

Closely related to external accessibility is the question of internal transportation and traffic facilities provided by the building. Movement of materials is of great importance in manufacturing. Except in extreme cases where the construction of the building actually obstructs movement, however, operations beginning on a small scale may subordinate this factor. Retail stores naturally wish customer traffic to be unhindered by columns, different floor levels, irregularly shaped buildings, and similar conditions. Movement of merchandise within the store may be important for items like furniture, heavy appliances, or especially bulky containers. In service establishments the nature of the process largely determines the importance as well as the type of internal transportation facilities. A beauty parlor and a job type of machine shop obviously have very different requirements.

Good layout often depends upon the nature of the building. At one extreme is the industry that almost requires a specially constructed building; at the other is the type of business for which any average building is suitable. An example of the former might be a power laundry; of the latter, the typical small retail store. This topic will be developed in greater detail later in this chapter.

Comfort and convenience are motives that account for a surprising amount of human conduct. The department store as well as the modern automobile are based on these consumer objectives. No businessman can safely neglect this pair of essential factors in the building and layout. In general, if the building will permit a desirable layout and economical modernizing, these objectives will be achieved.

Management methods change from time to time in keeping with changes in relative costs of land, labor, and construction and in response to new technological developments and changes in accounting, control, or supervisory procedures. A prospective building should be examined in relation to such management trends. Does it permit utilizing modern management methods, and can it be easily adapted to those that appear imminent?

Construction

Our concern here is less with architectural engineering factors than with existing conditions. Safety for customers, personnel, merchandise, and equipment comes first. Condition of the roof, foundation, supporting columns, and floors should be investigated, especially in the case of older buildings. Most cities prescribe acceptable types of construction to protect occupants. However, as is sometimes shown by insurance rates, a building constructed according to these requirements may not be safe at a later date.

Modern design as well as the use of improved construction materials should receive attention when a building is appraised. The former is more functional and less ornate than traditional architecture. It permits remodeling to secure a greater amount of glass for light and ventilation, or removal of supporting columns that obstruct internal movement or visibility. Load-bearing walls used in older buildings make certain types of remodeling difficult and constitute a hazard in case of fire. Modern design also develops a favorable corporate image among prospects and customers. However, wonders have been accomplished in modernizing many old buildings. It is not so much the age of a building as the feasibility of modernizing that is important. Naturally the tenant will want the landlord to bear the cost of modernization or other structural changes required to make the building suitable, and very often this can be arranged. Improvements are constantly under way in the field of floor coverings. Terrazzo, asphaltic tile, inlaid linoleum, hardwood or composition blocks, and special waterproof, rubber base, and antiskid paints are examples of fairly recent developments. Floors should be selected with their intended use in mind. Reinforced concrete reduces vibration and is ideal for heavy warehouses; resilient materials increase employee and customer comfort; nonslippery surfaces reduce accident hazards; some materials are resistant to special chemicals or unusual wear; and others are attractive and particularly suitable for lighting requirements. Areas visited by customers may have sales promoting features, guide lines, trade-marks, or "atmosphere" inlaid in the floor.

Will the building permit expansion or alterations that may be needed later? Is it flexible enough to be adapted to other possible uses? Potential growth and changes in the proposed business during the term of the lease and possibly for the next five to ten years should be considered. Will the occupant want to add new departments? Where can they be housed? If one is starting a service business and may contemplate adding retail sales later, is the building, as well as its location, suitable? Is the area or space such that he can use it economically? What about subleasing part of the building now in order to have it available later for expansion? Is extra space that can be used effectively during dull seasons available for recurring peaks of selling, storage, or processing? These are some of the many questions that should be investigated before a final decision is made, and many of them should be provided for in the lease.

Modernization[1]

The external appearance of the building is important in many ways. In the capacity of an advertising medium it should represent the character of the business, identifying it and at the same time distinguishing it from others. Some attempts to make the building represent the character of the business take extreme forms such as the massive columns and thick marble walls, floors, and fixtures of many bank buildings. However, modern architecture can achieve the desired impression of safety, stability, permanence, and dignity by less expensive means. Such a building may become a white elephant if the bank moves to different quarters and the building cannot be converted to other uses. A better example of representative character is the modern fronts of retail and service businesses operating on up-to-date principles and methods, the luxurious front of the exclusive shop being contrasted to the practical, economical appearance of the popular-price store.

The building, including the front, may distinguish a particular business merely by being different, yet fashionable, or by attempting to visualize the nature of the business or its name. The Brown Derby in Hollywood illustrates the latter case. For the small businessman entering a line of business in which such novel treatment of the appearance of the building is neither too costly nor too permanent, it may be a quick way to get started. If successful, the design may be patented and serve as the basis for granting franchises, as was the case with Clarence Saunder's unusual Piggly Wiggly store fronts, or it may be used to open additional stores of a similar nature. Often this idea of the theme of the business is carried out for the interior. A luggage shop in Little Rock, Arkansas, for example, was constructed in the form of a Pullman car. Unless watched carefully, these attempts to visualize the nature of the business may result in a single purpose structure with all the disadvantages of special purpose machinery.

[1] See: *Store Modernization Check List,* Small Marketers Aids No. 54 (Washington, D. C.: Small Business Administration, March 1960).

Three aspects of modernization are especially important: modern lighting, color, and air conditioning. Recent writings in each of these fields should be consulted as only a few comments can be included here. Modern lighting is both functional and decorative. At present three types of lighting units are used, each having its advantages and limitations: filament, fluorescent, and spotlight. Retailers often combine incandescent light for its pleasing customer effects with fluorescent lighting to show merchandise to advantage. Spot- or floodlights are used either to focus attention at a certain point or to furnish unusually intense illumination. Often colored lights provide certain desired effects. Local public utilities can give the businessman good advice on proper lighting.

Color conditioning implies that the effects upon people produced by the colors of walls, ceilings, floors, fixtures, and even merchandise may be controlled to secure desired effects. In general the trend is toward lighter colors, because they usually are more pleasing as well as more economical in light reflecting ability. Consumer surveys show the following colors to be desirable; ivory, blue, green, peach, rose, and other pastel colors. Warmth can be simulated, if desired, by the use of warm colors of the red and yellow varieties. Apparent size can be increased through the use of receding colors like white or decreased by use of advancing colors. Although blue ranks higher in abstract color preference, each color should be used to accomplish the particular result desired.

Air conditioning has become a virtual necessity in retail stores located in warm climates and has increased worker efficiency in many plants. It is now expanding to include odor conditioning. Not only are temperature and humidity being controlled but often pleasant or even sales-stimulating odors are provided.

THE STORE BUILDING—SPECIAL REQUIREMENTS

Most of what has been said about the appearance and interior of the building probably applies to retailing to an even greater extent than to the other main fields of small business. In addition, the retail store has several special requirements to make the store attractive and inviting to customers. Colors of walls, background, and fixtures should be selected to set particular kinds of merchandise off to greater advantage. In this manner lighting should be used as a silent salesman.

The store front, especially the windows and entrance, should be designed with care to be in keeping with the type of merchandise sold and the style of retail architecture prevalent in the community. Although the general trend is toward the all-glass front, this is not suitable in all cases. Paint, furniture, food, and wearing-apparel stores may use this open front to advantage, but jewelry stores and others dealing in small items may find the traditional window more desirable. Valuable help may be secured from the trade association in each field and from equipment manufacturers and store front engineering firms as well as from the Merchants Service Bureaus.

THE FACTORY BUILDING—SPECIAL REQUIREMENTS

In the case of buildings for small factories and for the processing type of service establishments, requirements center around the nature of work processes and types of machinery and equipment to be used. Adequate provisions for the economical installation of necessary piping, ventilating equipment, foundations for heavy machines, and similar requirements will vary according to the nature of the business. The trend is toward the rectangular rather than the U- or L-shaped building and toward single-story structures if ground values permit. Good lighting is important, with the elimination of glare and variations of light intensities according to the needs of each operation being performed as major objectives. Most of the remaining requirements are related to layout and will be discussed later under that heading.

Although very little has been written about the small factory, many companies have constructed decentralized branch plants throughout the country. Most of these would be considered small businesses if they were independently owned and operated. A personal inspection of these buildings in any area should provide a wealth of ideas on modern small factory building design.

THE SERVICE BUILDING—SPECIAL REQUIREMENTS

Service businesses are so diverse in nature that building requirements vary greatly. Certain consulting and other personal services may require nothing more than facilities for a telephone, desk, chair, and filing equipment. Personal services like beauty shops require an attractive, comfortable interior arrangement and provisions for adequate electric power, plumbing, and processes connected with the preparation of solutions used, as well as rest rooms for patrons and display space for the promotion of merchandise and services for sale.

Three considerations are important in the determination of service building requirements: (1) whether the service is of the merchandising or the processing type, (2) necessary facilities, and (3) legal aspects. Many service establishments sell enough merchandise to make provisions for adequate display, stockkeeping, and selling space important considerations. Examples of such services include shops that repair electrical appliances, radios, refrigerators, watches, and similar articles. Often shops such as these will need a building wired for heavy-duty electrical equipment.

Another group of service businesses with special plant requirements is composed of those working with heavy, bulky materials or products. Examples include automobile, truck, and tractor repair shops and storage places, and sheet metal and heavy machine shops. In general a single-story building without basement is preferable for such establishments. Large open spaces free of supporting columns and heavy, level, nonsagging concrete floors are also important. The latter may be essential for accurate welding and other operations commonly performed in sheet metal shops. The industrial, rather than commercial, type of building has many advantages for such shops. Exposed steel ceiling beams may be used for the suspension of hoisting and monorail overhead crane equipment. Steel columns may serve similarly for jib cranes and strong walls for supporting storage racks. Wide aisles and entrances are needed to accommodate delivery trucks as well as vehicles to be repaired. Frequently special facilities for ventilation may be necessary. Safety codes governing ventilation, exits, fire walls, floor loads, and similar conditions may introduce unusual building requirements.

Service stations will have some of the special requirements already discussed and in addition will need facilities for petroleum storage tanks, a hydraulic car lift or grease pit, and an appropriate exterior appearance for attracting motorists. Floors and service areas should be easily cleaned and resistant to grease, oil, gasoline, and other chemicals. Other types of service businesses that require work areas resistant to certain chemicals and fumes are battery repair shops, photo engraving plants, and electro-plating firms.

ARRANGING THE LAYOUT

Layout deals with the arrangement of machines, fixtures, equipment, and designated spaces *according to a plan*. A distinction must be made between "making" a layout and "planning" a layout. Too often machines are moved without a plan. Because of this it is important that qualified industrial engineers and retail executives supervise major layout revisions. Retailers can turn to Merchant Service Bureaus such as the National Cash Register Company, Dayton, Ohio; Rice-Stix Manufacturing Wholesalers, St. Louis, Missouri; or Butler Brothers, Chicago, Illinois, for additional aid. There are also many consulting firms which can supply helpful advice concerning factory layouts.

The purpose of plant layout is to (1) serve as a working medium for the interchange and development of ideas and (2) present a visual plan of the proposed organization as a basis for design and construction. Layout implies the most effective use of space for the particular business. A notable difference concerning space exists between manufacturing and retailing. Whereas in the former space is measured by area or volume, in the latter a fourth dimension is added—location. The same area or volume in one part of a store may be worth many times more than an equal area or volume in another part of the same store.

Layout starts with an analysis of activities involved in operating the business, objectives sought, and facilities for achieving them. In manufacturing and in many service businesses the primary objective is to facilitate productive operations. In the retail store it is to direct the flow of customer traffic for maximum profitable sales. The retail store is a machine for selling, and layout is properly regarded as a sales promotion device.

Certain factors must always be considered in arrangement and layout. They are:

1. *Logical and psychological arrangement of equipment and merchandise with reference to production flow for manufacturing and to customer buying habits for merchandising.* Having machinery in proper sequence and conveniently located saves factory workers much lost motion. Also, having merchandise in the right place at the right time increases sales per customer and reduces steps for salespeople.

2. *Maximum use of light, ventilation, and heat, to take full advantage of natural conditions resulting from the building construction.* Effective use of windows, doors, vents, and skylights will save eyes, improve work and health. Customers will also appreciate the fact that arrangements made with these factors in mind facilitate their personal comfort and their selection of proper merchandise.

3. *Maximum efficiency in the use of equipment.* Improper location of equipment may cause workers to do entirely by hand work that should be done by existing equipment. If the machine for putting "the finishing touch" on the final processing or packaging of goods requires extra steps, for example, employees may tend to do this work manually or to avoid it entirely.

4. *Location of materials or merchandise in such a way as to be readily available to workers or customers.* By thus reducing steps for workers or reminding customers of their needs, an orderly arrangement saves time in location for workers and permits customers to study and handle the merchandise.

5. *Maximum facilities for a clear view of the establishment by management, worker, or customer.* Management can readily observe all activities of customers and employees, workers can observe customers' presence and movements, and customers can readily see all the store's offerings and the location of particular groups of merchandise.

The same principles of arrangement apply to various types of businesses, since certain categories of factors are always present, namely:

1. People—workers, customers, management.
2. Equipment—machinery or fixtures.
3. Goods—materials, merchandise, or supplies.
4. The building and its features—windows, doors, stairs, and so forth.

To summarize, layout for any kind of business—merchandising, manufacturing,[2] or service—involves arrangement of equipment, machines, and

[2] For a list of objectives and methods for accomplishing them, see: Raymond C. Newton, *Principles of Plant Layout for Small Plants*, Technical Aids for Small Manufacturers No. 42 (Washington, D. C.: Small Business Administration, 1956).

other elements to secure maximum efficiency in use. The relative importance of meeting the needs of customers, workers, and management varies according to the type of business but must be considered in planning the layout.[3]

Store Layout

The retailer has three objectives for his layout: customer satisfaction, maximum sales, and economy. Customer satisfaction includes convenience, service, and attractive appearance. The objective of maximum sales involves proper selection of fixtures and placing of merchandise. Economy of operation covers both expenses and protection.

Stores vary in the relative amount of their business secured from telephone orders and from customers who visit the store. The former kind of sales demand a manufacturer's efficiency type of layout, usually of the process variety; the latter require a "selling machine" type. Finally, the amount of self-service compared to clerk service desired influences layout. The result is a compromise between these conflicting objectives for all stores except the few that concentrate exclusively on one type of selling, such as cash-and-carry self-service only.

Space locations within a store can be used more effectively in some ways than in others. It is usually poor business to try to increase the volume of a slow-selling department by giving it one of the best locations when that results in shifting another department better able to take full advantage of the good location. Figure 2 shows an approximate distribution of the total rent or value of space in a small store according to location on the main floor.[4]

When a one-floor store has entrances on two or more sides, such as the front and rear or front and one side, the relative amount of traffic through each door is the important consideration. In such cases the diagram can be used to indicate the relative value of space inward from each entrance if they have equal traffic volume; otherwise, it can be adapted in approximate proportion to the importance of each.

Whether the owner plans to make his own final layout or to call on the assistance of some member of the outside staff, such as a Merchants Service Bureau, he should make a tentative layout of his own as carefully as possible.

First, he should make a plan of the floor space to scale and divide it into areas as indicated in the diagram, noting the percentage value of each area in relation to sales potentials. Then he should list the space needs, and evaluate each in terms of several factors, such as need for particular locations, ability to capitalize fully on heavy customer traffic through impulse sales, ability to draw customers to remote sections of the store, and miscellaneous factors like employee conveniences and nearness to other activities.

[3] For further study see: John R. Immer, *Profitable Small Plant Layout,* Management Series No. 21 (Washington, D. C.: Small Business Administration, 1958).

[4] For a mathematical presentation of the "4-3-2-1 rule" see: Leo V. Aspinwall, *Are Your Merchandise Lines Paying Their Rent?* Small Marketers Aids No. 30 (Washington, D. C.: Small Business Administration, December 1957).

A preliminary step is to separate selling from non-selling activities. Non-selling work is in turn divided into essential store activities like office work, receiving and storing goods, display construction and "customer bait" like telephones, package checking, and postal substations. Facilitating activities may be assigned the least desirable locations from a traffic viewpoint. Customer service departments will be strategically located to lure customers past tempting selling displays of impulse goods.

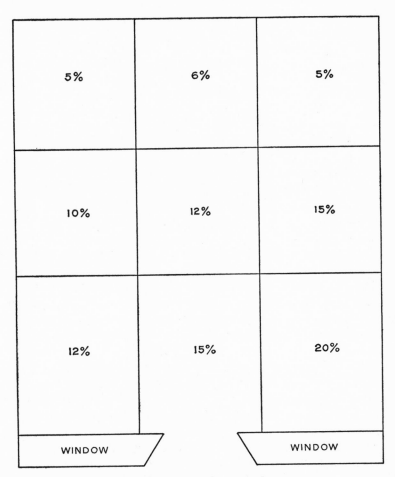

FIGURE 2. Plot of sales floor values.

Selection and arrangement of fixtures and merchandise within any store building will be determined in some part by the merchandise sold, the customers it seeks to serve, and the service it offers. As to fixtures, an exclusive shop selling but one kind of merchandise—apparel, furniture, or leather goods, for example—should possess an atmosphere of dignity, comfort, modernness, and perhaps even luxury. Stores selling primarily to men will need to present a rugged, masculine, "he-man," and businesslike atmosphere; those serving women will have "the feminine touch" characterized by carefully harmonized colors, decorative figures, and diffused lighting.

The first great division of merchandise from the viewpoint of arrangement is into "impulse" goods and "demand" goods; that is, goods which are bought on sight without previous deliberation and those which customers have in mind when they go to a particular store. This fact is frequently capitalized on. The druggist keeps patent medicines, hospital supplies, and his prescription department in the rear of the store. To get to these, the customer must pass many displays of impulse goods. The wise shoe store operator has his staple shoes in the rear; as the customer goes to them, he passes attractive hosiery, house slippers, and various sundries. Shoes will be bought in that store or in that kind of store without being prominently displayed, for competition on them is limited.

Some stores have found that having the wrapping desk in the rear draws people back, as they tend to follow the merchandise and the salesman as he moves in that direction. The value of this location, however, may be offset by the loss of the salesman's time in making the trip back that far for each sale.

Guiding traffic is helpful, and many devices are useful in managing this. Some stores, not fully relying on the "keep to the right" habit or perhaps wishing to counteract it, place obstacles in the way of customers in some paths and make wider entrances to others. A pile of boxes on display or a sizable showcase is an effective barrier to control traffic. People's tendency to act by habit and to follow the line of least resistance can be capitalized on by the alert merchant.

The success of the variety store, beginning with Woolworth, has been attributed to the use of open display.[5] The modern department store, having discovered the value of spaciousness, puts it to use in wide aisles and low display cases. Most store owners agree with the findings of one experiment which showed that open display in a drugstore doubled face powder sales, tripled soap sales, and increased candy sales over five times.

Should a selection of men's suits be arranged by price, by size, by line, or on some other basis? Arrangement by size seems to be the best plan, because the customer is not so likely to be attracted to a suit not available in his size and the mixture of price lines more readily permits trading up by showing and selling better lines. Placing the same colors together might make a more expensive suit look drab in comparison with a cheaper suit of a brighter shade. Also, if a merchant has a large stock of one style in different colors and sizes, he should not put them all on display, for this makes the garment look cheap and the customer feel that he would meet himself everywhere he went. This avoidance of large one-style displays is a rule that will

[5] See: *Will Self-Service Boost Your Profits?* Small Marketers Aids No. 45 (Washington, D. C.: Small Business Administration, June 1959).

apply generally to apparel. The problem may also arise in furnishings, appliances, paints, or shoes. Since shoes remain in boxes, ease in location for the salesperson is of major importance. In this connection it may be noted that, contrary to the common practice of keeping shoe stocks by lot number for convenience in reordering, one store found that keeping them by size saved salesmen many of the steps they had previously wasted in going from one lot number group to another looking for the size wanted. Similar reductions in effort and time may be made as the merchant opposes practical to traditional procedures.

Wrapping and cashiering facilities are frequently mislocated. They are usually together for employee convenience. They may be at the rear of the store to draw trade past other goods. Frequently, however, they comprise a rather bulky unit consisting of a large table and a large cash register. Many stores have found that small items may not have to be wrapped if "charged" facilities for the handling of such small cash sales may be arranged at other strategic points in the store. Under this arrangement only larger items or those sold on credit and requiring credit approval will require wrapping and the use of the larger facilities, which may be placed in space at the rear that is less expensive from the traffic viewpoint.

The manufacturers of store fixtures, recognizing the changing nature of merchandise and the desire of merchants to experiment, have for several years produced fixture units of such uniformity, mobility, and ready interchangeability that they permit various combinations. Although they are separate units, when properly placed they join together so readily as to appear to be one unit built to store specifications.

Layout in Wholesaling

Layout of the wholesale establishment is based on the primary function of the business, order filling. Optimum use should be made of the force of gravity, mechanical conveyors, and materials-handling equipment, since about 60 per cent of the cost of operation is likely to be payroll. Often forward stocks (say six to ten days' supply) of a frequently purchased item can be arranged along a conveyor or order assembly line. Major functions like receiving, "dead" storage, order assembly, breaking packages, packing and shipping, and office work should be physically separated. An exception might be combining receiving, packing, and shipping in the smaller plant. In general, the wholesale layout will resemble more closely that of a factory, and many good ideas can be adapted from factory layouts.

The following discussion, which is adapted from publications of the U. S. Department of Commerce, contains many suggestions applicable to the small wholesale house.

Most wholesale-warehouse activities are subject to a production-line type of operation. Unlike a manufacturer, who turns out goods that are identical, however, the wholesaler turns out orders of goods that are seldom alike.

The wholesaler's problem is to arrange an order-picking route and routine that will enable him to handle these unpredictable assortments without special adjustment for any of them. Therefore, both route and routine should be flexible enough to meet any reasonable contingency.

In a good many instances where the physical characteristics of the building have prevented the establishment of a basically sound layout, special mechanization has been substituted.

There seem to be many operational advantages in intermingling the full- and broken-case stocks for order-filling purposes. Some of these are:

1. Fewer work stations are needed and therefore fewer persons have to take the time to scan orders.

2. A smoother flow of orders is effected, since the fewer the work stations, the smoother the flow of work.

3. The amount of paper work is reduced, because an extra copy of the order or floor ticket from which to fill the full- and broken-case portions of the order is not needed and thus one operation is eliminated.

Although the selection of the basic order-pick-line pattern is determined largely by the character of the building, the wholesaler has some freedom of choice in its implications. He may arrange (1) a system featuring a short conveyor line with a long distance between the line and much of the merchandise, (2) a system featuring a long conveyor line with a relatively short distance between the line and all the goods, or (3) a system featuring push-buggies which carry the baskets to the merchandise at all times. If the wholesaler uses conveyors, he should have the shortest possible conveyor line which will carry the baskets close enough to the merchandise.

It is the usual custom to place the order-pick line around the perimeter of the shelf stock. This is a fault, no matter what the reason for the practice —whether it be to gain daylight for the order-picking process or to gain enough length of line either to reach all the goods or to accommodate all the baskets that might have to be placed on the line at any one time.

Drug wholesalers realize the importance of laying out the shortest average walk for order pickers. They know that these employees walk miles every day in the routine of order filling and that carrying goods from shelf to basket accounts for half of this distance.[6]

Progressive wholesale grocers have recently taken the view of the warehouse building as a machine for low-cost movement of merchandise as well as a storage facility. This new concept has brought about a separation of storage from order assembly. In the assembly-line type of operation the goods to be used in assembly are set up in a nearby space, preferably on one level. The "storage" stocks are in other parts of the building. Sufficient space must be specifically devoted to receiving and shipping docks for an efficient move-

[6] John R. Bromell, *Effective Use of Wholesale Drug Warehouses*, Industrial Series No. 68 (Washington, D. C.: U. S. Department of Commerce, July 1947), pp. 19 ff.

ment of goods in the receiving and shipping operations. In short, the warehouse building is "functionalized." Different parts of the building are specially designed for the functions to be performed in them. The results of this new concept of functional design are seen in the new streamlined one-story warehouse building.[7]

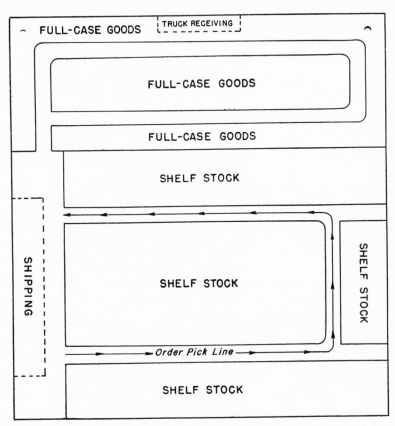

FIGURE 3. Illustrated above is a suggested location for shipping and receiving platforms where full-case goods and shelf stock are kept in entirely different places. It refers to a one-floor operation in a building that is almost square and in which broken- and full-case goods are picked into orders from different areas in the warehouse. (The floor plan is not drawn to scale.)

Source: John R. Bromell, *Effective Use of Wholesale Drug Warehouses*, Industrial Series No. 68 (Washington, D. C.: U. S. Department of Commerce, July 1947), p. 12.

The small wholesaler is likely to have the advantage of being able to select a modern one-story building and plan his layout accordingly. Naturally there will be variations from any plan that could be presented. Figures 3 and

[7] William H. Meserole and Charles H. Sevin, *Effective Grocery Wholesaling*, Economic Series No. 14 (Washington, D. C.: U. S. Department of Commerce, October 1941), p. 116.

4 show two layouts—one for a square building and the other for a long, narrow structure.

In the electrical goods and appliance field a committee recently studied the problem of warehouse building and layout. The following discussion is based upon some of the suggestions made by the committee, with particular reference to layout:[8]

1. Office or other facilities for shipping and receiving clerks should be close to shipping and receiving doors.

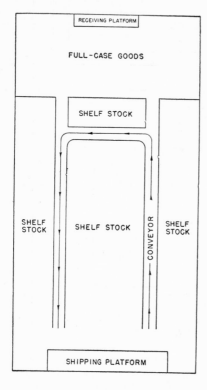

FIGURE 4. This shows a suggested location for the shipping and receiving platforms in a long, narrow building. In this case the full- and broken-case goods are picked into orders from different places in the warehouse. (The diagram is not drawn to scale.)

Source: John R. Bromell, *Effective Use of Wholesale Drug Warehouses,* p. 13.

2. The ceiling height in warehouses should be 16 feet where sprinklers are used and 14 feet where they are not. This will provide mezzanine space where required.

3. The building should provide adequate toilet and rest room facilities for all personnel.

4. In order to facilitate protection from theft, the number of building entrances and exits should be minimized.

[8] J. G. Johannesen, Chairman, Committee of National Electrical Wholesalers Association, *Warehousing, Deliveries, Installations, Freight Rates and Claims Committee Suggests Building Lay-outs; Offers Sample Plans.* Report to meeting held on May 14 and 15, 1945, by this committee in New York.

5. When the business includes distribution of major appliances and radios, the building should provide suitable display rooms and meeting space for salesmen and dealers.

6. Broken-package stock should be placed in bins directly behind the store counter in order to serve the sales counter as well as to fill broken-package orders out of stock. This stock should be enclosed. Aisles between bins should be 30 to 36 inches wide, with a main aisle 48 inches wide, and bins should be not more than 8 feet 4 inches high. Bins with dimensions in accordance with the type of stocks handled should be provided. The aisle space between bins and the store sales counter should be 4 to 6 feet, and the ends of the bins should face the counter.

7. When preparing warehouse layouts, wholesalers should investigate the latest mechanical devices and products available for materials-handling in order to take advantage of laborsaving ideas. Pallets and gravity chutes frequently offer a means of simplifying materials-handling under certain conditions.

Factory Layout

Most industries are of two primary types according to whether their products are diversified or uniform. Each type in turn has subdivisions. Some diversified industries, such as candy manufacturing or toymaking, turn out a variety of products; others perform a wide range of operations, such as those accomplished in a machine, or other kind of metal-working shop. This division results in two major types of layout: process, or job, layout and product, or straight line, layout. In the process layout, operations of the same type are performed in the same area—that is, machines of the same kind are grouped together and the material passes through these machine areas for processing. This type of layout is used for short-term standard items and specialties or products that cannot be standardized. It is the older of the two basic types of layout and still has many advantages. Among these are: superior control of intricate processes, greater utilization of machines, increased flexibility, low capital equipment investment, and adaptability to a wider variety of operations. However, it requires higher unit costs, greater movement of materials, more delays, difficulty of estimating costs and completion times on many jobs, and better daily planning and scheduling of work to avoid costly congestion at certain work centers. Since even a job shop will excel in certain types of work, the usual tendency is to find a few products or kinds of service increasing in frequency of demand. Sooner or later the advantages of product or straight line layout are realized for these cases. Under this system, operations are arranged in sequence so that material moves forward and successive operations are performed consecutively. It is partly for this reason that most layout specialists recommend the product or straight line layout whenever possible, even sacrificing certain advantages of flexibility and lower initial cost in many cases.

Although two examples from big business—automobile assembly and meat packing—both illustrate almost the ultimate in straight line layout, the former is an example of the assembly type of process, the latter of the analytical type. In spite of the little they seem to have in common, Henry Ford, the originator of continuous assembly straight line production, got his ideas from the meat packers. Small businessmen can find some of the best examples of layout and other "how to do it" ideas in big business concerns that have developed certain methods to a high degree of perfection.

Considering the foregoing variations in greater detail, we can first summarize some of the objectives as follows:

1. Materials and semifinished products should follow the shortest and quickest possible route from entrance to exit.

2. A minimum of physical handling, with as many operations being performed at each "stop" as possible, is essential.

3. Through layout, management must seek to eliminate "bottlenecks" in the production process caused by the slowing down of any one process at a strategic location. Although this may depend largely on the adequacy and care of machinery, the location of the machinery is a vital factor.

4. The misuse of space must be recognized as being of equal importance to wasted use of machinery and manpower.

5. Complete elimination of "backtracking," overlapping of work, and unnecessary inspection should be achieved through constant awareness of possibilities for new sequences and combinations of steps in processing or fabrication.

Efficiency in manufacturing layout will depend greatly on the nature of the work done. It is impossible to develop a standard layout pattern that will apply to all processes. The continuous process, such as that used in the sheet metal products field, where raw materials may flow in at one end of the plant and the finished products out of the other end, can be arranged in such a way as to achieve constant maximum efficiency day after day; however, once a product is designed, materials to make specific items are determined, and standards are set, the manufacturing sequence can usually be arranged once and for all until the materials, design, specifications, or methods are changed. In some plants production assignments are constantly changing in sequence and between machines and men. Smaller plants of this type will require that one man do the job through all operations; as plants grow larger, different phases of the work can be assigned to different machines. A third type of factory is the one where various kinds of work involving different materials are going on in different sections of the plant, sometimes interdependently. A pump factory may have one department casting iron, another turning out brass parts, and another cutting leathers. In this situation co-ordination of a group of continuous processes is paramount.

Layout for the Service Establishment

Service businesses may be divided into two broad groups as far as layout and physical plants are concerned, merchandising and processing. The former would include tourist courts and most personal service establishments. Customer convenience, pleasing appearance, and similar considerations would be of relatively great importance.

The second, or processing, type of service business has much in common with a factory. Here various operations, such as cleaning, repairing, or altering, are performed on articles owned by the customers. In many cases the customer never sees the work being done and may not even come to the plant at all. Factors governing productive efficiency are of relatively great importance in such cases with regard to both building and layout. Like manufacturing *operations,* most service businesses of the processing type can be classed as either job or continuous.

Principles and standards governing layout in manufacturing, as previously discussed, will be found to apply to processing service establishments if allowance is made for the greater diversity of activities carried on in the service fields.

In the well-established service fields trade associations and trade periodicals can be very helpful in solving problems relating to layout, equipment selection, and building construction. Many equipment manufacturers have an engineering or service division to assist in this work. There are also several independent firms and freelance specialists whose services may be obtained for a fee on a basis comparable to that used by the consulting engineers used by manufacturers.

Although management consultants may be needed to solve more complicated problems of layout, there is much the average service establishment operator can do by himself. First he should make a floor plan of the building and work areas to scale. After deciding which are the most important types of work done, he should go into the plant and observe the sequence of operations performed on each of these and draw a line representing the flow of work, using a different color for each. The result is a process or flow chart of the operations as they are actually being performed. It is important to limit the first chart to the most important types of work, for otherwise the diagram is likely to become hopelessly confusing. If the major operations are provided for first, most of the minor ones will usually be cared for. Any that do not fit the main pattern with only slight adjustments should probably be eliminated.

The flow chart should be examined against certain standards of desirable layout, the most important of which are maximum straight line flow, minimum backtrack flow, and minimum cross flow. The new layout can best be developed by experimenting with different flow charts. It is not always possible, even for one type of work, to achieve completely straight line flow because of the size and shape of the building or because of certain equipment that requires particular and relatively fixed locations. One solution is the U-shaped layout, according to which, processes on one type of work begin and end at the same side of the building. When two or more types of work are of approximately equal importance but require different sequences of operations at the same kind of workplaces, two solutions are possible. If the volume of work justifies duplication of equipment or work centers, several straight line flows may be used. In very small plants a compromise process and job layout may be necessary, planned for the maximum straight line flow and minimum backtrack and cross flows.

Even where straight line flow is used, in certain cases, back-tracking may also be present. This is true especially when the work is trucked between operations to particular equipment, such as to washers and then back along the same path to extractors in a dry cleaning plant. The flow chart will show such conditions, many of which may be corrected once they are discovered.

Cross flow resembles a street intersection. The voluntary or compulsory "stop-and-go" restrictions made necessary result in loss of time that could be avoided with proper layout. Careful study of the flow chart will disclose conditions that might continue unobserved indefinitely in the absence of planning of the type suggested. As mentioned earlier, layout is arrangement according to a plan.

CONCLUSIONS

Growth and change are essential parts of any business. The building, whether designed and constructed or adapted, should be regularly expanded or modernized as the business warrants such moves. Layout is most important in meeting this challenge. The trend in layout seems to point toward the concept of "flow"—flow of people through a store or flow of materials through a factory. This concept of layout should never be taken for granted since business is not static and both building and layout requirements change. An alert businessman will give continuous attention to these important profit-making tools.

For the small businessman valuable information is available in the trade press, from his trade association, and from other agencies mentioned in the chapter. However, he can often make worth-while improvements by analyzing his needs and studying operations as they are being performed to locate waste motion, uneconomical use of labor, and other weaknesses. By making a process or flow chart further improvements may be made. Often suggestions made by employees or customers will lead to valuable changes in layout, equipment, or construction. Planning layout is a fascinating undertaking that usually more than repays the effort and study given to it.

QUESTIONS AND PROBLEMS

1. How is the building related to layout in a small business?

2. Name and briefly explain the functions or aspects of a building that are important to consider.

3. Why is layout a continuous problem for most small businessmen?

4. Select some particular kind of business and tell how the best layout affects requirements of the ideal building.

5. Name and briefly describe five goals or standards for effective layout.

6. List separately the standards or principles governing layout for retailing, wholesaling, manufacturing, and service operations. Comment on similarities and differences in your four lists.

7. How, if at all, is retail store layout related to each of the following: display, advertising, personnel, location, customer services, buying?

8. Is it better for the retail store layout to accept the customers' habit of going to the right or to divert them to the left? Discuss.

9. Suggest methods for different kinds of stores to draw almost every customer to the rear of the store.

10. What developments in layout do you predict for the near future? Explain.

11. Make a list of the different things that could be done in a retail store to eliminate "blind spots." Discuss the practicality of each.

12. List several kinds of service businesses where the layout is based on factory layout principles, and do the same for those based on retail store layout principles. What types of service establishments have special layout problems of their own? Explain.

13. Is novel use of interior lighting more appropriate in certain lines of business than in others? Explain and illustrate from your own observations or material found in trade journals.

14. Make a list of all the ways odors could be added to particular business areas to produce desirable effects on customers and workers. What factors would tend to limit the use of each? Discuss.

15. Briefly summarize the main layout considerations for a small wholesaler.

16. What are the two main types of manufacturing processes? How is layout affected by each?

17. Examine the layouts of several chain and independent stores in the same kind of business and discuss your findings.

18. Visit a number of modern retail stores in different lines of business to study the colors used for backgrounds, walls, floors, and fixtures. What conclusions do you draw?

19. Visit several recently built small branch plants of large manufacturing or processing companies and study both building and layout. Discuss how your findings could be utilized by the small businessman in several different lines of business.

20. Tom wants to modernize his 30 foot front, 100 foot deep food store and convert it to self-service. He has ample funds for any justifiable alterations. Describe what he should do and give your reasons.

16 • Employee Relations

The reputation a small business acquires in the community is closely associated with its employee relations. Customers are quick to sense employees' attitudes toward their management. A contented, well-treated staff of workers will reflect loyalty and enthusiasm in their dealings with customers and with the public. Good employee relations therefore can be a major asset to the small business. Thus, good employee relations are an essential to good public relations. Every progressive business seeks some point of superiority or distinctiveness over its competitors. In the small business the major competitive advantage may well be its high-quality personnel.

Materials, equipment, machines, and other things used by business are available to all competitors at approximately equal prices. It is the firm's personnel that is unique and susceptible to the greatest individual management development. The result of good employee relations—a loyal, efficient group of workers—cannot be copied or purchased by competitors. Furthermore, the increased worker efficiency which usually accompanies good employee relations is of greater importance in the small business than in the large concern. In the manufacturing and service fields the latter is better equipped with more expensive machinery and mechanical aids. In merchandising the large stores have staff departments as well as better mechanical equipment to aid employees. The small business must rely more heavily on its personnel alone.

The human element in the small business is complicated by the close personal acquaintance that normally exists between the owner and his employees. It often happens that many of the employees are relatives or lifelong friends of the owner. The result may be an unwillingness to follow approved personnel practices as developed in larger organizations, either because the owner feels that they are too impersonal for his small group of intimately known workers or because he lacks understanding of modern personnel practices and their adaption to the needs of the small firm. Offsetting these obstacles in the small firm is the owner's greater knowledge of each of his employees and the feeling of mutual friendship that so often exists. These are *real advantages*. Actually one of the main reasons for the development of most so-called "modern personnel practices" has been the need of the larger organizations to make up for this lack of personal contact and understanding between management and employees. Yet the importance of separating business from personal and family relations should be a major incentive for using modern personnel methods in the very small company.

The methods to be discussed briefly are "standard practice" in large concerns but may appear to some readers as unnecessary in the small firm. But people are human beings, whether employed by large or small firms.

If the small fellow limits his choice of methods to those used by other small operators he will probably repeat their mistakes and make very little progress. If one small shop appears to have good employee relations without using any organized personnel procedures, the reason probably lies in the personality of the owner—something very difficult for other businessmen to duplicate. Another small business may have very little labor turnover and employees who seem to be contented and satisfied with their positions. Closer analysis might disclose an employer lax in his supervision and requirements of worker efficiency. Employees realize this and are satisfied to enjoy the easy going. A favorable lease may have made it possible for the firm to show a modest profit in spite of relatively inefficient but not disgruntled employees. Similar cases could be given to illustrate various ways in which a small business can exist without actually cultivating worker support, but they would prove only that inefficiency of operation is fairly common among many small concerns that have not as yet felt serious competition, or that many small businessmen are content with mediocre results. Good employee relations in such cases could convert these "average" concerns into more profitable, growing companies—to the mutual benefit of employer and employee alike.

Far too many beginning business operators, often being creative men, are by nature self-centered, driving ahead with only their personal goals and methods apparent to themselves and their employees. Authorities on business leadership agree that a significant measure of the business owner's success in utilizing, capitalizing on the talents of these others, is his ability to accept and use the ideas of his employees. A major obstacle is often that of incorporating them into his operational scheme of things as if they were his own, giving the employee full credit if they succeed and assuming the blame if they fail. Such courage begets contribution and co-operation of a high order, fosters a true group spirit of aggressiveness that can readily distinguish the small firm.

A logical starting point for any personnel program is job analysis and description. Job analysis involves for each position a study and recording of the nature of the work done, types of physical objects handled (such as machines, tools, equipment, materials, or merchandise), and how each job is related to others and to the entire organization. Job description translates job analysis facts into specifications relating to the skills, effort, responsibility, aptitudes, experience, knowledge, abilities, and physical and personality traits of the individuals best suited to perform the jobs successfully. Selection, placement, training, transfers, and remuneration of all employees should be based largely upon these job analyses and job descriptions.

In the company with relatively few employees each "job" will naturally involve more duties than would be expected of one individual in the large concern. In making a job analysis it is well to take all employees into one's confidence and explain the purpose of the study. Each individual is then asked to make a complete list of all his duties or responsibilities; kinds of work performed; machines, equipment, tools, or merchandise handled; relations with other individuals in the organization; and difficulties and problems commonly encountered. Often this listing will be made in cooperation with a supervisor or department head.

At this stage certain lost motion, inconsistencies, overlapping, or unsafe practices may be revealed. Thus it may be advisable to undertake some methods studies for the purpose of job improvement before actually preparing the job analyses and descriptions. Simply stated, methods study involves an earnest, intelligent effort to find the best way of doing the job. Depending upon the nature of the work, it may stress saving time, reducing risk, saving physical effort, examining motives, or determining the personal factors involved in selling or creative activity. Although large companies, where subdivision of labor is already highly developed, find it necessary to employ methods study "experts," the average small businessman can often make improvements resulting in a 50 per cent increase in efficiency by simple observation and analysis. The work can usually be done faster, better, and cheaper. Each time a method of doing a particular job is improved it should be made standard practice, and co-operation in using the new way should be secured from all employees concerned.

Job evaluation is the next logical step. In this procedure various jobs are evaluated with reference to one another and to their importance to the company in terms of skill, knowledge, effort, accuracy, responsibility, personality, and similar factors. Although used primarily to secure equitable pay for each job, it also provides a reliable basis for estimating labor costs and helps to reduce a common source of employee grievance—namely, a belief that he is underpaid relative to other workers. Job evaluation has many additional advantages to both management and employees. After many years' use in production, this personnel technique has spread to retailing, service industries, and many white collar occupations.

SELECTION

The small business is usually limited geographically in recruiting employees and is sometimes further handicapped by the fact that the best local talent may prefer employment in big business. By paying wages comparable to those offered by large employers and by stressing promotional opportunities or a better chance to learn the business, however, the small employer can largely offset this handicap. Aggressive solicitation and selling of the company by the small businessman can further lessen some of these limitations and help to secure an adequate supply of the right type of job applicants. His effort must be to cause his plant or store to be considered "a good place to work."

Another point of special importance to the small business is to seek out and select candidates rather than wait for applications. Under any circumstances, when applications for employment are received, standard employment procedures should be followed, though more informally in the small business than in the large one. The application blank to be filled out and studied by the prospective employer is the first of these. An application blank is a record of statements (presumably of facts) made at the time of seeking employment. It should include *all* information that will aid in deciding whether or not to employ the applicant, as well as certain facts that may later be useful if he is employed. Information concerning any circumstances peculiar to the particular company, if relevant, should be included, such as union membership or willingness to join if company policy requires this, family and financial status if these have been found to be important requirements for success in the organization, and a record of previous employment, with references.

Among the important uses of the application blank are to aid the interviewer, to furnish such information as references, to provide an initial record of employment if questions of fact later arise, and to serve as part of a permanent record in which added experience and training should find a place.

The wise employer does not take an application at its face value. References given should be investigated, either in person, by letter, or over the phone. The telephone check has gained in favor. Naturally, the applicant will select persons who he thinks will give him the best recommendations. Usually relatives, church officials, and politicians should be eliminated from further consideration, for the very nature of their positions precludes securing useful information regarding the applicant from them. Other references, such as former employers, school officials, businessmen, or acquaintances, require further appraisal. Two other situations sometimes arise, however, and deserve further consideration.

The logical references for an applicant to give are readily apparent to any employer: his present or former employer, banker, business associates, school officials (in the case of recent graduates), and possibly a few business acquaintances. An applicant's giving references other than these may indicate a desire to conceal certain "unfortunate" episodes in his past experience or it may indicate a thoroughly justifiable situation. In doubtful cases the prospective employer should exercise judgment supported by human understanding.

The other situation is more difficult to handle. Human beings, even supervisors and employers, are often wrong in their evaluation of an employee, and an unfortunate set of circumstances—personality conflicts, accidents, and so forth—may distort their opinions. In such cases the individual affected may justly prefer to give as references unbiased co-workers or others rather than his immediate "boss." Organizations of all types and sizes have "internal politics." Often publicity given to this condition in a particular organization or a knowledge of its existence by various individuals will give the clue needed as to which recommendations should be used by the prospective employer.

> In cities all over the country there are manufacturers, financial houses, retailers—all types of business firms—who have found a new way to make employee selections, a surer method of choosing between apparently equally-qualified candidates for an open position.
>
> These companies no longer rely entirely upon the naturally biased statements of job applicants. They eliminate practically all doubt as to whether a man of 42 has accidentally stated his age as 38, or whether a short and unsatisfactory employment period has escaped mention. They get all this and much more normally inaccessible information quickly and accurately in a "Personnel Report"—right from the local Credit Bureau.
>
> In its lowest-priced questionnaire form (in some areas as economically rated as $3.00) the Personnel Report reveals much helpful information on any type of prospective employee. In the more elaborate narrative forms (the cost of which may run to $100 or more, depending on the amount of detail desired) the Personnel Report presents a detailed and comprehensive history adequate for judging top executive material. In fact, there are a number of instances where men contemplating business partnerships have drawn such reports on each other.[1]

An example of a widely used form is No. 17, Personnel-Employment Credit Character Form. This report covers a specialized investigation on prospective as well as present employees designed to cover important antecedent questions such as peculiarities, educational advantages, ability to get along with other employees, home conditions, whether a steady worker or subject to considerable absenteeism, and related topics. An illustration of this form is presented in Figure 5.

The Use of Tests

Three general types of tests or examinations are often used during the selection process: mental tests, performance tests, and the physical examination. There are numerous varieties of the first category, some designed to measure intelligence or the ability to learn and others to rate aptitudes, interests, attitudes, and particular personality traits. Opinions differ regarding their value to the small firm although the availability of easily used tests

---

[1] *Service Provides Information on Prospective Employees,* Small Business Aids No. 231 (Washington, D. C.: U. S. Department of Commerce). Condensed from Bert Dale, "Pre-Test Your Employees," *Forbes Magazine of Business* (February 15, 1947). See also: "Better Selection of Personnel," available from the Retail Credit Company, Atlanta, Georgia, or their branch offices in principal cities.

is steadily increasing. The novice using psychological tests should be warned against the many charlatans offering testing services. No such test should be administered or interpreted without expert guidance, which is available from many educational institutions, personnel institutes, and practicing psychologists. Performance or achievement tests should be used, even in the small business, if the nature of the work for which an individual is applying permits. These need not be elaborate; often a mere tryout preliminary to actual employment is sufficient. The physical examination should be used much more generally than it is, especially when the job requires strength, good vision, hearing, ability to stand continuously, stamina, or other qualities above the average and wherever the health and safety of the public or fellow workers are involved.

The interview is the only selection procedure almost universally used. Although an interview is ordinarily necessary to determine such characteristics of the applicant as appearance, poise, and speech, it has many weaknesses. Chief among these is the exaggerated belief of the interviewer that he is a good judge of human nature. The interview can be made most effective when used in conjunction with an application blank and job description.

Before the main interview is started, the completed application blank should be studied and the job descriptions likely to be needed should be at hand. The interviewer should make a few reminder notes of important points to look for or ask the applicant about. He should have handy an interviewer's rating scale upon which he will enter evaluations of all the traits listed, which may be a few or many. This device is like a woman's shopping list, useful to insure complete coverage of essential items, to serve as a reminder, to guard against diversions, and to assist in directing and distributing effort.

The objective is to hire an individual who can satisfy the stated requirements of a particular position, performing certain predetermined functions.

The interview should be conducted in a suitable place, such as the office or a quiet part of the building. The applicant should first be put at ease. Often asking general questions designed to start the applicant talking and to "break the ice" is sufficient. Informality consistent with the dignity or importance of the interview is the goal usually sought. The trend in larger companies is to use two or three interviewers. Even the smaller employer may well have an applicant interviewed by different members of the organization. In addition to seeking information from him, the interviewer should furnish all important information regarding the company, the job, employment conditions, pay, company policies, and similar data, as well as answer questions the applicant may ask. If employed, the newcomer should be given specific instructions and encouragement. If rejected, he should leave with a feeling of goodwill toward the company.

Employment records are an important tool. An efficient but easy-to-manage record system makes use of an individual employee envelope measuring

Facthill REPORTS ARE BETTER

Associated Credit Bureaus of America
INCORPORATED
AN ASSOCIATION OF CREDIT BUREAUS SINCE 1906
CONFIDENTIAL

Personnel-Employment
Credit-Character Report
ACBofA No. 17
compiled by member bureau

1 REPORT ON:	POE	MR.	JOHN ALBERT	MARIE
	(Surname first)	(Mr. or Mrs.)	(Given Name)	(Spouse's name)

2 **RESIDENCE ADDRESS:** 4180 Maine   Anytown   Any   Anystate
(Street Number)   'City'   (County)   (State)

IDENTITY

3. Number of years covered: A. In file — A. 15 yrs.
   B. In investigation — B. 10 yrs.
4. A. Age (if near 21, confirm) — A. 38 yrs.
5. A. Marital status — A. Married
   B. Number of Dependents? — B. Wife, 2 sons and 1 daughter
6. Any disease, injury, deformity or peculiarity of appearance? — None with exception of glasses
7. How far did subject progress in school? — Grade and High School graduate

CHARACTER

8. Is subject well regarded as to character, habits, morals, etc? — Yes
9. Is relation with fellow employees, agreeable? — Yes
10. A. Is home environment favorable? — A. Yes
    B. Any domestic troubles? — B. No
11. Any suspicion of gambling, speculation, unfavorable associates? — None
12. Any suspicion of excessive drinking or use of drugs — None, social drinker only.

RESOURCES

13. A. Income from employment (state if estimate or exact) — A. $6,250 annually
    B. Estimate other income such as rentals, investments, etc. — B. Rent $30 mo. from upper apartment
    C. Estimate income of others in household — C. None
14. Own home, rent or board? — Owns home
15. Any items of public record in file? — None

CREDIT RECORD:

Trade Line	How Long Selling	Date of Last Sale	Highest Credit	Terms of Sale	Amount Owing	Amount Past Due	Manner of Payment
Department	5 yrs	11/2/6-	14.70	Open	00	00	30-60 days
Men's Clothing	3 yrs	10/14/6-	75.30	Open	00	00	60 days
Shoe	2 yrs	1/8/6-	7.50	Open	00	00	2 weeks
Ladies Wear	6 yrs	12/6/6-	15.64	Open	00	00	30 days
Hardware	7 yrs	12/18/6-	11.30	Open	00	00	30 days
Furniture	7 yrs	4/1/6-	160.75	Lease	00	00	as agreed

REMARKS: (A) Name and address of present employer. (B) Former employment history. (C) Amplification of incomplete information.

A) Mr. Doe is employed at the present time by the Pump Manufacturing Company, 531 S. First St., Anytown. He is in charge of production, and his duties are entirely of a supervisory nature. Has been employed by his firm since 9/12/4-.

B) He was formerly employed by Howald Machinery Company as clerk in the production department from 5/25/3- to 9/10/4-. Previously was office clerk at Stove Manufacturing Company at the time he graduated from high school, until 5/3-.

C) References report him to be a conservative type man, interested in his home and family. He is not active in civic or social affairs, with exception of his Church.

D) He owns his home, which is a two-story brick dwelling.

Report for Dakota Packing Company, Huron, Anystate

Date 11/15/6- **Prepared by** Credit Bureau   Anytown   Anystate
                    Name of member reporting bureau·   City   State

FIGURE 5. Personnel-employment credit character form.

9″ x 11½″ with the name of the employee on the tab and his application and birth and citizenship certificates inside. Personnel report forms are used by supervisors to report only when such things occur as an outstanding work performance, breach of discipline, progress of employee on the job, development of new skills, absence, change in work attitude, or any other important phase of the employee's work activity. This information is written on the personnel report form, dated, signed by the supervisor, and given to the individual in charge of personnel, who files it in the employee's envelope. This tool accomplishes two objectives: it keeps the personnel authority informed about the employee, and with a minimum of record keeping and red tape forms a permanent file of the employee for use in promotions, counseling, discipline, and any union negotiation of a grievance.

PLACEMENT

Many small employers could use their wage dollar more efficiently than at present by capitalizing fully on the special abilities of each employee when assigning duties. The man who would never wear an expensive new pair of dress shoes when digging a ditch might still be the man who would use a $100-a-week pharmacist or mechanical specialist to sell chewing gum or shoe strings. Since the time of either worker is worth at least $2.00 per hour, or at least three cents per minute, and selling costs are at least five per cent of sales, the employee would have to sell two packages of cigarettes each minute for the store to pay his wages. In most stores a salesman at that salary must produce 50 cents in sales volume every minute if his wages are not to eat into overhead beyond their proper share of ten per cent.

This example indicates that low-priced items must be sold by inexpensive help or self-service and that the expensive help required to sell cosmetics, dresses, dinner sets, and washing machines should devote their time to "big ticket" items exclusively. A store can carry both high- and low-priced items and have low-salaried people to sell one and qualified specialists to sell the other. Employee differentiation may be studied in the modern chain drugstore, although not all small retailers could carry the application of this principle to the same degree.

The production shop's problems along similiar lines are obvious. A competent mechanic's time can not be misspent with menial tasks, nor can the apprentice or handyman be entrusted with exacting technical work. The factors that constitute a job, which usually are discussed under job evaluation, must be considered here. Misspent payroll funds come directly out of profits. Profit is jeopardized whenever the wrong employee is assigned to the wrong task at the wrong wage rate. Furthermore, the job may not be properly performed, and the employee is likely to become discontented as well.

The one- or two-man business may not find this plan of labor specialization advisable. It may be that it must sell all price lines and that contacts in selling small items serve as "leads" for the sale of large ones.

There are many direct benefits from a workable training program. It reduces labor turnover, improves the quality of work performed, reduces absences, tardiness, and accidents, facilitates the discovery of promotion-worthy employees, and tends to lower the unit costs of labor. Yet the possibilities for efficiency in applying the principle remain and are nothing new, having begun, perhaps, when the father restricted his son, or the master his apprentice, to the handling of transactions in which no great loss was possible through mishandling, the craftsman applying his own and his journeyman's talents to the most profitable items.

The first few days in a new position are usually the hardest. A newcomer should be introduced to his fellow workers, shown the location of employee facilities, informed of any regulations, and encouraged to ask for additional information as it may be needed. A good plan is to assign an older, more experienced worker to act as sponsor until the introductory period is over. The "boss" himself should follow up on the new employee by occasional visits with him until he feels at home in the organization. Consideration and reasonable attention at this time are a good investment in employee relations.

TRAINING

The training of the beginning employee is an important part of his induction into the business. As with good selection, adequate early training will usually reduce the costs of getting the new person into profitable production and reduce personnel turnover. Probably the best known and most widely used method of teaching the individual a task is the procedure known as "Job Instruction Training." Ageless in principle, it was developed during World War II by the War Manpower Commission for improving the training methods of supervisors. It has since been effectively used in all kinds of production plants, banks, stores, and offices all over the world. The following series of teaching steps follows the basic assumption that "if the learner hasn't learned, the teacher hasn't taught." Careful study of them can be of great assistance to anyone having instructional responsibilities. Any employer will do well to study it and to master the principles of "Job Instruction Training," which has been aptly called "How to Teach Better the Things You Must Teach Somehow":

HOW TO INSTRUCT NEW WORKERS (OR OLD WORKERS ON NEW JOBS)

FIRST STEP: *Preparing the Learner*
Put him at ease.
Gain his interest and confidence.
Find out what he already knows.
Show task's importance, appeal to pride.
Show task's relationship to entire job.

SECOND STEP: *Presenting the Task, by Steps*
Tell, show, and explain patiently.
Be sure each step is understood.
Stress key points, one at a time.
Mention "tricks of the trade," knacks.
Welcome the learner's questions.

THIRD STEP: *The Learner's Tryout*
Have him perform the job himself.
Be ready to help avoid mistakes.
Keep him at ease, criticize diplomatically.
Have him explain steps as he goes.

FOURTH STEP: *Test and Follow-up*
Put him on his own, doing the job.
Check his performance after some practice.
Have him re-explain key points, knacks, and so forth.
Cause him to feel free to ask for further help.
Taper attention to him down to normal supervision.

MISCELLANEOUS SUGGESTIONS

1. Have a plan—something to shoot at!
   What do you want the learner to know?
   Have you considered time, ability, details?
2. Get the place and materials ready.
   Have the right supplies and equipment.
   Arrange things as they are under working conditions.
3. Get the job ready to be taught.
   Break it down to essentials, efficiency, safety.
   List key points and knacks in order.

Some preliminary training in company policies, system, work standards, and regulations is part of the introduction to the job. The need for improvement training, which should be offered as required, is fairly continuous in most cases. Training may thus be introductory, remedial or developmental.

Remedial training seeks to correct errors or mistakes made by individual workers regardless of how long they may have been employed. It is usually based on error reports of individuals, on reports by the immediate supervisor, or on indicators of the operations of each department, such as amount of spoiled work, rejects from the inspection department, lost sales, breakdowns, schedule delays, accidents, and similar measures of a department's deficiencies. Either group or individual training methods may be used in remedial training.

Development training assumes that every job can be done better, that there is always something more an employee can learn about his job, and in many cases that certain workers wish to prepare for advancement to better positions. Continuous on-the-job training is recognized as an integral part of the responsibility of every supervisor and executive. Unfortunately it is a responsibility often neglected.

There is no longer any need for the small business to neglect employee training because executives lack time or experience as teachers. Federal- and state-sponsored vocational training covering a wide range of jobs is available at no cost in nearly every community. Three such programs of interest to the small business are: Trade and Industrial Education, Distributive Education, and Diversified Occupations training. In certain cases the Vocational Agriculture program may be useful.

In general, training under the vocational acts is limited to employed persons and is related to the work they are doing and preparation for advancement to the next logically related occupation. Instructors are supposedly qualified by experience in the field and have received teacher training in vocational training methods. All courses are under public supervision and control; that is, they operate through the state's Department of Vocational Education and the public school system in each state.

In any of the three fields of small business, training of employees and management may be obtained if the Diversified Occupations program is operated in the state. In some states training assistance for the small manufacturer may be limited or unobtainable under the vocational programs except for members of his marketing division, salesmen, routemen, and others in customer contact positions. For the small business in the merchandising and many service fields the Distributive Education program should be available for all communities of the country.

Employee or group meetings weekly, monthly, or as needed should be part of training within the business. The manager, foremen, department heads, or other *qualified* members of the organization may lead these meetings. It is better to have no meetings than to allow an incompetent person to attempt to conduct one. Bring in outsiders if necessary—representatives from banks, wholesalers, manufacturers, the trade association, school system, or others.

Each meeting should have a definite purpose and one major objective. It might be to acquaint employees with some new development, product, machine, or equipment. Some contest or event planned by the firm might be the theme of another meeting. It is far better to make each meeting interesting and reasonably brief and to accomplish one single objective—something worthwhile to workers and management alike—than to have more ambitious objectives and risk a flop.

In many cases training films can be used to advantage in these meetings. They may be obtained from suppliers, government agencies, educational institutions, film renting concerns, or the trade association. Training films are of four types: sound motion pictures, silent motion pictures, and sound and silent strips. The latter resemble a continuity strip. Each frame or picture is a "still" projected on the screen for a few seconds or more before the next picture in the sequence appears. Sound film strips have a record played like a phonograph record on which each picture in the series is explained or discussed. Silent film strips are accompanied by an instructor's guide or manual so he can furnish comments needed for each picture. With a little practice they are easily used.

Many additional training aids are available, such as manufacturers' printed matter, charts or diagrams furnished by both governmental and commercial agencies, training articles on specific topics published frequently in trade journals, and "courses" sold by commercial training organizations. Whenever visual aids—films, charts, and so forth—or any of the prepared courses or aids are used, it is of the utmost importance that the person who is to conduct the meeting become thoroughly familiar with them in advance. Every film should be previewed. Even complete courses prepared in lecture form should be mastered by the leader before each meeting.

TRANSFERS AND PROMOTIONS

Neither employees nor jobs are static. They should be continuously adjusted to meet changing conditions of both worker and job. This phase of personnel work has at least three situations to deal with: transfers, promotions, and continuous worker-job adjustments involving no transfer or promotion.

Transfers are changes in the occupation of workers not properly considered as promotions. Need for transfers arises from one of four conditions: elimination of a job, request for change by an employee, belief by management that a worker has been misplaced, and fluctuations in the need for certain kinds of jobs.

When a job is eliminated through no fault of the worker, every reasonable effort should be made to place him elsewhere in the organization. If this is impossible, his employer should help him secure a satisfactory position with some other company.

For various reason employees sometimes ask to be shifted to another job. If the reasons given for the request are plausible, it should be granted if possible. In other cases management may take the initiative when it appears that a particular worker would be better suited to a different job. Usually a satisfactory transfer can be made in such cases if the reasons are discussed with the employee, but sometimes this is not possible. A surprisingly large number of workers resent any change in their job or duties, even when it involves a promotion, increases their income, or is otherwise to their own benefit.

In some cases certain locations for a desk or even a work place in the shop acquire "prestige" for employees, and those favored by such locations show resentment when moved. In making promotions provisions of the business personnel policy and factors discussed under Job Evaluation should be observed. Since merit and ability are of primary importance, provisions for evaluating these qualities are useful in measuring an individual's mastery of his present job. Operating reports should be supplemented by periodic ratings by supervisors or others in a position to make impartial evaluations of qualities like attitude, initiative, personality, self-development, and preparation for promotion. Often promotions may well be preceded by one or more trial periods in the new position for both experience and testing. Promotions will normally be accompanied by increased pay as well as greater responsibility and authority.

REMUNERATION[2]

The small firm is likely to find the simpler systems of payment better suited to its needs. These are straight salary or time payment, straight commission or piece rates, and simple bonus plans, such as regular salary plus a definite reward or bonus for achievement beyond a standard or quota agreed upon in advance.

Incentive systems based on time and motion studies or other measured output, with various formulas for calculating the incentive wage, may be used effectively in the small business if restricted to jobs where such plans are appropriate and if kept simple. Benefits to be derived from such systems must be compared with the added expense entailed and employee attitude toward the method. An incentive wage plan should give the worker more pay for the same amount of time worked, give management a lower labor cost (or a predetermined unit cost for pricing and budgeting), be understandable and acceptable to the worker, and be economical for management to operate.

The attitude of many workers toward incentive plans launched by management is sometimes difficult for the inexperienced manager to understand. Not all employees are ambitious. Many prefer their present income to prospects for a higher income if this involves changing established habits. Probably the majority of workers are suspicious and fearful of new plans to increase output even though they will share in the larger returns.

Probably more employees in small firms are interested in the stability and regularity of their incomes than in opportunities to enter higher income brackets. The following cases illustrate how this need can be met by good management.

Bottling soft drinks is a business affected by pronounced seasonal fluctuations. During the spring and summer the demand for salesmen is strong and remuneration high. When business declines in the fall, many salesmen have been in the habit of seeking positions with other companies, expecting their old jobs to be available again next spring. The Chase Company developed a plan that has enabled it to retain its salesmen throughout the year.

Analysis of the problem convinced management that salesmen became

---

[2] See also: *Using Deferred Compensation in Small Business,* Management Aids for Small Manufacturers No. 107 (Washington, D. C.: Small Business Administration, September 1959).

accustomed to the high standard of living made possible by the seasonally high incomes received during the warm months. When their incomes declined under the former method of paying salary plus commissions based on current sales, most men became dissatisfied and quit. The new plan provides for a stabilized drawing account that is paid weekly and is the same throughout the year regardless of seasonal fluctuations in sales. Under this plan each of the company's 12 salesmen draws a fixed sum of $60 per week throughout the year. This actually serves as a "salary," although it is charged against his commission earnings, and does not vary regardless of the salesman's actual earnings.

During the boom season for bottled drinks, some of the men earn more than $100 per week; but during three or four of the cold months sales go down considerably and the men's earnings fall as low as $30 per week. Chase salesmen, who draw their $60 a week right through the slow winter months, feel no particular temptation to seek other jobs, since their salaries do not slump with the season. The plan adopted by Chase might solve this phase of the wage problem for other small firms.[3]

In a different field of small business, rug cleaning, a similar problem of coping with seasonal fluctuations was solved by diversifying services offered and adding the selling of merchandise. During the seven dull months of the year one company promoted personalized cleaning and renovating services in private homes and institutions. The fact that such services brought company representatives inside these homes and institutions provided an opportunity for them to suggest the sale of remnants and other materials observation showed to be needed. Results were gratifying. After the adoption of the new plan, sales of merchandise represented 30 per cent of total receipts and the combined sales of merchandise and service have permitted retaining key personnel throughout the year.

Profit sharing, which has been gaining ground among small businesses, has many advantages, in theory at least. In many respects it is better suited to the small than to the large enterprise. For it to be successful, there must be a feeling of mutual trust and confidence between management and employees. The company's books must be open to inspection by those included in the profit sharing, although not indiscriminately. A basis previously agreed upon for sharing the profits must be established and followed, and a satisfactory wage and salary scale must be maintained. Profit sharing should not be used as a deferred wage payment plan.

There are certain basic questions regarding profit sharing, especially for all employees, that should be considered before adopting such a plan. Profit, which is a residual after all costs and expenses of the business have been paid,

---

[3] *Pay Plan Aids Men in Dull Season,* Small Business Aids No. 42 (Washington, D. C.: U. S. Department of Commerce). Condensed from Ruel McDaniel, "Pay Plan Aids Men in Dull Season," *American Business* (June 1946). See also: "Employee Security: Can Management Meet the Challenge?" *Management Review* (August 1954), pp. 493-494.

fluctuates widely, often as a result of causes external to the business, such as general economic conditions, competition, and government policy. Even under favorable conditions only a few employees are likely to be in a position actually to increase or decrease the company's profits. For these reasons, profit sharing is not a form of incentive wage, except in a limited sense for the few persons in a position to affect profits materially. Profit is the reward to owner managers for both risking their own capital and exercising good managerial ability. The owners bear losses when they occur; profit sharing does not contemplate loss sharing by those who participate in the profits when there are any. And finally, it is discouraging to employees who anticipate sharing in the profits and who may even have done extra work to help the company make a profit to discover at the end of the year that there are no profits to share.

Two interrelated uses of profit sharing have expanded in forward-looking small companies, to retain key employees and to expand retail concerns on the chain store principle. The latter plan was pioneered by the J. C. Penney Company over 50 years ago and appears to offer the solution today for many small retailers seeking safe but rapid expansion.

MORALE BUILDING

Nonfinancial incentives have a place along with incentive payment plans in stimulating and rewarding employees. Recognition by management of good work or of valuable suggestions by employees is an important example. Soliciting worker participation in management is another that has been receiving increasing consideration. Profit sharing, although often classed with payment plans, probably belongs equally well in the employee-management co-operation group.

An axiom in all human relations is that most major troubles result from neglected minor grievances. In the small business this is more serious than it appears. Employee grievances have serious effects on the community's attitude toward the employer concerned. Because of the very personal nature of most employer-employee contacts, many workers will be reluctant to talk about their "gripes." The checklist [4] on the next page may be used.

Big business has organized systems to secure and use employee complaints for better employee relations. The small businessman who relies upon his "close personal contacts" in this area is courting unnecessary risks. He has three main avenues to use in arriving at the best solution to this problem. First, he can make an objective study of all conditions in big business likely to be irritating to employees. A checklist will be a useful guide for this approach. Second, he can use the exit interview technique—that is, find out

---

[4] *Checklist for Industrial Workers' Complaints,* Small Business Aids No. 462 (Washington, D. C.: U. S. Department of Commerce), condensed from Lawrence Stessin, "Workers 'Griping'? Here's a Remedy," *Forbes Magazine of Business* (March 1, 1948).

CHECKLIST OF WORK CONDITIONS

Noise ☐ Average ☐ Should be lessened   How _____

Illumination ☐ Adequate ☐ Inadequate   Where correction is needed _____

Ventilation ☐ Good ☐ Fair ☐ Bad   How to improve _____

Access to snack bars, vending machines, drinking fountains ☐ Easy ☐ Difficult
How to improve _____

Dust ☐ Some ☐ None ☐ Too much   How to improve _____

Floors ☐ Clear ☐ Littered   How to improve _____

Monotony of jobs ☐ None ☐ Some ☐ Too much   Name jobs _____
How to improve _____

Parking facilities ☐ Good ☐ Fair ☐ Bad   How to improve _____

Toilets, wash basins, towels, soap, hot water ☐ Adequate
☐ Inadequate   How to improve _____

Time clocks ☐ Enough to prevent long waits ☐ Too far
Where to increase number of clocks _____

Arrangements for wage payments ☐ No long waits in line ☐ Present system inadequate
How to improve _____

Accident hazards ☐ Normal ☐ Need further correction   How, where _____

Lunch places (where no lunch rooms exist but employees eat on company grounds) ☐ Adequate ☐ Inadequate
How to improve _____

Tool boxes ☐ Adequate ☐ Too far—too long to wait   How to improve _____

Spacing of machines ☐ Adequate ☐ Too close   How to improve _____

337

from each employee who quits just what his complaints about the company were. And third, he can institute a continuous plan of employee suggestions with frequent conferences and requests for ways in which the firm can improve employee relations. If done sincerely, this procedure is really effective. Again the small businessman has the big advantage of being able to establish a close bond of confidence and trust with his employees if he will take the initiative in doing so.

PERSONNEL IN MERCHANDISING

The attitudes of employees are particularly important in the small organization, whether the business be a retail or wholesale establishment, a manufacturing firm, or service business. Persons who must be relied on to produce a given amount in a given period, or to face customers and, as such, to represent the firm in human relations situations, must not only be thoroughly familiar with the firm's policies, philosophies, goals, and methods of operation, but must share the opinion of management as to their desirability and justification. The fact that in the small concern each individual carries a larger share of responsibility makes these attitudes all the more important. In all phases of personnel administration, from selection through training and into normal supervision, the attitudes of the individual must be noted, evaluated, and cultivated constantly. Because of his importance to the organization, the dedicated nonconformist and the consistent malcontent—persons who may lower the quantity or quality of output, or damage relationships with clients or customers—cannot be tolerated and must be eliminated as quickly as possible if his attitudes cannot be changed. Most modern personnel administration experts agree that the way an employee thinks about his job makes or breaks him as contributor to the company's welfare.

Many things have been written concerning the need for employee loyalty to his employer. Perhaps the best known statement in this connection is by Elbert Hubbard, which reads as follows:

> If you work for a man, in heaven's name work for him. If he pays wages that supply your bread and butter, work for him, speak well of him, think well of him, stand by him, and stand by the institution he represents . . . If I worked for a man I would work for him; I would not work for him a part of his time, but all of his time; I would give undivided service or none . . . An ounce of loyalty is worth a pound of cleverness. If you must vilify, condemn and eternally disparage your employer, then resign your position; and when you are outside, damn him to your heart's content. But . . . so long as you are part of an institution, do not condemn it. Not that you will injure the institution . . . but when you disparage the concern of which you are a part, you disparage yourself.[5]

One authority and personnel consultant has these comments and suggestions:

[5] Elbert Hubbard, from "Get Out or Get in Line."

No simple ground rules for improving employee morale can be offered. Every situation is unique. No two individuals are exactly alike, nor are two companies identical. Nevertheless, from psychological research on morale and attitudes in business, certain practical suggestions may be made:

(1) Tell and show your employees that you are interested in them and would be glad to have their ideas on how conditions might be improved.

(2) Treat your employees as individuals; never deal with them as impersonal variables in a working unit.

(3) Improve your general understanding of human behavior.

(4) Accept the fact that others may not see things as you do.

(5) Respect differences of opinion.

(6) Insofar as possible, give explanations for management actions.

(7) Provide information and guidance on matters affecting employees' security.

(8) Make reasonable efforts to keep jobs interesting.

(9) Encourage promotion from within.

(10) Express appreciation publicly for jobs well done.

(11) Offer criticism privately in the form of constructive suggestions for improvement.

(12) Train supervisors to think about the people involved insofar as practicable, rather than just the work.

(13) Keep your people up-to-date on all business matters affecting them, and quell rumors with correct information.

(14) Be fair.[6]

Few lines of business compare with retailing in the wide fluctuations of need for personnel on an annual, monthly, daily, and hourly basis. The "stand by" capacity demanded of retail personnel is enormous. This is both a challenge and an opportunity to management. Because customers want prompt service when they do appear in the store, the merchant must always be prepared to handle unexpected busy periods. Fortunately, most fluctuations are regular and known in advance. On a daily and hourly basis, part-time employees can often be used to meet peak demands at certain hours of the day and on the busiest day of the week, usually Saturday. This arrangement gives the merchant an opportunity to try out or develop prospective full-time employees, but it also increases the work of training and personnel management. An excellent source of afternoon and Saturday workers is the local Distributive Education program operated in connection with the senior high school. The local superintendent of schools can furnish information on this program.

In addition to general sources of training material, the retailer in most lines will find excellent help in publications by the School of Retailing of the University of Pittsburgh and the School of Retailing, New York Univer-

[6] Martin M. Bruce, *Managing for Better Morale,* (Washington, D. C.: Small Business Administration, December 1958).

sity. *Better Retailing,* published by the National Cash Register Company, Merchants Service Bureau, Dayton, Ohio, is valuable for employee and management alike.[7]

Many trade associations also provide training for retail employees. The merchant should investigate such programs before completing his plans for training.

Retailers use special types of incentives for employees, among them discounts ranging from 10 to 30 per cent on merchandise purchased in the store and P.M.'s. The P.M. (premium merchandise, premium money, "spiff," or "stim") is used to encourage the sale of certain articles. When these are slow sellers, experience shows that a P.M. of from ten cents to a dollar will be up to four times as effective as a markdown in quickly disposing of the goods. However, it leads to pushing off poor merchandise on unsuspecting customers, usually to the detriment of the store. When used for "trading up," encouraging customers to buy higher-priced, better-quality merchandise, it may be justified in many cases.

PERSONNEL IN THE SMALL FACTORY

Large manufacturers have long recognized the importance of good personnel practices. At one time personnel management was widely considered as a preventive of unionization. More and more unions have taken part in working for better personnel management. Unions have been spreading their influence increasingly and have already entered many small factories. Some small manufacturers see in the introduction of a personnel program a means of forestalling the unionization of their plants. In the authors' opinion, this is the wrong approach; unions can be worked *with* to advantage.

Management has developed methods, tools, machinery, and skills to process and utilize materials efficiently. Little, and often nothing, is done to secure the maximum productive efficiency from the manpower involved. This should be the aim of a personnel program. Excessive labor turnover makes it difficult to achieve.

Labor turnover costs are not so intangible as many suppose. First, there is the direct cost involved in training new employees and in the period during which the employee is on the payroll but not producing at full capacity. This cost varies with the length of the training period. There are also costs from an increase in spoiled or wasted material, lowering of employee morale, and increased overhead. From this standpoint alone it is well to develop a personnel policy and program designed to attract the most desirable employees and to keep them with the company.

In a small shop there is a limit to specialization. It may be impossible to

---

[7] See also: R. E. Williams, *Employee Relations for Small Retailers,* Small Marketers Aids No. 4 (Washington, D. C.: Small Business Administration, 1955). Discusses essential elements as well as values of fringe benefits, incentives, and suggestion systems for achieving good employer-employee relationships.

have even one man whose sole responsibility pertains to personnel management. Hiring and training may be the responsibility of one member of the organization, whereas sickness benefits, employment records, and savings associations may be handled by the auditor or an accountant; or, as is frequently the case, each department foreman may do his own hiring and personnel record keeping. Yet it is important for employees to know who heads the personnel function. They must know who is responsible for their job relations and to whom they can take their problems.

Supervisors in the small shop must be called upon to give much of the preliminary on-the-job training. Training the new employee should begin with an explanation by the supervisor of company products, policies, regulations and an explanation of the importance, in their manufacturing setup, of the first job the employee is to learn. Key workers in each department should then take over the actual job instruction of the employee. Worker instructors should be carefully selected, not only for craftsmanship, but also for their loyalty and ability to explain and show how the job is done.

A safe shop is good business. Accidents are costly to management in lost time, in the weakening of employee morale, and in direct cash outlay. There are in general two causes of accidents, personal and impersonal. Personal causes account for accidents due to improper attitude, lack of knowledge or skill, physical handicaps, and poor health. Impersonal causes include hazardous work-handling arrangement or procedure, defective mechanical equipment, unsafe clothing, crowded aisles, improper lighting and ventilation, and inadequate guarding.

It is good practice for the executive in charge of plant safety to hold weekly meetings with his employee-safety inspectors. These inspectors should report to him on any unsafe conditions and careless workers in their departments. The individual employee is a large factor in safety engineering. Regardless of size or type of shop, good employee relations are vital to any organization. The human element in manufacturing has long been slighted as an important factor in production costs.

Small manufacturers who have their own sales organization are in danger of slighting this department because of their greater interest in production. The selection and training of salesmen is, therefore, of special importance. Since a high volume of sales and production is of industrywide concern, industrial groups and trade associations are co-operating in collective sales-training programs.[8]

PERSONNEL IN THE SERVICE BUSINESS

Good personnel is important in all service fields, but the special needs and problems vary for each of three main groups. In one group the service ren-

[8] Kenneth Lawyer, *Sales Training for the Smaller Manufacturers,* Small Business Management Series No. 11 (Washington, D.C.: Small Business Administration, 1955).

dered is highly personal and the caliber of employees may be the deciding factor between success and failure. Most professional services, such as medical and dental care, and many semiprofessional services are in this group. For our purpose the beauty shop may be used to illustrate the *employee relations* problem of this class of establishments.

Most states and communities have legal requirements governing employee's qualifications and sanitary working conditions for beauty shops and similar personal service establishments. These are minimum standards and the shop owner will endeavor to exceed them whenever possible. Usually operators must be licensed. Equipment and physical facilities must pass inspections. The owner, however, is more concerned with maintaining both personnel and plant standards well above legal requirements than with merely satisfying them.

Although *skill* is the greatest single ability required of a beauty shop operator, personality, voice, manners, and appearance are very important. The ability to sell both the services and merchandise offered by the shop is a valuable asset for most employees. Knowing when to be a good listener is often more desirable than skill as a conversationalist.

Personal service establishments will vary both in the degree of specialized service offered and in the extent to which individualized handling of each patron is encouraged. Beauty shop employees must be selected according to the shop policy of general or specialist service. Work should be assigned to each operator to take full advantage of special skills possessed. Most owners find it good practice to strive throughout the shop for standard procedures and methods, in which new employees should be instructed.

A second group of service businesses, considered from a personnel viewpoint, is composed of service stations, many repair shops, restaurants, and similar enterprises. This group shares to some extent the customer concern with the type of employees already noted for personal service establishments like beauty shops, but not to the same degree. Likewise many employees in this group have average working conditions and opportunities to meet the public. In these respects businesses in this group differ notably from those in the third classification as represented by laundries and dry cleaning establishments.

In general, service stations, repair shops, and restaurants have not played up the superior skill of particular employees. Rather, they tend to strive for reputations based on the quality of product or service rendered by the business. Surveys have shown frequently that factors relating to employees have been among the chief reasons why service stations have lost customers. Important reasons given include indifference, haughtiness, ignorance of products, overinsistence in sales efforts, and attempted substitution. Likewise, unless a restaurant has an outstanding reputation for superior-quality food, customers tend to be very sensitive to the appearance, personality, and general attitude of the hostess and food service employees.

As a class both service station and restaurant employees are likely to have frequent contacts with tourists and other strangers to the community. Employees usually need special training to be able to answer questions asked by tourists even though many of these inquiries relate to the employee's home community. In addition to receiving special training, employees in such positions may need simple aids like local maps, mileage charts, and folders describing and illustrating nearby places of interest.

In the restaurant business it is sometimes required that all applicants for employment pass a physical examination that gives special attention to venereal disease and the possibility that the applicant may be a carrier of diphtheria, typhoid fever, or other contagious diseases. Local regulations, such as the requirement that each food handler possess a health certificate, should be complied with.

Traditionally, the restaurant business has had a high rate of turnover among its personnel. Personnel turnover is, we agree, very costly yet it can be reduced and many organizations have proven this. In the Diner Drive-In business, which is particularly plagued with the turnover of employees, these techniques have worked:

1. Employment contract requiring one week's notice.
2. Increase in wage at the end of three weeks.
3. Premium wages for outstanding performance.
4. Benefit plans.

Obviously, laws of some states would forbid the use of methods quite acceptable in another state. It is well to check carefully with state or other labor authorities before setting up arbitrary rulings or provisions.[9]

Service industries have special problems of employee relations. Establishments such as laundries and dry cleaning plants illustrate the nature of these problems. Frequently the plant is located in a congested district of the industrial type; this by itself makes it difficult to attract and retain desirable employees. Working conditions are not likely to be pleasant and competition keeps wages relatively low. There are fewer opportunities for meeting the public than in retailing and for learning important industrial skills than in manufacturing. This makes it especially important in such cases to use all available personnel techniques as effectively as possible. Among these might be fair dealing, recognition of good work, friendly relations with employees, suggestion systems, employee service activities such as recreational facilities, and many others.

Although it is conceded to be difficult to make working conditions in service establishments and elsewhere as attractive to employees as those in many other lines of business, the situation can be improved in most cases. Probably

---

[9] Dr. Donald E. Lundberg (Food Service Consultant for Diner Drive-In and Head, Department of Restaurant and Hotel Management, Florida State University), "How to Reduce Personnel Turnover," *Diner Drive-In* (December 1959), p. 20.

one reason improvements have been slow in coming is the understandable tendency of the small plant owner to be so imbued with the pride of ownership that he has failed to see his shop as the employees see it. An objective appraisal would probably disclose antiquated rest rooms, inadequate dressing rooms, and no satisfactory place for employees to eat lunch. Improvements in ventilation and lighting also may be needed.

CONCLUSIONS

Although every business operates through its personnel, probably less has been done to utilize this valuable resource effectively than has been done for the other factors of production. Since payroll is usually a major and often the largest item of expense in any business, the opportunities for financial improvement through better personnel relations are great. In addition, a firm's personnel is one thing competitors cannot copy, duplicate, or equal without incurring equivalent trouble and expense. Materials, merchandise, advertising and display ideas, and even product designs are generally available to all businessmen on approximately equal terms, but this is not true of a good group of employees. Only the workers' time can be purchased or hired; their attitudes, loyalty, co-operation, and productivity must be earned. This is the aim of good personnel work. *The many advantages small business has over big business in handling employee relations should be developed to their fullest extent.*

Small business also has some special problems in securing and maintaining competent personnel. Fortunately the more important ones can be solved if they are recognized and given proper attention. Often apparent handicaps, like limited opportunities for promotion, can be turned into advantages by stressing the greater range of training and experience to be secured by employment in the small company. This has a strong appeal to men who later hope to enter business for themselves.

Many techniques of personnel management common in larger concerns can be used to advantage in the small business. A worker is a human being whether employed by a large or small concern. Carefully selected and well trained, he becomes an investment of value. Methods developed during World War II for training workers or supervisors, like Job Instruction Training, or for enlisting employee co-operation are available for use by the small businessman. In addition, material on personnel in both book and periodical (trade journal) form is extensive. Finally, the vocational programs in operation throughout the country can furnish practical and related training even to the smallest concern without cost to the owner-manager.

One of the authors[10] has developed an executive appraisal form, which has been successfully used by business firms for "describing" potential department superiors, branch managers, store managers, and others. The vari-

[10] Dr. Kenneth Lawyer.

SCALE FOR RATING MANAGERS

Possibilities for poorest ratings are at the left, the best at the right. Please note that while there are descriptions for only three scores, the horizontal line is divided into five parts and can be scored accordingly.

The *general pattern* is as follows:

1	2	3	4	5
Poor; not acceptable at all; failure to measure up.	*Fair;* barely acceptable, must improve; between 1 and 3.	*Good;* acceptable; only average. Can improve.	*Very Good;* better than average; between 3 and 5.	*Excellent;* top quality; commendable performance.

In most cases, as will be noted below, only three (1, 3, 5) degrees are described. Thus, 2 would indicate "between 1 and 3" and 4, "between 3 and 5."

1. PERSONAL APPEARANCE

1	2	3	4	5
Soiled apparel; hands dirty and face unshaven; "slovenly"; not correct for this business.		Acceptable only. Clothing not quite right for executive meeting public or for most business contacts.		Clean, neat, businesslike; "well-groomed"; looks and acts as a manager should at all times.

2. PERSONALITY, ENTHUSIASM

1	2	3	4	5
Not an agreeable person; apparently does not like *people*, as employees or as customers.		Luke-warm; agreeable but not very friendly; acceptable behavior in most situations.		Pleasing and congenial personality; contagious enthusiasm and inspirational manner.

3. ACCEPTANCE OF CRITICISM

1	2	3	4	5
Resents any criticism as personal; does not welcome instruction.		Accepts instruction and advice casually; reacts slowly, but takes advice as order, not aid.		Welcomes constructive help of any kind, anxious to learn from any likely source.

4. ABILITY TO LEARN

1	2	3	4	5
Slow to assimilate the job and to change his thinking—"set in his ways" or lacking in ability to understand and adjust to training and experience.		Able to adjust to change within reasonable time. Not particularly aggressive in thinking or in grasping new concepts and procedures. Learns slowly but retains well.		Grasps ideas and methods readily; growing with his job—analytical of situations and alert to changes. Retains and uses what he learns. Constantly eligible for advancement.

5. WILLINGNESS TO WORK

1	2	3	4	5
Puts in minimum of time and effort, avoids responsibility of extra work. Lays off frequently, arrives late, etc.		Does fair job, is faithful employee in routine duties of performing management; but not an aggressive worker.		Works early and late as needed to keep dept. at maximum efficiency; a conscientious and hard worker.

6. ADHERENCE TO POLICY

1	2	3	4	5
Resents business rules and standards; shows disagreement; critical in presence of employees; tolerates laxness.		Casual acceptance and reasonable conformity; no obvious lack of understanding and agreement.		Policies and regulations understood and enforced as essential; good interpretation in emergencies.

7. HANDLING DETAILS

1	2	3	4	5
Little respect for promptness, accuracy and completeness in reports or other detail matters. Often behind in obvious ways, affecting financial, equipment or personnel management.		Details handled as routine, under pressure of job requirements. Usually reminded, but cooperative in manner. Willing but not a natural handler of business detail.		Methodical and thorough in work involving detail, by nature. Seldom needs reminding or correction concerning mdse, supplies, maintenance, reports or service.

346

1	2	3	4	5
Does little thinking for himself. No originality, little resourcefulness or imagination. Not a creative person.		Occasionally has a good idea, but may not try it, until encouraged. Follows line of least resistance.		Resourceful, inventive and self-reliant; can usually work himself out of difficulties without assistance, gets good ideas, puts them into action.

9. PRODUCTION EFFICIENCY

1	2	3	4	5
Dept. seems to lack speed and efficiency; breakdowns frequent, cannot meet emergencies in stride.		Occasional failures but generally good performance under ordinary conditions.		Efficient operator, keeps dept. operating at good pace; can run at top speed, smooth in emergencies.

10. PLANNING ABILITY

1	2	3	4	5
Frequently caught "short" or "over" with equipment, personnel, supplies—many late or emergency orders.		Occasionally runs short or over-orders, does generally fair job of planning and provisioning—acceptable.		Correct amounts of materials and personnel, etc, on hand whenever foresighted planning is possible—good organizer.

11. LEADERSHIP

1	2	3	4	5
Figurehead only; tolerated by coworkers but not respected as leader or supervisor.		Handles major responsibilities effectively; routine usually followed; friendly associates; may not delegate well.		Obtains top performance from all employees; inspires loyalty to company and self; can delegate authority.

12. ABILITY TO TRAIN

1	2	3	4	5
Neglects instruction, lets employees learn "the hard way."		Does some training in essential spots; avoids costly errors when expedient.		A good teacher; dept. produces good workers who stay with company.

ous topics concerning employee and employer characteristics reviewed in this chapter are very similar to many items listed as vital considerations on this rating scale. A high score on this sheet might indicate greater promise of success as a small business owner-operator. In any case, it may serve as a guide to the employer in selecting his associates or in promoting others to more responsible assignments.

QUESTIONS AND PROBLEMS

1. Compare the opportunities for management to maintain good employee relations in large and small companies.

2. What is meant by "job analysis"? In what ways is it of use to the small businessman?

3. How can a small businessman obtain well-trained employees who might otherwise go to a large concern for employment?

4. How can a businessman evaluate the answers on an application blank?

5. Do you think tests or examinations are worthwhile to the small concern? Why or why not?

6. Describe the nature and purpose of the Personnel-Employment Credit Character report.

7. What advantages can you see in the Job Instruction Training program over traditional methods?

8. In what respects are *all* supervisors and executives responsible for personnel activities?

9. Discuss the different aspects of Trades and Industries, Distributive Education, and Diversified Occupations. Give the disadvantages and advantages of each and the conditions under which each thrives.

10. In your opinion does each company have more of a monopoly on the quality or characteristics of its own personnel than it does on advertising ideas, production processes used, or merchandise handled? Discuss.

11. Are the non-financial incentives, as compared to wage and bonus payments, relatively more important in the large or in the small company? Explain.

12. Do you think a small business has a better chance of making a success of profit sharing or of the guaranteed annual wage? Discuss.

13. Do you think that a Labor-Management Committee would solve most management-personnel problems? Discuss fully.

14. What are the opportunities for and limitations of employee-management committees in each of the three fields of small business?

15. How do you explain the need for high quality personnel, the good salaries paid to retail executives, and the low esteem many people have for retail employees?

16. Compare the relative importance of and problems connected with maintaining good employees in each of the three main fields of small business.

17. Explain how management and personnel relations are connected. How do policies fit into this relationship?

18. Select some job and outline in detail how you would make a job evaluation for this position.

19. Interview as many small businessmen as possible who are engaged in retailing, manufacturing, and service to find out their: (1) experience with profit sharing, (2) attitudes toward it, and (3) current use or plans to use it. Analyze and report your findings and conclusions.

20. Ted's men's store depends on part-time student employees from the university from which it also draws 60 per cent of its business. Price competition from the larger stores in the district emphasizes Ted's limited buying power. The university has an excellent School of Retailing. What should Ted do, and why?

17 • *Relationships with Resources*[1]

The aim of successful buying is to obtain the best goods for the intended use. Favorable relationships with resources helps in achieving this goal. It also facilitates other aspects of buying. Although buying is a function that must be performed in all businesses, maintaining favorable relationships with sources of supply is one characteristic of successful buying that is particularly important in the small enterprise.

RESOURCES AND POLICIES AVAILABLE TO THE SMALL BUSINESS

Before the small businessman can effectively formulate his buying policies or undertake the actual purchase of goods needed to operate his business he must be familiar with the different types of suppliers available to him, the advantages and limitations associated with each type, and the conditions under which it is better to concentrate most of his buying with one or a few suppliers as compared to making purchases from many sources.

Types of Resources

Three groups of suppliers are usually recognized and most small businesses will find that they must make some of their purchases with representatives of each group: producers, merchant middlemen, and functional middlemen.

Producers. Manufacturers, miners, farmers, or processors of natural products all may be classed as producers. With the exception of farmers, the business units so classed usually may be of any size, ranging from very small to very large. Naturally, advantages claimed for concentrated purchasing would not apply with respect to purchasing from many of the smaller producers. An-

---

[1] Business terminology is not well standardized, and "resources," "supplier," and "vendor" are words commonly used to refer to the sources from which a business secures its merchandise, materials, or supplies.

other consideration is that many businesses, especially the larger manufacturers, have their own methods of distribution and may not be available for direct dealings with the small enterprise. Their products may be purchased, but only through middlemen or representatives used by the particular manufacturer.

Merchant middlemen. Merchant middlemen will constitute the chief source of supply for most small firms in any field. These are marketing institutions that buy and take title to goods, for resale. Familiar examples are wholesalers or jobbers, supply houses, and merchant truckers. In many "hard lines," especially where the goods carried are used both by industry and retail-service businesses, "supply houses" are comparable to wholesalers. In the laundry and dry cleaning fields resources are called the "allied trades."

Wholesalers, especially in the general merchandise fields, are classified as service and limited function wholesalers. Cash-and-carry is one example of a limited function middleman.

Many service wholesalers also operate cash-and-carry departments. Since small businessmen often patronize local wholesalers, the opportunities available through purchasing by the cash-and-carry method are significant.

The fundamental reason for the use of the cash-and-carry policy is to reduce prices to retailers by lowering some of the wholesaler's operating expenses. The method also enables the buyer to inspect his purchases, keep his payments up to date, and eliminate the clerical work necessary for buying on a charge basis. However, cash-and-carry takes the buyer away from his business where he may be needed, involves more working capital than many small businessmen have, and is usually confined to a more limited assortment of merchandise than that carried by the service wholesaler.

Advantages claimed for the service wholesaler were recently stated to include the following points: ability to purchase from a single source products made by hundreds of producers; assurance at all times of a supply of new items made available locally through the wholesaler's constant scouting of all markets; quick delivery of goods as needed; opportunity to buy on credit; service and advice rendered through salesmen who visit the store; assurance of the wholesaler's interest in the retailer's success because this is the only basis upon which the wholesaler can continue in business.[2] The last advantage listed would also apply to the cash-and-carry wholesaler.

In merchandising, the small independent retailer has learned from experience that a reliable wholesaler is one of his best assets. The amount of confidence most retailers have in their wholesalers would surprise anyone not familiar with the field. This trust and confidence has been earned by the ever increasing interest wholesalers have exhibited in the welfare and success of their retail customers.

[2] *The Services of the Service Wholesaler,* Small Business Aids No. 198 (Washington, D. C.: U. S. Department of Commerce). Reprinted from article of the same title, *Modern Merchandising* (December 1945), National Association of Tobacco Distributors, New York.

Merchant middlemen differ in their product specialization, such as general wholesalers versus drug houses, as well as in the range of services offered. Some wholesalers of this type give all services expected—credit, delivery, advice, salesmen calls and order taking; others, especially in the grocery field, offer only limited services, such as cash-and-carry. The majority of merchant middlemen wholesalers do not have any well-organized plan of voluntary co-operation for buyers such as the voluntary chain, although many will work more closely with customers who concentrate their purchases than with those who do not.

Merchant truckers, another type of wholesaler, operate in many lines of goods, such as raw and processed foods, bottled drinks (route men), and some hard lines. Some are erratic sources of supply, but often they have "good buys," whereas others carry regular lines and follow fairly definite schedules of calling on buyers.

Functional middlemen. Small businessmen may also have occasion to purchase from functional middlemen. These are suppliers who do not take title to the goods for which they perform certain marketing functions such as selling, buying, or transporting. Familiar examples are brokers, selling or buying agents, manufacturers' representatives, resident buyers, purchasing agents, and freight forwarders. A broker serves either a buyer by seeking out sellers, or a seller by locating buyers. He brings buyer and seller together, and often has a wealth of market information available for both parties.

Small enterprisers will ordinarily use brokers when: (1) brokers are traditional in the field, such as in the canning and certain subdivisions of the textile or food industries; (2) the goods of a particular producer are available only through brokers (or other sales agents and manufacturers' representatives), and (3) on certain occasions when they are trying to locate a seller of goods not readily available in the established channels of trade. Resident buyers or purchasing agents are used by retailers and smaller wholesalers.

Apart from providing market information, most functional middlemen are not in a position to offer merchandising plans, although in some fields they are highly respected as technical advisors regarding uses of the product with which they deal.

One or Several Suppliers?

Retailers or service businesses holding dealerships or franchises, service agreements, or a voluntary chain affiliation usually are under obligation to concentrate purchases with the co-operating supplier. Only one resource is used by manufacturers where a monopoly of supply exists or where the nearest supplier is traditionally the least expensive source of materials. Other businesses should decide whether to concentrate their buying with one or a few suppliers or to "play the market."

In selecting suppliers, most small businesses free to choose will have several objectives in common: among these will be the following:

1. Obtaining goods of the required quality, type, or model.

2. Availability of goods at desired prices and terms and in quantities needed.

3. Reliability—goods should be continuously available.

4. Reasonable and customary protection of the buyer's interests should be provided—quality guarantees, right to make legitimate returns, protection against likely risks from resale or use, limited agency or similar franchise rights all are important.

5. Good service, not only in making deliveries, but also in handling transactions and making adjustments.

6. Appropriate provisions for managerial or merchandising aids and technical assistance when needed.

7. Suppliers' representatives should be the type with whom the businessman can work and co-operate successfully.

Whether to diversify or concentrate purchases will involve additional considerations, many of which are special applications of the foregoing standards. In any instance where the owner is a shrewd buyer who enjoys trading and procurement activities, when he wants various suppliers competing for his business, and believes that he is in a position to take advantage of any variations in lines, prices, or services different suppliers may offer, diversification would be the logical policy to follow. Another advantage is that this policy enables the business to match popular lines carried by competitors, with the exception of exclusively franchised or otherwise restricted lines. Finally, it protects the small business in case any one supplier should cease business, change its lines, or change its business policies.

To the small businessman advantages of concentrating purchases may be stated briefly as follows: By carrying the same lines continuously, his customers are not shifted from brand to brand, nor his employees from materials of one kind to another. As a good customer of one resource he may receive special favors or cumulative quantity discounts, valuable advice and assistance in merchandising the goods, tips on market changes, and special considerations during times of difficulty.

Those are the advantages on each side. There are, however, disadvantages not directly implied in either of the lists. Dangers encountered in diversification include stocking too many lines, perhaps attended by difficulty in maintaining complete stocks in any one, and inability to capitalize fully on the advertising program of any one brand of merchandise or on technical advice regarding the use of certain materials or supplies.

The businessman with a close working relationship with his resource must acknowledge these drawbacks to such an arrangement: inability to take advantage of unusual offers in other lines; some loss if the supplier changes policy or becomes poorly managed; and the risk that the merchandising advice, assistance, and guidance offered may become irritating or of no use.

Experience has shown the last weakness to be present, unfortunately, in some voluntary chain groups. During the scarcities of recent wars, some resources, unfortunately, used their available supplies to get new accounts instead of serving their regular customers adequately.

FUNDAMENTALS OF BUYING FOR THE SMALL BUSINESS

The art of careful buying involves six basic processes: (1) determining needs, (2) locating suitable sources of supply, (3) negotiating terms, (4) maintaining favorable relations with resources, (5) receiving, checking, and marking, and (6) follow-up. Often the last two are considered separately, but in the small business they are so closely related to actual buying that they are discussed briefly here.

Determining Needs

Too much buying in the small business is based on hunches instead of adequate information. Often it is spasmodic rather than planned. However, neither of these undesirable conditions need exist, even in the one-man business.

Determining needs means finding out the kind, type, quality, brand, size, or other varieties needed, and the quantities of each. For the merchant this involves a study of the demand of his particular customers. Even for the same class of trade, demand may be quite different in two locations even though they are not far apart. Customer wants change, and the alert merchant will keep abreast of these changes—anticipating them whenever possible, perhaps by reading the same magazines and seeing the same shows as do his customers. Wholesalers and trade journals are valuable aids to the small merchant in anticipating customer demand.

For the small manufacturer and service operator the intended use for materials, parts, and supplies is the important factor. Even when the small enterpriser knows the technical side of his business thoroughly he should watch for opportunities to use new, improved, or even less expensive materials that will do the job equally well. Trade journals, suppliers' representatives, and manufacturers' catalogs or descriptive printed matter will help him in this task. Also, his own production workers often offer valuable suggestions if they are consulted.

In determining the correct quantities to buy, the close relationship between inventory or stores control and purchasing becomes apparent. Estimated needs minus quantity on hand (from inventory control records) gives quantity to buy. In merchandising the usual guides are followed: basic stock list and past sales records for staples, the model stock for shopping goods or other lines involving an assortment like size or color, and sample tests before placing complete orders for novelties.

In manufacturing, estimated sales or planned production of each article is the starting point. Then a list of materials and parts is used to determine the quantities needed for each unit. By multiplying planned production in units by the quantity of each material or part required per unit, the various quantities to purchase are calculated. Other factors like transportation charges, if any, quantity discounts, and manufacturer's packing amounts would be considered before deciding the specific number of each item to order at one time.

Locating Suppliers

Once needs have been determined, the next step is to locate suitable sources of supply. Resources available to the small businessman usually are more limited than those for the big company. Often the former is restricted to the particular market representatives or channels of trade used by the producers from whom he wants to buy. Sometimes he is limited to the immediate area in which his own business is located. Regardless of these limitations, he will nearly always have some choice between competing suppliers.

In selecting a resource, he will consider which supplier carries the quality and variety of goods best suited to the needs as previously determined. Other important factors will be price for the quality needed, time required for delivery, transportation costs, services rendered by the resource (including willingness to sell in the quantities desired), and market strategy. An example where consideration of the last factor plays an important part is a furniture retailer in Fort Smith, Arkansas—a furniture market—who does almost all of his buying in Chicago so as to have merchandise different from that offered by his competitors. Too much attention is often paid to price. Goods should also be bought with an eye to quality, past performance, and customer needs. The aim should be to obtain the lowest price, the most favorable terms, and the most adequate service, all consistent with satisfactory quality.

Both in selecting a resource and in choosing particular items, the buyer should be as well informed as possible regarding important properties of the goods. In merchandising, the following points are considered important: materials, construction, reasons for different qualities, comparative values, intended uses, and care required. These are the factors of greatest concern to intelligent consumer buyers. When style or fashion is characteristic of the merchandise, its stylishness may be of even greater importance than other elements. It is not necessary for the merchant to be an expert on all kinds of materials, nor for him to attempt tests. Reliable suppliers provide this information through their salesmen, on labels, in descriptive advertising, or by other means.

Small manufacturers and service operators will be concerned with the way different materials and supplies act in their production processes. Again, suppliers' representatives will give valuable information if requested, or permitted, to do so.

Buying Techniques

In negotiating prices and terms, the small buyer will do well to steer a middle course. If he really is an expert on the goods purchased, he needs no advice, but the average man should try to be a careful buyer, to keep as well informed as possible on current prices, and to insist on fair treatment. Any attempt to pose as a know-it-all, however, or a reputation for trying to beat down prices, is likely to invite trouble. Nearly always the salesman is better informed on qualities and prices than is the small purchaser, and some salesmen enjoy "putting it over" on the "smart" buyer. The exact quality needed for the purpose, at a fair price, should be the standard to follow.

Terms available to the small buyer are of two principal types, cash discounts and "datings," or the length of time before the net amount of the invoice is due. Often the trade will have its customary terms, or they will be fixed for the little fellow. When opportunity for bargaining does exist, however, too many small businessmen are more interested in datings—that is, the length of credit extended—than they are in the cash discount. Unless a business is in dire financial straits, the cash discount is usually more important than the length of credit extended.

Maintaining Favorable Relations with Resources

The topic of this chapter is not "Buying," but "Relationships with Resources." Merely to buy goods is easy. To maintain favorable relations with vendors seems, at times, to be especially difficult for the small businessman. But it is always worth the effort. The smaller the business, the greater the importance of cultivating friendly relations with resources. In contrast to the big buyer, the small operator has far less to offer vendors in the way of total profits. But he can be considerate of salesmen, prompt in paying his bills, and fair in all his dealings with suppliers.

Receiving, Checking, and Marking

Receiving, checking, and marking goods purchased are routine activities in most cases, and they may be performed carelessly unless provisions are made for their proper handling. In the small business this involves recognizing the importance of careful checking on quantity, condition, and transportation charges. Quality should be inspected in most cases. An alert small buyer has a good opportunity to build a desirable reputation, and to cement favorable future relations with his resources, by the way he handles these activities. All overages as well as shortages should be reported promptly to the seller. All too often the only report vendors receive from small buyers is a complaint about shortages or damaged goods. Damage claims should be made, in so far as possible, to the party responsible—either the vendor or the transportation company. In either case they should be made promptly and supported by adequate proof. Care in observing little details like these will help considerably in setting the small operator apart from the vendor's other customers, and stamping him as a "big businessman on the way up."

The way goods are marked upon receipt varies by type of business, the firm's policy, and other factors. Merchants should always mark each item or container with the date received. Whether size, cost, selling price, vendor's identification, or other data are marked on the goods will depend on many factors. Small manufacturers and service operators may need very little marking, unless points like identification of kind or grade and source are significant.

Follow-up after Purchase

It seems to be characteristic of most Americans to exert strenuous efforts to get something which when once received loses most of its former interest. Since in a small enterprise the man *is* the business, this trait frequently shows itself in buying for the firm. Goods once purchased and received are likely to be forgotten. Thus a bad buy is often repeated, and merchandise or materials already on hand in ample supply are reordered.

Follow-up relates to the history of the goods once they have been received. In merchandising it includes data on how the article sold, rate of turnover, markdowns, customer complaints, returns, adjustments, and allowances. It is an always up-to-date moving picture of the item from the time it entered the store until it was finally disposed of. The small wholesaler will watch this record closely in terms of re-orders by his retail customers. In either case, retailer or wholesaler, one of these situations will develop: The article will be a "hot" item to be re-ordered at once; it is an average piece of merchandise; or it is a "buyer's mistake."

In small manufacturing and service establishments follow-up is more difficult and more frequently neglected. Of course, if a particular purchase turns out to be a "dud," appropriate action is taken. However, in the small firm most purchases are moderately satisfactory and too little effort is exerted toward tracing the success of each. Small operators could well give more consideration to their follow-up, on the purchase of materials and supplies especially.

When any firm has reached the size at which purchase records beyond those required for legal and accounting purposes are needed, a "resources file" is indicated. In this file is kept a card for each supplier that carries a complete record of the success of all transactions with him. It also contains data on prices, unit packages, discounts, and other purchasing information. Such a file serves as a current history record, which is a valuable guide to re-ordering.

BUYING BY THE SMALL RETAILER

Buying for the retail store has been developed to a highly skilled occupation, utilizing many aids and scientific methods—but it is still an art based on individual ability and supported by all available information. Buying is the foundation for success in retailing. Small-scale retailers, since they are, at best, handicapped because of limited experience and buying power, should capitalize on the experience of larger stores, use the outside staff, or affiliate with some reputable voluntary and co-operative group. Our discussion will follow this plan, first considering proved buying guides, and then the voluntary and co-operative groups.

Consumer demand for many goods varies from one community to another as well as from time to time for the same group of people. The successful retailer understands the dynamic nature of consumer wants and makes strenuous efforts to keep his merchandise offerings adjusted to current demand. To do so usually involves anticipating what his customers' needs will be so that goods will be on hand when they are needed.

Determining Customer Wants

Three main methods are used to determine what merchandise customers are going to want:

1. Analyzing sales records.
2. Making consumer surveys.
3. Studying trade information.

Chain stores that deal in staple merchandise, such as grocery and drug chains, have developed a simple system of maintaining adequate stocks of articles in steady demand. Headquarters first prepares a list of the items each store should carry. Once a week the store manager compares his actual stock on hand with original quantities for each item on the checklist. For example, if the stock on hand of one brand of soap is ten bars and the entry for the previous week shows twenty-two were on hand, one dozen were sold during the week if none were received. Thus, without recording sales daily, the manager knows the rate of sale of each item and orders goods to keep his stock in balance with sales. Small retailers can use this checklist system by securing basic stock lists from their suppliers.

A different system is needed to provide information about the sale of merchandise whose style changes rapidly. Retailers who handle such goods find it advisable to record each sale and to make frequent (sometimes daily) analyses of these sales records. Thus they know what styles are selling rapidly and should be reordered at once, as well as the styles for which demand is declining. For the latter a small price reduction made in time may help to sell the goods before customers have lost all interest in the merchandise.

Small merchants will not ordinarily make formal consumer surveys but may accomplish approximately the same objective by observing and talking with customers in the store. Trade journal staffs sometimes conduct surveys of consumer buying habits and report their findings.

Studying trade information. A retailer has available to him many sources of information about developments in his field. Examples are trade papers written for other dealers like himself, fashion magazines, bulletins prepared by Merchants Service Bureaus, special market services that undertake to keep retailers informed about new merchandise and trends, manufacturers, brokers, and other salesmen. Many of these sources of trade information may reveal a customer demand in other localities before the merchant's own customers have expressed themselves.

Trade papers are especially helpful for informing a merchant of new goods for which there is as yet no active consumer demand, but which are likely to become popular later on. Such information is presented both in the form of articles and as vendors' advertising. If he is to avoid costly mistakes in buying unwanted goods, each retailer must know his own customers well enough to judge what new merchandise will, and what will not, be acceptable to them.

For style goods, and other lines where balanced assortments are of great importance, the model stock is the usual buying guide. A model stock plan means carrying a predetermined assortment of merchandise that is in proper balance by types, sizes, and colors with the sales of the line of goods. If the model stock plan were perfect, it would include the exact quantities of the right sorts of goods in relation to the desired rate of sale. In other words, if the estimates of the model stock plan were entirely correct, the merchant would sell all the goods projected in the plan; and in doing so, he would achieve exactly the stock turnover rate for which he had planned.

Changing consumer wants make past sales far from a perfect guide to what and how much a retailer should purchase. Changes in trading areas, such as increases or decreases in population, make it impossible to use past sales alone as a reflector of future demand for certain sizes and for staple articles. A change in business conditions also to some degree nullifies the past as a guide for the future, except with respect to sizes and staples. When prices are changing rapidly, past records in terms of units sold should be used, instead of dollar sales volume, to forecast future needs. Changes in demand with respect to fashion, color, and material likewise weaken past sales records as a barometer for future purchases. The retailer should use market trends and sales forecasts to modify his decisions based upon past sales records.

Determining Market Trends

Several of the sources discussed as useful in determining customer demand will be helpful in forecasting market trends—especially trade journals and manufacturers. The latter are in a favorable position to aid dealers in this activity because producers must forecast such trends for themselves if they are to experience profitable operations. Also, like wholesalers, manufacturers are continually receiving orders and inquiries from many territories. This furnishes them with the data needed to observe important trends.

During the 1960's pronounced changes in the composition of our population will be significant. The importance of teenagers and people past sixty, both with ample purchasing power, deserve attention. Higher levels of education, more working wives, and locational changes of various groups will be important. In the later 1960's the bulge in our labor force will be especially important.[3]

Salesmen who call upon the retailer are usually well informed about trends, particularly changes affecting the line of goods carried. Suggestions given by traveling salesmen are often very helpful to the small merchant. Of course he should be careful not to let himself be oversold on certain goods an unscrupulous salesman may want to dispose of. Salespersons in the store also can furnish information on current trends in customer preference for certain merchandise.

Some retailers have each salesperson record every customer request for merchandise that is not in stock. Want slips are frequently used for this purpose, although some merchants, especially druggists, prefer to use a want book. Care should be exercised in using information recorded on want slips. First, it is important to be sure that requests come from regular customers rather than from transients or from shoppers employed by other stores or even by vendors. Next the retailer should be satisfied that there are enough calls for the merchandise not in stock to indicate a trend and to justify placing an order for such goods.

Competitors, especially progressive large stores, may be studied by the small retailer to determine market trends. The advertising and displays of such stores provide many cues both as to increasing and declining popularity of certain merchandise. In using this method, the merchant should select a store that is normally slightly in advance of his own in the merchandise acceptance curve. This means that the customers of the store selected for observation usually buy new merchandise before his own customers do. Even if such a store is not available in the community, the method suggested will be useful provided a large, progressive store is selected for observation.

Voluntary and Co-operative Groups

Especially since the rise of the chain store, which has brought the efficient merchandising methods of big business into direct competition with the independent retailer in his own home town, there is more need for outside assistance in management and merchandising than is realized by many small-scale retailers. Since the chain stores, along with other types of large-scale retailing, tend to go around the wholesaler and buy direct from manufacturers, the wholesalers are also concerned about their loss of markets.

A development of major importance has been the formation of many co-operative arrangements, either between a wholesaler and a selected group

[3] See: *Markets of the Sixties* (New York: Harper & Brothers, 1960), by the Editors of *Fortune*.

of his retail customers or among a group of retailers in the same line of business. The former arrangement is called a "voluntary chain"; the latter is a "co-operative chain." Although both types of organizations were formed originally for the primary purpose of buying merchandise in larger quantities and on terms more nearly comparable to those offered large-scale competitors, extensive experience has proved that managerial and merchandising aids made available by the central headquarters for each store are usually of an importance to the members at least equal to the buying advantages. Another lesson learned by these groups is that the retail outlets all must be of one kind. This means that the various retail stores comprising the group must be approximately similar as to class of trade, merchandise carried, and other factors that would have a bearing upon joint merchandising and management through common policies. Size differences are less important than the quality of management, provided extremes are not included. Examples of such extremes would be stores too large to need group aid, or those too small to appreciate and use it.[4]

There are four different types of organizations classified as voluntary and co-operative groups: (1) retailer co-operatives or co-operative chains,[5] (2) wholesaler-sponsored voluntary chains, (3) manufacturers' voluntary chains, and (4) agency or franchise stores sponsored by the corporate chains, and others. The retailer co-operative is owned entirely by the retail merchants, operates entirely for their benefit, usually has its own warehouse, and sells exclusively to member stores. In some respects, such as in the use of patronage dividends, it resembles the consumer co-operative type of organization.

Wholesaler- or jobber-sponsored voluntary chains usually carry the wholesaler's own or "private" brand merchandise, have a common name and appearance of the store front, and offer advertising and other merchandising aids that vary with each organization. The retail stores are individually owned but agree in joining the voluntary to assume certain obligations such as to feature the company's merchandise, to co-operate in advertising, and to maintain acceptable standards of appearance for the store front and interior. Most organizations specify the minimum amount of merchandise that must be purchased through the sponsoring wholesaler.

Voluntaries sponsored by manufacturers operate principally in the auto accessory and shoe fields. Considerable expansion has taken place recently in the former. Products not manufactured by the company may be purchased through its buying organization more economically than if the local retailer were to buy them independently. The large tire companies that have gone in for this type of expansion also purchase related merchandise for franchised stores and follow a policy of giving preference to the locally owned

---

[4] Gordon Cook, "The 1947 Position of Voluntary and Co-operative Groups," *The Voluntary and Co-operative Groups Magazine* (February 1947), p. 37.

[5] Organizations in this field seem to prefer the term "group" to "chain" in describing their type of operation.

store whenever one that meets their standards can be found. It is only when the company desires an outlet in a town where this condition does not exist that company-owned stores are operated.

Several years ago some of the corporate chains appeared to be interested in launching their own voluntary or agency groups. A few did so. One large mail-order house chain, after arranging for agency outlets, later abandoned the plan because results were not satisfactory. It now concentrates on its own stores exclusively. However, two prominent examples of chain store-sponsored voluntaries in such diverse fields as auto accessories and drugs (The Western Auto Authorized Dealer Plan and the Walgreen Agency), as well as many cases that closely resemble such combinations, point to the possibilities of this type of distribution. Those resembling this type of operation include the large tire manufacturers that have both their own retail chain and agency stores, and large wholesalers like Butler Brothers, who operate company-owned and voluntary chain outlets.

A survey conducted in 1947, covering all four types of chains mentioned, led to the conclusion that most corporate chains of the regular merchandising (nonmanufacturing) type were not interested in establishing voluntary or agency affiliates. Information received from 33 of the best-known corporate chains disclosed that only four were operating independently owned retail affiliates, and one other was considering doing so (men's furnishings). The four operating voluntaries were: Walgreen's in the drug field, Western Auto Stores in auto accessories and general merchandise, United Cigar-Whelan Stores in the tobacco and drug fields, and one shoe manufacturer who had a plan for women's shoe departments in specialty and department stores, as well as in its company-owned chain stores. By commodity fields the others were distributed as follows: junior department and general merchandise, 7; variety, 7; grocery, 4; shoes, 3; women's wear, 3; food service, drugs, candy and cigars, 1 each.

It is interesting that two of the three companies having plans for independent affiliates are also manufacturers who distribute their products through company-owned chain stores as well as through voluntaries. At least in one case, that of Walgreen's, a major reason for the agency plan is to increase the outlets for company-manufactured products, especially in towns of less than 20,000 population, where a company-owned store could not be justifiable. Large tire companies, like B. F. Goodrich and Goodyear Tire and Rubber Company, that operate both company-owned and voluntary chains are also concerned primarily with maintaining outlets for their own brands of products.

The following brief discussion of several of these voluntary plans for independent merchants, from a representative selection of fields, is intended merely to present the outstanding features of the four types of programs. All descriptions have been adapted from printed material published by the sponsoring organizations or from letters addressed to the authors.

Groceries. Clover Farm Stores, with headquarters in Cleveland, Ohio, a wholesale-sponsored voluntary group, was begun in 1926.

The Clover Farm field representatives help wholesalers and retailers with their individual problems—finances, selling, operating efficiency, and so on. Headquarters publishes a monthly magazine, *The Clover Farm Bee,* which contains articles, editorials, and advertisements. It also publishes the *Four-Leaf Clover* for advertising to the home; this newspaper, although edited by the main office, is printed and distributed without cost by the various divisions. The retailer receives the *Clovergram,* a mimeographed publication containing information about store operations, promotion, merchandising, and clerk training. In addition to this, Clover Farm headquarters sends posters, price cards and pennants, and other advertising material to the various divisions.

Other well-known retail food voluntaries include A. G. (Associated Grocers), St. Louis, Missouri, with 467 members; Jack Sprat Food Stores, sponsored by the Western Grocer of Marshalltown, Iowa; I. G. A. (Independent Grocers Alliance), with headquarters in Chicago and several thousand retail and wholesale members; and H. G. F. stores, sponsored by the H. D. Lee Company of Kansas City, Missouri. Organizations such as these have membership contracts and usually collect dues; they feature their own private brands, but also carry national brands; and they furnish merchandising and management assistance in varying amounts to franchise members. Advertising and promotional aids, as well as some help on layout, accounting, and sales clerk training, are furnished in most cases, but the use of supervisors varies among the different firms.

Variety and general merchandise. Butler Brothers entered the voluntary field in 1927, revised their plan in 1943, and again during the 1950's. In 1958 they had over 2,400 variety merchants using their Distributor Store program. During 1959, 92 new Ben Franklin stores were opened. These stores had returns on: sales of 10 to 15 per cent, and on investment of 20 to 35 per cent. The plan is so complete that Butler Brothers claims no retail experience is necessary to success.[6]

Before recommending that a prospect invest in a particular store, Butler Brothers make a careful study of facts pertaining to his background, experience, likes, and dislikes. Every precaution is taken to see that each prospect is a perfect "fit" for the store he takes over. Special attention is given to an owner's retail suitability, to the type of community for which he is best suited, whether or not he has the proper personality for meeting the public, to his ability to meet capital requirements for stores of the size under consideration, and to similar factors. A prospective merchant without sufficient experience in retailing is given an opportunity to take a complete course in operating a store under the supervision of experienced re-

[6] *Today's Most Timely Business Opportunity: Owning a Ben Franklin Store* (Butler Brothers, Chicago, 1958.)

tailers. Detailed surveys and analyses are made of recommended towns to determine their exact mathematical opportunity for success. Population, trade areas, shopping habits, spendable income, scientific traffic counts, building required—these are only a few of the many important factors studied before establishing a Distributor Store. Butler Brothers lease-location men are responsible for sound lease protection to provide each Distributor Store owner with security and the certainty of having an adequate building at a fair rental. This Distributor Store organization is serving a growing list of store owners in exactly the same way the Butler chain stores headquarters serve their individual units. The Distributor Store organization matches—man for man, function for function—the organization and supervision found in the chains.

Distributor Store men—experts in retail management, merchandising, advertising, display, and sales promotion—now devote their entire time to servicing this proved program and to keeping retailers abreast of the best that competition can offer. Today's trend of rapid development in retailing makes professional guidance for individual store owners as imperative as having a dependable merchandise source. Store superintendents make periodic calls on each independent owner in order to give him every assistance possible on any problems of merchandising, financial control, personnel, displays, and other management duties. The total charge for this printed and personal service amounts to about $3/4$ of one per cent of the store's annual volume.

Upon entering the Distributor Store plan, the owner agrees to purchase merchandise of the type and quality offered by Butler Brothers, and to put into practice all the guidance and retail know-how provided by the program. Currently they are advising self-service.

The merchandising division makes available almost all of the well-known nationally advertised brands. In addition, Butler Brothers has a packaging and brands department for the purpose of providing Distributor Store owners with exclusive brands that can be obtained only in their stores. Since these brands cannot be purchased from local competitors, it is to the owner's advantage to create a demand for them.

Butler Brothers has regional offices located in Chicago, St. Louis, Baltimore, Minneapolis, Dallas, and San Francisco. Distributor Store headquarters are in Chicago. If a person is interested in becoming a Ben Franklin owner, he should contact the Development Manager in any of the above regional offices.[7]

In 1949 the Baltimore house changed over to 100 per cent franchise operations with such success that the company decided to shift its other four wholesale houses to the same plan.

---

[7] Comments regarding Butler Brothers adapted from letters of May 12, 1947, and October 27, 1953, by Mr. K. C. Meyer, Assistant General Production Manager, Butler Brothers, Chicago.

Auto accessories. Western Auto Supply Company of Los Angeles started in 1916, when the first store was opened in Los Angeles, and it had 173 stores in the chain by 1935 when the Western Dealer Plan went into effect. Later the company merged with Gamble-Skogmo, Inc., sponsors of Gamble Stores voluntary chain.

During and since World War II Gamble-Skogmo, Inc., with headquarters in Minneapolis, Minnesota, expanded their lines to include staple clothing, shoes, and furniture, and now stress the combination store. By 1953 they had four regional divisions in the United States and affiliates in Canada, 2,086 authorized dealers, and 486 company-owned stores in operation from Ohio to the Pacific Coast. Popular nationally advertised brands and private label merchandise are provided for each store. Company-owned test stores try out new merchandise. Private label goods are made by their manufacturing affiliates as well as purchased on specifications developed in their experimental laboratory.

A complete plan of merchandising and management aids has been developed that are now provided through field men in each region. No charge is made to franchised dealers for these services.

Western Auto Supply Company of Kansas City, Missouri, retailing auto supplies, sporting goods, electrical appliances, and related lines, had over 3,600 Western Auto Associate stores by 1959, when they launched their Western Auto Agency Program. The Agency plan is for stores in small towns. Plans called for 450 agencies by the end of 1959.[8]

Several large tire companies, including Goodyear, B. F. Goodrich, Firestone, and others, have authorized dealer plans operated on a franchise basis with merchandising and management aids comparable to the voluntaries in other fields. These companies manufacture thousands of products that are sold through their dealers' stores. In addition, many of the tire companies have secured distribution rights for other well-advertised companies' lines, such as General Electric and Kelvinator refrigerators, for sale through dealer stores.

The following excerpts from a letter from Goodyear Tire and Rubber Company are sufficiently representative of these plans:

> Goodyear is a dealer company and our distribution has always been primarily through dealers. We have approximately 12,000 direct franchised dealers.
>
> The essential provisions of our plan as to qualifications of retailers for affiliation are primarily that the dealer have or be capable of developing the proper reputation in the community, the necessary management and merchandising ability, and sufficient finances, to warrant his being extended the proper line of credit. We make no charge to our dealers for the Goodyear franchise.

[8] Letter from Charles M. Wilson, Jr., Sales Research Manager, Western Auto, November 17, 1959.

The buying advantages offered consist of our supplying our dealers with products we manufacture bearing our own name and with certain other lines of nationally advertised merchandise which we do not manufacture, but which we offer to our dealers in order to round out their selling opportunities and to give them a complete business franchise.

Many merchandising and management aids are available to our dealers— these include the personal advice and counsel of our field representatives, special representatives on certain products (such as truck tires, farm tires, batteries, and brake linings), district operating managers, district credit managers, district sales managers, and budget supervisors.

In addition to the personal advice and counsel by the qualified people just mentioned, our dealers get the benefit of comprehensive employee training programs, both in meeting form (consisting of movies, sound slide films, charts and quizzes) and of printed booklets, folders, etc.

The obligations or responsibilities assumed by our dealers consist primarily of taking full advantage of the sales and profit possibilities of our complete business franchise, backed up by the merchandising helps available, and of seeing that the people to whom they sell Goodyear products are given the right kind of service to assure the products delivering all the service mileage and value built into them.

It is expected that our dealers will buy from Goodyear those lines of merchandise we have which the dealers want to handle. We have no objection to a dealer handling lines of merchandise which we do not carry, and these, of course, he may buy from any source he desires.[9]

Usually the tire companies encourage franchise dealers to capitalize the installment credit business, and often furnish a company representative to develop this department in the dealer's store. In contrast to voluntaries in other lines, the nature of tire products leads to a dual system of dealer outlets —the retail store and the service station.

Drugs. Probably the most comprehensive real voluntary in the drug field is the Walgreen Agency Plan, inaugurated in 1931. It is a complete merchandising plan for independent druggists. There were well over 1,500 Walgreen agency drugstores functioning late in 1953, and applications are constantly being processed.

The Walgreen agency may be established in registered drugstores, if they fulfill the requirements of the plan and conform to certain standards. All the merchandising facilities of the company are available to the agents— construction and layout plans, advertising, display, and merchandising helps. Other services may also be obtained on an advisory basis.

Agents operate under a franchise for the exclusive sale of Walgreen merchandise within their trade area. Selected sundry items are also sold. A minimum purchase requirement is stipulated, based on population or sales. The usual term of an agency agreement is ten years.

During 1953 the largest percentage of the Walgreen agencies were located

[9] Excerpts from letters of May 12, 1947, and November 13, 1953, from Mr. J. A. Lewin, Manager, Dealer Department, The Goodyear Tire & Rubber Co., Inc., Akron, Ohio.

in smaller towns. However, a recent change in policy has made it subsequently possible to establish agencies in most of the large cities. They must bear approved identification and are urged to merchandise to make their stores higher volume units. Recommended displays and advertising services are furnished by headquarters at a nominal charge. Agencies are invited by the company to join in certain sales promotion and merchandising events throughout the year. The Walgreen Agency Plan does not disturb the regular jobber-retailer relationship in so far as national brands are concerned, but Walgreen merchandise is stocked in addition as an exclusive.

Working in co-operation with Walgreen, the agents secure standard store installations. Because concentration of purchases of fixtures and equipment allows mass production methods, agents usually can lower the cost of improving their stores.

Figures volunteered by agents indicate increases up to 40 per cent in total store volume after conversion of the typical nonaffiliated store to a Walgreen agency.

Hardware. The largest chain of franchised stores operating in the hardware field in 1954 was the 500-store group of the Marshall-Wells Company of Duluth. In 1952 Hibbard Spencer Bartlett & Company of Chicago launched a franchise dealer plan, using the owner's name on individual store signs and the identifying line "True Value Hardware and Housewares."

Foods. In the restaurant and candy fields, franchising independents has expanded greatly in postwar years. Over half the Howard Johnson of Boston restaurants operate as franchise holders in various cities. Where several units are located on the same turnpike, they are usually company owned. Late in 1959 the Frank G. Shattuck Company announced plans to franchise their Schraffts chain of restaurants on a national basis to be operated chiefly in connection with new motels.[10]

The Russell Stover Candy Company of Kansas City, Missouri operates its own chain of retail candy stores in leading cities and franchises selected drugstores to distribute its packaged lines.

Chicken Delight and several varieties of the soft ice cream, or custard, field operate largely through franchise dealers. Well-known examples are Dairy Queen, Dari-Delight and Tastee Freez.[11]

Miscellaneous. Combined services and product fields are prominent in franchise operations, such as Midas Mufflers. In services, Service Master and Duraclean (carpet sweepers), National Homes Corporation, (the largest prefabricated house company), and National Car Rental System are examples. Also most brand name oil companies franchise their service station operators.[12]

---

[10] *Business Week* (November 28, 1959), p. 75.

[11] "Franchise Selling Catches On," *Business Week* (February 6, 1960), pp. 90-94.

[12] David Schwartz, *The Franchise System for Establishing Independent Retail Outlets* (Atlanta, Georgia: Bureau of Business and Economic Research, Georgia State College of Business Administration, 1959).

Market Representatives

Both large and small retailers located at some distance from the main central markets find it highly desirable to maintain contact with a representative situated there from whom they secure a large part of their merchandise. In the "soft lines"—wearing apparel, dry goods, and department store merchandise—these representatives are referred to as "resident buying offices." In hardware and "hard lines" the term "purchasing agent" is frequently used.

With proper modification the following discussion will apply to purchasing agents as well as to resident buyers, although it deals primarily with the latter. Important differences between "hard" and "soft" lines are: a larger number of manufacturers, greater weight per unit of merchandise, and fairly stable styles for the former; and frequent style and price changes, light unit weight, many new producers, and a somewhat smaller number of manufacturers for the latter.

Resident buyers of interest to the smaller merchants are of two principal types—the paid buying office, and the merchandise broker. The latter were formerly called "commission buying offices."

Paid buying offices. The paid or independent offices maintain continuous contacts with a selected group of retailers on an annual fee and contract basis. In addition to buying merchandise for subscribing stores, the paid office furnishes a wealth of market information and forecasts. Many stores large enough to afford a paid office seem to be more interested in this market information service than in actually buying much merchandise through the office. However, when buyers from these stores go to market they work closely with the merchandise experts in their resident buying office, which saves the buyer's time as well as keeping him in touch with the latest trends and best resources. The buying office is normally used as the store buyer's temporary headquarters when in the market.

Although there are several hundred resident buying offices in New York City, and many in other major markets, such as Chicago, St. Louis, Los Angeles, San Francisco, and Dallas, about 17 have long been in operation and are widely known throughout the country. In general, these offices serve only one client (subscribing retail store) in any community. The usual practice is to charge an annual fee of approximately one-half to one per cent of the subscriber's net sales. In pricing their services to individual stores, a few of the offices consider, in addition, the relative amount of the merchandise experts' time needed by the store. Some offices have minimum fees, which have been as low as $900 to $1,200 per year. Even the smaller of these figures would indicate a store volume of $90,000 or more per year to keep this fee within the customary one per cent standard. Recently an organization located in New York City has been advertising itself as a paid buying office for small stores doing a volume up to $250,000.

The Association of Buying Offices, composed only of paid offices, recently stated its objectives as follows:

1. To keep our member stores informed through timely bulletins of the latest fashion and market trends, as well as opportunity purchases and new items presented in the various markets.

2. To assist our member stores in the screening of resources and values.

3. To act for and represent member stores in the market in the interim period between buyers' trips.

4. To follow up and speed deliveries on outstanding orders.

5. To assist our member stores in the planning of promotions and regular selling events in line with prevailing market trends.

6. To foster good relationships between trade factors and our member stores.

7. To provide merchandise in adequate quantities and increasingly improved quality, as reasonably as possible to the ultimate consumer.

8. To counsel and advise with the management of our member stores in planning their stock and merchandising operations.

9. To consult with store managements on their organization problems, their personnel programs, and analyze store figures in many constructive ways.

10. To offer through branch offices a nation-wide knowledge of important markets and merchandise.[13]

Merchandise brokers. Merchandise brokers buy for retail stores, securing their revenue as a discount or brokerage commission from the vendors; they make no charge to their retail clients for their buying services. As of 1949, there were nearly 200 merchandise brokers with offices in the New York City market, as listed in the Manhattan Classified Telephone Directory. J. S. Phelon and Company, 32 Union Square, and Nugent's Directories, published by the Chelton Company at 100 East 42nd Street, both in New York City, are other sources of information about merchandise brokers. The following description, furnished by Arthur Mincer Company, Merchandise Brokers, of New York City, is probably representative of the work done by these representatives.

A Merchandise Broker usually has one customer in a city. This situation is brought about by the fact that the broker represents a great many sources of supply and the retail merchant would want to be the broker's only customer in the specific town in order to avoid conflicts with his competitor.

The predominant factor in selecting or accepting a retail account is the credit standing. Merchandise Brokers occupy the peculiar position in the market of having a reputation of choosing their customers carefully, look-

[13] The Association of Buying Offices, "The Buying Office Faces the Future—and the Facts," *Women's Wear Daily* (December 26, 1946).

ing into their credit standing and financial condition, and the wholesale markets therefore deal with brokers with confidence.

There are no agreements or contracts between the Merchandise Broker and his retail customer and could not be because the Merchandise Broker's contractual relations are with the source of supply.

There are a great many advantages for a retail store to use a Merchandise Broker's office, for the broker saves him a great deal of time on his market trips by presenting such a large number of lines from which he can make his selections. The broker also sends him bulletins and flashes on merchandise that is available from the source of supply with whom there is a contractual relation.[14]

The following additional points were provided by Bernstein and Wolff, Manufacturers' Representatives for Wholesale Ready to Wear, New York City:

1. The commission is paid to the office by the manufacturer at a stipulated rate of commission on the net amount of merchandise shipped and paid for by the retailer. When purchasing goods through a commission office, the service is rendered "gratis" to the retailer.

2. There are some offices which will accept accounts with purchasing power from $3,000 and up a year—then again, there are offices which will not take on any accounts below the figure of $25,000 per year.

3. Market bulletins are sent to the stores showing outstanding lines and keeping the account informed of new items from time to time. The office also advises the account of the best time to come to the market to make his purchases, if he plans on a trip.

4. The offices specialize in various lines of merchandise. For instance, one office may buy only millinery, another men's wear, but one like Bernstein and Wolff handles ladies' and children's ready-to-wear, such as coats, suits, dresses, millinery, bags, undergarments, and kindred lines.

5. In the event that the buyer of the store is in town, the office takes her to the outstanding houses and aids her in selecting her merchandise, and makes sure the best values are obtained at all times.[15]

Merchandise Marts. In the general merchandise fields even small retailers find it desirable to "go to market." Recently "markets" are often held in a single building or mart where the leading vendors have displays and representatives. The few mentioned here are merely illustrative. The Merchandise Mart in Chicago contains seven miles of display corridors with the offerings of some of America's best-known manufacturers. Atlanta's Merchandise Mart, after three years of operation in 400 lines of furniture, home furnishings, juvenile and gift wares, planned a new 22-story building for more space and to add appliances, luggage, jewelry, and wearing apparel.[16] The Trade

[14] Excerpts from a letter of June 5, 1947, from Mr. Arthur Mincer. Confirmed, November 18, 1953.

[15] Items 1 through 5 are adapted from a letter of April 15, 1947, from Mr. Morris M. Bernstein, President, National Association of Merchandise Brokers.

[16] *Business Week* (July 25, 1959), pp. 88-100.

Mart in Dallas has 160 showrooms for 1,000 lines of furniture and accessories.[17]

BUYING BY THE SMALL WHOLESALER

As a class, wholesalers are supposed to have large businesses. Actually many small wholesalers find it difficult to purchase in carload lots or other quantities of sufficient size to secure the low prices and economical transportation needed to justify their status as wholesalers. This has often led to the use of pooled buying, ordering through resident buying offices, and transportation arranged by freight forwarders or shippers who consolidate several less than carload shipments into car lots to secure lower transportation rates. Actual examples of practices followed by small wholesalers known to the authors are described in the following paragraph.

Three brothers, each operating an independent, noncompeting wholesale grocery, pool their buying to secure a five-per cent discount permitted for purchasing in car lots. A feed and flour wholesaler pools his buying with a few large retail customers. Another seed wholesaler buys on contract from growers, sends scouts out to locate sellers, and orders from catalogues. A produce dealer uses truck drivers to scout for "good buys"; a small packer sends his buyers to the local stockyards on sale days; a radio wholesaler waits for visits by salesmen but does some ordering by mail. One small hardware wholesaler does not stock heavy, bulky, expensive items but buys them only on customer orders. These few examples illustrate the diversity of buying methods likely to be found among small wholesalers in many average towns. Several of these practices are quite similar to those followed by retailers.

In at least one other respect many small wholesalers resemble retailers; by virtue of it, they are, in fact, both retailers and wholesalers. Throughout the country, but especially in the small towns in the less densely populated states, small businessmen in fields like groceries, meats, hardware, electrical supplies, and some others, function as both wholesale and retail distributors. In such cases the wholesale division is influenced greatly by the needs and policies of the retail in matters such as brands carried, price lines, and quantities to order. Much less frequently the wholesale activities have set the pattern for the retail store.

Policy decisions regarding brands to carry, assortments, number and completeness of merchandise lines, when to add new items, and the extent of quantity buying, are much more acute for the small than for the larger wholesaler although similar for both. Limited financial resources and a smaller market are the chief reasons for this condition. Also, the relative importance of short-run considerations as compared to long-run factors is greater for the small wholesaler.

[17] *Business Week* (July 25, 1959), pp. 88-100.

In gauging demand, the small retailer-wholesaler may have a slight advantage over his large counterpart. Consumer demand is immediately reflected through the retail store. However, the man who is exclusively a wholesaler would anticipate this demand and would have stocks on hand to fill orders of retail customers as they come in. In practice many wholesalers try to maintain continuous contact with consumer demand and trends by means of frequent visits of their representatives to retail stores. In addition to this firsthand observation, small wholesalers should use all available sources of demand forecasting, including the advice of their resident buying offices, reports on market trends, and tips received from manufacturers' representatives.

At least partly because of this need to forecast market trends further in advance than retailers, wholesalers are more tempted to engage in speculative buying. For the small operator this is especially dangerous. *One wrong guess and he may be wiped out.* A study disclosed opportunities for improved buying as follows. The buying mechanism might well be improved, since the buyer must examine the records to decide when and how much to purchase. Moreover, the records do not provide a tickler for timing the buying action. Except where the standing order is actually in effect, the buyer has to await advice from the warehouse as to when to buy. He decides only on how much.[18]

In selecting resources the small wholesaler finds that available ones vary by lines of goods, methods of distribution used by particular manufacturers, and location. The wholesaler's buying power may also have a bearing on the best sources of supply to use. Concentration is more common for staples, limited lines, and exclusive agencies. Orders are placed through selling agents. Diversification exists when there are a large number of small producers, such as in dry goods, and where style changes are frequent.

Another factor that may be of relatively greater concern to the small wholesaler is the distribution policies of competing manufacturers. Some producers sell directly to chain stores and other cut-price retailers, thus undermining the market for the wholesaler. Others protect their independent wholesale distributors.

Additional factors that enter into the choice of resources are transportation rates and the vendor's speed of delivery, ability to supply quantities desired, prices, services rendered; also his financial standing, credit policies, reputation, and types of protection he may give to small wholesalers.

To a greater extent than do retailers, small wholesalers order from catalogues and price lists by phone or mail. In the hardware and grocery fields, and for some electrical goods and other similar lines, this is common practice. Soft goods wholesalers seem to prefer market visits or salesmen's calls.

The small wholesaler is actually a relatively small operator and a newcomer in an established field where the age and size of the average concern

---

[18] *A Study of Tobacco Wholesalers' Operations*, Industrial Series No. 62 (Washington, D. C.: U. S. Department of Commerce, Office of Domestic Commerce, G. P. O., 1946).

are both quite large. Accepted business practices are well established. Confirming a small telephone order in writing, for example, may seem like a waste of time to the small wholesaler. Failure to do so would be acceptable in many retail fields, but in wholesale it is a serious mistake. All orders should be in writing, with proper duplicate copies as needed. Other well-established business practices, such as the use of purchase schedules, card indexing of vendors, prompt discounting of all invoices, dealing ethically with vendors, and observing trade customs, are expected to an even greater extent from small wholesalers than from retailers.[19]

The importance to the small wholesaler of maintaining favorable relations with his resources was aptly stated by Mr. Charles E. Woodward, Executive Secretary, Farm Equipment Wholesalers Association, in a letter to the authors as follows.

> The thousand or more factories who are the suppliers for our members usually call not less than once a year on their present and prospective wholesale customers. A small wholesaler who wants to grow, however, must return the favor by calling on the factories whose lines he would like to handle. Trade connections between manufacturers and wholesalers are not made in slap-dash fashion, but often follow an extended courtship. By the same token, these connections usually continue, some of them for many years. We know of one case where a distributor in California has handled for 52 years a line made in Philadelphia.[20]

An alert wholesaler will seek out appropriate sources of supply, secure and file catalogues, and aim at being informed in advance even if actual buying is done at the warehouse. Several compilations are used, such as the *Thomas Register of American Manufacturers* (published annually in three volumes), *McRae's Blue Book,* and specialized directories such as the *Thomas Wholesale Grocery and Kindred Trades Register.* These directories are in addition to the usual trades press articles and advertisements. At first the very small wholesaler may want to consult a directory or register in the purchasing department of some large nearby institution until he feels financially able to obtain his own.

BUYING BY THE SMALL FACTORY AND SERVICE BUSINESS

All manufacturing and most service establishments require materials and supplies to carry on their operations. Whereas the merchant buys for resale and frequently will purchase new items on his judgment that they can be sold at a profit, purchases for a factory or service establishment are made only in response to the expected needs of using departments. Assuming these needs to be reported or estimated accurately, purchasing aims at keeping the inven-

[19] Theodore N. Beckman and Nathanael H. Engle, *Wholesaling* (New York: Ronald Press Co., 1937). See also 3rd ed., 1957, Chap. 21, "Buying Policies and Procedures."

[20] Excerpt from letter of August 6, 1948, from Mr. Charles E. Woodward, Executive Secretary, Farm Equipment Wholesalers Association, Minneapolis, Minnesota.

tory of materials, parts, and supplies in proper balance with the needs of the company.

Many shops, during the beginning years especially, do not confine their operations exclusively either to manufacturing or to rendering certain services. The small business doing processing or performing a service, frequently also sells some parts or merchandise. A manufacturer of metal products needs raw material and supplies like fuel and oil. Because he maintains a stock of various kinds of metals, or parts, he often sells some of these with or without processing. Plumbing contractors, repair shops, beauty parlors, and other small establishments often derive a sizable proportion of their total income from the resale of materials, parts, or merchandise used in their kind of business.

To some degree at least, these small businessmen have a dual purchasing problem—buying for use, and buying for resale. Purchasing for these small operators usually is not a specialized function requiring the full time of one man or department. It is ordinarily done by the owner or under his close personal supervision. Because the owner-manager is more likely to be interested chiefly in the processing side of the business, buying may easily be slighted or carelessly handled. Unless the owner is capable of doing the job properly himself, and is willing to do it, definite responsibility for purchasing should be vested in one person who is also given adequate authority and facilities to do the job correctly.

Although the same fundamentals of buying operate—determining needs, locating suitable sources of supply, using approved techniques, maintaining favorable relations, receiving, and follow-up—their application to different fields varies to some extent. In the following discussion several fields have been selected to illustrate these differences as well as to call attention to important considerations in each. Except for the comments regarding the small factory, most of the material has been adapted from Department of Commerce small business manuals cited in the footnotes.

Purchasing for the Small Factory

Purchasing for the small factory aims to maintain inventories that are balanced in terms of production needs. If only one product is made and the rate of production is fairly constant, purchasing can be simplified to become nearly a routine operation once the qualities needed and the identity of suitable suppliers have been ascertained. Even in such a case some of the following purchasing techniques may be useful.

When items needed can be obtained regularly as wanted within a predictable time limit, it may be sufficient to establish maximum and minimum stock limits and the quantity to order at one time. However, when deliveries are uncertain, two additional guides may be needed: "lead time" in placing orders, and "not before" and "not after" dates. On these two methods one author has commented:

As to "lead time," if the purchasing agent is on a sound footing with his suppliers, it is perfectly proper for him to write to them and say, "You know the internal operating conditions in your plant and we don't. So that we can get our supplies from you on a proper scheduling basis, please tell us how far in advance we must place our orders with you. We shall give you whatever notice you ask for, but we shall not stand for 'dumping' ahead of our delivery schedule." This leads us to a consideration of the "not before" or "not after" principle. If these two dates are not set too close to one another, no supplier can properly object to making deliveries in the scheduled period provided the "lead time" is correct.[21]

Purchasing by the small producer can sometimes be limited to materials actually needed for orders already on hand. For example, a small dress factory located in a town of 13,000 and several hundred miles from its nearest supplier has solved the problem satisfactorily. This company manufactures dresses that are sold from a catalogue by two agents. An inventory of material amounting, on the average, to only $400 is carried. Most materials are purchased as soon as an order comes in from one of the agents. Deliveries are made so that materials needed are on hand by the time actual work on the order is about to start.

Purchasing for the Small Service Business

At least three factors will influence the importance of purchasing in different kinds of service establishments: (1) the percentage of total revenue obtained from the resale of merchandise, (2) the ratio of material and supply costs to labor costs, and (3) the range of qualities available from different suppliers. All three factors will be present in varying degrees in most cases.

Many service establishments secure almost half of their total revenue from the resale of merchandise. It is likely in such cases that materials, parts, and supplies used in conjunction with services performed will also make up an important part of the total "service" charge to customers. Examples include television, radio, and electrical repair shops, plumbing contractors, and some beauty parlors. In establishments of this type purchasing is a function of major importance. In many personal service types of business, such as bookkeeping or advisory services, the cost of materials and supplies used bears such a small ratio to labor costs as to reduce the importance of the purchasing function to a minimum. Whenever the service is performed upon the person of the client or upon his property that is of high unit value, there may be significant quality variations in available materials and supplies that would lead to considerable differences in the quality of the resulting "service." An expensive garment cleaned with a cheap solvent that was inadequate for the task would be one example. By contrast, some establishments, such as sheet metal shops, work with materials that are so close to a standard that considerable improvising or substitution is possible.

[21] L. W. Scott Alter, "Purchasing at the Management Level," *The Stove Builder* (July 1947), p. 45.

In the following examples many of the foregoing points will be developed. It is well to remember that even where purchasing is of minor importance in a certain type of business, it must be performed efficiently for the firm to be continuously profitable.

Service stations. The service station operator has a different set of conditions with which to deal. At the time of starting business he probably selects the brand of gasoline and other petroleum products to handle. This choice may depend upon the location selected as well as upon the brands available.

Two general types of suppliers may be used in buying products for resale—producers, and wholesalers who specialize in this type of merchandise. Petroleum products will probably be purchased from an established and reliable oil company or jobber. Tires, batteries, automotive accessories, replacement parts, and supplies for service stations may be obtained from either type of supplier. In any case, a reliable company should be selected; one that guarantees the quality and performance of its products, provides advertising, prompt and efficient delivery service, and the assistance of a capable and experienced sales force to help in solving merchandising problems is recommended. In buying petroleum products, the service station operator who deals with a reliable supplier is protected against over- or understocking, product obsolescence, and similar problems often encountered in buying other merchandise. Oil companies and jobbers have solved these problems through systematic deliveries of gasoline and almost obsolescence-proof packaging of other products.[22]

Electrical appliance, radio, and television business. In contrast to the service station operator, the owner of an electrical appliance and radio and television shop cannot safely neglect matters of price level, obsolescence, overbuying, and transportation. Demands for types and quantities of appliances differ greatly in various communities, influenced principally by one or more of the following factors: (1) size of average family income, (2) size of average home, (3) type of community—industrial, mining, urban, suburban, or farm, (4) extent to which electrical or gas appliances are used, (5) activity of the electric or gas utility in promoting the use of appliances.

In gauging consumer demand in a community, it is advisable for the beginner to consult the local banker, utility company, electric or plumbing contractors, and friendly competitors. The banker knows incomes and buying power of residents; the utility company knows the number and location of prospective customers. Contractors know consumers' needs; friendly competitors know many peculiarities of the community that they have learned from experience. These four sources have the background of knowledge and experience that beginners opening a new appliance and radio and television

[22] Charles H. Sevin, in co-operation with the members of the petroleum industry (under the direction of Walter F. Crowder), *Establishing and Operating a Service Station,* Industrial (Small Business) Series No. 22 (Washington, D. C.: U. S. Department of Commerce, 1946), pp. 97-98.

store lack, and which they badly need if they are to avoid mistakes in buying a stock of merchandise.

Cases that illustrate unexpected differences in consumer demand include an appliance company that had operated successfully in Washington, D. C., for several years before opening a store in Baltimore, only 40 miles away. The same type and brand of appliances were stocked, the same sales policy and methods of operation were followed in both stores. However, it was necessary to close the Baltimore store after two years because losses were so great. Consumer demand had not been analyzed. The average family income and buying habits were different in the two cities.

In addition to frequent reordering to maintain staple stocks, the proprietor may want to place orders for seasonal items and new models when these are introduced by the manufacturers. He may also decide to add new items to his stock from time to time in response to customer demand. Both in buying new models and adding new items the small shop owner should be guided by what his customers will accept rather than by his own preferences.

A study of alternative methods of transportation may be important to the shop owner because of the ease with which radios, television sets, and electrical appliances are damaged in transit. Several choices may be available, including railroads, motor freight companies, and carloading companies, and possibly express, parcel post, and air express for emergency orders. Usually there will be differences in time required for deliveries, in the care with which goods are handled, and in the speed and fairness exercised in adjusting damage claims. Once the most appropriate transportation agency has been selected, it is well to concentrate all possible business with one company and to play fair in all dealings with it.[23]

Restaurant. In the restaurant business cost of food is the largest expenditure. To it is allocated from 35 to 50 per cent of total income. Because of the perishable nature of food, and the sanitary requirements, careful buying is of the utmost importance.

In deciding what and how much to buy, the following factors should be considered:

1. The menu.
2. Prices.
3. Geographic location, local habits, and food tastes.
4. Market supply.
5. Availability of seasonal and out-of-season goods.
6. Storage facilities and refrigerator space.
7. Frequency of deliveries.
8. Inventory of staples.
9. Quantity and quality standard of the restaurant.

[23] Donald S. Parris, and associates (under the direction of H. B. McCoy), *Establishing and Operating an Electrical Appliance and Radio Shop,* Industrial (Small Business) Series No. 28 (Washington, D. C.: U. S. Department of Commerce, 1946), pp. 55-56.

Once the general guides to be followed as formulated in accordance with the foregoing factors have been decided upon, actual purchasing should follow recommended practices relating to quality, quantity, and trade customs.

In each purchase the quality selected should be suited to the intended use. Products to be chopped up for salads, such as green peppers, need not be so uniform in appearance as those to be used for stuffing; a less expensive quality is satisfactory. Commercial grades have been established for all important foods and should be used in buying whenever practical. The grade indicates the quality of a product at the time of grading as compared to certain standards. In the case of perishables the condition at the time of sale may be different for products of the same grade. Some fresh fruits and vegetables, especially those grown locally, may not be graded before they are offered for sale. The food buyer must know enough about the goods he is buying to judge quality and condition for many of his purchases.

For many foods, especially milk and dairy products, the sanitary conditions under which they were produced and distributed are very important.

Buying should be done by specifications formulated in terms of commercial standards. A specification is a statement of particular in specific terms, for example: "peas—Extra Standard, 3-Sieve, Early June, No. 10 cans." Specifications will be used to define the specific variety and type of a product to be purchased so as to secure the exact quality desired when placing orders by telephone or with salesmen who call at the restaurant. Specifications and grades are useful both for comparing competitors' prices and for studying the yield obtained from different products. It will frequently be found that the best grade gives the greatest total yield and that the more expensive items on the basis of the unit of purchase prove the least expensive from the standpoint of cost per serving.

Successful food buyers prefer to purchase by weight rather than by quantity measures like bushel, box, bag, or crate. When count is used, size and minimum weight should be included for such items as citrus fruits, apples, tomatoes, and melons.

Small restaurants, even though ample storage space may be available, should aim at keeping reserve stocks just large enough to meet normal requirements. Thus they may obtain satisfactory turnover and keep the risk of loss from spoilage to a minimum. Each type of product should be stored under proper conditions of temperature, humidity, and other variables.

Upon receipt, goods should be inspected for quality and checked for quantity by a competent person. Scales should be located in a convenient place so as to encourage their use. The vendor should be notified promptly of any products that do not meet the standards specified in buying.

Buying may be done by visiting the market, placing orders with salesmen who call at the restaurant, by telephone, or by mail. In smaller towns seasonal products grown locally may be purchased from farmers who call on the buyer with samples. Merchant truckers may be another good source of supply in many cases.[24]

Beauty parlor. Operating a beauty shop offers many opportunities for brand selection and for the purchase of profitable merchandise for resale. Supplies needed will be determined by the services to be rendered. One of the easiest ways to find out what will be required is to list, under departments, the various services the shop is to offer, and then to itemize the supplies necessary for each department. Also, it is advisable to consult catalogues of beauty shop suppliers. These catalogues present complete lists of supplies for all types of service. In the reference given at the end of this section a fairly complete checklist of these supplies is presented.

The shop owner may buy from beauty supply houses or jobbers, mail order beauty supply houses, and from many manufacturers. Certain supplies, such as shampoo soaps and oils, wave-set solutions, nets, combs, hairpins, and other items in constant use, should be purchased in large enough quantities to take advantage of quantity discounts as well as to maintain adequate stocks on hand at all times.

In selecting cosmetics for resale it is advisable to choose a line that is complete as well as one that has an established reputation in the community. Such a line can be featured in the shop, can be made the source of repeat business, and is more economical to order and to handle.[25]

In the preceding discussion little has been said about two aspects of purchasing in the small factory or service shop. Too many small operators buy supplies as needed at retail instead of arranging for their purchase at wholesale prices and planning needs well enough in advance to warrant such consideration. Often group buying is also possible. In several instances small noncompeting shops have successfully pooled their buying of many items.

CONCLUSIONS

Businessmen have a wide range of choice available to them in purchasing materials, merchandise, and supplies. This fact often leads to overbuying, and to dissipation of the already limited buying power of the small business. Although good arguments may be presented in favor of distributing orders among many suppliers, *it is usually better policy for the small business to concentrate and work closely with one major resource.*

Moreover, for the small business, buying is so often associated with valuable assistance from the supplier in many management activities that the im-

[24] Mary de Garmo Bryan, Alberta M. MacFarlane, and E. R. Hawkins, *Establishing and Operating a Restaurant,* Industrial (Small Business) Series No. 39 (Washington, D. C.: U. S. Department of Commerce, October 1946), pp. 129-132.

[25] Edith E. Gordon, *Establishing and Operating a Beauty Shop,* Industrial (Small Business) Series No. 25 (Washington, D. C.: U. S. Department of Commerce, February 1946), pp. 58-63.

portance of purchasing from him is further increased. Voluntary and co-operative chains in the merchandising fields enable the small independent to compensate for his smaller buying power through headquarters aids. Relationships with resources for most businesses are fully as important as relationships with customers or employees.

QUESTIONS AND PROBLEMS

1. Discuss the relative importance in small business buying of quality and price alone, as compared to other considerations, such as services rendered by various suppliers.

2. Compare the arguments for and against concentration in buying for each of the fields of small business. What conclusions do you draw from these?

3. What factors should a small independent consider in selecting his resources?

4. What is meant by "relationships with resources"?

5. How, if at all, does the relative importance of buying and selling differ among the major fields of small business? Explain.

6. How do a small firm's relations with its resources vary in relative importance during periods of good times compared to periods of business depression? Why?

7. Which type of resident buying office would be better for a retailer just large enough to use either? Discuss.

8. If you were starting in a business where voluntary chains were in existence, would you prefer to affiliate with one or to "go it alone"?

9. Why have "voluntaries" not developed in the manufacturing fields? Why have they been slow to develop in the service fields? Name some organizations in either of these fields.

10. Explain how buying and inventory control are: (1) more closely related, (2) less closely related, for: (a) manufacturing, (b) merchandising.

11. What additional discussion not included in the chapter would be of value to the small wholesaler? Explain.

12. From the viewpoint of member independent merchants in the same field, would you expect a corporate chain or a manufacturing wholesaler to be the more useful sponsor of a voluntary chain? Explain.

13. Why do retailers, but not manufacturers, add expected markdowns when calculating what goods are to be purchased during a certain period of time?

14. Explain each of the following as used in retailing: basic stock, model stock, checklist, markdowns, style, fashion, staple goods.

15. What do you think of the opportunities for a qualified person to start a small business as a "voluntary" headquarters? Discuss.

16. Assume you plan to enter a particular kind of small business. Describe how you would decide whether to diversify or to concentrate your buying.

17. Talk with several different men in one kind of business about what factors each considers to be most important in buying. Analyze the results and report your conclusions.

18. Interview several retailers who are members of voluntary or co-operative chains as to the relative value of them for buying and other services rendered by headquarters. Compare your findings with the comments made in this chapter.

19. Fred's independent superette competes with both corporate and voluntary chains on price and service. Recently, frequent out-of-stock conditions have become serious although business conditions are normal. Fred knows that many customers have started buying those items which he is out of from competitors. What should he do, and why?

18 • Sales Promotion

The term "sales promotion" is self-explanatory. It simply means to promote sales. Since advertising and display and personal selling constitute the major activities of selling, they are, with public relations, the major tools and methods of sales promotion. Perhaps the best definition, then, of sales promotion is that which describes it as the *effective coordination of all marketing activities having to do with the performance of the selling function.* The effectiveness of this coordination, the effective use of time, effort, and money in achieving the efficiency with which the sales dollar is thus used, is the measure of success in sales promotion. As such, sales promotion is of vital importance to the business; but it must not be overemphasized to the neglect of the other functions, and it must be long range as well as short range in its viewpoint and approach. There are always certain dangers involved, among which the following are of special importance: overemphasis on pushing immediate sales to the neglect of long range objectives; misdirected efforts; and the slighting of adequate records, expense control, and planned results.

Sales promotion methods fall logically into two main groups: direct and indirect. Direct methods include a wide range of special sales promotions, personal selling, merchandising aids by manufacturers, publicity, advertising, and display. Indirect sales promotional devices are represented by customer services, favorable customer relations, product styling, packaging, and good public relations. Indirect methods pave the way for the increased effectiveness of direct methods. One of the latter, advertising, has been so highly developed that it is made the subject of the next chapter. Most of the others are considered here.

To be continuously successful, sales promotion must be based on customer satisfaction, good customer relations, sound policies, and real values as business ideals and goals. Only when customer relations are the best will advertising and other direct sales promotional efforts be most successful. Effective sales promotion thus seeks to build goodwill as well as immediate sales.

While "razzle dazzle" plays its part, the long-run philosophy of management, as expressed in policies and practices, must always prevail.[1]

CUSTOMER RELATIONS

That the person who buys (or fails to buy) the product or services offered is the true employer of every businessman and his employees must always be foremost in the minds of the latter. Those people from among the public who are attracted, who decide to buy, and later to re-buy, are the very life of a business. The objective, then, is to attract and maintain a supporting clientele of satisfied user-customers.

Customer satisfaction is the basis for the continued success of all business; however, casual observation of a large number of companies, big and little, will show the extent to which this fundamental is neglected. A large part of goodwill, that intangible asset which may be worth anything from less than nothing to several million dollars, is the result of maintaining favorable customer relations. In big business this usually accrues to the company or brand name; in the small business personal attributes of the owner are of relatively greater importance. Good customer relations should be planned as carefully as any other major objective of the business.

An initial step is to define the company's customers so that proper steps can be taken to comply with their likes, dislikes, and interests. Coordination of policies and the activities based on them will be an important means of building and maintaining good customer relations. For example, if a small manufacturer's distribution policy aims at enlisting the support of one class of customer, such as individual retailers, or a particular income group of consumers, it may easily be weakened by attempts in the company's advertising or publicity to gain the support of such other groups as chain stores or consumers in a different income class.

Other ways in which securing the desired customer relations will involve different aspects or activities of the business include the following: training in proper customer attitudes for all employees who come into contact with customers personally, over the telephone, or through correspondence; strict observance of the company's product or merchandise guarantees; servicing the product after purchase when required; care and courtesy in handling customer accounts; efforts to provide convenience and services desired by customers, such as parking facilities; prompt answering of all inquiries; and scrupulous care in observing delivery dates and other promises.

It is sometimes difficult for the employee to realize that to the patron or customer, he, the employee, is the store, the company, the firm, as of any moment of their relationships together. In the customer's mind, and in reality, the employee is delegated by management to represent the firm—in fact, to

---

[1] See: "Lucky Winner of Franchisers' Contest Gets a Business—and a Trip to Russia," *Business Week* (April 16, 1960), p. 76.

be management at that moment. Thus his behavior, being management's behavior as the customer sees it, can be constructive or destructive of the goals of the business.

Modern management provides routines and channels through which information regarding customer relations is continuously obtained. Some of these will be impersonal, such as periodic analyses of returned goods and of customer complaints and correspondence, suggestion systems (including customer suggestion contests), and service shopping or other customer surveys; in addition, executives as well as salespeople and other employees have personal customer contacts.

It has been said that the success of the businessman is in direct proportion to his desire, determination, and motivation to serve his fellow man. This need for devotion to service and for concern with the welfare of others, when combined with a respect for detail, gives that "something extra" that makes the customer-buyer desire to do business with one businessman rather than another.

Perhaps the most familiar example is the gas station proprietor who offers a maximum of service, as compared with his competitor who offers a minimum. The one offering the maximum anticipates the wishes of his customers. The one offering the minimum, or, shall we say, grudgingly giving the minimum, must be *asked* to make the necessary or the desirable checkups for the customer.

The electrician, when called into the home on a repair job, has two choices: he can do the minimum, charge a maximum, and go away having taken care of the situation temporarily, having done his business with the customer on a strictly temporary basis; or he may use the opportunity to build a long-term relationship by working the maximum for the future well-being of the householder, and charging a minimum as an investment toward a future relationship which can be profitable to both parties.

Those of us who buy coal, fuel oil, or bottled gas for heating know that there are two kinds of purveyors in these fields. In one instance, when the supply runs out, the householder frantically places a phone call to the supplier, who frantically, but sometimes grudgingly, comes to fill the tank or repair the line or to do whatever else is necessary to keep the service going. The more successful operator anticipates the need with careful records—seeing to it that at anytime the supply or the reservoir is almost exhausted, it is refilled. Thus the problem of being out of the commodity never arises—nor does the question of whom the user should patronize.

There are all kinds of insurance men. One kind annoys, may eventually sell a policy, then leaves and forgets his client. The other kind carefully analyzes the client's financial situation, makes his recommendations accordingly, and writes and sells the appropriate policy. He calls back on the client at a later date to see if changes in the family or personal situation have brought needs for any adjustment in the insurance program. Similarly the dentist or the druggist can become an associate in business relationships for life if he will, by a sincere interest and ample evidence of that interest, build himself into a personal working relationship with his client-customer.

Many people feel that the status of the automobile business and of the automobile salesman has deteriorated considerably over the past several years —especially since World War II. Others would say that the typical clothing salesman is a routine employee selling suits and overcoats to those who happen to come in and ask for them. Yet there are outstanding dealers and salesmen of both automobiles and clothing. One automobile dealer we know keeps such careful records of his client's purchases and of repairs on those cars that he usually knows before the user that it is time for a new car.

Typically, a successful clothing salesman may make $100 per week in the United States. This man serves customers in his turn, as they arrive in the store in response to an ad, or when they feel they need a new suit. However, several men we know, such as Joe Gilchrist of The May Company in Cleveland, exceed $15,000 per year salary, year after year. This kind of salesman has a clientele, built up over the years as his professional following. When any of his clients needs new apparel, this salesman's name comes first to mind automatically. When his store receives new merchandise, this salesman immediately identifies certain items with the tastes, preferences, and characteristics of individual customers. Most important of all, this kind of salesman keeps records.

Why do we continue to patronize a given service station, insurance man, barber, or clothing salesman? It is because he knows what we want; he knows us and our possessions; he knows what we like and need. He makes our buying easier and safer, and he gives us a feeling of confidence and of security. What he does for us is done for the individual; he has dignified us by setting us apart from the crowd. Like a physician or a dentist, he has our "history," his services to us, our likes and dislikes on record.

The keeping of sales records and service records, and their constant analysis and use as guides to the offering of further service to the individual customer are the "secret weapon" of many successful small businesses in sales promotion. The satisfied customer of long standing is the most valuable possession any business can have.

MERCHANDISING[2]

The small retailer's close personal contact with his customers provides many advantages in developing a well-co-ordinated program of sales promotion, since this should be based, here as in other fields, on customer satisfaction and good customer relations. The right merchandise and services consistent with the store's policies, backed up by qualified personnel, competent sales-

[2] See: *Is Your Store a Sales Builder or Barrier?* Small Marketers Aids No. 41 (Washington, D. C.: Small Business Administration, April 1959).

manship, and a suitable physical plant, furnish the framework for effective sales promotion.

Most of the retailer's problem in this area may be aptly summarized in the often quoted definition of good retail salesmanship, "selling goods that won't come back to customers who will." Improving the quality of retail salesmanship seems to be a never ending process. Surveys made by trade associations, schools of retailing, and others dealing with customer likes and dislikes and why sales are lost, have consistently shown the importance of the salesperson, the influence of economic conditions, and results of effective training or its absence.[3] In addition to utilizing results of such surveys made by his trade association, the small retailer can secure help in sales training from representatives of his suppliers and from the Distributive Education program if presented through the public schools in his community. Everything about the physical plant and equipment—its appearance, "atmosphere," air conditioning, proper lighting, attractive displays, absence of accident hazards, facilities for rapid, uncongested transportation between floors, and other conditions that contribute to customer comfort and convenience—will influence the clientele's attitude toward the store.

The care and courtesy exercised by nonselling employees will also contribute to the customer's attitude. Having merchandise delivered in good condition at the promised or expected time by courteous, neat-appearing employees using attractive delivery equipment is one example. Customer irritation may be reduced through proper planning by providing for such special situations as the following: what to do with "charge send" packages when the customer is not at home at the time of attempted delivery; what procedure to follow on C.O.D. sales when the customer offers a personal check or does not have quite enough money to meet the payments but insists that he needs the merchandise at once. These are merely suggestive of the situations that may arise. It is well in such situations that the representative, whether he be delivery man, credit officer, shipping clerk, installer, or repairman, remember that in the customer's thinking, and as of that contact, he is the company.

Alert retailers follow definite guides in their efforts to build favorable customer relations. Some years ago one investigator compiled sixty of these, including the following which cannot be greatly improved upon:

1. We greet as many customers as possible by name.

2. We have a personal word or two with customers, when possible.

3. We greet customers immediately when they enter the store even if we must keep them waiting before serving.

4. We take the greatest of care to assure the utmost courtesy in handling customers, even the difficult ones. All staff members avoid giving a flat "no" to a request for merchandise not in stock.

5. We give special consideration to the tired shopper.

[3] See: Wenzil K. Dolva, *Continuing Studies on Salesmanship,* Study No. 7 (St. Louis: Washington University, Department of Retailing, July 1953).

6. We avoid the patronizing phrase "we can let you have" and use instead "we will see that you get."

7. We express genuine regret when unable to supply customer's requirements.

8. We consult customers regarding ways of improving service.

9. We refer customers to a competitor when we are out of an item and are not afraid to express praise of a competitor.

10. We will do favors for customers gladly, not grudgingly.

11. We pay special attention to newly married couples.

12. We study the methods used by chain stores and other stores in nearby towns and cities to see what methods can be adapted to our own store.

13. We maintain spacious aisles, not crowded.

14. We arrange merchandise to encourage self-selection.

15. We set up a self-serve section where it is feasible.

16. We review stock regularly to find out why certain lines are not selling.

17. We display odd and broken lines for quick sale and eliminate all old goods.

18. We add a certain amount of novelty merchandise to brighten up current offerings.

19. We bring prices into line with current competition.

20. We change window displays at regular intervals to avoid a "tired" appearance.

21. We keep making attractive innovations in the store, featuring one section after another to give customers something new to look at.

22. We make use of empty shelving for display purposes by use of display alcoves.

23. We maintain local advertising.

24. We join the organization of merchants for improvement of local merchandising, and to assist in local work.

25. We attend meetings of farm forum radio programs to keep informed on farmers' problems.

26. We influence town officials to provide parking space for farmers and others.

27. We avoid extremes in shortening store hours, having due consideration for farmers' and workers' shopping time.[4]

Although the small retailer is in close personal contact with his customers and thinks that he understands what they want, he may be wrong in this reasoning because (1) many customers do not express their wants or even dislikes, and (2) potential customers may be avoiding the store for causes unknown to the merchant. It is good business to study surveys of customers' wants as well as to analyze causes of complaints.

---

[4] Adapted from *60 Ways to Gain Goodwill*, Small Business Aids No. 82 (Washington, D. C.: U. S. Department of Commerce).

Many studies have been made relating to the causes of customer complaints. The following is a representative list of causes disclosed by such studies:

I. *Selling Department*

1. Wrong merchandise
2. Defective merchandise
3. Merchandise left out
4. Mistakes in price
5. Misunderstandings of price
6. No record of sales
7. Order not filled
8. Delay in filling order
9. Overcharges due to error or claim of customer that goods are sold for less elsewhere
10. Incorrect delivery or shipping instructions
11. Merchandise out of stock
12. Broken promises
13. Improper alterations or repairs
14. Failure to credit return merchandise

II. *Wrapping and Packing Departments*

1. Wrong merchandise wrapped up
2. Merchandise left out
3. Sales check lost
4. Improper wrapping, marking, or addressing
5. Delay in wrapping
6. Damaged in wrapping

III. *Delivery*

1. Delay in delivery
2. Loss in delivery
3. Damaged in delivery
4. Delivered to wrong address
5. Packages sent which should be handled as "will call"
6. Failure to make truck call as promised
7. Goods lost in transit
8. Overcharge or error on C.O.D. sales
9. Complaint about driver; lack of courtesy or attention

IV. *Accounts and Records*

1. Goods charged or credited to wrong account
2. Errors in billing
3. Remittances not promptly acknowledged
4. Bills sent which have been paid
5. Failure to change address when notified
6. Bills sent in wrong envelopes
7. Cash credited to wrong account
8. Correspondence not promptly or correctly answered
9. Dunning letters sent when claim is pending
10. Credits not entered for goods returned
11. Mail incorrectly addressed
12. Refusal of credit in error

13. Goods sent C.O.D. instead of charge
14. Statement sent in error

V. *Miscellaneous*

1. Lack of courtesy or attention
2. Goods sent but not ordered
3. Not at home for package
4. Poor telephone service
5. Poor mail-order service[5]

These surveys are interesting, but the small retailer is more concerned with complaints made by his customers. One merchant had been using a "man on the street" type of radio program for the rural trade in front of his store on Saturdays with apparent success. When discussing this advertising before a group of his regular customers, he was surprised to find that it had annoyed them to the extent that many had already shifted their patronage.

WHOLESALING

Recently it was found that in the wholesale drug trade good service and favorable relations with customers were more important factors in causing merchants to buy than were low prices and large discounts. Top-ranking reasons for patronizing their major wholesaler were given by customers as follows: quicker deliveries, "bought from him for years," fewer "shorts," more interest, "like salesmen," "like house employees." The same survey disclosed as one of the chief complaints that wholesale salesmen lacked knowledge in pharmaceuticals, drugs, chemicals, and other related items. The salesmen also needed above all, according to the survey, *training in retail sales promotion;* next in importance was training in "deals," stock prices, product knowledge, and retail store management, as well as an interest in retailing.[6]

In a survey by Dun & Bradstreet covering retailers' preferences and practices in the distribution of dry goods, 46 per cent expressed interest in wholesalers' plans to modernize the store, to set up basic competitive stocks, and to follow a planned merchandising and promotional program based on close teamwork with the wholesaler. The majority favored selective distribution, even among the small store group. Preference for nationally advertised brands on a quality and style basis over unbranded merchandise on a price basis rated a 70 per cent majority vote. About 14 per cent of the retailers, faced

[5] Paul H. Nystrom, "Causes of Customer Complaints," Small Business Aids No. 227 (Washington, D. C.: U. S. Department of Commerce). Condensed from "Retail Store Service," Chapter 16 of *Retail Store Operation* (New York: Ronald Press Co., 1937). See also: "How Do You Handle Complaints?" *Bedding Merchandiser* (November 1953), pp. 11-12.

[6] *What Retail Druggists Want From Their Wholesalers,* Small Business Aids No. 165 (Washington, D. C.: U. S. Department of Commerce). See also, "The Retailer Looks at His Service Wholesale Druggist," National Wholesale Druggists' Association, 1954.

with loss leader competition, look to their suppliers for defensive assistance, although not necessarily for competitive loss leaders.[7]

Wholesalers in other fields have experienced a similar need for assistance by their retail customers. One co-operative study found the principal cause of failure among 15,000 retail candy and confectionery stores to be lack of sufficient advice and assistance from their wholesale salesmen. The merchants needed help on store management, especially with reference to advertising, display, buying, stock control, and sales promotion.[8] Probably the most striking characteristic of those wholesalers who have been successful in withstanding corporate chain competition is the dealer-assistance program, which often approaches the voluntary chain relationship. As one wholesale firm's president explained, "We have learned that our job is to help the retailer move the merchandise out the front door. Only then will there be a demand for us to bring more in through the back door."

MANUFACTURING

Small manufacturers may sell direct to final consumers, to dealers, or to both types of customers. In either case the following suggestions for the factory owner will be helpful:

1. Are telephone calls answered promptly and courteously?

2. Are telephone inquiries brushed off with the old "I'll call you back" excuse, only to have the call never returned?

3. Is it possible to obtain price information by telephone without long waits and some impatience on the part of the employee who answers? (It might be well to make a test.)

4. Are letters answered promptly?

5. Send your own company a letter asking two questions. When the answer comes, see if it ignored one question.

6. Is it possible to obtain accurate information of deliveries to customers, shipping dates, or similar information from your employees?

7. Do your salesmen answer inquiries promptly and intelligently?

8. How do your truck drivers and deliverymen act toward customers? If you don't check this point, your customers may be leaving you for one of your competitors.

---

[7] *Retailers' Preferences and Practices in the Distribution of Dry Goods,* Small Business Aids No. 350 (Washington, D. C.: U. S. Department of Commerce). Adapted from "Retailers' Preferences and Practices in the Distribution of Dry Goods," *Survey of Dry Goods Distribution,* prepared by Marketing and Research Service, Dun & Bradstreet, Inc., for The Wholesale Dry Goods Institute, Inc., New York.

[8] *How the Candy Wholesaler Can Increase Retail Sales,* Small Business Aids No. 409 (Washington, D. C.: U. S. Department of Commerce). Condensed from "Balanced Selling —A Guide to Master Salesmanship for Wholesale Candy Distributors," Published by the National Confectioners' Association, Chicago 2, Illinois, in co-operation with the Business Education Service, U. S. Office of Education, Washington, D. C. See also: *Sales Contests for Wholesalers,* Small Marketers Aids No. 47 (Washington, D. C.: Small Business Administration, August, 1959).

9. Does it make your credit department angry, and do they show it, when a customer slips slightly behind in his payments?

10. Is it common talk among the trade you serve that you favor the bigger buyers and neglect the little fellows? [9]

The small manufacturer can make especially good use of informative labels, if they are appropriate to his products, in building both dealer and consumer goodwill as well as in supplying salesmen with selling facts. The larger concern may accomplish these objectives through extensive publicity and training programs not available to the small operator. The large firm may have a tremendous investment in past advertising featuring the brand name or particular selling points that would not be well suited to the use of informative labels, but the small manufacturer "on the way up" has no such restrictions.

One feature of the informative label that recommends its use to the small manufacturer struggling to establish a favorable reputation for his product is that salespeople do not always tell the customer how to use and care for a product and the customer sometimes forgets even when told. Extensive experience with the use of informative labels shows that they increase the proportion of customers who buy better-quality products. This helps the small producer with a superior quality product to overcome some of the effects of extensive advertising by large competitors.[10]

In the average plant or other small business many valid complaints may not come to the attention of the owner unless provisions are made to insure that they do. Experience shows that systematic procedure in handling complaints is desirable.

Good complaint handling by any company entails three steps: (1) making rapid and reasonable adjustments; (2) gathering facts about the complaints; and (3) using the facts to improve production and operational methods. One food company, merchandising a product of low unit cost, adjusts all complaints directly and quickly by multiple replacement (sometimes double the original quantity, often more) of the product.

A single complaint may not be significant, but a concentration of complaints on a single subject is almost certainly so. Various methods are used to ferret out concentration, such as encouraging dealers and salesmen to pass on product complaints to the manufacturer. Forms for easy forwarding of complaint information may be supplied to them and to customers.

Repeated experience shows that unless a company obtains, analyzes, and acts upon the facts about its products and service that a good complaint system turns up, a significant opportunity for good sales promotion is being missed.

[9] Adapted from *Customer Relations Checklist,* Small Business Aids No. 81 (Washington, D. C.: U. S. Department of Commerce).

[10] *Informative Labels Do a Job,* Small Business Aids No. 232 (Washington, D. C.: U. S. Department of Commerce).

SERVICE BUSINESS

Selling intangibles like services has long been recognized as more difficult than selling physical goods. Often it is difficult to convince customers of their need for the service and to prove to them that it has actually been performed. Many small automobile repair shops have a worn parts panel. Customers can actually see how bearings, breaker points, and other parts of their car look after considerable wear. It is then easier to "sell" prospects on the need for installing new parts, as well as on the importance of preventive maintenance. Radio and television repair shop operators often keep the replaced parts to show the owner why it was necessary to replace them as partial proof that new parts were actually installed.

Since services are performed upon the person or property of the customer, the qualifications of the operator are important to patrons. When life or health may be endangered, state laws usually restrict practice to those of proved competence. Signs displayed in the shop assure customers that all operators are certified to be competent. Even in fields where laws do not require such certification, many service operators employ this device for promoting sales. Examples that might be cited include AAA and other approval signs in hotels, tourist courts, and restaurants, United Motor Service signs in auto repair shops, and Master Barber certificates in tonsorial establishments. Many trade associations have established standards of operation which, when accepted and practiced, permit the individual business owner to display a distinguishing sign.

For three weeks a Phoenix carpet shop laid a nylon carpet in front of the gas pumps of a nearby service station for cars and trucks to drive over, dripping oil and grease. The carpet was then removed, half of it cleaned, and put on display for customers to see. An ad heralded the laying and removal of the carpet. They proved that the carpet looked like new after being cleaned and sold a good volume of this carpeting following the promotion.

A Sioux City furniture store decorated its premises with balloons for one of the firm's most successful promotions. Inside each balloon was a discount slip guaranteeing the customer a discount on his purchase. After a customer made a purchase, he was allowed to select one balloon to puncture. Inside he would find a slip discounting his cost, ranging from 5 per cent to one balloon with 100 per cent discount. They named the promotion the "Count Down" and customers were encouraged to be at the store for the "blast off." An eight-column newspaper advertisement promoted the event and guaranteed "no duds."

The key letter in a Cleveland department store's page ad was the "s" in "Foundation Departments." Designed to attract teen-age shoppers, the ad applied to both the junior intimate apparel and the foundation departments. Announcing a drawing for a free ski weekend in the Laurentians, the ad also invited girls to drop in for a free figure analysis and booklets on grooming. Registration was open for a full week in both departments. The merchandise included girdles and bras from standard lines. These were not special teen sizes but regular merchandise isolated for special promotion aimed at teen-age customers.

The closed door "party" promotion held on the sales floor is becoming very popular. A limited group is invited to a "party" after normal store hours. Ice cream, cake, sandwiches, coffee, and the like are served while the group watches product demonstrations and learns about merchandise features.

To encourage self-service in the electric housewares section, one store uses elaborate "Tell all" fact tags and large posters which graphically compare the various brands regarding features, cost, performance, and so on.

The stereo demonstration room, well separated from the noises of the main floor, is proving essential in moving higher priced stereo equipment. Many retailers serve coffee or soft drinks in this room.

Few stores capitalize sufficiently on the news value of new merchandise. One store features "just arrived" fashion merchandise in a main window. Another outlet has a special section set aside for new items.

For lunch hour shoppers, one store stages fast-moving, ten-minute fashion shows every half hour. The schedule permits attendance regardless of when the shopper's lunch hour begins and still leaves time for shopping.[11]

Another aspect of promoting the sale of services is the importance many customers attach to little "extras." Hotels often find that a flower for lady guests or a free newspaper for the men pays big dividends in greater spending and repeat business.

Quality is important in the work performed by the service establishment, but the business must not stop at quality service: it must have quality salesmanship state honestly that the business desires to please the customer.

Salesmanship for the service establishment as well as for the retail store requires that the salespeople understand the working of the business. Even the stenographer who answers the telephone in a plumbing firm should be able to give the approximate time necessary to complete a repair job and should be instructed in the use of an appointment book. The salesman, whether in the office or doing delivery work, should be able to give a good sales talk. Any changes in prices or any "special" for the week should be immediately relayed to all employees.

SPECIAL ASPECTS OF SALES PROMOTION

Without increasing his expenses a small businessman can promote sales through free publicity, timeliness, displays, special sales, and other means.

An alert businessman will use publicity to impress his public with the fact

[11] Courtesy of "Marketing & Merchandising Data," *Chicago Daily News* (March-April 1960).

that he is continually seeking ways to give them better service. Dry cleaners in towns all over the country who attend the national convention to learn about new methods have their home town newspapers carry news items to this effect. An apparel store in a southwestern town of 13,000 is operated by a man and his wife who make several trips to market each year. News items in the daily paper always report these trips with comments regarding the fashion showings to be attended. When the store became affiliated with a Los Angeles buying office a few years ago and the wife attended showings of California designers, the local newspaper publicized this step forward. Later, when their display director received high honors in a southwestern display convention in Dallas, Texas, the award was given ample free publicity to impress the "home folks" with the progressiveness of the store personnel. When the owner-manager of a small retail-wholesale jewelry business in the same town took several weeks away from his business to attend a school for advanced training in watchmaking and repair work, the paper carried an account of this fact and all employees in the store found ways to comment favorably on it to customers. Many local broadcasting stations have home town news periods on which the activities of small businessmen and their employees are reported. A company picnic for employees, the promotion of John J. Jones, Jr., from salesman to buyer for the store, a new machine for testing radio and television sets installed in the local repair shop—these and similar items should be reported by the small businessman to his local paper or radio station. But they must be items of real news value even though the reason for giving them publicity is to keep the name of the business before the public in a favorable light.

An interesting example of the power of publicity may be seen in the case of a woman who had been making artificial flowers in her home two miles out of town on a main U. S. highway. A news release written about her by a reporter for the local newspaper was picked up by A.P. and reprinted in hundreds of newspapers throughout the country. Letters and orders began pouring in, and within a few weeks it was necessary to buy land across the road to construct a new "factory," secure a business manager, start training employees to do the actual production, have form letters printed to answer the avalanche of inquiries and orders, start the process of taking out domestic and foreign patents on the production process, adopt a brand or trade name, and begin seeking advice on the methods used by big business. All this was accomplished without the expenditure of one penny for advertising.

Special Events

The distinguishing feature of successful promotions is their timeliness, either when planned in advance for certain days or seasons or when opportunistic in capitalizing on some unexpected development. Merchants have available to them calendars of promotional events, usually prepared several months or more in advance by the trade association in the field and giving all important dates likely to be useful in staging promotions. Most of these are published in trade journals and in dealer material released by wholesalers' Merchants Service Bureaus.[12]

Sometimes the kind of business provides seasonal merchandise for timely promotions regularly throughout the year. Feed dealers time their promotions with the planting, cultivation, or marketing of customers' (farmers') products; auto accessory stores time their promotions to the weather and the popular use of the family car.

Games and contests primarily of local interest afford opportunities for timely tie-ins, often through displays in the small business. High school or local college football and basketball games are of this type. A score board displayed in the store may keep customers informed on the progress of the game. Some merchants place a radio in the store for customers to hear reports of important games that are broadcast. Local elections and other political campaigns often arouse intense interest. Many small stores, shops, and newspapers attract customers by reporting election returns or other events likely to have a bearing on the outcome of such contests.

Another group of promotional ideas, such as anniversary sales, relate to the company itself. The established business should keep records of each promotion and consult them in planning future events. Contrary to popular belief, previously successful promotions of a seasonal or recurring nature are more likely to be effective when repeated than are entirely new ones. Each new promotion is an experiment that may or may not prove successful. Since the customers of one store do not change greatly from year to year, an event that has proved its appeal to the customers once is very likely to succeed several times more. Of course details may be changed, but the basic idea of the promotion will remain the same. This should not discourage careful experimentation, but it should be a warning against seeking change merely to be different.

The range of themes or ideas useful in building sales promotions is unlimited. Each issue of the trade journals contains suggestions and stimulating ideas from nearly every field of retailing. Often ideas developed by large city stores can be used to advantage by the small store, such as having customer juries select 100 perfect gifts for Christmas from the store's offerings. A useful approach to planning sales promotions is to follow a checklist of steps to be taken to provide for all details and proper timing. Important points, even to the obvious ones, should be included:

1. Opening and closing dates.
2. Name of promotion and any explanations needed.
3. Merchandise to be featured.
4. Complete plans for advertising and window and interior displays, seek-

---

[12] *Annual Time Table of Retail Opportunities* (New York: Bureau of Advertising, American Newspaper Publishers Association, Inc.), suggest ad timing and practices for advertising. (Published annually and available from member newspapers.)

ing co-ordination of media and use of all appropriate devices—signs, price cards, window streamers, banners, special layout, and display.

5. Organization plans—staff meetings, employee incentives, and provisions for extra help or special training.

Moving Slow Items

Every store will at times have some slow-selling items that can be sold through proper promotions before they result in a loss. The following methods are useful in the order stated: (1) showmanship, (2) bargain atmosphere, (3) reduced prices. Several methods in each group are presented to suggest the possibilities in this approach.

1. Mass-display the product at the best traffic spot, even if it means separation from other brands of like classification.

2. Give a premium with large quantity purchases of specified "cats and dogs." One retailer offered a scarce aluminum cooking utensil at cost with each $5.00 purchase.

3. Use hanging banners and pennants, strung from wall to wall, to promote shelf-warmers.

4. Place arm bands bearing red question marks on all clerks. Clerks then tell inquiring customers about special offerings.

5. Emphasize slow movers on the shelves with differently colored price tags.

6. Focus colored spotlights on special mass displays.

7. Advertise that customers get a package of the featured item free if a clerk forgets to tell her about it. This makes both consumers and employees conscious of the product.

8. Offer free movie matinee tickets with every quantity purchase of shelf-warmers. These tickets usually can be bought by the roll at reduced prices from the neighborhood movie.

9. Pile "cats and dogs" in bushel baskets placed at traffic spots. Change baskets daily.

10. Mass-display full cases offered at discounts of 5 per cent or 10 per cent on case lots.

11. Sell a "pig-in-a-poke" bag of slow movers for 49¢.

12. Tell the truth in advertising or display material. Say "I want to get rid of this stuff, so here's a bargain"; "We made a mistake and bought too much. Take some away and we'll give you a bargain"; "The quality is good, but we no longer can get this brand. Clean out what's left."

13. Advertise "Certified Bargains." Produce the original bills showing what you paid for goods now offered as bargains. Also show what you charged for them previously.

14. Gather all items that can be offered at a uniform price. Emphasize: "Look what 19¢ will buy," or "Look what 10¢ will buy."

15. Hold a penny sale like "One can for 18¢—two for 19¢."

16. Put slow movers alongside of fast movers. Contrast the two by sharply cutting prices of the merchandise you are trying to move.

17. Advertise "Surprise Sales." Whenever a crowd gathers in the store announce that, "For the next ten minutes the such-and-such shelf-warmer will be sold at half-price."

18. Set up an automatic price system. Keep reducing prices by a fixed percentage every week until the merchandise is sold.[13]

Trading Stamps[14]

The trading stamp has become an increasingly important means of attracting trade in recent years. The idea is very old and its popularity has risen and fallen, over the past 50 years particularly. Basically, it is a payment of a sort of "commission" to customers on their patronage through the issuance of stamps, usually one stamp for each ten cents of purchases. These stamps are saved by the customer and pasted in a book provided by the merchant. A completed book of several hundred stamps may be exchanged for cash, for gifts, or for merchandise.

The actual cost to the seller of stamps issued to customers is very low, even in those few cases where stamps are carefully saved and redeemed by great numbers of customers. Not all customers request or even accept the stamps, and in most instances do not bother to accumulate and bring in completed books. The popularity of stamps varies by areas and may be influenced by income level of the community or by the competitiveness of rival merchants and service businesses.

Arguments for and against trading stamps are plentiful. The purveyor who considers them as a means of cultivating and maintaining patronage may well ask himself these questions:

1. Would this promotional expense be in addition to an established program or would it replace a part of it?

2. Would the addition of this cost to each sales transaction call for increased prices?

3. What types of stores in the area are now using this kind of stamps and what levels of income, taste, do they attract?

4. Are there already great numbers of people in the area familiar with this "brand" of stamps, or would advertising the idea of stamps be an expensive undertaking in itself?

Trading stamps can be, and apparently are in most cases, a valuable device for attracting and maintaining patronage.[15] In general, it would seem that results depend on the popularity of the stamps, the degree to which the

[13] *Some Ways to Sell Shelf-warming Food Items,* Small Business Aids No. 298 (Washington, D. C.: U. S. Department of Commerce). Condensed from "40 Ways to Get Rid of Cats and Dogs," *Food Topics* (April 7, 1947), Topics Publishing Co., Inc., New York.

[14] See: "New Flurry Over Trading Stamps," *Business Week* (February 27, 1960).

[15] Their exponents claim that 77 per cent of U. S. families save stamps (Sperry & Hutchinson Co., from a survey by Dr. Eugene Beem, company economist, as announced March 24, 1960).

prospective buyer chooses to make his purchases in those establishments which offer them primarily because they are offered there, and the degree to which they can be offered by the seller as a normal advertising expense without interfering with other promotional activities, with his prices, or with his profits.

CONCLUSIONS

The broad field of stimulating increased sales may be divided into three areas: customer relations, special sales promotional ideas, and advertising.

Any effort to increase sales is more effective when relations between the business and its customers are favorable. Very often sales promotion or advertising ideas that have been successful in one business are failures in another because the "environment" is different. A news release that Mr. Jones is attending the district convention of a big oil company will interest many people who will later come in and discuss the trip with him while having their car serviced. A similar item reporting Mr. Smith's trip to the laundry convention may arouse such comments as, "Well, it's about time Smith snapped out of it—I hope he learns something at the meetings."

In most small businesses the sales personnel, including the owners, are very important in determining how favorable relations with customers will be. Most of the effectiveness of advertising or other special promotions that may be undertaken can be destroyed by poor quality of salesmanship. Consequently, our approach has been to emphasize first conditions that influence the customers' attitude toward the store, including quality of salesmanship. Next, a few ideas to illustrate various special aspects of sales promotion were considered. It will be noted that many suggestions come from trade publications and associations. For this reason, and others previously stated, we suggest that every beginner in any field should be a regular subscriber to, and reader of, at least one trade publication, and that as early as possible he should become a member of his trade association. The ideas he will garner in sales promotion alone will soon justify the expense, time, and effort.

QUESTIONS AND PROBLEMS

1. Why are good customer relations of greater importance in sales promotion than in other activities?

2. How do you account for the fact that the trade press gives so much attention to sales promotion?

3. Is sales promotion, including advertising, of greater importance to the merchant, the manufacturer, or the service operator? Explain.

4. How, if at all, does sales promotion differ for each of the three major fields of small business?

5. State frankly your own opinion as to the importance of good customer relations in determining the effectiveness of sales promotional efforts.

6. Why is it no longer possible for any business to succeed without sales promotion?

7. In view of the fact that most producers who have adopted informative labels up to the present time are large concerns, evaluate the statements made in this chapter that the small business is in a better position than the large firm to make maximum use of informative labels.

8. What are the special problems and needs of the small wholesaler that might be at least partially solved by sales promotion, including better customer relations? Discuss.

9. Do you think the average small businessman can make effective use of survey results obtained by the trade association in his field? Explain.

10. Is personal selling or advertising more important to the small business? Discuss and give concrete examples.

11. Select several types of services and analyze each for sales promotion themes, using the major marketing instruments as a guide.

12. For some kind of small business of particular interest to you, name four or five unusual ideas that could be used for effective sales promotion.

13. Select some product suited for manufacture by a small firm and write out an informative label for this product.

14. After using traditional promotion ideas for many years with only moderate success in his general merchandise store, which caters equally to wage earner and college faculty families, John is considering featuring grade and informative labels on all appropriate merchandise. Evaluate this proposal and suggest what he should do to make it successful.

19 • Advertising for Profit

Advertising includes those activities by which oral and visual messages are directed to the public for the purpose of informing and influencing them either to buy or act favorably toward the subject featured. Profit-minded businessmen use advertising because it is a cheap, quick, and convincing way to increase sales. Although advertising has been referred to as an area in which big business has many advantages, it can be a powerful tool for the small businessman too.

Since advertising is a message to a group of people, a basic principle is to aim your shots. Careful selection of the logical prospects for a particular advertisement should be one of the first steps in planning. The message or theme and its form of presentation in copy, illustration, and layout, as well as the appropriate media to use, all depend primarily upon the particular group to be reached by each advertisement.

Before buying a new car, refrigerator, television set, or any other article involving a considerable investment, the average businessman (as a householder) makes some effort to be certain the article is the best obtainable for the price. A great deal of advertising would be much more effective if the same businessman exerted equal effort to make certain the objective of his advertisement is right before promoting it. The principle is to make it right *before* advertising.

Probably the greatest single waste in modern advertising results from the careless preparation of many advertisements and campaigns. Recognition of this fact has led an increasing number of businessmen to take steps toward testing and measuring the effectiveness of their advertising. Keeping adequate records of all advertisements, including weather and other relevant conditions at the time each is released, is important. Some retailers make a practice of asking each new customer how he happened to come to the shop. An analysis of these results as a basis for planning future advertising increases the number of successes and reduces errors.

Frequently it is possible for the small businessman to pretest advertisements before they are released on a large scale. This may be done by using a less expensive, more easily controlled medium like display, handbills, or direct mail to improve the effectiveness of different elements of the advertisement before completing it in final form for use in such media as newspapers. Another plan, sometimes called "elements research," is an adaptation of split-run testing as used by national advertisers. If the element to be tested is the headline, one half of a sample mailing will receive the circular with one headline and the other half with another. On the next mailing the "heads" will be reversed. Results of each mailing will be carefully recorded, either by inquiries received or by calls in the store if a retailer is working the test. Comparison will show which headline is the more effective. Copy, illustration, or the theme to use may be tested in a similar manner.

Two types of advertising are recognized, according to primary purpose or objective, as *institutional* (selling the business) and *direct action* (selling the merchandise, product, or service the business has to offer). Both are necessary, although the small businessman will usually devote most of his limited advertising funds to the promotional or direct action type. Selling the business and selling the goods are in many respects similar. Some businesses will wish to sell all the many things there are about a business to be sold; others will emphasize only one or a few. Some of the business attributes that advertising sells are:

Services	Prestige
Integrity	Location
Brands carried	Size
Courtesy	Price
Business success	Quality
Credit terms	Fashion policies

PUBLIC RELATIONS

The matter of "public relations" comes early into the problems of every business. This is "a diverse and complex intangible even in the hands of experts," according to one authority. Described as "doing the right thing at the right time in the right way at the right place," it is an attitude toward the public expressed in business behavior. Consequently, since every business act or contact is a matter of behavior in a situation, every business has a public relations program, whether or not it knows it.

These generalities may be observed concerning public relations efforts and results:

1. Every person who in any way has anything to do with attitudes toward or contacts with the public, is creating good or bad public relations.

2. Public relations results or their status, as of a given time, can be

measured to a degree by objective inquiry among customers and others affected.

3. Public relations, as such, cannot be bought, except as advertising is a vehicle or business communication. But advertising is only one of many such vehicles.

4. Public relations need not be expensive. It (or they) must be built continuously and systematically, in terms of well-developed philosophy expressed in well-planned policies.

5. The public relations job is never finished.[1]

In the field of advertising and public relations, the words "corporate image" are frequently noted. We are inclined to think in terms of the efforts of tremendous corporations so familiar to us through the magazines, television, and radio. Yet, a small company can create a desirable corporate image, as indicated by John H. Rice, President of A. H. Rice Co., industrial sewing braid and thread manufacturers.

The Rice Company, on a small budget ($14,000 per year), created a new corporate image by:

1. carefully analyzing what they wanted to accomplish and whom they wanted to impress

2. eliminating scattered ineffective advertising schemes

3. realistically selecting the media

4. using this corporate image program to supplement and support their salesforce.

This program made a definite contribution to their financial strength as evidenced by the fact that they sold to many new accounts and increased sales to many of their regular accounts.[2]

Some businesses seek to set themselves up in the public mind as possessing all virtues. As this is difficult to do, the wise business operator stresses one or two at a time. Likewise, in presenting merchandise it is easier to convince the prospective buyer that it has the one or two outstanding things he really wants than that it is the paragon of all virtues. This is an application of the principle "Aim your shots."

BASIC FACTORS TO CONSIDER

There are several basic factors a small businessman in particular should bear in mind about advertising:

1. Advertising is much more than simply laying out an effective advertisement or writing a clever sales talk.

---

[1] Raymond W. Miller and Robert W. Miller, *Public Relations for Small Business Owners,* Small Marketers Aids No. 27 (Washington, D. C.: Small Business Administration, September 1957).

[2] John H. Rice, President, A. H. Rice Co., Pittsfield, Mass., "Can a Small Company Afford a Corporate Image Program?" *Industrial Marketing,* Part I (June 1959), p. 54.

2. The kind of advertising that is best for some types of businesses may not be right for others.

3. Money can be wasted in advertising by failing to have adequate information about potential customers, by lack of experience or judgment, by spending too high a proportion of gross income, by lack of adequate planning, and in other ways.

4. Finally, the purpose of advertising is to sell or help to sell. Advertising that doesn't do this, directly or indirectly, should be avoided.

Although an advertisement should be regarded as the end result of considerable research and planning rather than the starting point of advertising, it is advisable to know in advance what each advertisement is expected to accomplish. Checking each advertisement before it is released will enable the advertiser to preview such requirements.

An Advertising Check List[3]

(To appraise effectiveness of retail advertising)

This advertising check list was worked out for appraising the effectiveness of retail advertising. Copy which gets 70 points or better has proved to be satisfactory. Sample checking of your advertisements against this table occasionally is suggested.

	Rating
1. Does the headline contain news value?	15
2. Is there a promise to the reader's self-interest?	15
3. Is there an appeal for direct action?	10
4. Is the advertisement of proper size for the importance of the offer and for its most favorable presentation?	10
5. Is the advertiser's signature clearly displayed?	5
6. Is the merchandise or service mentioned in the headline?	3
7. Does the headline include the name of the firm?	2
8. Does the illustration show the merchandise or service in use?	5
9. Does the illustration invite the reader to project himself into it pleasantly, profitably, or favorably?	3
10. Does the layout locate elements logically and eye-invitingly?	5
11. Is the layout exciting or attention compelling?	3
12. Does the copy tell what is new, different, or better about the merchandise or service, especially from the style angle?	3
13. Does the copy inspire enthusiasm for the merchandise or service?	3
14. Does the copy have a definite ring of truth and sincerity?	5
15. Does the copy tell that the merchandise or service is priced to save money?	2
16. Does the copy tell that the product is guaranteed, lasting, and gives good service?	3
17. Does the copy develop and appeal to price?	2

[3] Roscoe R. Rau and Walter F. Shaw, *An Advertising Check List,* Small Business Aids No. 278 (Washington, D. C.: U. S. Department of Commerce). Condensed from Selling Home Furnishings, Appendix F, Vocational Division Bulletin No. 216 (Washington, D. C.: U. S. Office of Education, 1941).

18. Does the copy or illustration imply the merchandise increases sex appeal? 3
19. Does the copy tell why the merchandise is so priced? 1
20. Does the copy tell of the seasonal appeal of the merchandise? ... 1
21. Does the copy describe the merchandise or service with reasonable completeness? 2
22. Does the copy indicate a personal loss for not buying or using the product? 1
23. Are all negative thoughts connected with the product eliminated from the copy? 2
24. Does the copy indicate enthusiasm of users, such as testimonials? 2
25. Does the copy bring out superiorities of the merchandise or service over competitive products? 1
26. Is the urge to action repeated three times—in the heading, in the first paragraph, and in closing? 5
27. Is the price displayed so it will command sufficient attention? ... 3
28. Is there a free deal, free offer, free trial, or something free included? 3
29. Have all details to facilitate action been included? (Phone number, order blank, store hours, mention of air conditioning, parking, etc.) 2

THE GROUNDWORK FOR ADVERTISING

The first step in advertising, as in anything else, is to do the groundwork. A businessman can begin by asking himself these questions:

1. Who are my potential customers?
2. How many are there?
3. Where do they live?
4. Can they get to me conveniently?
5. Are they the kind of people who want charge accounts and delivery service?
6. Where do they now buy the things or services I want to sell them?
7. Can I offer them anything they are not getting now? What? How?
8. How can I convince them they should do business with me?

A businessman should never cease to "survey" or study his customers. Neighborhoods and customers' habits change. If a customer drifts away, he should try at once to find out why.

Consumers may not realize a need for certain products until "educated" by advertising. This is nearly always true of new products for which extensive pioneering advertising may be required. This explains in part why advertising expense may be higher during the first few years. However, if consumers do not want a product or service, advertising alone cannot *make* them buy.

Advertising has a cumulative effect. Response is slow at first but increases with time. Sporadic splurges rarely pay. It is much better to advertise regularly and continuously on a small scale than to use large advertisements infrequently.

By "merchandising" advertising, a company can achieve maximum co-operation from its employees. Road salesmen, for instance, should be convinced that the firm's advertising helps them make more sales more easily.

How Much to Advertise

Determining the right amount to spend for advertising is important because this expense often ranks among the highest. For the small business it is especially important that limited funds be used to the best possible advantage. Once the amount available for advertising is decided upon, a more intelligent campaign can be planned covering such factors as items to promote, prospects to seek, media to use, and frequency of releases.

For a business in an established field, operating ratios are valuable guides in determining how much to spend. However, these are guides, not absolute standards. Many profitable stores and shops spend more than the standard for their fields. The correct amount of money to budget for advertising will depend upon the job to be done and the funds available.

OUTSIDE STAFF ASSISTANCE

Since advertising is one of the most highly developed fields of business, there are specialists in every division of the work. Many sources of assistance are available even to the very small business. These services are referred to in this text as the "outside staff." An understanding of the field's organization is necessary to make the most effective use of modern advertising.[4]

Free lance specialists or independent small businessmen specializing in copywriting, layout, commercial art or illustration, photography, research, and display work will be found in many cities. Their services may be secured for a fee as needed. This group forms an important segment of the outside staff for small businessmen, providing services similar to those of public accountants, bookkeeping firms, and others. For certain types of advertising, such as signs, handbills, and circulars and other direct mail pieces, additional agencies stand ready to help the advertiser.

One of the most valuable aids in many cases consists of the various mat services. A mat is a heavy-paper impression of an advertisement or of some such element as illustration, headline, or copy from which the local printer can make the stereotype or metal plate from which the advertisement is printed.

Mats are prepared by two types of concerns, manufacturers and commercial mat services. Producers often help dealers who handle their products by furnishing them with mats to use in local advertising. These may be dis-

[4] *How Advertising Agencies Serve Small Businesses,* Management Aids for Small Business No. 38 (Washington, D. C.: Small Business Administration, November 1953).

tributed direct to the retailer or through the wholesaler, trade association, or resident buying office. Usually they are available to the local merchant free of charge. Since they are prepared centrally for nationwide distribution, advertising specialists may be employed and information about the product and its selling features incorporated in the advertisement much more effectively than the local advertiser could do it. Mats are flexible, permitting the local advertiser to make such changes as he needs or desires. Even when little or none of the actual mat is used, valuable suggestions for advertising themes, copy, illustrations, and layout may be obtained from it. Trade journals and the publications of Merchants Service Bureaus often present suggested advertisements based on centrally prepared mats that may be obtained by the retailer on request.

Commercial mat services are available to the small advertiser either by direct subscription or through the advertising department of his local paper. Most lines of retailing and service businesses may find adequate the mats furnished at no extra cost by services subscribed to by the newspaper. These mat services are very comprehensive in covering the lines of business that do local newspaper advertising. Each month the subscribing paper receives a large book illustrating all the accompanying mats and making it very easy for the small advertiser to select material appropriate to his needs.

In addition to a score of mat services of broad business coverage, there are many more that serve particular lines of business, such as fashion apparel, furniture, foods, and some service fields. Subscription to one of these services by the small businessman may be a good investment when similar material is not available through his local paper, trade association or other organization.

ADVERTISING MEDIA

Newspaper and radio advertising, the chief forms referred to so far, are considered "mass" media. Often they are not suited to the advertising needs of the small businessman, primarily because of the high cost of waste coverage. Although this is true in many cases, even very small-scale businesses may find limited amounts of advertising in both media useful. On the radio this may involve "station break" commercials or announcements. In the newspaper an especially valuable but often neglected form is advertising in the classified columns.

In appraising advertising media, or comparing them as to effectiveness, the prospective advertiser may well bear these considerations in mind:

1. Cost per contact—how much is it actually costing to get the right persons? How much effort is being wasted on persons who are not logical sales prospects?

2. How frequent are these contacts or message deliveries? In this busi-

ness, is the single powerful impact preferable to a series of constant small reminders, or vice versa?

3. Does the medium in question offer full opportunities for appealing to the appropriate senses, such as sight and hearing in presenting design, color, or sound?

4. Selectivity—to what degree can the message be restricted to those people who are known to be most logical prospects?

There are many such considerations and questions which must be faced and answered. There are many contracting possibilities in media. The newspaper and radio offer broad geographical coverage of the general public, while direct mail can be the utmost in selectivity. The radio commercial may reach hundreds of thousands, only a few of whom are possible customers. An expensive direct mail piece may reach only a limited number, yet the cost per contact may be the same. The question often revolves around the extent to which the prospect can be readily identified beforehand. If unidentifiable, newspaper, radio, or TV advertising may cause him to reveal himself; if identifiable, the expensive direct mail piece might be the best investment. These considerations are some of those fundamental to decisions concerning advertising media.

Newspaper Advertising

Small stores in medium-sized and small communities have found the newspaper to be particularly valuable. Mr. Forrest Arthur of Buttrey Associates, Inc., of Great Falls, Montana, a department store, stated not long ago:

> If I were suddenly restricted to one and only one advertising medium I would board up the display windows, discontinue all internal and departmental selling displays, eliminate all sales meetings, and sales incentives, stop all telephone selling and continue an aggressive business building advertising investment in the newspapers . . . the final selling of any product must be done locally—by the local newspapers.[5]

With a given amount to spend for advertising, the following are some of the many things that can be done to make it profitable:

Buy space at the best rates. Often advertising will cost less if more space is purchased. For example, if the campaign calls for 985 lines at a rate of 10 cents, the cost will be $98.50. A study of the publication's rate card might reveal that 1,000 lines can be run at a rate of 8 cents or a total cost of $80.00.

Do not scatter advertising. Skipping around from one publication to another seldom gets results. It destroys the effectiveness of consecutive advertising and, most important, loses the handling and consideration privileges afforded the consistent advertiser. This makes a great deal of difference when it is desirable to secure a favorable position for the advertisement.

---

[5] NAEA Report: "Retail Merchant Urges More Newspaper Ads." Appeared in *Editor and Publisher* (January 24, 1959), p. 20.

Check circulation figures closely. The smaller the newspaper, the more chance of padded circulation. It is good business practice to demand certified statements as to how the total circulation figure is broken down. The Standard Rate and Data Service gives the total net paid circulation of a paper as well as the circulation by city zone, by retail trading zone, and by city and retail trading zones together. Run checks to see which of the local media pays best. It never pays to guess about which publication is bringing the best returns.[6]

The classified sections of most local newspapers present an opportunity for the businessman with a limited advertising budget. The classified pages of a single paper sometimes contain as many as 55 sections, including automobiles for sale, electricians' services, electrical supplies, mattresses remade, boats and equipment, awnings and shades, and the like.

Because this form of advertising is not used by the large, integrated store operator, we may conclude that the "little fellow" has obtained his money's worth from it, for if the medium had failed to produce results, its use would have been discontinued.

The newspaper representative will assist the inexperienced advertiser in his selection of space, copy, and layout at no extra cost. These salesmen are usually highly skilled in planning classified advertisements.

Telephone-book Classified Advertising

Most telephone directories have a special section usually called the "yellow pages" in which the local businessman may advertise his goods and services. Such advertisements are little different from those in newspapers except that they are more likely to be illustrated and to depart in other ways from a straight, agate line appearance.

One insertion in a telephone book continues to function as an active advertisement until the next issue appears, usually six months later. The telephone book stays in the home or office, ready to serve as a source of information on where to buy anything. Every business that has a telephone receives without charge a one-line insertion in the classified section of the book. Any further advertising must be paid for.

Radio Advertising

One form of advertising that is often neglected by the small businessman is radio; yet it can be one of the most effective and far-reaching of all media.

It can and does sell goods for the small retail merchant. What many little fellows do not know is that "spot" announcements cost as little as $3.50 each on some of the small local stations that reach a large proportion of the local market. These, now comprising the majority of the commercial stations in

---

[6] Adapted from *Make Your Ads Pay Off*, Small Business Aids No. 252 (Washington, D. C.: U. S. Department of Commerce). Condensed from "Make Your Ads Pay Off," by Ernest W. Fair, *The Jewelers' Circular-Keystone* (January 1947), Chilton Co.. Inc. Philadelphia, Pa.

the United States, have a power of less than 1,000 watts and are therefore unable to reach beyond a limited geographical area. This limitation is an advantage to the small retailer, because when he buys time on such a station he has little waste circulation. The programs of the local station are directed to the market in his area. The best way to get the complete story of radio costs is to visit the radio broadcasting office, examine the station's rate card, and have a talk with an authorized representative of the station. In addition, *The Standard Rate and Data Service,* which is published monthly in Chicago and found in many libraries, will furnish the prospective radio advertiser with cost information.

The advertiser must give attention to the type of person he wishes to reach —including age, sex, and profession—before selecting the kind of program he wants and the time to put it on the air. Information of this type is provided by the A. C. Nielson Company of Chicago. The Nielson Service Report includes (1) the weekly audience of each station for each county or other economic area, (2) the composition of the weekly audience with respect to economic status, race, home ownership, and so on, (3) out-of-home listening, (4) homes reached per minute by large, network-affiliated radio stations, and (5) radio and TV ownership.

In numerous surveys made throughout the nation it has been proved that programs featuring stories, music, news, and public services continued from day to day have the highest rating among women for daytime listening; at night, comedy and musical shows attract the largest audiences of men and women.

The age of the listener might be important to a candy store, theater, teenage dress shop, or snack shop advertiser. The best time to appeal to children is in the late afternoon or on Saturday morning. Record shows in the afternoon or night appeal to teen-agers and college students, providing the record or snack shop with a chance to benefit from "spot" commercials.

There are certain hours that are recognized as the best broadcast time, and consequently carry a higher advertising price than others. For example, Class A radio time on some stations is from six until ten at night; this means that, according to surveys, more people listen at that time than at any other time. These are the so-called "family hours." [7]

Another factor determining the price of an announcement, "spot" commercial, or entire program is the power of the station. This is very important for the small businessman, because if his products are sold in one city or to nearby customers, a small 250-watt station will reach prospective customers satisfactorily but if he covers the state or a larger area with his service or product, a 5,000-watt or larger station would be more effective. The question will be whether the less expensive station can meet the advertiser's needs as

[7] Current advertising rates and related information for every newspaper and broadcasting station may be obtained from the latest issues of *Standard Rate and Data Service* (monthly), 333 N. Michigan Avenue, Chicago, Ill.

well as the larger station. Also, the population of the area covered by a certain station will influence the price of commercials; a station in a large town will reach more people and be more expensive than another station of the same power in a less populous area. In addition, the price will be affected by the number of times a week and the number of weeks a "spot" commercial or a program is put on the air. The longer the commercial and the more often it is on the air the cheaper it will be per unit of time.

Use of public service features is an excellent way to promote goodwill for an advertiser. Such an announcement as, "Through the courtesy of Blank's Department Store we bring you a report on the activities of the Red Cross," is a "plug" for Blank. The department store has no commercials on this type of program other than the statement in so many words that the store is paying for the time to bring listeners some important civic information.

Unless the advertiser uses an agency, usually all he need do as far as writing the commercials is concerned is to tell the radio station time salesman that he would like to publicize a certain sale or a product that day or week. The station man gathers the details and writes the commercials without any extra cost to the advertiser.

If the businessman wants an entire program, the radio station will suggest popular types that may be sponsored, or the advertiser may suggest a program himself. The national networks have "co-op" shows that are originated by the networks themselves but these may be sponsored locally. Commercials are inserted by the local announcer when the network gives the cue.

It is not advisable to accept a show to sponsor unless one has seen some national radio ratings of the type of program under consideration. In addition, it may be well to ask relatives, friends, and acquaintances of different ages and professions, especially those representative of the audience desired, what their favorite type of radio entertainment is. An advertiser may also decide upon the most effective place for a commercial by using this method. He should listen to his commercials or programs on the radio and try to judge them as he would an advertisement in a newpaper.

Television Advertising

Television is the fastest growing medium available to the advertiser. Up to the mid 1950's its cost to the potential small advertiser was prohibitive. However, the rapid growth and use of television have caused the small enterpriser to focus new attention upon it. The mere fact that in 1959, 86 per cent of all homes in the United States had one or more TV sets provides evidence of its usefulness.[8]

Spot announcements or some type of co-operative sharing of program expenses are probably feasible in large cities. For example, a 10-second spot

---

[8] A. C. Nielson Company, *Television 59,* A booklet prepared by the A. C. Nielson Company, 1959.

announcement on a Cleveland TV station costs approximately $200. Other possibilities are:

1. Dual or Co-sponsorship
2. Alternate-Week Sponsorship
3. Participating Sponsorship
4. Regional Sponsorship[9]

Television costs when prorated against the coverage of a potential market may be lower than many other media. For this reason, even the small advertiser cannot afford to overlook this powerful force.

Sign Advertising

Signs used to identify the place and kind of business represent one of the oldest advertising media. This type of advertising is well suited to reaching the buyer while he is traveling about the neighborhood on foot, by bus, or by automobile.

Some authorities consider the ideal outdoor advertising medium for the small retailer to be the hand-painted sign on a board located as near to his store as possible, preferably on the side of his building. Such a sign has the advantage of relative permanence, but it also has the disadvantages of fixed copy, since it is more difficult to change a hand-painted sign than a poster panel.

The outdoor poster is made in two sizes, the 24-sheet poster and the 3-sheet poster. The 24-sheet poster, when assembled, measures 8 feet 10 inches by 19 feet 8 inches. These are the familiar large signs that may be seen along any highway, mounted on a substantial steel or heavy wooden poster-panel structure 11 feet high and 25 feet long.

The 3-sheet poster can be effectively displayed on the side of a building. It is well suited to use by the small retailer. A space 4 feet 10 inches by 8 feet 7 inches is required for the whole display including the frame. Such a poster makes a good point-of-purchase reminder or a colorful supplement to mail, newspaper, and handbill advertising. There are approximately 12,000 poster plants set up to handle such work in this country.

At one time or another nearly every member of the family uses the bus and reads the bus cards for lack of something more interesting to do. Certainly the small enterpriser whose business is located near a bus terminal should be able to use the bus card as an advertising medium.

Storefront signs are often provided by some manufacturer whose product or equipment is carried or used by the small establishment. Such signs naturally contain the name of the manufacturer as well as that of the local businessman. Many small retail and service establishments and most factories prefer to erect their own building sign featuring the name of the firm or its business

[9] Albert Wesley Frey, *Advertising* (New York: Ronald Press Co., 1953), p. 389.

exclusively. It may feature package reproductions, neon lights, or other attention-getting displays.

Point-of-purchase signs may easily be used to excess, especially when the small businessman is too lenient in permitting every salesman to put up his own signs. The cluttered appearance of many small shops is testimony to this danger. Useful guides to follow are: make each sign justify its space in terms of sales volume or profit to the business; require that it harmonize with the "atmosphere" and over-all appearance of the establishment; and reserve all spaces needed for the firm's own signs or other business uses.

Handbill Advertising

Handbills can be a very effective and inexpensive form of advertising for small businessmen. They are especially useful for announcing the opening of a new neighborhood business, for periodic reminders of the merchandise or services offered, and for advertising special sales. Handbills should be planned carefully as to layout, message or appeal, headline, and appearance. A good printer can give advice on the quality of paper to use, over-all appearance, size, cost and similar factors, but should not be depended on for the sales message or copy of the advertisment. The printer however, should be carefully selected since he can render many valuable services to the beginning advertiser.

Since the use of handbills is likely to be undertaken partly because of low cost, there is a real danger that efficient distribution may be neglected. It is advisable to select reliable distributors and pay adequately for the work. Either the owner or some other competent adult should supervise distribution. In many cities organized handbill distributors may be employed who will guarantee effective circulation.[10]

Direct Mail Advertising

Direct mail can be defined as *the controlled distribution of a written message to a selected audience.* Compared with other media it allows the advertiser to be very *flexible* in promotional costs, highly *selective* in choosing prospects, and quite *personal* in his sales message.

Generous postal laws in this country provide businessmen with extensive opportunities for using this highly effective medium.

Most people like to receive a friendly, interesting letter. The small businessman can capitalize on this human tendency and should make his direct mail advertising as personal, informal, and selective as possible. Careful study of charge account and delivery records, as well as the owner's personal knowledge of his customers, should make it possible to classify most of his clientele

---

[10] For further study see William L. Doremus, *Handbill Advertising,* Small Business Aids No. 313 (Washington, D. C.: U. S. Department of Commerce). Condensed from *Advertising for Profit—A Guide for Small Business* (New York: Pitman Publishing Corporation, 1947).

into several groups based on their common buying interest. Direct mail pieces can be thoughtfully worded in such a way as to have a strong appeal to each customer and create the impression of individualized attention.

Although as many as ten different forms of direct mail advertising are recognized, the most important for the average small businessman are envelope enclosures, mailing cards, and post cards. Envelope enclosures include the direct sales letter, self-addressed return card or envelope, and folders or booklets to supplement the letter.

A mailing card can be used to advantage for making an announcement in a dignified manner. It may be printed either with or without illustration on stock of good quality. Appropriate uses include announcing the addition of a new line of goods, the arrival of new models, or a change of business address. A mailing card of superior quality should be enclosed in an appropriate envelope and first-class postage should be used.

Many small-scale advertisers have made effective use of the lowly post card. It is an ideal direct mail form for the retailer with a good prospect list and a limited budget. A good layout that combines well-selected type with a line-cut illustration presents a concise sales story on a post card and can carry on an excellent and economical sales campaign. A series of such messages mailed on a systematic follow-up basis is likely to produce a telling effect. The postal card (government printed) has been used successfully by many small enterprisers.

Within each merchandise or service group appropriate *themes* should be chosen to appeal to strong human desires, such as health, comfort, security, and advancement, or to any of the consumer wants the advertised good is especially intended to satisfy. In the presentation of the message, consumer benefits should be stressed in a friendly person-to-person manner. Each letter should contain all the essential information necessary to make the prospect want the offering. Descriptive folders or small booklets may be enclosed to supplement the letter.

Nearly two dozen shapes and sizes of enclosures are used in direct mail work. Each variety has its advantages and special uses. For example, the "broadside" (a large sheet of paper, usually 25 by 38 inches) is very effective for creating "impact" or dramatic effect. The large size of broadsides makes it possible to use showmanship methods effectively. When the nature of the advertisement makes a reply by the prospect desirable, make it easy for the recipient to act by enclosing a return post card or envelope. Whether to use a stamped, self-addressed card or envelope or to take advantage of postal provisions permitting "postage guaranteed" returns should be studied. The former is cheaper per letter, but the latter often costs less in the end, since usually not all the cards or envelopes are returned.

Direct mail is more expensive per message delivered than publication advertising, but when used properly it can be an inexpensive method of reaching selected groups. The mailing list is of the utmost importance. If it is necessary to economize, most authorities recommend using a less expensive mailing piece and the best possible mailing list. Each name on the list should represent a live prospect for the goods advertised. It is important to keep the mailing list current and to make every effort to have titles and first names correct.

Repetition will ultimately drive home the message. One piece of direct mail advertising may bring results, but it is a proved fact that regularly repeated mailings will do a better selling job.

ADVERTISING FOR THE SMALL RETAILER

For the retailer, timeliness, selection of the right merchandise to advertise, the best theme to use, and window and interior displays are important points to consider in addition to those already discussed. Timing the release of advertising should be related to the store's position in the merchandise acceptance curve or fashion cycle. Fashion leaders in the community advertise heavily at the very beginning of the selling season; those catering to the middle class advertise just before the peak of the selling period; and stores in the "economy" group put out their ads just after the selling crest has been passed.

For staple merchandise and special sale events, advertising should be timed to fit in with pay days and shopping habits of customers for stores in the lower and average income groups; those catering to the upper income brackets will be more concerned with tax dates and special customer preferences.

Selecting the right merchandise to advertise is of great importance to the retailer because only about 15 to 20 per cent of all goods carried are suitable for the purposes of external advertising. Not only should goods selected produce enough sales of the advertised articles to cover the direct cost of advertising, but they should also attract to the store customers who will buy quantities of unadvertised merchandise. In other words, advertising should attract shopping traffic of regular customers rather than bargain hunters or specific item buyers exclusively.

Selecting items to advertise may be done in many ways. Preference should be given to goods representative of the store's character and of proved clientele appeal. The store's records of past sales, advertising, want slips, customer complaints, and adjustments may be used for selecting the product to advertise. For new items customer response to display is considered the best guide. Opinions of buyers and salespeople are useful guides if time will not permit test displays before advertising.

To help in deciding upon the theme or appeal to be used in advertising, buyers should state the features about each article that caused them to buy it for the store. Current practice is to require each buyer at the time he purchases new merchandise to secure from the vendor the "sizzle" or selling story for each article. Salespeople should also be able to give valuable suggestions as to what features of the merchandise would be most attractive and interesting to customers.

The relationships between purchasing and selling are obvious. The dangers of making any business decision, particularly a purchase for stock on a strictly personal taste basis, are outlined as follows:

Compare your impressions with others. In sizing up an article for possible purchase, get the reactions of some other knowledgeable people. If there is general agreement with your favorable view, you have grounds for going ahead with the order. If there is general disapproval, reconsider soberly before deciding one way or the other. Where opinions vary widely, your own best judgment is the only guide.[11] The suggestion here is that the question "What advertisable features does the merchandise have?" is best asked when it is being considered for inventory.

Naturally, certain merchandise suggests its own theme, such as fashion rightness, authenticity, or economy. Experience has shown, however, that such "obvious" points of appeal as durability, strength, economy, or assumed use of the article may differ widely from the *real* reasons why customers buy particular merchandise. Careful and continuous investigation is the safest course to follow.[12]

Coordination of Sales Effort

Customers can be encouraged to buy additional merchandise by attractive displays, informative signs, point-of-purchase advertising, and circulars, handouts, or lists of unadvertised items placed in convenient traffic locations throughout the store. Interior displays and advertising material should be representative of the store and its merchandise in appearance and merchandise selections. These should represent articles of real value (not "bargains") selected from various departments in order to encourage customers to visit all parts of the store. Apealing displays of impulse items adjacent to each listed item, as well as to merchandise advertised externally, will give real meaning to the expression "It pays to advertise."

Most authorities agree that windows are usually an indispensable advertising medium although several supermarkets have constructed large stores completely free of windows. External advertising presents a message about the merchandise; displays the merchandise itself. "Atmosphere" can be used with equal effectiveness in both. Showing the merchandise in three dimen-

---

[11] Harry Lipson, "Profitable Buying for Small Retailers," *Alabama Retail Trade* (bulletin), Vol. 30, No. 1 (September 30, 1959), Bureau of Business Research, School of Commerce and Business Administration, University of Alabama, University, Alabama. See also Jean C. Halterman and Bert C. McCammon, *Individuality in Retail Advertising,* Small Marketers Aids No. 23 (Washington, D. C.: Small Business Administration, May 1957).

[12] *Advertise to Promote Your Business to Sell Your Goods* (Dayton, Ohio: Merchants Service, National Cash Register Company, 1958), shows essentials for preparing ads and for effective advertising. (Available on request.)

sions, in all its true color and beauty, is a strong point. Since they are at the point-of-sale, displays serve as reminder advertising in addition to stimulating impulse buying.

If any merchandise in the window fails to result in the volume of sales expected, it should be replaced at once—even in the middle of a busy selling day—by items that will produce the desired results. Not only is window display space the most valuable space in the store, but goods on display help to make up the "face" of the store that impresses traffic.

Displays should be tied in with national advertising whenever possible. This may be accomplished in many ways, such as by timing displays to appear during national campaigns and by including pages from the national media or placards stating "As advertised in *Vogue*" and the like. Seasonal displays are usually effective, offer many opportunities for originality and related item selling, and help to build the store's reputation for merchandising alertness. Important promotions in the community, such as National Cotton Week, Mardi Gras, Mother's Day, or Days of the Forty-Niners, can offer profitable advertising themes.

Interior displays should always have price cards and usually informative signs. For impulse and convenience goods, mass displays are very effective, especially the jumbled type with nothing for the customer to knock down when selecting articles from the display. Grocers have found that the effectiveness of mass displays is noticeably increased by the addition of advertising placards calling attention to featured goods and giving the price. If the offering is a special-price feature and there is a time or quantity-per-customer limit, this information should also be given.

As a rule, the display cards and other dealer helps offered by manufacturers and distributors should be utilized, because they provide authentic sales information about the goods and provide space for pricing. Such dealer helps represent extensive and often expensive study to discover the appeal that will be most effective in presenting a product to the public, and they contain tested catch lines that are bound to help sell the goods.

ADVERTISING FOR THE SMALL WHOLESALER

Small wholesalers do relatively little advertising. For most lines of wholesaling, considering large and small firms together, the expense of personal selling is from ten to twenty times as much as the amount spent for advertising.

For our present purpose, small wholesalers may be divided into two classes, those who do "floor selling" and those who do not. Buyers often visit those in the former group to inspect merchandise displayed in the sample rooms or on the selling floor. Since these buyers are mostly small retailers, the wholesaler can use appealing displays both to increase immediate sales and to show the retailers how to present the merchandise effectively in their own stores.

Whether display rooms are operated or not, some small wholesalers do a limited amount of external advertising. Practically all of them use signs over the store front and on the side of the warehouse if possible. Most other advertising is directed to the trade rather than to consumers. Only when a wholesaler has an exclusive franchise line or is trying to promote his own brand does he use consumer advertising.

Catalogues, price lists, sales letters, and some dealer aid material that is usually furnished by the manufacturer constitute the principal forms of advertising used. The objective is to pave the way for personal selling or to economize the salesmen's time. Almost no direct merchandise advertising is undertaken by the wholesaler himself.

ADVERTISING FOR THE SMALL FACTORY

The small factory will usually direct its advertising either to consumers or to dealers or business users (other manufacturers) of its product. Manufacturers of consumer goods selling only in the local market, whether through local dealers or direct, may often use newspaper, radio, outdoor sign, and direct mail advertising effectively.

In some small factories the nature of the business permits advertising through the appearance of the building as well as through use of the windows. A small candy factory that was recently opened in a town of 13,000 illustrates these ideas. Merchandise displays as well as several candymaking processes are visible from the sidewalk through the glass store front. The interior is done in bright red and white "candy stripes" on the walls and ceiling, with varicolored glass blocks in one partition transmitting bright colors from a hidden source of illumination.

Sometimes a small factory located near a highway can make good use of highway displays. A small artificial flower plant displays orchids and gardenias in transparent individual packages ready for sale to customers. The plant itself is not visible from the highway but is close enough to service the highway displays. When the product made is attractive, has impulse appeal, and may be sold profitably direct to consumers, such a plan should be useful for other small manufacturers.

Small factories selling through dealers or to other businesses will select as their media principally direct mail and trade publications read by their prospects. When the area covered or sought to be covered is regional or national in scope, trade journal advertising will probably be the best. Space rates are relatively low and the circulation is selective. Small advertisements inserted frequently may be most effective. The purpose will be to solicit inquiries or secure leads to be followed up by direct mail, samples, or personal selling.

In either situation direct mail is the suggested medium when prospects are relatively few in number and form a highly selective group or when the advertising message requires a great deal of description and explanation. Lists for direct mail advertising should usually include: present active customers, former or inactive customers, and prospective customers.

The manufacturer, particularly, has the problem of budgeting the amount to be spent for advertising. He has no standard ratios as established for retailing. He will have ideas as to how much of his selling job can be done by advertising as compared with the results he can expect through salesmen. The budget is the result of these considerations and is essential as a plan of action. A logical approach to the problem is stated as follows:

> 1. *The percent-of-sale method.* Some companies determine in advance the amount they will spend for advertising and promotion even before they have determined the year's objectives and before they have analyzed the problems to be surmounted. This allotted sum is generally set at a fixed percentage of (a) estimated sales for the forthcoming year, or (b) the current year's sales volume (not so common).
>
> 2. *The per-unit-assignment method.* Others arbitrarily establish a figure for each product based upon what they think they can afford to spend next year. Again little attempt is made to relate the expenditure directly to practical requirements.
>
> 3. *The job-requirement method.* To some advertising managers, this technique (also called the task method) is the most practical one for deciding what the advertising budget should be. However, while it may be good, it has a weakness in the fact that it is sometimes difficult to determine what funds are required to accomplish given objectives; for example, the schedule of advertising needed. Nevertheless, this method does bring into the open the issue of the *amount to be spent.* Thus, it tends to make people think clearly in justifying expenditures for advertising. It is necessary to determine the job to be done, the problems to be solved, the tools needed for solution, and the method of accomplishment. The job requirement method recognizes the importance of the carefully developed program, emphasizing high efficiency and low expenditure. This method is based on marketing research and media investigation.[13]

Although radio is used by small manufacturers less frequently than direct mail, "spot" announcements may be an effective way to get a new product off to a good start, to draw attention to other advertising media used, and to gain dealer acceptance and distribution for the product because it is being supported by consumer advertising.[14]

---

[13] Raymond P. Wiggers, *Profitable Advertising for Small Industrial Goods Producers,* Small Business Management Series No. 18 (Washington, D. C.: Small Business Administration, 1956).

[14] For further study see: *How Small Manufacturers Can Maintain Lists for Direct Mail Advertising,* Small Business Aids No. 415 (Washington, D. C.: U. S. Department of Commerce), condensed from "Mailing List," Section Forty-Four, *The Sales Manager's Handbook* (Chicago: The Dartnell Corporation); *Using Spot Radio Ads to Increase Sales,* Small Business Aids No. 383 (U. S. Department of Commerce), condensed from "16 Ways to Back Sales with Spot Radio in Selected Markets," by Thomas Cox, Jr., *Sales Management* (December 15, 1946); "Consumer Advertising for the Small Manufacturer," by J. Howard Westing, *Michigan Business Review* (University of Michigan, Ann Arbor, July 1949).

Advertising themes will usually be found in one of the major marketing instruments. Such themes might be: the product itself if it is new or superior to competing products; the package; the price, which may be favorable to the small producer either because of low costs or because he is entering a field of well-advertised brands where his competitors have already incurred the expense of demand creation; or availability in terms of prompt deliveries and nearness to customers. Other themes may of course be used if certain unusual services are offered, the product is better for certain special uses than those now on the market, or other particular circumstances prevail.

ADVERTISING FOR THE SERVICE BUSINESS

Too many small service establishment operators are in doubt as to just how they can improve their advertisements. What can a laundry do? A laundry is just a laundry; if the customers like the service, they will come back. This is true to a certain degree, but it shows a rather short-sighted outlook. How can new customers be won in the face of so much competition? Other laundries may have quality service too. How can the housewife be persuaded that it pays to send her family's textiles to the laundry rather than do them herself? How can a reputation for quality service be built? Why do people desire the particular service offered? Why do customers prefer to trade with one shop rather than another? These questions must be kept in mind while the promotional campaign is being planned by the proprietor if his plans are to be effective.

To answer them he must take the customer's view in advertising. He must tell in a truthful manner what the customer wants and needs to know about the service. Both emotional and rational motives of the consumer play an important part in service organization patronage.

Experience has shown that small laundries and cleaning establishments can make effective use of one or more of the following forms of advertising: signs on trucks, strikingly clean appearance of trucks and store front, distinctive bags and wrapping paper that carry a short advertising message, and inserts that tie in the firm name with trade association or other general advertising. If a window trimming service operates in the city, dry cleaners especially may use this service effectively. These methods are in addition to the use of common media like newspapers, radio, and directories.

Restaurants find interior signs especially effective because of the impulse nature of customer buying. In addition to promoting the sale of particular dishes, signs can build confidence in the quality of food served. One small restaurant has two such signs. The first, which carries the slogan "Good Food For Good Health," states that the firm is a member of the National Restaurant Association; the other reads, "Member—American Restaurant Association—An Approved Restaurant." The same restaurant has two "Ultra Violet Purifyers" and a Salad Bar with identifying signs, all visible to customers. The result is to convince patrons that the owner is doing everything possible to protect their health and best interests.

Pride in the appearance of person or property, distinctiveness in taste, health, and cleanliness are all emotional buying motives used by various service establishments. Rational buying motives include quality, dependability, durability, enhancement of earnings, and economy.

Professional services, although they do not "advertise," feature the qualifications of the practitioner by his degree, title, or badge of approval of the certifying agency. Examples are such designations as C.P.A., M.D., A.I.A., and Realtor. A list of professional association memberships and past or present offices held is also used to support the title. There is a trend to expand this practice to other service fields.

Window displays may be one of the best and yet the most undeveloped promotional media in service industries. A shoe repair shop could show the steps in manufacturing or repairing a shoe. In San Diego, California, a fur storage plant displayed a piece of valuable fur being eaten by moths.

Open displays of machinery showing the service actually being performed give customers confidence in its quality. Examples can be seen at Coca-Cola Bottling Companies throughout the country, where one can stand on the sidewalk and watch, through a large window, the bottles being inspected, filled, and capped. In Little Rock, Arkansas, a laundry used this idea by installing a plate glass window that enabled passers-by to watch employees iron the various garments. In Akron, Ohio, a bank spent $6,000 to build a large showcase in the lobby for displays of its customers' wares, with the idea of keeping its clients "sold" by helping them to sell.[15]

The owner should reaffirm the appeal to buying motives in planning his advertising schedule. Too many think that word-of-mouth publicity and past performance should be the main promotional efforts of the service shop. Both newspaper and radio will help at the time of the grand opening, when prospective customers are informed of the presence of the shop and some free offers are made to help get it off to a good start.

CONCLUSIONS

Advertising is one of the most important "mass production" tools of big business available to the little fellow. However, like dynamite and other powerful forces, its effective use requires understanding and skill in handling. Trade associations and advertising agencies specialize in solving their members' and clients' advertising problems.

With increased intensity of competition in recent years, marketers have

---

[15] *Banks Profit Through Glamour, New Services,* Small Business Aids No. 88 (Washington, D. C.: U. S. Department of Commerce), condensed from "Banks Make Glamour Pay," by Keith Monroe, *Nation's Business* (Washington, D. C.: Chamber of Commerce of the United States, May 1946).

sometimes resorted to methods of advertising and selling which, if not illegal, have been unethical and injurious to the public interest. Deceptive promotional methods not only harm individual buyers but undermine the public's faith in all business.

Better Business Bureaus and various trade associations have long been concerned with these practices, as have been various state and Federal agencies. The impact of Vance Packard's *The Hidden Persuaders,* the quiz show scandals, and "payola" investigations are the results. Local advertising is coming under increasingly intense scrutiny. That the Federal Trade Commission, usually concerned largely with national advertising methods, has recognized the dangers involved is illustrated by the following quotation from *Dun's Review and Modern Industry:*

> A look at last year's FTC operations suggests stepped-up activity where the manufacturer and retailer are hardest-hit—at point of sale. For many surprised manufacturers, this has meant cutting out special prices, deals, discounts, and volume and advertising allowances for favored customers. For retailers, it has meant eliminating traditional advertising practices that have now been branded by the FTC as deceptive or bait advertising.[16]

Perhaps such warnings should not be points of major emphasis in the closing lines of the chapter on advertising in a book on small business. They are covered in depth in another chapter. Yet they are reiterated here because one of the major temptations of the beginner, particularly at times when business is "slow," is to forget previous plans, policies, and long-run profit and in blatant advertising to flash forth with wild claims, descriptions, or promises in desperate appeals to the public for patronage. The simplest way to prevent such departures, as with other possibilities of error, is to know of their dangers and to remember that the great names in industry were built through consistent and unfaltering integrity in all dealings with the public, including those involved in advertising.

QUESTIONS AND PROBLEMS

1. State, explain and illustrate the three basic principles of advertising.

2. Explain how the small business can pretest advertising. Is pretesting worth the time and expense required? Discuss.

3. How should an enterpriser determine the amount to spend for advertising?

4. If the standard expense for advertising in your chosen field were 4 per cent, would you be justified in spending during your first year in business 6 per cent? 10 per cent? 25 per cent? Explain.

5. If a retail store has to dispose quickly of a limited quantity of some item of

[16] Paul A. King, "Living With the Law," *Dun's Review and Modern Industry* (January 1960). See also: *Guide for Retail Advertising and Selling,* 5th ed. (New York: Association of Better Business Bureaus, Inc., 1956), for information of federal trade rules and regulations and how to avoid misleading practices. This guide covers general rules as well as particular merchandise and service groups.

outer wearing apparel representing good value, what medium or media would be best to use? Why?

6. What advantage, if any, does the characteristic of privacy give direct mail? Discuss.

7. Upon what bases may the costs of different media like the newspaper, radio, and direct mail be compared? Discuss each.

8. If the budget for direct mail advertising is limited, is it better to economize on the mailing list or on the mailing piece? Explain.

9. One limitation on retail advertising is that it cannot succeed without the backing of the entire organization. Explain fully why this is true.

10. List a number of ways in which a firm's policies will influence or limit its advertising. Give examples of each.

11. How should a retailer select the merchandise for external advertising? Discuss.

12. Mention additional uses for direct mail advertising in each of the fields of small business.

13. Compare the post card with the postal card for advertising use by the small businessman.

14. Compare and contrast appropriate advertising for the small manufacturer and service establishment.

15. What "sizzle" or advertising theme would be best for each of the following: A new record changer, a child's picture story book, an electric-clock-operated radio, a launderette with adjoining beauty parlor, a home study high-school course?

16. For some kind of small business of interest to you study the current advertising available, analyze it and suggest improvements. Explain.

17. For a period of at least two weeks be alert for every example of national advertising in all available media that offers a good opportunity for retail store tie-ins. Report your findings together with your advertising suggestions for the retailers.

18. Ed advertised several slow selling items over the radio and in the newspaper. Many people asked about these items but none bought them. What errors are apparent here? What should Ed do, and why?

20 • Pricing for Turnover and Profit

That price, turnover, and profit are related seems reasonable to most businessmen, but the specific relationships among these three are not always clearly understood. Profit does not depend upon either price or rate of turnover alone nor only on both together. It is the result of the combined effects of price, volume, and expenses. Since the usual tendency is for expense to decrease percentagewise as turnover increases, many small businessmen think that increasing turnover is a sure road to greater profits. In general this is true only when increased turnover can be achieved without loss of sales volume and without either a proportionally greater increase in total expenses or higher purchase prices as a result of buying in smaller quantities.

Furthermore, the usual tendency for sales volume, and consequently turnover, to increase as price is lowered does not always hold true in specific cases. Correct pricing of the product or service of a particular business depends upon many factors, such as company policy, nature of the product or service, location, costs and expenses, competition, market strategy, business conditions and trends, and distribution.

According to one authority, the optimum selling price is one that will net the most dollars (after allowing for applicable selling costs) during the time the product is on the market. It depends in part on whether you have a short- or long-run item. Also, it represents the profit-margin concept on the basis of standard replacement cost.[1] Company price policy will normally be influenced by casual factors like location, size or position in the field, nature of the product, customer services rendered, and the owner's preference for a particular market or reputation. Certain businessmen seek a particular class of trade and consequently follow a price policy intended to appeal to this group. For the small business this may be either a matter of owner preference

[1] Jules E. Anderson and Earl C. Gassenheimer, *Pricing Arithmetic for Small Business Managers,* Management Aids for Small Manufacturers No. 100 (Washington, D. C.: Small Business Administration, February 1959).

or of business experience and ability. It is well known that certain individuals can cater successfully, especially in the retail and service fields, only to one of the three major income groups.

An individual may set out to establish a reputation for having either the lowest or the highest prices in his field. In such cases the level of prices set is the starting point; expenses, location, organization, and policies other than pricing must be adjusted to conform. For most beginners, however, a policy of price strategy is best. This involves selecting prices that appeal to markets not already served by existing firms.

The casual factors are dominant in the majority of small businesses. A merchant will adjust his prices as location characteristics change and compe- tition increases. A manufacturer will normally change his prices to correspond to changes in cost. Any intelligent businessman will price each product or service according to customer reaction, using a low price when demand is highly elastic, a "class price" for luxury items, and so forth.

It is important to understand how certain characteristics of marketing costs and even the method of distribution used may influence appropriate pricing, especially for the manufacturer and in some cases the service busi- ness. Distribution or marketing costs, relative to production costs, are "sticky" and do not change quickly with small changes in price. Since market- ing costs for most consumer goods make up almost half of the price paid by the final consumer, this rigidity tends to lessen the benefits received by the producer who reduces his prices when costs of production are lowered. An- other important consideration for the small business is that distribution costs may increase per unit with increased sales, at least up to the point where large-scale methods, such as extensive advertising, can be used. Some exam- ples will clarify these points.

Two situations will be examined—examples of indirect and direct market- ing. First, assume the existence of a factory producing 10,000 units per month of an article sold through several dealers to consumers; manufacturing cost is $0.50 per unit, net profit $0.10, factory selling price $0.60, and retail price $1.00. Thus, marketing cost is $0.40 per unit. A way is found to reduce pro- duction costs 10 per cent or $0.05. If factory price is lowered by this amount from $0.60 to $0.55 and dealers pass along the full amount of this reduction, retail selling price will be reduced by only 5 per cent. If this increased retail sales in units by only 5 per cent, sales will now be 10,500 units with a retail value of $9,975 and factory value at selling price of $5,775. The manufac- turer would thus be selling 10,500 units for $225 less than he formerly re- ceived for 10,000 units and his net profit would be increased by only $50. The retailer would receive $25 less in total sales for 10,500 units than he for- merly received for 10,000. Even an increase in retail sales of 6 per cent to 10,600 units would mean sales at retail of $10,070, or only $70 more than when the price was $1.00. To the manufacturer this would be only $5,830 in sales, a decline of $170, and $1,060 profit, an increase of only $60. Had price not been reduced, profit to the manufacturer would have been increased by 50 per cent, or from $1,000 to $1,500, with no change in sales volume. However, such a static condition is usually undesirable and likely to be unstable.

Assume, as a second example, that the $500 gained by lower cost plus an additional $500—a total of $1,000—is used for effective sales promotion. If an additional 10,000 units were sold, advertising cost would be only $16\frac{2}{3}$ per cent of the increased sales or $8\frac{1}{3}$ per cent of total sales (both figured at the factory price of $0.60). This would double profits to the manufacturer, over and above his advertising expense. It would probably increase dealers' profits sevenfold by reducing expense per unit. Probably the dealers would begin to lower prices, thereby further stimulating sales. Larger volume would very likely lead to still lower production costs, and the cycle of expansion typical of most manufactured consumer goods would be under way.[2]

The foregoing example may be presented in tabular form as shown in Table 6.

TABLE 6. Effect of Advertising on Profits

	Before Cost Reduction	After Cost Reduction and Expenditure of $1,000 for Advertising
Manufacturer:		
Units sold	10,000	20,000
Total sales	$ 6,000	$12,000
Cost of production	5,000	9,000
Advertising expense		1,000
Net profit	$ 1,000	$ 2,000
Retailer:		
Units sold	10,000	20,000
Total sales	$10,000	$20,000
Cost of goods sold	6,000	12,000
Gross margin	$ 4,000	$ 8,000
Expenses (estimated):		
Fixed or overhead $2,500		$2,500
Variable or selling 1,000		2,000
Total	3,500	4,500
Net profit	$ 500	$ 3,500

[2] See: Samuel Berke, *Break-Even Point Studies for Small Marketers,* Small Marketers Aids No. 50 (Washington, D. C.: Small Business Administration, November 1959).

Another situation likely to be present for the small factory is direct sale to consumer or user. The principal difference in this case is the ability of the manufacturer or service operator to set the final price. Otherwise, the following three factors are important in determining price and promotion policies, whether distribution is through dealers or direct to consumers, namely: elasticity of demand, expansibility, and distribution costs. Elasticity of demand refers to the change in dollar value of sales that accompanies price changes. If a lower price alone increases total revenue, demand is elastic; if it decreases total revenue (even though the number of units sold increases), it is inelastic; if price changes do not change total revenue, the elasticity is unitary. Different products and services vary greatly in the amount advertising increases sales. This property is known as expansibility or advertisability. An article that sells only slightly better when well advertised has a low coefficient of expansibility; one that sells much better has a high coefficient. The latter is often called a "natural" for advertising. In most cases both price reductions and advertising will be used simultaneously but in amounts proportionate to the product's relative elasticity and expansibility.

Distribution cost is more complicated than either elasticity or expansibility alone. One of three situations is likely to prevail. First, distribution costs per unit sold may remain constant within fairly wide ranges of amounts. This was illustrated in our first example, in which marketing costs remained at $0.40 per unit when both factory and retail prices were reduced and the quantity sold increased. Such a condition is probably characteristic of most situations. Second, distribution often takes place under conditions of increasing unit costs. This is especially true after a certain volume point is passed. It explains why department store expenses usually become a larger percentage of sales as volume increases and also why selling costs to final consumers remain fairly constant while production costs are decreased.

A small manufacturer may sell his initial production at a profitable price to local customers with relatively little expense. If he seeks to expand his market, all distribution costs tend to rise until it reaches a volume sufficient to justify mass distribution methods, especially extensive advertising. This was illustrated in our second example, in which advertising by the manufacturer helped to reduce the retailer's total expense from 35 per cent to $22\frac{1}{2}$ per cent of sales of the advertised article.

The third situation is that in which distribution operates under conditions of decreasing unit costs. This occurs less often than might be expected. The best example is a staple product that can be sold and distributed to one or a few buyers in ever increasing quantities. The belief that such a concentration of buyers is a dangerous marketing policy to follow, plus the fact that such situations occur very infrequently, has made this type of cost condition relatively unimportant. However, opportunities in this direction should be cultivated. Small business, as the characteristic present-day pioneer in other fields, might experiment and find a solution to this extremely important problem.

A firm's price policy under direct marketing conditions will be strongly influenced by the representative situations just discussed. With constant costs, a policy of lowering prices requires a fairly high degree of elasticity of demand. With constant or only slightly increasing costs, sales promotion should be used with greater vigor in proportion to the expansibility of demand. For example, imagine two products, A and B, each selling for $1.00 per unit above production costs and having a constant total distribution cost of $0.90 per unit. Assume that 10,000 units are being sold; A has a very slightly elastic demand where B is highly elastic. Experiments with different prices might yield results as follows:

Price		A	B
$1.00	Number of units sold	10,000	10,000
	Total sales	$10,000	$10,000
	Total expenses	9,000	9,000
	Net profit	$ 1,000	$ 1,000
$0.97	Number of units sold	11,000	20,000
	Total sales	$10,670	$19,400
	Total expenses	9,900	18,000
	Net profit	$ 770	$ 1,400

Under the conditions assumed, it would be profitable to increase sales by lowering price for product B but not for A. If A has a high expansibility the procedure indicated for it would be to use extensive advertising while keeping the price constant.

When both production and distribution take place on a decreasing cost basis, an ideal combination of conditions exists for the small business that plans on expanding rapidly. In the short run, when distribution operates on a decreasing cost basis, the small businessman may well lower his price and push sales promotion to the maximum limit of his capacity to produce. His attention in this case should be directed primarily toward reducing production costs and expanding facilities, and next toward devising plans to continue this most fortunate condition.

Turnover will receive more particular attention later in discussions relating to each major field. What should be re-emphasized at this point is that turnover is merely one of the factors that can lead to an increase in profit. Its importance varies by type of business and by commodities handled, as well as by the most important consideration of how an increase in it is achieved and at what cost.

Today pricing is closely related to certain Federal and state laws, to social control within most business fields, and to custom. Each of these will be considered in their applications to the three major fields of small business.

Price is one of five or six devices so often used in various combinations by businessmen to expand their market that these relationships should be understood. These major marketing instruments are: price, advertising, personal selling, availability, the product itself, and the package or container if one is used. The result—greater volume—may be achieved by varying the combination of these marketing factors to meet different situations, but careful study and forecasting must be done. The foremost factor is pricing, and it should always be considered as a means of expanding sales.

PRICING IN MERCHANDISING

Merchants handle a wide variety of goods under varying conditions of location, clientele, competition, and operating expenses. Legal regulation of some retail pricing, first appearing in the middle 1930's, often affects individual prices that may be charged. Fair Trade, or resale price maintenance, laws exist in nearly every state. These permit the maker of a branded or identifiable article sold in commerce to enter into agreements with dealers governing the price at which it can be resold. One resale price agreement may apply to all dealers in the state. Some states have anti-loss leader laws intended to prevent selling at a price lower than landed cost plus six per cent.

Next to legal limitations on pricing, certain store policies are of greatest importance. Among these are policies regarding the store's reputation, clientele desired, competitors, and market strategy. Most independent retailers try to sell at current market prices, recognizing differences in services, location, and quality of goods handled. For staple merchandise this is probably the best policy. Retailers handling luxury or specialty items with no direct local competition often sell at "market plus" or "class" price. Many small retailers attempt to sell at less than current market prices, but few if any succeed with this policy. Whenever the local situation permits, it is better for the small retailer to select merchandise lines that can be priced to avoid direct competition.

Retail pricing is complicated by several factors. An important one is the fact that the cost of handling each item, out of thousands carried, cannot be determined with sufficient accuracy and speed to be valuable. Demand and competitors' prices therefore become dominant factors.

For pricing purposes most merchandise can be divided into seven major classes: Fair Trade items, items with prices suggested by the manufacturer or nationally advertised, staple convenience goods, shopping goods, fashion and seasonal merchandise, novelties or specialties, and leaders. Correct pricing will be somewhat different for each class. Pricing of items under Fair Trade laws is done for the retailer by the manufacturer, usually through the local wholesale distributor. Each item has either a fixed price or a minimum price that usually becomes the market price whenever competition is active.

When vendors suggest retail prices or quote prices in national advertising, small retailers usually conform to them unless the store policy is to cut prices. For staple convenience goods, which are fairly well standardized items available in a large number of stores, either customary prices or the going market price is used. These are usually the lowest prices at which such merchandise can be handled profitably. A serious danger in cutting prices on such items is that all competitors will quickly reduce their prices and no permanent increase in volume or traffic will result.

Shopping goods are unstandardized items that change frequently in both quality and style. Before retailers adopted price lining, prices changed frequently. Customers formerly compared the offerings of two or three stores before purchasing goods in this class, although this practice has been declining for several decades. Retail districts vary in the extent to which customers actually shop, and each merchant should understand his trading area. Some branded lines of shopping goods, especially in the wearing apparel fields, are sold through exclusive or selected agency agreements according to which prices are set or suggested by vendors. In most cases, however, the retailer has a certain amount of freedom in setting prices. It is here that price lining, or the reverse demand curve, and elasticity of demand are especially important to the individual merchant.

Before 1920, merchants often carried a bewildering array of prices and brands with little analysis of the rate at which each sold. Since Filene popularized price lining in his book, *The Model Stock Plan*,[3] extensive studies have proved that customers of any store handling shopping goods prefer a small number of prices within each merchandise classification. Often 65 to 85 per cent of all purchases will be made at three prices even if six, ten, or more prices are offered. This is the reverse demand curve in action. Since food is not usually considered a shopping good subject to price lining, the following quotation was selected to show both the basic nature and widespread application of this concept:

Briefly, price-lining is nothing more than having quality merchandise at prices customers want to pay. Experience shows that when a grocer carries 7 to 9 different lines of the same quality item with prices ranging from 15 cents to 27 cents, the bulk of his sales will be concentrated in 2 or 3 prices. Knowing the prices that sell, the grocer can deduct his margin and know what prices he can pay for such items.

Along with price lining, the grocer must consider brand lining, in order that both price and brand desired be available. This is especially true in grocery items where the price differential is negligible. It was found in one store where the retailer stocked a complete variety of canned milk, by brand, that the sales broke down in the following manner:

[3] Edward A. Filene, *The Model Stock Plan* (New York: McGraw-Hill Book Company, Inc., 1930).

Brand	Percentage of Total Sales	Amount of Display Space (Per Cent)
A	34	20
B	30	20
C	17	20
D	9	10
E	4	10
F	3	7
G	2	7
H	1	6

Obviously, by cutting down the number of brands and utilizing total available display space in a manner best suited for merchandising properly those brands which consumers desired, total sales were increased, faster turnover was achieved, and higher profits resulted. There was no noticeable consumer dissatisfaction over the elimination of slow sellers.

The most effective way of breaking down consumer indifference is by offering reasonable values on merchandise she needs daily. If the housewife can walk into a clean, friendly store and find bright, fresh displays of items she needs—at the right price and in the brand she likes—that is the store that will get her business.[4]

Although most fashion goods and seasonal items are subject to price lining, they show the additional influence of the time factor in relation to pricing. Store policy will determine whether fashion merchandise is first offered at the very beginning of the season or somewhat later after the risk element and retail prices have been reduced. Initial fashion offerings should be high enough to allow for greater amount of risks, subsequently larger markdowns as the fashion cycle develops and price becomes competitive.

A store catering to the middle or upper middle class but not to the fashion leaders in a community would price merchandise relatively high early in the season expecting to take markdowns as the fashion cycle progresses and before the more popular-priced stores enter into competition. Initial prices would be somewhat higher than those in volume or "promotional" stores but substantially lower than prices in fashion leadership stores. Markdowns to be considered in the initial price would be normal for fashion (not high fashion) goods and would be similar for different styles, because the fashion acceptance of all styles carried would be assured before this type of store begins promotions. By contrast, the high fashion store will offer many styles that do not receive public acceptance. These may be difficult to sell at any price, often even well below cost. Consequently, the few fashionable lines must bear the loss of less successful numbers. Also, predicting even what percentage of styles offered at the very beginning of the fashion cycle will become fashionable is

[4] *Keeping a Balanced Grocery Inventory,* Small Business Aids No. 330 (Washington, D. C.: U. S. Department of Commerce). Condensed from "Clear Your Decks for Action," *National Grocers Bulletin* (May 1947), The National Association of Retail Grocers of the United States, Inc., Chicago, Ill.

far more difficult than estimating markdowns for the more conservative store.

Two methods are used to arrive at the initial price when retail reductions are a major item. One is the simple, noncompetitive, or approximate method which most small retailers will find adequate. The initial price is the sum of cost of goods plus total expenses, profit desired, markdowns, discounts to employees, and estimated stock shortage. The last three are called "retail reductions." The formula to use for this method is:

$$\text{Initial retail price (\$)} = \text{landed cost of goods} + \text{expenses} + \text{profits} + \text{shortages} + \text{markdowns} + \text{discounts to employees}$$

The second method, markon (sometimes called initial markup) is figured as a percentage of the initial retail price, but markdowns, shortages, employee discounts, expenses, and profits are figured as percentages of net sales. Adjusting for this shift in the basis of percentages, we have the formula:

$$\text{Markon (\%)} = \frac{\text{Expenses} + \text{profits} + \text{markdowns} + \text{shortages} + \text{employee discounts}}{\text{Net sales} + \text{markdowns} + \text{shortages} + \text{employee discounts}}$$

Regardless of which formula is used, the final price set is the nearest or most appropriate price line. For example, if use of either formula gives an initial retail price of $1.66 and the store has price lines for such goods of $0.98, $1.39, and $1.79, the article would probably be priced at $1.79.

Novelties or specialties usually carry a relatively high markup. Also, they may often be selected with price strategy, or dovetailing, in mind. Since novelties are likely to have a short selling season, prices may be high at first but often must be lowered as the novelty demand wears off. As with seasonal or fashion items, drastic markdowns may be needed to close out stocks as the demand drops toward zero. Careful daily watching of prices is important with goods of this type.

Leaders are items priced low enough to attract price-conscious customers and, in addition, for shoppers to buy regular merchandise. Small retailers affiliated with voluntary groups often use leaders furnished by their sponsoring vendors, especially in the grocery and drug fields. In general, the trend has been to use fewer leaders than formerly. Price regulating laws, especially state anti-loss leader or unfair practice laws, restrict their use. Unfair practice laws resemble the anti-loss leader laws discussed previously except that they require a vague "cost of doing business" instead of some small percentage to be added to landed cost in determining retail price. However, economic conditions that make customers extremely price conscious may cause an increase in the importance of the loss leader price policy.

Although the retailer is not ordinarily able to price each item to cover its landed cost, expenses, retail reductions, and a fair margin of profit exactly, he should always consider these factors and aim to average the results of a line or class of goods, or at least a department, to achieve this goal. In the case of unstandardized goods, the small retailer's intimate knowledge of his customers will often enable him to select different styles for two or more retail prices from a lot of goods that all cost the same, or he may find it possible and necessary to sell for the same price lots of goods having different landed costs. These are both cases of averaging to achieve the desired gross margin.[5]

The size of the town in which a store is located often has a bearing on price policies. Contrary to uninformed popular belief, prices on most items sold in retail stores (chain stores included) are lower in larger cities than they are in small towns.

High fashion goods, which are not ordinarily handled by retailers in the smaller towns, are an exception to this generalization. However, merchants in small towns have two serious dangers to contend with that are all too frequently ignored—out-of-town shopping and mail-order competition.

Shopping out of town is a more serious and extensive problem than the vast majority of retailers in small towns of 10,000 or less realize. Numerous important studies have proved this fact, but few of the retailers affected will face the facts. Because the larger-margin, more expensive items are usually purchased out of town, the local merchants lose most of their business on the more profitable items.

PRICING BY WHOLESALERS

Wholesale pricing in many lines is still influenced by the traditional trade discount system, as illustrated by the manufacturer's use of chain discounts from list prices. This practice was originally based on the relatively constant margins required for dealers in each stage of distribution. Thus in the farm equipment line the wholesaler may expect to receive a discount of "less 25 less 20." His price to retail dealers is list price less 25 per cent which is considered adequate to enable retailers to pay all expenses and have a satisfactory margin. When the list price used is actually the retail price at which the article is sold to the consumer, when each discount in the chain represents the gross margin actually needed currently for dealers in the respective stages of distribution (retailer, wholesaler, or broker), and when the discounts are large enough or changed frequently enough to keep them in line with gross margin changes, the chain discount system is usually satisfactory to the dealers. If conditions and prices are subject to great changes, the small wholesaler who has any choice in his pricing will do well to investigate the relative merits of this fairly rigid type of pricing as compared to alternate methods.

In general, wholesale as well as retail prices are based on the markup or gross margin necessary to handle each line of goods profitably. Competition

[5] See: E. L. Anthony, "Pricing and Profits in Small Stores," concerning relationships between price, volume, profit, various price policy considerations. Small Marketers Aids No. 21 (Washington, D. C.: Small Business Administration, 1957).

tends to keep margins small on staples, but larger margins are needed on lines affected by fashion or other influences resulting in large markdowns. Since wholesale prices are much more sensitive than retail or factory prices, they may change frequently in many fields, daily in some.

Sometimes the wholesaler wants to suggest a list or retail price, either at the request of the manufacturer or as management counsel to the retailer. An extreme example of this practice is merchandise sold under Fair Trade agreements. When Fair Trade pricing is used, margins for both wholesaler and retailer are usually adequate. With other goods the wholesaler has the problem of pricing to the retailer in such a way that the latter will have sufficient margin and still be able to keep his prices competitive. This is probably the major pricing problem for most small wholesalers today.

In setting his prices low enough to enable retailers to handle each item profitably, the wholesaler must consider the effects on his margins and business methods. This is one reason for the great interest in cost accounting and expense control among wholesalers in recent years.

Another decision the wholesaler must make is what basis to use for determining the cost of goods. Three methods of arriving at this cost are used: (1) landed cost for each shipment—the "first in, first out" method, (2) last purchase, and (3) replacement cost. Since even small wholesalers purchase in large lots and prices may fluctuate greatly before the wholesaler has sold all of any one shipment, selection of the best methods to arrive at cost is a matter of considerable importance. There is no one best way that would apply to all fields under the various conditions that may exist at a given time.

Even small wholesalers are likely to follow the varying price policy—that is, quoting different prices on the same merchandise to different buyers depending upon bargaining ability, size of order, and similar factors which can be substantiated under the legal requirements. Even under the one-price policy, actual prices may vary according to the services extended, such as credit and delivery. This condition is not so troublesome, because usually a uniform discount schedule can be used or a price schedule prepared for each grouping of services.

Under the varying price policy it is desirable for the wholesaler's salesmen to have maximum and minimum prices for each good and some incentive to sell at or near the maximum price whenever justifiable.

PRICING FOR THE SMALL FACTORY [6]

In manufacturing in general the price of each product is closely related to its cost of production. When only one product is made, unit cost is easily calculated by dividing total expenses plus total costs of materials and parts for a given period by the number of units of products made during the same period. To this must be added distribution or selling costs per unit plus a fair margin

[6] See also: *Pricing Arithmetic for Small Business Managers, op. cit.*

of profit for a minimum price to be determined. Sometimes whether a higher price than the minimum should be charged will be determined by other conditions, such as lack of competition, a demand greater than the company is able at present to supply, or the desire to create a prestige reputation. In setting a price above the calculated minimum there is always the danger of inviting competition. Usually it is better for the small business to figure a fair profit in the minimum calculation and price at that point.

When two or more products are manufactured, cost accounting becomes necessary to arrive at the approximately correct minimum price for each product. Expenses are divided into two groups, fixed or overhead, and variable or direct; the sum of these two is the total unit cost. As volume increases, fixed or overhead expenses remain approximately the same in total amount but decrease per unit. Variable or direct expenses increase in almost direct proportion to increased volume but remain fairly constant per unit of output. Consequently, the cost of production can be decreased, per unit, in proportion to the relative importance of overhead or fixed costs. When additional products of a different nature can absorb some of this overhead, the effect is similar to that of manufacturing one product in greater volume. When certain variable costs, such as that of raw materials, are small or even decrease with increased volume, as they may in the utilization of waste or by-products, actual additional costs of production for the by-product may be relatively very low. Finally, when several products are made in the same factory, the determination of unit costs becomes somewhat arbitrary and standards for pricing should be shifted from so-called "cost of production" to other factors like competition, nature of demand for the product, and company pricing policy.

In pricing to meet competition the first question to decide is what competition the firm plans to meet. This may be viewed in two ways, either as to other manufacturers' products or as to temporary price reductions or cut-price wars. In general, it is inadvisable for the small manufacturer to attempt to meet all such price cuts as special promotions and those resulting from competitors' price wars. Selection of the manufacturers' products for competitive pricing should recognize the extent to which the firm's product differs from those of other companies. If a company has successfully differentiated its product, the pressure to meet direct price competition is greatly reduced. Probably the two best guides are, first, those products that most nearly meet the same need as the company's product and, second, from this group those that are most popular in the marketing area.

Another factor especially important for the small businessman to consider is the way competitors are likely to respond to price changes. If pricing is keenly competitive and price changes take place frequently, it may be risky for the small business to take the lead in offering lower prices. This leads logically to a consideration of the general nature of pricing accepted in the field. At one extreme is a policy of administered prices, by which the leaders set their prices and stay with them for considerable periods of time. At the other extreme is the policy of meeting all price reductions and keeping prices at the lowest possible point. Between these extremes will be found the policies followed by the majority of companies.

Within the more important limits on pricing set by competition the effects of two important factors should be considered: nature of demand for the product and cost of production. Products vary widely in customer response to small changes in price. This property is commonly known as elasticity of demand for the product. The importance of lower price as a method of market expansion naturally varies directly with the degree of elasticity or the price alertness of customers. It is well to remember that price is only one of the six major marketing instruments and should be emphasized only when it is more effective in expanding sales than one or more of the others. Frequently experimentation with customer response to different possible prices may be necessary to determine the relative importance of the price factor. In this experimentation competitors' actions should be noticed and care taken to avoid starting a price war.

Very often some pricing must be done before actual production takes place. This involves the necessity of estimating costs fairly accurately, because the price set will influence volume of sales; this in turn will react upon unit cost of production. Thus it is desirable to determine for each product the break-even point, beyond which further price reductions should not be made under existing conditions. It means that point at which the extra revenue obtained from increased volume just equal additional production plus marketing costs.[7]

Another condition likely to be encountered by the small business is that involving differential pricing, which may be desirable when the company's products are sold through two different types of outlets. For example, a small factory may contract to sell approximately half of its output to one large distributing organization, such as a mail-order house, chain store, or department store. Since these large firms perform the wholesaling functions and selling to them usually involves a low selling cost per unit of product, a low price can be quoted on this part of the plant's output. Pricing the rest of the product will follow the principles already discussed, except that in calculating costs of production allowance must be made for the fact that a large share of indirect or overhead expenses has already been absorbed by the sale of the large order. It is considered a violation of the Robinson-Patman Act to price the product to the large buyer so low that it does not include a proportionate share of overhead costs. A second consideration in such cases will be the effect of this dual distribution on the price necessary to induce individual dealers to handle the product. For the small manufacturer this may not be

---

[7] For further study see: *Figuring and Using Break-Even Points,* Management Aids for Small Business No. 37 (Washington, D. C.: Small Business Administration, October 1953). Also see: Frederick G. Disney, *Are You Kidding Yourself About Your Profits?* Small Marketers Aids No. 25 (Washington, D. C.: Small Business Administration, July 1957).

serious because the large distributor will probably resell the product under its own private brand name. It is only when the product is offered by the large distributor in easily identifiable form and in direct competition with individual outlets that pricing to the latter becomes a serious problem.

Another consideration in pricing by the manufacturer relates to the use of list prices from which discounts are granted, as compared to quoting direct net prices each time a sale is under consideration. The use of list prices has at least three advantages: (1) it suggests the retail price to the dealer; (2) it is often useful to the dealer in selling to the final consumer; and (3) it permits more flexibility in making price changes and quoting different prices to different buyers. A closely related question is the extent to which individual salesmen are to be given authority to determine prices at which the company's product will be sold. This is mainly a matter of price and organization policy. The company price policy should further provide for any recurring decisions not already discussed in this section.

In 1958, fictitious list pricing became so serious that the Federal Trade Commission required compliance to the nine-point guide published by the FTC. For example, the FTC discovered that one manufacturer provided dealers with a choice of several price tags for the same product so that they could tailor their discount policies to the local competition.[8]

A small dress manufacturer, located away from a market center, sets his prices as follows: A card file contains the cost of materials and labor for each garment, and to this is added a 40 per cent markup as well as 10 per cent for selling costs and .093 per cent overhead.[9]

Small factories, located in market centers for their type of product, often find it desirable to use wholesale price lines. When the goods produced are sold through retail stores that use price lines, as is the case with many articles of popular women's wear, this method of pricing is used. Wholesale price lining is also desirable when the products are sold through fixed price or even price concerns like variety stores. In either case the manufacturer has his prices determined for him, within narrow limits, and his problem is the profitable manufacture of goods to sell at these price lines.

Pricing by the Service Business

The variety of businesses classified as services is enormous and pricing will be quite different in some fields from what it is in others. In professional and many semiprofessional lines like insurance, real estate, and advertising agencies, prices are usually based on a customary fee or percentage of the value of the transaction handled. Splitting commissions with clients and

---

[8] See also: *FTC and Guides Against Deceptive Pricing,* Small Marketers Aids No. 42 (Washington, D. C.: Small Business Administration, April 1959).

[9] "Manufacturers Pricing Practice Under Attack," *Dun's Review and Modern Industry* (April 1959), p. 75

similar price-cutting tactics should not ordinarily be considerered in these fields. It is always unethical and frequently contrary to law.

Another broad class of services may be represented by personal service establishments like beauty parlors and barber shops, and common repair or reconditioning plants like appliance repair shops, laundries, and dry cleaning plants. In most communities there will be several establishments of each kind with currently accepted prices for the basic or more standardized services.[10] Pricing in these fields is usually based on a fairly stable price for a few of these services in each kind of business. For example, in dry cleaning plants a lady's plain dress and a man's three-piece business suit are commonly used. Appliance and other repair services may take the typical cleaning and tuning-up job for a popular model of car, refrigerator, or radio, as the case may be, for the basic price. In barber shops a haircut is the same price whether it is an easy or complicated job. From these basic service prices a price schedule should be set up for other important and fairly standard services. Special jobs are frequently priced at some standard rate according to the amount of labor required. In all cases adequate allowance must be made for wide variations in the amount of materials and supplies needed.

Many small repair shops in the automobile, radio, appliance, and similar fields find that customers like flat rate pricing. It can be used on 80 to 90 per cent of the jobs that come to the average shop. Company agencies will ordinarily use the list prices suggested by the manufacturers they represent. Others may use published lists or subscribe to a price reporting service like those used by plumbing and heating contractors. When published lists are used, an average wage rate is the basis. Flat rate prices are calculated by applying to the average hourly wage rate some multiplier, such as two or two and a half, for overhead and expenses other than direct labor.

The tendency with many small operators is to use hourly rates that are too low. For example, a list may give the standard time for a particular job as four and a half hours, the multiplier as two, and the average hourly rate as two dollars. Thus the standard flat rate price would be eighteen dollars plus cost of materials used. A small operator may figure his price as follows: $4\frac{1}{2} \times 2 \times \$1.50$ (his hourly rate in dollars) = a flat price of \$13.50. If his labor at \$1.50 per hour is fully as efficient as the average \$2.00 per hour worker, he will be in the clear. However, the standard time is usually based on efficient labor skilled in the particular kind of work being priced.

One illustration of relating price to cost is the two-price system used by some dry cleaners. Under this plan, price is based on the cost of labor and materials used rather than on the value of material worked on. For example, cleaning a pair of \$10 drapes with hooks would cost more than a \$20 pair without hooks, and a man's suit that was badly stained would cost more than a similar suit requiring a minimum amount of labor and materials.

[10] In some states minimum prices that may legally be charged for many kinds of personal services are set by state boards.

Although prices should be set high enough to cover processing and marketing costs, the relationship is not so simple as total cost plus a fair profit. In fact it is more likely in these fields for the small operator to accept prevailing prices and try to keep his costs low enough to make a profit since custom and competition tend to set the basic price. To attempt to cut prices for service of comparable quality may result in a price war which would place the small operator at a distinct disadvantage.

Even when the small businessman would be able to sell at reduced prices, it is not certain that it would be desirable to do so. Assuming that competition merely meets his prices, the lower level may or may not increase total use enough to make it profitable. It is usually better for the small business to stress quality of service, being careful to maintain an above-average quality at all times. The personalization of services and of conveniences to the patrons —such as quicker delivery, friendly advice regarding services, and special inducement on less frequently used or unused new variations of services— should be capitalized and featured as a reason for patronage. Although prices for services of the type under discussion here tend to be customary and competitive in each town, they vary considerably in different towns and parts of the country due to labor costs and general level of incomes of each area. Also, the volume of business and relative efficiency of management will cause costs to vary considerably among different concerns even in the same town and kind of business.

The remaining group of service industries are those in which direct quality competition is absent. The important factors to consider in setting prices are: the willingness and ability of customers to pay; the extent to which users are unable to judge the quality of the service directly and consequently tend to use price as a guide to quality or desirability; nature of the service itself; whether larger volume lowers unit cost or does not affect it; whether expansion is definitely limited by the time of key men; and the danger of inviting competition to enter the area. Most of these are self-explanatory. In general, prices for services of this type will tend to be high—well above nominal "costs of production"—but tempered by opportunities to expand at decreasing costs or by the threat of competition.

For the service field as a whole, costs tend to be less powerful in determining price than in either merchandising or manufacturing. If costs are near the prices that can be successfully charged, they must be reduced to meet customary or competitive prices. In all cases the quality of services is of prime importance and should not be so competitively reduced as to jeopardize the future of the business from an operating-costs standpoint.

CONCLUSIONS

Inasmuch as modern business operates through a price structure or system, correct pricing is of great importance in the success of a concern remaining in business or maximizing profits. Price is one of a few major marketing instruments commonly used by most firms to expand their markets or volume; its importance relative to the others varies widely under different circumstances. At one extreme lower prices may result in no appreciable increase in sales or may even cause sales to decline. At the other extreme even small decreases in price result in large increases in sales. However, even in this case it is not always wise for the small business to take the lead in cutting prices. At least two additional factors must be considered: total unit costs at the new price and probable action of competitors. *Pricing for profit is important but not simple.*

Many factors in addition to costs and competition need to be considered in successful pricing. Two important factors are company policy regarding the reputation and class of trade desired and the customers' attitude toward price. In a surprisingly large number of cases customers—especially household consumers—tend to judge quality primarily by price. When quality determination or comparison is difficult or troublesome, as it is for some consumer goods and many services, this situation is likely to be present.

For the manufacturer who distributes his products through dealers the additional factor of marketing costs is often important in correct pricing. Sometimes a policy of maintaining prices at the factory and putting any available funds into increasing sales promotional efforts, improving packaging, or restyling the produce is much more desirable than lowering prices to dealers.

In general, price is the most dangerous of the major marketing instruments for the small businessman to use aggressively. This should not discourage carefully directed experimentation in pricing, but it should emphasize the need for careful study and understanding before changing prices or price policies.

QUESTIONS AND PROBLEMS

1. Describe the usual relationships between price, turnover, and profit. Why are these relationships not always reliable as a guide to pricing? Discuss.

2. Explain and illustrate how the nature of marketing costs affects a manufacturer's pricing for profit.

3. Name the major marketing instruments and briefly explain each.

4. Explain, or define, each of the following and describe how it affects a firm's pricing: (a) elasticity of demand, (b) expansibility of demand, (c) price-lining, (d) customer acceptance curve, (e) markdowns.

5. Describe the two methods of calculating initial retail prices when markdowns are important and discuss the significant aspects of each.

6. Is the popular belief that prices are lower in small towns than in large cities true? Explain.

7. Why do merchants, but not manufacturers or service establishments, consider markdowns in setting their prices? State any qualifications.

8. What are the advantages and dangers to the small businessman of experimenting with his prices? Are these the same for each main field? Explain.

9. For each main field compare the discussion of price policies in Chapter 8 with the corresponding discussion of pricing contained in this chapter and explain why certain topics considered in this chapter were not discussed in Chapter 8.

10. Which is more likely to lead to business failure, selling at too high or too low a price? Discuss.

11. How important is forecasting the trend of future prices as an aid in correct pricing by the small businessman? Explain and illustrate.

12. Name as many products and services as you can think of in regard to which consumers rely chiefly on price as a guide to quality. Suggest probable reasons in each case.

13. Is the business selling at a "class" price (well above total costs or intrinsic value) or one selling at market price on firmer ground? Explain and support your conclusion.

14. What attitudes among businessmen are likely to influence pricing by the small businessman? Discuss.

15. Describe the conditions under which it might be advisable for a small business to initiate price cutting.

16. Give several examples of the pricing tactic of "dovetailing" in a competitive market.

17. How do the most important factors in pricing differ for each of our three main fields, merchandising, manufacturing, and service? How do you explain these differences?

18. If you were starting an entirely new kind of business, explain how you would endeavor to determine the most profitable prices to charge.

19. Examine the prices in several stores from the viewpoint of price lining. If you find examples of more than four price lines, find out the proportionate sales of each.

20. In Bill's store dresses are keenly competitive. Prices featured are: $4.79, $7.49, $9.95, $14.75, and $19.75. The dress department data are: expenses, 30 per cent; profit, 6 per cent; and retail reductions, 12 per cent. Landed cost of two dozen dresses just received is $120. At what initial retail prices should they be offered? Explain.

CASE PROBLEM

A small artificial flower shop makes a high-grade, realistic product and has acquired a good reputation for orchids and gardenias. The flowers have often been mistaken for live ones, even by florists. With reasonable care they will last indefinitely. The shop is small but is in the process of expanding. It is owned by the lady who originated the process and her partner, a young college graduate with about five years of successful business experience. Four girls, who are artistically talented, make the flowers by hand. However, there is a possibility of subdividing operations somewhat along the usual factory assembly line principle.

The principal raw material is obtained from Japan through an importer. Other materials and supplies are purchased from American manufacturers and wholesalers. At present the average total cost per orchid of materials and supplies is about $0.90, direct labor $1.00, and overhead $0.20, making an average total cost per orchid of $2.10. All sales are made direct to consumers with no advertising or selling expense. At the current price of ten dollars each the firm is behind on filling orders actually on hand. With the new organization of production it will just about be able to supply present demand, and production costs will probably be lowered to about $1.80 per unit. Further cost reductions are possible with increased volume, although it is doubtful if real mass production would ever be possible.

The buyer for a large group of department stores has offered to take the entire output of the plant or any part of it up to an expanded output of twenty times its present capacity on a five-year contract basis at a factory price of $2.30 per unit, all packing and delivery expense to be paid by the buyers. He contemplates that the individual department stores would sell the orchids at prices between $3.75 and $5.00. If his offer is accepted, output would have to be increased fourfold and he would prefer an increase of from ten to twenty times present capacity. At such a volume unit production costs could probably be reduced to about $1.60.

The owners believe that most of the department stores would find a better market for the orchids at prices of $7.50 or $10.00 each, or even more, than at prices under $5.00. This belief is based on previous experience with department store selling. There is also some question as to the effect upon their mail-order sales to consumers at $10.00 if department stores were to offer the same flower at prices under $5.00. A buyer from California suggested that the price be raised to $15.00.

There are no serious questions concerning financing expansion or securing raw materials and an adequate supply of workers who could be trained to turn out a quality product. The only questions are those relating to pricing and price policies with reference to the future and profits of the business.

Analyze this problem carefully and decide what you think the management should do. If you decide they should sell to the department store group, at what price should the orchids be sold? Should a minimum resale price be part of the contract? Why or why not? Justify all your decisions.

21 • Expense Control

Whatever measure must be employed in the determination of whether or not a business is successful, the degree to which it makes a profit is usually the final criterion; that is, the degree to which it continues to serve its customers so satisfactorily that they continue to support it as an enterprise. Profit may be described as that which is left over for the businessman after the goods are paid for and the bills are met.

Until the 1920's, emphasis on expense control was largely directed at efficiency in production, the manufacturing of the highest quality product at the lowest possible cost per unit being the common business goal. In more recent years the spotlight of attention (with reference to expenses) has been placed on office operations, on warehousing, and more and more on the various marketing aspects of business operation—all of the costs of *moving* goods. It is contended by most business authorities that during the next decade the greater opportunities for the reduction of expenses, and thus for the increase of profits, lie in this realm.

For the small business, expenses are of two broad types: actual and imputed. Examples of actual expenses are payments made for utility services, labor, interest on loans, and, if the building is not owned by the proprietor, rent. Imputed expenses are those that would be charged for property or services of the proprietor if secured from someone else; they include interest on the proprietor's own capital invested in the business, rent for the premises he owns that are used for business purposes, and a fair salary for his own services as manager of the business.

Many small businessmen fail to appreciate the importance of the difference between gross margin and net profit. The common practice of referring to the former as "gross profit" is in part responsible for this careless attitude. In addition, failure to keep adequate records showing *all* expenses that must be deducted from gross margin to ascertain net profit has caused much vague and, perhaps, falsely optimistic thinking on this subject. With a margin of 30

442

per cent, too many operators think of their net profit as being almost that much, after allowing for a few of the more obvious expenses such as rent, utilities, and so forth. In manufacturing, a common weakness is to focus attention on the cost of raw materials and the expense of direct labor without giving much thought to other expenses.

The profit and loss statement is the basic accounting record that brings sales, material costs, expenses, and profit (or loss) into their logical relationships, usually, and should be familiar to every entrepreneur. Modern management requires adequate records, and the profit and loss statement and balance sheet are basic to all records. Both must be analyzed and used for management decisions as well as for purposes of taxation.[1]

The following approach to expense control seems to the authors to be a logical one: The owner of the business, in order to operate it once it is established, must have, as items or "tools" with which to work, a building, equipment, cash funds, materials or merchandise, personnel, and potential customers. The effectiveness with which he utilizes each of these, singly or in combination, determines his profit or loss and, therefore, his business success or failure. Over the years experience has shown that the importance of each of these is measurable in terms of what it produces, to be sure, but its value to the organization may also be measured in terms of the costs of its use. Thus effectiveness of use means profitableness of use. After a business has been in existence for a reasonable length of time, these costs, if the business is successful, tend to become rather fixed portions or percentages of the expenses of the business, and in many industries desirable ratios (the percentages that these things have come to cost in representative successful firms) are well established. There is, therefore, a minimum percentage that each can cost and still provide proper service, and a maximum that each can cost before it reduces or prevents profit. While this is merely an explanation of "standard ratios," it seeks to emphasize the premium placed on the effective use of tools, and the need for expense records to check one's effectiveness against these norms.

Expense Budget[2]

An expense budget is a control device used by management to predetermine what each major class of expenses should be for the period of time covered, and to aid executives in conducting the business in line with these expenses as planned. It is a valuable management aid.

In modern business, control is always exercised in relation to some goal. There must be a desired objective, certain standards set or predetermined,

[1] A good primer on cost control is Glenn A. Welsh, "Cost Control Pointers for Small Marketers," Small Marketers Aids No. 34 (Washington, D. C.: Small Business Administration, July 1958).

[2] A useful article on starting budgeting in a small company is "Budgeting for Small Business," by I. W. Keller, from *The Journal of Accounting* (January 1959), pp. 44-49.

current reports or records for comparison with these standards, and prompt executive action to keep in line with planned figures. This applies to every division of the business, including sales, production, raw materials or merchandise purchases, personnel, and financing; but our attention here will be confined to business expenses. To repeat for emphasis, control requires: predetermined standards, current comparable reports, and prompt, intelligent executive action.

As applied to the expense budget, the objective may be to achieve a certain volume of business at minimum cost or to expand volume rapidly even though the cost of doing so will be high temporarily. In either case standards will be set in terms of anticipated expenses appropriate to the objective planned; operating reports that show at frequent intervals what expenses have been actually incurred will permit comparison with planned figures. Appropriate action taken in time will prevent an unsatisfactory condition from continuing. In some cases it is possible to require authorization before certain expenses are incurred and thus to increase the degree of expense control exercised. One example is to require prior authorization before a department head can add an additional employee.

An expense budget is a "must" for every business. One author says: "Few, if any, techniques are more vital to the sound management of a manufacturing enterprise than budgeting. But many smaller companies unwisely neglect or ignore this simple, effective tool. Yet, smaller companies have a great need for it because of a pressing need for proper utilization of working capital, and for the development of sound plans for meeting future competition and for expanding." [3] In launching a new enterprise, it is the basis for deciding whether the venture should be undertaken, or for satisfying the banker that the enterpriser has a good proposition for a loan. To the established business it means the difference between success and failure. It should be made in terms of an accepted expense classification for the particular business field and in line with available data from other successful firms. If a businessman aspires to higher goals, he should provide for improving on industry standards by reducing his expense percentages through better management.

1. Budgetary control allocates responsibility. It forces the small businessman to define areas of responsibility.

2. Budgeting makes for co-ordination and teamwork of those concerned with the process. Affected personnel should be consulted in order that the budget be truly effective.

3. Judgments and opinions of management are crystallized through budgeting and through the formulation of such a plan of action.

4. An advance study of all essential needs for equipment, materials, and manpower is required for budgeting and for adequate financing plans.

[3] Howard Ellsworth Sommer, *Budgeting in the Small Plant,* Management Aids for Small Business No. 23 (Washington, D. C.: Small Business Administration, October 1953).

5. A budget sets a target which if attained should result in improved operations and financial position.

The term "control" means something affording a standard of comparison, a means of verification, or a check. In small business management, control can be illustrated by these three situations:

1. A sales manager dictates a letter acknowledging receipt of an order and promising shipment before a certain date. He then asks his secretary to send a copy of that letter to the shipping room with a note: "Please date and return to me when order goes out." That's a control system.

2. A plant superintendent knows that to meet production requirements, he needs a reserve supply of about 100 small metal castings which go into his product. He buys in lots of 500 whenever his stock drops to 100. To relieve himself of this detail he has the storage bin divided into a small section which holds just 100 units, and a big section which will take up to 500. Then he assigns the job of keeping tabs on the castings to a stock clerk. . . . That's a control system, too.

3. A new president takes charge of a small company which produces four separate product lines. The president divides the company into semiautonomous divisions, each one charged with a specific share of the total invested capital. A system of internal records and reports is set up . . . [another "control"].

In devising effective controls in your small business, you must cope with two basic problems. First, to be of practical value, your system cannot be very costly because a small company cannot afford to be burdened with excessive personnel and overhead charges. This means that your control system should be simple and sparing of manpower.

Second, you must face the fact that almost everybody not only resents the idea of being controlled but also objects to being judged. More often than not the targets of a control system regard the devices as personal report cards. According to studies made by the Controllers Institute, standards and budgets can be highly unpopular. . . . Those points are clear evidence that your control system should be simple, inexpensive and installed with patience and tact so as to be accepted by those who will operate under it. Otherwise, it may not have much success.[4]

Expense Classification

If a firm is well established, the standard expense classification accepted for that particular line of business should be set up in the firm's accounting records. Usually, for the very small establishment, a simple breakdown of

[4] Edward L. Anthony, Chief, Management Methods Division, Small Business Administration, Washington, D. C., "Effective Control for Better Management." Originally published as Management Aids for Small Manufacturers No. 79.

expenses into a few major divisions is suggested, with progressively detailed subdivisions recommended as the size or volume of the business increases. In so doing one will inherit the benefit of previous experience in the field. He will also be able to use current operating ratios and expense data published by the trade association, the Department of Commerce, Dun & Bradstreet, and other reporting agencies as a continuing guide to the success of his operations. If he selects his own expense accounts, definitions, or classifications, he will have no assurance that they are comparable to published data. For example, does the expense for advertising include only payment to newspapers and other media, or also payroll, "donations," and other such items? Are the same items included in the delivery, credit, or other expenses for customer services that other businessmen in the field include? Discrepancies in expense classifications such as the few suggested here will render comparison with average data for the field worthless.

With an accurate, complete record of the expense items which make up the totals in standard expense accounts, an operator can immediately tell whether one item that is too high can be cut down in future operations. Suppose one of the accounts is lower than standard. Ordinarily he would experience a certain amount of satisfaction over this, but he should examine it anyway. Perhaps something is wrong. If this was his advertising account, he might have brought in a larger sales volume and a correspondingly higher profit if he had spent more for advertising. In studying expense control it is well to know how much can wisely be spent to increase profitable sales volume and where adjustments, up or down, can be made to increase net profit in the long run.

There are two major classes of expenditures in operating expense: fixed (such as licenses, franchises, taxes, and usually rent) and variable (such as payroll, utilities, supplies, and advertising).

Fixed expenses are those that cannot be changed a great deal, although, of course, minor reductions can usually be made. These expenses often represent only a small part of the total operating expense.

Most of the important expense items are variable expenses, which are those which change as volume changes—or, in other words, are dependent on volume. Even rent, for example, may be reduced in a number of ways as previously stated by discussion with the landlord, or by subleasing a part of the premises. Sales volume may be too low for the amount of space or the location occupied. If this be the case, sales may be increased by more aggressive promotion.

The cost of utilities can be reduced by turning out unneeded lights in storerooms, by a periodic check of heating equipment and making any possible changes that would result in a lower fuel cost over a period of years. It might be more profitable over a long period of time to substitute a new, more economical heating plant.

Salaries and wages may be reduced by employing fewer workers, or they may be reduced as a portion of total expenses by increasing productivity per worker.

Advertising expense can be reduced in proportion to sales by making the advertising result in more business. This can be done by carefully selecting one's message so that it will appeal most strongly to those you wish it to reach, and also by carefully selecting the media to reach these people so that you receive the largest possible exposure per dollar expended.

Bad debts can be reduced by keeping accurate, up-to-date records on all charge sales and following them up immediately when they become delinquent. Credit applicants should be interviewed and their past credit records should be checked. The terms to be granted should be carefully explained to the customer to prevent any misunderstanding.

Delivery costs can be reduced by a periodic inspection of delivery equipment. An inexpensive grease job on the pickup truck could very well save the much greater repair cost of having a universal joint replaced. Sometimes savings can be made on delivery costs by hiring delivery services instead of maintaining company equipment.

Miscellaneous expenses, which are all expenditures that cannot be classified under any of the other expense accounts, can often be cut down to some extent.

Methods Studies

Methods studies are careful analyses of the way some activities are being performed, usually for the purpose of reducing the expense involved or making other improvements in the way the work is done. For repetitive operations that take a short time to perform, time studies may be used to assist the analyst in selecting more efficient methods. For most situations in the small business, however, critical observation and good judgment in making changes will usually be sufficient.

To repeat, expense control means *control;* if any item is too expensive, something should be done about it. This is the primary purpose of methods studies.

If a retailer cannot make a profit selling cereals with clerk service, he should put them on a self-service basis. If a product costs too much to manufacture, production expenses must be reduced or the business turned over to competitors. If a store is unable to operate a needed millinery department at a profit, it can lease it to one of the millinery syndicates.

To illustrate applications of the fundamentals of expense control further we shall now examine the major fields of small business. It must be remembered that within each major field there will be variations in application, different standard methods of expense classification, and similar adaptations to be made for each particular line of business.

EXPENSE CONTROL IN MERCHANDISING[5]

To the retailer certain items of expense are of major importance. They are: labor, rent, advertising, and those items relating to inventory or investment in merchandise. In some lines customer services also account for large expenditures. Store policies regarding the class of customers desired and services to be rendered may affect expenses greatly.

A merchant can keep his payroll under control by employing the amount and kind of help needed. More use should be made of part-time employees such as former employees who resigned to get married, who would be willing to work occasionally when needed but who would not accept regular employment. Although the small retailer is not usually able to employ workers specially trained and skilled for each kind of task to be performed, he can try to secure more reliable and better qualified employees than those frequently hired. To do so will involve paying higher wages but may actually reduce labor costs because of the greater productivity secured. Once qualified workers are employed, it is a good policy to assign duties to each worker to take full advantage of special skills and abilities. Proper supervision and use of the other techniques of good labor management will help to keep this largest item of expense under control.

In some cases retailers can reduce expenses by employing outside agencies to do work that would not justify investment in equipment and payroll. For example, deliveries can be made through a mutual or consolidated delivery system. For infrequent small deliveries Western Union messengers may be used. Sometimes delivery trucks may be rented, maintenance and depreciation costs being borne by the renting firm. Purchasing such services as bookkeeping or window display may be good business when they are performed by experts for a modest charge.

Store policy determines how rent, which is usually the second largest item of expense, can be controlled. Continuously adjusting policies to capitalize fully on all changes in the characteristics of the store's location will help to keep this expense in line.

Studying location trends in the region closely and planning future adjustments to them will provide for the long-run needs of the business. Usually a fundamental decision is involved, whether to remain on a particular site and adjust to changes in shopping traffic or to keep changing sites to follow the original class of customer.

Advertising is an example of an expense that can often be controlled more effectively by increasing than by decreasing the amount spent. A merchant whose advertising expense ratio is below the standard could probably increase his sales and profits by spending more money for effective advertising.

[5] See, for example, "Departmental Merchandising Results in Small Department Stores, 1956-1958," by Edgar H. Gault, *Michigan Business Reports*, No. 30 (1959).

Electricity is an item in regard to which expense reduction may be accompanied by better service. Frequent cleaning of all light fixtures and replacement of bulbs when necessary should be standard practice. Walls and ceilings should be painted white or a very light color and kept clean if maximum returns are to be secured from the lighting bill. In the use of electrically operated equipment, such as refrigerators, deep-freeze units, or fans, conservation should be studied and practiced. Frequent inspection to keep motors at peak efficiency may be needed.

Other opportunities for economy can be found in the use of supplies, as well as in most divisions of the business. Although a "penny pinching" attitude is unwise, continual alertness to ways of making major expense reductions is often one of the surest roads to profits. A good example of this is the case of fire hazards, especially during busy months like December.

The merchant's problem of expense control is unique because he carries a large number of articles of merchandise, many of his employees do several kinds of work, and he must continually defer to customer wishes or demands. In place of using cost accounting for particular products, as is done in manufacturing, the merchant "costs" entire lines or classes of goods. Since the functions performed by various retailers remain basically the same regardless of location, class of customers, kinds of merchandise handled, or other variables, and since many of the expenses incurred, such as those for labor, rent, and equpiment, serve two or more functions, a dual system of expense classification and control has been developed, especially for the department store and general merchandise fields.

Expense Classification

Retail expenses, under this dual system, are classified as either natural or functional. The natural groups include all expenses, such as payroll, utility bills, rent, and travel, as they are actually incurred and recorded, regardless of what functions are served. The functional classification assigns to each function the proportion of these natural expenses it accounted for. To illustrate, the National Retail Merchants Association recommends for small stores seventeen natural classes of expense as follows: payroll, property rentals, advertising, supplies, services purchased, travel, communication, pensions, taxes, interest, insurance, depreciation, professional services, donations, bad debts, equipment rental, and unclassified. These were distributed among five major functional classifications: administration, occupancy, buying, selling, and publicity. From 1955 on, expense centers replace the functional classifications, but are recommended only for larger stores. Further breakdowns are used in both types of classification. Operating data assembled and published by the Controllers' Congress, National Retail Merchants Association, and the Harvard Bureau of Business Research use these standard expense classifications. Merchandising departments are also standardized and numbers are assigned to each so that a given number always refers to the same department in every store anywhere in the country. Such departmental operating data as turnover, stock-stales ratio, and total expenses can then be compared accurately with national averages.[6]

Closely resembling these expense classifications for department and general merchandise stores is an effort by the Department of Commerce to develop a system of cost accounting for retail stores, especially those handling such convenience goods as groceries, drugs, and hardware. Although somewhat complicated for the average small retailer, this system is recommended for study.[7]

Operating Ratios

Ratios constitute an important device for comparing data when two factors vary, such as sales and rent, payroll and size of city in which the business is located, or manufacturing expense and type of order (stock, special, rush, or preseason). There are three types of ratios: those which refer to the relationship of various items in the balance sheet (showing how the business stands at a given moment); those which show the relationships of expense accounts and income (operating ratios); and those which show the relationship of a balance sheet item to one in the profit-and-loss statement (summary of results over a period of time). It is with the latter two that we are dealing. Operating ratios serve as the yardstick or measuring device for many business activities. They are averages of the results achieved by thousands or hundreds of thousands of businessmen striving to do the same thing—namely, make a profit. Some fail and show very poor ratios. A few excel and provide ratios for the most ambitious to use as guides or bases for comparison. Many published operating ratios are presented in these three groups: those for unprofitable, for average, and for very profitable concerns. Operating ratios are usually compiled annually and published by the trade association in each field. In recent years, retail operating ratios by store and town sizes have been published by the U. S. Department of Commerce in the *Business Information Service*.[8] There are many sources of ratios. These include the Business Service Bulletins published in 1954 by the U. S. Department of Commerce and the

[6] See also: *The Lilly Digest of Retail Pharmacy Income and Expense Statement* (Indianapolis, Ind.: Eli Lilly and Company), covering a summary of individually owned drugstores' income and expense statements. This booklet includes operating costs and ratios by sales, cost trends, and analysis of prescription department operation. (Published annually and available upon request.)

[7] An excellent summary of the kinds of material available from the U. S. Government, and ratios for 15 retail trades, 8 wholesale trades, and 7 service trades, is found in *Guides for Business Analysis and Profit Evaluation* (Washington, D. C.: U. S. Department of Commerce, 1959), pp. 23-54. Operating ratios are treated in at least two publications of the Small Business Administration: *A Handbook of Small Business Finance,* Small Business Management Series No. 15, by Ralph B. Tower (January 1957); and *Ratio Analysis for Small Business,* Small Business Management Series No. 20, revised 1960.

[8] *Expenses in Retail Businesses* (Dayton, Ohio: Merchants Service, National Cash Register Company), a periodically published booklet showing a collection of operating ratios for retail and service trades. (Available upon request.)

Small Business Administration; Robert Morris Associates at the Philadelphia National Bank Building, Philadelphia 7, Pennsylvania; Dun & Bradstreet, Inc.; various trade associations; banks, or one's suppliers; a number of universities, including Harvard, Pennsylvania State University, Stanford University, and Indiana University; and certain trade magazines, such as *Progressive Grocer, Printer's Ink, Drug Topics,* and *Supermarket Merchandising.* Two excellent sources are the National Association of Credit Men and the New York Credit and Financial Management Association, both in New York, which develop articles on nearly every subject relative to financial and operating ratios and their analysis. Although operating ratios are more highly developed in the retail than in other fields, their use is recommended for small businessmen in other fields whenever they are available.

Comparison analysis, and intelligent, timely action is the proved formula for expense control. Operating ratios help in this respect just as does the budget for the individual store. After comparing your ratios with those of your trade, it is important, before taking steps to correct an out-of-line ratio, to find out why a ratio is different and to realize that the difference may be balanced by a difference in another ratio.

At the end of the year the retailer may find out whether he has made as much profit as he should have or if he has operated efficiently by comparing his business with others in his line of trade. If he finds that his expenses are too high, a comparison of his figures, item by item, with the expenses of profitable firms will enable him to ferret out those that are guilty of eating up the profits. Also, he may find that he is losing business by not spending enough along some lines or is raising other expenses by more than the amount he is saving on the low items.

To use standard operating ratios, the retailer should first list the different items in his profit and loss statement under the headings used in tables available for his line of trade. He should then work out the ratios by dividing the total of all the items shown under each heading by his net sales.

It is the total of all expenses that affects net profits; should one item be too high, some other must be decreased to keep profits at the average ratio. For example, a high delivery cost ratio may be balanced by a low rent ratio. Also, increasing one expense item may cause a reduction in another that was formerly too high.[9]

To illustrate the use of operating ratios, Table 7, which shows typical operating and merchandising ratios for dry goods and general merchandise stores in 1957, may be analyzed. An individual retailer in this field would, of course, compare his ratios with those given in the table.

As the table shows, the most profitable concerns had a combined salary and

[9] G. A. Welsch, *Cost Control Pointers for Small Marketers,* Small Marketers Aids No. 34 (Washington, D. C.: Small Business Administration, 1958). This booklet gives insight into organizing a structure for cost control, becoming cost conscious, and effecting profits for the firm.

wage expense of 14.4 per cent, whereas unprofitable concerns had a ratio of 19.4 per cent, or 5 per cent higher. Occupancy expenses were 4.2 per cent and 5.1 per cent respectively, or 0.9 per cent more for unprofitable concerns. Thus, of the difference in total expenses, 8.2 per cent between the profitable and unprofitable groups, about 60 per cent consisted of higher payroll and 72 per cent of payroll and occupancy expenses combined.

TABLE 7. OPERATING RATIOS FOR STORES GROUPED BY PER CENT OF NET PROFIT*

| | NET PROFIT ON NET SALES | | | |
	Un-profitable	0.1% to 3.0%	3.0% to 6.0%	6.0% and Over
Number of Concerns	79	59	56	46
Typical Net Sales per Concern	$68,990	$111,540	$92,055	$88,435
Net Sales	100.0%	100.0%	100.0%	100.0%
Cost of Goods Solds	71.6	70.4	70.5	68.3
Gross Margin	28.4	29.6	29.5	31.7
Expenses—*Owners' Compensation*	10.9	8.3	7.3	7.8
Employees' Wages	8.5	9.0	8.3	6.6
Occupancy Expense	5.1	4.7	3.7	4.2
Advertising	1.5	1.4	1.2	0.8
Bad Debt Losses	0.0	0.0	0.0	0.0
Buying Expense	0.2	0.4	0.2	0.0
Depreciation, Fixtures	0.7	0.8	0.7	0.6
All Other Expense	4.0	3.6	3.9	2.7
Total Expense	30.9	28.2	25.3	22.7
Net Profit Before Income Taxes	− 2.5	1.4	4.2	9.0
Net Profit on Net Worth (%)	− 4.2	2.9	9.1	17.2
Net Worth Turnover (*per year*)	2.1	2.8	2.3	1.9
Inventory Turnover (*per year*)	2.1	2.5	2.7	2.4

* Source: "Cost of Doing Business," A Dun & Bradstreet, Inc. survey by Elmer T. Silvertsen; Dry Goods and General Merchandise Stores, Operating Results in 1957 (New York: Dun & Bradstreet, Inc., 1959).

It will also be noted in the merchandising ratios that the gross margin was 3.3 per cent larger for profitable than for unprofitable stores. This suggests the possibility of poor buying accompanied by heavy markdowns. Although inventory turnover was lower for unprofitable concerns, it was so nearly the same for both groups that it does not appear to be an important factor in this case.

Further analysis shows the largest difference to be for owners' compensation that was 3.1 per cent higher for unprofitable concerns—indicating excessive withdrawals.

As this analysis shows, expense ratios do not show how a retailer may be failing to obtain an adequate return for some of the money he pays out. Even when the retailer's ratios compare favorably with the standard expense ratios, individual items may in reality be too high if he gets less for his outlay of money. For example, one retailer may deliver fewer packages than another who spends the same amount for this service. The remedy may be found in cost analysis based on the cost of doing a given piece of work, such as either cost per package, in the case of deliveries, or cost per average sale. This type of cost accounting requires that overhead costs be charged to lines of goods or to departments. How much of the rent bill for the store should be charged off to delivery expense, for example, might be figured out by estimating the percentage of total floor space occupied by the quarters devoted to preparing packages for delivery and loading them on trucks.

The ratio of net profit to sales should be interpreted in the light of sales volume and capital invested. A low ratio on a large volume may mean a good profit. Likewise the same ratio is more satisfactory when volume is the same but investment less.

The following comments of the Senate Special Committee to Study Problems of American Small Business are pertinent to the subject of using operating ratios effectively:[10]

> Even though the standard ratios are based on the figures of a group of stores more or less like your own, there are sound reasons why the ratios for your store may vary considerably from the standard ratios. Some of the reasons why variations between your ratios and the standard ratios may be either favorable or unfavorable are discussed under the headings which follow.
>
> *Gross-Margin Ratio.* A high gross-margin ratio may indicate either purchases at low prices, or sales at high prices, or both. A low gross-margin ratio, on the other hand, may indicate either inadequate markups, or high merchandise costs as a result of poor buying judgment and heavy inventory writedowns. Or, it may be the result of a deliberate merchandising policy (or campaign) of selling at low prices in order to obtain a large sales volume. To be profitable, such a policy must result in large sales volume and be accompanied by low operating costs.
>
> *Total Operating-Expense Ratio.* A higher-than-average total operating-expense ratio does not necessarily reflect any unfavorable conditions in the store. If it is accompanied by a high gross-margin ratio, and a satisfactory net-profit ratio, it may reflect the character and policy of the store. For example, a better-than-average type of merchandise, or sales based on additional service to customers, may yield extra gross margin to cover the extra expense involved, and to provide a satisfactory net profit.
>
> Nevertheless, a store with a total expense ratio much higher than that for similar stores is quite likely to be unprofitable. The typical unprofitable store has a high total expense ratio for its kind of business. This may be owing to small sales volume as compared with the profitable store, and not necessarily because it pays higher wage rates or higher rent rates. More frequently, however, a higher-than-average total operating expense ratio in an unprofitable store indicates low efficiency; that is, poor management in controlling expenses.

[10] An excellent example of use of operating ratios is found in *Guides for Business Analysis and Profit Evaluation, op. cit.,* pp. 8-13.

Net Profit or Loss Ratio. The profit or loss ratio reflects the net results of the operation of the store. This ratio indicates the effectiveness of the management of the store and measures the efficiency of its operation. The net profit or loss ratio is influenced by many factors. A profitable store is usually the result of efficient management which, on the one hand, succeeds in maintaining a satisfactory dollar gross margin—from purchases at low cost and from sales at prices that are neither too high nor too low—and, on the other hand, succeeds in keeping all expenses under control.

Proprietor's Wage Ratio. Since many retailers do not make a distinction between money withdrawn for their wages and that which is a withdrawal of profits, a proprietor's wage ratio which varies from the average may have no significance. A higher-than-average ratio may indicate either that the store earns large profits, or that excessive wages are being paid to the owner. It is important that excessive portions of capital not be withdrawn, for this is limiting future growth.

A low owner's wage ratio, accompanied by small withdrawals of profits and a satisfactory net profit ratio, indicates that the retailer is building up his capital by leaving his profits in the business. On the other hand, a low wage ratio, accompanied by a low net profit ratio, indicates that the owner is getting a small total return from the operation of his store.

Employees' Wage Ratio. A relatively high employees' wage ratio is ordinarily an unfavorable sign. A high wage ratio may be the result of inefficient use of help, a poor store arrangement, the employment of too many clerks for the sales volume being obtained, or it may be the result of other factors. Like a high gross-margin ratio, however, a high wage ratio may be the result of a carefully thought-out management policy. It may indicate the retailer's policy of obtaining sales by providing more or better clerk service instead of spending more on rent, fixtures, or advertising. The degree of success of this policy can be determined by studying the sales volume, the gross-margin ratio, the rent and other expense ratios, and the net profit or loss ratio.

A low employees' wage ratio is usually evidence of efficient management, especially if it is accompanied by a low total operating-expense ratio and a satisfactory net-profit ratio. It may mean, however, that the store is not employing enough workers or not employing the right kind of clerks. An unsatisfactory sales volume may indicate that the latter is the case.

Rent (or Occupancy) Expense Ratio. A high rent ratio may be the result of the store being larger than necessary to handle the present sales volume. On the other hand, a high rent ratio may mean that a favorable location has been obtained which makes it possible to obtain sales without high expenditures for advertising which might otherwise be necessary.

A low rent (or occupancy) expense ratio may mean that the retailer has been able to secure the store building at a low rental or purchase price. Or it may mean that the building is too small for the volume of business. A mutual comparison can be made with a rent-to-gross-margin ratio.

Advertising-Expense Ratio. An advertising-expense ratio that is in line with a standard ratio may not necessarily be favorable. The advertising may have been successful in increasing dollar sales volume, so that the added dollar advertising expense represents no greater percentage of sales than normal. But, if the added sales volume consists mainly of staples or low-margin goods, the advertising may not be profitable. To be profitable, advertising must result in added dollar gross margin more than sufficient to cover the added dollar advertising and other expenses. That is, the advertising should sell goods carrying high gross-margin rates as well as staples.

On the other hand, a low advertising-expense ratio, which is accompanied by small sales and net profits, may possibly mean that one of the causes of the unfavorable results is insufficient advertising.

Delivery-Expense Ratio. Unless the proportions of delivered sales to total sales are known, no worthwhile comparisons of delivery-expense ratios can be made. A store with two-thirds of its sales delivered will almost necessarily have a higher delivery-expense ratio than a store with only one-third delivered sales, and any difference between the ratios of two such stores will be of no significance. Only when a store has approximately the same proportion of delivered sales as that of the group with which it is being compared can significant comparisons be made. A high ratio will then indicate inefficiency in the delivery operation, and a low ratio the opposite.

Bad-Debt-Loss Ratio. One of the factors to be considered in analyzing the bad-debt-loss ratio is the proportion of credit sales to total sales. Just as in the case of the delivery-expense ratio, a more worthwhile comparison can be made if the proportion of a store's credit sales is approximately the same as that of the group of stores with which it is being compared.

A low bad-debt ratio is usually evidence of a credit and collection policy that has been carefully planned and strictly enforced. Or it may be an indication that too much caution is being used in the development of credit sales. A high ratio usually indicates laxness in extending credit and in making collections.[11]

Other Expense Ratios. Higher-than-standard ratios for any of the other expense items on the profit and loss statement usually indicate an opportunity for expense reduction. Heat, light, power and water, store supplies, and miscellaneous expenses, may be higher than average because of a deliberate merchandising policy of rendering extensive service, but more often they are high because of a lack of expense control. Depreciation of store equipment, being a noncash expense, may be high because of the methods of computing depreciation. A cash-shortage ratio that is too high is almost always the result of improper methods of safeguarding cash. Taxes and licenses may not be subject to the control of the retailer, but a high miscellaneous-expense ratio probably arises from carelessness in expense control.

Inventory Turnover Rate. The inventory turnover rate is calculated by dividing the cost-of-goods-sold item on the profit and loss statement by the average of the beginning and ending inventories at cost. For example, assume the cost of goods sold was $17,595, the value of the inventory at cost on January 1 was $3,569 and the value of the inventory at cost on December 31 was $3,606. This means that the inventory was "turned" approximately five times during the year—$17,595, divided by $3,587.50 equals 4.9.

A high inventory turnover rate is commonly considered to be favorable, but its importance may be exaggerated. In fact, a turnover rate that is

---

[11] An excellent primer on establishing a credit system and policy is *Building Sound Credit Policies for Small Stores,* by Clyde William Phelps, Small Marketers Aids No. 6 (Washington, D. C.: Small Business Administration).

too high may be just as unfavorable as one that is too low. A high rate sometimes means that the retailer has concentrated his attention on carrying small stocks of "fast movers." This practice may result in the loss of potential sales because of the increased risk of being "out of stock" and because of the lack of a sufficient variety of goods to satisfy customers. Also, the practice of buying fast-moving merchandise in small quantities may merely deprive the retailer of the wholesaler's lowest prices for quantity purchases, and increase the time he spends in ordering and receiving goods.[12]

On the other hand, an inventory that turns over too slowly is probably loaded with slow items, that may not only tie up needed working capital, but also may lead to loss of sales because of the lack of fresh stocks of merchandise.

The foregoing discussion indicates that the profit and loss statement of any store should be analyzed. As an aid in your analysis you may compare your operating results with those of similar stores, by means of standard ratios. This comparison must be made, however, with a knowledge of the ways in which the operating conditions of your store differ from those in the stores whose operating results are reflected in the standard ratios. Such critical analysis can point the way to larger profits.[13]

Financial and operating ratios provide guides, not precise measurements, with which businessmen can analyze business operations and compare results with firms operating under similar conditions. Although variations from standard or average results should be investigated, they do not necessarily point to weakness. . . . The user . . . should understand that operating results vary according to size of business, location, type of ownership, credit and delivery policies, rate of profit earned, and other factors.[14]

EXPENSE CONTROL IN WHOLESALING[15]

In wholesaling materials-handling is a major target for expense reduction. Clerical expense can easily get out of line, since almost every transaction involves some paper work. Other common methods of expense reduction are: simplification of stock, reduction in selling costs through closer co-operation with retailers, manufacturers' co-operation in packaging small units to eliminate the wholesaler's "broken package" room expenses, and selective distribution.

Stated differently, the wholesaler must help his independent retailer cus-

---

[12] The costs of storing goods may be excessive, and this problem is covered in *More for Your Storeroom Dollar,* by Erick M. Hauer, Management Aids for Small Manufacturers No. 83 (Washington, D. C.: Small Business Administration).

[13] Charles H. Welch and Charles H. Sevin, *Small Business Problems; Record Keeping for Small Stores,* Senate Committee Print No. 2 (79th Congress, 1st session), Rev. ed. (Washington, D. C.: U. S. Government Printing Office, 1945), pp. 50-53.

[14] "Guides for Business Analysis and Profit Evaluation," (Washington, D. C.: U. S. Department of Commerce, 1959), p. 5.

[15] A bibliography and brief resume of this subject is found in "Operating Costs and Ratios—Wholesale," by Richard M. Hill, Small Business Bulletin No. 11 (Washington, D. C.: Small Business Administration, June 1959).

tomers meet the growing competition of chains, mail-order houses, manufacturer-controlled retail outlets, "supers," and new kinds of low cost retailers in a market where price competition will be an important factor. Many wholesalers are setting goals for expenses that will enable them to sell to independent retailers at prices low enough to permit the retailer to meet mail-order competition or at chain store prices adjusted for the difference in customer services. The more important wholesaler's expenses can be reduced only if retailers co-operate. This is especially true with reference to selling expense. Also, unless wholesalers can aid many of their retail customers in reducing expenses the retail margin will offset most of the lower prices made possible by expense reduction.

Wholesalers share the advantages of manufacturers and most service businesses in being able to control expenses on an impersonal basis. Wholesalers should discover useful adaptations by studying cost reducing techniques and equipment as developed in manufacturing.

Distribution unit cost studies, a technical application of the methods studies technique already discussed, have been used by wholesalers in connection with expense control. The following procedures in particular illustrate this approach: determine the cost of rendering service to individual customers, the cost of handling orders of various sizes, and the cost of selling per dollar of sales or for a certain number of orders received by each company salesman. The last is a common function of sales management. The first two deserve some special comment.

Experience shows that many retailers buy in such small quantities from any one wholesaler and often demand so much service that their accounts are found to be handled at a loss when all valid expenses are charged to the servicing of their accounts.

When a wholesaler has determined the minimum he can handle at a profit, expense control can be used more effectively in dealing with small order buyers. Efforts are usually made to bring every order accepted up to the minimum, allowing for a few exceptions in the case of normally good customers whose annual volume would justify an occasional small order. Repeated small orders below the minimum may be refused. Usually the salesman can show the small buyer how he can plan his purchases to meet this standard. A few new customers who show promise of expanding may be carried at a loss temporarily. In general, however, it is better to refuse orders below the minimum and to reduce the expense of trying to serve "hopeless" customers.

EXPENSE CONTROL FOR THE SMALL FACTORY

Although some of the best opportunities for small business in the field of manufacturing are in totally new or noncompetitive lines, expense control is important in such cases for several reasons. No matter how new, different, or so-called "noncompetitive" the product being made seems to be, it must compete on a price-usefulness basis with all other objects of consumer expenditures. Interindustry competition exists regardless of the size of business units involved. In test factories and pilot plants or in pioneering the manufacture of a new product, the ultimate criterion of the commercial value of the item is the cost at which it can be made and sold. And finally, a new article that clicks with the market will soon be copied by competitors making price competition based on production and selling costs inevitable.

During the first few years, while a new product is being perfected in design, expenses may be considered second to quality only if they are (1) in line with the owner's ability to pay, and (2) capable of future reduction to meet the inevitable competition that will quickly develop once the product gains market acceptance.

Fortunately for the small manufacturer highly developed techniques for expense control have been perfected in this field. Cost accounting, methods studies, and almost every other tool of modern management were inaugurated in the field of production and later adapted to other fields.[16]

For example, standard costs as used in estimating, pricing, and budgetary control have been well developed for most kinds of manufacturing. Although specific standard, or average, costs are developed for each concern and consequently are not so useful to other firms as the standard operating ratios discussed for retailing, methods of arriving at standard costs and their appropriate uses may well be studied and applied to any kind of business.

No matter how small the factory, certain costs can be controlled from the first day of operations. One of these is plant maintenance.[17] Maintenance should be systematized, planned, scheduled, and controlled as carefully, cost-wise, as production. The same principles of careful assignment of duties and responsibilities, good supervision, and budgetary control of expenses may be used to advantage. Providing maintenance workers with efficient tools and equipment is good economy. Work should be so scheduled that it does not interfere with productive operations.

Many other expenses are significant to the small producer, such as packing and shipping costs and selling expense. Several references are mentioned in this connection elsewhere in the book. The same basic techniques are used: careful selection of the best materials, methods, and equipment; adequate records; simplification and standardization; and planning, supervision, and control.

Distribution or selling costs for the small manufacturer are subject to

[16] Certain pitfalls to avoid in setting up a system, and suggested forms for doing so are in *Pitfalls in Estimating Your Manufacturing Costs,* by Orville T. Wood, Management Aids for Small Business No. 40 (Washington, D. C.: Small Business Administration, December 1953). Basic steps in cost control are outlined in *How to Reduce Your Operating Costs,* by Virgil Rotroff, Management Aids for Small Business No. 51 (Small Business Administration, June 1954).

[17] One similar expense has been written about in *Controlling Inspection Costs in Small Plants,* by Robert E. Heiland, Management Aids for Small Manufacturers No. 96 (Small Business Administration, July 1958).

essentially the same types of expense control. It may seem strange to insert a caution against "volume-itis" for the small producer, but practical considerations make this advisable. All too often the beginning or small concern goes after volume by means of seeking additional orders regardless of their immediate profitableness, hoping for future repeat business at a profitable price. Granting that some pioneering must be done, it is still good business to watch expenses on all orders and follow up closely on those of questionable value. One of the popular methods of exploiting the small producer is to get him to accept orders at or below cost by making glowing promises (never contracts) for future business at highly profitable figures.

Marketing costs are generally allocated (when a direct relationship is observed) to appropriate functional cost groups—groups broken down according to a marketing function. These in turn are assigned to individual territories, products, customers or other desired marketing segment. Here is a way in which the allocation can be made:[18]

	BASES OF ALLOCATION	
FUNCTIONAL COST GROUPS	*To Commodities*	*To Customers*
1. Investment in finished goods	Average inventory value	(Not allocated)
2. Storage of finished goods	Floor space occupied	(Not allocated)
3. Inventory control, finished goods	No. of invoice lines	(Not allocated)
4. Order assembly (handling)	No. of standard handling units	No. of invoice lines
5. Packing and shipping	Wgt. or No. of shipping units	Wgt. or No. of shipping units
6. Transportation	Wgt. or No. of shipping units	Wgt. or No. of shipping units
7. Selling	Time studies	No. of sales calls
8. Advertising	Cost of space, etc., of specific product advertising	Cost of space, etc. of specific product advertising
9. Order entry	No. of invoice lines	No. of orders
10. Billing	No. of invoice lines	No. of invoice lines
11. Credit extension	(Not allocated)	Average amount outstanding
12. Accounts receivable	(Not allocated)	No. of invoices posted

Expense control for the average small manufacturer involves good management in at least seven areas: (1) demand forecasting, (2) direct production costs, (3) indirect costs, (4) material and supply costs, (5) transportation costs, (6) costs of methods used for market promotion, and (7) miscellaneous costs such as financing.

Keeping in mind that expense control does not necessarily involve expense reduction, there are ways in which a small operator can improve the accuracy

[18] From *Analyzing Your Cost of Marketing*, by Charles H. Sevin, Management Aids for Small Manufacturers No. 85 (Small Business Administration, July 1957).

of demand forecasting. By subscribing to the trade journals in his field and possibly in certain cases to those in his customers' fields, he can keep better informed of future conditions likely to affect the demand for his product. There are numerous forecasting services available, one or more of which should be helpful. It is possible to co-operate with business neighbors in subscribing to some of these services and thus reduce their cost to each plant. Attending meetings of trade associations, at which trends in the industry are frequently discussed by representatives of large companies that spend a great deal of money on their forecasting research, should pay the little fellow. Monthly reports of the Federal Reserve Banks for each district report major trends that can be used to forecast demand. Many state universities publish a monthly bulletin analyzing economic and business conditions within the state, often undertaking to forecast demand and supply conditions likely to have a bearing on the sales plans of local businessmen. The charge for these bulletins, when there is any, is seldom much more than the cost of printing and mailing. Every small operator should write to the College of Business or Bureau of Business Research of his state university to have his name placed on the mailing list for monthly bulletins and other useful publications. In many industrial fields the U. S. Department of Commerce, Washington 25, D. C., publishes monthly analyses and forecasts of conditions. This material too is either free or so inexpensive that no small businessman can afford to neglect using it.

What direct production costs involve is pretty evident in the small factory. Their control involves the determination of a fair day's output for men and machines or the man-hour and machine-hour amounts required to produce each article. These become output standards with which actual production is compared to secure control. Before adopting such a standard, the operator of even a small factory should study ways of improving productivity. Perhaps subdividing the work and letting each worker become more skilled in performing a smaller number of tasks would increase total productivity, or a new layout might accomplish the same result.

Indirect costs, as the words are used here, include such overhead expenses as management salaries, utility bills, rent, and similar rather fixed costs that do not change directly with varying quantities of production, although such office items as management salaries and excessive utility bills may be partially controlled. In small factories the number of employees engaged in paper work, maintenance, and other activities involving indirect expense may be small relative to the number of direct production workers, and it is easy to be careless about efforts to control such costs.

Managers of larger plants are giving increasing attention to both the control and reduction of indirect costs and have developed methods to direct and check on such work. These guides should help the small plant operator do a better job of controlling indirect costs in his factory.

Control over material and supply costs involves much more than shrewd buying. It starts in the factory with a careful study of production needs and processes. One small manufacturer found that a slight change in design enabled him to use an unfinished moulded metal part at less than half the price formerly paid for a similar part with finished surfaces. In another case investigation and the advice of a local technician showed one plant operator how he could use a slightly more expensive lubricant for his machines and actually reduce total supply expenses 20 per cent because the new lubricant was especially made for the type of work involved. Since new materials and supplies constantly appear on the market, many designed for special purposes and others less expensive than ones traditionally used for the same purpose, the small operator always has opportunities for expense reduction. Also, few small operators are so well informed that they know the properties of all materials and supplies already on the market that they might use.

The small factory usually has some transportation costs, with good opportunities for expense control. Careful study of the methods in use, alternate routes, comparative rates, "extra" charges, services required compared to those being used and paid for, auditing of invoices, packing procedures and materials used, damage claims, and use of more costly emergency methods or small order shipments, will usually disclose ways of cost reduction and control. Careful stock control can avoid emergency ordering and expensive special freight costs. In some cases an alternate method of transportation, such as trucks instead of railroads or leased instead of company-owned trucks, may result in reduced costs.

Market promotion offers many opportunities for expense control. At the start personal solicitation of orders may be necessary. Later the expense of personal selling may be lessened by using brokers or selling agents who operate on a very small margin, by selling through established middlemen like wholesalers or supply houses, or by using some of the many forms of advertising. Solicitation of repeat orders can often be done by mail or telephone. Although both methods are cheaper per unit than salesmen's calls, they may actually be more expensive per order received than the latter.

Miscellaneous expenses such as costs of financing in the small factory resemble those for market promotion in this respect: during the initial stages of the business, or while its operations are on a very small scale, only the most expensive methods are likely to be available. As the small manufacturer becomes better established and expands his operations, he may easily secure needed capital at more attractive interest rates.

This discussion of expenses in manufacturing concludes with the advice to use all the regular methods of expense control already discussed, including working closely with the trade association in the field. In manufacturing, the opportunities for expense control are relatively greater than in other fields, because the producer is dealing mainly with materials and processes. He should learn all he can from the extensive writings on industrial management and adapt to his business every idea and technique possible.

SERVICE ESTABLISHMENT EXPENSES

Well-established service fields have standard accounting systems and expense classifications useful to the small operator. For instance, in the laundry business, the American Institute of Laundering (A.I.L.) has developed three systems for plants of each size group. For smaller plants the simplified system is used. There are eight expense accounts: (1) productive labor, (2) productive supplies, (3) power plant costs, (4) building overhead, (5) laundry machinery overhead, (6) indirect overhead, (7) collection, delivery, and sales promotion costs, and (8) office and administrative costs. For expense control purposes, however, each of these is further subdivided. For example, 1.1 is a productive labor (laundering), 1.2 productive labor (dry cleaning), 4.2 is rent of laundry building, and 4.3 repairs and maintenance. For each size group operating ratios that may be used for comparison by individual plant operators are compiled each year.[19]

It is not always necessary to engage outside industrial engineers for a cost analysis, although sometimes their objective approach and specialized knowledge may be needed, as the following cases illustrate.

A failing dry cleaning plant was taken over by a firm of management engineers. Investigation showed labor costs to be excessive and rigid. Whenever business increased additional workers were added, but when volume declined man-hours were not reduced. Lack of supervision and the absence of performance standards were apparent. Production was poorly scheduled and work centers were not properly balanced, so that work piled up at certain points while employees at other production centers were idle. The engineers devoted special attention to making methods studies, established labor output standards, and promoting sales more effectively. Results were gratifying. Plant output per worker doubled, labor costs were greatly reduced, and both store cash-and-carry and route sales increased.

Two case histories selected from many available for the hotel field will illustrate opposite methods used for expense control, namely, cutting down and increasing expense.

One hotel had two bellboys on duty during the period from 8 A.M. to 8 P.M. Because patrons demanded early morning delivery of mail, one boy was sent to the post office to pick it up. This trip and sundry other duties took the boy off the floor for an hour and a half at the most critical time of service. Instead of employing a third bellboy, management investigated the work loads of other employees and was able to assign a relief elevator operator to do the work formerly performed by the bellboy.

In another hotel the manager was payroll-conscious. Investigation showed, however, that the kitchen staff were overworked and unable to perform their

19 V. H. Kramer, *Establishing and Operating a Laundry,* Industrial (Small Business) Series No. 37 (Washington, D. C.: U. S. Department of Commerce, 1946), pp. 100-101.

duties efficiently. Overtime payments alone offset the economy of a small basic staff. By employing two more workers and improving the scheduling of work, an actual reduction in total payroll expense was made.[20]

CONCLUSIONS

Expenses must be incurred to operate any business. Activities relating to management of expenses involve accounting records, expense control, and usually expense reduction. Control operates through standards, comparable reports, and prompt executive action. It does not have expense reduction as a necessary objective. Expense control may involve: the use and operation of machines, equipment, and supplies, and methods studies or similar research to discover less expensive ways of performing essential operations. *Since business costs are directly related to profits, efficient management of all expenses is essential to success.*

QUESTIONS AND PROBLEMS

1. Distinguish actual from imputed expenses and give several examples of each.

2. Is it important to include both imputed and actual expenses to secure effective expense control? Discuss.

3. Explain and illustrate why expense control is not the same as expense reduction.

4. Name and illustrate the three essential elements of budgetary control.

5. What are the two major types of expense classification used in retailing? Give some examples of each.

6. Why should methods study be a part of expense control?

7. What are the three largest expenses in nearly every retail store? How, if at all, does this generalization need qualification?

8. Explain the nature of and several uses for operating ratios.

9. Compare the operating ratios for the following retail fields and explain any similarities and differences: grocery, hardware, drug, jewelry, wearing apparel.

10. How could some of the ways of reducing expenses in manufacturing and service industries be applied to retailing?

11. Summarize the points of similarity and of difference in expense management for each of the three major small business fields.

12. What mechanical aids to expense control are used in the line of business in which you are interested?

13. What machinery, equipment, or other mechanical aids could be used by a retailer who finds the expense of operating certain necessary divisions of the store to be too high? Be specific in your answer.

14. What would you classify as indirect labor in retailing? in wholesaling? How important are these expenses? Can output of such workers be measured and expense control applied to their activities? Discuss.

[20] Sanford E. Maus, "Payroll Studies Eliminate Costly Labor Waste," *Southern Hotel Journal* (July 1947), pp. 26-32.

15. Suggest and discuss several ways expense control should involve deliberate efforts to increase certain expenses.

16. How would the topics discussed in this chapter be of use in appraising a business for possible purchase? In justifying a new business?

17. List in two columns the conditions under which expense control is of greatest, and of least, relative importance. Discuss.

18. Select some kind of business and prepare a budget for the first year of operation based on an assumed volume of business.

19. As the new owner of a store that has been declining in sales and profits for several years, Joe finds that ratios for advertising are 20 per cent, and for bad debt losses 5 per cent below the standard ratios for the field. What should he do, and why?

22 • *Inventory or Stores Control*

Every business requires some inventory of goods. In most lines this inventory of merchandise, materials, parts, or supplies represents a sizable investment of the owner's capital. In general, the merchant invests a larger proportion of his capital in inventories than the small manufacturer, and the service businessman invests a smaller proportion than either. Extensive experience in all fields has shown that unless these inventories are controlled they tend to get out of balance and result in loss to the business. It is the primary purpose of inventory control to maintain the balance that permits most profitable operations.

A major purpose in business is to have the right goods at the right place at the right time. This means having adequate merchandise on call and available to meet the demands of customers. Merchandise represents an investment in funds, an investment which can be well or poorly controlled, well or poorly guarded and guided in use. In any measure of business efficiency the degree to which the wants of customers are satisfied readily, the degree to which capital funds are used effectively, careful and constant adjustment of inventory must be considered.

In terms of economic considerations as to any given time period, and increasingly in terms of taxation factors, inventory control can be a major business activity. It is not a production problem, but a problem of over-all coordination of business activities in which this phase of marketing activity plays a very important part, reflecting as it does a return on investment and expenses in giving adequate service to customers, and an effective use of money, people, equipment, time and space in operation, as shown in operating ratios at the end of any period.

A well-controlled inventory may be said to be in good balance—in balance as to capital, usage, and productive facilities, and in balance as to customer needs. This means that each kind or class of merchandise reflects the best available current facts and, therefore, is, insofar as is possible, "just right"— in proper balance.

Any inventory may be out of balance in either direction; that is, it may be too large or too small. This applies to the investment in total inventory carried as well as to investments in each subdivision or classification of inventories. It is especially important with reference to the lack of balance among different items of merchandise, materials, or parts.

Under different economic conditions the relative importance of the value aspect—that is, the amount of capital invested in total inventories—varies in importance. An inventory may be well balanced in terms of number of units of each item within a total amount, but be dangerously out of balance with regard to the dollar value invested. This is true especially (1) at the peak of a rising price trend, (2) just before a pronounced upward swing in prices, and (3) when shortages with controlled prices are imminent. Each of these three important but unusual situations requires management policy decision and lies beyond the normal scope of inventory control, although each may influence management's concern regarding present conditions of the firm's inventory.

In addition to its use as a buying guide, inventory control may result in maintaining small stocks and thus reduce taxes, lessen interest and storage expenses, and secure other benefits.

An analysis of the effect of increased stock turn on an inventory investment on annual sale of goods costing $100,000 (assuming annual carrying cost of 25 per cent) brings out these interesting reductions in costs and freeing of capital for other uses:

Turns per year	Inventory Investment	Costs Reduced	Capital Released
One Turn	$100,000	24,000	—
Two Turns	50,000	12,000	50,000
Three Turns	33,333	$4,000/8,000	16,667
Four Turns	25,000	$2,000/6,000	8,333
Five Turns	20,000	$1,200/4,800	5,000
Six Turns	16,667	$ 800/4,000	3,333 [1]

Profit would automatically decrease as ten stock turns were achieved. In each business there is a proper amount of inventory to be on hand, available or on order, in terms of best use of capital, space, and labor, as well as other considerations such as deterioration, price changes, or new materials available.

SCOPE OF INVENTORY CONTROL

Five topics are usually included in the scope of inventory control: (1) information required, (2) system, (3) basic data, (4) storekeeping, and

[1] Andrew V. Ackerman (Cherry-Burrell Corp.), *Purchase and Inventory Control,* Small Business Bulletin No. 6 (State of New York: Department of Commerce, 1958), p. 7.

(5) inventory taking. For our purpose the last two will be discussed principally in connection with each of the major fields of small business.

At this point we are concerned with a preview of the scope of inventory or stores control, as well as with some general comments that will apply to all fields and conditions. Variations by field and particular applications will be considered later.

Inventory control requires information. Whether records are used to secure this information depends upon the size of the business and particular internal conditions. Many very small businesses have good inventory or stores control without maintaining more than a few records, if any.

Effective inventory control requires accurate information from the using departments (sales in the case of merchandising, processing in the case of manufacturing or service businesses) concerning such requirements as kind or quality of goods and quantity of each variety, as well as when they are needed. It is not the function of inventory control to forecast needs, but it does help in making these forecasts more reliable. Forecasting, in turn, is a guide to quantities required for inventory, for inventory requirements and sales expectations are inseparable.

Some system must be used if inventory control is to be even moderately efficient. An early question in establishing a system is whether value or quantity is the factor controlled. In merchandising, especially, we observe both dollar control and unit control systems. Any "system" requires intelligent human effort to be successful. Systems or methods used to secure the information essential for inventory control will usually operate through observation, physical checks, or a perpetual inventory record.

Any form of inventory or stores control works with the following basic data: quantities needed, amounts on hand, additions to stock (purchases), subtractions (sales or issues), goods on order, and critical points at which action is needed. The last are usually expressed as maximum and minimum amounts. Whenever the quantity on hand reaches either the maximum or the minimum, steps must be taken if the inventory is to be kept in balance. Two other elements frequently included among the basic data are quantities allocated to known needs and the quantity to order at any one time.

Storekeeping, or the physical handling and storage of merchandise, materials, and parts, must be performed efficiently if good inventory control is to be achieved. This requires adequate facilities to store each item in such a way that it will be protected and can be located quickly as needed. If some items are carried on consignment, storekeeping should provide for their special identification.

Finally, inventory taking, or the counting of articles on hand, must be carried out from time to time. When the physical count or frequent check system of inventory control is used for all items stocked and each count is recorded on the inventory control card (or ledger), it may not be necessary to take additional inventories. However, if the perpetual inventory system is used, actual counts must be made from time to time to correct the book figures. The small businessman must not mistake the system, which is merely a labor- or time-saving device, for the goal, which is balanced inventories.[2]

INVENTORY CONTROL IN MERCHANDISING

The small retailer's biggest investment is his inventory of merchandise carried. When this can be kept at the optimum amount, profits are increased. When inventories are well balanced at all times, the investment in merchandise is working most effectively. Among the major advantages of inventory or merchandise control in retailing is the fact that it enables the retailer to do the following: (1) balance stocks as to value, size, color, style, and price line, in proportion to sales; (2) "play the winners" as well as move slow sellers; and (3) secure the best rate of stock turnover for each item. Expenses and markdowns are reduced. The store's reputation for always having new, fresh merchandise in wanted sizes and colors is one of the major long-run benefits of good merchandise control.

Information provided by a good system of merchandise control that will improve both buying and selling activities includes the following:

1. Price preferences of customers.
2. Right quantities to buy.
3. Amount of a given item sold.
4. Season or time a given item sells.
5. Time to stop buying seasonable goods.
6. Kind and style of goods customers want.
7. Items no longer popular.
8. Time to display and promote certain items.
9. Particular item for which demand is falling off.
10. Best buying sources.
11. Best buying prices.
12. Possibilities for new lines or kinds of goods.

A control system giving this information will eliminate guesswork and memory—both unreliable guides to prosperity.

Every store that has tried a stock control system for the first time has found that the greatest number of items in stock are rarely asked for or sold. Difficult as this is to believe, it has been found that from 20 to 24 per cent of the items in a poorly controlled store produce from 75 to 80 per cent of sales.

Efficient, profitable merchandise control need not be difficult, complex or expensive. Many agencies, organizations and associations can furnish good control systems to store owners in their respective fields. These system forms are economical, simple, and easy to operate. They are easy

---

[2] See: D. J. James, *Basic Stock Control for Small Stores,* Small Marketers Aids No. 5 (Washington, D. C.: Small Business Administration, 1955), a basic control system which will aid management on what stock control will and will not do. See also: *Stock Management in Small Stores,* Small Marketers Aids No. 26 (August 1957).

to install, can be brief or extended to fit the need and can be handled in a few minutes each day.[3]

To illustrate how stock control may aid in buying to meet customer demand, the following representation of unguided buying may be used.[4] Data furnished by inventory control could have reduced A and C in the table.

If AB represents what you buy	A	B	
And BC is what customers want		B	C
Then B is what you sell		B	
A are the "sleepers"	A		
C represents the "outs"			C

Since inventory control tends to increase the rate of stock turnover, it may be well to illustrate how important this advantage may be to the small retailer. Figures and operating ratios used are representative of many small general merchandise stores. Consider a store with annual sales of $50,000, stock turnover 3 times a year, rent 5 per cent of sales, and gross margin 40 per cent. If a turnover of 4 times a year is standard in the field, the situation can be summarized as follows:

Present Condition:

$50,000 \div 3 = $16,667 .... average inventory at retail

$16,667 \times 60\% = $10,000.............. average inventory at cost

Goal or Standard:

$50,000 \div 4 = $12,500................ average inventory at retail

$12,500 \times 60\% = $7,500............... average inventory at cost

Excess inventory: $10,000 - $7,500 = $2,500

Interest on excess investment: $2,500 @ 6\% = $150

Approximate rent for space used to store surplus inventory:

$50,000 \times 5\% \div 4$ ($2,500 is $\frac{1}{4}$ of $10,000) = $625

The smaller inventory, turning more rapidly, might reduce markdowns, shrinkage, and handling costs by 2% of sales (estimate):

$50,000 \times 2\% = $1,000

Total Probable Gain $1,775

Average net profit for stores of this class might be 3%; $50,000 \times 3\% = $1,500. Therefore, the total gain from increased turnover in this example is greater than the average net profit. The more rapid turnover might change a losing concern into one with average or better than average profits.

In the illustration it is assumed that the turnover of 4 times could be accomplished with no increased expense, that the space occupied by the 25 per cent surplus stock accounted for 25 per cent of the total rent, and that

[3] *Controlling Merchandise* (Dayton, Ohio: Merchants Service, National Cash Register Company, 1958), presents information on physical inventory, stock turnover, and rates of turnover for different businesses, unit control, and sources for stock records.

[4] Nelson A. Miller, *Establishing and Operating a Variety and General Merchandise Store,* Industrial (Small Business) Series No. 35 (Washington, D. C.: U. S. Department of Commerce 1946), p. 143.

when this space was released it could be used effectively for merchandise of average turnover. These would be reasonable assumptions in most cases. They are mentioned merely to caution the reader against overemphasizing the magic of increased turnover by failing to take related factors into consideration.

For most types of inventory control, as well as for other purposes, it is desirable to classify the goods carried into merchandise departments, i.e. to departmentize the store. Similar and related items are grouped together both in the store layout and in merchandise control records. Standard departmental classifications should be used as recommended by the trade association in the field.

Methods Used[5]

Methods of inventory control used by small retailers include: observation, physical check, On hand—On order—Sold record, and perpetual inventory. Observation may be sufficient in a very small store in which the variety of

FIGURE 6. On hand—On order—Sold record.

LIST NO. *D-253* NAME OF SUPPLIER STREET ADDRESS CITY AND STATE TERMS: *Net 30* *#420 Ladies' F.F. Hose 48¢*			ON HAND - ON ORDER - SOLD							
PACKED *½ doz. $8.75 doz.* MINIMUM SHIPMENT *15 doz.*	O.H. 8-16	O.O. 9-14 REC'D	SOLD	O.H. 9-18	O.O. 9-28 REC'D	SOLD	O.H. 9-18	O.O. 11-1 REC'D	SOLD	SEASON SOLD
Dawnblush size 8½	3	3	2	4	6	7	3	9		
9	8	6	5	6	12	12	6	15		
9½	12	9	13	8	18	20	6	24		
10	5	6	7	4	12	12	4	15		
10½	2	3	4	1	6	5	2	9		
Rose Nude 8½	2	3	2	3	–	1	2	–		
9	4	6	4	6	–	3	3	–		

Explanation: O.H.—On hand on date noted.
                O.O.—On order, same date.
                Rec'd—Rec'd on date noted.
                Sold—Number on hand on first date, plus number received, minus
                      number on hand on next date.
Note: Tally on 6 (½ doz.), not on 5. All figures are units.

merchandise is not large, the rate of sale is fairly constant, and the owner keeps in very close daily contact with all goods. Usually, however, a physical check or count is necessary at intervals that vary according to the rate of

---

[5] *Merchandise Control in the Retail Pharmacy* (Pullman, Washington: Bureau of Economic and Business Research, Bulletin No. 30, State College of Washington, 1957), presents a study of retail and hospital pharmacies control systems in use in Washington.

sale and importance of the merchandise. It may be a simple or approximate check, as in the case of volume control of staple hardware items, or a careful and accurate one for higher-value shopping goods. The On hand—On order—Sold record enables a retailer to know how to order sizes, colors, or styles in proper proportion. The form shown on page 470 is one filled in like in actual practice.

This control supplies the information needed to order in quantities that will sell out evenly, as illustrated in the example.

		Lot number				
		1	*2*	*3*	*4*	*5*
On hand	8/1	12	17	14	11	10
Received	8/11	..	12	24	12	..
On hand	9/1	3	14	16	6	2
Sold	8/1-30	9	15	22	17	8

The quantity sold is obtained by adding together the number on hand at the beginning and the number received, and deducting the number on hand at the end. The amount needed to bring stock up to normal is estimated and the order made out. Assuming that no seasonal change in sales is anticipated, that 30 days' supply is sufficient to order, that six is the minimum packing per lot number, and that 48 is the minimum shipment, the order is estimated thus:

		Lot number				
	Total	*1*	*2*	*3*	*4*	*5*
Sold 8/1-30	71	9	15	22	17	8
On hand 9/1	41	3	14	16	6	2
Needed to replenish stock	30	6	1	6	11	6
Necessary to order 9/1	48	6	6	12	18	6

True, 18 units more than are required for the next period are being purchased, but the merchandise is needed at once. Stocks will be balanced again at the time of the next check and order.

When the shipment is received, the contents should be checked against the on-order figures. If there are variations, the on-order figures must be changed to correspond if the next calculations of figures are to be accurate.

The On hand—On order—Sold form is flexible and adaptable to all types of goods handled in limited-price variety and general merchandise stores. Varying the checking interval does not detract from the usefulness of the information obtained.[6]

[6] Adapted from *Establishing and Operating a Variety and General Merchandise Store, op. cit.*, pp. 144-46.

Perpetual inventories are not likely to justify their expense in most departments of an average small store unless the complete Retail Method is used or the perpetual inventory is confined to an important line of goods of high unit value and pronounced demand changes. With such a system the merchant knows at all times the amounts of goods that should be on hand, either in dollar value or in units, or both.

Control Systems

Stores having a very small volume of sales and limited amounts of merchandise may not need much of a merchandise control system. Continuous first-hand contact with stocks on hand may be sufficient. Even in larger stores where persons responsible for inventory control are in training for positions as buyers or managers, emphasis is often placed on daily personal familiarity with merchandise on hand and merchandise needed. However, in most cases the small retailer should take advantage of a suitable merchandise control system as an aid to his numerous managerial duties.

Before deciding what type of merchandise control system to use, at least the following factors should be considered: (1) what information is needed, (2) what uses will be made of it, (3) by whom it will be used, (4) how much detail is necessary, (5) what expense is justified to obtain this information, (6) the type of merchandise involved, and (7) what systems are used by other stores of a similar type. The last consideration may enable the merchant both to profit by the experience of other retailers in the same line of business in selecting the best system and also to compare his operating data with their results.

Basically there are two types of merchandise control systems: dollar and unit. In the former standards are set, operations are reported, and corrective action is taken in terms of the dollar value of the inventory concerned. Thus, planned sales for a department might be $10,000 for a six-month season; actual sales and purchases are reported in dollar value, usually at retail, and adjustments needed are made in terms of dollar value. This makes the buyer responsible for converting dollar amounts into specific items and quantities of goods. In unit control the same steps are carried out in terms of number of items of each kind of merchandise or inventory. Dollar control is ordinarily used for all departments and kinds of merchandise; unit control is employed primarily when an assortment or variety is included under one class or line of goods. Unit control frequently involves some form of perpetual inventory to cover in physical quantity each important variation within the line of goods concerned. The type of unit control to use depends upon: regularity of the relative sales of each variety, unit value of the merchandise, length of the selling season, store policy, and possibly other factors.

When each variety within a line or class of goods sells at a fairly constant rate throughout the year, a model stock system with periodic physical counts is sufficient. A checklist may be used with clerical assistants to do the checking. Or maximum and minimum stock systems may be employed. In the case of seasonal goods or of others with a short selling period, such as skates, staple housecleaning items, or rubbers, checking should be more frequent and greater attention should be given by the buyer to prevent loss from "outs" or end-of-season overstocks. When the unit value of each item is small, unit control can be operated in terms of reserve stock or full cartons rather than of individual items. This is sometimes called a "requisition system."

The most valuable area for unit control is in shopping goods and especially in fashion merchandise of fairly high unit value, such as wearing apparel, shoes, furniture, and many house furnishings and appliances. For such merchandise, unit control is obtained by keeping a daily running record of sales and stocks of each variety of each item within the line or class of goods. Two types of systems are in general use: merchandise tag and clerk tabulation. In the former each piece of merchandise has attached to it a tag of some sort, usually perforated and ordinarily with two duplicate parts. Each time an article is sold, one part of the tag is removed and either sent in to the office with the salescheck or deposited in a special container by the salesclerk. Small stores often have each salesclerk record or tabulate the specific size, style, color, and other characteristics of merchandise as each item is sold. Sometimes this information is included on the salescheck instead of being kept as a separate record. Modern cash registers furnish stubs that are often used for unit control records. In all cases a unit control clerk, who may be the proprietor himself in a very small store, should summarize the data at least once a day so that a perpetual inventory in units of each variety may be kept.

To the small or beginning merchant, unit control seems like an unnecessary amount of trouble. However, it is the basis of modern merchandising. To be out of a particular size, style, color, price line, or other variety of a line or class of goods is the same as for a carpenter to have a saw but no hammer, a plumber to have pipe but no wrench, or a stenographer to be without a pencil. One merely lacks what it takes to do the job. Not only does the merchant lose the sale, but he helps his prospective customer acquire the habit of trading with competitors. There is probably no greater error in merchandising than to be out of wanted items, even occasionally! Naturally, however, this does not mean that a retailer should stock every item asked for by customers no matter how infrequently.

Our emphasis on unit rather than dollar control has been deliberate. The whole trend of merchandising for three decades has been toward greater unit control. Dollar control is necessary, especially for the huge organization with hundreds of merchandise departments and scores of buyers; but it is unit control that spells merchandising success or failure in the small store. If the unit control is right, dollar control will take care of itself—to the merchant's profit.

Staple or Fashion Goods?

Merchandise differs as to the type of inventory control system most suitable. Stability of demand and regularity of sale are major factors. For staple items, such as pins, needles, brooms, nails, tooth paste, bread, milk, chewing gum, and cigarettes—products which rarely change and have fairly regular sales—simple routine merchandise control systems are best. Certain items are staples for particular seasons, such as fireworks, Easter eggs, Santa Clauses, overshoes, skates, and water wings. These differ from year-round staples principally in the timing aspect. Inventories should be large at the beginning and as small as possible to secure maximum profitable sales during the closing days of the season. Whether to close out or carry over an inventory is a matter of store policy. In either case the inventory of seasonal merchandise should be at a minimum at the end of the selling period.

Staple items are fairly well standardized. In modern merchandising many staple goods consist of a series or assortment of individual items that are not substitutes for one another and that sell at different rates. Three types of variation are especially important: size, kind, and brand. Others that often operate are color, price, quality, or characteristics peculiar to certain merchandise. There are few varieties or sizes of pins but many of needles and still more of nails. With cigarettes, brand is important. In staple canned goods, brand, size, grade (quality), and price are major variables. Many items are staples with fashion-affected varieties, such as thread, bias tape, and most yard-goods. White and black in popular sizes are likely to be staple, with other colors and patterns, as well as types of construction, affected by the current fashions.

Although it is not the function of merchandise control to predict demand or fashion changes, it is necessary to use different control systems when demand is erratic or subject to fashion influence. Information is needed concerning (1) the quantity of merchandise to be on hand at each time and (2) reports or warnings to be sent to buyers in case the inventory changes from that planned. If proper information is furnished by the buyers, the inventory can easily be controlled, for a balance can be maintained or due notification sent to buyers. Appropriate action is their responsibility.

Assortments or variations within one line or kind of merchandise is one of the constant factors even for fashion goods. The proper inventory of staple goods in relation to sales is called a basic stock; that of fashion goods is called a model stock. Use of a good basic stock list should keep a store supplied with items demanded well over 90 per cent of the time; a model stock list will help keep wanted items on hand about 80 per cent of the time. In either case the inventory control must keep goods on hand for each size, pattern, color, style, price line, or other basic variable in proportion to its rate of sale. Unit control is often necessary for this purpose.

Inventory Taking

In retailing the trend has been to take physical inventories more frequently, at least twice a year and sometimes monthly or even weekly. With proper planning and organization this is not too difficult in most stores, and experience proves it to be well worth the extra trouble. A tickler, or reminder, file may be set up showing the dates to inventory each department. Thus faster sellers can be counted more frequently than staple items.

A serious weakness of many small retailers is regarding a physical inventory as a necessary evil. Actually this should be a major source of profitable ideas. Proper planning, cleaning out old stock, remarking certain items, having forms on hand, and training counters will reduce the drudgery of actually taking the inventory. It should be taken carefully by important lines or classes of goods at retail and cost, if the older cost method is used, and by age or length of time each article has been in stock. Then *use* the inventory records for sales planning and promotion, especially to clean out old stocks and reduce overstocks, and for future buying, as well as to calculate profits and net worth.[7]

Shrinkage, or losses due to merchandise becoming unsaleable for one reason or another, can be costly. Butler Brothers, variety goods distributors and sponsors of the Ben Franklin Stores, famous voluntary chain, warns its member stores as follows:

1. Cut down on shrinkage by the careful handling of understocks . . . keep items that are easily soiled or damaged carefully boxed.

2. Inaccuracies are responsible for big losses. Give accurate measurement on yard goods and accurate weight on candy.

3. Be sure that items are marked correctly, prices quoted correctly and that displays carry correct price signs.

4. Arrange displays carefully. Don't pile items that are easily damaged or dog-eared . . . customers want FRESH merchandise.

5. Handle carefully all fragile or easily soiled merchandise.

6. Straighten and dust counters and understock regularly. Refill displays . . . put new goods on the bottom and sell from the top.

7. Separate merchandise that comes folded or nested together.

8. Cover counters at night.[8]

Conclusions

Most small retailers hope some day to be big operators. Before we leave this analytical discussion of merchandise control, attention should be called

[7] Clyde Bedell, *Seven Keys to Retail Profits* (New York: McGraw-Hill Book Company, Inc., 1931), pp. 139-143.
[8] From *Ben Franklin Store Manual*, prepared by G. L. Rothermel (Butler Brothers, Chicago, 1957), p. 262.

to a method that was originally confined to such control but now embraces the whole area of retail accounting.

The Retail Method of accounting control, which is discussed in Chapter 24, is the only method that the authors recommend for most stores in view of its many advantages and continuing spread to additional fields. However, a beginning retailer might keep both retail and cost inventory records to advantage during the first few years. Under the Retail Method a perpetual inventory must be maintained at retail prices and careful records kept of all changes in the retail price. This gives a record of markdowns, discounts, and other changes that is a valuable management aid. It is independent of the unit control and has other limitations that should be understood by the proprietor. In particular, it must be used by departments or by merchandise classification, not on a storewide basis. In contrast, dollar control in retailing may include the total store inventory, or any subdivisions as needed. Usually the following subdivisions for dollar control are useful: departmental, price line, merchandise classification, and others in particular cases. Control should observe the rule of the golden mean—enough, but not too much.

Different merchandise control systems should be used as needed. The Retail Method is not suited to "manufacturing" departments like food service or alterations. Although some form of dollar control (physical or perpetual inventory) should be used for all merchandise, unit control may be needed to supplement dollar control in certain fashion lines. The use of several systems in a small retail store is illustrated in the following description of recommended practice.

Stock control for retailers of phonograph records has been selected for discussion because it illustrates how a merchant may need three different systems, each appropriate for one kind of merchandise. In retailing phonograph records these are: a perpetual inventory system for albums, a weekly physical inventory for popular records, and a "stock envelope" system for standard records.

The basis of the perpetual inventory is a filing card that contains such fundamental information as the title of the album, the name of the artist, the supplier, and the album number. The rest of the card is usually arranged in columns, with a heading for each; in the columns are recorded the date and the numbers ordered, received, sold, and remaining. When the clerk in charge places an order, the number ordered is set down. As the albums are received, this fact is recorded on another line opposite the date received. When one or more albums are sold, the date is listed, the number of albums sold is recorded, and the number remaining on hand is computed and set down, usually the first thing each morning for the transactions of the previous day.

To increase the accuracy of recording, salespeople make out a sales slip with the album number written on it for every album sold. The sales as indicated on the sales slips are then posted on the perpetual inventory cards.

Another common but less satisfactory method is to place "markers" similar to book marks in each album when it is received and put into stock. Each marker carries the number of the album in which it is inserted. When the album is sold, the salesperson removes the marker and drops it in a drawer. The next morning the clerk who keeps the inventory cards need only collect and tally the album markers to learn the daily sales. This is an adaptation of the stub system used for wearing apparel. Disadvantages of the system are that the markers get lost easily and careless clerks forget to remove them when they make sales.

The weekly physical inventory system is preferred for controlling stocks of the 25 or 50 "pops" carried in most stores. Inventory cards similar to those described for albums are used for recording weekly counts and computing the previous week's sales of each title.

For standard records the stock envelope system provides adequate information with a minimum of effort. The factory envelope is removed from one record of each title and the record is placed in a bright-colored stock envelope. Other records of the same title are placed by it.

On the stock envelope is placed a sticker bearing the catalogue number, title, and maker of the record. The beginning inventory is listed, with the date, and subsequent entries are made when more records of that title are received. It is a simple matter for the clerk to count the number of records on hand for any title and subtract it from the original inventory and receipts to learn the sales volume to date.

The sticker has room for the clerk to record the date and the number of records ordered whenever he places an order for a particular title. Most dealers use the semiannual inventory as a time to review every album and standard or classical item in their stock.[9]

STOCK CONTROL IN WHOLESALING

Wholesalers buy in large lots and carry heavy inventories. In the grocery field from 30 ot 50 per cent of the wholesaler's total assets are investments in inventory. This is his largest single asset item. The trend toward widespread acceptance of the low gross margin and high turnover principle, evident for many years in wholesaling, increases the need for accurate current information on inventories and good stock control. The aim of many wholesalers to supply to their independent retail customers all goods needed at prices

[9] *Stock Control of Phonograph Records,* Small Business Aids No. 39 (Washington, D. C.: U. S. Department of Commerce), condensed from "Disk Stock Control," *Radio & Television Retailing* (Caldwell-Clements, Inc., New York, September 1946). See also: Harry A. Lipson, "Practical Stock Control for the Smaller Store," University of Alabama Business News (July 15, 1954), p. 1-8; R. D. Lewis and D. Stote, How to Keep Merchandising Records, Rev. ed. (New York: Fairchild Publications, 1954) ; and Lester R. Nathan, "Merchandise Management Profitable to the Small Retailers," *Journal of Retailing* (Summer 1951), pp. 86-108.

competitive with those of chain stores and mail-order houses can be effectuated only with good stock control.

In the wholesale hardware field the United States Department of Commerce found some years ago[10] that concerns using unit control had a maximum percentage of capital in inventory of 50.3, whereas the maximum of others was 75 per cent. Other significant findings in this survey were as follows:

> Establishments using a stock control system get a higher turnover. No establishment in this group had a turnover less than 2.5 times a year, and five of them had more than 4 turns. On the other hand, those with no system of stock control had as low as 0.9 turn a year, and five had an average turnover of less than 3 times.
>
> Establishments with a careful system of stock control were able to operate on smaller gross margins. One establishment using a stock control system was operating on a margin of 14.5 per cent, and yet it gave a return to stockholders of 6.8 per cent. Nine establishments using a unit control system operated on a margin of less than 20 per cent, and the highest margin for the group was 20.8 per cent. Seven of the eleven establishments recording no systematic stock control had a margin of 20 per cent or larger.
>
> The maximum percentage of capital in inventory in establishments with unit control system was 50.3 per cent, whereas the maximum in the others was 75 per cent. Four firms with poor or no systems reported inventory over 50 per cent of capital. The practical measure of the effectiveness of stock control, however, is on the basis of earnings and profits. In both items the earnings of those establishments with unit control systems were much more stable than establishments with no control system.[11]

Inventory control is continuing to receive the attention of wholesalers. A committee of the National Electrical Wholesalers' Association in a report to the membership recently stressed many of the advantages of maintaining an adequate warehouse stock record system. The advantages mentioned, in addition to the value of reliable inventory records in case of fire, include: (1) convenience of having a continuous record in the office of items on hand and the quantity available for shipment; (2) ability to place replenishing orders without taking a physical inventory: (3) use of information contained on stock record cards to calculate rates of turnover and quantities to order for each item; (4) prompt filling of back orders when goods are received by placing a "rider" listing customer back orders on the stock record; (5) reduction of costly errors in ordering by including on each card such essential information as complete and accurate catalogue numbers, description of the

---

[10] Although the specific data contained in the report of this study may not represent current conditions, the authors believe its findings have permanent validity; and they are supported in this by the Managing Director of the Southern Wholesale Hardware Association, Orlando, Florida, who has referred to the report as one of the most practical books published regarding hardware wholesaling.

[11] "Buying the Wholesale Stock," *Hardware Distribution in the Gulf Southwest,* Domestic Commerce Series No. 52 (Washington, D. C.: U. S. Department of Commerce, Bureau of Foreign and Domestic Commerce, 1932), pp. 72-73.

stock item, manufacturer's full name, standard package quantities, terms of shipment if minimum list value or minimum weight factors are needed by the manufacturer to establish the most advantageous discount or most advantageous F.O.B. point; (6) use of the cards as a cross reference to indicate substitute items for "out of stocks"; (7) saving of the time of the sales manager, manufacturer's representatives, and salesmen by using the stock record cards to review inventory conditions; (8) "costing" of sales from data on the cards at the time of taking physical inventories; and (9) disclosure of misappropriation of merchandise, especially of small stock items.

Even in the small wholesale firm the "office" where ordering is done and customer orders are received is usually physically separated from the warehouse where goods are stored. Thus, the accuracy and frequency of reports on inventories on hand are especially important. In the warehouse it is often desirable to store part of a shipment in "dead storage" rather than with that part used for current order filling. This introduces the danger of overlooking part of a lot of goods when securing information for stock control reports.

In wholesaling, as in retailing, merchandise is usually classified into departments for stock control, layout, and other purposes.

Before discussing methods and systems used for inventory control, we may call attention to the key position occupied by this activity as illustrated in Figure 6.

Although small wholesalers use the same three basic methods of keeping track of inventories mentioned earlier—observation, physical count, and perpetual inventory—there are some variations by lines of business. One authority lists six methods suitable for small wholesalers: (1) actual physical inventory, (2) physical inspection, (3) continuous stock taking, (4) tickler method, (5) purchase record system, and (6) real perpetual inventory.[12] The last term, as it is used in wholesaling, usually refers to a perpetual inventory in terms of units (cases), not merely in terms of value.

In the grocery field the observation method is commonly used in small houses and by some larger firms. No record is made of the amounts on hand. Either the manager or the warehouseman is responsible for observing stock frequently. If the warehouseman notices that a pile of merchandise does not diminish in size, he notifies the manager and the latter decides what to do. Another duty is to guard against out-of-stocks. When a stock gets low, he has to report to the manager. Even in the smallest houses observation methods place great dependence upon the observation of warehousemen and the memory of buyers.[13]

In the hardware field the observation method is supplemented by the use

[12] Theodore N. Beckman and Nathanael H. Engle, and Robert D. Buzzell, "Inventory Control," *Wholesaling,* 3rd ed. (New York: Ronald Press Co., 1959), pp. 490-491.

[13] "Inventory Control," *Effective Grocery Wholesaling,* Economic Series No. 14 (Washington, D. C.: U. S. Department of Commerce, Bureau of Foreign and Domestic Commerce, 1941), p. 145.

of "short lists" or "outs," and "getting low" reports sent in to the office.[14] "Short lists" are records of lines usually in stock but temporarily out, for which orders have been received that cannot be filled.

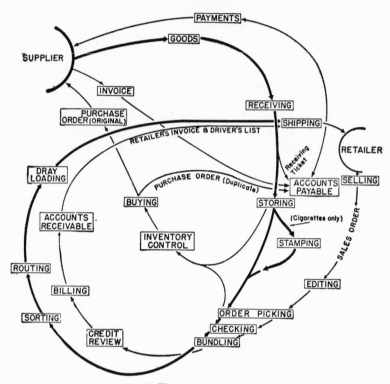

FIGURE 7. Flow of goods and records.

Source: W. H. Meserole, *A Study of Tobacco Wholesalers' Operations,* Industrial Series No. 62 (Washington, D.C.: U. S. Department of Commerce, 1946), p. 52.

Periodical stock count methods are widely used in the grocery and other wholesale fields and are recommended for drug wholesalers to replace their more expensive case labeling method.

The periodical stock count system is based on a periodic count, fast-moving items being counted frequently and slow-moving items being counted less often. This means that some items may be counted daily and others only monthly. Like purchases and goods received, the counts are entered in a stock book, usually one for each department. The pages in the stock book may provide for any desired number of items of information. However, the simpler the form, the easier the operation.[15]

[14] "Buying the Wholesale Stock," Hardware Distribution in the Gulf Southwest, Domestic Commerce Series No. 52 (Washington, D. C.: U. S. Department of Commerce, Bureau of Foreign and Domestic Commerce, 1932), pp. 70-71.

[15] *Effective Use of Wholesale Drug Warehouses,* Industrial Series No. 68 (Washington, D. C.: U. S. Department of Commerce, 1947), p. 31.

Often "in and out" cards are used to record inventory counts as well as purchases, or a simple inventory card on which merely the date and amount of each count are recorded may be used.

Few of even the larger wholesalers in the grocery and drug fields use a perpetual inventory system (by units) because of the extra expense entailed. An interesting analysis of stock controls used by hardware wholesalers was prepared by the U. S. Department of Commerce. Out of 76 establishments of all sizes, 30 had unit control, 13 used perpetual inventory control, and others relied upon devices as follows: 7 on buyer's records, 7 on a system of warehouse reports sent in by men in charge of the stock, 5 on reports of "shorts" from the warehouse, 1 on "want lists," 6 on special individuals such as warehouse foremen who were appointed to take the responsibility for watching the stock, and 7 on no system at all. Although every wholesale house had some system of stock control, 23 per cent of the wholesale-retail firms had no system at all. It was usually the larger firms that used unit control.[16]

An adequate inventory control system makes it possible to establish certain standards useful in controlling inventory and purchasing activities. Such standards include order points, which indicate when to buy; maximum and minimum stock standards, which are safeguards against out-of-stocks and overstocks; and standard-order quantities, which indicate how much to buy. These standards can be set up for each item in stock.

The order point will be based on the average time lapse that occurs between purchase and receipt of the merchandise and the maximum rate of sales during that interval, so that sufficient stock will be in the warehouse at the time of ordering to avoid out-of-stocks before the new goods are received. The minimum stock, which represents a margin of safety against out-of-stocks, can be computed by subtracting the average sales during the time required to fill an order from the quantity established as the ordering point. The maximum quantity of stock is, of course, the maximum old stock expected to be on hand when a new shipment is received plus the standard-order quantity. An example will clarify the concept of these standards:

Minimum Stock

Cases

Order point (maximum amount likely to be sold during the time in which order is being filled as shown by the inventory control) 50

Less: Average amount sold during time in which order is being filled (as shown by the inventory control) 25

Minimum-stock standard 25

Maximum Stock

Order point 50

Less: Minimum amount sold during time in which order is being filled (as

16 "Buying the Wholesale Stock," *op. cit.*, p. 71.

shown by the inventory control) 10

Maximum amount likely to be on hand when new order is received 40
Plus: Standard order 300

   Maximum-stock standard 340

The order point and the minimum stock standard are based on (1) the time required to fill an order and (2) variations in sales during this period. These are relatively easy to determine. The maximum stock standard depends largely, of course, upon the size of the standard order. Although a good inventory control system permits setting the order point at lower levels of warehouse stock without incurring the danger of out-of-stocks, the size of standard order has a greater influence in determining the average inventory and thus has a greater influence on the expense of carrying inventory.[17]

Forms for use in stock control are prepared to be used with equipment made by many well-known companies. Many electrical wholesalers prefer some of the visual methods. Many stationery dealers can supply standard forms.

INVENTORY CONTROL IN THE SMALL FACTORY

The frequency with which production would be slowed down or even stopped if some essential material or parts were not in stock led manufacturers years ago to recognize the importance of inventory control. Before stores control was introduced, an "out" condition of some important but inexpensive part was often accompanied by from one to ten years' supplies of other items.

In the small factory the variety of different materials and parts may not be large and inventory control need not be complicated or expensive. But it is always important.

Some control is likely to be needed for raw materials, fabricated parts, and finished products. A common plan is to use a certain number of days' supply as the standard. Quantities of individual items to have on hand are derived from this. For example, each unit of a certain product requires two pounds of material A, three feet of part B, and one fabricated part C. Planned production is 12 units per day and the desired quantity on hand is set at 10 days' supply. Obviously the ideal inventory would consist of 240 pounds of A, 360 feet of B, and 120 units of C. Quantities to order each time would depend on the usual factors, such as time required for delivery, supplier's shipping units, transportation costs, quantity discounts, stability of demand for each item, storage space available, price fluctuations, and company policy.

The results of a survey of inventory control in 37 small companies are summarized as follows:

[17] Adapted from "Inventory Control," *op. cit.*, pp. 156-158.

Information Needed for Inventory Control. One of the most important types of information which a company needs is that which will give it effective control over its inventory. The following information is necessary. In some companies, it may be so simple to obtain that no records are required.

(a) The amount of stock on hand—raw materials, goods-in-process, fabricated parts, finished goods.

(b) Amounts on order (either production or purchase orders).

(c) Amounts allocated for certain jobs or customers.

Findings in Survey of Companies. Of 37 small companies surveyed by the author, 12 companies did not maintain a perpetual inventory of any kind. Nineteen companies had perpetual inventories for raw materials, 15 for finished goods, and seven for fabricated parts. Where there were no perpetual inventories, physical inventories were taken monthly in about half the companies. The remainder of the companies were divided rather evenly among those which took quarterly, semiannual, and annual physical inventories.

Only one company maintained inventory control records in terms of both dollar value and physical units. The other companies kept the record in physical units only. When it was necessary to compute inventory values for the financial statements, the number of units was multiplied by the unit cost.

When perpetual inventories were maintained, some method for comparing the inventory records with the actual goods in the stock rooms had to be used. In a few cases, the only comparison was made by quarterly or annual physical inventories. It was more common, however, to make spot checks of a certain number of items each week. In this way, each item would be checked at least once during the year. Sometimes this method had proved the perpetual inventory to be so accurate that the physical inventory at the end of the year merely consisted of some more spot checks of the items shown in the perpetual inventory records.

In many cases the perpetual inventory of raw materials was maintained only for certain important items. For instance, the manufacturer of molds and machinery kept a perpetual inventory only for steel, and the knit goods manufacturer kept the inventory only for yarn and thread. Other items were treated as supplies and were controlled through monthly or quarterly inventories with visual observation in between.

Inventory information usually was kept on cards. In most cases these cards were in drawers of the so-called visible card type where the bottom of each card protruded enough so that the item could be indicated in the margin. The simplest forms of such cards showed only the order number, issues, receipts, and balance. About half the inventory cards showed not only this information but also information concerning the amounts on order (either production orders or purchase orders). When the order information was shown, it was common to have two cards instead of one.

In five or six companies, the cards showed allocations of material to certain jobs or certain customers' orders, thus preventing the use of the stock for other purposes.

A large proportion of inventory cards had spaces to record the minimum and maximum amounts beyond which the stock was not supposed to go. Several companies also had spaces to show the monthly usage. Both types of information were being entered very irregularly. Those who operated the systems felt that such figures were useful, but under the pressure of getting the work done these bits of indirect information were sacrificed in order to record primary information.

Why Inventory Information Was Kept. The executives interviewed mentioned a variety of reasons for wishing up-to-date information concerning inventories. In the case of raw material inventories, the executives wished to avoid running out of any important item and thus interrupting the production process. In those companies which performed assembly work, perpetual inventories of fabricated parts were considered necessary in order to make sure that enough parts were on hand to start the assembly. Another reason for wishing accurate information concerning the inventory of fabricated parts was to reduce the possibilities of losses when changes in design or materials made some of the items obsolete. In those companies where stocks of finished goods were maintained the executives wished to keep track of finished stocks so as to minimize the number of back orders, and at the same time avoid accumulation of slow-moving items. When the materials or products were of such a nature as to tempt the workers to smuggle some from the factories, inventory control was desirable to detect thefts by showing the exact numbers that should be on hand.

In addition to these reasons for keeping track inventory, the executives wished to make sure that the amounts invested in inventory were kept within bounds. This information seldom was used during the month: perpetual inventories were not employed for such purposes. Ordinarily, the financial statements were used to determine whether the amounts invested in inventory were becoming too high.

Use of Visual or Card System. Whether inventory information was obtained by visual inspection or by using perpetual inventory cards depended upon the size of the company, the number of items in inventory, the number of stock rooms, whether the production was for stock or to order, and whether the production process included assembly. For companies in the early stages of growth the visual system was more common than perpetual inventories. The mere fact of growth, regardless of other factors, tended to force the keeping of perpetual inventories. As companies grew, there were larger volumes of goods on hand so that it became more difficult to count or estimate the amounts. Likewise, growth meant that more persons could take items from stock and forget to mention it.

In most of the companies that did not maintain perpetual inventories, adequate control apparently was achieved by visual methods. For the small companies with simple processes it was easy for the president to step into the stock room and look at a relatively small number of barrels or bins. In a few minutes he could tell whether he was getting low on any of the items in stock. To adopt inventory records under such circumstances would be foolish. It soon would be discovered that the records showed what easily was visible. Actually, such records, if started, invariably are suspended when some rush period occurs, or when somebody becomes sick, and are never reinstated.

Determining Amounts on Order. Inventory records showing the amounts on order are useful only when perpetual inventories are kept. After a company becomes large enough, and has a sufficiently large number of items to warrant a perpetual inventory, the chances are good that the order information should be written rather than kept mentally. The amounts on order change the whole significance of the amounts on hand. Experience indicates that information concerning purchase or manufacturing orders should be very simple in order to minimize possibilities that the data will be omitted when the clerks are rushed. A brief note on production or purchase orders, however, can show the whole picture without recourse to thumbing through the order files.

Determining Allocations of Materials. The same general considerations apply to the presence of columns showing allocations of materials to certain jobs or of finished goods to certain customers. In companies where the amounts involved approach the magnitude of the amounts on hand, the need of showing allocations is definite. On the other hand, in some companies the amount of any material or finished goods that will be withdrawn for one order is only a small fraction of the amounts on hand. In such cases the information concerning allocations may well be omitted from the cards.

The use of a perpetual inventory for certain critical items provides a large proportion of the desired inventory control information with a minimum amount of work. The main consideration in employing such a system is to make sure that all critical items are included. Production, of course, can be stopped by the absence of minor parts just as thoroughly as the absence of more valuable material.[18]

As the findings of this survey brought out, small manufacturers are concerned with the control of inventories in units, not in terms of value. The basic record is the balance-of-stores card. An example of a simple perpetual inventory balance-of-stores record form is illustrated below. If material allocated to future production jobs but not yet disbursed is recorded in a different color, the balance on hand will indicate actual quantities available.

PURCHASING RECORD —— MATERIALS AND SUPPLIES

SOURCES OF PURCHASE:
1. ________ USUAL QUANTITIES PURCHASED:
2. ________ MAXIMUM ________
3. ________ MINIMUM ________
4. ________ TERMS:
5. ________ FRT. PREPAID ☐ FRT. COLLECT ☐

ORDERED				RECEIVED						USAGE		BALANCE ON HAND	
SOURCE	DATE	P.O. NO.	QUANTITY	DATE	QUANTITY	INVOICE AMT.	FRT.	DEL'D COST	UNIT COST	MONTH	QUANTITY	MONTH ENDED	QUANTITY

DESCRIPTION UNIT DEPT. ACCT. NO.

FIGURE 8. Simple balance-of-stores record.

Source: Stuart F. Heinritz, *Purchasing,* 2nd ed. (Englewood Cliffs, N. J.: Prentice-Hall, Inc., 1951), p. 388.

If the small factory carries stocks of different materials that vary widely in relative importance to production, in price, or in other significant ways, inventories should be classified and appropriate methods of control adopted

[18] "A Survey of Inventory Control in 37 Small Companies," Small Business Aids No. 264 (Washington, D. C.: U. S. Department of Commerce), from Paul F. Lawler, *Records of the Control of Growing Manufacturing Enterprises* (Cambridge: Harvard University Division of Research, Graduate School of Business Administration, 1947), pp. 80-93; and *Materials Control for Small Plants,* Management Aids for Small Business No. 35 (Washington, D. C.: Small Business Administration, August 1953).

for each classification. For example, staples may be controlled by a simple maximum-minimum system when both their price and rate of use are fairly constant. If some raw material, such as cotton or grain, that has large and frequent price fluctuations is an important item in the cost of the finished product, a very exacting type of inventory control operated under the close personal supervision of the owner may be required.

Inventory control in the small factory must be synchronized with production on the one hand and with purchasing on the other. This may involve more "paper work" than the small manufacturer cares to undertake. Some firms will handle these details for him and provide counseling service in addition.

Small factories that operate on a customer order basis, such as millwork companies, may require special inventory control methods. It is usually necessary to be able at any time to identify the customer for whom each article is being made and to know what items are still to be delivered on each incompleted order.

FIGURE 9. Customer's order card.

Name *John J. Doe*	Millwork Co.'s Order No.
Address *256 West 5th Avenue*	Order No. *7296*
City *Washington, D. C.*	Order Rec'd *4-30-6-*
Phone No. *926-M*	Date Promised *—*

Delivery Instructions *Bin until notifies us. Then delivers to new house at 1015 East Douglas.*

Pieces		Size		Description	Deliveries
*5/19	6	24 x 24	2 Lt.	Wd. fras. D.C. B17	
5/19	1	24 x 18	"	" " B17	
6/19	1	36 x 18	"	" " B17	
	1	3/0 x 6/8	1 3/4	R dr. fr. **	***
	1	2/8 x 6/8	1 3/8	R " "	

* Date of arrival of material.
** Bin No. in which material is stored.
*** When delivery is made date will be placed in this column.

A simple inventory system that keeps all this information and more on two record cards, eliminates losses and duplicate orders, and expedites shipments from the mill has been developed by one company.

The system is based on a customer's Order Card and a Delivery Record such as those shown here, and on a three-compartment Order File.

When millwork is ordered for a given construction job, the routine followed from receipt of order to actual delivery of the mill work to the customer gives complete stock control at every stage, as described in detail in the footnote reference.[19]

Unless stores control makes it possible to locate each item quickly when needed, it is useless for current production. This requires some systematic plan for storing each item so that it can always be located. Various systems are in use, including: (1) numerical storage—storing each item according to a parts number; (2) storage by type and, within each type, by size; and (3) location systems. The last are the most flexible and seem to be gaining increasing favor in spite of the extra paper work required.

DELIVERY RECORD						
Date of delivery	Order		Material	Buyer	Disposition	No.
	Date	Number				
5/19	4/20	6212	doors	Samson	deliver	122
5/19	4/30	7296	Wd fra.	Doe	bin	123
5/19	5/2	6315	Wds	Peterson	deliver	124
	—					

FIGURE 10. Delivery record.

A location system operates by assigning location symbols to all storage space used. For example, "A10b" might designate aisle A, stack 10, shelf b. Usually similar materials are stored in the same section or area, but this is not essential. Card records show: (1) for each item, where it is stored, and (2) for each storage area, extent to which space is in use and available. Each item must be correctly described according to some standard nomenclature, and identification is facilitated by putting this identification mark on each item or container. Again symbols are often used. Whether to mark with pencil, rubber stamp, or tag, depends upon the type of material and similar factors.[20]

INVENTORY CONTROL IN THE SERVICE ESTABLISHMENT

Both in manufacturing and in service businesses, in contrast to merchandising, inventory control is entirely in terms of units and physical quantities. Naturally, the accounting records show the cost of materials and supplies purchased. In general, materials used in further production are of greatest

[19] *Stock Control for Millwork,* Small Business Aids No. 362 (Washington, D. C.: U. S. Department of Commerce), condensed from "Fingertip Stock Control for Millwork," *Building Supply News* (Industrial Publications, Inc., Chicago, November 1946).

[20] *Simplifying Stock Room Problems,* Small Business Aids No. 237 (Washington, D. C.: U. S. Department of Commerce), condensed from "Simplifying Stock Room Problems," by Benjamin Melnitsky, *Distribution Age* (Chilton Co., Inc., Philadelphia, February 1947).

importance to the manufacturer; supplies are the major items in the service business. However, repair shops and wood- and metal-working shops use parts and materials much as a factory does. To illustrate certain aspects of stores control in two types of service business, the following advice for a laundry and for a metal shop operator is presented:

> Supplies should be stored in a locked place with one person in the plant responsible for their issuance. The supply room should be kept clean and orderly, and if possible, a separate section should be assigned for each type of goods. Scales and measures available for the accurate measuring of all supplies used is one way to keep the supply cost down. Guesswork is always costly. Make sure that the place in which the goods are stored is not damp, and guard strictly against all fire hazards.[21]

Stocks of fast-moving items are depleted quickly unless replenished frequently. Perpetual inventory control arranges for almost automatic reordering. This system involves determining the maximum stock which should be on hand or on order at any one time and the minimum amount below which stocks cannot, with safety, be allowed to drop. Between these extremes is the reordering point.

Unit of Issue:			Description:		
Location:		Unit Value		Time required to obtain:	
Maximum stock:	Minimum Stock:		Reorder Point	Minimum Ordering Point: (Quantity)	
Date:	Quantities in terms of units of issue:				Remarks
	On order	Rec'd	Del'd	Bal. on hand	

FIGURE 11. Perpetual inventory card.

These data should be recorded on an inventory card placed in a bin or tacked on the wall near where each item is stored. The card also contains the amount to reorder each time, the date of each order placed but not yet received, and the running totals of orders received and of removals from the bin or rack. It therefore shows, with reasonable accuracy, the stock on hand. A simple form such as shown here is the only stock control record needed for the small business.

Several times a year the card total should be checked against the actual

---

[21] V. H. Kramer, *Establishing and Operating a Laundry*, Industrial (Small Business) Series No. 37 (Washington, D. C.: U. S. Department of Commerce, 1946), p. 55.

count for all stock items. Occasional spot checks (a few scattered items at a time) in between regular inventory periods should be made to make sure that employees are noting removals on the card and that smaller items are not disappearing.[22]

CONCLUSIONS

Properly handled, inventories of merchandise, materials, and supplies, which are one representation of the owner's capital, may be his major asset. The peculiar thing about many businesses, both large and small, is the extreme care with which cash is guarded and the lack of care exercised over "cash" in the form of inventories. A good rule for the small businessman is to regard his supplier as his banker as far as materials are concerned.

Good inventory control depends in part upon whether the businessman can rely on receiving shipments within an allotted time. Good vendor relationships, fair treatment of suppliers in matters of claims, and prompt payment of bills will help to make this possible. In spite of excellent inventory control, emergencies will arise when unexpectedly depleted inventories must be replaced quickly. In such crucial times the value of good vendor relations is of the utmost importance.

QUESTIONS AND PROBLEMS

1. State the five topics usually included in the scope of inventory control and briefly explain each.

2. Why does the merchant emphasize the value of his inventory, whereas the manufacturer and service operator are concerned primarily with the number of units of theirs?

3. What is the fundamental purpose or objective of inventory control?

4. What, if any, conventional accounting records are used in inventory control? What other records are used? How do you explain these differences? What conclusions can you draw from this situation?

5. Discuss the various ways inventory control in each of the three major fields is related to other departments or functions in each field. Be specific and give illustrations.

6. Assume that you have just bought a going business, and describe how you would proceed with your inventory control.

7. How, if at all, does the importance of inventory control vary with each of the following conditions: (a) size of town, (b) price trend, (c) age of the business, and (d) size or type of business?

8. Give several reasons why the distinction between inventory control and inventory control system is important.

9. Summarize the main points of similarity and of difference between inventory control as used in merchandising and in manufacturing. Discuss.

[22] Adapted from William H. Meyer, and Associates, *Establishing and Operating a Metal Working Shop,* Industrial Series No. 16 (Washington, D. C.: U. S. Department of Commerce, 1945), pp. 119-22.

10. Does the importance of inventory control in each of the three fields of small business vary directly with the relative amounts of total capital invested in inventories? With any other factors? Discuss.

11. Review the discussion in the chapter concerning the risk of inventory losses in manufacturing as compared to merchandising. What management aids in addition to inventory control could be used to minimize these risks in each field? Explain.

12. In separate columns list the ways good merchandise control in the retail store can aid (a) buying, and (b) selling.

13. Would a location system as described in this chapter for a factory be useful for control of reserve stocks in a retail store? Under what conditions? Discuss.

14. Assume that you are starting a small business of a type not discussed specifically in this chapter. Outline an adequate inventory control system for this business and give any needed explanations.

15. Select a particular kind of business for an intensive study of inventory or stores control. After learning all you can from reading and talking to men in the field, see if you can find ways to simplify the paper work needed, reduce the time required to store and to locate items, and reduce losses common in this field.

16. During his first year as owner-manager of an inherited general merchandise store doing $200,000 a year, Tom introduced the Retail Method in the clothing department. Initial opposition and confusion had been overcome by the end of the year, and Tom debated whether to convert the entire store or to add, gradually, certain departments to the Retail Method. Which plan would be better, and why? If the department plan is chosen, in what sequence should departments be taken?

23 • *Credit—A Sales Tool*

The use of credit in business has often been described as representing "man's faith in man." Since the beginning of time, provision for the postponement of payment by seller to buyer has characterized business transactions between responsible parties. Certainly, if in these times all business or domestic transactions were handled on a strictly cash (or C.O.D.) basis, the wheels of business would be slowed down appreciably.

Most businesses in determining their capital requirements include the need for funds representing goods sold but not paid for. The money represented in the cost of the goods may be regarded as being loaned to the buyer. Because the use of capital must be compensated for and because of the record keeping involved in the maintenance of credit accounts, the handling of credit relationships by the seller represents a business expense. As with any other tool or device or method whereby business is facilitated or expedited, the credit function must be carefully controlled if its use is to be a profitable one for the business.

The granting of credit between business firms is traditional, as noted, and in most countries a substantial amount of credit business is done also at the retail level as a service to consumers. In the United States, however, it has become a dominant characteristic of retail merchandising to the point that almost all consumer service businesses (even the variety stores, which a few years ago would never have thought of extending credit!) are now offering it as a means of attracting trade. In other countries, particularly in Northern Europe, considerable momentum is being established which once started and going well will probably become as strong as it has in this country.

TYPES OF CREDIT

Two types of credit are thus recognized according to the purpose implied: *consumer credit* and *mercantile credit*. The former is extended to consumers for the purpose of facilitating the sale of consumption goods, which may be either merchandise or services. The latter, often called commercial or production credit, has as its purpose the encouragement of production, which may be of either a physical or a business nature, as in manufacturing and merchandising, respectively.

Experience shows that, in the retail field, credit-granting firms are more profitable and do a larger volume of business than strictly cash stores. This is true in spite of the also well-known facts that credit stores sell for slightly higher prices than cash stores, that some firms fail because of unwise credit extension, and that the long-time trend in retailing is toward more cash sales —"minimum service" stores.[1]

Mercantile credit is that usually extended by a manufacturer to a wholesaler, distributor, or retailer, or by a wholesaler to a retailer, or by a manufacturer or distributor to an industrial consumer. It may be less of a lending or financing device than a means of simplifying payment. A frequent buyer finds it quite convenient to postpone payment until a number of purchases and deliveries have been made, usually over a period of a month. In this way, when each party adds the figures on his copies of the invoices, including any returns, they should agree, and the obligation is settled by the buyer with one check.

The financing aspect, that is, the lending factor, may on the other hand be the uppermost consideration in the extension of credit. A retailer may not be able to pay until a part of the shipment is sold and paid for. A wholesaler may be unable to pay until his retailer clientele has paid him. A manufacturer is quite often unable to pay until the materials or parts purchased are assembled into the finished product, sold, and paid for. Thus we have a situation where creditor is dependent upon creditor and debtor upon debtor—a basic fact in business life.

A second important classification is that based on characteristics of the credit instruments used—namely, legal aspects and methods of payment. In addition to open account or charge credit, installment credit, and coupon books, prepayment plans may be included, for, although they are not strictly a type of credit, they are used frequently in retailing as a substitute for other forms of credit extension. The various and increasingly varied types of credit arrangements provided by retailers, hotels, restaurants, and service establishments are discussed in detail later.

In most fields of business we find both cash and credit firms, with a sizable proportion of the concerns selling both for cash and on credit. The small businessman will consider his preferences and those of his customers, balance the cost and risk of credit extension against the extra business to be expected, and

---

[1] Albert J. Wood, "A Charge Customer is Worth Nearly Four Times as Much as a Cash Customer," *Credit World* (December 1953), pp. 5-7; Joseph L. Wood, *Better Sales Through Credit* (New York: Vantage Press, Inc., 1954).

compare the capital needed for a credit business with his own resources before deciding which policy he will follow.

After the decision to grant credit (a matter of policy) is made, the question of how much credit to extend arises. The businessman should weigh both the advantages and disadvantages. Among the former are:

1. A more personal relationship can be maintained with credit customers, who feel they are part of the firm.

2. Credit customers are likely to be more regular than cash customers, who tend to go where bargains are greatest.

3. Credit customers are more interested in quality and service than in price.

4. Goodwill is built up and maintained more easily.

5. Goods can be exchanged and adjustments made with greater ease. If necessary, goods can also be sent out on approval.

6. A list of credit customers provides a permanent mailing list for special sales promotions.

Some disadvantages are:

1. Capital is tied up in merchandise bought by charge customers.

2. If the merchant has borrowed the extra money required when credit is granted, the interest is added to the cost.

3. Some losses from bad debts and customers with fraudulent intentions are bound to occur.

4. Some credit customers, knowing they do not have to pay for the goods at the time of purchase, overestimate their ability to pay in the future.

5. Credit customers feel more at liberty to abuse the privileges of returning goods and having goods sent out on approval.

6. Credit increases operating and overhead costs by adding the expenses of investigation and of the bookkeeping entailed in keeping accounts, sending out statements, and collecting payments.

The relative importance of credit in a particular field and customers' basic needs are also necessary considerations. To illustrate, manufacturers selling to the trade may do over 80 per cent of their volume on credit, but one firm selling almost entirely to a few large buyers could dispense with credit because it would not be needed. The type of credit called for will be influenced by the custom in each field as well as by the nature of the goods.

The basic considerations as to credit extension to a given customer begin when his first order is received and must continue uninterrupted from then on. On receipt of each order, the person granting credit must make a decision as to the probability of the merchandise being paid for. This decision can be no better than the facts on which it is based.

Sources of information on which the individual credit decision may be based include:

1. A complete credit application form, properly filled out and checked, utilizing any references available
2. Local, state, or national "professional" credit agencies
3. Trade association facilities insofar as they provide reliable credit information
4. Banks; officials, credit departments, general and special reports as available
5. Trade and general business bulletins and publications; newspaper articles on business changes and legal decisions
6. Records within the firm; salesmen's reports; information from other customers.

Every customer will therefore have, as a part of his listing by the firm, a credit record and rating, which, being constantly subject to change, must be re-evaluated with equal constancy. While considerations regarding individual regular customers will vary, many businesses require that the credit status of most buyers be checked quarterly and that record of these "checks" be noted for management's protection. Obviously, some customers will require a recheck on the occasion of every purchase.

Many mercantile credit agencies and most retail credit bureaus have available a standard credit application form. Manufacturers, wholesalers or others may have models for distributors and retailers. A credit application form for mercantile use should gather the following information:

1. Name of firm (or proprietor if unincorporated)
2. Street address and telephone number
3. Kind of business.
4. Number of years in operation
5. Other firms who have granted this firm credit
6. Banking connections
7. Other financial references
8. Personal credit data on owners or management—previous connections, home ownership, and so on
9. Amounts of credit and terms desired.

Adequate space will be provided on such a form for credit administrators to note pertinent information as to decision, current limits, any changes, new information, and date of last check on this customer's credit status. The quality of factual evidence used as the guide must be unassailable. Refusal of credit, or overzealousness in collections, can be as dangerous as it can be protective. Refusal of the order not only alienates the customer but depresses the morale of salesmen or other sales representatives. The credit manager, if any, can be most embarrassed professionally through such an error. All refusals should be accompanied by documented reasons therefor, and presented in an organized manner.

To summarize, credit is a facility provided by the business whereby the customer can buy more conveniently. It is a means of selling and often is employed as a device for sales promotion.[2] For this reason it is most important that credit departments and sales departments, or persons representing those functions, understand the purpose of the business which each represents. The credit person must recognize the fact that his job is to see to it that selling is made easier because buying is made more convenient. The salesman must recognize equally well that the credit department function is to protect the financial interests of the business. Thus, they must work hand in hand in providing and exercising this important function of distribution.[3]

CREDIT AS A SALES TOOL

Small businessmen who do a credit business are losing most of the advantages of this method if they fail to capitalize on the information their credit records provide for additional sales promotion. This is particularly true of open-account customers. Stores call this "customer control analysis" and manufacturers and wholesalers regard it as "sales analysis." In the small business it simply means watching each customer's account (1) to discover opportunities for suggesting the purchase of certain items considered appropriate in the light of previous purchases, (2) to gather material concerning sales by departments or by salesmen, and (3) to detect any decline in purchases that might suggest a drifting away from the firm. When such a trend is discovered in time, an alert merchant can often investigate the cause and take appropriate steps to prevent what would otherwise result in the permanent loss of regular customers.

There are three major ways the small enterpriser can secure extra business as a result of credit extension:

1. By offering special services with the account, customers will be more anxious to open an account, to maintain their credit standing, and to make greater use of the account than they would if it is merely a means of deferring payment. Most stores will cash personal checks and order special merchandise more readily for charge than for cash customers. Manufacturers and other small businessmen who want to expand their credit business should investigate special services that could be used to make an account more attractive. Naturally, care should be exercised not to alienate any of their cash customers.

2. By using the information available in the records of past purchases management may develop case histories for each customer, showing his purchasing power, buying habits, time of purchasing, special merchandise preferences, hobbies, and similar data. Similarly, as indicated, failure to purchase

---

[2] Pearce C. Kelley and Norris B. Brisco, "Credit Sales Management," Chapter 18 in *Retailing, Basic Principles,* 3rd ed. (Englewood Cliffs, N. J.: Prentice-Hall, Inc., 1957).

[3] See: "Ten Keys to Basic Credits and Collections," Dun & Bradstreet, Inc., (1956), prepared by W. H. Kuehn, Director of Education, for use of D&B subscribers.

over a period may be noted and acted upon. This sales analysis information available from the records may be supplemented by that obtained directly from each credit customer at the time application is made for an account, through personal contacts and by means of a judicious use of questionnaires. Such information can be used for direct-mail advertising, special sales promotions, timing buying and merchandise showings, selecting small lots of special merchandise for particular groups of customers, and in many other ways.

3. Management research based on closer contact relations is another way to secure extra business. This, in most small concerns, should not, of course, be confined to credit customers. There are sound reasons, however, why the charge customers constitute a better group than cash customers for management research purposes. Two objectives deserve careful study by management. First, charge customers as a class are usually steady repeat patrons of the company. Management action based on what this group wants is likely to be on firmer ground than that based mainly on other sources of information. Second, a fundamental principle of successful credit business is to keep the charge customer on the books. To do so requires continuous knowledge of the customer's needs, changing status, interests, and so forth. Successful management in any area of business involves forecasting and continuously adjusting to conditions, especially those relating to major groups of present customers. Beyond these criteria are more complex but also more revealing credit and collection control indexes for measuring the effectiveness of credit granting. These include the following:

1. *Rejection Percentage*—numbers of persons refused credit, reasons analyzed.
2. *Number of Accounts*—new accounts, closed accounts, total.
3. *Credit Sales Volume*—increase or decrease, by month or vs. year ago.
4. *Credit and Total Sales*—credit sales as percentage of total sales.
5. *Accounts Receivable Outstanding*—changes and trends, credit sales volume.
6. *Inactive Accounts to Total Accounts*—trends in use of credit by customers.
7. *Turnover of Charge Customers*—customers lost during the year or other period. Collection control (percentages) indexes include the following:
8. *Collection Percentage*—amount collected divided by amount outstanding at month's opening.
9. *Volume of Collections*—percentage of change in dollar volume of collections.
10. *Delinquency Percentage*—proportion of past due accounts.
11. *Age of Receiveables*—Percentages past due by periods—30 days, 60 days, etc.
12. *Bad Debt Losses*—Percentages of volume written off as uncollectable.[4]

[4] Clyde William Phelps, "Credit and Collection Controls For Small Marketers," Small Marketers Aids No. 33 (Washington, D. C.: Small Business Administration, May 1958). See also by the same authority: "Improving Collections from Credit Sales," Small Market-

COLLECTIONS [5]

It would be difficult to overemphasize the importance of collections for the small business that extends credit. This is the "make or break" area. Although credit business can be very profitable, too many slow accounts will probably cause the firm to suffer a loss and prevent making a profit because:

1. The older an account becomes, the harder it is to collect.
2. Attempts made to collect the money due take time away from other duties.
3. Formerly good customers avoid the firm because it is embarrassing to meet the one to whom they owe money.
4. Slow accounts tie up funds needed to operate other divisions of the business. As a result, the firm's own credit suffers and the firm is not able to take advantage of cash discounts.

FORM FOR DETERMINING AVERAGE AGE OF ACCOUNTS

Date	Last week's charge sales	Amount due today	The number of days' business on the books*
Feb. 7	410 —	740 —	$10\frac{1}{2}$
14	446 —	770 —	11
21	390 —	800 —	$11\frac{1}{2}$
28	420 —	840 —	12
Mar. 7	450 —	730 —	$10\frac{1}{2}$

* Amount due today divided by average charge sales per day last month.

Experience shows that unless the firm extending credit is continually alert to the danger of slow accounts its owner may find himself in a hopeless situation before he realizes that something is wrong. Two basic methods are used to measure the trend toward slow accounts: (1) charge sales compared to collections, and (2) charge sales compared to the amount owed by customers. When a retailer's charge sales during a week amount to more than his collections on charge sales, it may mean either that his charge business is increasing or that his collections were poor. There should be a close relationship between

---

ers Aids No. 49 (Washington, D. C.: Small Business Administration, No. 49, October 1959). A basic reference in retail credit matters in C. W. Phelps, *Retail Credit Management* (St. Louis, Mo.: National Retail Credit Association, 1949). See also: T. N. Beckman and R. Bartels, *Credits and Collections In Theory and Practice* (New York: McGraw-Hill Book Company, Inc., 1955), and W. J. Schultz and H. Reinhardt, *Credit and Collection Management* (Englewood Cliffs, N. J.: Prentice-Hall, Inc., 1954).

[5] See also: *Improving Collections from Credit Sales,* Small Marketers Aids No. 49 (Washington, D. C.: Small Business Administration, October 1959).

collections and charge sales. The danger sign is when collections lag behind charges week after week.

Bad debt losses, normally, are deductible from income before taxation. The full amount of the debt may be written off if it can logically be assumed uncollectible, or a part of it, if collection appears to be only partially possible. Losses taken on debt settlements are normally deductible from income. Common sense must prevail here, with adequate proof of loss essential. Naturally, debts written off but later collected are considered as income. Once an account becomes past due, there is a twofold objective to accomplish: (1) getting the money and (2) retaining the patronage and goodwill of the customer. Prompt followup after the due date is desirable, whether by letter, telephone, or personal call. Telephone conversation or personal contact permits ready adjustment of the caller's approach to the debtor's reaction. The collection letter calls for most careful preparation. It must possess certain qualities which will collect the bill yet maintain goodwill with the customer. One authority offers these suggestions:

> The requirements of collection mail do not differ from those of any other business communication. Actually, every letter written is a selling letter. The writer is either trying to sell himself, his product or his company, to the recipient. Consequently, there are certain fundamental features that each letter should contain. These are:
>
> 1. Positive Approach—Avoid the use of negative words. They create a bad impression on the reader. Thus, avoid such words as: refuse, unfavorable, wrong, unsatisfactory, dishonest.
> 2. Directness—Write to the person to whom the letter is addressed. Make your words personal—use the YOU approach.
> 3. Spirit—Put life, friendliness and enthusiasm into your letters. A warm feeling will always have a good effect on the reader.
> 4. Care—Do not be too demanding or pressing. Use tact in asking for what you want.
> 5. Brevity—Do not clutter up your letters with big words or long sentences and paragraphs.
> 6. Above all, avoid glittering generalities. Be specific, precise, down-to-earth.
>
> The success of any collection mail program lies in the care that is given to keeping letters and notices current. It is advisable to change the wording of your form letters frequently. This is especially necessary when studies of your mail indicate that a particular letter has lost its pulling power.[6]

The question often arises as to who must eventually "pay" for credit—for the use of funds involved, for collection procedures, for the risks involved, and for losses. Some authors in the field of credit feel that the credit department should support itself and indeed this is true where credit extension is limited to that of the installment type. In the typical retail store, the regular

---

[6] Harold A. Wallace, *Starting and Managing a Small Credit Bureau and Collection Service* (Washington, D. C.: Small Business Administration, 1959).

30-day charge account still comprises a large percentage of the credit volume although the percentage appears to be declining. The major portion of credit department upheaval and, therefore, of expenses in handling the 30-day accounts is caused by those not paid within that period.

These added expenses must be reflected either in increased prices or losses by the merchant; if in increased prices, the burden is on the "good paying" customer. For such reasons, it has been suggested recently that more firms should charge a penalty fee for past due regular accounts as is done in mercantile credit. If this were done (assuming the customer had been advised to that effect at the time credit was requested) it should considerably reduce the overall cost of retail credit extension.

The *1958-59 Credit Management Year Book* of the National Retail Merchants Association makes this statement:

> A recent single development has occurred which will enable stores to solve the problem of the past due regular account and at the same time enable the credit department to be self-supporting. I refer to the type of account which has flexible terms. Such an account enables a store to combine its regular and soft-goods accounts into one account—the terms of which are simple—30 days or at the option of the customer one-fifth or one-quarter of the balance owing. Under the terms of the account as soon as the customer decides to pay partially instead of in 30 days, a service charge is added. The service charge no longer becomes a penalty charge but is an integral part of the terms of the account. The approach is extremely logical to the customer because she becomes her own credit manager. For the first time credit managers now have the technique by which their departments can become self-supporting.[7]

CREDIT IN RETAILING

For many years, until recently, the trend in retailing had been toward less and more closely controlled credit. The rise of strictly cash stores in many lines of retailing had demonstrated that credit was not the essential customer service it was earlier considered to be. Credit losses incurred in the great depression of the 1930's had encouraged cash business. The "cut-rate" store, the supermarket, the discount house, and almost all retail chains were founded as cash institutions. Most voluntary chains encouraged member stores to sell only for cash. Now, however, the American business scene, as previously noted, is obsessed with the use of credit as a tool of sales promotion.

Many factors have contributed to this, including the broadly increased income of the average citizen, the general ineffectiveness of selling at the retail level, the development of novel credit plans by retailers, the improved status of the loan companies, and the aggressive entry of banks into the small-loan field. These and related changes have caused all retailers to seriously recon-

[7] Charles H. Dicken, Assistant Controller, Gimbel Brothers, Philadelphia, Pa., "Should the Credit Department Be Self-Supporting?" *1958-59 Credit Management Year Book* (New York: National Retail Merchants Association).

sider credit matters and many have accepted and promoted use of credit in self-defense.

Federal laws concerning personal and business expenses as income tax deductions have popularized the use of consumer credit for transportation, food, and lodging, because complete records of charges and payments are thus made available. There is no doubt but that the laws have encouraged the "charging" of many items by these business and professional people.

Generally speaking, the following reasons explain and summarize why small merchants have employed credit in their efforts to attract, accommodate, and retain profitable customers:

1. To secure additional business that can be handled at practically no extra expense
2. To attract new customers who need or want credit
3. To expand his sales rapidly up to his optimum capacity, and thus to reduce unit costs by using alternately with advertising or cut prices as a sales promotional device
4. To draw customers from cash stores by offering them the advantages of credit
5. To build goodwill and a desirable reputation by the way he handles his credit accounts
6. To compete with large-scale retailers such as chain stores, mail-order houses, and "supers" who do not extend credit
7. To secure a financial return over and above his merchandising profit in certain lines like durable consumers' goods that are purchased on installment contracts
8. To increase customer traffic by encouraging customers to pay their accounts in person in the store
9. To take advantage of the mine of valuable customer information available in the list of charge customers

How much credit business is to be accepted or even encouraged will depend upon particular circumstances in each case. First, the local situation is important. It is not always necessary to follow competitors' policies, but if credit is extended by all other stores in the same line of business in the community, customers will probably expect it or some other inducement for paying cash.

Second, and of probably even greater importance, the class of trade desired and what they expect in the way of credit. This is not always the simple relationship so often assumed. The fact that people in the upper income bracket do not *need* credit is no assurance they will buy for cash. Rural customers may be in the habit of buying on credit, but when agricultural conditions are favorable they might prefer to pay cash. The retailer may find that even customers who think they want credit because of habit, convenience, pride, or financial need will discover the desirability of buying for cash when the right inducements are offered.

Some merchants encourage the payment of cash by cashing customers' personal checks. This is equivalent to changing from one type of credit business to another, but it has two advantages. If purchases are paid for at the time by check, the period of credit extension is reduced from an average of about 45 days to two or three and the risk is greatly lessened. In the second place, even customers who are habitually dilatory about paying their charge accounts are hesitant about writing a bad check.

The final determinant will be the retailer's financial resources. Credit extension of any amount requires more capital and involves greater risks for the small retailer than most other activities. Total costs of open account credit extension are likely to be from three to well over five per cent of credit sales.

Using a Controlled Credit System

Properly controlled, credit can increase sales and bring the merchant steady, well-satisfied customers; handled in a slipshod manner, it can cause an over-investment in accounts receivable, large bad debt losses, and perhaps eventual failure of the business. The basic principles of a sound or controlled credit system are:

1. Thorough investigation of applicants for credit.
2. Carefully made decision.
3. Limit set on credit.
4. Terms of payment defined.
5. Account controlled by the merchant.
6. Delinquent accounts followed up promptly.

1. The first step in the investigation should be an interview with the applicant. During the interview the merchant's appearance, friendliness, and manner of obtaining information can help to gain the applicant's goodwill and confidence. Since an applicant usually will speak more freely when relaxed, the interview should be in complete privacy, if possible, and in a pleasant atmosphere. In order to have a record of the desired information, the merchant should have the customer fill out and sign a credit application, whether the customer takes the initiative in seeking credit or the store solicits the account. This is a good time to secure information to be used later in promoting sales, such as birthday dates of members of the family, hobbies, likes, and dislikes.

"Most credit offices find the following information sufficient: (1) full name; (2) home address; (3) if less than two years at this address, previous place of residence; (4) business affiliation and address; (5) name of one or two personal references; (6) trade references (other accounts); and (7) bank." [8]

[8] *Setting Up a Credit System in a Men's Wear Store,* Small Business Aids No. 421 (Washington, D. C.: U. S. Department of Commerce), condensed from "Setting Up a Credit System," by J. Gordon Dakins, *Apparel Arts* (July 1947). Copyright 1947 by Esquire, Inc., Esquire Building, Chicago, Ill.

The National Retail Credit Association, which is composed of over 21,000 local credit bureaus, has adopted a standard form that should be used if possible.

Three general methods are used in distributing credit applications. The most common plan is to have the applicant fill out the blank in the credit department, to which customers inquiring about credit are referred. In other stores salespeople give the application blanks to customers who are interested or appear to be good prospects. Some stores enclose the credit application with merchandise that is wrapped for certain customers. If the customer applies at the credit department in person—a procedure which in the small store may mean merely talking to the executive in charge of credit—a preliminary interview is usually held at this time.

During the interview the store's credit policy and terms will be explained. A skilled interviewer can get some clues to the applicant's character, capacity, and capital—the three "Cs" of credit. Each of these may be investigated further from information given on the application blank.

The next step should be to obtain credit information on the applicant from the local credit bureau or, if there is none in the community, from other stores and businesses, the applicant's place of employment, and his bank and neighbors.

2. After completing his investigation, the merchant should make a careful decision on the application. In this he should consider the applicant's character and credit record, his earning power and ability to pay, and his capital and property. Along with these factors the merchant must take into account the personal background of the applicant—his social standing, general reputation in the community, and business career.

3. The merchant should not decide to open an account without considering the dollar amounts involved. The amount of credit granted to a customer should be based largely on his income and will vary, of course, with the type of store. A credit limit is usually set so that a customer will not buy beyond his capacity and in doing so jeopardize his credit record. To let him know that his account has been accepted, the store writes him a friendly letter telling how pleased they are to count him as a regular customer and also restates the conditions under which credit is granted.

4. As a safeguard against bad debt losses, the merchant should have a definite understanding with the customer as to the credit terms. He may stipulate that payments are to be weekly, monthly, or on pay days. The time for which credit is extended on open accounts is frequently one month for salaried workers and weekly for wage earners, especially in food and other convenience goods stores. Usually payment by the tenth of the month for the previous month's account is customary on regular open accounts.

5. From the day the account is opened, the merchant should control it carefully to see that the customer upholds his part of the agreement. If credit is on a monthly basis, some merchants permit no further charges on an

APPLICATION FOR CREDIT

ADOPTED BY AND FOR MEMBERS OF THE

NATIONAL RETAIL CREDIT ASSOCIATION

NUMBER_____ DATE_____

FULL NAME (SURNAME FIRST)	FULL GIVEN NAME	INITIAL	AGE	GIVEN NAME, HUSBAND — WIFE'S MAIDEN NAME	
RESIDENCE	MAIL ADDRESS			TELEPHONE	HOW LONG
FORMER ADDRESS					HOW LONG
BUSINESS OR OCCUPATION	BY WHOM EMPLOYED			BUS. ADDRESS	HOW LONG
FORMER BUSINESS OR OCCUPATION	BY WHOM EMPLOYED			BUS. ADDRESS	HOW LONG
WIFE OR HUSBAND EMPLOYED?	CAPACITY		BY WHOM		

OWN REAL ESTATE	(GIVE LOCATION)	MORTGAGED TO	AMOUNT
			$

RENT	FURN. APARTMENT? UNFURN. APARTMENT? RESIDENCE?	OWNER	MONTHLY RENTAL	CHILDREN AT HOME	EMPLOYED

NAME OF NEAREST RELATIVE AND RELATIONSHIP (OTHER THAN HUSBAND OR WIFE)   ADDRESS

PERSONAL REFERENCE

BANK	(NAME OF BANK)	(CHECKING) (SAVING)	BRANCH

LIFE INSURANCE	NAME OF INSURANCE CO.	APPROX. INCOME	
$		$	PER

TRADE REFERENCES

FIRM OR STORE	KIND OF MDSE. BOUGHT	ACCOUNT IS NOW	
		OPEN	DATE PAID

LIST ON REVERSE SIDE OF THIS APPLICATION ANY UNPAID BALANCES ON INSTALLMENT ACCOUNTS AND MONTHLY PAYMENTS THEREON.

THE ABOVE INFORMATION IS FOR THE PURPOSE OF OBTAINING CREDIT, AND IS WARRANTED TO BE TRUE. I AGREE TO PAY ALL BILLS UPON RECEIPT OF STATEMENT OR AS OTHERWISE EXPRESSLY AGREED.

SPECIAL TERMS IF ANY.

SIGNATURE_____

AMOUNT CREDIT	APPROVED
$	

FIGURE 12. Application for credit.

account if it is not paid by the end of the month in which payment is due. Others insist on giving personal approval to additional purchases on such accounts.

Credit control involves adequate records and prompt collections. For a small business, the best system of records has to be decided upon by the proprietor. The important provisions are an individual record for each customer, a filing system to keep the records straight, and a follow-up file to take care of delinquent accounts. The credit limit is often placed on each account record. It is important to keep up with customers at all times—to know just how they stand and how they pay. Cultivate the best customers and if possible gradually drop the poor ones, remembering that they can frequently be converted into good cash customers.

6. Prompt follow-up is likely to show delinquent accounts to be the result of (a) oversight on the part of the customer, (b) temporary financial difficulty, or (c) unwillingness to pay. In the first case, a reminder by the merchant will usually result in prompt payment. In the second case, on the re-tailer understands the customer's difficulty a mutually agreeable payment plan can be arranged. The third situation may be the result of customer dissatis-faction that could be settled agreeably if understood and acted upon promptly, or it may represent the typical "dead beat" charge customer. When the dealer has determined the reason why each account is delinquent, the appropriate action to take is usually apparent. Aggressive collection procedures should be instituted if necessary, but should be delayed in favor of remedial action when the latter is indicated.

Charga-Plates and Credit Cards

There is one exception to the usual procedure of starting the credit process by securing a credit application. Sometimes the local credit bureau takes the initiative and issues "Charga-Plates" to a selected number of individuals who have already established good credit records. Certain stores have formed an association under an agreement to extend credit to all customers to whom a Charga-Plate is issued. Co-operating stores all accept this Charga-Plate as evidence of credit approval.

The "credit card," as developed by the oil companies, hotels, and others, has become a popular means of gaining the advantages of consumer credit for both buyer and seller. The individual operator of a service station or repair shop has the benefit of professional screening of applications at the headquarters of his resource, which also assumes liability for loss unless formal warning has been issued to the contrary.

Credit card service of this type is also available to other sellers of consumer goods or services on a percentage of sales basis. The American Express credit card, the Hilton "Carte Blanche," and the Diner's Club, for example, are used by stores and restaurants of all kinds all over the world, and thus have been particularly helpful to travelers. Although bearers of these cards are welcomed by all subscribing vendors, some of the latter resent the charge, approximating 6 per cent, levied on them by the card-issuing agency.[9]

[9] See: 'The Credit Card Spree," *Life* (June 1, 1959) ; "Credit—For Everything," *Time* (March 23, 1959), p. 83 for discussion of increasing credit facilities of banks; "The Coming Turn In Consumer Credit"; *Fortune* (March 1956), p. 99; "Credit Caution," *Time* (November 9, 1959), p. 91 concerning dangers of over-expanded consumer credit; "Keeping Consumer Credit In Line," *Business Week* (June 27, 1959), p. 160.

"Revolving Credit" and "Option-Terms" and similar variable plans for facilitating buying through credit have been introduced by larger retailers, particularly department stores and chain organizations such as Sears Roebuck & Company, Montgomery Ward & Company, and even Woolworth's. Revolving credit is said to have the conveniences of an open charge account plus the privileges of installment payment. Users are under a fixed credit limitation, with interest or service charges on payments delayed beyond 30 days. The option-terms plan is similar, calling for arbitrary portions of larger amounts to be paid at time of purchase, with a planned schedule for payments also involving an interest or carrying charge. Various arrangements or combinations of plans can be projected.[10] Most smaller firms will find the complexities of devising, experimenting, controlling, and adjusting beyond the limitations of their record-keeping facilities. Also, the job of educating the public to the advantages and intricacies of such "different" devices can be rather formidable.

Credit Bureaus

Credit bureaus are service agencies organized to gather, compile and distribute information concerning the identity, history, character, resources and paying habits of consumers. They serve all types of retail credit granters, banks and loan companies, service businesses, physicians and dentists, hospitals and clinics, real estate agencies, insurance companies, employment departments of industries, local, state and national government agencies, and law enforcement departments. Their master files contain complete credit histories consisting of facts obtained from the ledgers of at least the principal and representative credit granters of the community, as well as information from public records, the press, and employers.

Merchants, professional men, and hospitals are the chief supporters of the bureau. Since more than 1,800 retail credit bureaus belong to a national trade association, the Associated Credit Bureaus of America, a newcomer's credit record may be obtained easily and rapidly by a local bureau although the independent businessman would have a difficult time doing this for himself. Each member of the bureau agrees in his membership contract to supply ledger information concerning his customers, including those who are in arrears on their accounts. Thus, the bureau secures and can furnish much more information about customers than any businessman could obtain on his own.

Two methods, generally, are used to determine membership fees, the meter plan and the flat rate. Under the meter plan, credit reports are purchased at so much per report. Many smaller bureaus use the flat-rate plan by which each member is classified according to the approximate amount of service the business will use and is charged a flat monthly fee. In return for this fee, the member is entitled to as many telephone credit reports as he

10 For extended discussion, see Delbert J. Duncan and Charles F. Phillips, *Retailing, Principles and Methods,* 5th ed. (Homewood, Ill.: Richard D. Irwin, Inc., 1959) p. 675.

Facktitt
REPORTS ARE BETTER

ASSOCIATED CREDIT BUREAUS OF AMERICA
INCORPORATED
AN ASSOCIATION OF CREDIT BUREAUS SINCE 1906
CONFIDENTIAL

INTER-BUREAU
REPORT
ACBofA No. 1
compiled by member bureau

1 REPORT ON:	ROE	MR.	JOHN JAMES	MARY
	(Surname first)	(Mr. or Mrs.)	(Given Name)	(Spouse's Name)
2. RESIDENCE ADDRESS:	162 Pine Street	Utopia	Rose	Any State
	(Street Number)	(City)	(County)	(State)

IDENTITY

3. Number of years covered: A. In file	A.	10 years
B. In Investigation	B.	10 years
4. A. Age. (If near 21, confirm)	A.	46 years
B. Racial extraction (White, Black, Red, Yellow, Brown)	B.	White
5. A. Marital status	A.	Married
B. Number of dependents?	B.	Wife and 4 children

HISTORY

6. A. Name of employer	A.	Comm'l. Radio Co., 512 Main St.
B. Type of business	B.	Radio & Appliance, Sales, etc.
7. A. How long so employed	A.	10 years
B. Position held	B.	General Sales Manager
8. A. Does applicant have record of steady employment?	A.	Yes
B. Any recent employment change? (If yes, explain in remarks)	B.	No
9. Any suits, judgements or bankruptcies? (If yes, explain in remarks)		No

Character

10. Is applicant well regarded as to character, habits and morals?	Yes
11. Is applicant favorably regarded by employer?	Yes
12. Any suspicion of illegal practice past or present?	No

RESOURCES

13. A. Estimate monthly Income from present employment	A.	$500 & $1000 annual bonus
B. Estimate other income such as rentals, investments, etc.	B.	$800 from investments
C. Estimate income of others in household	C.	None
14. Own home, rent or board?		Owns home at above address

CREDIT RECORD: (If feasible include whether subject has satisfactory bank checking account.)

Trade Line	How Long Selling	Date of Last Sale	Highest Credit	Terms of Sale	Amount Owing	Amount Past Due	Manner of Payment
Grocery	8 yrs	1/16/6-	70.00	Open	35.00	35.00	Pays monthly
Hardware	5 yrs	8/28/6-	253.00	Install	55.00	none	$20 mo.
Shoes	9 yrs	1/2/6-	22.50	Open	none	none	30 days prompt
Department Store	8 yrs	1/13/6-	115.00	Open	70.00	none	30-60 days
Electric Supply	2 yrs	2/16/6-	174.00	Install	none	none	$15 mo.
Drug	8 yrs	11/3/5-	25.00	Open	14.25	none	30-60 days
Automobile	5 yrs	3/9/6-	400.00	90 days	none	none	satis.

REMARKS: A. Give brief word picture of subject's history, explaining any unusual condition.
B. Amplify any incomplete or adverse information in answers above. Use other side also for full details.
C. Include estimate of net worth if possible.

Subject is also director and owns stock in Empire Specialty Company, dealers in electrical equipment. His house and lot are assessed for $5700 on basis of 40% actual value. Good citizen and active in civic and business affairs. Report from previous place of residence, Fairville, New State, indicates prompt paying record and good moral integrity. No court or derogatory record; subject is estimated to be worth between $15,000 - $20,000. Assets consist of home, personal property, car and stocks.

Report for   Credit Bureau of Excelsior, Excelsior, Other State

Date 2/15/6-   Prepared by   Credit Bureau of Utopia   Utopia   Any State
                               Name of member reporting bureau   City   State

FIGURE 13. Inter-bureau report.

ASSOCIATED CREDIT BUREAUS OF AMERICA
INCORPORATED

AN ASSOCIATION OF CREDIT BUREAUS SINCE 1906

CONFIDENTIAL

Facbilt REPORTS ARE BETTER

PREVIOUS RESIDENCE
REPORT
ACBofA No. 5
compiled by member bureau

1 REPORT ON:	DOE (Surname first)	MR. (Mr. or Mrs.)	WILLIAM E. (Given Name)	SARAH (Spouse's Name)	
2 RESIDENCE ADDRESS:	343 Tulane Avenue (Street Number)	Any (City)	Any (County)	Anystate (State)	

3. Number of years covered: A. In file	A.	26 years
B. In investigation	B.	14 years
4. A. Where did applicant move to?	A.	Hope, Blankstate
B. How long has he been gone?	B.	10/31/5–
C. If other cities have inquired, please name	C.	Blankville, Southstate
5. A. What is approximate age now? (If near 21, confirm)	A.	47
B. Racial extraction (White, Black, Red, Yellow, Brown)	B.	White
6. A. What was his (her) marital status?	A.	Married
B. Number of dependents?	B.	Wife and 2 children
7. A. Name of former employer	A.	Dupont Co., Wilmington, Otherstate
B. Type of business	B.	Welding
8. A. How long so employed?	A.	3 years
B. Position held?	B.	Welder
9. Did applicant have record of steady employment?		Not Steady
10. Any suits, judgements or bankruptcies? (If yes, explain in remarks)		Yes
11. Was applicant well regarded as to character, habits and morals?		Good
12. Was applicant favorably regarded by employer?		Fair – repeated wage assignments
13. Any suspicion of illegal practice or business?		No
14. What was estimated monthly income from employment?		Approx. $300 to $340
15. Did applicant receive any income from other sources such as rentals, investments, etc.? (If yes, explain in remarks)		No
16. Did applicant own home, rent or board?		Rent

IDENTITY / HISTORY / Character / RESOURCES

CREDIT RECORD: (If feasible include whether subject has satisfactory bank checking account.)

Trade Line	How Long Selling	Date of Last Sale	Highest Credit	Terms of Sale	Amount Owing	Amount Past Due	Manner of Payment
Loan Company	3 yrs	8/15/6–	$150.00	Install.	$125.00	$50.00	Very slow
Dairy	1 yr	current	11.00	Open	9.00	9.00	Always slow
Department Store	3 yrs	8/26/6–	20.00	Open	17.00	17.00	60 days slow
Furniture	5 yrs	5/15/5–	156.00	Install.	125.00	125.00	repossessed
Coal & Fuel	10 yrs	195	90.00	90 days	90.00	90.00	sued
Gas & Oil	6 yrs	10/30/6–	15.00	Open	10.00	10.00	closed a/c
Physician	9 yrs	5/20/6–	300.00	Open	114.00	114.00	coll. effort
Hospital	3 yrs	3/15/6–	220.00	Open	32.00	32.00	collection

REMARKS: A. Give brief word picture of subject's history, explaining any unusual condition.
B. Amplify any incomplete or adverse information in answers above. Use other side also for full details.
C. Include estimate of net worth if possible.

Subject was resident of Joliet and Wilmington, Otherstate for 20 years, starting to
work as apprentice welder and part time truck driver. Record became slow in 194–
and has continued as indicated. Prior to your inquiry, this office showed subject
in "skip" file and has had several requests for address. Two suits pending and 3
unsatisfied judgments. Estimate of net worth is $500, consists mainly of household
goods and 195– H_____ car.

Report for   Credit Bureau of Any, Any, Anystate

Date 11/20/6–   Prepared by   Credit Bureau of Othercity   Othercity   Otherstate
Name of member reporting bureau   City   State

The confidential information given in this report is in answer to a request for same. This report is compiled simply as an aid in determining the propriety
of extending credit, or the value or condition of an existing credit and is based upon information obtained from sources deemed reliable, the accuracy
of which, however, is in no manner guaranteed. The inquirer, in accepting this report, agrees to hold same in STRICT CONFIDENCE for his own exclusive
use, never to be communicated, and to be personally responsible for any damage arising from a violation of any of the above provisions. (Printed in U.S.A.)

PATENTED—MOORE BUSINESS FORMS, INC., NIAGARA FALLS, N.Y.

FIGURE 14. Transfer of record report.

needs. The vast majority of credit reports are requested and given over the telephone. Precautions are taken to insure identification of the inquiring credit granter and to give reports only to authorized persons.

The credit bureau does not give opinions. It is never a forecaster of the future. When information is called for, the prospect's credit record is given. The decision as to whether to extend credit is left to the credit granter. Only information applying to the subject's credit standing is given in such reports. The credit granter has an interest in the subject of a report when that subject is a user or prospective user of credit privileges, and credit information requested comes legally under the title of "privileged communications," and must be respected as such by all recipients. Information obtained from the credit bureau should be treated confidentially by the member and never disclosed to the subject of the report or to anyone outside the firm's credit department.

Some credit bureaus offer a valuable aid to members in the form of a "pre-collection service." This usually consists of a personal letter or other mailing piece appearing under the letterhead of the credit bureau and addressed to customers whose accounts are past due. The message may outline the purpose of the credit bureau and show how it benefits customer and store alike. The debtor is told that the past-due account is about to be, or already has been, placed on record in the credit bureau. The name of the creditor, the amount past due, and the due date are given. The customer is advised to pay the amount due immediately in order that the proper disposition of the account may be recorded in the credit bureau's files.

Surveys of ethical collection services indicate that the following are approximate commissions charged for collecting consumer accounts: over $10 and less than two years past due against debtors living in the trade area, thirty-three and one-third per cent; accounts under $10 and those against debtors who have moved from the trade area, 50 per cent. Fifty per cent is charged on accounts which must be forwarded to collection services out of town.

The National Retail Credit Association

The National Retail Credit Association, with headquarters in St. Louis, Missouri, publishes a variety of useful material that may be purchased through local member bureaus or direct from headquarters. The application-for-credit form has already been mentioned. Over three dozen different stickers and inserts each dealing with some aspect of credit administration are available at a very low cost. These are attractively printed in color with an appropriate message for such purposes as thanking the customer for a remittance, informing the customer that the store knows his account is paid in full, inviting the use of inactive accounts, and warning politely that accounts are overdue. The following wording on one of these stickers is representative of several used to keep customers reminded of the importance of their credit record: "Your Credit Record is an Open Book. By the way you pay, you write your own record in the files of the Credit Bureau. Millions of cards in the files of the Credit Bureaus of the United States and Canada, form the basis of credit reports—used by creditors and employers to judge the trustworthiness of individuals. Prompt Payments Make a Good Credit Record."

An illustrated insert contains the following wording, the purpose of which is self-evident:

> We have Your Name in this Who's Who. As a member of the Credit Bureau we are called upon to report, at frequent intervals, the credit standing of our customers. This report is available to every merchant or professional man who is a member of the Credit Bureau.
>
> Your account with us at the present time is Past Due. To maintain a good credit record, you should make a payment Now or arrange for an early settlement.
>
> Customer's Name.....................................
> Firm Owed ....
> Balance $......................Past Due...........
> Date...
>
> Guard Your Credit as a Sacred Trust..
>
> A new letter-writing service ("Effective Credit and Collection Letters") was recently offered to members at a nominal charge. It is intended to be usable by all types of business, and by small and large concerns.[11]

Correspondence courses in various aspects of credit management are offered by the National Institute of Credit, 1 Park Avenue, New York 16, New York, and by extension divisions of certain universities. Ample material in book and pamphlet form is available to the small businessman who cares to learn more about this subject.

Installment Credit

Installment selling involves different methods from those used for open accounts, although procedures of credit application and investigation are similar. To protect the seller, two forms of legal devices are usual in extending installment credit: the conditional sales contract and the chattel mortgage. The conditional sales contract states that the title remains with the seller until the full price agreed upon has been paid, even though the goods have been sold and delivered to the purchaser. In case of failure to make payments, it is easy from a legal standpoint for the seller to repossess the goods. This device is more convenient from the seller's point of view. Under the chattel mortgage, title passes to the buyer at the time of sale, but he either transfers it back to the seller, on the condition that he will get it back when he has fulfilled all the provisions of the mortgage, or gives the mortgagee a first lien on the goods.

Installment credit should be used by the small retailer only for articles that

[11] "Announcing a New Service in the Letter-Writing Field," *Credit World* (St. Louis, Missouri, July 1954), p. 27.

have repossession value; and only after checking with the credit bureau to determine that the applicant is not already overloaded with debt payments; and when the following principles are observed:

1. Merchandise should be priced sufficiently high to cover all costs, including the possible cost of repossession, reconditioning, and reselling.

2. Merchandise—not terms—should be sold. When terms are emphasized, the customer tends to think less of the merchandise and is more likely to return it.

3. Adequate down payments should be obtained to prevent the account from becoming bad. When a customer pays a sizable part of the price he feels that he is the owner and the merchandise will more than likely be paid for in full.

4. Terms should be made as short as possible, and within the customer's ability to pay.

5. Collections should be made regularly. Installment payments require more attention than regular accounts.[12]

In the small business installment credit is likely to be called for if fairly durable goods of high unit cost are sold. Even wearing apparel is sold on the installment plan. When lay-away sales are encouraged, a variation of installment credit is employed. In the past, small stores have not made extensive use of coupon books good for purchases within the store, the books being paid for by small weekly installments. However, this may be a good way to secure regular payments from customers of limited income who want to buy on the same basis as credit patrons. Provisions made by state laws for each of these legal devices vary. Carrying charges usually must be added to installment purchases because of the extra bookkeeping and other costs involved in carrying the account. The common practice is to charge one-half of one per cent a month on the unpaid balance, The customer pays for part or all of the added installment credit expense, whereas open-account costs are levied against cash and charge customers alike.

Many retailers prefer to have installment payments made in person at the store. This enables the merchant to keep in touch with the customer and offers further opportunities to sell additional goods.

Obtaining Financial Assistance

Two types of agencies assist the merchant in financing his installment sales, sales finance companies, and banks. The latter are also used frequently for other working capital needs.

Sales finance companies. Five plans are commonly used by sales finance companies: the "Cash Availability" plan, the "Direct Collection," the "Cooperative" or "Indirect Collection," the "Revolving Fund," and the "Schedule" plans. Basically, these plans are all alike. The sales finance company pur-

---

[12] "Installment Selling Principles" from the booklet "Credit and Collections," one of 17 booklets making up *Better Retailing* (Dayton, Ohio: National Cash Register Company, 1941), p. 226.

chases the retailers' accounts receivable, advances a certain percentage in payment, and retains or holds back another percentage as a "deferred payment reserve" that serves to increase the security of the advances made by the sales finance company.

Although charges to the retailer for this type of financing vary from store to store and from territory to territory, sales finance companies may charge as much as $\frac{1}{30}$ of one per cent per day plus six per cent interest per year on the unpaid balance. In special cases, the rates are much higher because of the character of the receivables being financed. On the other hand, some companies have charged as little as four per cent discount on the face value of the note plus eight per cent interest per year, or less. In some cases sales finance companies purchase the accounts receivable outright, pay the retailers the full value of the notes immediately, charge a five per cent flat rate on the accounts payable over 12 months, and assume the complete risk and the job of collecting from the consumer. When the retailer himself collects from the consumer, the amount of money advanced to him immediately by the sales finance company may range from 70 to 100 per cent.

Banks. Banking services to finance accounts receivable differ from those of the sales finance companies principally in a somewhat tighter credit policy on the part of the banks and elimination of some of the controls deemed necessary by sales finance companies.

Bank charges for services to retailers tend to be low. In certain large cities a fairly usual rate is three and one-half to four per cent discount on the face amount of the accounts receivable. When the retailer does the collecting from the customer, many banks charge a three per cent discount plus six per cent interest per year. Advances to the retailer by the bank range from 75 to 90 per cent of the face amount of the accounts receivable. The bank usually requires that the retailer himself be entirely responsible for payment of the accounts.

Although we have discussed elsewhere the use of banks in business financing, it should be recognized here again that (1) the credit grantor may find a bank loan necessary, as noted, to finance his "lending" at times; also (2) the customer may find the bank a more convenient or agreeable creditor than his resource; and (3) the seller and buyer may go to the bank together to solve the buyer's financing plan. Under this latter arrangement, the seller may or may not find himself obligated in the buyer's borrowing agreement.

Bank Credit Plans

An important development for small businessmen in many communities is a bank credit plan started in New York and now available in an increasing number of places throughout the country. It is variously viewed as an effort to aid small merchants to meet the credit promotion competition of large department stores, to encourage people to buy in their neighborhood or hometown, to separate financing from merchandising, and to furnish additional revenue for banks. One or several co-operating banks in a retail area may sponsor the plan.

In this plan the bank makes a credit investigation of an applicant for consumer credit, whether the application is made at the store or the bank. If approved, an embossed plate is issued that henceforth becomes identification and authorization when used for charge purposes in any co-operating store up to the floor limit. If a customer wants to charge more than the floor limit the merchant telephones the bank and secures the information needed immediately. Sales checks are furnished by the bank and retailers record each charge transaction on these, insert the plate in a stamping machine, and usually secure the customer's signature if the purchase is made in person. Each day one copy of these charge sales checks is deposited with the bank, which then credits the merchant's account with the total amount less service charges. These are usually five per cent for open accounts and six per cent for two- or three-payment budget accounts up to 90 days.

The bank does the recording and once a month sends a single statement to each customer accompanied by copies of all charge sales checks from all co-operating stores. The account is due and payable to the bank within ten days after billing. It is a nonrecourse plan since the bank assumes full responsibility for approving credit applications and making collections.

Advantages of the plan to the retailers, according to its proponents, are:

1. It increases sales volume as much as 50 per cent.
2. It provides immediate cash.
3. It provides retailers with several thousand prospective customers whose credit has already been approved by the bank.
4. It builds goodwill among regular customers.
5. It attracts new customers.
6. It enables merchants to meet the credit competition of larger stores.
7. It enables the merchant to take advantage of merchandising opportunities.
8. It adds prestige to the store among shoppers.
9. It gives the retailers the benefit of the bank's extensive advertising of the service.

The retailers gain all of the foregoing advantages without:

1. Investigating the customer's credit.
2. Setting up a credit bookkeeping system.
3. Billing customers.
4. Having to dun slow-paying accounts.
5. Incurring bad debts.
6. Tying up his own capital.
7. Giving time and money that could be more profitably devoted to merchandising.
8. Incurring possible ill will or loss of sales by refusing credit.[13]

[13] Lawrence Freeman, "New Business for Banks—Through Shoppers Service," *The Oklahoma Business Bulletin* (Norman, Oklahoma: Bureau of Business Research, College of Business Administration, University of Oklahoma, July 1953), pp. 3-4.

CREDIT IN WHOLESALING

Wholesalers sell principally to small retailers, about 90 per cent of whom need credit. The credit manager of the wholesale house is also one of the most valuable advisors for retailers who will consult with him. By granting or refusing retailers credit, he exerts a powerful influence on trade. If by extending credit he carelessly encourages a new business to start or a nearly defunct one to continue the hopeless struggle, the wholesaler does an injustice to all concerned—including innocent competitors. The latter usually suffer when the failing business is forced to run closeout sales at a loss. Because of their strategic position in commerce, wholesalers are probably better able than any other type of businessman to give sound credit advice to retailers.

Since the small wholesaler has the dual responsibility of protecting his own investment and encouraging promising small merchants while discouraging hopeless ones, a customer analysis is highly desirable. The following examples and related advice should make this point clear.

> One wholesale house in the hardware trade made a simple and inexpensive analysis and was surprised at the information which it revealed. A number of policies and many operating procedures were eventually changed as a result of this study.
>
> The bases of the investigation were confined to company records and the knowledge of the officers regarding customers. All records needed and used were:
>
> 1. Name of each credit customer (cash business was negligible and ignored in the study).
> 2. City or town in which customer was located and his distance from wholesaler's warehouse.
> 3. Type of business of the customer (hardware store, filling station, and so on).
> 4. Number of each customer's purchases over a six months' period.
> 5. Total dollar value of each customer's business during this period.
>
> Where the kind of business was not apparent from the records, the information was supplied by the general manager, credit manager, or salesman.
>
> The information from the records necessary for the analysis was placed on 3" by 5" cards, one to a customer. These cards were sorted and classified according to the subject under investigation at that moment. For example, in order to determine the number of small orders and their value, the cards were sorted into three piles: those for which the total sales of the customer for the period of six months were less than $100; those for which the sales were between $100 and $499; and those of $500 and over.
>
> After this sorting was complete, the number of customers and the value of their purchases were added up on an adding machine separately for each of the three groups. A similar method was employed to determine the other figures presented below in this statement.
>
> Examples lifted from the report of the hardware wholesaler will illus-

trate the kind of information which any wholesale house can expect from such a customer analysis.

A large proportion of your customers buy very little from you, place small orders and probably cost you a great deal of service. An example would be:

Total sales to each customer per period	Number of customers percent	Value of wholesale sales percent	Average value per order in dollars
Less than $100	55.6	5.2	$11.18
$100 to $499	28.4	20.8	16.94
$500 and over	16.0	74.0	31.56
	100.0	100.0	

A further detailed breadown can be made if desired, to show smaller dollar purchase groups and their relation to totals. These figures will show the large number of customers whose total purchases are so small that their value is doubtful. While startling, these figures are probably not unusual.

Your salesmen are calling upon types of business for which you are not either a primary or secondary source of supply. Our hardware house found that its salesmen were calling upon 71 different kinds of business *in addition* to hardware stores, garages, filling stations, general stores, lumber yards, furniture stores, tire stores, and drugstores. These eight kinds of business, however, accounted for 80 per cent of the number of customers and 88 per cent of the value of their orders.

On which types should selling efforts be increased, and on which discontinued? It is fairly simple to determine the number of customers of each type and the value of wholesale sales in percentages for each type. You then have relative values in terms of dollars of sales for all types of customers.

Some of your salesmen may be traveling territories which are too far from the warehouse to be profitable. The locations of customers are important. It costs more to call on the customers two hundred miles away, than those twenty miles away. At what distance is it unprofitable to solicit business?

One hardware house found its breaking point at 175 miles. About 75 per cent of its customers were located within such a radius and these customers accounted for 83 per cent of sales volume. If other records are available, sales volume, gross margin and operating expenses can be studied to secure a more refined answer to this question.

A great many customers place small orders very infrequently. A wholesaler can take steps to increase sales effectiveness or he can discontinue soliciting small buyers if he is not convinced that the small buyer will eventually become a larger and more profitable one.

The significance of this question is shown on the records of our hardware house by the fact that 51 per cent of its credit customers placed four or fewer orders during a six-months' period and accounted for only slightly more than six per cent of the dollar volume of that period.

At the other extreme, three per cent of the customers ordered 75 times or more and accounted for slightly more than 29 per cent of the total volume. Without any additional information, steps might be taken to change the buying habits, or eliminate customers who bought too infrequently, or whose orders were plentiful but too small to be profitable.

These examples may bring to mind other analyses which would be valuable. The study could go further and determine accounts that show the greatest gross margin or the accounts that are least expensive to service. The opposite will also be shown. A concentrated effort could then be made to increase gross margins and decrease selling expenses on those accounts that are least profitable. If these accounts do not warrant those efforts, then solicitation can be discontinued with the full knowledge that only unprofitable business is being eliminated.

First determine what figures and comparisons will help you. Then get them with the least possible delay. Above all—use them. Carefully planned and selective selling will eliminate unnecessary expense, secure more profitable sales, and increase net profits.[14]

Mercantile credit differs from consumer credit in many respects, two of which are our immediate concern: ratings, and insurance. The financial standing of many business firms is rated by agencies like Dun & Bradstreet. Since a favorable credit rating is highly desirable, businessmen strive to safeguard this precious asset. However, "ratings" are not always up to date, and many small-scale or newly established retailers do not have one. These facts limit the value of the mercantile agency's service in many cases, especially as far as the wholesaler is concerned. However, the agency may still be employed effectively in the case of doubtful credit prospects to secure special credit reports that are likely to be somewhat more reliable than the wholesaler's independent appraisal.

The second difference between commercial and consumer credit is credit insurance, which is available only for the former. It is guaranty of accounts receivable as additional security for loans to business concerns. Briefly stated, credit insurance is a form of insurance to protect the merchant against loss arising from sales on credit to debtors who have one of the stipulated mercantile agency ratings. Credit insurance coverage is limited to manufacturers, jobbers, or wholesalers who sell to the trade. Experiments are under way for insuring retail credits.

The insurance policy provides protection against all known forms of debtor insolvency and guarantees the payment of all past-due accounts filed with the insurance company within 90 days after due date in accordance with the provisions of the policy.

The insurance company does not attempt to replace the credit manager of a concern, but rather aims at widening the efficient credit work of businessmen and to educate them in the importance of building up well-equipped credit departments. The policyholder is required to bear a small percentage of the

---

[14] Wilford White, *Wholesalers' Customer Analysis*, Small Business Aids No. 451 (Washington, D. C.: U. S. Department of Commerce, 1948).

covered loss as coinsurance. The insurance is only against loss in excess of this normal loss, which is borne by the merchant himself. In practice, the merchant's expected loss is regarded as an expense of doing business.[15]

CREDIT IN THE SMALL FACTORY

Credit management in the small factory has certain conditions in common with that in wholesaling. Both deal in mercantile credit, except when the small factory sells direct to consumers exclusively. Uses by both of commercial ratings and other sources of information on the financial standing of business firms are similar, although the nature of their customers may introduce significant differences. For example, the small wholesaler is more likely to have a preponderance of retail store customers who either are not rated or whose ratings are less reliable than those of the small manufacturer's customers. Offsetting this is the wholesaler's more favorable position in becoming personally familiar with his customer's business.

Customers of the small factory will usually be other businessmen. Merchants or service establishments to which direct sales are made will be either established firms with ratings or small concerns in the vicinity of the factory. Other factories that make purchases are likely to be larger concerns. In any case it is well to be familiar with sources of information and the various services available in the field of mercantile or commercial credit.

A very excellent source is Dun & Bradstreet, Inc., which publishes reference books containing ratings of business concerns, issues special reports to members, supplies analytical reports, provides a continuous report service, offers a limited credit-checking service, prepares business analyses, may collect overdue accounts, will conduct special surveys, and publishes *Dun's Review and Modern Industry*. Except for a subscription to the last named periodical, the services mentioned are rendered on a contract basis to members or subscribers of Dun & Bradstreet's services. It has been the experience of this agency that nonmembers may easily be misled by partial information secured indirectly because they do not have access to the full service.[16]

Information on new or prospective customers may be obtained from other creditors through direct exchange, either personally or by correspondence. Credit bureaus maintained by associations of credit men for the exchange of ledger experience and information are another source, and trade credit bureaus operated by trade associations are also useful. Information may be obtained from sales representatives who are familiar with the company under investigation, and salesmen of creditors, attorneys, and banks may be able to tell if the

[15] H. Lloyd Jones, "Credit Insurance—Boon to Small Business," *The Casualty and Surety Journal* (March 1945), pp. 37-44.

[16] Letter to the authors dated April 20, 1953, from Mr. W. H. Kuehn, Director of Training, Dun & Bradstreet, Inc. See also: *Credit Management Handbook* (Homewood, Ill.: Richard D. Irwin, Inc., 1958), a guide on commercial credit for financial and credit management use.

firm is a good risk. Other sources of information are corporation manuals, corporation financial services, trade and financial publications, credit character reports, and the *Credit Manual of Commercial Laws,* which is published annually by the National Association of Credit Men. Before giving credit, of course, the manufacturer may wish to have a personal interview with the prospect and perhaps secure a financial statement directly from him.

Various special agencies provide credit services to business, many of them being of particular interest to smaller concerns that have no established credit department. Some are affiliated with trade associations. Many of these agencies are specialized as to industry, such as furniture, plumbing, textiles, shoes, paint, produce, and the like. Various state and local facilities also exist. They issue rating books regularly or from time to time, which are distributed to subscribers, and ordinarily provide a collection service as well, on a percentage fee basis. Among leaders in special agencies are the National Credit Office of New York City, the Manufacturers Clearing House, the Iron and Steel Board of Trade, the Credit Clearing House (a Dun and Bradstreet service), Lyon Furniture Mercantile Agency (eight branches), and the Shoe and Leather Mercantile Agency.

The rating books published by such agencies usually indicate, by symbol, the listee's general credit standing, current capital resources, and paying habits and method, supplemented by any pertinent special information. Such special items include evidence of continued unethical or troublesome practices, excessive returns of merchandise, chronic complaints without justification, disregarding of sales-contract terms such as deduction of discounts not earned, or unreasonable requests for service.

All such data is accumulated from field reports conducted by the agency.

These public agencies, as noted, provide a variety of services, from simple reporting of "slow pay" firms, through listing of firms who have sold to a listee, to those who give credit data in extreme detail—some even providing insured recommendations. The strength of many lies in their specialization and the pertinent detail resulting, and the currency of their reports. The weaker ones are generally to be blamed for lack of this detail or currency. The national or state trade association, to which the small businessman should belong, can refer him to a reputable and profitable credit agency. Local chambers of commerce often include a credit bureau as a part of their facilities.

If we consider the bank as a factor in commercial credit, as apart from financing the business establishment, the possibilities of the warehouse receipt or of field warehousing can not be overlooked. A producer of seasonal goods, having produced for months but sold little, may require more funds, probably for more materials and further labor. He can store his manufactured goods in a public warehouse and receive a negotiable receipt approximating their value; the bank or his resource will honor the receipt as collateral for further credit. Field warehousing, a service provided by licensed warehouse firms, permits similar arrangements under sealed, guarded storage on the premises of the maker or elsewhere; negotiable receipts are issued and employed as before.

Credit Terms

If the prospect seems to be a good risk, credit is extended and an account opened for him. Terms must be decided upon at the beginning. Slow accounts are just as dangerous in a manufacturing concern as they are in a retail or service business. Not only do they tie up working capital, but if they are not collected over a period of time they will slow down production. In most trades, cash discounts are offered for payment within a certain length of time, otherwise the total amount must be paid. Such terms are stated "2/10, net 30," which means that a 2 per cent discount is allowed if payment is made within 10 days and that the total amount must be paid within 30. Some businesses buy in small quantities and frequently. In such cases the man-ufacturer may extend M.O.M. or E.O.M. terms. Under M.O.M. (*middle of month*) terms, all purchases bought before the middle of the month are billed as of the fifteenth; if such a discount as that granted in the terms "2/10, net 30" is allowed, it can be taken through the 25th of the month. For example, an invoice dated March 3, terms 2/10, net 30, M.O.M., could be discounted at 2 per cent if paid on or before March 25, the net amount of the invoice being due April 15. An invoice dated March 16, with the same terms, could be discounted up to April 25 or paid net May 15. E.O.M. (*end of month*) terms are very similar to M.O.M., except that all purchases are billed as of the end of the month instead of the middle and discount periods as well as due dates are based on that date. Other terms often used are: R.O.G. (*receipt of goods*), which means that the discount period starts only after the goods have been received; *extra dating,* which indicates that the discount period is extended for so many days after the regular allowed term; and *season dating,* which is another form of *extra dating* but is for a much longer period of time, because buyers are reluctant to pay immediately for goods purchased as much as seven or eight months in advance of demand.

A misuse of credit in so far as cash discounts are concerned may occur when some firms remit the amount of the bill less the cash discount even though the discount period has passed and, in some cases, the net period as well. Per-mitting such a practice would certainly be unfair to the prompt-paying cus-tomer. Sometimes the remittance must be accepted, but no further credit should be extended. The amount of the discount may be added to the next bill, or the check may be returned with a note reminding the debtor that the discount was not to be taken and asking him please to remit the proper amount. Laxness in enforcing terms will only bring loss to the company.

Both wholesalers and manufacturers have occasion at times to sell on a C.O.D. (*collect on delivery*) basis. Goods sent C.O.D. are usually sent to credit risks that are known to be undesirable or to simply unknown firms. Instead of sending merchandise C.O.D. and letting the shipping company collect for the merchandise, the manufacturer may wish to send a sight draft with a bill of lading attached. A bill of lading is evidence of title when the goods are shipped by a common carrier. When the merchandise arrives, the buyer is notified and he comes down to pay the amount of the draft and receive title to the goods. This applies only to a cash transaction.

Manufacturers often find it desirable to relate credit terms to the size of the order. This procedure has a dual purpose. By this limitation of credit to orders above a minimum quantity, customers are encouraged to place orders of sufficient size for economical handling; furthermore, encouraging the larger orders favors the better-established firms and thus tends to reduce the risk of granting credit.

CREDIT IN THE SERVICE BUSINESS

Because services are by their very nature intangible, nonreturnable, and "consumed" when rendered, credit extension is more risky and less common in this than in the other fields of small business. However, small service establishments with regular customers and frequent repeat sales, such as laundries and dry cleaning establishments, often find credit extension a convenience that is attractive to many customers. This is especially true when it is accompanied by pickup and delivery service. Naturally, prices will have to be higher than if the business were run on a cash-and-carry basis.

Personal service establishments like beauty parlors and many types of repair services find credit extension an aid to increased business. In all such cases, credit is primarily a customer convenience and is based on the willingness and ability of customers to pay. There can be no reliance on tangible goods as security except in such special cases as when the law permits a hotel to retain the baggage of nonpaying guests.

Except for these differences, credit for the service business is similar to that for the retail store. Usually only open account credit is appropriate, although major repairs on durable goods may be paid for on the installment plan. Account solicitation, sources of information, investigation of applicants, record keeping, and credit control are very similar in both fields.

Probably the typical service business has more to gain and less desirable business to lose by striving to reduce its credit business to a minimum than do firms in other fields. Since the quality of service rendered is of major importance, this will often be a more powerful means of attracting business than the credit extension.

CONCLUSIONS

Although credit carelessly handled can ruin any small business, carefully controlled credit has two major advantages. In many cases business gravitates to the credit-granting firm. *The mere availability of credit is sufficient to attract and hold many customers who would not trade with the firm if credit were not extended. Furthermore, information furnished by the credit customers' records can serve many purposes of management.* This aspect deserves more attention in the small business than it usually receives. Although credit is primarily a customer service, proper handling can make it also a powerful tool of management.

Many surveys show the total cost of consumer credit extended by retail stores to be close to three per cent of net sales, bad debt losses accounting for about one-half of one per cent. Credit-granting stores, however, tend to be more profitable than strictly cash stores.

Certain principles governing credit extension have been well established and should be observed. One is that the length of the credit period should not exceed the useful life of the merchandise.

Credit bureaus and many other sources of useful information are available to small businessmen. Experience shows that using them greatly reduces losses resulting from credit extension.

The bank credit plan described in this chapter appears to be an ideal opportunity for independent enterprisers to secure all the advantages of extending consumer credit economically and safely while avoiding any disadvantages. Resembling the bank credit plan is a recent expansion of credit card organizations. People may use these cards practically anyplace to purchase meals, lodging, gasoline and other goods, and receive a monthly statement that serves both for payment purposes and as an expense and tax record. Certain types of small businesses should find this method of credit extension advantageous.

The purpose of credit extension is to help the customer to buy; but the purpose of business is to make a profit. Thus credit must insure payment as it facilitates sale. As a "payment insurance" facility, it is an accounting financial control activity. As a buying convenience for the customer, it is a sales and marketing activity. The difficulty arises when the temptation is to sell at all costs, forgetting the true "day of reckoning"—that the transaction is profitable only if the bill for goods or services is paid promptly.

That this lack of realism is one of the beginning businessman's greatest hazards is evident in all business history. To say that profitable credit decisions often call for "nerves of steel" is no great exaggeration. One's friends or relatives, his former business associates, the big name, the large order, the "ground floor" approach—all constitute pressures and obligations to friendship and family harmony, and resistance to jibes, smirks, and even dares. The party who will suffer most through loss must defend profitable operation, which can be based only on logical thinking and actions.

As we criticize the banker's traditional "coldness" in lending situations, we must remember that the emotional warmth of friendly enthusiasm or blood ties has been an expensive luxury for many a businessman; better to be rational and objective and profitable in business than emotional and subjective and bankrupt. Those who have suffered believe that it is better to lose a friend quickly through refusal of credit to him than slowly through the long trials surrounding his refusal to pay.

QUESTIONS AND PROBLEMS

1. Differentiate between consumer and mercantile credit, showing why each point of difference is significant to the small businessman.

2. What factors should an enterpriser consider before deciding on his credit policy? Discuss.

3. From the retailer's viewpoint compare open account with installment credit.

4. Briefly describe the purpose of and services rendered by retail credit bureaus.

5. For each of the four major fields of small business, explain *fully* how the records of credit customers can be used as a tool of management.

6. Credit extension in the small business may show bad debt losses ranging from less than one per cent of sales to an extent that could put the firm out of business. Why is the danger of reaching this upper limit much greater for the small than for the large business?

7. Select some line of business in which customer credit is widely used and show how you could profitably operate in this field on a strictly cash basis.

8. What other divisions or activities of a business are closely related to its credit policy and administration? Discuss these relationships.

9. Explain how, if at all, the desirability of credit extension varies for manufacturers of different kinds of products as it does for different types of retail and service businesses. What conclusions do you draw from this?

10. If credit is a customer service, explain how, if at all, a policy of no credit could also be a customer service.

11. Assume that you have purchased a going business in which liberal credit has been the policy for years and that you want to operate on a strictly cash policy. Explain how you would proceed.

12. Explain how the same approach of customer control as used in a retail store could be applied to a service establishment and to a small manufacturing business.

13. Under what conditions would it be advisable for the small businessman to promote deposit account credit (that is, having customers deposit in advance the amount they plan to spend at the store for a certain period) to replace open accounts? Discuss.

14. As a small manufacturer selling entirely to small retailers, explain how you would (a) get many customers to buy for cash, and (b) reduce credit losses from other customers to a minimum.

15. How is cost accounting as used by a wholesaler or a manufacturer related to his credit department? Discuss.

16. If you were to start a collection agency in a town of 50,000, describe exactly how you would proceed.

17. Since most surveys show that credit-granting stores are more profitable than stores selling only for cash, how do you explain the steady expansion of cash-and-carry retailing?

18. Look up in some good retail advertising or management text, like *Retail Advertising and Sales Promotion* (by Charles M. Edwards, Jr. and William H.

Howard, Englewood Cliffs, N. J.: Prentice-Hall, Inc., 1943), the topic of "customer control." Prepare to discuss the ways a credit-granting store could use its customer ledger information for other objectives of management. Discuss how a customer control analysis could also improve credit administration.

19. From department stores, large mail-order house chains, and others, obtain all data on their newer credit plans, such as the revolving account, flexible limit, and similar plans that involve carrying charges to customers. Compile and analyze your findings, computing actual costs to customers, advantages and disadvantages of such plans. Formulate a plan whereby small independents could either (a) use such plans, or (b) compete successfully with the strong customer appeal of these forms of credit.

20. Sam's small department store did 45 per cent of its volume on open account credit, 15 per cent on installment, 5 per cent on semi-credit plans, and 35 per cent in cash. An increasing proportion of customers were younger families in their early twenties. Sam had complete records on all credit sales since 1945. Sales had increased rapidly from 1945 to 1952, then a declining rate to mid-1956 when they were $2.3 million. Sam suspected that credit plans recently being promoted aggressively by several of his larger competitors were responsible for his failure to progress. What should he do and why? Consider at least three significant lines of approach. Analyze and justify each.

24 • Simplified Record Systems

As a Dun & Bradstreet publication says: Two and two make four in any store, shop or factory, even in a "papa and mama" grocery enterprise. Good recordkeeping, a constant and detailed knowledge of expenses, income and profit or loss, is the first step toward profitable management of any business.[1]

Basically two groups require data from the records of a business, its own management, and outsiders. The latter include tax collectors, creditors, suppliers, and the insurance company in the event of a loss. For small manufacturers their customers often insist on knowing the financial condition and probable permanence of the enterprise.

Most of the necessary records and their proper use have been discussed in the chapters concerned with managing the major divisions of business and need not be considered again here. However, three groups require additional consideration: accounting, tax, and miscellaneous records. These are dealt with under three major heads in this chapter. Certain information provided by the accounting records is used for expense control and has been discussed in the chapter on business expenses, and use has been made of data secured from the accounting records in other places throughout the book. There is little need to elaborate on the superiority of factual information over rule of thumb or guessing. Mistakes in judgment, when the latter is based on the best obtainable facts, will be less serious and less costly than errors resulting from ignorance.

Some enterprisers believe recordkeeping takes more time than it is worth; others avoid it because of a dislike for figure work, a feeling that other duties are currently of greater importance, or a lack of knowledge as to the information needed and how it may be obtained. Since facts must be secured for purposes of taxation and regulation, and additional data are often needed for intelligent operations, it is easy to prove that properly planned records cur-

[1] "Profitable Management For Main Street," Dun & Bradstreet, Inc., New York (1959), p. 24.

rently maintained actually save time in the long run, in addition to their other advantages. Fortunately for those holding the other opinions mentioned, there are many ways they can secure the benefits of recordkeeping with a minimum of effort. A major objective of this chapter is to explain how this may be accomplished.

We shall also review briefly the basic accounting statements, profit and loss, and balance sheet. From these records analyses can be made to obtain financial ratios and operating ratios, both having many internal and external uses, which we shall examine.

ACCOUNTING RECORDS

Any experienced businessman knows that it is just common sense to keep an accurate, written record of every transaction. The man who has no oil pressure gauge on his automobile would have no way of knowing whether his motor was being properly lubricated until a knock in the motor or the mechanical failure of some moving part showed that it was not. Similarly, the lack of proper accounting and recordkeeping in the business concern makes it impossible for the manager to know how his enterprise is functioning, and in the majority of cases the first indication that something is wrong comes too late. Failure is already upon him.

Small business operators tend to keep their records in a single entry memorandum style, with no system of checks or balances and without preparing financial statements that reflect the condition of the business and warn of impending failure. They do this because, failing to realize the importance of accurate recordkeeping and its relation to efficient business management, they try to economize by eliminating the expense of double entry records and bookkeeping advice. Actually, this is false economy, for there can be no wiser expenditure than money spent to maintain complete records. In many cases the amount saved in bookkeeping expenses is more than balanced by the amount lost in overpayment of income taxes due to the lack of adequate records.

Needs met by accurate records. The following are only a few of the more common questions to which a businessman may be called upon to furnish the answers:

1. What was your income last year? What were your expenses?
2. What article is your best seller? Which is your worst?
3. What are your assets, liabilities, and net worth?
4. How much cash business do you have? How much credit business?
5. Are you carrying too large or too small an inventory?
6. What is the current value of your building, delivery equipment, and other fixed assets after deduction of depreciation allowance?
7. How much did you lose last year from bad debts?

8. What was the net gain realized on that piece of store equipment you sold last year as "used equipment"?

In addition to these, a proprietor should consider the following questions in order to take care of his business in the most efficient manner:

1. How much do my charge customers owe me now? How much of this is overdue, and how long overdue? When does the remainder fall due? Am I extending too much credit or could I stand some more accounts?

2. How much ready cash do I have with which to meet my obligations? Will my income during the next 30, 60, or 90 days be sufficient to take care of obligations I have assumed?

3. How much money do I actually have invested in my business, and what rate of interest am I earning on my investment?

4. How do the trends of sales, purchases, expenses, and other items in my store compare with those in similar stores? How do they compare with my own operations during previous years? Does the present trend of my sales justify an increase or decrease in any of these items, such as advertising?

5. In what ways can I cut down or eliminate some of my last year's expenses?

Simplicity of recordkeeping. Many small businessmen labor under the misapprehension that bookkeeping is difficult and complicated. Nothing is further from the truth; keeping a set of simple records that will be fully adequate for small businesses is an easy matter. Illustrated and explained later is the record known as the "one-book" system in which all records of income and cash payments are combined in a single book. This type of record is very popular among small retailers who prefer to use as few separate books as possible.

Sales records. Properly kept sales records are very definitely a requirement for successful business management. Regardless of how small or how large the business is, the owner will want to know the answers to one or more of the following questions, which apply with slight modifications to any field:

1. *Departmental information.* Which department in my store is making the most profit for me? Which department operates on the closest margin? Should I hold a clearance sale or do some type of special advertising to close out slow-selling articles?

2. *Efficiency of salesclerks.* Which one of my salesclerks is making the most sales for me? How do their individual selling records compare with their wages?

The answers to all these questions are easily found in the sales records if they have been properly made and preserved. Illustrations of simple forms for the analysis of sales figures will be presented later. Monthly sales totals are merely transferred at the close of each month from the sales column of the "one-book" record to the sales analysis statement, which may be totaled at the end of the year. Daily sales figures may be obtained in one of several ways: by totaling the sales slips which are made out for each sale, by taking the total as recorded by the cash register, or by having salesclerks keep individual records of sales on a form designed for that purpose for the particular store. The total daily sales of each department can be checked by using individual sales slips for each department, by using departmental keys on the cash register, or by keeping an individual cash register in each department. Sales of each clerk can be kept separate by requiring the clerks to initial their sales slips or to use the identifying letters assigned to them when ringing up sales on the cash register. In some businesses it might be practical to assign an individual cash register to each clerk; some registers have a key for charge sales.

Both cash and charge sales are recorded daily from the sales slips in stores that use the sales slip system. Sales may be posted from cash register totals by having the customer sign the register slip retained by the store, or by posting charge sales from the sales slips in order to arrive at total sales. Totals of individual sales slips are posted daily to the customers' ledger sheets in the customers' ledger. Many small retailers have found that an easier way to maintain the customers' ledger is to purchase a filing device designed especially for filing sales slips. One device has a number of hinged shelves that contain spring clips to hold the sales slips in place. When the clerk makes a sale on credit, he merely itemizes the articles on the sales slip and files the slip away in the special file. Many small business managers require the customer to sign the sales slip as evidence of his having received the goods, but this is a matter of the individual store's policy. All subsequent sales to the same customer are handled in the same way, all sales slips being pinned together. When the account is paid, the slips are given to the customer and his charge account file is empty. If merchandise is returned for credit, a credit memorandum is issued and a duplicate is filed in the customer's file at the close of the day. With this system it is unnecessary to maintain a separate accounts receivable ledger for charge customers, since the file is in itself an accounts receivable ledger, and much bookkeeping detail is eliminated.

Accounting for cash payments. Questions like the following are continually arising to challenge the proprietor, and the man who keeps careful records is the man who is going to have the advantage, other things being equal. If it became necessary for you to furnish a statement of cash disbursements showing in detail what happened to every sales dollar you took in last month, how much work would the preparation of such a statement entail? Could you account for every dollar spent without having a sizable amount in a miscellaneous account? If you find that your expenses are running too high, which ones are you going to reduce?

One of the best methods of accounting for cash disbursements and receipts in modern business is to deposit to a checking account in the bank all money taken in and to write a check for each and every expenditure except for very small items (costing, say, two dollars or less) like postage, window cleaning, or express charges. The bank helps to keep the firm's records, because canceled checks furnish a complete record of each disbursement. Each check is a written receipt for the payment and may prove very useful it the Bureau of Internal Revenue calls for substantiation of some expenditure.

The matter of small cash disbursements is easily taken care of through what is known as a "petty cash fund." A small fund of from $10 to $50, depending upon the need, is set aside to cover minor expenses. Each time an expenditure is made, a petty cash form is filled out for the amount of the expenditure in order to provide information for charging it to the proper expense account. When the fund is exhausted, a reimbursement check is drawn on the checking account, with the expense accounts being charged as indicated upon the petty cash forms. The manner of recording expenditures in the "one-book" system will be explained later.

Purchase records. Almost all small businesses do a certain amount of buying on credit. It is more convenient than having to pay for merchandise when ordered because the owner can make his purchases as often as needed during the month and settle for all purchases at one time at the end of the month. This eliminates the detail involved in paying for each purchase individually, and it permits the manager to check the merchandise for quantity and quality before paying for it. Another advantage of credit is that it actually amounts to an addition to working capital during the credit period. When the businessman buys on credit, he can make purchases that he could not have made if it had been necessary for him to pay cash, and usually by the time the account becomes due he has sold enough of the merchandise to pay the bill.

Since credit is such an important asset, it is important that it be diligently safeguarded at all times. Invoices must be paid promptly when they become due. A good plan to insure prompt payment is to keep an invoice file with a section for each day of the month. As invoices come in, they should be filed under the date upon which they fall due or when they should be paid to secure cash discounts if these are offered. It then becomes a relatively easy matter to check this file daily and make payment on all matured invoices. After payment each invoice is filed in an alphabetical file under the name of the company concerned. In the case of payments for which no invoices are available, a memorandum invoice should be prepared, giving the name of the person, the amount, the date, and the article purchased or service rendered. In this manner, a complete record of all purchases is made instantly available at all times. Invoices should always be marked with the check number and date of payment in order to eliminate the possibility of duplicate payment. Credit memorandums should be attached to applicable invoices upon receipt so that they will be deducted from the invoices before payment is made.

Equipment records. Regardless of the type or size of business operated, the owner will need a certain amount of equipment. In many cases he will have to purchase new equipment each year in order to keep up with competitors and with the trends in his type of business. Many times this equipment will be rather expensive and its use will raise operating expenses, but if it brings in enough additional business at a gross margin greater than the increase in expenses, it will prove to be a good investment.

Equipment records should be maintained on all equipment owned by the business. These records may be kept in book form or on cards in a card file. On a separate sheet or card for each piece of permanent equipment should be shown the following:

> Cost of equipment
> Amount of down payment
> Monthly payments
> Balance due
> Yearly depreciation

Each time a payment is made on a piece of equipment, it should be entered on the equipment record card. Also, at the end of each year depreciation should be computed and entered on the card. This depreciation is an expense of the business, just as much as rent, utilities, or salaries. The simplest and most practical method of computing depreciation is the straight-line method, an example of which follows:

Original cost of equipment	$500.00
Estimated trade-in or scrap value	50.00
Amount to be depreciated	$450.00
Yearly depreciation (estimated life: 10 years)	$ 45.00

The declining balance method should be used whenever quicker recovery of the investment is desirable.

Centsless accounting is increasing as a method of saving time, saving space on forms, and reducing errors. For a firm's own summaries all amounts are rounded to the nearest dollar, $1.49 becomes $1.00, $1.51 becomes $2.00, $1.50 is totaled as $2.00, $2.50 as $3.00, and so on. For amounts ending in $0.50 they may be rounded consistently to the nearest even or odd dollar. Customer and supplier accounts must be kept in exact amounts, and a variance or reconciliation account may be used to achieve a final accurate balance of the books, although even this step may be dispensed with when experience shows the variances to be small.[2]

Interpretation of financial statements. If the records are complete and accurate, it is a small matter to draw up the two basic statements universally used in successful business management, the balance sheet and the profit and loss statement. The latter statement, as the name implies is a summary of business transactions that have taken place during the year (or month),

[2] For further study see: E. S. Barnard, "Whole dollar accounting, an application," *NACA Bulletin,* August 1955), pp. 1704-10.

resulting in either a profit or a loss. It is like a motion picture of business operations during the period covered by the report; by careful analysis of the profit and loss statement, one can clearly see what has happened and determine why the business is now where it is. The balance sheet is the statement that shows exactly where the business stands; it can be thought of as a snapshot of the business as it stood on the last day of the accounting period. The balance sheet shows where the business is; the profit and loss statement shows how it got there. Used wisely, these two statements will give a good indication of what may be expected in the future.

The profit and loss statement summarizes the business transactions as follows:

Sales	$5,000.00
Deduct Cost of Goods Sold	3,500.00
Gross Margin	$1,500.00
Deduct Expenses	1,000.00
Net Profit	$ 500.00

The records make readily available all these amounts except the cost of goods sold, which is easily computed as follows:

Inventory, beginning of period	$2,000.00
Add Purchases of Goods during period	4,500.00
Goods Available for Sale during period	$6,500.00
Deduct Inventory on Hand, end of period	3,000.00
Cost of Goods Sold	$3,500.00

Now that we have the profit and loss statement, we are ready to proceed with the analysis. In analyzing a set of figures we want to compute certain ratios. These may be expressed as percentages of a common base—usually the total net sales figure—to make them comparable. These percentages are obtained by dividing the amount of each item in the statement by the net sales figure and multiplying by 100. To keep the illustration simple, we will take the previous example for our computation, although in practice the various types of expense would be listed and the percentage of net sales computed for each.

		Per Cent
Sales	$5,000.00	100
Deduct Cost of Goods Sold	3,500.00	70
Gross Margin	$1,500.00	30
Deduct Expenses	1,000.00	20
Net Profit	$ 500.00	10

What significance do these percentages have? How can they be of use in the determination of policies for future operation of the business? First, the owner can compare the ratios of his business with standard ratios. These can be obtained from publications of Dun & Bradstreet and the trade association in his field, or from the local banker, who usually has access to these or similar publications. Of course, there will be some items on the profit and loss statement that will necessarily be different from standard ratios because of peculiarities of the individual business. One company might have some expense item not commonly found in this type of business or might not have some expense that is commonly found. By making adjustments for unusual items, one can readily see how his business compares with the average business. In addition to this, he can measure his success by comparing his ratios with those of a successful, profitable business similar to his own. If he notices certain items in which the percentages of his business vary considerably from those of others, he should make an immediate investigation to ascertain the cause of the differences; by so doing, he may stop a leak somewhere in the business that would lead to ultimate failure unless corrected. Many businessmen also find it helpful to management to compare their ratios for the period under scrutiny with their own ratios for previous periods. If profits are declining, they can quickly check their ratios and ascertain the cause for the decline. If the ratios are not checked, a businessman might be misled by comparison of dollar figures. It is altogether possible that increased sales volume may produce a greater dollar profit from one month to the next although profit in relation to sales might be down by a rather large percentage.

By analyzing his balance sheet, the owner can see how much cash he has in his cash register and in the bank, how much inventory is on hand, how much the customers owe the firm, the value of his equipment, how much is owed to creditors, and the "net worth," the latter being the difference between what he owns and what he owes. Here is a simple balance sheet:

Assets

Currents Assets:

Cash on Hand	$150.00	
Cash in Bank	800.00	
Accounts Receivable	650.00	
Merchandise Inventory	900.00	$2,500.00

Fixed Assets:

Furniture and Fixtures	300.00	
Building	3,000.00	3,300.00
Total Assets		$5,800.00

Liabilities and Net Worth

Current Liabilities:

Accounts Payable	$375.00	
Notes Payable	125.00	$ 500.00

Fixed Liabilities:	
Mortgage Payable	2,500.00
Net Worth:	
Capital	2,800.00
Total Liabilities and Net Worth	$5,800.00

This is called a "balance sheet" because the total assets balance with, or are equal to, the total liabilities and net worth. It is very closely related to the profit and loss statement, in that almost any entry made in the financial records affects both statements. An addition to cash in the balance sheet is usually an addition to an income account in the profit and loss statement. A deduction from cash in the balance sheet is usually charged to some expense account or to the cost of sales in the profit and loss statement. And when the two statements are drawn up at the close of the accounting period, the amount of net profit or net loss for the period as shown in the profit and loss statement is exactly the sum that is needed to effect a balance between the capital account plus liabilities and the total assets as shown in the balance sheet.

The balance sheet should be used in conjunction with the profit and loss statement in the management of a business. As in the case of the latter, ratios make it easier to analyze and use the data contained therein. The current ratio, which is one of the most common, is the ratio between total current assets and total current liabilities. In other words, does the business have enough customers' accounts coming due to enable it, when they are added to its cash and to the income it will realize from sales during the next two weeks, to pay all the accounts that will fall due to creditors within the same period? Dividing total current assets by current liabilities will provide a current ratio that can be compared with the standard ratio or with former ratios of the business. A current ratio of two to one is usually considered a satisfactory but not in all cases a necessary indication of ability to pay current obligations.

In order to guard against purchasing too many fixed assets, a businessman should try to keep his ratio of net worth to fixed assets around one to one. In other words, he should have enough capital invested in the business to pay for most, if not all, of his fixed assets.

He can determine the amount his investment is earning for him by finding the ratio of net profits to average net worth as shown on his balance sheets at the beginning and at the end of the period.

Another analysis that should be made when a business extends credit is one according to the age of accounts receivable. Those that are past due should be divided into suitable groups, such as those that are 30, 60, 90, and more than 90 days past due. Separate ratios are then computed for each group. This analysis will disclose important trends and danger signals very useful for successful credit management.

Dun & Bradstreet suggest 14 important ratios that experience shows to be most useful in keeping a business in financial good health. They have published median figures for these ratios covering 70 lines of business activity including manufacturing, wholesaling, and retailing, thus providing standards for comparison for enterprises in any of these fields that compute similar ratios. The ratios are:

> Current assets to current debt,
> Net profits on net sales,
> Net profits on tangible net worth,
> Net profits on net working capital,
> Net sales to tangible net worth,
> Net sales to net working capital,
> Average collection period,
> Net sales to inventory,
> Fixed assets to tangible net worth,
> Current debt to tangible net worth,
> Total debt to tangible net worth,
> Inventory to net working capital,
> Current debt to inventory,
> Funded debts to net working capital.[3]

TAX RECORDS

Regardless of what kind of business one may decide to take up, he will always be confronted with the preparation of tax returns for the state and Federal governments. Since the laws of the different states vary, it would be impractical to attempt to give in detail the requirements for any individual state or states. Some of the taxes that may be expected in most states are sales taxes, income taxes, workmen's compensation, and unemployment taxes. Before going into business one should check with the managers of a few stores and service establishments in the community in which he expects to locate, and find out what state taxes he may expect to encounter. It would be wise to write to the state revenue department to inquire as to what forms must be submitted to comply with the law.

Federal tax requirements, on the other hand, are uniform throughout the United States, and it would be well at this point to consider some aspects of Federal income and excise taxation. Since the income tax laws change from year to year, the businessman should supplement the general discussion that follows by studying explanations of each important change. If an owner keeps his records in good shape throughout the year and prepares a standard profit and loss statement at the end of the year, it will be a simple matter to copy the figures from the profit and loss statement onto Income Tax Form 1040.

---

[3] For a more detailed study of ratios see: Roy A. Foulke, *Practical Financial Statement Analysis,* 4th ed. (New York: McGraw-Hill Book Company, Inc., 1957); and Richard Sanzo, *Ratio Analysis for Small Business,* Small Business Management Series No. 20 (Washington, D. C.: Small Business Administration, 1957).

The instructions accompanying this form usually are helpful in answering questions that arise in a business connected with income tax procedure. One particularly important point that is often misunderstood is that depreciation of equipment used in an enterprise is just as much a business expense as cash paid for rent or salaries. Accurate and complete depreciation records should be maintained.

Some of the important facts about Federal taxes which should be studied by persons operating small businesses are: deductions allowable for research and development work, the terminology used in tax reports, dates for filing various tax reports, bad debt rules, differences and reconciliations of tax laws with standard accounting, and tax laws pertaining to proprietorships and partnerships.

In recent years simplification of terminology has resulted in many of the former complicated terms being eliminated. Now only three logically related ones are needed: "gross income," "adjusted gross income," or gross after taking allowable deductions such as necessary expenses, and "taxable income," the result of taking all allowable deductions.

Most businesses operate on the accrual instead of the cash basis. Standard accounting procedures have recognized this distinction, and allocated advance payments to the period they were for and during which expenses to earn them would be incurred. In the past tax collectors have not accepted this concept, leading to the old quip about businessmen needing two sets of books, one for approved accounting, the other for the tax collector. Now advance payments may be accepted and spread over the period during which expense deductions to earn them are allowable, thus bringing tax requirements in line with business accounting practice.

Many former controversies over alleged tax inequality between corporations and unincorporated firms should be dissolved by the provision permitting proprietorships and partnerships of less than 50 partners to choose among the three forms of organization as to how they will be taxed. Certain limitations are included and the decision should be made only after competent counsel. Also, specific statements in the law define partnerships as income-reporting, and not income-paying, entities.

Withholding tax—This is another Federal tax requirement that will give an employer many headaches unless watched carefully. This is a tax that is withheld from the wages of all employees (regardless of how many employees one has) before salary or wage payments. It represents an installment on each individual employee's income tax liability for the current year. Withholding tables, which one may use in determining the exact amount to be withheld, are furnished by the Bureau of Internal Revenue. By making these deductions an employer is acting as an agent of the Federal government, and he is required to account for all money withheld. The information of the greatest importance that his records should show in connection with the withholding tax is: (1) number of persons employed during the year, (2) amount of wages paid to each person subject to withholding, (3) periods of employment of each person, and (4) amounts and dates of wage and salary payments and withholding tax deductions therefrom. In addition to these records, he must keep in a safe place copies of all withholding exemption certificates and notices of changes in exemptions for all employees.

There are three different reports that must be filed with the Commissioner of Internal Revenue in connection with withholding tax procedure. These are:

1. Quarterly return of income tax withheld on wages (Form 941).
2. Annual statement of income tax withheld on wages (Form W-2).
3. Reconciliation of quarterly returns of income tax withheld with statements of income tax withheld (Form W-3).

Specific filing dates, forms, procedures and penalties are subject to change, and should be ascertained from the Commissioner of Internal Revenue for your district, or from your accountant or accounting service if you use one.[4]

Sales tax—This is another type of tax about which a businessman will need to secure information. Various states and cities levy such taxes, with the rate varying from place to place. One should contact the state or local revenue office for information that will acquaint one with the applicable law; having done so, one can adapt one's records to the requirements.[5]

If such taxes were always levied upon gross sales, they would present no appreciable difficulty. But in almost all of the states or localities having retail sales taxes there are specific exemptions, either on a certain class (or classes) of merchandise, or a particular group of customers. In most states the applicable road tax on gasoline does not apply to fuel used by farmers in their tractors. In many instances cigars, cigarettes, and tobacco are exempt from sales tax because a specific tax already has been levied upon them. Because of such exemptions, in keeping his records, a manager will need to devise some type of control by which he can distinguish tax-exempt sales that will be deducted from his total sales at the end of the taxable period.

In most cases there will be certain other items that may be deducted from gross sales after tax-exempt sales have been subtracted. Some of these are:

1. Cash discounts to customers and refunds for returned goods.
2. Bad debts charged off.
3. Finance and interest charges.
4. Allowances on trade-ins.
5. Freight and transportation charges.

One should be sure to study carefully the deductions allowed by the particular state and/or city in which his business is located in order to prevent the overpayment of sales taxes.

[4] Information concerning Federal income and withholding taxes is obtainable in the *Prentice-Hall Federal Tax Service.*

[5] Information concerning state taxes may be found in the *Prentice-Hall State and Local Tax Service.*

Some business enterprises will find it necessary to keep records of the sales of certain items that are subject to Federal excise taxes. Under provisions of the Federal Revenue Act in force at a given time certain rates will apply to articles taxed and certain procedures will be required for recordkeeping and making returns. The same sources of information mentioned earlier should be consulted and their recommendations followed.

In regard to the computation of the tax on an article, the amount of the Federal excise tax is not considered to be a part of the sales price of the article before tax. In other words, if the price the retailer wants to get for himself is $2.00 and the Federal tax is 10 per cent, the sale price will be $2.20. The Revenue Act may provide however, that any retailer who represents to his customers that he is absorbing the tax (not charging it to them) shall be liable to penalty. Thus if a seller does not charge the tax to his customers as a separate amount, he should not make any written or oral statements that will cause any person to believe that the price of the article does not include the tax.

When a state or community retail sales tax is imposed on an article subject to the Federal excise tax and billed as a separate item, it may be excluded from the taxable price. Thus in our previous example a five per cent state or local tax would raise the price to the consumer to $2.30, not to $2.31 as it would if the 10 per cent tax were figured on the retail price including the state sales tax. Whenever such a state or local sales tax is excluded from the taxable sales price of the article, the merchant must retain a copy of the invoice or other record of sale rendered to the purchaser that will prove to the Commissioner of Internal Revenue that the retail sales tax so excluded was stated as a separate item.

Occupational taxes and retail excise taxes apply to governmental agencies, and in respect to the latter tax the United States government, or any of its instrumentalities or agencies, must collect the retail tax on the sale of any article generally subject to the tax unless sales by such agencies are specifically exempted.

A retailer may be allowed a credit or refund of a tax paid on an article when the price on which the tax is based is later readjusted as a result of return or repossession of the article, or by a bona fide discount, rebate, or allowance. The allowable credit or refund is limited to the overpayment of the tax when calculated on the adjusted price. For example, if a $2.00 article subject to the 10 per cent Federal excise tax is sold for $2.20 and later a discount or allowance of $1.00 is made (plus $0.10 excise tax), the retailer is allowed this $0.10 tax refunded as a credit or refund.

If in a business the owner is liable for the collection of excise taxes, it will be necessary for him to make provision in his accounting setup for an adequate record of taxable sales or of the actual amount of tax collected from customers so that his records will be in order for inspection by Federal officials at any time.

RETAIL METHOD OF INVENTORY

A widely used method common in department and specialty stores for determining the cost value of the inventory without taking a *physical* count is the Retail Method. This technique has been approved by the Treasury Department for income tax purposes.

The Retail Method is suitable for use by any store or department that has as its primary function the selling of merchandise without processing or alteration. In addition to providing a closing inventory at "cost or market whichever is lower," it is a means of maintaining a perpetual merchandise inventory and of keeping records of markdowns, additional markups, and employee discounts. It also discloses stock shortages when the physical inventory is compared with the book inventory. However, our concern here is with its use for inventory valuation.

TABLE 8. THE RETAIL METHOD OF INVENTORY VALUATION

		Cost	Retail
Beginning Inventory		$27,000	$ 45,000
Purchases		49,400	76,000
Add Freight and Express (cost column only)		460	
Add Net Markups (retail column only)			1,000
Goods Available for Sale (at cost and at retail)		$76,860	$122,000
Markup (retail minus cost)	$45,140		
Markup of $45,140 divided by merchandise at retail of $122,000 = 37 per cent markup			
Net Sales	$50,000		
Add Markdowns, Discounts to Employees and Shortages	3,000		
Goods Sold or Disposed of (at retail)			53,000
Retail Value of Goods on Our Shelves			69,000
Cost percentage (100 per cent minus 37 per cent)			.63
Inventory at Cost		43,470	
Cost of Goods Sold (cost of goods available for sale minus inventory at cost)		$33,390	
Net Sales	$50,000		
Deduct Cost of Goods	33,390		
Gross Margin	$16,610		

The beginning inventory and all subsequent purchases are recorded at both cost and retail prices. Freight and express charges are added to the cost column and net markups are added to the retail column. The resultant column **totals** are the cost and retail prices of goods available for sale during the period. The *cost* value of this merchandise is then deducted from the *retail* value to get the markup in dollars. Dividing the markup in dollars by the *retail* value of the merchandise available for sale and multiplying by 100 will result in the markup as a percentage.

The next step is to add markdowns, discounts to employees, and shortages, in dollars, to net sales in dollars for the period. This sum, representing the retail price of the goods sold or disposed of otherwise, is then deducted from the total retail price of the goods available for sale to give the *retail* price of goods still on the shelves. The *cost* price of these goods is the objective. The retail price is multiplied by the cost complement of the markup per cent (100 minus per cent markup) to give the final figure for this ending inventory at cost.

Cost of goods sold is easily calculated by deducting the inventory at cost from the cost of goods available for sale. The explanation is that from the total cost of goods available for sale, the cost of goods still on the shelves has been deducted, the resulting figure being the cost of goods sold or disposed of.

It will be noticed that the markup percentage used (37 per cent) was calculated without including markdowns, discounts, and (estimated) shortages, but these were added to sales as recorded to get the total value at retail of goods disposed of. Therefore, the calculated cost value of the closing inventory is less than actual cost, and this is proper because some of the goods were marked down. If, however, the price trend had been upward and additional markups (rather than markdowns) had been taken, these *would* be included in calculating the markup percentage and the caluclated cost would more closely approximate actual cost.

MISCELLANEOUS RECORDS

A small retail lumber dealer has for many years maintained records of contractors and of carpenters in his area in such a way as to be able to tell at any time what each one is doing. For example, he knows that contractor Smith has just started construction on a duplex apartment house and will be needing eight or ten carpenters in about two weeks. From past experience he knows that Smith will soon be asking him where he can find them. When this time comes, he can immediately refer to his carpenter file and learn which ones are ready to start to work at once and when each employed man will be available. Most of the men now take the initiative in informing him of their status. By making his office a clearing house for employment, this service has built up goodwill with both groups; and by keeping construction moving forward at a more regular rate, it has helped to increase sales.

A job printer who has several presses and employees but is still a small businessman solved many of his problems by maintaining efficiency and activity records of each machine and of each employee. In this way he has instituted a miniature production control and costing system which enables him to plan jobs well in advance, make more accurate bids on competitive jobs, go after additional work whenever needed to keep his plant busy, and thus maintain greater stability of output and employment.

A small wholesale grocer secures published crop forecasts and prepares his own charts to help in planning and timing his buying. From his sales records he prepares a daily commodity breakdown to show buying trends. By analyzing past sales to each customer, many of whom are large farmers and poultry and stock growers, he has a record of the seasonal buying habits of each regular customer. These records are used in buying, sales promotion, and inventory control.

A small dress factory selling through agents to retail stores maintains a customer record card for each store showing the date and types and quantities of each purchase. These records are useful in planning production, in checking on the agents' solicitation of repeat business and as a follow-up on the success of styles previously made and sold.

An insurance agent keeps records of all customers' policies, present and lapsed, showing renewal dates, reasons for changes, and similar data. By watching current news items, he sometimes secures reinstatement of a lapsed policy when circumstances have changed for a former customer. Naturally, customers are reminded of renewal dates, but this agent also studies each client's current needs and suggests changes to provide policy coverage better suited to present conditions. He also maintains records on prospective customers that are used for solicitation of new business.

These are just a few examples of particular small businessmen who have made effective use of records other than the standard accounting ones. In any small business a judiciously selected set of records will make possible increased sales, more regular and improved operations, and better customer and public relations.

SERVICE RECORDS

Another type of record system not properly classified elsewhere may be illustrated by the records needed for a repair service.

Certain kinds of business in each of the three main fields must meet the repair problem. Manufacturers may have their products returned to the factory for repair or in certain cases may furnish repair service at the customers' locations. Merchants handling items like household appliances, radios, television sets, furniture, and jewelry must make provisions for necessary repairs after the product has been sold. The need may arise either before or after a guarantee period has expired. If the former, repair costs will be borne by the merchant or charged to the manufacturer. Where and by whom such repairs are made is a matter of policy and agreement with the manufacturer. In any case, records are needed to handle the transactions efficiently, to prevent loss of goods, and to assure collection from the customer or manufacturer. Finally, an important segment of the service field is that concerned with repair services of various kinds.

Sale and installation dates usually determine the status of a guarantee and this in turn determines who is to bear the cost of repairs. This information is also useful to a merchant who may be called upon to repair or service goods purchased from him without any specific guarantee. Most retailers want to make good any merchandise defects but should not be expected to provide maintenance against normal wear and tear.

A complete record should be kept of each service call or of all work done on articles brought in for repair.

An adequate supply of essential repair parts is necessary to render efficient service. A simple bin card will help maintain this inventory. When parts are added to the bin stock, the amount is added to the bin tag, and the process is reversed as parts are removed.

It is a good practice to establish standard appliance repair charges for as many run-of-the-mine repair jobs as possible. This will not only establish a fair profit basis for the repair work, but will help the bookkeeping department and increase customers' confidence in the fairness of the service charges.

Dealers and merchants rendering repair service on most kinds of mechanical products may secure suggested customer charges for recurring types of repair jobs. Whether followed exactly or not, these lists are useful guides.

For each type of business certain additional records may be needed. Even though a situation in a particular business is out of the ordinary, sufficient thought given to planning the essential records will usually lead to the development of a simplified system like those illustrated throughout this chapter.

Paper Work and Office Procedures

When the small businessman first starts his own business, he will always have some paper work, whether his office is merely a table top and a letter file or a separate, well-equipped room. It is necessary to have some organization of the paper work to be performed, such as the writing of business letters, filing of records, opening and sending out of mail, and filling out of orders and invoices. Perhaps the owner-manager will do all of this work himself. If so, he will need to have this paper work so organized that it will not interfere with his obligation to serve his customers. The small businessman who sits back at his desk in the rear of the store checking invoices, writing orders, and so forth, during business hours while his customers stand around waiting, is sacrificing goodwill for the sake of work that should be done either during slack periods of the day or after business hours.

In the organization of office procedures, no single important activity that should be performed daily can safely be neglected. Letters must be answered promptly, accounting records must be kept up to date, and all the records necessary for the carrying on of the business should be filed daily.

Records must be arranged so that they will be available when they are needed for reference. The plan for filing each kind of record will depend upon the needs of the business. Correspondence, for example, may be filed alphabetically by name, location, or subject; the most practical method for the small businessman would probably be alphabetically by name. Equipment houses supply standard sets of alphabetical guides that will probably serve the needs of a small business if used with manila folders.

Printed or typed material containing useful information from trade journals, trade associations, or suppliers should be kept for future reference. This material should not be piled on a desk or in a drawer in the hope that it can be found when needed, but should be filed by subject or name in an alphabetical file, for this method might save hours of searching some busy day.

Sales records should be filed at first by customer's name and later, when the business is large enough, by territories. Purchase and pricing records, as well as quotations, could be filed alphabetically by commodity. Catalogue indexes can be filed by commodity for easy reference. Mailing lists for advertising pieces should be filed by location.

Personnel records should be kept whether employees number one or fifty. These should be filed alphabetically by name with such material as application letters, letters of reference, social security records, and the like in each employee's folder. When an employee leaves, a notation of his reason for leaving should be made. This information will serve to jog the memory of the owner in case he is asked for a letter of recommendation or the employee again applies for a position with the business.

When a letter or paper might be filed in one of several possible places, the material should be filed in the most likely place and cross-reference sheets like the sample one shown below should be filed in the other locations. By this simple method of cross-referencing, the location of papers can be greatly facilitated.

```
┌──────────────────────────────────────────────────────────┐
│                  CROSS-REFERENCE SHEET                     │
│                                                            │
│   Name or                                                  │
│   Subject:   Joe Doakes                 Date: 8/25/—       │
│                                                            │
│   Regarding: Complaint                                     │
│                                                            │
│                                                            │
│   SEE                                                      │
│                                                            │
│   Name or                                                  │
│   Subject:   New Supply Company                            │
└──────────────────────────────────────────────────────────┘
```

After the small businessman has been in business for a year or two, his files will begin to grow out of bounds. For the small business, once a year will be often enough to transfer records to inactive files. The decision to retain all records may be expensive over a period of years, for adequate storage boxes and storage space must be made available. The more general practice for small business firms is to destroy certain material every year. Some general factors have an influence in determining what material should be immediately destroyed and what should be stored. State and Federal regulatory bodies have handed down complete instructions regarding the length of time that correspondence and records shall be kept by insurance companies. The Commissioner of Internal Revenue has ruled that, in general, records bearing on income taxes must be kept five years. The statutes of limitations in the various states, relating to the period during which suits may be brought, have much to do with deciding how long to keep records and correspondence concerned with contractual relations. Any record that may be involved in a case of fraud should not be destroyed. Generally speaking, the test of the advisability of transferring or destroying material is the number of references to past material and the need of protection in legal and tax matters.[6]

In many cities small firms may have permanent records microfilmed for economical storage in small space.

In a small business some type of calculating machine will probably be a good investment, depending upon the amount and complexity of the book-keeping system used. By talking with experienced men in the business and with suppliers, a suitable machine can be selected. Whether or not the purchase of a typewriter will be necessary will depend on the type of business.

In a small office it is often advisable to send certain work out to agencies, particularly duplication work that cannot be performed economically by the small office staff. There are so-called letter service companies that specialize in typing letters or in mimeographing, multigraphing, or printing material for small concerns that do not have the necessary equipment to do their own work. Prices for a particular type of service can be obtained from several agencies and may then be compared with the probable cost of doing the work in one's own office.

BETTER RECORDS WITH LESS RECORDKEEPING

Three major ways an enterpriser may secure proper records with a minimum of effort are: (1) to have a part-time bookkeeper or accountant keep his records for him, (2) to affiliate with an accounting service (such as Mail Me Monday which has franchise offices in all leading cities), or (3) to use an approved simplified one-book system.

Subscribers to the Mail Me Monday service may choose among several options ranging from a minimum for accounting and tax purposes to very complete systems. Fees compare favorably with the cost of alternate services

[6] John J. W. Neuner, *Office Management and Practices,* 4th ed. (Cincinnati, Ohio: South-Western Publishing Co., 1959), Chapter 24.

and the organization does have the advantage of nation-wide experience and current data for comparisons and advice. Interested persons may contact their local Mail Me Monday office or write to the Accounting Corporation of America, 1929 First Avenue, San Diego 1, California.

Simplified and One-book Systems

Standard double entry accounting as developed for large corporations may be unduly cumbersome for many small enterprises. Especially since labor and other costs of paper work have increased so greatly, many small businessmen have sought and found simplified systems adequate for their needs. Many of these operate on the one-book principle and economize through columnar entries based on appropriate classification of items, thus avoiding duplication of writing and re-entering frequently recurring transactions.

The adequacy of simplified systems, especially those prepared by commercial agencies or by the businessman himself, is still a controversial subject. Accountants understandably prefer a system tailor-made by themselves to fit each enterprise, whereas the commercial agencies claim that their extensive experience makes possible the design of forms and systems adequate, if not superior to, those locally prepared. A person should be able to make his own decision if he will withhold judgment until he has made a fair investigation of his own specific needs.

Considerable misunderstanding exists regarding simplified and one-book systems. They *are* based on approved double-entry accounting in spite of the one-book designation often used. Students are often confused on this point, and relatively few are familiar with the systems available or those that can be self-designed.

Several commercial agencies produce simplified one-book systems that may be purchased in most office supply stores. Three will be briefly described here for purposes of illustration. In addition, most stationery stores carry ruled blank forms that may be adapted to a firm's recordkeeping needs, and the Department of Commerce has published guides for their use. In many cases, however, the best solution to a firm's needs is to adopt, with possible adaptations, the recordkeeping system prepared by the leading trade association in the field.

Although the systems prepared by the latter group and by leading commercial associations for use by members embody the double entry principle of checks and balances, it is well before adopting any system to be certain that it is based on sound accounting principles, and that you understand and observe its recommended use. Systems prepared by commercial companies may usually be inspected in your local office supply store. If you decide to design your own one-book system be especially careful of these admonitions so as to avoid an oversimplified single entry system lacking accurate checks and balances. In addition, make certain your system will furnish in easily accessible, usable form all data you need for purposes of taxation and insurance, and what you actually need and will use for intelligent operations.

One of the most complete lines of simplified bookkeeping and tax record systems on the market is the Johnson System. Systems are available which are designed to meet the needs of various particular types of businesses. These books are available in standard sizes and at moderate prices. Each is a complete one-book system, and instructions are included.[7]

Another well-known system is the Blackbourn System, which is also designed for particular types of operations. This system is a bit more complicated and is recommended for those with prior accounting or bookkeeping experience. It is also a complete one-book system which sells for a moderate price.[8]

If investigation of record and tax systems available shows none to be suited to an enterpriser's needs, or if for other valid reasons he prefers to design his own system, it would be a relatively easy matter to purchase ruled columnar sheets in blank and supply his own headings. By doing this, he could make his records as simple or as complex as desired. For instance, the following form represents utter simplicity:

		CASH RECEIPTS		CASH PAYMENTS			
		Cash Sales and Rec'd on Acc't	Other Income	Mdse. for Resale	Operating Expenses	Other Payments	
Date	Remarks					Account	Am't
(a)	(b)	(c)	(d)	(e)	(f)	(g)	(h)

These columns would be used as follows:

(a) Enter the date on which the transaction took place.

(b) Write a brief description of the transaction.

(c) Enter total cash receipts from cash sales and customers' payments on account. This could be entered as one total for the day's transactions on one line, or, if desired, individual entries could be made on separate lines under the same date.

(d) Enter any other cash receipts in this column.

(e) Enter total amount (or individual amounts) spent during the day by cash or by bank check for merchandise for resale.

(f) Enter total payments (cash or check) for expenses.

(g) Write in this column the nature of any other payment made which could not be classified under (e) or (f).

(h) Enter amounts of items listed in column (g).

This simple record, if well kept, would provide the small operator with general information and would be better than no records at all. However,

---

[7] The Johnson System, 828 N. Broadway, Milwaukee, Wisconsin.
[8] The Blackbourn System, 230 South Cedar Lake Road, Minneapolis 5, Minnesota.

it has serious limitations, for it lacks columns that an owner will need from time to time to record other transactions. For example, if he extends credit, it will be necessary for him to have two columns in the journal for customers' accounts, one for charges and one for credits. Otherwise, this information will have to be laboriously scheduled from the customers' tickets each time he needs to know his total accounts receivable. Similarly, a column should be provided for creditors' accounts payable—that is, accounts representing bills owed but not yet paid by the firm.

The record keeping system for a retail store, which is described below, is designed to provide: (1) guides for good management; (2) a measure of profitability; (3) a systematic record of the progress of the business; and (4) the necessary facts for computing required Federal and state taxes. After the system has been installed and has been in operation for a short period, it should not require more than a few hours each week to keep it up to date, with some additional time for the preparation of monthly, quarterly, and annual tax reports and statements.[9]

The principal parts of the system include:

1. A daily cash report to provide a check on cash receipts and payments and a summary and classification of cash received and paid out for entry into the cumulative one-book summary.

2. A cumulative one-book summary covering cash transactions, credit transactions, and payments by check to provide most of the information necessary to prepare statements of profit and loss and required tax reports.

3. A monthly statement of profit and loss, illustrating the use of operating ratios as a management tool.

4. Adaptation of the cumulative one-book summary to provide analysis of gross margin by departments if desired.

5. An annual profit-and-loss statement, illustrating its relationship to the cumulative one-book summary and the Federal income tax return.

6. Employee tax records and reports covering Federal withholding, social security, unemployment, Federal excise, and state sales taxes.

7. A record of fixed assets, including information for making depreciation charges and determining the current value of fixed assets for preparation of a balance sheet.

8. Recommendations concerning the handling of charge sales, collections and accounts receivable.

9. A balance sheet, to be prepared at the close of each calendar or fiscal year.

10. A statement of the proprietor's net worth, adjusted for withdrawals and accumulated profit or loss.

[9] *Record Keeping for Retail Stores,* Industrial Series No. 80 (Washington, D. C.: U. S. Department of Commerce, 1948).

Many of the refinements generally included in the accounting system of large concerns have been omitted to achieve maximum simplicity. The records are kept on a cash basis; other income is included with sales; purchases and charge sales are recorded net of all refunds and allowances; and only major end-of-period adjustments are made. A daily cash report and cumulative one-book summary replaces all journals and ledgers except for accounts receivable, employee records, and records of fixed assets.

The daily cash report items which are entered in the cumulative one-book summary are indicated by the arrows. At the time this information is entered in the one-book summary, total charge sales, less returns and allowances, should be entered on the same line. If the cash register provides sufficient keys and totals, charge sales can also be rung up and included in the daily report. Otherwise information must be obtained from the charge slips, or from a separate listing of charge sales. If the cash register does not provide a separate key and total covering cash received on account, a separate record of such receipts must be maintained.

The daily cash report form may be mimeographed on an $8\frac{1}{2}'' \times 11''$ sheet and punched for filing in a ring binder or printed on the front and back of a manila envelope. All supporting papers, including paid-out receipts, cash-register tapes, carbons of deposit slips, should be attached or inserted and the reports filed by day for future reference.

A one-book summary will supply a cumulative record of all cash transactions (including payments by check) and of all charge sales. The monthly (or quarterly) totals will provide almost all of the information necessary for the preparation of a statement of profit and loss. The totals may be transferred to an annual summary, in the same form, to obtain totals for the annual statement of profit and loss and income tax return.

Any number of columns may be used in the summary with any expense breakdown desired. It should conform with the classifications to be used in the profit-and-loss statements. Expenses paid infrequently may be grouped in one column to reduce the number of columns required. However, in this case separate totals must be obtained for use in the profit-and-loss statement. If no credit sales are made, columns A, B, and D should be omitted. If operations are recorded on a departmental basis, additional columns for purchases and sales should be inserted.

None of the items listed in column R (other payments) are used in the profit-and-loss statement. This column, with space for explanations, is included for recording payments which are not for purchase of merchandise nor operating expenses. Such payments include owner's cash withdrawals, repayments of loans, and purchase of assets.

The cumulative one-book summary may be prepared on any columnar pad secured from a stationery store. The blank column headings may be cut from enough top sheets to last for a year and the column headings written in on the last sheet. This will avoid the necessity of writing the column headings more than once during the year.

CONCLUSIONS

Modern business must be operated on the basis of adequate records. Financial records are necessary to determine *profit or loss, return on investment, owner's equity, assets, liabilities, and other pertinent facts. In addition, good accounting is an important tool of management.* Information obtained from records furnishes the basis for managerial decisions ranging in scope and importance from policy formation or revision down to day-to-day decisions regarding routine operations.

Both financial and closely related records are required for many tax uses. Often Federal or state laws require that certain records be kept and that reports based on these records be made. Penalties are imposed for failure to comply with these statutes.

Although financial (or accounting) and tax records were emphasized in this chapter, additional records are desirable in many cases, even in the small business. The more important of these are treated elsewhere in the text in connection with the particular management functions to which they are related.

Keeping the necessary records for a small business need be neither complicated nor time-consuming. Simplified record systems have been developed for recording the essential accounting information needed, such as the one-book system described in this chapter. Whenever certain transactions occur frequently as do sales in a retail store or service calls in a repair shop, the necessary recording can be reduced to a simple system. When the transaction is common to other businesses in the field, prepared record keeping systems are usually available from either local stationers or suppliers.

Since a strong urge to keep accurate and complete records does not seem to be characteristic of most small businessmen, *the owner-manager should be on guard against neglect of this important function.* To make it easy to maintain essential records, the system installed should be as simple as possible, provided it does the job. At the start, at least, this may justify seeking competent advice or even employing a specialist to select the best system and get it started properly.

The owner should remember that *in the long run time spent in keeping adequate records actually saves time* that would otherwise be necessary to secure essential information required for measuring progress, paying taxes, or financing. The results will be more accurate and the efficiency and profitableness of the business will tend to increase when decisions are based on reliable information that is available only through a system of adequate records.

QUESTIONS AND PROBLEMS

1. Why is recordkeeping not merely desirable but absolutely necessary in modern business?

2. What information could be obtained from the balance sheets of a business drawn up at the end of each of ten consecutive years? Could the same information be obtained from the profit-and-loss statements for these years? Discuss.

3. What records would be most useful to you in deciding whether or not to buy a particular business that is offered for sale? How, if at all, could you verify the accuracy of these records? Discuss.

4. If a business has adequate records, what advantages are there in having an audit of the books made annually by a public accountant?

5. In what ways did the contents of this chapter show the influence of Federal and state laws upon the records a business must keep? Would all these records be made unnecessary if the laws you thought of were eliminated? Explain and discuss.

6. How would you use the contents of this chapter in starting a new business? In justifying a business opportunity? In refinancing a going business?

7. Do all businessmen keep all the records they know they need? Explain.

8. In general, which small businessman is more likely to keep adequate records, the one whose background was primarily in production or the one whose background was in selling? Are you sure? Explain.

9. In what ways, if any, are the following people interested in the records kept by a particular business: its customers, its suppliers, its creditors, and its competitors?

10. If you were called in to assist a small business that was getting into financial difficulties, explain how you would use records and recordkeeping.

11. What important records are needed in the small factory but not in the retail store? In the retail store but not in the factory? In either of these but not for the service business, and vice versa?

12. In what respects do the records needed for the proprietorship, partnership, and corporation differ? Discuss.

13. How would customer control be affected by a retail store using the spring clip method of filing sales checks for charge transactions instead of customer ledgers? Discuss.

14. Explain how a simplified one-book system applies the double entry principle. Illustrate.

15. Visit a local stationery and office-supply store to find out what simplified record systems are available. What systems are designed for such special purposes as keeping certain tax records, production control in the factory, and identification of each customer's goods in the service establishment? What conclusions do you draw from your investigations?

16. Bill had a minor in accounting for his degree in business. After serving two years as his own accountant for his own enterprise, he felt his time could be used better for top management duties. His firm makes a line of products sold directly to retailers and to consumers. Most sales to retailers are on open account, those to consumers for cash. All purchases are for cash. Bill wants to install a simple but adequate recordkeeping system that will relieve him of all routine paper work. What should he do, and why?

25 • Independent Professional Practice

More college students plan to enter one of the professions than any other occupation. The survey by *Time*[1] showed that 50 per cent of college alumni were engaged in all types of professions combined, and limited surveys by the authors confined to business school graduates showed from 30 to 40 per cent in the various professional fields. A larger proportion of professional men and women aspire to independent practice than do majors in other fields. Where a small business or independent enterpriser course has been offered in more than a hundred business schools of the country, students training for the various professions outside the business school enroll if permitted to do so. For these, and several reasons more directly related to the typical small businessman, this chapter should be of considerable value.

For all practical purposes the representative professional man in independent practice today is essentially a small businessman or independent enterpriser. With due respect to certain differentiating factors, policies and procedures, professional and independent business enterprisers have essentially the same basic factors and problems. Both must keep records, pay taxes, maintain an office or headquarters, meet their expenses, secure and satisfy a clientele, and obtain gross receipts in excess of total expenses. Both must perform all of the operating functions associated with their kind of enterprise, service, or service and retail.

Concepts change, especially in a dynamic economy such as ours. We have many more professions today than formerly, and our concept of professional conduct is also changing. Operation of the "adopt and adapt" technique mentioned often in our text is quite evident in the area embracing the accepted professions and aspirants to professional status. The *modus operandi* in this area should be useful to independents in either of these subdivisions. It represents a fundamental long-time trend of both extremes toward the middle:

[1] E. Havemann and Patricia Salter West, *They Went to College* (New York: Harcourt, Brace & Company, Inc., 1952), p. 27.

former nonprofessional fields now seek professional status because of its prestige and many other advantages, while the accepted professions seek dignified ways to apply business techniques to their own advantage. This concept should be better appreciated as we progress with the discussion in the chapter.

WHAT IS A PROFESSION?

Webster recognizes this changing concept in giving several definitions of a profession as "an occupation, if not commercial, mechanical, agricultural or the like, to which one devotes oneself, as the profession of arms, of teaching," and the "learned professions," theology, law, and medicine. The word "professional" is also explained as observing the standards of a profession such as its code of ethics, as contrasted to amateur, and as contrasted to the opinion or belief of the laity or layman, namely anyone not belonging to the profession. Although historical, these descriptions indicate certain features associated with the professions, reflect the origin and problems of many, and are concepts widely held even today.

Our approach must be concurrently pragmatic, because this is a practical book with definite economic objectives; and idealistic, because many of the characteristics claimed by the professions are asymptotic or theoretical limits of perfection, sought constantly but rarely completely achieved. The following are generally conceded to be the five major characteristics of a profession:

1. An organized body of knowledge, tested and accepted as the best currently available for *application* to some field of endeavor. This usually consists of one or more of the sciences and/or disciplines of knowledge. This organized body of knowledge should permit testing applicants for competence, and appraising the work of practitioners in case of doubt. In many nonprofessional fields there is too much uncertainty as to the one best way to accomplish an objective, and a lack of agreement even among authorities to meet these standards. In fact, there may be several methods all equally effective when used by different individuals, or under different sets of largely uncontrollable circumstances.

The professional man, or woman, engages in the practice of applying his knowledge and skills to some area of human wants. Thus we have the psychologist (the scientist) who seeks to learn more and more about his field, and the "professional" psychologist who engages in applying his knowledge to aid people with their problems; the economist (the scientist) who seeks further knowledge of casual relationships in economics, and the "professional" economist who applies what he knows to particular business, government, or personal problems. Essentially, the professional man diagnoses, then prescribes a remedy; the scientist may diagnose or analyze a problem, but he is not expected to prescribe a remedy to solve an individual's problem.

This distinction is sometimes blurred in the older professions by including research workers, teachers, and academic administrators in professional schools as members of the profession. For our purposes we shall limit our consideration to those who seek to practice (*diagnose and prescribe*) in an area of human wants or immediate problems.

2. Certification of those qualified to practice the profession, evidenced by some insignia or title, and based on tests of competency. This provision recognizes the inability of the public to judge a person's qualifications or competency in a professional field and their need of protection against incompetents, as well as the self-interest of members of the profession to protect both their market and the reputation of their field. The certification technique is valuable to all concerned but so frequently counterfeited that it requires the force of law or extensive public education for general effectiveness.

3. Efforts to limit professional practice to members in good standing in the profession. In areas where the public interest is great, such as medical care and the practice of law, the power of government is used to prohibit nonmembers of the profession from practicing or representing themselves to the public as qualified to practice. Thus it is illegal for the nonprofessional to practice medicine. In many of the newer professional fields a certification mark or term secures legal backing through copyright procedures, and the profession itself assumes responsibility for self-regulation, testing, certifying and policing its members. Examples include the Certified Public Accountant (C.P.A.), Mortician, Professional Engineer, Realtor, and many others. The Federal Lanham Act grants service and certification marks protection comparable to trade-marks.

4. Needs and interests of clients or patients take precedence over those of the practitioner, except with reference to diagnosis and prescription. The exception refers to cases where a patient or client may want something that would conflict with professional standards—a patient who wants a cavity in a decaying tooth filled to ease the pain in spite of the dentist's conviction that to do so would cause autoinfection, a confessed criminal who wants his attorney to distort the evidence or "forget" his confession so that he may escape punishment, or a woman who wants an interior decorating scheme that would be an atrocity to accepted standards of taste. In such cases the practitioner is expected to forego a fee he could receive for unprofessional conduct. He could also be censured and often expelled from the profession if he accedes to the client's wishes.

The affirmative standard first stated implies that a professional man should serve those in need regardless of their ability to pay. While this ideal is still observed to some extent in the medical and legal professions, the trend has been to shift the financial burden of the needy to society, the latter then reimbursing the practitioner for his services. In the newer professions only the sliding scale of fees, or differential pricing aspect has been used to any extent. Even in these fields the tendency is strongly in favor of uniform pricing based on the amount of work involved or value of the project. The latter indirectly recogniezs ability to pay, such as a realtor's higher fee for selling a more expensive house, or an architect's higher fee for designing one, even though in both cases the same or a slightly declining percentage may be applied to different values, but the higher dollar fee may often more than compensate for the additional work required.

5. A close personal, often highly confidential, relationship between practitioner and client. This characteristic has many facets. It emphasizes the importance of the practitioner's knowledge, skill, and experience in making an accurate diagnosis of the true or fundamental cause of a difficulty, in contrast to an inadequately informed snap judgment based on more apparent symptoms; and his skill in prescribing the best remedy after considering all individual aspects of the case, for "one man's medicine may be another's poison." Were it not for the numerous variables involved, such as the same apparent symptoms being associated with many different causes, and the fact that for the same ailment different prescriptions may be required best to remedy each individual case, a large amount of professional practice could be mechanized and reduced to standard formulas.

That some standardization in formula practice exists in many professional fields is well known, and this may be a contributing factor to "self-medication" or attempts to diagnose and prescribe for one's own ailments and problems whether in the field of health, law, accounting, architecture, or elsewhere. It may also account for the general resentment or reluctance to pay for professional services, and the tendency to economize by copying from apparently similar cases.

A patient may pay a physician $5.00 for a brief diagnosis that involves merely asking him about his symptoms, checking his weight, and then writing a prescription in Latin which is duly filled by the pharmacist for another $2.00. Said patient may see the druggist pour a few pills from a bottle, type a label, and complete the transaction. If he learns later, as he sometimes does, that he paid $2.00 for a standard drug available to anyone under its technical or trade name for $0.20, and that this prescription is a standard home remedy widely in use, he may feel resentful and exploited.[2] Likewise, an architect's client may be displeased when he learns later that he paid a generous fee for his "individually designed" house, the plans for which he could have secured free or for little more than printing charges from commercial organizations, and that his "protective contracts" were standard forms with merely his name, address, and the date inserted. Of course, in both cases the intangible personal contact, and the selection to suit individual needs were present, but these facts are hard for the client to appreciate.

The foregoing comments are not to depreciate the value of professional

---

[2] In 1960 physicians were being urged to write prescriptions for welfare patients using the generic name rather than a pharmaceutical company's brand name. The price differential was indirectly involved.

services even in cases such as those used in the illustrations. Had it not been for the physician's and architect's opportunity to utilize standard aids and formula analysis, their fees would have been much higher and the resulting benefits to the clients probably less. But the illustrations should emphasize certain problems connected with professional practice: the value of individualized diagnosis and prescription, and the need to protect the practitioner's "stock in trade" as well as the public against ill-advised attempts to be their own "professionals." The characteristic under discussion permeates many areas of professional practice and gives rise to various devices employed to protect the practitioner as well as (in many cases) the public. An example of protection for the practitioner is the contract which stipulates that the realtor's fee shall be paid during a specified time in excess of the "listing" and his promotional efforts, or if the property is later sold to any prospect first contacted by the realtor. The medical practitioner's use of Latin or some other code unfamiliar to the public may at times be an attempt to capitalize on his knowledge, but generally is also intended to protect the public. Many professions must contend with possible public ill will in their efforts to protect their own (often undervalue) status as well as the public.

Many of the characteristics of a profession are embodied in a code of ethics, which is considered by some people to be one of its basic features. Such a code is primarily a formulation of the standards of conduct or moral responsibilities that members accept and agree to observe. In recent times it has become one symbol of fields aspiring to professional status, a technique widely used in nonprofessional fields for such diverse purposes as to court public favor and ward off government regulation, and to coerce ambitious innovators who dare to deviate from traditional practices and prices in some well-established field. Although ethics is a branch of philsophy concerned with right versus wrong, or moral conduct, when it comes to practical applications, in contrast to academic discussion, many problems arise. The term "unethical" has invariably been applied to innovations that later are hailed as the salvation of their field, or to anything new that disturbs the *status quo*. In view of the diverse viewpoints, objectives, and almost universal attempts to formulate codes of ethics in every field, the mere adoption of a code of ethics (or assumption of the symbol often without its true content) is not considered by the authors as a unique characteristic of the professions.

Once the five essential characteristics of a profession are understood it should be possible to appraise any occupation as to the degree to which it measures up to these standards. In practice this is complicated. Is a particular segment of one of the original professions to be denied professional standing because the majority of its members appear to be concerned primarily with their dollar incomes, as is sometimes alleged? Are some of the newer specialists in the older professions to be denied professional status because the "old-timers" control licensing? Are business occupations like accounting to be accorded professional status while denying such to advertising agents, free-lance commercial artists, management consultants, financial advisors and others? Where does the dividing line appear between architects, landscape architects, tree surgeons, gardening counselors and so on? The authors prefer to avoid the endless controversies possible in cases such as those suggested by the foregoing questions. They are relatively unimportant for our purpose. By the same token any complete cataloguing of the professional fields would be unnecessary here, probably challenged, and out-of-date too soon to warrant such an undertaking. Our main purpose in the following brief discussion is to suggest bases and fields that may suit our concepts of independent professional practice.

The original professions dealt respectively with man's relations to God, nature, and government or society. As society developed other fields appeared that met professional standards. Some dealt with manipulation of the forces of nature and aesthetic concepts, as architecture, engineering, and art. Later others appeared, as landscape architecture and interior decorating. Specialization developed as conditions warranted, as naval architecture, commercial, and residential architecture; civil as distinct from military engineering. Civil engineering then branched out into hydraulic, mechanical, electrical, petroleum, and atomic engineering. Within each branch are specialists, as automotive, aeronautical, marine, internal combustion, turbo-jet engineers, and others.

As industry and business expanded in size and complexity, certain functions developed far enough to attain professional stature, as accounting, industrial management, and personnel administration. These, with several specialties within each, are generally accepted as professional fields today. Certain other functions, although similar in many respects to those mentioned, appear to have had greater difficulty in winning professional acceptance. Examples include advertising, finance, insurance, brokerages and other agencies which concentrate on the buying or selling functions.

Certainly many individuals and firms specializing in the functions enumerated have maintained high ideals and fine codes of moral conduct. Whether their dilemma is the result of one or more of the following factors could well be debated: (1) the stigma still associated with financial, business, or commercial pursuits; (2) the fact that exchange or promotion of the buying and selling functions is either their goal or has been aggressively used, as inducing people to buy insurance protection; and (3) the absence of formal training and competency tests as requirements for admission to the field. In varying degrees each field has developed an organized body of knowledge and formal higher education as preparation for those planning careers in the field, but whether or not such knowledge is comparable in scientific content to that of the established professions, or represents mainly an accumulation of methods that have been successful, is sometimes questioned. For example, the mathematical basis of insurance, or actuarial science, has its professional actuaries; and advertising is often based on results obtained by professional market or consumer research agencies. But insurance and advertising agents are still in the doubtful zone. Another possibility, and probable clue to the difficulty, is that in each of the doubtful fields mentioned, no adequate system of control has developed to insure that all members of the occupation are fully competent and actually do abide by recommended codes of ethics that seek to embody professional standards. For our purposes we shall accept those segments of such fields that claim to observe and enforce professional standards as among the newer professions.

Before concluding our discussion in this section we should note that accompanying our rising standard of living many fields of personal service have appeared and expanded. Some involve operators who work on the persons of clients, as beauticians, barbers, and masseurs; others render counseling services, as insurance counselors, financial advisors, and family relations consultants. The urge to achieve professional status by many of these fields makes it advisable to recognize the ones that have met enough of the characteristics of a profession to be generally accepted as such, which we shall include with the newer professions. Thus cosmetologists (performing services only) are included, barbers and masseurs are not, at present; insurance counselors and financial advisors who counsel only but do not participate in the sale of policies and securities are accepted in the newer professions category.

There are other service fields, many concerned with the repair and maintenance of certain kinds of personal property, that may before long be on the threshold of the professional arena. If the current rate of progress in applications to consumer goods of electronics and atomic fission continues, it would not be surprising to see fields develop where the scientific and technological training required is great enough, the value of articles worked on and safety of the public sufficient to warrant a whole new field or fields of professional practice. Further speculation along this line is left for the student's research and contemplation.

Professional Adaptations of Business Techniques

The trend mentioned earlier for professional fields to seek applications of proven business techniques warrants examination. Our economy is a pecuniary, market-oriented system, regardless of one's occupation. Physicians, and even ministers, must eat, have shelter and educate their children, as well as provide attractive physical plant and equipment, often air conditioning, for their adherents. They must cope with "inter-industry" competition and other economic activity, as do all others.

A brief excursion into etymology should emphasize a significant change in professional-public relations. The former "patient" has become less patient and more selective. He no longer endures his pain or ailment until the only available "doctor" can help, nor is he content with a depressing environment while waiting or being served. Moreover, "clients" are no longer a dependent class attached to some patrician nobility. Both competition and custom in other fields have made the typical patient or client one to be courted as well as served. A "buyers' market" with practitioner and client belonging to the same social and economic class, has replaced the former class-mass relationship, but century-old customs have remained. It is at least debatable whether practitioner-client relationships representative of conditions during the Roman Empire deserve the sacrosanct reverence accorded them in many professional fields. Probably not a few professional men realize this situation and believe the benefits of their services could be more widely distributed to those who need such services, but dare not openly employ modern promotional methods. But they seek to achieve similar goals indirectly. Undoubtedly policies of no advertising or client solicitation, no persuasive selling tactics, and similar professional standards help to maintain dignity and to lessen intraprofessional competition. But they also deprive most professions of many opportunities to utilize some very effective promotional methods developed in business. While individual advertising is condemned, seeking the same goal of personal publicity through club memberships, speaking engagements and similar time-consuming methods is acceptable. Whether this represents effective use of a highly trained professional man's time is often questioned. These restrictions also make the *adaptation* of commercial methods more important.

Market promotion, and especially advertising, is used effectively in business to accelerate a new firm's acceptance and to shorten the time until operations become profitable. Being deprived of this timesaving device, many professional men launching their own practice may have several years of near idleness, except for paying expenses necessary to maintain their facilities. To relieve the financial strain during this waiting period beginning physicians, dentists, lawyers, and some in the newer professional fields have operated a small business on the side. How widespread this practice has been is unknown, but several cases have been disclosed in alumni surveys by the authors and a few reported in published case histories and biographies. In later years many professional men branch out by investing in a small business under their ownership and supervision. Diversification of interests, preparation for retirement and other motives prompt such moves. They are different from the traditional physician's ownership of the local hospital or drugstore, in being unrelated to the field of professional practice.

As to advertising, its use by individual practitioners is taboo in the older professions, but co-operative or association advertising has been gaining in favor. The goodwill type of publicity by suppliers, and even less directly related companies in other fields, often using paid advertising, has been quite prominent in recent years. Examples include drug and pharmaceutical companies' advertising to the public advising the greater use of ethical medical services, life insurance companies' advertising that encourages frequent medical examinations, and a recent campaign dealing with the opportunities and requirements for success in selected fields including many of the professions.

Returning to advertising and publicity by the individual practitioner, in the older professions it is restricted to "name announcements," professional cards, name plates at the place of practice, listing in the classified telephone directory and in association directories. Some of the accepted professions approve of institutional and prestige type of purely informative, in contrast to direct selling, advertising. Semipromotional advertising that calls attention to benefits clients may receive from the service, merely mentions the sponsor's name, convenient location, modern facilities, and experienced staff, but carefully avoids self-praise or comparisons to competitors, appears to be gaining acceptance. It would not be surprising to see further expansion along all of these lines. In several professional business fields advertising and personal solicitation are used. Basically, professional advertising aims at (1) educating the public regarding their possible need for the service, (2) seeking to build confidence in the advertiser or the profession, and (3) notification of availability. It is not competitive like much commercial advertising.

A type of indirect market promotion of recent origin may experience appreciable expansion in the near future as it is adopted by and adapted to different professional fields. Its prototype is the prepayment or group plans for hospitalization and medical care, although also used to some extent by banks, family finance organizations and insurance companies. A few features of such plans suggest their probable spread. The cost of professional services has undoubtedly limited their use by many people in need of these services, and plans to ease or facilitate financing should expand the market. This has already been demonstrated in fields where the plans have been used. Direct, forceful sales promotional advertising can be used by an organization engaged in the financing of, but not itself in the practice of, professional services. Telephone and other personal solicitation has recently been part of these extensive advertising and promotional campaigns. Since all three parties benefit, the public, the financing organizations, and the members of the profession, it seems like a happy trio. Because the advertising and sales promotion are conducted by a third party, they may be even more effective than similar campaigns by professional associations. There appear to be no good reasons why similar plans could not be adapted to nearly any profession.

Another market promotion device suitable to many professional fields combines the budget payment and preventive service concepts. Large corporations use this idea by paying retainer fees to legal counsel and other professional men, consulting them in advance of any major decision. Physicians and attorneys know that numerous individuals wait too long before seeking professional aid. Many businessmen do the same before calling in a management consultant or "business doctor." One feature of many professions is that clients seek their services only when unable to solve their own problems. Periodic consultations, audits or check-ups *before* trouble actually appears would prevent many difficulties from developing. But most people are reluctant to pay for professional guidance until some serious problem arises. F·

limited studies made in a few professional fields there is good reason to believe that the long-run cost of services paid for on a regular budget or periodic basis, and used to prevent trouble, would be cheaper than the traditional method. Nonprofessional service fields have used this plan, as the monthly charge for complete maintenance of the family car or company fleet of trucks. Independent practitioners in many professional fields should be able to adapt such a plan to their particular situations to the mutual advantage of their clients and themselves.

Market research techniques have several applications in professional fields. These include (1) measurement of market potentials, (2) location of under-developed areas or communities, and (3) determination of clients' wants, likes and dislikes. Judging from the heavy concentration in large cities and wealthy communities of practitioners in the specialties of medical care, of management consultants, advertising agencies, and some other fields, total market potential has received ample consideration in selecting locations, but whether the potential available to each practitioner is more or less than it would be in other communities is uncertain. The fact that median incomes of practitioners in these areas is above the average for the entire country indicates that they are doing all right, but tells us nothing about what the situation would be if less concentration existed.

Closely related to the foregoing discussion is the uneven distribution of professional men in relation to population or potential clients without direct regard to relative purchasing power. That some tendency toward concentration in the centers of largest purchasing power is to be expected, whether in business or professional fields, is well known. But frequent criticism of the unequal geographic distribution of physicians and certain medical specialists led the Bureau of Medical Economic Research of the American Medical Association to launch a comprehensive medical trading area research in 1946 that was still under way seven years later. Publications resulting from this study are obtainable in the literature on the subject. Our concern here is to note that applications of market research are being made by the professions, location of underdeveloped areas are disclosed by such research, and additional information needed by prospective entrants as independents in the field may now be available for more intelligent planning and decisions.

The third application of market research, determination of client or consumer wants, likes, and dislikes, is especially pertinent in a small business book such as this. A significant aspect of small independent enterprise is meeting consumer wants neglected by other agencies. An equally significant feature of professional practice is individualized services suited to each client's needs. But many professions have been so engrossed in their technical aspects and so imbued with the traditional disdain for "lay" opinion that schisms have often developed, such as public ill will, or at least avoidance of the use of their services.

Examples from the medical and architectural professions should serve to illustrate this point and its bearing on our present discussion, namely that in America the public will be served. They also show that professions can meet consumer wants. Similar examples could be cited from other fields that have been slow to keep tuned to changing client wants, but these two will serve our purpose here. In the medical field, despite its enormous contributions to human welfare, public antagonism became so great that Grievance Committees were set up by various local medical societies, comparative in many ways to Better Business Bureaus. The movement is too new to appraise its value but reports released indicate progress, and it does show that no field can safely disregard public attitudes and wants. The railroads tried to, as did many banks before the 1930's, and neither field has fully recovered from the resulting impact of social control.

Since the architectural profession has been less "affected with a public interest" and in continuous competition not experienced by the other fields mentioned, the indirect effect of public reaction is demonstrated in this field. Prior to World War II the profession had been reluctant to accept the wants of American home builders in preference to their professional training in classic styles and similar concepts. Many home builders wanted a place designed for comfortable living, with convenient arrangements, and constructed so as to avoid common annoyances. When the profession failed to provide for these wants the people sought and found aid from practical builders, class magazines, and their own ingenuity. Recently the situation has changed for the better, but most of the lost patronage could have been avoided by greater sensitivity to client wants.

Some professions have found suitable adaptations of techniques of organization and specialization of effort developed extensively in business. Medical clinics, accounting, law and management consulting firms are a few examples. It is possible, with the help of modern diagnostic equipment and technology, standard procedures and similar aids, to make a more thorough diagnosis of a patient's or client's difficulty without any major practitioner actually meeting the subject personally, than could be done by former close practitioner-client procedures. Even the prescription or appropriate remedy may often result from these impersonal studies, although there is more likelihood that personal contact will be used to explain what is needed, with some explanation of reasons or objectives, and possibly to employ follow-up supervision. There appears to be no valid basis for criticism of these impersonal procedures, although some people dislike the lack of personal attention, and results achieved have often been outstanding. In fact, many businesses could learn considerable of value for their own use by careful study and adaptation of these techniques.

In the area of payment for services, many professional men now belong to their local retail credit bureau and use its services—at least much more so than only a few decades ago. The general trend in most fields toward more cash transactions and closer control over credit that is extended is noticeable in the professions as in business. Time payment plans on a formal prearranged periodic basis have increased in both professional and non-professional fields. This is just one additional manifestation of our changing times and attitudes, as well as of the trend already mentioned of extremes toward a common middle ground.

The older professions were concerned with professional services and did not deal in the sale of merchandise, although as noted earlier in some places physicians have owned a local drugstore, but never to the authors' knowledge were patients required to have prescriptions filled there. Many clinics also have a pharmacy attached but do not require that patients use this service.

Even when a professional service required the use of some tangible goods, it was formerly considered desirable to keep prescribing and vending separate. This custom also appears to be undergoing modification. Some of the newer professions, such as optometrists and cosmetologists, develop around professional help in selecting, fitting, or aid in using appropriate merchandise, with the profit from merchandising representing a significant proportion of total revenue. Realtors and members of the National Association of Food Brokers are agents who concentrate on performing the buying or selling function for property they do not own, and belong in a different category.

Optometry has several specialties, optometrists or practitioners licensed in most states to examine a person's eyes and prescribe the exact type of glasses that may be needed. They may or may not be equipped to grind lenses and fit them into frames selected by the client, but many larger firms render a complete service and stock a wide selection of styles, colors, and sizes of frames for the client's choice. In other cases a separate optician fills the prescription by grinding the lenses and fitting them into frames either specified in the prescription or, as is more common recently, from ones selected by the customer from the stock maintained and attractively displayed by the optician. In some states efforts have been made to restrict the sale of glasses, and fitting lenses into frames selected by the customer, to licensed members of the profession of optometrists, but the legislatures and courts have not always acceded.

Pharmacy, or the filling of prescriptions according to physicians' instructions, represents the most pronounced combination of professional practice with the sale of merchandise. Pharmacy is recognized as a profession and a license is required to practice in all states of the Union. The modern pharmacist fills a large proportion of prescriptions brought to him with standard drugs prepared in pharmaceutical laboratories, and merely measures out, packages, and labels these in the store. He is also the druggist who usually owns and operates the "junior department store" familiar to Americans as the local drugstore. Most states require at least one registered pharmacist to be on duty in a drugstore, whether chain or independent. Receipts from filling prescriptions range from less than ten per cent to over 40 per cent of total sales in representative drugstores. The modern druggist must be a good retail merchant as well as a licensed pharmacist, although the drugstore owner may hire either a merchandiser or a pharmacist, as needed, to complement his own qualifications.

Employment or Independent Practice

Some men with professional training prefer to remain as employees in teaching, research, or various activities for government agencies or private corporations. In most professional fields a larger proportion than in commercial occupations seek independent practice after their necessary "internship" or period of practical experience. Some do this by becoming partners with established practitioners as a method of getting a quicker start. The percentage of self-employed varies by different fields and no comprehensive survey reports have been published. About 74 per cent of physicians were in private practice during the early 1950's, although this figure would probably be much lower for engineers and accountants, but higher for architects, cosmetologists, osteopaths, and realtors.

From meager data available, the income pattern seems to be similar in the professions to that in business, somewhat higher for employed professional men, and business *executives,* than for all proprietors, including very small enterprises but excluding the more profitable close corporations. However, these are averages and usually do not compare like abilities. In both fields the extremely large number in independent practice or small business in the lower income brackets pulls the average down. For comparable abilities, ambitions, and conditions, self-employment probably results in higher incomes in both fields for those who desire larger incomes. What distorts the impression many people have is the tendency to report incomes, often before all expense deductions, of the largest income professions like physicians and dentists, and to publicize the dire financial straits of large numbers of marginal small businessment. Also, little is ever publicized about the incomes of beginning professional men or those who have less than average success.[3]

Since the law change in 1951 that brought self-employed businessmen under social security, proposals have been made to allow professional practitioners to build up some form of retirement income. The form or forms ultimately decided on may be different from recent proposals but the development seems certain.

Because of the long period of formal training required, usually on a college or postgraduate level, and frequent internship requirements, most men by the time they become eligible for practice have a good basis for deciding between employment and independent practice. In many cases the decision for independent practice precedes the formal training and is an important reason for entering the professional field. This is probably true in medicine,

[3] For further study see: Milton Friedman and Simon Kuznets, *Income from Independent Professional Practice.* (New York: National Bureau of Economic Research, 1954); and postwar studies of professional incomes released by the U. S. Department of Commerce.

pharmacy, law, architecture, and similar fields. In other cases, such as engineering, management, and often accounting, both the opportunity for successful private practice, usually as consultants, and the decision to become self-employed come fairly late in such careers.

It is equally difficult to generalize on financial requirements for independent practice in such a diverse area as that of the present-day professions. The expense of a professional education is usually large, often more than that for a normal college education, partly because of the longer period of formal training and larger professional library required. For the business professions, accountancy, advertising, real estate, insurance and the like, the formal training and personal library requirements are comparable to other college majors. In some professions a college degree is not a requirement, but these are in the minority.

Once a person is eligible to practice, financial requirements to launch out as an independent vary more widely for different fields than do the costs of professional training. An accountant, attorney, or realtor may need little more than an address or telephone number, some stationery, and either capital or a side-line source of other income to defray expenses until his fees exceed his relatively low break-even point. Physicians, dentists, and medical specialists usually require equipment costing from a few hundred to over $20,000, plus capital for expenses until their practice is on a paying basis, which may take several years. A beauty parlor operated by a cosmetologist requires a few thousand dollars invested in equipment, very little in merchandise, and some working capital. A pharmacist, however, requires very little investment in professional equipment but substantial amounts for inventory and operating expense until the enterprise becomes self-supporting. This assumes a drugstore type of operation.

Operating Functions

Most of the functions involved in operating small businesses of the service and retail types already discussed will apply to independent professional practice, if the limitations placed on many professions regarding advertising and aggressive solicitation, restriction of practice in one profession to licensed practitioners, and other features explained earlier, are observed. For example, druggists are often asked by customers to prescribe for certain supposedly minor ailments. To do so could in many cases involve them in the illegal practice of medicine. Up to fairly recently druggists often removed dust and similar particles from a person's eye, thus quickly relieving intense pain, but today this is illegal in some states, and the unfortunate victim is compelled to wait until he can locate a doctor licensed to practice medicine. The important point for our immediate purpose is that in any area bordering on professional practice the independent is much more circumscribed in what he is legally permitted to do than in other fields of entrepreneurship.

In personal service fields in general, but especially in most professions, the entrepreneur has an excellent opportunity to secure considerable information of value from each client. How did he happen to come there? Who recommended the practitioner or firm? Also personal data may easily be obtained that most customers of business enterprises would consider "none of your business." Custom apparently has caused most clients of professional firms to accept this type of preliminary interviewing and to be willing to furnish freely even highly personal information. Although, contrary to business practice, professional men can rarely use this information for direct market promotion or "customer control," they can use it effectively to guide certain policies and procedures. When a particular class of clients is most frequently mentioned as recommending new ones the practitioner knows the class he has been able to please and those most likely to send in new clients. He knows where to "play the winners" for future patronage. He also learns the classes where he has either not rendered satisfactory service or who have limited opportunities or desire to recommend new clients.

The preliminary interview is usually the best time to secure information regarding the patient's or client's plans for payment, except, of course, for emergency cases in dire need of immediate relief or medical care. Services once performed, as explained earlier, are nonreturnable and have no repossession value. Services of physicians and dentists are often peculiar in four important respects: many people believe that services will or even must be performed regardless of ability to pay, the thrill of acquiring new merchandise is absent, no tangible product remains to remind them of benefits received, and once pain is relieved or some ailment cured, certain people seem unwilling to pay even moderate fees.

While professional ethics in the medical profession require practitioners to render emergency aid if at all possible, and to place patients' real needs above their own income goal, even the most idealistic interpretation of these provisions must recognize certain limitations. No private practitioner can hope to serve all patients without charge, unless he has unlimited resources, because many people would prefer not to be obliged to pay if they could receive high quality services gratis, and the practitioner would be swamped with free patients. Each practitioner decides for himself the amount of time he cares to devote to free or charity patients. In the preliminary interview patients incapable of paying for service needed can be directed to free clinics or for free service by the practitioner himself. In many cases the patient's ability to pay will suggest the type of care he should be advised to have, and on a time schedule that corresponds to his ability to pay. Even certain medical and dental care may be deferred or spread out over a period of time suitable to the patient's capacity to pay for them. These two alternatives—choices among several types of service from a cost standpoint—and scheduling on a payment basis, will apply to most fields. Differential pricing may be used at the practitioner's option in fields where some free service is not customary.

As early as possible during initial contacts with patients or clients, the amount of charges should be explained, payment plans ascertained, alternatives discussed if appropriate, and if credit is contemplated, all essential credit data written on the client's personal record. If credit is to be extended, standard procedures as explained in Chapter 23, should be followed, especially a definite agreement on a payment schedule, and careful credit control. Use of the local credit bureau is probably the best known way to achieve proper credit management. Partly because of the peculiarities of credit extended by medical practitioners, and partly because beginners in the field are often short of funds, it may be advisable to secure notes from a patient seeking considerable amounts of credit, and these signed notes should be acceptable for discounting.[4] Where the local bank credit plan is in operation professional men are usually eligible and invited to participate in the program, and normally would be well advised to do so.

In contrast to the typical small businessman's training and attitudes, the professional man has been drilled in maintaining detailed records and using the information they provide to guide his future decisions and procedures. On several occasions earlier in this book we have commented on the lack of adequate recordkeeping and factual management by many small businessmen. While it might be too much to hope that independent businessmen could find ways to secure the detailed personal information from customers that the professional man secures from clients, such a goal is at least worth encouraging. Also worthy of encouragement is for professional men to find ways of effectively utilizing for mutual personal gain and patron benefits the information they can so easily obtain from their clients.

Professional training naturally tends largely toward scientific and technical subjects. Even in the area of recordkeeping, as just discussed favorably for the professions, whether or not the performance of independent practitioners is superior for accounting and tax records to the rather inadequate showing of many small businessmen is unknown to the authors. No doubt professional associations in the major fields have developed accounting and tax recordkeeping systems, and public accountants can install adequate systems. One alternative is to adopt an appropriate accounting and tax system designed and distributed by one of the commercial organizations, such as the Ideal System for Professional Service Bookkeeping and Tax Record (No. 3421). This particular system is designed for architects, engineers, artists, optometrists, photographers, public stenographers and notaries, small advertising agencies, brokers, employment agencies, collection, and other agencies. It is a simplified one-book system that may be started at any time of the year. This, and other systems, may be inspected in your local office-supply store.

---

[4] For further study see, George B. Allen, "Credit Problems of the Dentist," *Credit World* (August 1954) p. 1:17.

CONCLUSIONS

The line of demarcation between professional and other occupations of interest to college graduates has been receding for some time. Just as earlier beliefs that each kind of business was so different from every other that each constituted a separate study and, hence, no one can learn from a different field, or that big and little enterprises differed so greatly that even management had nothing in common; in the same way, many former beliefs regarding an absence of similarity between the professions and some other occupations are disappearing with better understanding and appreciation.

Discussion in this chapter should enable the independent enterpriser in almost any field to understand certain features characteristic of all professions and how he may adopt and adapt many of these to his own needs. The professional man already in or contemplating independent practice should also be able to see his economic problems more clearly and to recognize possible adaptations from the field of business that would be advantageous to him without jeopardizing his professional status.

QUESTIONS AND PROBLEMS

1. What are the various meanings attached to the word "profession"? Briefly explain each.

2. Briefly describe and illustrate how professional and nonprofessional fields are tending toward a middle ground.

3. Name, and briefly explain, the accepted characteristics of a profession.

4. In your opinion is the formulation of, and subscription to, a code of ethics a characteristic of a profession? Discuss.

5. How, if at all, have professions sought to limit their market to their own members? Evaluate and discuss.

6. State, and illustrate or describe, as many examples of the "adopt and adapt" procedure mentioned in the chapter as you can. Suggest others not mentioned.

7. Discuss the pros and cons of the use of modern advertising by individual professional men or firms.

8. Explain the advantages and limitations of third party financing of prospective users of professional services.

9. How can the professions make most effective use of market research? Should they use it? Discuss.

10. Explain and illustrate the trend to combine professional practice with the sale of merchandise.

11. Compare and contrast decisions regarding independent practice in the professions with similar considerations in business or other fields.

12. In what important respects, if any, do the functions involved in entrepreneurship differ between professional and business fields? Discuss.

13. Compare and contrast the professional and businessman's attitudes toward the use and keeping of records.

14. Formulate a practical plan for third party financing and promotion of some professional services not now covered by such plans.

15. Formulate a practical plan for professional men to use patient or client personal record information for "customer control" or similar purposes as used in business.

16. Les was married and had two children by the time he was able to start on his own as a practicing attorney. He owned a service station close to his office that he had been operating part-time himself, and another station operated by a hired manager. Les needed the income from these enterprises but wondered about their effects on his legal practice. What should he do, and why?

26 • Small Business and the Future

The steady postwar expansion in the number of small businesses continues but less rapidly than in early postwar years. In 1960 we had well over four million small firms in operation. About 1,000 new concerns are launched each day. Although nearly twice that number are liquidated or change ownership, only a small fraction of these—less than 1,200 a month—actually fail.[1]

The future of American small business has never been more encouraging. Trends and problems discussed in this book have both contributed to this condition. The trend of expanding interest has been supplemented by a growing effort to secure more facts about independent enterprisers and their problems and needs.[2] One result of the findings of such investigations has been to expand training for owner-management. A second has been to make more and more agencies, such as schools of commerce and business administration, vocational education administrators, manufacturers, and other business organizations, aware of their responsibilities to present and prospective small businessmen.

Another significant development has been the high failure rate of many small concerns that were started during the post-World War II influx by inadequately prepared individuals. This has not only left those who survived the early "recession" on a sounder basis, but has also emphasized the importance of adequate preparation *before* undertaking business ownership. Accompanying the increase in failures of many ill-advised small businesses have been reports of the outstanding success achieved by other well-managed small enterprises.

Predictions are hazardous at best and are especially difficult in the rela-

[1] "Why Businesses Fail," sixth in a series on "A Business of Your Own?" *Changing Times, The Kiplinger Magazine* (March 1960), pp. 13-15.
[2] For further study see Pearce C. Kelley, *What Commerce Majors Do After Graduation,* Special Studies Series, Bureau of Business Research, University of Mississippi (1949).

tively uncertain area of economic or international conditions for specific periods of time. It is not our intention in this chapter to forecast the position of small business for the next year or for any other particular time. We are concerned with long-time trends and with an examination of fundamental factors that will continue to influence the position of small business regardless of what conditions may develop.

The best approach to this problem seems to be to review briefly certain points about small business developed in this book and then to examine the probable effects on small business of different conditions that may appear at some time in the future. Finally, we hope to show that the surest way to insure an enduring place for small business is through continued study and application of the ideas and methods suggested throughout this book.

We have seen that small business occupies an important and unique place in our economy. Not only was every important big business of today started as a small enterprise, but also well over 90 per cent of all businesses are still properly classified as small. That this situation will continue in spite of conflicting and often confusing trends is the accepted belief of all well-informed observers.

Small business is unique in many respects. It has advantages, limitations, and problems that differ from those of large concerns. It is necessary to have a large number of small enterprises if true competition is to exist, if freedom of initiative and business enterprise is to be maintained, and if we are to continue our progress in extending more goods and services to an ever increasing number of people. Big business alone cannot provide these things.

Of course, many limitations and problems accrue to certain enterprises merely because of their small size. Inability to operate in the fields of mass production where heavy investment in machinery is required is one of these. Particularly in the field of manufacturing, a given industry usually achieves maturity only by developing machinery and the subdivision of labor to an extent that seriously limits the opportunities for small-scale enterprise.

In general, the fields of natural monopolies are not for the small enterprise. The so-called "heavy industries" are represented by large concerns, although many small firms operate in service and facilitating capacities as well as in the distribution of some of these industries' products. Although a small enterprise can operate successfully in the vast majority of business areas, in most of these fields branches of large concerns may also be operated. It is principally when the potential volume is too small to be of interest to big business that the little fellow has the field to himself.

Of the many problems of small business, probably the most important are: (1) limited time of the owner-manager, (2) wide range of managerial ability demanded of one or a few men, (3) difficulty in making effective use of research, and (4) the problem of securing access to adequate financial resources. Some of the other problems, as we have seen, arise principally because of the type of individual normally attracted to business ownership;

others plague a business of any size but seem to bear more heavily on the little fellow.

One advantage of a study of *small* business is that the recognition of its special problems stimulates efforts to solve them. We have seen many ways in which the independent businessman can conserve his precious time for important matters by adapting to his needs well-developed managerial aids, including policies, organization, modern personnel practices, and the fundamentals of modern management. He may share managerial duties with a partner or a few well-chosen members of a closed corporation. In certain retail fields he may affiliate with one of the voluntaries and thus economize his own time as well as secure the benefit of additional managerial abilities. And finally, for certain functions of management he may utilize the outside staff discussed in the text. Many ambitious beginners have found one of the expanding franchise plans that furnish know-how along with the well publicized product or service suited to their needs.[3]

The White House Conference on Technical and Distribution Research for the Benefit of Small Business discussed in Chapter 10 has expanded the suggestions given in the business press to meeting the research needs of independent enterprisers.

Already several groups of small firms are reported to have made satisfactory progress in meeting their research needs. In some cases the research facilities of governmental agencies are aiding; in others, by pooling research efforts the facilities of private research agencies have been employed; and in a few cases large companies may make their research departments available to small firms. It also seems reasonable to expect that experience during World War II, when know-how was furnished to subcontractors, will be utilized more and more in helping to solve this problem. The basic fact that all industry is interdependent suggests that it is entirely logical to expect efforts in this direction even within the framework of a competitive economy.

We have seen many free lance operators in the field of management, marketing and marketing research offering their services to small businessmen. Because even fairly large concerns need these services on a part-time basis, they are free to engage in professional practice for themselves some of the time.

Financing, which was mentioned as the fourth important problem, is at least in part a corollary of the more basic management problem. As noted on several occasions in the text, the agreement seems to be pretty general among bankers and others concerned with the financial needs of small business that the real need is for management counsel. Given good management, most of the financial problems of small business become of minor importance, because (1) good management includes efficient handling of finances and (2) lenders are usually anxious to invest money in a well-managed business.

There are, however, three other types of financial problems confronting small business for which it is not so easy to suggest solutions.

[3] "Get a Franchise?" *Changing Times, The Kiplinger Magazine* (May 1959), pp. 7-11.

1. Most important is the fact that small-scale financing is always more expensive per dollar than large-scale financing. Whether the lending or investing process can be analyzed, simplified, and organized in such a way as to overcome this inherent handicap remains to be seen. Several interesting but as yet untried proposals have been made. One approach involves separating the various cost elements, such as risk-bearing, investigation, negotiation, paper work, and contact, to mention a few for purposes of illustration. The cost of each of these elements would be reduced to a minimum through use of whatever plan is appropriate; for example, the principles of underwriting and insurance might be applied to risk-bearing. This has been done in reducing the cost of financing home ownership through the F.H.A. as well as the cost of temporary unemployment to the worker through unemployment insurance. The principle of guided self-declaration used in American income tax procedure with appropriate penalties for falsification might be applied to reduce the cost of investigation. Costs of paper work and of contact could probably be reduced greatly by centralization and use of machine methods. Harebrained as these proposals may sound to a person familiar with the difficulty and expense of small-scale financing, they are probably no more ridiculous and impractical than were the original ideas that started most of our large modern technical industries when first proposed. This does not mean that the particular proposals listed above represent a solution to the problem, but it does suggest that a solution can be found no matter how impractical it seems to the "experts" at first. Such is progress!

2. The second type of problem relates to what small businesses should be financed through loan or investment capital. Recently established SBIC's combine both by making their debentures convertible into stock of the small company. The principle is generally accepted under our system of free enterprise that any individual should be permitted to invest his own capital in any business venture no matter how unsound it may appear to others, provided he does not break the law or transgress the rights of others. However, creative imagination, or "brains," and adequate capital do not always go together, at least at the inception stage of a new idea. There may be ten to a hundred freak ideas launched by hopeful enterprisers that fail for one that succeeds, but who can pick the successful one at the start? In a given market that appears to be overcrowded with businesses of a particular kind, the right individual can succeed when scores around him are failing. The authors do not propose a solution to the problem of forecasting the winner out of hundreds of contestants beyond advice already given in the text. The chapter on justification is intended to offer helpful suggestions in regard to this type of problem.

3. Financial problems in a third and final group relate to building and maintaining adequate financial reserves. Not only is the first thousand—that is, the initial capital to start business—usually the hardest to get, but the effects of both the business cycle and our tax system lays additional financial burdens upon the beginning small business. Heavy taxes on personal incomes

in the lower brackets affect the typical small business, which is usually a proprietorship or partnership, although they have no serious effect on larger corporate units. Also, whenever the tax system imposes heavy rates on low business profit brackets, the effects are more serious to small than to large business units.

The effects of the business cycle, especially on the downswing, bear more heavily on the capital structure of small than of large businesses. However, small business has some compensating advantages, especially greater flexibility and relatively lower fixed overhead expenses. Also, the very nature of the recession period of the business cycle—a period of contracting over-expanded business facilities at current prices—may make this pressure on many small businesses desirable. Being more flexible than their large competitors, they may be able to reduce costs and prices to justify continuing operations. If this is not possible and ability to stay in business depends upon using accumulated capital, small business may actually take a lesser loss by retiring early in the recession period of a prolonged business depression. In some cases it may even be possible to make a second start later at bargain prices. This resembles the procedure of going through a reorganization of the capital structure as big firms sometimes do.

It is in connection with changing economic conditions that the two basic points discussed often in our book are of great value, namely, the importance of studying small business as such and of adapting methods developed in one field to use in other lines. The small business has special needs and problems that differ from those of big business when economic activity is changing, either for better or for worse. The fact that limited capital makes it harder for the little fellow to withstand a decline in business activity is not always an unmixed evil; but it also restricts his ability to expand rapidly to capitalize fully on opportunities resulting from an upswing of the business cycle. Once we appreciate this and other needs and problems characteristic of small business, we see the importance of profiting by the experience and methods of big business. Adequate reserves, well-formulated policies governing expansion and contraction, proper timing, the use of options instead of long-term commitments, and various other methods could be mentioned. The fundamental facts remain the same. Only the "dress" changes with different stages of the business cycle.

PERMANENCE OF SMALL BUSINESS FIELD[4]

Our examination of small business in each of the three major fields—merchandising, manufacturing, and service—has established (1) that the field of independent business operation is important and distinctive enough to warrant special study of small business as such and (2) that any business,

---

[4] See: *The Persistence of Small Business* (Kalamazoo, Michigan: The W. E. Upjohn Institute for Community Research, March 1958).

large or small, can profit by the experience and methods developed in other concerns regardless of their size or field of operations. The former is the justification, the latter the major thesis of this book. The two belong together. The interdependence of all business has been stressed and illustrated throughout the book. Our purpose has been to study the small enterprise, not as an isolated segment, but as a part of the entire interrelated and interdependent business structure. Not only is the little fellow a part of the whole economic system, but he learns from and contributes to the entire field of economic activity.

These two points are important when we consider the future of small business. Economic conditions change; attitudes and interests of the government, the public, and individuals shift; international conditions vary and influence national policies and business activities. In this respect change is the only constant factor. However, regardless of economic conditions, small business will continue as an important part of our economy. Each of the three types of changes mentioned affects both the immediate or temporary position of small business and its long-run or permanent position.

The number of small concerns tends to decrease during depression and increase during prosperity both absolutely and relatively, although the same tendency operates for employment, wages, profits, rents, and other economic elements. Offsetting the somewhat greater problems of small business during hard times are the many opportunities such conditions afford to buy or to start a business on a safe foundation. Also, were it not for these cyclical fluctuations in business activity, the study of small business would be much simpler but also less interesting.

The long-time trend in American business history has been favorable to small business, especially in terms of new opportunities and number of concerns. Each new industry, although it may soon be dominated by large concerns, brings in new opportunities for small firms and results in a great increase in the total number of establishments. Electronics and semiconductors are recent examples.[5] In wholesaling the trend has been toward a larger number of small concerns. Nearly the entire field of service businesses was unknown a century ago. Only in farming has there been a decline in the number of small enterprisers relative to either population increase or total number of units in operation. In fact, it is primarily the rise of many large industries and a steady increase in the use of capital goods and modern technology that have made it possible for us to have an ever-increasing number of small business units in operation.

Probably one reason for confused thinking on this point is the failure to compare similar periods of the business cycle. Naturally the number of small businesses will be smaller during the depression stage than during the preceding boom stage, and usually small units represent a smaller percentage

[5] See: "Business Week Reports on: Semiconductors," *Business Week* (March 26, 1960), pp. 74-121.

of the total number of firms in operation during hard times than during good times. However, if successive years of boom or of depression times are compared separately, the long-time upward swing in favor of small business will be evident.

Even during the years of World War II the number of small manufacturing firms showed a steady increase. From 1940 to 1945 small manufacturers also showed greater proportionate gains in net worth and net working capital than did large concerns. In addition to the enormous increase in our productive capacity that took place during the war period, we had 40,900 more manufacturers in June 1946, than in June 1945. About 60 per cent of the new manufacturers in business in 1946 had four or fewer employees.[6] We have noted earlier in the book that the vast majority of the nearly one million new firms starting business in all fields during the first two postwar years were small concerns. Economic conditions cause the number and kinds of small businesses needed at particular times to vary but do not change the long-run trends of the increasing number and importance of small independent operators.

Changing attitudes and interests on the part of the government and of the public are to be expected from time to time. These need not affect the position or permanence of small business and should not weigh too heavily in determining our interest in this field. During the closing years of World War II and the first postwar years, attention was naturally directed to problems of reconversion, including those relating to small business. Once the period of great influx into business has passed, it is reasonable to expect attention to shift to other fields. Also, it is always possible that propaganda campaigns in progress at any particular time will have undue influence on government attitudes and public interests. However, this very shifting of government and public attention to new "topics of the hour" should intensify rather than lessen our serious study of the needs and problems of the independent enterpriser.

More small firms are in operation today than ever before in a similar period of our history. Many of them were launched hastily often by individuals none too well prepared for the inevitable competition to develop sooner or later. Certain fields appear to be overcrowded and readjustments will be needed. The more obvious opportunities for starting a small business have been taken up. Prospecting and seeking out new and justifiable opportunities will require increasing attention by entrepreneurs of the future. These conditions all point to the ever greater importance of a careful study of small business organization and operation such as that suggested in the text.

Since the rise of our industrial economy, developments in the international situation have always affected small business as well as the rest of our economic activity. However, they have never lessened the ultimate importance

[6] A. M. Sullivan, "Small Business—It Can Go Places—And Without a Free Ride," *Printers' Ink* (October 31, 1947), pp. 94-108.

of the individual enterpriser nor invalidated the fundamental principles relating to small business. Merely the emphasis as to type of needs and problems is shifted.

The point of emphasis here is that the study of small business is justifiable in its own right at all times. It should not be viewed opportunistically as something of importance only during a period of rapid business expansion or "easy going." Small business has certain advantages, limitations, problems, and opportunities that shift in emphasis with changing conditions but remain surprisingly constant in fundamentals throughout all types of economic conditions.

And finally, if certain economic or international situations enforce a delay in starting the kind of business an individual ultimately hopes to own, the result may be actually to strengthen the business when it is finally started. Several examples of such semivoluntary delay have been cited in the book; it has been pointed out, for instance, that prospective retailers often work for years to secure a particular location before starting on their own. In other cases individuals with one type of know-how, such as technical training, have deliberately planned several years of business experience or training in management before launching their own enterprises. Usually the interval between deciding to enter business and starting the enterprise can be used profitably in planning, accumulating capital, and developing trade connections.

A long-range view of any type of business should include consideration of its probable status under changing conditions. In the past, at least, during a 20- or 30-year period a particular business went through all the varieties or conditions discussed in the preceding paragraphs. Small business, in spite of ups and downs, has stood the test of operating under every variety of economic conditions and is stronger today than ever before. The long-range future prospects seem bright, regardless of temporary setbacks that will probably appear from time to time.

IMPROVING THE OUTLOOK

That the future prospects of small business can be improved is implied in every effort to study the field, in every proposal to solve some of the problems of the little fellow, and in the growing recognition of the importance of this segment of our economy. Self-improvement is usually the most desirable. In general, the plan recommended in this book stresses self-improvement by present and prospective small businessmen as the surest road to future progress.

Two organizations launched during the 1950's have this objective: The Society For the Advancement of Independent Enterprise (Iota Epsilon) for prospective entrepreneurs, and The Council For Small Business Management Development for incumbent businessmen.

We have suggested that a potential business owner should first determine if he is better suited to being his own boss than someone else's employee. After selecting the kind of business to enter, he should determine the requisites for success in the chosen field and acquire as many of the ones he lacks as possible before actually starting the business. Questions of when to launch, where to locate, and how to formulate sound policies complete the "getting started" stage. Once safely launched, the new business can be reasonably sure of success if the modern management methods discussed throughout the book are applied.

No better concluding advice could be given to the small businessman, present or prospective, than to keep in close touch with information provided through his trade association, trade press, suppliers, mercantile agencies, and local banker.

SMALL BUSINESS FOR OLDER PEOPLE

Looking toward the future should include some consideration of self-employment for people past their prime of life and those approaching the traditional retirement age of 65. In 1960 we had about 16 million people 65 and older, or one out of eleven, and four times as many as we had 50 years earlier. Life expectancy at 65 is double what it was a generation ago and is likely to continue increasing as more attention is devoted to the needs and problems of the older folks. But the earning years of employed people have been shortening because of longer periods of formal schooling, defense needs at the beginning of their careers, and earlier retirement.

It is not likely that defense needs will be reduced appreciably and there is little the young men can do about it. The economic value of a higher education seems to be well established by numerous studies. The *Time* survey found that male college graduates had higher incomes almost from the beginning (median $3,547) than the peak incomes of all males in the United States (median $2,845). Median incomes of the college graduates increased sharply to $6,152 for ages 40 to 49, then rose slightly to $6,244 for those 50 and over; whereas median incomes of all males declined after 44 to $2,344 for the 55- to 64-year-old group. Part of the explanation may be that 50 per cent of the graduates were in professional fields and an additional 34 per cent were proprietors, managers, and executives; compared to 3 and 13 per cent respectively for all males in the United States.[7] Income from current employment tends to decline sharply after age 65, but much less so for college graduates and other highly educated workers, who also stay employed more frequently and longer after 65 than the average male.

[7] E. Havemann and Patricia Salter West, *They Went to College* (New York: Harcourt, Brace & Company, Inc., 1952), Chap. 3, "The Matter of Money."

The foregoing comments should be encouraging to the college student, but they are only part of the picture. Among the 84 per cent of male college graduates included in the *Time* survey in professional and higher positions in business, we do not know what proportion were self-employed. We may assume from other information that most of those with top incomes in the past 50 group, or at least past 60, were self-employed. In most professional fields this is the typical pattern: to acquire sufficient employment experience early, build up capital and contacts, then to enter self-employment, making room for more recent graduates. In business, large corporations understandably want to start their future executives fairly young, and the policy of retirement at 65 is widespread, even though some progress has been made in rehiring after retirement. In general, older employees begin to feel the effects of their age in lower salaries and wages for some years before actual retirement.

Our concern here is not with the older men who are already self-employed, except to note that their income security is much greater than others, and that their position is more flexible. They can delegate increasing responsibilities to relieve themselves, or even sell the enterprise and buy or start a smaller one better suited to their abilities and needs.

The average young college-trained person is naturally optimistic. At the age of 25 to 35 he expects by 65 to have provided amply for later years, and a few, but very few, have done so. Regarding the first point, if he will take time to compute the percentage of his current income during his earning years that would be required to provide a satisfactory income for the number of years after retirement, he may modify this goal. This computation should be made realistically, allowing for the long-time decline in the value of the dollar, the steady rise in our standard of living that makes corresponding demands for larger consumer expenditures both before and after retirement, the time preference tendency to undervalue future benefits relative to more immediate ones, the increasing life span after 65, and similar considerations. No student or young alumnus could make this calculation honestly without realizing that providing adequately for his older years entirely from current savings is practically impossible. There are rare exceptions, of course, where lucky investments and the like solved the problem, but as we shall see they are of very minor importance.

People retire for many reasons. A fairly comprehensive study made by the University of California in co-operation with the Census Bureau for the year 1951 produced some interesting data that agree closely with a general understanding of the problem. This study showed that for males over 64 years of age, 46 per cent had retired voluntarily, 14 per cent involuntarily, and 41 per cent were still in the labor force. Of those retired, 57 per cent gave poor health, and 13 per cent formal retirement systems as the reason for their retirement. These percentages vary considerably for major occupational groups. The general tendency to demote older men even before they are re-tired appeared in this as in other studies.[8]

The California study found couples, and individuals, with some earnings to be substantially better off financially than others. About 10 per cent used savings in an amount of $200 or more, but such savings rarely accounted for as much as 10 per cent of the total receipts of those with savings. According to the principal source of receipts for couples, the following tabulation shows the percentages that had each source as their major means of livelihood, and the mean receipts of each group.

Major Source of Receipts	Percentage Having This as Major Source	Mean Total Receipts
Earnings	42.1	$3,260
Assets	8.6	2,268
Savings	4.4	1,989
Pensions including Social Security	22.6	1,536
Public assistance	17.0	929

During 1951 median earnings of those 65 and over who were employed was $1,681, compared to $3,046 for all ages. Employment income of the over 65 group was less than half that of the 35 to 54 group (average of medians $3,435), and only slightly over half that for all ages ($3,046).[9]

Material presented so far supports that from other sources, which indicate that (1) older folks are at a pronounced disadvantage in opportunities to earn income except in self-employment; (2) earned income is the major factor in providing adequately for the financial needs of older people; and (3) those fortunate or provident enough to have assets and savings (a major source of receipts for only 13 per cent combined) are moderately well provided for at about a $2,000 income level at 1951 prices, but some of this was from current earnings. In general, incomes of most couples 65 years and over have been inadequate to meet the wants of our rising standard of living regardless of the fact that people past 64 years of age usually need less than younger folks, and budgets for older couples show it is possible to live but hardly to enjoy many economic goods on incomes of $2,000 and less.

Three general solutions to this problem have been widely discussed: (1) increased employment of older men, (2) larger social security and other pension benefits, and (3) directing energies, interests and abilities of retired folks into community activities, hobbies, and other endeavors to keep them occupied as well as to give them a sense of usefulness, and possibly to provide society with some benefits. The last would probably be of no help to the financial needs of retired people. A survey of management publications will

[8] Robert Dorfman, "The Labor Force Status of Persons Aged Sixty-Five and Over," *American Economic Review* (May 1954) pp. 634-44.

[9] Peter O. Steiner, "The Size, Nature, and Adequacy of the Resources of the Aged"; and Melvin W. Reder, "Age and Income," *American Economic Review,* (May 1954) pp. 645-70.

show very few references to self-employment for older folks, although a few periodicals discuss this topic, and a recent address by James C. Worthy, Assistant Secretary of Commerce, does an excellent job of pointing to the self-help, self-employment solution.[10] Our aim now is to consider this alternative, namely self-employment suitable to older people.

Regardless of a person's age, moderate infirmities and handicaps common to older people, a well selected small business or independent professional practice may easily mean the difference between happiness and longevity, or despair and premature death. But three points warrant major emphasis: (1) not all older people should attempt self-employment, (2) financial risks are more serious because of the irreplaceable nature of invested capital in the event of failure, and (3) advance planning and preparation are prerequisites to probable success.

For entrepreneurs in general, age is a personal matter. Most continue as independent enterprisers to suit their own convenience and conditions. The wide range of self-employment opportunities makes it possible to select one to suit almost any set of needs, and as his own boss the self-employed person can set his own pace. What he might be unable to do consistent with the time schedule of dependent employment he could often do on his own. The fact that his major goals are moderate supplemental income, purposeful activity, and an increased feeling of security, rather than an ambition for large and increasing income, puts the older enterpriser in an entirely different category from younger ones.

For the college graduate with 20 to 40 years of successful employment, a logical approach would be to seek to capitalize on his training and experience. But unless he studies the situation carefully, or happens to have been employed in a field where large and small firms do equally well, an opportunity to capitalize on his background may not be readily apparent. An executive in charge of some function in big business, such as personnel, production, sales, or research, may see few if any opportunities to make direct application of his experience in self-employment. One in charge of a branch plant, warehouse, or chain store, however, may see many chances to shift to self-employment in the same or a closely related field.

Older people who have not devoted considerable study to the opportunities for self-employment often appear to need counsel and advice even more than younger college graduates. The latter are more likely to be better informed on the latest developments that open up opportunities for independent enterprises. Records of the Department of Commerce and SBA show hundreds of cases where consultation with older people contemplating self-employment resulted in the Department's informing them of recent discoveries or developments that were far superior as bases for self-employment appropriate to

---

[10] "Our Present Challenge: Creating New Opportunities," at the University of Michigan's Sixth Annual Conference on Aging (July 10, 1953). Also: The First Oklahoma Conference on Aging, University of Oklahoma, Norman, Oklahoma (June 1960).

their situations than were their original selections. Hardly any one person today, especially one having a full-time job, can keep informed of all technical, scientific, and other progress. Often an experienced engineer, sales manager, or personnel director of a large company is just the person to develop some recent innovation that will make maximum use of his special skills and experience. So the best advice is to seek advice and counsel from all logical sources.

In general, the older person should follow recommended practices discussed throughout our text, but give special consideration to his peculiar needs and interests because of his age, possible limitations not characteristic of younger men, his much broader background to draw upon, and the greater probability that if he fails he is less likely than a younger person to have a second chance. The last assumes, of course, that a major portion of his resources would be capital invested in the enterprise.

CONCLUSIONS

Our growing older population in an economy that gives employment preference to youth and requires "buying a living" on an ever-increasing standard raises many problems for both old and young. With over 2,700 reaching age 65 on the average every day, and a life expectancy of over 13 more years, the financial problems of this group are significant. In the absence of currently earned income most older people are forced to lower their plane of living drastically from what it was during their years of employment. As a group, only the self-employed have been able to maintain their economic status well past the traditional retirement age of 65 years.

As a little explored alternative to higher retirement benefits, or increased employment at lower salaries for those 65 and over, our discussion has dealt with the many opportunities for, and the advantages of, self-employment during the later years of life. Any attempt to catalogue specific types of entrepreneurship appropriate for this group was deliberately avoided because such opportunities change continuously and vary so much according to each individual situation. But the probable need and basic principles discussed are likely to remain sound at least for the present generation.

QUESTIONS AND PROBLEMS

1. State the four most important problems of small business. For each, briefly outline a practical solution.

2. In what major ways does small business differ from big business during changing economic conditions?

3. As compared to large concerns, what advantages have the small firms during the decline and rise of the business cycle?

4. How, if at all, may enforced delay in launching a small enterprise strengthen its chances for success?

5. How can you justify compulsory retirement from big business employment at age 65 while also justifying self-employment for many of those retired?

6. From data presented in the chapter what is the major reason people retire from paid employment. How should this knowledge be used by a young person in planning for his later years?

7. For a man age 65 who has the ability and opportunity either to remain employed or to become self-employed, what factors should he consider so that he makes an intelligent choice?

8. Assume any reasonable conditions such as the following: (a) college graduate age 25, (b) normal family life and consumer expenditures of the same per cent of current income as others in similar income brackets, (c) paid employment for 40 years at median income for each age bracket, (d) retirement income for life after age 65 at 40 per cent of average purchasing power of income during employment plus the additional five years his widow will live and need income. Prepare a specific plan for retirement income in certain dollars adjusted for probable future purchasing power—that is, guaranteed dollar income of the required number of dollars, not some uncertain investment. Use any or all devices, such as savings, any form of insurance and annuities, purchase of federal government bonds, or similar certain dollar return channels.

1. Tabulate and report your findings and conclusions.

2. Do you plan to use this method? Why, or why not?

9. A married veteran graduating from college at 29 has accepted a position as assistant production manager of a big corporation having a compulsory retirement policy at 60. Ted and his wife want to have four children, a good standard of living until retirement, and ample provisions for the 15 to over 20 post-retirement years. What would you advise them to do? Be specific and practical.

27 • Small Business International

A fortunate combination of circumstances makes the present a unique period in world history in opportunities and challenges for independent enterprise. For the first time all countries of the free world believe they can improve their lot. Most of them are actively seeking to do so. But they need the managerial experience, technical know-how, and capital available only from the leading industrial countries, chiefly the United States.

The phenomenal rebuilding of Western Europe in early postwar years as a result of Marshall Plan technical and financial assistance is well known. Less well appreciated is the great contrast between these countries and the underdeveloped ones regarding education, training, and industrial experience. Also, many of the new and underdeveloped nations have had unpleasant experiences with colonialism and other foreign intervention.

They have seen the rapid industrialization of the Soviet Union under Communism, and heard fantastic boasts of progress from Red China. Few are in a position to appreciate the terrific social cost of these ventures. But the Soviets have declared an economic war—as well as other aspects of the cold war —on the Free World. Private enterprise thus faces challenges as well as opportunities. In view of conditions such as these it is not surprising to find in most countries that the government plays a more dominant role than in the United States, and that safeguards to protect nationals and natural resources are widespread. Although big business continues its participation in this Free World struggle there are many opportunities for small business to make its contribution within the framework of private enterprise.

At least three features highlight the importance of the international aspects of small business: (1) greater profit potentials, (2) the trend toward globalism, and (3) the cold war—especially its economic and related aspects. It is fitting that a comprehensive small business text give attention to this increasingly important interest in international business.

SCOPE AND EMPHASIS

Small business international divides itself logically into two distinct areas (1) international marketing—both importing and exporting, and (2) establishing a business in a foreign country. Just as there are similarities, but significant differences between small and big business, so does the same dichotomy exist between domestic and international business. In most cases even the two distinct areas of international business—marketing and establishing a business in a foreign country—share a common problem, that of foreign exchange or a country's balance of payments.

Within a huge monetary area, such as the United States, this problem has not been present in recent times. But international business—both trade and entrepreneurship—even when the United States is one of the parties involved, has in postwar years had to contend with this problem of the availability of foreign exchange to carry out the project. Thus a U. S. importer from Pakistan, Italy, Japan, or France should have no difficulty in making payment because dollar exchange is in short supply throughout the world, but a U. S. exporter to any of these and all other countries would be limited by the respective importer's ability to obtain dollar exchange.

In establishing a business in a foreign country it is also the shortage of dollar exchange that plays a dominant role. For a foreigner to launch a business in the United States it is primarily a problem of converting his local money into dollars. For almost all other countries of the world it is also the impact of the proposed venture on the host country's balance of payments. Thus an American with sufficient capital to establish a business in some foreign country, even if he has the nonfinancial requirements, and even if the country stands to gain by the proposed venture, must still contend with certain aspects of the country's foreign exchange situation. These are mainly two: need to import equipment, materials and supplies from countries where foreign exchange is in short supply, and the ability of the proposed enterprise to generate through exports foreign exchange needed or desired by the host country.

Our emphasis on foreign exchange difficulties as an introduction to our subject has been deliberate because it is a universal problem of international business, but one not too familiar to Americans. Also, by stressing this problem in the beginning we may avoid repetition in later discussion. We have also assumed familiarity with terms commonly used in international business for the sake of space economy. Selected references cited at the end of this chapter should be consulted by readers who need the basic foundation of terms, principles and practices of international business.

INTERNATIONAL MARKETING

Importing

Many small businessmen import products for domestic distribution. These include automobiles; electrical, electronic, and other mechanical articles; wearing apparel of either distinctive design or economy appeal; gifts, novelties, and other impulse items; foods and others. A few small producers import some of their raw materials or parts. Although many of these goods are purchased from importers or wholesalers, other methods are common. Some retailers have friends abroad with whom they deal directly. Many make initial contact with foreign vendors through responding to international advertising either in mass media or direct mail. Others buy from foreign representatives present at trade fairs or exhibits. And some are solicited by foreign producers seeking distribution in different countries. The last is common where franchised dealers merchandise and service products such as automobiles and sewing machines.

A small businessman importing direct may engage a customs broker and freight forwarder to handle technical details and expidite the shipment.[1] Governmental agencies, such as the Bureau of Foreign and Domestic Commerce, and Small Business Administration, as well as trade associations, many banks, and others can also assist the importer. International marketing is often complex and should not be undertaken lightly by the uninformed or inexperienced.

Exporting

A small business engaged in exporting is likely to be a manufacturer or other producer.[2] Again the simplest method is to sell to an export merchant. Import merchants in foreign countries, or direct dealing with the foreign buyer may be used. In either case the exporter must assume responsibility for proper packing, marking and meeting all legal requirements, arranging transportation and collection of payment. In addition to the agencies rendering assistance to importers already mentioned, the exporter may consider foreign advertising, personal solicitation, or representation abroad, and participation in trade fairs and exhibits. These are topics covered adequately in standard references on foreign trade and need not be elaborated on here. But one topic warrants further comment: merchandising to the foreign market.

As used here merchandising refers to adapting the product to each market. This refers primarily to manufactured goods, and to some extent to their packaging, colors and symbols used. In many countries the people have beliefs

[1] See: Walter J. Mercer, "A Look into the roles of . . . The Customs Broker and Freight Forwarder," *American Import and Export Bulletin* (July 1959).

[2] See: Stuart W. McFarland, "Foreign Trade Activities of Atlanta Manufacturers," *Atlanta Economic Review* (April 1960), pp. 17-19.

and preferences regarding certain colors and symbols. Important ones are known to the authorities on each country. Through inquiries they can be ascertained. Other features of the product may be less obvious but should be determined before foreign marketing is undertaken.

While it would be an endless task to detail all features about every product for all countries, a few suggestions as to what to investigate are in order. If some seem obvious, please remember that the obvious often account for failures in foreign marketing.

For mechanical and electrical goods sources and kinds of power available are important: United States 110 volt electrical goods are unsuited to countries where 220 volt current is standard. Electrically powered products may be unsuited to regions where electric current is not available, too expensive or unreliable. Gasoline powered products may be unsuited in areas where gasoline is very difficult to obtain or too expensive.

Availability of repair and maintenance service as well as of repair parts and supplies are important for most mechanical products. If proper installation and instructions on use and care are relevant they should be provided. In many countries potential customers may not be able to read or understand even simple printed instructions. Tools required for repair and maintenance may not be available. What we take for granted in industrialized countries may be nonexistent elsewhere. Even many industrialized countries have not yet adopted international standards for bolts, nuts, screw thread pitch and similar factors.

The nature of user or consumer may be important. Does he, or often she, have the strength, intelligence or adaptability to use the product? Will normal hazards be recognized or cautions observed? Will beliefs or even prejudices prevent or hamper proper use? Wide differences in beliefs, superstitions and prejudices, exist in many parts of the world. Although these may at times seem silly to an exporter and actually run counter to well founded scientific knowledge, he can not safely disregard them. Similar conditions still exist in many technically advanced nations including the United States.

For satisfactory consumer use certain products depend upon local factors such as character of the water supply, climate, temperature, and others. At one time European furniture was found to be unable to survive the overheated stuffy American apartments. Pumps and other products may function efficiently with soft water, but poorly with hard water, and hardly at all with sea or heavily saline water. Additional conditions that may hamper a product's proper functioning include: humidity, sand, dust or other air pollution, excessive temperatures, terrain, and many others. Relevant ones for each product should be investigated.

The character of distributors and channels in each foreign country should be studied. Often they are very different from those in the exporter's country. In general, distributors outside the United States tend toward two patterns of divergence (1) belief that a good product will sell itself, and (2) lethargy or even familytis. The exporter should bypass personal evaluations of these attitudes and concentrate on what his foreign distributors need in assistance. This may vary from persuasive demonstrations to dealers in industrialized countries of the importance of aggressive sales promotion, to appropriate incentives, prodding and assistance in the less developed countries. But it is essential.

ESTABLISHING A BUSINESS IN A FOREIGN COUNTRY

There are many reasons why a person may want to establish a business in a foreign country. Some are based on first hand experience, such as travel or temporary residence abroad. Others may be founded on reading or hearsay. First hand experience offers the best basis even though it should be supported by sound background knowledge.

At least four groups of reasons often encountered are: (1) personal, (2) economic, (3) escape, and (4) noneconomic.

Personal reasons include a liking for the environment, altitude, climate, scenery, nearness of water or beaches or mountains, character of residents, tempo or pattern of living, and character of government or society. Many Americans have returned from France, Germany, Italy, Japan, some Pacific Islands or country in Latin America with such a liking for the place and people they want to return to live there. If they are the "own business" type, establishing their own enterprise is a natural. In most countries it is also easier than securing dependent employment.

Economic reasons account for most big business operations abroad, often in spite of some difficulties.[3] Since an increasing number of large corporations in the leading industrial nations have been expanding their foreign operations in recent years, they must have faith in the profit prospects. In many cases it may be the only feasible way to be competitive in promising markets protected by tariffs and similar barriers. This has been true of companies opening branch plants in one of the six Common Market Countries, and to some extent elsewhere. For most prospective small businessmen the decision will involve starting with a single establishment in a foreign country rather than opening a branch, although the latter is possible. When a branch, franchise, or royalty agreement is under consideration, the possibility of taking profits or fees out of the country needs careful study. Whereas Mexico and a few other countries do not at present restrict such movements, most countries do. Thus investment may be for the distant future. While the enterprise may be profitable and expanded from profits it may be years before any money can be withdrawn. Our assumption is the typical case where the entrepreneur plans to live in the country and operate the business himself.

Faith in the growth prospects of a country is one reason for establishing a

[3] See: "Going Into Business Abroad: Some Things Americans Learn," Special Report, *U. S. News & World Report* (December 14, 1959), pp. 82-85.

business there to grow with the market. An enterpriser with managerial ability, experience and capital may believe he can obtain a greater excess of profit over his living expenses than he could at home. This tends to be true because of higher profits and lower living costs in many foreign countries. Sometimes a favorable exchange rate may give the prospective enterpriser greater purchasing power for his capital when it is transferred abroad. In addition, a business may be launched successfully with less capital in some countries than in others. Sometimes special financial incentives are offered, such as tax exemption, provision of land and buildings, government loans on favorable terms. This seems to have been partly responsible for the phenomenal postwar industrial expansion in Puerto Rico.[4] Some men with military pensions or other continuing incomes from United States sources believe they can supplement these payments with a business in a foreign country of their liking better than they could at home.

Another economic reason is to process some local raw material for the domestic market, or possibly to cushion the wide price fluctuations characteristic of the world market for many raw materials. Underdeveloped countries often export raw materials and import products made from them.

Sometimes a person's occupation may be crowded at home but in strong demand abroad. Many skilled technicians from Germany, France, Great Britain, and Switzerland have opened successful businesses in the United States and other countries. A man may believe in some idea or innovation that would be difficult to make the basis for an enterprise at home but very welcome in other countries.

A foreign branch of a large American company sometimes needs parts or services they experience difficulty in securing. Either foreign exchange is not available for importing or local sources are unsatisfactory. A competent person from an industrialized country willing to establish a local business may be the answer. For the enterpriser, having an established demand may give him an assured start for a business that may later be expanded. Some countries permit this only when the authorities are convinced that nationals cannot furnish the materials or services needed. On the other hand, in most countries where such a situation is likely to develop the host country welcomes the establishment of a new business, but may require that nationals be employed below the management level.

A desire to escape onerous conditions in one country has caused many people to emigrate and establish a business in the host country. Forces causing such migrations may be religious and racial discrimination or other forms of oppression. Mass migrations in world history are familiar examples: displaced persons and those escaping from Communist-dominated countries, both Russian and Red Chinese.

Social, humanitarian and political motives have accounted for an unknown,

---

[4] "Private Investment and the Industrialization of Puerto Rico," *Monthly Review,* Federal Reserve Bank of New York (April 1960), pp. 65-67.

but appreciable, number of enterprises established abroad. Social and humanitarian reasons appear most often in fields associated with health and medical care. They may or may not be partially subsidized. Political reasons are likely to be prompted by espionage and world conquest ambitions of the two giant Communist countries. Our concern is less with these groups than with traditional private enterprise ventures.

As a caveat it is worth repeating that personal experience—or actually living—in the country of proposed domicile should precede actual launching of a business. Conditions vary so greatly among different countries that reliance upon even the most carefully prepared published material is unwise. Too many personal factors not covered in published reports are involved. On the reverse side of the coin personal experience will not reveal many factors that will be disclosed in the reports of reliable studies such as those of the U. S. Bureau of Foreign and Domestic Commerce in their, "Establishing a Business in . . . [close to sixty countries of the Free World]." Copies of those still available may be obtained for ten cents each from the Superintendent of Documents, Washington 25, D. C. Although these are recent reports and many have been revised, it should be remembered that since the last publication a country may have changed its (colonial) status as well as its name. These reports cover the following countries:

Angola	Dominican Re-	Venezuela	Luxembourg
Argentina	public	Italy	Malaya
Australia	Ecuador	Hong Kong	Mexico
Austria	Ethiopia	India	Monaco
Belgian Congo and	France	Iran	Morocco
Ruanda Urundi	Fed. Rep. of Ger-	Iraq	Netherlands
Belgium	many	Republic of	New Zealand
Brazil	Gold Coast	Ireland	Norway
British East Africa	Greece	Israel	Panama
Burma	Pakistan	Jamaica	Portugal
Canada	Peru	Japan	Spain
Ceylon	Rhodesia	Jordan	Sweden
Chile	Sudan	Lebanon	Tunisia
Colombia	Thailand	Liberia	United Kingdom
Denmark	Turkey	Libya	Viet-Nam

As in domestic business a country or community tends to welcome an outsider who plans to engage in manufacturing or processing more so than one going into retailing or wholesaling, although branches of "big name" chains are an exception.

In establishing a business abroad the entrepreneur becomes the foreigner. He must abide by the laws of the host country and generally conform to local customs. In some countries, such as Argentina, aliens may own land. In others, such as Mexico, land ownership is restricted to nationals. However, in many cases foreigners are permitted to own land and buildings if they agree to act as nationals and not to invoke their native government in case of disputes. Complete naturalization is the extreme, although not unusual. In many countries, such as West Germany, nationals and aliens have the same legal rights and privileges.

Mexico and several other countries reserve certain rights for the federal or provincial governments. These usually include: transportation, mass communications, extraction of petroleum, and sometimes electric power. Under license such countries frequently permit exploration for oil deposits.

Countries vary as to the percentage of nationals in ownership from 100 per cent in Mexico for broadcasting to none in many countries. For other than the restricted fields most countries permit alien ownership or top management but tend to emphasize employment of nationals at lower levels. In nonindustrialized countries underemployment tends to be high and great stress is placed on employment of nationals. A common provision is that no alien may be employed if local talent is available. Industrial countries vary in this respect from West Germany with no restrictions to Japan with some. For underdeveloped countries a major reason for welcoming businesses established by aliens may be as much to provide employment for nationals as it is to develop foreign exchange and promote a country's industrialization. Competent managerial ability among nationals is scarce or nonexistent.

Labor laws in many countries, especially in Latin America and some Asiatic countries, tend to stress continuity of employment. Mexico requires dismissal compensation of three months pay plus 20 days for each year of employment. In some countries it is almost impossible to dismiss an employee for any cause after ten years of employment. Even when dismissal is legally allowed, local disapproval, as in Japan, may cause a company to prefer to lose business during periods of peak demand rather than to add temporary employees.

One aspect of the labor provisions of less developed countries requires the employer to provide suitable housing for his employees if the plant is located away from population centers.

In the majority of countries permission must be secured before a business is established. Important considerations for approval are: contribution to the economy in terms of local employment, appropriateness to the country's expansion goals, and effects on the country's foreign exchange. Most countries welcome a *new* industry if it does not impose a burden on their foreign exchange or threaten to deplete scarce natural resources. Some governments have published lists of desired industries, usually included in the Department of Commerce series previously mentioned.

Taxes, especially avoidance of double taxation, may be important in establishing a business abroad when the enterpriser does not plan to seek naturalization. The United States has concluded treaties on this point with many countries, and others are in progress.

CONCLUSIONS

Our discussion so far should make clear that (1) a prospective foreign businessman needs to be familiar with the policies, laws and similar conditions in the host country, and (2) that these vary for each country. The best sources of published material on a country-by-country basis is the U. S. Department of Commerce series, World Trade Information Service publications, already mentioned. In general each publication covers the basic information needed. Some include government expansion policy as well as relevant basic laws. The following Table of Contents for the issue on Panama should furnish an overall perspective of these publications.

CONTENTS

Government Policy on Investment
> Regulations, Laws, Development Plans—Government Monopolies and Businesses—Foreign Ownership of a Business Entity—Foreign Ownership of Real Property—Expropriation.

Entry and Repatriation of Capital
> Screening Procedure and Criteria—Exchange Controls—Industrial Investment Guaranties.

Trade Factors
> Tariff and Trade Concessions—Advantages of Location in Panama.

Business Organization
> Types of Business Organization—Laws and Regulations Governing Business Enterprises—Organization of Foreign Firms—Organization Costs—Patent Licensing—Accounting and Correspondence.

Regulations Affecting Employment
> Employment of Aliens—Labor Legislation—Social Insurance Legislation.

Taxation
> Income Taxes—Real Estate Taxes—Stamp Taxes.

Tax Agreement with United States

Colon Free Trade Zone
> Buildings and Facilities—Taxes.

Bibliography
> Government of Panama—Other Reports.

QUESTIONS AND PROBLEMS

1. What important differences are there between the two basic areas of small business international?

2. Why and how is a small business likely to import?

3. Under what circumstances is a small business likely to export?

4. Compare and contrast the reasons small business desires to establish a business in a foreign country with the reasons big business does so.

5. Select any one of the major groups of reasons why individuals want to establish a business abroad and elaborate on the chapter discussion, giving illustrations.

6. Why is foreign exchange a problem when an alien wants to establish a business?

7. Why do most countries welcome new businesses established by aliens while restricting dependent employment of aliens from the same countries?

8. Why is government control over business greater in most countries than in the United States.

9. From the list of countries for which the Department of Commerce has published "Establishing a Business in . . . ," select one country, secure and study the publication. Report with your reasons what you would do relative to establishing a business in this country.

10. During his military stint abroad Bob spent considerable time in Spain and acquired mastery of spoken and written Spanish. He has $15,000 which he would like to use to start a business in Brazil because he has heard of its potential for expansion and beautiful scenery. What would you advise him to do and why?

SELECTED REFERENCES

American Marketing Association, *Successful Marketing at Home and Abroad,* edited by W. David Robbins, Chicago, 1958.

Fayerweather, John, *Management of International Operations,* New York: McGraw-Hill Book Company, 1960.

Horn, Paul V. and Gormey, Henry, *International Trade; Principles and Practices,* 4th ed., Englewood Cliffs, New Jersey: Prentice-Hall, Inc., 1959.

Kramer, Ronald L., *International Marketing,* Cincinnati: South-Western Publishing Co., 1959.

Myrdal, Gunnar, *An International Economy,* New York: Harper & Brothers, 1956.

U. S. Bureau of Foreign and Domestic Commerce, World Trade Information Service: "Establishing a Business in . . . [almost 60 countries]," Part I.

Appendix A

TABLE A-1. COMMERCIAL FAILURES, 1900-1958*

Year	Failure Rate per 10,000 Concerns	Year	Failure Rate per 10,000 Concerns
1900	92	1930	122
1901	90	1931	133
1902	93	1932	154
1903	94	1933	100
1904	92	1934	61
1905	85	1935	62
1906	77	1936	48
1907	83	1937	46
1908	108	1938	61
1909	87	1939	70
1910	84	1940	63
1911	88	1941	55
1912	100	1942	45
1913	98	1943	16
1914	118	1944	7
1915	133	1945	4
1916	100	1946	5
1917	80	1947	14
1918	59	1948	20
1919	37	1949	34
1920	48	1950	34
1921	102	1951	31
1922	120	1952	29
1923	93	1953	33
1924	100	1954	42
1925	100	1955	42
1926	101	1956	48
1927	106	1957	52
1928	109	1958	56
1929	104		

* *Commercial Failures in an Era of Business Progress, 1900-1952* (New York: Dun & Bradstreet, Inc., 1953), p. 8, and *The Failure Record Through 1958-1959*), p. 3.

TABLE A-2. AGE OF BUSINESS FAILURES BY FUNCTIONS IN 1958*

Age in Years	*Total All Concerns*
One Year or Less	3.5%
Two	17.4
Three	16.2
Total Three Years or Less	37.1
Four	11.4
Five	8.7
Total Five Years or Less	57.2
Six	6.5
Seven	4.8
Eight	3.7
Nine	3.6
Ten	2.8
Total Six-Ten Years	21.4
Over Ten Years	21.4
Total	100.0%

* *The Failure Record Through 1958* (New York: Dun & Bradstreet, Inc., 1959), p. 10.

TABLE A-3. CLASSIFICATION OF CAUSES OF BUSINESS FAILURES IN
U.S.—YEAR 1958*
(Based on Opinions of Informed Creditors and Information
in Dun & Bradstreet's Credit Reports)

Total Underlying Causes	Apparent Causes		Mfg.	Whol.	Ret.	Const.	Com. Ser.	Total
3.4 Neglect	Due to:	Bad Habits	0.6	0.7	0.8	1.1	1.2	0.8
		Poor Health	1.3	2.9	2.0	2.0	1.5	1.9
		Marital Difficulties	0.2	0.2	0.4	0.4	0.4	0.4
		Other	0.2	0.2	0.4	0.2	0.4	0.3
2.1 Fraud	On the part of the principals, reflected by:	Misleading Name	—	0.1	0.0	—	—	0.0
		False Financial Statement	0.3	0.3	0.4	0.5	0.25	0.4
		Premeditated Overbuy	0.0	0.7	0.1	—	0.1	0.1
		Irregular Disposal of Assets	1.5	2.0	1.1	1.2	1.1	1.3
		Other	0.3	0.8	0.2	0.2	0.25	0.3
12.3 Lack of Experience in the Line	Evidenced by inability to avoid conditions which resulted in:	Inadequate Sales	58.5	50.2	53.7	38.5	56.2	52.2
		Heavy Operating Expenses	6.8	5.1	3.5	9.1	6.2	5.2
		Receivables Difficulties	14.3	20.3	6.3	17.6	6.0	10.7
17.0 Lack of Managerial experience		Inventory Difficulties	5.4	11.1	11.2	2.0	2.3	8.1
		Excessive Fixed Assets	10.8	3.7	6.1	5.4	17.2	7.5
		Poor Location	0.5	1.0	4.6	0.3	1.6	2.7
18.6 Unbalanced Experience		Competitive Weakness	14.6	20.1	21.8	28.8	19.1	21.1
		Other	4.9	4.8	3.4	7.0	3.1	4.3
44.1 Incompetence								
1.3 Disaster	Some of these occurrences could have been provided against through insurance:	Fire	0.8	0.3	0.8	0.0	0.2	0.6
		Flood	0.2	0.3	0.1	0.1	0.1	0.1
		Burglary	0.0	—	0.1	—	0.2	0.1
		Employees' Fraud	0.2	—	0.1	0.0	0.1	0.1
		Strike	0.1	—	0.0	0.1	—	0.1
		Other	0.2	0.4	0.4	0.3	0.4	0.3
	Per Cent of Total Failures		17.9	9.6	50.2	14.4	7.9	100.0

* *The Failure Record Through 1958, op. cit.*, pp. 12-13.

TABLE A-4. Sources of Initial Capital and Forms of Organizations Used By University of Mississippi Alumni Entrepreneurs*

Per Cent of Initial Capital Furnished by Enterpriser	DISTRIBUTION BY FORM OF ORGANIZATION AND SOURCES USED FOR REMAINDER OF INITIAL CAPITAL								
	Proprietorship			*Partnership*			*Corporation*		
	No.	Source of Funds	%	No.	Source of Funds	%	No.	Source of Funds	%
80	1	Relatives	20						
51-75	1	Banks	25	1	Partners	30			
				1	Friends	33⅓			
26-50	2	Banks	60	3	Partners	50	1	Stockholders	50
	1	Banks	50	2	Partners	66⅔			
				1	Banks	60			
10-25	1	Relatives	50	1	Partners	80	1	Stockholders	90
		Banks	40	1	Partners	75	1	Stockholders	75
				1	Partners	25	1	Stockholders	50
	1	Relatives	50		Banks	50		Relatives	25
		Banks	25						
				1	Partners	11			
	1	Relatives	25		Banks	27			
		Banks	50		Suppliers	36			
					Relatives and Friends	15			
	1	Banks	90						
	1	Suppliers	90	1	Relatives	75			
None				4	Relatives	100			
				3	Partners	100			

*Compiled from Pearce C. Kelley, *What Commerce Majors Do After Graduation.* Special Studies Series, Bureau of Business Research, University of Mississippi, University, Mississippi, 1949.

Appendix B

CHECKLIST FOR ORGANIZING AND
OPERATING A SMALL BUSINESS

The following checklist should be completed satisfactorily before any person is ready to enter business for himself. It follows the general plan and recommended procedures of the text *How to Organize and Operate a Small Business*. An important consideration for any prospective business owner is to plan carefully and to work out every major requirement for success *before actually starting the business*. It is not enough merely to read the text and to have good intentions of applying its recommendations as each need arises. Not only is there danger that some important matters will be overlooked unless this checklist is followed seriously, but once the business is in operation the pressure of daily work greatly reduces the likelihood that the best practices will be adopted and the best decisions made on all important questions.

The plan of the checklist is simple. Each topic is presented as a question intended to stimulate analysis concerning some important point. An honest affirmative answer to most questions means that the topic has been considered and provided for to the best of the enterpriser's ability. When further attention to a topic is needed, an attempt to answer the question should convince the prospective businessman of this need and also suggest what further action is called for. Requirements thus discovered should be recorded and checked off as completed.

TOPIC QUESTIONS

I. *Place of Small Business*

    1. What are the most serious problems for the small businessman?

    2. How would these affect *you* as a business owner?

II. *Factors in Business Success*

    1. Have you rated yourself and had some acquaintances rate you on the qualities necessary for success as your own boss, using scales such as those presented in the text?

    2. Have you taken steps to improve yourself in those qualities in which you are weak but which are needed for success?

    3. Have you saved money, made business contacts, taken special courses, or read particular books for the purpose of preparing yourself for business ownership?

4. Have you had experience in your proposed line of business or in one similar to it?

5. Have you employed and supervised workers?

6. Are you (a) good at managing your own time and energy? (b) easily discouraged? (c) willing to work harder in your own business than as an employee?

III. *Employment or Your Own Business*

1. Would you worry less as an employee or in business for yourself?

2. What is the principal reason why you want to enter business on your own?

IV. *Appraising a Going Concern*

1. Have you checked the proposition against the lists of warnings issued by Better Business Bureaus and other authorities as discussed in Chapter 6?

2. Have you honestly compared what it would take to start a similar business of your own with the price asked for the business you are considering buying?

3. Has your lawyer checked to see that the title is good, that there are no liens against the business and no past due taxes or public utility bills?

4. If it is a bulk sale, has the Bulk Sales Law been complied with?

5. Have you earnestly investigated possible developments, such as those discussed in Chapter 6, that might affect the business adversely?

V. *Justifying the New Business*

1. If your new firm will be similar to established businesses, have you checked statistical data as recommended in Chapter 7?

2. If your business will be based on an entirely new idea, have you attempted to secure actual contracts or commitments from potential customers instead of merely getting their polite approval of your idea?

3. Have you discussed your proposition with competent advisors who are in several different occupations or who have different, but important, viewpoints?

VI. *Establishing the Business Policies*

1. Have you made an honest, objective investigation of the probable success of your proposed policies?

2. Have you written down the main provisions of your general and major policies?

3. Have you discussed your proposed policies with competent advisors to counteract the beginner's tendency to offer what *he* likes and wants instead of what his potential *customers* like and want?

4. Have you written down an adequate statement of the reputation you want your business to acquire with customers, suppliers, and competitors?

5. Have you made adequate provisions to insure that your policies will be understood and enforced and that you will receive ample warning of the need for policy adjustments?

VII. *Management and Leadership*

1. Have you planned the way you will organize duties and responsibilities?

2. Have you made up a tentative plan or schedule to guide the distribution of your own time and effort?

3. Have you planned ways to conserve your time and energy by using management aids such as policies, standards, budgets, schedules, and others discussed in the text?

4. Have you provided some check on your own actions to insure that you do

adequate management planning before making commitments or important decisions covering future activities of the business, as illustrated by the cases in Chapter 9?

5. Have you arranged to use periodically some checklist (such as that presented in Chapter 9) covering detailed activities regarding customer relations, maintenance, safety, or whatever type of activity will require close attention to details in your particular business?

VIII. *Financing and Organizing the Business*

1. Have you written down a complete, itemized list of all capital needs for starting your kind of business, including a fair allowance for operating expenses and your own living expenses until the business is able to support itself *and* a substantial reserve for the one serious error most businessmen make during their first year of operation?

2. Have you discussed this financial prospectus with a banker and a successful businessman in your proposed field?

3. If available for your kind of business, have you used as a guide: (a) the appropriate U. S. Department of Commerce publication *How to Establish and Operate* manual? (b) the standard operating ratios for your business in calculating your capital requirements? (c) the "Worksheet for Determining Capital Needs" prepared by the U. S. Department of Commerce?

4. Are you sure you have made ample provisions for your personal and family needs during the period when no funds should be withdrawn from the business?

5. Have you considered all the factors for and against each legal form of organization?

6. If you plan to secure much of your initial capital from friends or relatives, are you *certain* that your business will remain free of "friendly" domination?

IX. *Regulations and Taxes*

1. Have you ascertained from reliable sources all regulations that must be complied with for your business?

2. Have you provided for an adequate system of recordkeeping that will furnish essential information for all taxation purposes?

3. Have you checked the police, health, fire, and other safety regulations that apply to your business?

4. Have you provided for securing all information from employees required by law?

5. Have you obtained a social security number?

6. Have you checked with competent advisors systems you plan to use in paying sales, excise, and similar taxes?

7. Have you complied with regulations governing the use of a firm or trade name, brand names, or trade-marks?

X. *Selecting the Profitable Location*

1. Have you compared several different possible locations before making your final choice?

2. Have you used one or more detailed checklists to guide your selection?

3. Have you arranged for legal counsel before signing the lease and any similar contracts?

4. Are you, and the members of your family affected, satisfied that the community in which you plan to locate will be a desirable place to live and rear your children?

5. If your proposed location is not almost ideal, are there sound reasons (not merely your impatience to get started) why you should not wait and begin working to secure a more nearly ideal location?

6. Have you considered significant recent developments and trends?

XI. *Building and Layout*

1. Have you studied your proposed building with function, construction, and modernization in mind?

2. Have you made a personal inspection of the physical plant of other successful businesses similar to the one you plan to start, including both independents and branches of large organizations?

3. Have you planned your proposed layout for the building to scale on paper?

4. If the proposed building does not meet all of your important needs, are there any *good* reasons for deciding to use it?

XII. *Employee Relations*

1. Have you investigated thoroughly the advisability of employing friends and relatives as compared to employing persons only on the basis of objectively determined qualifications?

2. Have you planned working conditions to be as desirable and practical as possible? Are you sure that what *you* think will be pleasant to your employees?

3. Are you certain the employee incentives you plan to use represent the workers' viewpoint rather than what *you* think they want?

4. Have you planned your employment, induction, and follow-up procedures?

XIII. *Relationships with Resources*

1. Have you considered each of the desirable objectives in choosing a particular supplier as discussed in Chapter 17 before selecting the companies you plan to deal with?

2. Have you carefully analyzed the points for and against concentrating your purchases with one or a few vendors, taking into account your personal skill and ability as well as conditions in your line of business?

3. Have you given adequate attention to each of the fundamentals of buying discussed in Chapter 17 in making your plans for this function?

4. Have you investigated your field of business with reference to the presence and advantages of voluntaries or co-operative buying groups?

XIV. *Sales Promotion*

1. Have you analyzed your probable competition in connection with the direct and indirect sales promotional methods you plan to use?

2. Have you planned definite ways to build and maintain superior customer relations?

3. Have you defined your potential customers so precisely that you could describe them in writing?

4. Have you decided how you can measure and record the degree of success achieved with each sales promotion so that you can repeat the "hits" and avoid the "duds"?

5. Have you made provisions to secure a sales promotional calendar applicable to your kind of business?

6. Have you considered different features of your business that would be appropriate for special promotions timed to your customers' needs and interests?

XV. *Advertising for Profit*

1. Have you put in writing your own list of *dos* and *don'ts* to guide your advertising?

2. Have you made a list of all the media suitable for use in *your* business with some evaluation of each?

3. Have you selected the most promising reasons why people should patronize your business and incorporated them in plans for your opening advertising?

4. Have you made use of all appropriate sources in the preparation of a good initial mailing list?

5. Have you given careful thought to the advertising value of the proposed names for your firm, products, and services?

6. Have you made plans for some unusual gesture of welcome and appreciation for all customers during the opening days of your business?

7. Have you planned how you can measure the effectiveness of your advertising?

8. Have you arranged to use an advertising checklist, such as the one presented in Chapter 19.

XVI. *Pricing for Turnover and Profit*

1. Have you thought through the desirability of and difficulties connected with acquiring the price reputation you plan for your business?

2. Have you considered the probable reaction of competitors to your pricing practices?

3. Have you compared the relative importance in your business of each major marketing instrument, including price?

4. Have you investigated possible legal limitations on your pricing plans?

5. Have you considered possible applications of price lining and brand lining to your business?

6. Have you decided on the formula or method you will use in pricing each class of goods and services?

7. Have you decided how and to what extent you will meet probable price competition?

XVII. *Expense Control*

1. Have you investigated the standard systems of expense classifications used in your field and selected the most appropriate one for your use?

2. Have you determined what are usually the largest items of expense for your type of business and made definite plans for controlling these expenses from the very beginning of the business?

3. Have you determined which, if any, expense items, though normally small for your type of business, very easily become excessively large unless carefully controlled *at all times?*

4. Have you prepared on paper a *flexible* expense budget for two or three different probable amounts of volume of business, including provisions for frequent operating expense reports to be compared with planned figures in your budget?

5. Have you determined the standard operating ratios for your field that you plan to use as guides?

6. Have you compared the expense of "farming out," or having certain activities of the business done by outside agencies, with what it would cost you to do the work yourself?

XVIII. *Inventory or Stores Control*

1. Have you determined carefully what constitutes a *balanced* inventory for your business?

2. Have you recorded on paper the exact information you will need for effective inventory control?

3. Have you planned the best methods for securing this information?

4. Have you selected the most appropriate inventory control *system* to use?

5. Have you planned the best procedures to use for stock or stores-keeping?

6. Have you listed the purposes and uses of information you plan to secure from your inventory or stores control system?

XIX. *Credit and Collections*

1. Have you carefully investigated the need for credit extension by your business?

2. Have you planned specifically the various ways you will secure and use information obtainable from your charge account customers?

3. Have you made a personal investigation of the services and costs of affiliating with the local credit bureau?

4. Have you planned the basic procedures you will *always* follow before extending credit to any applicant?

5. Have you formulated plans to *control* all credit accounts?

XX. *Records*

1. Have you decided what records will be adequate for each division and need of your business?

2. Have you secured the necessary forms to enable you to start keeping adequate records from the first day of operation of the business?

3. Have you planned your record system so that appropriate use will be made of standard operating ratios?

4. Have you investigated the possibilities of using simplified record-keeping systems for some of your needs?

5. Have you considered applications of the "one-book" system to your business?

6. Have you decided when and by whom each record needed will be kept?

7. Have you investigated the advantages and cost of using some outside agency, such as the "Mail Me Monday" system?

8. Have you made plans for keeping essential records in addition to your accounting records?

9. Have you investigated the record-keeping system recommended by the trade association in your field?

Bibliography

Throughout the book the best references available have been listed in the footnotes to each topic. These are not repeated here. This bibliography is limited to publications covering broad areas of small business, a few of special importance mentioned in the footnotes, and some very recent publications.

Allan, George Howard, Editor. *Individual Initiative in Business*. Cambridge: Harvard University Press, 1950.

Bain, Joe S., "Economics of Scale, Concentration, and the Condition of Entry in Twenty Manufacturing Industries," *American Economic Review*, Vol. XLIV, No. 1, March, 1954, pp. 15-39.

Banning, Douglas, *Techniques for Marketing New Products*. New York: McGraw-Hill Book Company, Inc., 1957.

Black, Nelms, *How to Organize and Manage a Small Business*. Norman: University of Oklahoma Press, 1950.

Burck, Gilbert, "So You Want to Make Money," *Fortune*, June, 1953, pp. 112, 234.

Christensen, C. Roland, *Management Succession in Small and Growing Enterprises*. Boston: Division of Research. Graduate School of Business Administration, Harvard University, 1953.

Donham, Paul and Day, John S., *New Enterprises and Small Business Management:* (Text and cases). Homewood, Illinois: Richard D. Irwin, Inc., 1959.

Dun & Bradstreet, Inc.:
Getting Ahead in Small Business, New York, 1954.
How to Build Profits by Controlling Costs, New York, 1959.
How to Control Accounts Receivable for Greater Profits, New York, 1959.

Ellis, Jessie Croft, *Small Business Bibliography*, Boston, Mass.: F. W. Faxon Co., 1951.

Favor, Homer E., *Are You Going Into Business?* 100 Representative References on Starting or Expanding a Small Business. Pittsburgh, Pennsylvania: Bureau of Business Research, University of Pittsburgh, 1956.

Fitch, James W., "A Study of Employer Companies," *Harvard Business School Bulletin*, Winter, 1953, pp. 216-218.

Foulke, Roy A., *Behind the Scenes of Business,* Revised Edition. New York: Dun & Bradstreet, Inc.

———, *Inventories and Business Health.* New York: Dun & Bradstreet, Inc.

"Get a Franchise? . . . Way To Go Into Business For Yourself," *Changing Times,* the Kiplinger Magazine, May, 1959, pp. 7-11.

Gotterer, Malcolm H., *Profitable Small Plant Management,* New York: Conover-Mast Publications, Inc., 1954.

Haas, Kenneth B., *Distributive Education,* 2nd ed. New York: Gregg Publishing Company, 1949.

Holtzman, Robert S., and Livingston, A. Kip, Editors, *Big Business Methods for the Small Business.* New York: Harper & Brothers, 1952.

Kaplan, A. D. H., *Big Enterprise in the Competitive System.* Washington, D. C.: The Brookings Institution, 1953.

Kuehn, W. H., *Pitfalls in Managing a Small Business.* New York: Dun & Bradstreet, Inc.

Lasser, J. K., *How to Run a Small Business,* 2nd ed. New York: McGraw-Hill Book Company, Inc., 1955.

Marting, Elizabeth, Editor, *Management for the Smaller Company,* New York: American Management Association, Inc., 1959.

National Council for Small Business Management Development: Papers and Proceedings of the Fourth Annual Conference, Urbana, Illinois: University of Illinois, 1959.

Osborn, Alex F., *Applied Imagination, Principles and Procedures of Creative Thinking,* New York: Charles Scribner's Sons, 1953.

Pederson, Carlton A., "Twenty-five Years of Business School Graduates," *Stanford Business School Alumni Bulletin,* July, 1953, pp. 3-10.

The Retailer Looks at His Service Wholesale Druggist. New York: National Wholesale Druggists Association, December, 1953.

Schoen, Sterling H., *Personnel Management in Small Manufacturing Companies.* Bureau of Industrial Relations Bulletin No. 21. Ann Arbor: University of Michigan, 1954.

Select Committee on Small Business, United States Senate, 85th Congress, 2nd Session, *Briefing on the Investment Act,* Washington, D. C., G.P.O., 1959.

Select Committee on Small Business, United States Senate. *Shopping Centers—1959,* Washington, D. C., G.P.O., 1959.

Select Committee on Small Business, United States Senate, 85th Congress, 2nd Session. *Small Business Tax Adjustments* (Contained in the Technical Amendments Act of 1958). Washington, D. C., G.P.O., 1958.

Select Committee on Small Business, United States Senate. *The Right to Buy—and Its Denial to Small Business,* Washington, D. C., G.P.O., 1957.

"Should You Go Into Business for Yourself?" Series of six articles in *Changing Times,* the Kiplinger Magazine, October, 1959-March, 1960.

Small Business, Winter, 1959 issue of *Law and Contemporary Problems.*

Small Business Administration, What It Is, What It Does. Washington, D. C. Small Business Administration, December, 1959.

Small Business Administration, *Starting and Managing a Small Business of Your Own.* Washington, D. C., G.P.O., 1958.

Small Business Administration Publications. Washington, D. C.: Government Printing Office, November, 1959, or latest release.

Small Business Bibliography, Bureau of Business Research, University of Pittsburgh, 1955.

Small Marketers Aids, Annual No. 1. Washington, D. C.: Small Business Administration, 1959.

Sullivan, A. M. *Profitable Management For Main Street,* A Small Business Handbook. New York: Dun & Bradstreet, Inc., no date.

U. S. Department of Commerce Publications, published by the U. S. Government Printing Office, Washington, D. C.

A Report on the Survey of Collegiate Education for Small Business, Spring, 1950.

Proceedings of the President's Conference on Technical and Distribution Research for the Benefit of Small Business, 1957.

United States Government Organization Manual (Annual). Federal Register Division of the National Archives and Records Service, General Services Administration, Washington, D. C.: U. S. Government Printing Office.

Weaver, Robert A., Jr. "Equity Financing for the Small Firm," *Harvard Business Review,* March-April, 1956, pp. 91-102.

What New Industrial Jobs Mean to a Community. Washington, D. C.: Chamber of Commerce of the United States, Economic Research Department, 1954.

Zimmerly, Isabelle M., *Newspaper Advertising for the Small Retailer.* Urbana, Illinois: University of Illinois Bulletin, Vol. No. 51, No. 42, January, 1954, Business Management Service Bulletin, No. 851.

Index